HTI+ Guide to

Home Networking

Quentin Wells

THOMSON
™
COURSE TECHNOLOGY

Australia • Canada • Mexico • Singapore • Spain • United Kingdom • United States

THOMSON
COURSE TECHNOLOGY

HTI+ Guide to Home Networking
is published by Course Technology

Senior Editor:
William Pitkin III

Senior Editor:
Lisa Egan

Product Manager:
Amy M. Lyon

Developmental Editor:
Jill Batistick

Production Editor:
Brooke Booth

Technical Editors:
John Bosco, Warren Wyrostek

Product Marketing Manager:
Jason Sakos

Manufacturing Coordinator:
Trevor Kallop

Quality Assurance Team Leader
John Bosco

Associate Product Manager:
Nick Lombardi

Editorial Assistant:
Amanda Piantedosi

Cover Design:
Nancy Goulet

Text Design:
GEX Publishing Services

Compositor:
GEX Publishing Services

BRIEF

Contents

PREFACE   xvii

CHAPTER ONE
Introduction to HTI   1

CHAPTER TWO
Home Technology Network Basics   27

CHAPTER THREE
Home Network Design and Configuration   71

CHAPTER FOUR
Installing Central Components and Low-voltage Wiring   113

CHAPTER FIVE
High-voltage Wiring   151

CHAPTER SIX
Video and Audio Fundamentals   185

CHAPTER SEVEN
Audio and Video Installation and Setup   225

CHAPTER EIGHT
Security and Access System Fundamentals   267

CHAPTER NINE
Security System Installation and Setup   303

CHAPTER TEN
Telecommunications Fundamentals and Installation   335

CHAPTER ELEVEN
Home Lighting Control   371

CHAPTER TWELVE
Heating, Ventilation, and Air-Conditioning Management   407

CHAPTER THIRTEEN
Water System Management   437

CHAPTER FOURTEEN
Miscellaneous Automated Control Systems   463

APPENDIX A
CompTIA HTI+ Examination Objectives   497

APPENDIX B
State Codes and Standards   513

APPENDIX C
Integration Case Studies   515

GLOSSARY   525

INDEX   545

TABLE OF

Contents

Preface   **xvii**

CHAPTER 1

Introduction to HTI   **1**

   What Is Home Technology Integration?...2

   What Can a Home Technology Integration System Do?...4

      Internet Connectivity...4

      Audio and Video Reception and Distribution.......................................5

      Telecommunications 5

      Home Security and Access Control..6

      Home Automation and Control...7

      Utility and Resource Management...7

   The Benefits of HTI..8

      Technology on Demand..8

      Technology to Save Time 8

      Technology to Save Money...9

      Assisted Living Functions...9

      Home Office Enhancement...9

   Basic Components of HTI Systems..10

      Processors..12

      Communication Links...13

      Sensors..13

      Control Devices..15

      Display and Monitoring Devices..15

      Recording and Storage Devices...16

   Designing and Installing HTI Systems—the Professionals.....................................16

   How Much HTI is Enough?...18

   Chapter Summary...18

   Key Terms...19

   Review Questions..22

   Hands-on Projects...24

   Case Projects..26

CHAPTER 2

Home Technology Network Basics   **27**

   What Is a LAN and How Does It Work?..28

The OSI Model..28

Data Packets..29

Network Architecture..30

Ethernet..31

Ethernet Data Control..33

Token Ring 35

Wireless Networks..36

Fiber-optic Cable Networks...39

Receiving and Sending External Information on a LAN..39

How Data Travels on the Internet..39

The Role of Routers..40

Connecting a Home Network to the Internet..41

Transmitting Internal Information on a LAN..44

Major Hardware Components of a Home Network...45

Computers...45

Monitors..46

Printers..49

Network Interface Card (NIC)..53

Server..55

Router...55

Switches and Bridges...56

Wireless Access Hub 58

Firewalls..58

Chapter Summary..60

Key Terms...61

Review Questions..64

Hands-on Projects...66

Case Projects...69

CHAPTER 3

Home Network Design and Configuration   **71**

Home Information Distribution Requirements..72

Wired Network Types...72

Wiring an Ethernet or Token Ring Network...72

HomePNA or Phone-line Network..76

AC Power-line networks..80

X10...84

Wireless Protocols and Standards...87

Unlicensed Shared Use of Wireless Frequencies...89

Interference Potential...90

Wi-Fi (Wireless Fidelity)..90

Home Radio Frequency..91

Bluetooth...92

WiFi5... 92

Which Wireless Technology Is Best?...93

Network Configuration and Settings for a Home Network.. 94

TCP/IP Addressing..94

Domain Names...96

Dynamic Host Configuration Protocol 97

Network Addressing Translation.. 97

Security Firewall Configuration and Filtering... 99

Threats to Home LANs Security... 99

Proxy Server... 103

Chapter Summary... 103

Key Terms.. 104

Review Questions.. 106

Hands-on Projects... 108

Case Projects... 111

CHAPTER 4

Installing Central Components and Low-voltage Wiring   **113**

Planning a Home Network... 114

Where Will the Network Be Built? 115

What Nodes Will Be on the Network?.. 116

Where Will Each Node Be Located?..118

How Will Each Node Be Connected?...119

Do I Have a Diagram of the Home LAN?..121

Is My Diagram Correctly Labeled?.. 122

Basic Central LAN Components.. 123

Patch Panel... 123

Straight-through and Crossover Cables...124

Residential Gateway..126

Wiring a Home LAN... 127

Wiring in New Construction.. 128

Tips for Working with Concealed Wiring 129

Tips for Surface Wiring..130

Working with Wiring Connectors and Terminating Jacks.. 132

Installing a Home Run Cable 135

Configuring the Hardware and Cables... 140

Chapter Summary... 141

Key Terms.. 142

Review Questions..144

Hands-on Projects..146

Case Projects...148

CHAPTER 5

High-voltage Wiring **151**

High-voltage Electrical Safety Standards..152

    Organizations that Develop Electrical Standards 152

    Avoiding Electrical Safety Hazards...153

Calculating AC Load Requirements...154

    Electrical Use in the Home..155

    Calculating the Load..156

    Checks for Inadequate Home Wiring...157

Planning and Installing New AC Circuits...158

    Plan the Electrical System Upgrade..158

    Install Outlet and Switch Boxes...159

    Install AC Wiring...160

    Wiring New Circuits..163

    High-voltage Electrical Components...164

    Service Panels..167

Circuit Protection..169

    Ground Connections..169

    Surges and Spikes..169

    Minimizing High-voltage Interference..171

Chapter Summary..174

Key Terms..175

Review Questions...176

Hands-on Projects..179

Case Projects..182

CHAPTER 6

Video and Audio Fundamentals **185**

From Analog Recording to Digital Transmission..186

Audio Recording and Broadcasting..188

    Audio Recording...189

    AM Radio Broadcasting..190

    FM Radio..191

    Digital Radio...192

    Digital Audio Recording..193

    CD Audio Recording...194

    Computer Audio Recording...195

Television Recording and Broadcasting..196

Analog Television..197

Analog Video Recording..197

Digital Video 199

Digital Television Compression...200

Changing Video Formats...203

Standard Definition Television...203

Sources of Audio and Video Services..204

Broadcast Radio and Television...204

Cable Television..205

Digital Satellite Television...207

Video Storage Files and Formats..208

Internet Video..208

Stored Video Media..209

Connected Audio/Video System Design...210

Chapter Summary...212

Key Terms...213

Review Questions..216

Hands-on Projects...218

Case Projects..222

CHAPTER 7

Audio and Video Installation and Setup   **225**

Audio and Video System Components..226

Audio System Components...227

Audio Players...232

Television System Components...233

Installation and Setup of Audio and Visual Systems...................................238

Termination points..239

Receiving Components...241

Audio Components..241

Video Components..243

Control Components..246

Configuration and Settings for External Audio and Video..........................247

Audio Systems..247

Television Systems...249

Configuration for Internal Video/Audio...252

Monitoring and Maintaining Video/Audio Systems...................................253

Chapter Summary...254

Key Terms...255

Review Questions..258

Hands-on Projects...260

Case Projects..264

CHAPTER 8

Security and Access System Fundamentals   **267**

Security Design and Installation Factors...268

     Existing Home and New Construction Environments...269

     Security Zone Layout..270

     Home Utility Specifications and Capacity...272

     Security System Integration with Home Utility Systems 273

     Safety and Code Regulations...274

Security System Types..274

     Hardwired Security Systems...275

     Wireless Security Systems..276

     Remote Access Systems...276

Security System Equipment Locations..277

     Lock and Keypad Locations...277

     Sensor Locations..278

     Camera Locations...279

Security System Components...280

     Access Devices..280

     Cameras and Recorders...283

     Monitors...285

     Sensors...285

     Security Panels...289

     Alarms..290

     Call-in Devices..290

Chapter Summary..291

Key Terms...292

Review Questions...294

Hands-on Projects..296

Case Projects..300

CHAPTER 9

Security System Installation and Setup   **303**

Security System Installation 304

     Low-voltage Wiring..304

     Wireless Security Systems..307

     X10 Security Systems...308

Component Installation and Setup...309

     Wired System Components..309

Wireless System Components..312

X10 Power-line System Components...314

Accessory Security Components...317

Outside Alarms..317

Controlled Access Components...317

Uninterruptible Power Supply...319

Backups and Fail-safe Systems...319

Security System Programming and Settings..320

Keypad Access Devices 320

Security Panel Programming...321

Time and Notification Settings..322

Maintenance, Servicing, and Recovery..322

System Service and Maintenance...322

System Recovery...323

Chapter Summary..324

Key Terms..325

Review Questions..326

Hands-on Projects...329

Case Projects...334

CHAPTER 10

Telecommunications Fundamentals and Installation   **335**

Telecommunications System Types and Characteristics 336

Analog Telephone Communication Systems...336

Digital Telephone Communication Systems...338

Local Telephone Systems...339

Centrex Systems...339

PBX Systems...340

Key Systems...342

Hybrid Systems...343

Voice over IP (VoIP)...343

Remote Access Methods, Standards, and Protocols..................................344

Telephone Components and Features...345

Telephone Fundamentals...345

Extension Dialing...347

Phone-line Extensions and Splitters...347

Intercom...348

Caller-line Identification...348

Call Conferencing...349

Video Conferencing...349

Call Restriction..349

Voice Mail..350

Fax Machine Communications..351

Telephone Installation and Configuration..352

Connecting Telephone Equipment.. 352

RJ-11 Connections..354

Connection Blocks..356

External Services... 357

Caller ID...357

Call Blocking..358

Three-way Calling...358

Call Waiting..358

Emergency Response System...358

Chapter Summary... 359

Key Terms... 360

Review Questions..362

Hands-on Projects...364

Case Projects 368

CHAPTER 11

Home Lighting Control   **371**

Automated Home Lighting Design...372

Load Requirements and Grounding... 372

Lighting Zones and Scenes..375

Home run-connected Lights and Daisy Chains...377

Types of Automated Lighting Systems.. 379

Power-line Control Systems...380

Wireless Lighting Controls..382

Wire Runs and Wireless Zones.. 383

Lighting Control Components.. 384

Command Modules and Controllers..384

Remote-access Controllers...385

Outlets..386

Light Switches and Dimmers...386

Fixtures (Luminaires)..387

Automated Window Treatments.. 387

Sensors..387

System Installation and Setup.. 388

Cautions While Wiring and Connecting Lighting Components................................388

Installing Interior Lighting Zones... 388

Installing Exterior Lighting Zones.. 390

Installing Security Lighting Zones... 390

Programming the Automated Lighting System 390

Troubleshooting the Automated Lighting System...392

Chapter Summary...393

Key Terms..394

Review Questions..396

Hands-on Projects...398

Case Projects..404

CHAPTER 12

Heating, Ventilation, and Air-Conditioning Management   **407**

Design and Operation of Zoned and Nonzoned HVAC Systems 408

    Space Heaters, Room Air Conditioners, and Evaporative Coolers.........................408

    Central Heating Systems..408

    Fuels within Furnaces..410

    Central Air Conditioning (A/C)..411

    Single and Multiple-Unit HVAC Systems..411

    Zoned and Nonzoned Systems...412

    Ventilators...413

HVAC Components..414

    Furnaces..415

    Refrigeration Air Conditioners..416

    Thermostat..417

    Sensors..418

    Air Handlers..418

    Damper Controls...419

    Duct Boosters...420

    Controller Panels...420

HVAC Controller System Installation...422

    Controller Wiring..422

    Termination Points..423

Setting and Programming HVAC Controllers and Sensors...424

    Sensor and Thermostat Settings...424

    Zone Programming..425

    Time-of-Day Programming..425

    Seasonal Presets...426

    Remote Access...426

Chapter Summary...427

Key Terms..427

Review Questions..429

Hands-on Projects...431

Case Projects...434

CHAPTER 13

Water System Management   **437**

Water Control System Design..438

Zoned Water Systems..438

Interior Zones..440

Timed Water Systems..440

Watering Scenes...441

Remote Access..442

Water Control System Components..442

Solenoid Valves..442

Controller..443

Sensors..446

Pumps...447

Water Control System Installation and Programming..448

Locating the Controller..448

Low-voltage Wiring..449

Programming 451

Chapter Summary...453

Key Terms..453

Review Questions...454

Hands-on Projects..456

Case Projects..460

CHAPTER 14

Miscellaneous Automated Control Systems   **463**

Automated Interior Furnishings..464

Automated Audio and Video Furniture...464

Installation of Mechanical Systems...467

Automated Window and Door Systems..468

Window Shades and Blinds...468

Drape and Shade Pulls..469

Shade Lifts..470

Door Openers...471

Skylights...472

Automated Fan...474

Automated Lift Systems..474

Dumbwaiter..475

Elevators...477

Hydraulic Lifts...479

Stair Lift..480

Installation of Lifts..481

Automated Heating Systems...482

Fireplace Igniter...482

Heating Cables...484

Chapter Summary...487

Key Terms...487

Review Questions...489

Hands-on Projects...492

Case Projects...495

APPENDIX A

CompTIA HTI+ Examination Objectives

497

APPENDIX B

State Codes and Standards

513

APPENDIX C

Integration Case Studies

515

Case Study #1: Discussion...516

Case Study #1: Solution..516

Case Study #2: Discussion...516

Case Study #2: Solution..517

Case Study #3: Discussion...517

Case Study #3: Solution..517

Case Study #4: Discussion...517

Case Study #4: Solution..518

Case Study #5: Discussion...518

Case Study #5: Solution..518

Case Study #6: Discussion...519

Case Study #6: Solution..519

Case Study #7: Discussion...519

Case Study #7: Solution..520

Case Study #8: Discussion...520

Case Study #8: Solution..520

Structured Wiring Installation Background Information...................................521

Case Study #9: Discussion...521

Case Study #9: Solution...522

Case Study #10: Discussion...522

Case Study #10: Solution 523

Case Study #11: Discussion...523

    Scenario 1: No Demarc Evident...523

    Scenario 2: Demarc is Evident..524

    Scenario 3: Homeowner Moves in, but Demarc Is Not There!...........................524

Case Study #11: Solution...524

Contributors to the Case Studies..524

Glossary   **525**

Index   **545**

Preface

Data technologies and automation systems for home and home business use have expanded exponentially over the past few years. As is always the case when multiple independent developments occur in a free market economy, integration of the various hardware and software components to function seamlessly as an automated home network has lagged behind. This book is designed to provide basic knowledge of all the major home technologies and help the reader develop the necessary skills to install and configure these technologies so that they function as a unified system to the maximum extent possible.

Some technologies, such as wired and wireless networks, work together easily; others, such as home entertainment systems and security systems, require sophisticated interfaces to connect and function with a home data network. To install and configure multiple technologies in a unified system, the home technology integrator must understand not only the operation of each technology, but also the communication methods (wired or wireless) it uses, the protocols that govern its data flow, and the specific hardware and connection devices it employs. Home technology is by definition a broad field, and one that is expanding daily. Every reader will need to study constantly in order to keep current with new developments.

Each section dealing with a specific technology provides basic knowledge about how the technology functions and the operation of its components, as well as practical information for connecting these components into a working system and integrating them to the maximum extent possible with the overall home technology network. The book starts with an overview of all the technologies that can be installed and integrated in a home system, then concentrates for several chapters on the design, installation, and configuration of high speed, hardwired and wireless local area networks in the home. Successive chapters add detailed knowledge about other technologies that can be linked to or controlled by a home LAN. These include audio and video transmission systems, security systems, telecommunication systems, lighting systems, and numerous automation systems. The pedagogical design of the text provides an interactive learning experience that gives students sound theory and hands-on activities in each technology area to prepare them for the working world. Each chapter also provides case studies that challenge the student to develop solutions to real-life problems likely to be found in the work environment.

One of the main objectives of this book is to prepare you to pass the CompTIA HTI+ Certification exams (see *www.comptia.com*). Obtaining this unique certification will demonstrate to employers that you have the theoretical and practical knowledge needed to work in all areas of home technology. Successfully completing the two-part HTI+ certification process is a challenging task, but it qualifies you for wide employment opportunities in this growing area. Whether you work for one of the specialized firms that install and service only one or two home technologies (cable and satellite television hookups, for example, or security and fire alarm systems), or a broad-based systems integrator that supplies total network solutions, the knowledge in these chapters, confirmed by the CompTIA HTI+ Certification, will assure you multiple career opportunities in an expanding technological field.

Appendix A provides the most detailed information about HTI+ Certification available and ties each exam objective to the appropriate section of the book where information about that subject will be found.

The Intended Audience

This book is intended for students and professionals who plan to install and configure home technology systems. It is an ideal text for introducing students to all the home technologies, and provides an excellent base of knowledge for more intensive study of individual specialties. It assumes that students have an elementary knowledge of electricity, some mechanical systems, and computer operation using Microsoft Windows, but the function of each home technology is explained in depth so that those with no experience can quickly grasp both the conceptual and practical aspects of its operation.

Chapter Descriptions

The chapters in this book discuss the following topics:

Chapter 1, "Introduction to HTI," identifies the major data transmission and automation technologies that are part of home technology, and explains how the integration of these technologies into a unified system can benefit the homeowner.

Chapter 2, "Home Technology Network Basics," identifies the major types of Local Area Networks and explains how they function. This chapter also describes the various components in a computer network and how each item operates as part of an integrated system.

Chapter 3, "Home Network Design and Configuration," describes the protocols used in computer networks, the wire types, connectors and hardware pieces employed to build networks, and the standards that must be followed when wiring them. This chapter also describes how to set up and configure wired and wireless network hardware.

Chapter 4, "Installing Central Components and Low-voltage Wiring," tells how to plan a home network and install low-voltage wiring and other components. It also describes how to connect the components, test them, and configure them into a working network.

Chapter 5, "High-voltage Wiring," presents the safety standards for high-voltage AC wiring, and details how to calculate current loads. This chapter also explains how to install new AC circuits including wiring, breakers, outlets, fixtures, and safety equipment.

Chapter 6, "Video and Audio Fundamentals," includes analog and digital recording, broadcasting of both audio and video signals, and how each of these processes works. In addition, analog and digital standards for audio and video transmission, how these signals reach a home network, and how audio and video programming can be integrated in a home network are also covered.

Chapter 7, "Audio and Video Installation and Setup," details how audio and video system components function and how they are combined into systems that display the various types of audio and video signals. The setup and configuration of audio and video systems as part of a home network are also covered.

Chapter 8, "Security and Access System Fundamentals," outlines the factors that must be considered in home security and access design, as well as the different types of home security systems available. Security and access system components are described in detail, along with the locations where each can be effectively used.

Chapter 9, "Security System Installation and Setup," presents more information about installing low-voltage wiring for security and access systems and how to set up components for both wired and wireless systems. It also details how to configure and program security systems and access devices, the accessories that are available, and how these systems must be maintained and serviced.

Chapter 10, "Telecommunications Fundamentals and Installation," explains the development of analog and digital telecommunications systems and the services these central systems provide. Local telephone systems and their internal services are described along with their component parts. Telephone system wiring, connection, and configuration are also covered.

Chapter 11, "Home Lighting Control," illustrates how home lighting is constructed and discusses the systems that are used to control lighting automatically. Wired and wireless lighting control components are detailed. The reader also learns how to install, configure, and program master controllers to direct them.

Chapter 12, "Heating, Ventilation, and Air-Conditioning Management," describes the design and operation of zoned and nonzoned HVAC systems, the components that are included in them, and the control systems that automate them. The chapter also describes how to wire, install, and program automation controls on the major types of HVAC systems.

Chapter 13, "Water System Management," describes the components of water management systems and how they function. Sprinkler system automation is explained in detail, including wiring, component installation, accessories, and programming.

Chapter 14, "Miscellaneous Automated Control Systems," presents several home features and appliances that can be automated for greater utility and convenience. Four automation system types are described: interior furnishings, windows and doors, lifts and elevators, and auxiliary heating devices.

Appendix A, "CompTIA HTI+ Examination Objectives," lists certification objectives for the CompTIA HTI+ certification with corresponding references to chapters and headings within this book where the related material is presented. Check *www.comptia.org* to see if updated certification objectives have been announced.

Appendix B, "State Codes and Standards," contains a listing of Web sites where you can obtain up-to-date information on each state's electrical codes and other standards that must be followed when installing electrical wiring and components.

Appendix C, "Integration Case Studies," presents a variety of cases built on actual scenarios from the home technology industry. With these cases, you can begin to appreciate and understand the complexity of networking the modern home.

Features

To aid you in fully understanding networking concepts, this book includes many features designed to enhance your learning experience.

- **Chapter Objectives.** Each chapter begins with a detailed list of the concepts to be mastered within that chapter. This list provides you with both a quick reference to the chapter's contents and a useful study aid.

- **Illustrations and Tables.** Illustrations are provided to step you through various networking commands and installation procedures. Extra graphics are included to explain complex technology concepts and the use of specialized tools. Tables are provided to detail useful information about various technologies.

- **Chapter Summaries.** Each chapter's text is followed by a summary of the concepts introduced in that chapter. These summaries provide a helpful way to recap and revisit the ideas covered in each chapter.

- **Key Terms.** All of the terms within the chapter that were introduced with boldfaced text are gathered together in the Key Terms list at the end of the chapter. This provides you with a method of checking your understanding of all the terms introduced.

- **Review Questions.** End-of-chapter assessment begins with a set of review questions that reinforce the ideas introduced in each chapter. These questions ensure that you have mastered the concepts.

- **Hands-on Projects.** Hands-on projects are provided at the end of each chapter to give readers practical experience in the installation, wiring, and configuration of actual equipment used in each of the HTI technologies.

- **Case Projects.** Located at the end of each chapter are case projects. To complete these exercises, you must draw on real-world common sense as well as your knowledge of all the technical topics covered to that point in the book. Your goal for each project is to come up with answers to problems similar to those you will face as a working home technology integration technician.

Text and Graphic Conventions

Wherever appropriate, additional information and exercises have been added to this book to help you better understand the topic at hand. Icons throughout the text alert you to additional materials. The icons used in this textbook are described below.

The Note icon draws your attention to additional helpful material related to the subject being described.

Tips based on the author's experience provide extra information about how to attack a problem or what to do in real-world situations.

The Caution icon warns you about potential mistakes or problems and explains how to avoid them.

Each hands-on activity in this book is preceded by the Hands-on icon and a description of the exercise that follows.

The Case Project icon marks case projects, which are more involved, scenario-based assignments. In these extensive case examples, you are asked to independently implement what you have learned.

Instructor's Resources

The following supplemental materials are available when this book is used in a classroom setting. All of the supplements available with this book are provided to the instructor on a single CD-ROM.

Electronic Instructor's Manual. The Instructor's Manual that accompanies this textbook includes additional instructional material to assist in class preparation, including suggestions for classroom activities, discussion topics, and additional projects.

Solutions. These files provide solutions to all end-of-chapter material, including the Review Questions, and, where applicable, Hands-on Projects.

ExamView®. This textbook is accompanied by ExamView, a powerful testing software package that allows instructors to create and administer printed, computer (LAN-based), and Internet exams. ExamView includes hundreds of questions that correspond to the topics covered in this text, enabling students to generate detailed study guides that include page references for further review. The computer-based and Internet testing components allow students to take exams at their computers, and also save the instructor time by grading each exam automatically.

PowerPoint Presentations. This book comes with Microsoft PowerPoint slides for each chapter. These are included as a teaching aid for classroom presentation, to make available to students on the network for chapter review, or to be printed for classroom distribution. Instructors, please feel at liberty to add your own slides for additional topics you introduce to the class.

Figure Files: All of the figures in the book are reproduced on the Instructor's Resources CD in bit-mapped format. Similar to the PowerPoint presentations, these are included as a teaching aid for classroom presentation, to make available to students for review, or to be printed for classroom distribution.

Photo Credits

The following figures were used with permission, as indicated:

7-10	Courtesy of Microsoft Corporation
9-2	Courtesy of Smarthome, Inc.
12-7	Courtesy of EWC Controls, Inc.
13-4	Courtesy of WGL & Associates
13-5	Courtesy of RCI Automation, LLC
14-3	Courtesy of Smarthome, Inc.
14-8	Courtesy of Inclinator Company of America
14-9	Courtesy of Inclinator Company of America
14-11	Courtesy of Inclinator Company of America

ACKNOWLEDGMENTS

Home technology integration is such a broad field that no one could write a book about it unless multitudinous assistance and support were available. Fortunately for me, both have been provided of excellent quality and in unlimited quantity. The Course Technology team headed by Senior Editor Lisa Egan has been a pleasure to work with, despite the complexity of the project and the constant deadlines. Product Manager Amy Lyon has been an excellent guide through the production process, and Developmental Editor Jill Batistick has done more to improve the clarity and style of my writing than any editor I've worked with. John Bosco and Warren Wyrostek have both provided tremendous help in making the book technically accurate and in assuring that the activities actually work as the instructions say they will. Production Editor Brooke Booth has asked and answered all the technical production questions about formatting, style, grammar, and graphics that drove me crazy when I was a printer, but make the book a pleasure to look at as well as to read. I would also like to thank the two peer reviewers, Mark Brown of Polk Community College, and Ken Quamme of Williston State College, who provided valuable market and classroom feedback during the development of this book. Last, I would like to thank the two contributors to this book: Avi Rosenthal, with Digital Living of CompUSA; and Brandon Blankeship, with Home Director.

I'm indebted to many people for their expertise, and I've called freely on all of them for technical guidance in writing this book. I'm especially grateful to my colleagues, both faculty and staff, at Salt Lake Community College who have contributed significantly to my understanding of technical subjects. Among them are Bill Bradford, Randal Chase, Dick Darnell, Chris Fielding, Win Jensen, Art Kanehara, Stephen Rose, and Chad Thomas. I've also learned much from Richard Meyer and Carl Gundestrup, with whom I spent many years working in the audio and video production business. And lastly, I thank the most technically accomplished person I know, whom I taught until he was about eight years old and who has been teaching me ever since: my son Nicholas. The accuracy and completeness of this book are mostly due to the input of these talented and knowledgeable people; the errors are solely mine.

CompTIA Authorized Quality Curriculum

The logo of the CompTIA Authorized Curriculum Program and the status of this or other training material as "Authorized" under the CompTIA Authorized Curriculum Program signifies that, in CompTIA's opinion, such training material covers the content of the CompTIA's related certification exam. CompTIA has not reviewed or approved the accuracy of the contents of this training material and specifically disclaims any warranties of merchantability or fitness for a particular purpose. CompTIA makes no guarantee concerning the success of persons using any such "Authorized" or other training material in order to prepare for any CompTIA certification exam.

The contents of this training material were created for the CompTIA HTI+ Exams covering CompTIA certification exam objectives that were current as of August 2003.

How to Become CompTIA Certified:

This training material can help you prepare for and pass a related CompTIA certification exam or exams. In order to achieve CompTIA certification, you must register for and pass a CompTIA certification exam or exams.

In order to become CompTIA certified, you must:

1. Select a certification exam provider. For more information please visit *http://www.comptia.org/certification/general_information/test_locations.asp*

2. Register for and schedule a time to take the CompTIA certification exam(s) at a convenient location.

3. Read and sign the Candidate Agreement, which will be presented at the time of the exam(s). The text of the Candidate Agreement can be found at *http://www.comptia.org/certification/general_information/candidate_agreement.asp*

4. Take and pass the CompTIA certification exam(s).

For more information about CompTIA's certifications, such as their industry acceptance, benefits, or program news, please visit *http://www.comptia.org/certification/default.asp*

CompTIA is a non-profit information technology (IT) trade association. CompTIA's certifications are designed by subject matter experts from across the IT industry. Each CompTIA certification is vendor-neutral, covers multiple technologies, and requires demonstration of skills and knowledge widely sought after by the IT industry.

To contact CompTIA with any questions or comments:

Please call: 630-268-1818

Or email: questions@comptia.org

Read This Before You Begin

The Hands-on Projects in this book help you to apply what you have learned about Home Technology Integration. The following section lists the minimum hardware requirements that allow you to complete all the Hands-on Projects in this book. Because HTI+ covers many technologies, each of which requires hands-on experience as well as theoretical knowledge, the list is extensive.

In order to provide detailed and precise instructions in the Hands-on Projects, specific brands and models of hardware have been chosen for each project. Although the instructions are tailored for the equipment specified, other similar equipment can be substituted, if more conveniently available, with the understanding that some of the instructions may need to be modified for the substitution.

Note that programming instructions for automated devices, in particular, are usually very specific and must be followed precisely in order to obtain the desired results. If other equipment is substituted, however, it will always have instructions provided by the manufacturer for programming and configuring it. These instructions should be used, as appropriate, in place of those provided in the Hands-on Projects. If the instructions for a piece of hardware are lost, they can usually be obtained as a printout from the manufacturer's Web site, or an additional copy can be ordered there.

Minimum Lab Requirements

Hardware: Many devices listed here are used in multiple hands-on activities. Numbers in parentheses indicate the number of activities for which each piece of equipment is used. If no number is shown, the equipment is used in only one activity. Those devices that are used in multiple activities are described with all the features they will require to complete every activity, even though all features will be not be used in every activity.

- (15) Two computers, each with Windows 2000 operating system, network interface card, CD-burner/player drive, sound card, microphone, Internet access, and a Web browser

- Single color ink jet or laser printer and spare ink or toner cartridge for the printer

- Crossover patch cable to connect both computers in a network

- Laptop computer with wireless interface for public access wireless networks

- (3) Simulated stud wall section at least eight feet wide and six feet high, or real wall with open studs

- (3) Three stud-mounted outlet boxes

- (3) Simulated finished wall section at least eight feet wide and six feet high, or a real wall with finished surfaces
- (2) Surface-mounted outlet box
- Cable raceway parts sufficient to run a finished raceway for a distance of eight feet with at least one elbow or T junction extending one foot from the main raceway
- (2) Roll of Romex 2 conductor #14 cable
- Roll of Romex 3 conductor #14 cable
- (3) Standard AC duplex outlet
- Single-pole AC switch
- (4) Twenty twist-on electrical connectors for AC wiring
- Two double-pole, double-throw AC switches
- (7) Two plug-in lamps
- (5) NTSC television with antenna reception and input jacks
- (3) Video cassette recorder (VHS standard)
- (4) Ten RCA-type video connector cables
- Blank VHS video cassette
- (2) Commercially recorded VHS cassette
- (4) Stereo audio system with amplifier, monaural select button, FM radio receiver, tape cassette recorder, and CD player
- (2) DVD player
- Commercially recorded music cassette tape
- (4) Commercially-recorded music CDs
- Commercially recorded DVD
- X10 wireless heat sensor and transmitter
- X10 security control panel
- (4) X10 mini-controller
- X10 Wireless Security Console (Model PS561 or similar)
- (2) X10 Wireless Camera system (model VR36A or equal) with power supply
- (8) X10 MS14A or MS13A Motion Sensor and transmitter
- X10 RF transceiver (Model RR501 or TM 751)
- (3) X10 wireless remote control module (Model 4000 remote and base or similar)

- (6) Two X10 plug-in lamp modules (Model 2000 or similar)
- X10 mini-timer controller module (Model 1100X or similar)
- PBX (DataLabUSA Model 308 or similar)
- Two telephone extension sets
- Cordless telephone set
- Telephone patch cable with RJ-11 or RJ-14 plugs on both ends
- One working telephone line accessible through an RJ-11 jack
- Fax machine
- Splitter
- (4) Roll of Category 5 cable
- (3) Roll of Category 3 two-pair telephone wire
- (4) Roll of single strand wire
- Twenty twist-on connectors for low-voltage wire
- Two RJ-14 plugs
- Two RJ-14 jacks
- Three RJ-11 or RJ-14 patch cables eight feet in length
- Two RJ-45 jacks
- Four RJ-45 plugs
- Two surface-mounted RJ-14 hand-wired jacks
- Wall area or board on which to mount surface telephone jacks
- (2) Real or simulated three-way switched electric circuit in a classroom mockup
- Leviton 2202 WI DHC X10 500 Watt Dimmer Switch with cover plate
- Leviton 22081 Slave Switch with switch cover plate
- Leviton DHC Split Receptacle with receptacle cover plate
- (5) Room with 3 or more live AC outlets
- (2) Thermostat (manual)
- 24-volt motorized damper
- (2) 24-volt AC transformer
- Drinking glass (glass, not plastic)
- Small plastic plate
- Cardboard box large enough to hold plate

- Ice cubes
- Automatic thermostat (Dayton Fuel Trimmer Model T-110 or similar)
- 9-volt electric light in a socket
- Five enlarged copies of Figure 13-10
- Automatic sprinkler controller (Rainbird Model ESP 6SI or similar)
- Four 24-volt electric lights in individual sockets that can be wired
- Eight-foot heating cable
- Six-foot pipe section with at least one bend
- Fiberglass wrapping tape
- Binding twists
- Eubank Remote Control Door Mechanism kit
- Entertainment center with 20-inch sliding doors (or doors only that can be mounted on a table edge)
- Mounted loop pull curtain rod (with curtains preferred, but not required)
- Smarthome Model 44 Drapery Motor kit
- Mounted window blind
- Auto Tilt Blind Control kit
- Four AA batteries
- Four AAA batteries

Tools: The only tools listed are specialized items. It is assumed that labs will have standard tools available.

- (2) RJ-45 punchdown tool
- (3) CatX combination cable stripper/crimping tool
- (4) Power drill and ½-inch speed bit for wood
- (4) Hair dryer

1

INTRODUCTION TO HTI

After reading this chapter, you will be able to:

- ♦ Understand how Home Technology Integration (HTI) is used in today's consumer market
- ♦ Describe the major technology areas that make up a complete HTI system
- ♦ List some of the important benefits that HTI systems provide to users
- ♦ Identify the main components from which all HTI subsystems are constructed and the function of each
- ♦ Define some of the knowledge and hands-on competencies needed by professional technicians who design and install HTI systems
- ♦ Discuss how much HTI is enough for a given situation

In this chapter you learn the meaning of **Home Technology Integration (HTI)** and what it can do. You also learn the technology areas that form subsystems in HTI and the basic categories of components that make up each of these subsystems. You will understand how the **network** enables each part of the HTI system to share data with the others so that all can provide better service to the user. You will also understand how the benefits of HTI are making it increasingly popular and how the need for professionally qualified technicians who can design, install, and maintain HTI systems is growing.

WHAT IS HOME TECHNOLOGY INTEGRATION?

HTI is the concept of a connected home environment in which a central computer system, programmed or otherwise directed by the homeowner, manages and distributes incoming and outgoing Internet and audiovisual **digitaldata**, and controls the network, **appliances**, security, and utilities of the home.

HTI management and control can be minimal or extensive, depending on the preference of the individual and the amount of investment in equipment and **infrastructure**. A complete HTI system requires a variety of **subsystems**, which are linked together and centrally controlled, but some degree of HTI can be accomplished with individual control modules linked to various devices and appliances in the home. Figure 1-1 shows a diagram of a large HTI system with arrows indicating the bidirectional flow of data to and from the various subsystems. Note that data flowing outside the network must pass through the gateway that protects the LAN from outside attacks and from the release of unauthorized information.

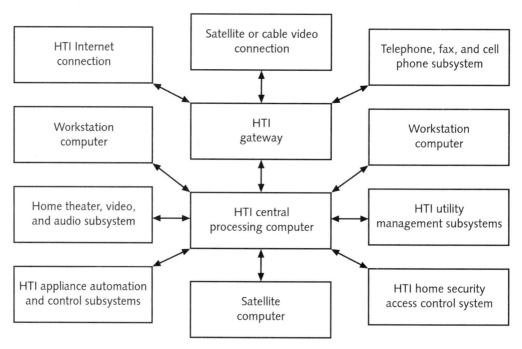

Figure 1-1   Block diagram of a large HTI system

HTI systems are generally used to provide, manage, and control six broad areas of the home technology environment:

- Internet and network (within the home) connectivity

- **Video** and audio signal reception and **distribution**

- **Telecommunications**

- Home security and **access control**

- Utility management (electricity, heat, air conditioning, and water)

- Appliance **automation** and control

Consumer demand for HTI systems that incorporate some or all of these features is increasing. To provide the needed services, homes require a complete, automated home control network that integrates the computer-based systems with entertainment, heating and cooling control, water management, home security, and other systems.

The complexity of networking a variety of electronic products into one home control network calls for trained home networking and integration professionals who are skilled in the design, installation, and troubleshooting of HTI computers, infrastructure, and subsystems. Consumers who employ HTI professionals want to be assured of their technical qualifications in the field. To help provide this assurance of competence, the industry has developed a **credential** called HTI+ Certified Professional.

The HTI+ Certified Professional credential is designed for technicians who install and network digitally based security, audio and video, computer, heating and air conditioning, cable and satellite, and telecommunications systems. To earn an HTI+ **certification**, professionals must pass two computer-based exams: HTI+ Residential Systems and HTI+ Systems Infrastructure and Integration.

HTI+ was developed jointly by **CompTIA** (*www.comptia.org/*) and **Internet Home Alliance (IHA)** (*www.internethomealliance.com/*) in response to the growing need for qualified technicians to install and maintain networked home entertainment, environment, and security systems, including the integration and distribution of the following:

- Communications network

- Entertainment network

- Security network

- Home control network

- Services and subscriptions

- Commercial wiring and cabling

- Ethernet, token ring, or other LAN topology

This book is designed to prepare technicians to pass the two HTI+ exams and become credentialed as an HTI+ Certified Professional.

WHAT CAN A HOME TECHNOLOGY INTEGRATION SYSTEM DO?

This section takes a closer look at the particular data and services an HTI system can provide for a home and its occupants. No single HTI system would likely include all the features described here. Although each system's parameters reflect the individual needs and wants of its owner in the data and services it provides, all the functions noted here are presently available and new ones are being developed continuously.

Internet Connectivity

An Internet connection gives the home access to the **World Wide Web (WWW)** and to literally millions of sites on every imaginable, and some unimaginable, subjects. The usual home connection to the Internet is by means of a **modem** connected to a telephone line. The telephone line connects the home user's computer to a **service provider** who, in turn, connects it to the Web. A standard telephone line connected through a modem serves adequately for most home users of the Internet, but it has limited data-carrying capacity. For this reason, many users lease a larger capacity Digital Subscriber Line (DSL) or use a cable modem for their Internet service. These types of connections cost more than the regular telephone link, but provide correspondingly greater **transmission** capacity (**bandwidth**).

The Internet connection from the home computer to the service provider is an important part of the HTI configuration because the type and capacity of that connection influences how the HTI system distributes and uses Internet data. When the home LAN has Internet connectivity through a gateway or directly to the main network computer, either of these devices can perform the following specific tasks on the incoming data:

- **Scan** the data to detect **viruses**, which can then be blocked from entering or affecting the system.

- Detect illegitimate attempts by outsiders to "hack" into the user's computer system and prevent them from accessing any information on the system behind its **firewall**.

- Distribute Internet access to other computers within the home using a network setup.

- Block or **password**-protect access to some Internet sites, either on all computers on the network or on specific units designated by the system **administrator**.

- Manage all of the services available through Internet access, including e-mail, chat rooms, home or business Web site, etc.

Within the home, the central processing computer can also manage network services for other computers and **peripherals** connected to the system. A home network permits all connected computers to swap data directly, share files, use common printers, play games, etc. Maximum use of computer resources is achieved along with maximum speed of communication within the network environment.

Audio and Video Reception and Distribution

Incoming video data usually comes to the home via cable hookup or **satellite transmission**. Cable television requires a direct wire connection to the transmission facility. Most, but not all, areas of the country now have access to cable connection and those (mostly rural) areas which don't have cable are declining in number as the cable providers' wiring networks expand.

Satellite television access is available nationwide because the signal transmissions originate from several satellites positioned in geosynchronous (stationary in relation to the ground) orbits in space above North America. The satellites **downlink** (transmit) a coded audio/video signal to a dish receiver mounted on the home and aimed directly at the satellite.

Both cable and satellite digital transmissions must pass through a **decoder** or **translator** unit before they can be displayed on screen. The decoder is set by the service provider to decode only those channels to which the user has subscribed.

The type of incoming television signal selected by the user influences the configuration of the HTI system that uses the signal. Cable hookups can be split and the incoming signal shared among several television displays. Each television can be set to a different channel and a recorder can record one channel while the user views another. Satellite hookups require a separate decoder for each television display connected to the system.

The HTI system that receives the decoded digital television signal can do any or all of the following with it:

- Distribute the signal to the various television receivers in the home.

- Monitor and control access to selected channels or programs on a channel for all television receivers or for selected receivers.

- Direct selected programs to recording devices for storage and later use.

Telecommunications

Telephones are the most universally installed technology in America, and an HTI system can extend the utility and expand the functions this established service performs. The voice telephone line, which is standard in almost every home, can be made available in every room, either through hardwired extensions or through **wireless technology**. The latter also allows telephone service to extend into the yard so that a convenient receiver can be carried while gardening or kept near the pool.

Telephone lines also provide the Internet access point in most homes. A separate line is preferable for this purpose, although one line can provide both data and voice transmission, but not simultaneously. When a line is used for data transmission, voice calls into or out of the home are blocked. The same is true of data transmission when a voice call is in progress.

A separate data line managed by the HTI system provides much better Internet service and can also be used as a fax line with messages being routed to fax software in the home computer or to a separate stand-alone fax machine. HTI systems can also use a data line as an emergency alarm line connected to the **home security system**. The system can be programmed to take control of the line in the event of an emergency and summon immediate assistance. Voice and data transmission service can be expanded still further by the installation of a **Digital Subscriber Line (DSL)**, a high-speed data transmission telephone line that also has the ability to transmit voice and data simultaneously.

The security system can also be programmed to use a cell phone, which isn't subject to localized power failure or cut wires, for outgoing emergency calls. This is just one of several ways in which cell phone technology can also be integrated into the HTI system to provide better communication service to the home.

Home Security and Access Control

An HTI System can provide a wide variety of security measures for the home. It allows access to the home and its surroundings and other security measures to be centrally controlled and monitored for maximum protection of the occupants and their property.

Security and monitoring features that can be included in an HTI system include all of the following:

- **Cipher locks** on exterior doors. These require **keypad** entry of a **numeric code** to open, and some types can be time coded to block entry during specified hours.

- **Sensors** on windows and other vulnerable entry points that trigger an alarm if intrusion occurs. These can be taped circuits on the glass, laser beams, or motion/vibration **detectors**.

- Heat and/or motion sensors that monitor the immediate area around the home or specific traffic corridors within it and trigger an alert if anyone enters the space.

- Video surveillance **cameras** that monitor both exterior and interior areas of the home for intruders.

- Strategically placed pressure-sensitive pads that respond either to pressure being applied (weight) or pressure being relieved (object picked up).

Any of these sensing and monitoring devices trigger a variety of responses, including the following:

- Summon the police or other assistance, either by telephone or by radio.

- Activate an audible alarm.

- Activate additional lighting.

- Activate additional security procedures such as lockdown devices, circuit breakers, dropdown security doors, etc.

Home Automation and Control

HTI automation and control systems offer tremendous convenience and labor-saving comfort for most owners and truly essential technology assistance for certain groups, such as those with limited physical mobility and those with sensory impairment. For these groups, home automation can often be the key to living independently.

Home automation is accomplished by means of **remote-controlled systems** activated at will by the homeowner from a convenient location, or by systems that can be programmed on a preset schedule to self-activate at specified intervals or times. Many automation features are available, including the following:

- Centralized control of lighting throughout the house and outdoor lighting fixtures as well.

- Control of window shades and curtains.

- Control of electric appliances such as coffee makers, radios, alarm clocks, dishwashers, etc. Almost any appliance operating on standard house current can be controlled remotely.

- Control of safety systems such as swimming pool covers, driveway and sidewalk heating systems, and roof de-icing systems.

- Management of personal safety devices such as baby **monitors**, fall alarms, and vital sign monitors.

For persons with limited mobility, having as many home systems as possible automated and controlled from a central location is essential. If physical movement is severely restricted, control systems can often be adapted to function easily using whatever motion is available to the user or by using voice commands.

Utility and Resource Management

An HTI system can help minimize energy waste, increase efficiency, and reduce costs by continuously monitoring and managing utility usage. The system can turn off lights and other electrical devices when not in use. Lights left on in a room can be turned off automatically when a sensor detects that the room is unoccupied for a preset period of time. When anyone enters the room, the lights come on again, controlled by the same sensor.

Sensors and timers can control heating and air conditioning systems. This provides maximum energy efficiency while maintaining comfortable temperatures for the home's occupants. Heat can be turned down at night and when the home is unoccupied during the day, then turned back up just before the occupants awaken or return home. Air conditioning can be similarly adjusted to fit the schedules of those in the home.

Efficient home use of water includes the controlled watering of landscaped areas, which usually requires far more municipal water than any other consumer use. By adjusting sprinkler systems to provide only the needed amount of water for each part of the landscaping, and programming them to operate after sundown and for only the necessary time, an HTI-managed system can use less water and be far more effective in maintaining the land-scaping.

An HTI system can also assist in managing a swimming pool. An automated pool cover that covers the pool when not in use prevents evaporation, helps hold heat in the pool, and provides a safety barrier against anyone falling into the water. Pool filtration systems can also be timed to clean and backflush (part of the cleaning process in most pool filtration systems) at night, and in some locations, the waste water used for these operations can be directed to the landscaping.

THE BENEFITS OF HTI

The main benefits of HTI are simple: it makes the user's life more convenient, safer, and more fun. It provides maximum use and enjoyment of electronic media, Internet, and telecommunication systems. HTI makes technology available where and when the user wants it. Automated systems that function on demand or by programmed direction to meet predetermined needs in a timely manner often become essential services rather than mere conveniences. Similarly, HTI's ability to make communication and data sharing easy to use throughout a home enables users to make maximum use of technology to save time while accomplishing more. When that increased productivity is utilized in a home business setting, the payoff occurs not only in time efficiency, but in increased profitability. When technology extends the senses and physical abilities of the physically challenged, while at the same time monitoring their safety and health, it becomes a critical, life-enhancing, if not life-saving, necessity.

Technology on Demand

Hardly anyone who has watched a **home theater** system featuring a 60-inch screen with high-definition television viewing and surround sound audio reverberating from high-quality speakers will be content to go back to a small screen with standard resolution and a single 6-inch monaural audio speaker. Similarly, no one who has come home on a snowy evening to find the driveway and sidewalks clear of ice, the garage door opening as the car's front bumper approaches it, and the house warm and brightly lit, is anxious to return to the "good old-fashioned days" of snow shovels and manual lift doors. In other words, HTI makes life a lot more pleasant and a lot less work.

Technology to Save Time

Users also save time with HTI. Its automated features eliminate the need for many household tasks to be done manually and make services available on demand throughout the home with no need to move or alter equipment setups. With HTI, each room in the house can be connected so that telephones, Internet, television, radio, and network services are all available wherever and whenever they're needed or wanted. Whole-house connectivity also means no waiting for multiple users, each of whom can log on simultaneously. The system apportions bandwidth and delivers data efficiently so that everyone can perform their desired tasks using the shared resources.

HTI saves the user time by automating the performance of routine tasks and functions using a set of programmed instructions. With HTI, custom programming is available that permits a very sophisticated level of control in many automated systems simultaneously. There's no need for the user to think about or perform any of these daily tasks.

Technology to Save Money

By taking over the management of home functions, HTI can make them more efficient and therefore more cost effective. The automated system won't leave the water running too long or forget to turn off the lights when rooms are empty. It always turns down the heat or the air conditioning at night and activates the security system to make sure the occupants' rest is undisturbed. Standardizing household functions for time of performance and duration minimizes the amounts of energy and resources these operations use, which saves the homeowner money.

A sprinkler system can be programmed to water the yard from midnight until 3:00 a.m. on Mondays, Wednesdays, and Fridays from April 15 to October 15, and also add a Saturday or Sunday watering whenever the preceding five days include two or more with daily high temperatures above 90 degrees. Operating on those instructions, the HTI system can keep the yard green throughout the spring and summer. The homeowner may never see any evidence of the process and probably won't need to alter or adjust it unless there's a breakdown in the equipment.

Assisted Living Functions

HTI can provide genuine security for the home and the family living in it. With that security comes a feeling of peace and comfort that's hard to quantify in cash terms alone. HTI security can protect people and property not only against break-ins, burglaries, and other criminal activity, but also against the danger of fire, electrical malfunctions, and water damage. The system can alert the homeowner to danger and quickly summon assistance. It may also be able to shut down faulty power circuits, close gas valves, or activate sprinklers to help control a fire.

HTI can also provide some protection for children. The protective devices include individual cell phones or location monitors that children can carry with them. They also include protective devices such as security gates and pool covers, and quick, easy access to communication links that they can use to get help in the event of an emergency. Similar systems can be set up to monitor the welfare of individuals in customized ways so that assistance is automatically requested if any injury is suffered or a health-related problem occurs.

Home Office Enhancement

Whether someone is operating a small business or telecommuting to a distant office or other location, HTI benefits the person working from a home office. HTI makes maximum services and functions available for business use just as it does for home use. Some of the costs of HTI can be taken as business expenses if they're used in a home office, and some services whose cost can't be justified for home use only become economical when their use is shared among personal and business functions.

A DSL, for example, which is usually provided at a fixed monthly cost regardless of the amount of use, is often required for business use in a home office. After hours and on weekends, when the business use of the line is minimal, it provides greater bandwidth for home use than would otherwise be available.

BASIC COMPONENTS OF HTI SYSTEMS

Although HTI can be used for an almost endless variety of data functions and control of devices and operations, all automated home technology systems consist of combinations of six basic components:

- Processors

- Communication links

- Sensors

- **Control devices**

- Display and monitoring devices

- Recording and **storage devices**

A desktop or laptop computer contains all six of these components and is, therefore, an example of an integrated technology system. Figure 1-2 shows a diagram of a computer system with several input and output devices sending information to and receiving information from the central processing unit, which is the "brain" of the system and performs all the manipulation of its data.

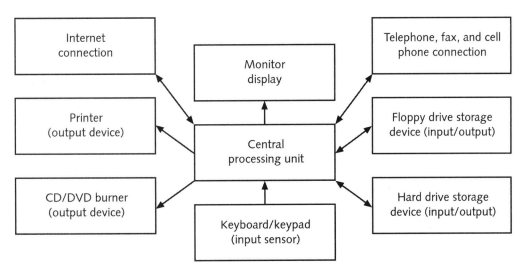

Figure 1-2   Computer system block diagram

HTI simply expands the scope and the scale of these components so that their functions can be extended over a wider geographic area—the whole interior and exterior of a home and its surrounding yard—and to a much larger array of output and storage devices than just the computer's display screen and its hard drive. Figure 1-3 shows a small HTI system that extends the input and output reach of a computer by providing it with input from other segments of the home LAN and allowing the central computer to remotely control automated systems in distant segments of the LAN.

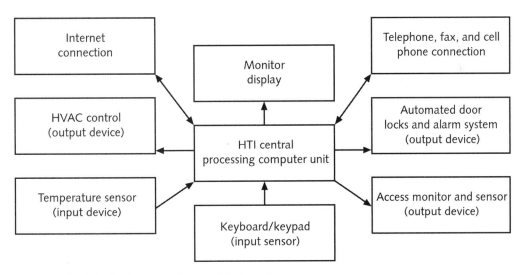

Figure 1-3   Block diagram of a small HTI system

Processors

Processors are electronic devices that receive digital information (input), process this information according to a set of stored instructions (program), and send the results of their processing (output) to another device which can either display it, store it for future use, or perform a preprogrammed action using the information or based on it.

A computer's central processing unit programmed with word-processing software constitutes a processor. It receives input data from the **keyboard**, processes the input according to its programmed instructions into a finished document, and sends the results to a printer, which displays the data as a printed page.

In an HTI system, a processor may receive many different types of input from a variety of input devices such as cameras, sensors, **microphones**, telephone links, etc. The input data may be processed in a variety of ways, according to the manner in which the processor has been programmed, and the results of that processing may be output to various storage, display, and action devices in equally diverse ways.

Input to a processor, for example, could come from a digital thermometer, which is one type of temperature sensor. If the sensor sends data to the processor that the outside air temperature has fallen near the freezing point of water, the processor might compare the temperature information it receives with a preset schedule of instructions and, as a result, output instructions to subsystems throughout the home. It might send instructions to perform any or all of the following actions:

- Shut down the sprinkler system.

- Cover the swimming pool.

- Turn on the driveway heating system.

- Turn on the rain gutter de-icing system.

- Close vents and windows in the home.

- Turn on the space heater in the doghouse.

In HTI, a single central processing unit is usually sufficient to operate and control the entire system, although some subsystems may have smaller processors to perform localized functions. Centralized processing permits the greatest degree of integration among all subsystems and helps ensure that they aren't acting in conflict with one another. It would be counterproductive, for instance, to have one automated function turn on the air conditioning system, while another opened windows and vents to the outside at the same time. If one processor controls all automated functions, its programming can be integrated for maximum beneficial effect.

Communication Links

Communications links are the infrastructure of an integrated technology system and work to tie that system together as a functioning unit. These links are the wires, cables, connectors, wireless transmitters, receivers, routers, **switches**, and other devices that connect the components of a system and permit them to transmit and receive data both among themselves and to the outside world.

These bits and pieces of hardware and lengths of wire are usually quite simple and mundane objects, but they are critically important parts of every integrated technology system. Correctly designing, installing, and maintaining communication links can do more to assure the reliability of an integrated system than any other facet of the system's creation.

In a computer, all of whose components are housed in a single case and closely wired together, communication links are made up of the integrated circuit boards, buses, sockets, and cables that connect the parts electronically so that data can be transferred among them. HTI systems use similar links, but because their components are usually farther apart, the communications links are longer and need to be more robust. Because they are usually built-in as part of the home's structure and are difficult and expensive to repair or replace, the cables, connectors, plugs, and other infrastructure of an HTI system must be durable over time and able to resist the effects of weathering, outside interference, and other factors that can degrade their performance.

HTI communications links can be hardwired using a variety of cable types and sizes and suitable end-point connecting devices. Hardwiring is performed most conveniently and at the least cost as part of the construction process when a home is built, but it can be done after the home is completed using a process called retrofitting. Retrofitting a home for HTI may cost more than new construction wiring and may be less pleasing in appearance because of the difficulty of entirely concealing wiring and connectors after the finished surface of the home is complete.

Wireless connection of HTI is often preferred for retrofitting existing homes and even for some new construction. There are several wireless technologies that can provide connectivity for an HTI installation. Most require the installation of one or more radio transceivers within the home, which communicate with all the components of an HTI system via high-frequency radio transmissions. No wiring is required for this type of installation except a power connection for the transceivers (hubs) and hardwired connections for Internet and television data coming into the home.

At least two other technologies, the **X10** system and the Home Plug system, use the existing electrical wiring in the home to carry digital data in addition to the standard electric current flowing through these circuits to power lights and appliances. Still another technology, called HomePNA, also requires no new wires to be installed in the home because it uses the existing telephone wires to carry data to devices on the home network.

Sensors

Sensors are devices that convert human activity or environmental conditions into data. A keyboard that reacts to finger pressure on each of its keys is a type of sensor. It senses pressure applied to each key and converts it into corresponding digital data, which goes to the computer's central processing unit. A microphone is another type of sensor that reacts to the air pressure of sound waves and converts voice commands or dictation into digital data for the computer.

Sensors in an HTI system can be the same keyboard, microphone, or mouse found in any computer system. They can also be other much more diverse devices, and they can be separated by much greater distances from the **central processor** to which they send their data.

In an HTI system, keypads can be located near the home's entrances where they serve as input devices for the codes to open cipher locks on doors. Other keypads can be located throughout the home and may control entertainment systems, lighting, curtains and shades, garage doors, and others functions.

Environmental sensors are devices that react to some aspect of conditions around them. A temperature sensor, for example, continually sends the current temperature to the processor, which then determines whether to adjust heating, air conditioning, or other systems, based on the data it receives.

A light sensor measures the light level in a room and sends the data to the processor, which can turn the lights in the room off, if another sensor indicates the room is unoccupied. Alternatively, the processor may open window shades and curtains to increase a low light level during daylight hours. A light sensor placed inside a normally dark cabinet or case can even be used to shut down a system for safety reasons or trigger a security alarm if the door to the cabinet is opened, letting in light. Figure 1-4 shows a diagram of a lighting control segment of a home LAN, including sensors to detect interior and exterior light levels and control modules to adjust shades, curtains, and lighting both inside and outside the home. Arrows show the direction of data flow to and from the various devices. From the keyboard, the LAN administrator can **program** the system parameters and set any of its features by time, as well as by sensor input.

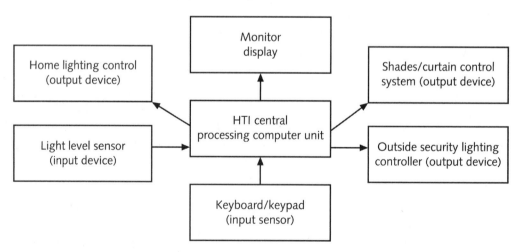

Figure 1-4   Block diagram of a light control segment of a home LAN

Other types of sensors include the following:

- Smoke detectors

- Heat (infrared) sensors

- Motion (vibration) detectors

- Pressure or weight pads

- Water level sensors

- Chemical sensors such as carbon monoxide monitors

All of these devices send data to the processor about the particular environmental condition that they monitor. The processor compares this information to its programmed instruction set and directs the system to respond accordingly.

Control Devices

Sensors collect information about conditions around the house and send it to the processor. The processor evaluates that information and issues commands to the appropriate control devices. These devices are the action components in an HTI system. They act on the processor's instructions to turn off, turn on, or adjust the level of subsystems in the home.

Control devices come in many forms:

- Switches, which turn electrical appliances on or off

- Electromagnetic valve controls in water systems

- Magnetic lock controls

- Electrical **relays**, which act as switches in circuits

- Electromagnetic mechanisms that perform linear movements such as pulling curtain and shade lines or drawing a pool cover open or closed

All control devices in an HTI system have the ability to receive digital instructions from a processor and convert those instructions into some form of action or movement. Many control devices can also be operated manually so that the instructions they receive from the processor can be overridden, and the subsystems they control can be operated or shut down on site in the event of an emergency or a system failure.

Display and Monitoring Devices

Display and monitoring devices are usually computer screens or television screens that display video and audio signals brought into the home via the Internet, by cable, or from satellites. They also display software programs running on home computers, recorded programs from video recorders and DVDs, and data generated by the processor about the status of other systems throughout the home.

Speakers and earphones are audio devices that "display" sounds to our ears. They play the music of recorded CDs, allow users to speak with one another in separated parts of the home, and output the conversations of audio chat rooms. The processor can also use speakers to sound warnings or alarms if the HTI system detects danger or other problems within its programmed parameters.

NOTE   Other types of monitoring devices include continuity lights, which monitor circuits, and space monitors, which can use motion, heat, or pressure sensors to monitor a given area.

Recording and Storage Devices

Recording and storage devices save digital data so that it can be retrieved and used again. Computers typically store their data on magnetic devices such as hard drives, floppy disks, Zip disks, tapes, and memory sticks.

CDs are storage devices that store data in a form readable by a beam of light reflecting off the disc as it spins in a player. Television programs and movies are usually stored on videotape cassettes and DVDs by recorders, which can also play these devices to recover and display the data.

Entertainment programs, video and audio, will nearly always be on videocassettes, CDs, or DVDs. These media can also record images from security cameras and other monitors in the HTI system. Storing images and data from system monitors, especially those devices in the home's security subsystem, allows any significant event to be reviewed after the fact, often a critical advantage in investigating crimes or settling disputes. Home residents can use recorded data to determine the time and date of events that occurred while no one was at home.

The type and amount of data to be stored usually determines the type of device used. Video programs and high-resolution photographic images are the most data-intensive types of files, and so usually require the largest capacity storage devices. Next in size are sound files followed by graphic files. The smallest files are usually those composed of text or numerical data.

DESIGNING AND INSTALLING HTI SYSTEMS—THE PROFESSIONALS

The need for professionals skilled in integrating home networking equipment is growing as a direct result of rising consumer demand for home networking products and Internet-enabled devices for entertainment, voice, and data systems. Homes with complete, automated control networks that integrate computer-based systems together with entertainment, heating and cooling, water management, home security, and other systems are being constructed or retrofitted in growing numbers.

The HTI+ credential was jointly developed by the Computer Technology Industry Association (CompTIA) and Internet Home Alliance (IHA). According to John Venator, president and CEO of CompTIA, the certification was deemed essential "in response to the growing need for qualified technicians to install and maintain networked home entertainment, environment and security systems."

"During the next few years, as we're connecting products beyond the home computer—products like intrusion alarms, furnaces, air conditioners, and the next generation of smart-appliance, families will want to be assured that technicians are qualified."

"The goal of the HTI+ certification program is to establish a recognized standard for the men and women who install and service home-networked products."

The certification is designed for technicians who install and troubleshoot integrated residential subsystems, beginning from the demarcation (d-mark) point, which is where the homeowner's network equipment and the external network service provider's equipment meet, to where the regulated signal stops.

The CompTIA HTI+ Certificate is a cross-industry credential providing recognition that a Home Technology Integrator (HTI) professional has attained a standard of excellence in the integrated home networks industry. The certification is based on a set of standards designed to measure the knowledge and understanding of core competencies regarding the installation, integration, and troubleshooting of the following subsystems:

- Home security

- Audio and video

- Computer networks

- **Heating, ventilation, and air conditioning systems (HVAC)**

- Cable and satellite

- **Broadband**

- Telecommunications

- Service provider wiring (external)

- AC electrical wiring

The required knowledge and skill sets addressed through the HTI+ certification program are extensive. To provide the necessary thoroughness in evaluating the competency of the certification candidate, the knowledge content has been spaced over two unique exams. Each HTI+ certification exam focuses on specific content (tasks) and domain content.

The content of this book has been carefully coordinated with the knowledge required to pass both exams and obtain the HTI+ certification.

How Much HTI is Enough?

The answer to this question is about the same as the answer to the question: how much equipment should mountain climbers carry? Enough to reach the summit they're ascending, but not so much that carrying it is a burden. Similarly, a home technology system should provide the entertainment, communication, and automation the user needs and wants, but should not be so expensive that its cost outweighs its usefulness, nor so complex that the home owner finds it difficult to use or maintain.

There is no ideal HTI system. Each installation is a balance between features and costs. Each person has his or her own preferences about how many subsystems an HTI design should have and what features and level of performance each of them should have.

That said, it's evident that the first major step in creating an HTI system is to develop an overall design. The design should start with a list of objectives describing what the system should be able to deliver in data and services, and what it should be able to do in automation, monitoring, and control.

Specific, detailed objectives allow HTI technicians to design a system in the most economical way. Of course, when planning for wiring or wireless installation, whether in new construction or as a retrofit, it's a good idea to design for more capacity than you think you'll need. Doubling the required number and capacity of communication links over what the design indicates are actually needed is generally a good investment in the future. The reasons for building in such excess capacity are twofold:

- First, installing wiring and other infrastructure in the walls of a home is the most difficult and expensive part of creating an HTI system, but installing multiple wires requires very little additional effort and costs very little more. The wire and other hardware parts aren't expensive. It's the labor of stringing and pulling them through finished walls that takes time and costs dearly. Hence the axiom: never pull a single wire; always double it. Even if you have no need for the second wire at present, chances are good that you will later.

- The second reason is that when the user sees how useful, how convenient, and how downright essential HTI is in the American home, the system as originally designed may begin to seem inadequate. To many HTI consumers, if some is good, more is better.

Chapter Summary

- HTI is the concept of a connected home environment in which a computer system manages and distributes Internet and audiovisual digital data, and controls the network, appliances, security, and utilities of the home.
- HTI systems provide, manage, and control six areas of home technology environment:
  - Internet and network

- Video and audio reception and distribution
- Home security and access control
- Telecommunications
- Utility management
- Appliance automation and control

❏ HTI makes home life more convenient, safer, and more fun.

❏ HTI provides maximum use and enjoyment of electronic media, Internet, and telecommunication systems, and makes technology available on demand.

❏ HTI systems consist of combinations of six categories of components:

- Processors
- Communications links
- Sensors
- Control devices
- Display and monitoring devices
- Recording and storage devices

❏ Trained professional technicians certified in HTI design, installation, and maintenance are increasingly needed to meet the growing demand for home technology systems.

❏ HTI systems should be carefully designed to accomplish the specific entertainment, data transmission, security, and automation objectives that the user desires. Provision should be made for expanding initial designs.

KEY TERMS

access control — Restriction on who has the right to use a computer system or to enter a physical location.

administrator — A person designated to maintain and control a computer system or subsystem.

appliance — Any piece of equipment that performs a specified task.

automation — Performing a task or function by means of a programmed device or system without the need for human supervision.

bandwidth — The size of a digital data stream that determines the amount of data that can be transferred in a given amount of time.

broadband — Any method of transmitting large amounts of data in a short time span. Usually accomplished by using multiple frequencies or data streams; a large (or wide) bandwidth technology.

camera — A device that creates a video image in digital or analog form. Cameras can produce still images or moving images.

central processor — The main computer in an HTI system or, alternately, the component in a computer that performs calculations on data.

certification — The process of attesting to the qualification or competence of a person to perform certain services.

cipher lock — A door lock that opens only when a numeric code is entered on a keypad mounted near it. The code can also be placed on a memory card that is swiped through a reader to open the lock.

CompTIA — Computer Technology Industry Association, a global information technology (IT) trade association with more than 13,000 members in 89 countries. It works to advance the IT industry, promote IT public policy, and develop standards for training of professionals in the industry.

control device — Any device which initiates a process, directs equipment to perform a function, or responds in a preset manner to remote commands.

credential — A written certification that an individual has specified qualifications, abilities, or expertise.

decoder — A device for rendering data received in an encrypted form into a form that can be used by a computer or displayed by a video or audio system.

detector — A sensor that is designed to react to a certain event such as pressure, motion, heat, or light.

digital data — Data in the form used by computers and that consists only of the binary numeric digits 1 and 0. Nearly all forms of information can be rendered into digital form for processing or transmission and then rendered back into a form that can be displayed or understood by people.

Digital Subscriber Line (DSL) — A telephone line used for high-speed digital data and voice transmission and always available for the subscribing user's exclusive use.

distribution — The process of transmitting data throughout a system so that it is available to all components.

downlink — Digital data being transferred into a ground-based system from a satellite.

firewall — Hardware or software that controls the data entering or leaving a computer system. Used to maintain the security of the system.

Heating, ventilation, and air conditioning systems (HVAC) — Heating, ventilation, and air conditioning; a specialized field in the construction industry that installs and maintains the equipment and infrastructure of these systems.

home security system — An HTI subsystem of hardware and software designed to prevent unauthorized persons from entering a home or yard, using any of its data systems, or removing anything from them.

Home Technology Integration (HTI) — A connected home environment in which a computer system manages data and controls subsystems in the home.

home theater — An HTI subsystem for displaying television programs and recorded video programs. Similar to a home entertainment center, but usually specialized primarily for video viewing.

infrastructure — Any of the wiring, conduit, connectors, wireless hubs, switches, routers, and other hardware that enable the subsystems of an HTI system to communicate with one another and the outside world.

Internet Home Alliance (IHA) — An industry group whose objective is to develop the market for home technologies that require a broadband or persistent connection to the Internet.

keyboard — An alphanumeric data input device for a computer. It may contain additional keys that input specific commands or run sequences of data.

keypad — A numeric data input device for a computer or other hardware in an HTI system.

microphone — A device that converts sound waves into digital or analog data, which can be transmitted over distances and replayed or stored.

modem — An electronic device that converts digital data into a form that can be sent over a telephone line. Modems are the most common method of connecting a home computer to the Internet through a telephone line to a service provider.

monitor — A device for displaying data in text or picture (graphic) form. Also, a sensor that monitors one or more environmental conditions.

network — A group of computers, information sources, and peripheral devices connected by cable or radio so that they can share data and communicate with one another.

numeric code — A group of digits that serves as a password and must be entered into a cipher lock to open it.

password — A group of letters and numbers that must be entered into a security system in a home or into a computer system to gain access.

peripheral — Any input or output device connected to a computer that sends or receives data from the processor. Examples of input peripherals are floppy drives and microphones. Examples of output peripherals are printers and control devices.

program — A set of digital instructions that a computer executes in sequence to perform functions.

relay — A remotely operated electric switch that is controlled by a small current, but that controls a large current flow.

remote-control system — A combination of hardware and software that allows a person or a computer to direct the operation of a subsystem from a distance.

satellite transmission — Digital television signals beamed to receivers on the ground from a stationary satellite orbiting Earth in space.

scan — Survey of a data set, space, or sensors to determine if particular data or a set of conditions is present.

sensor — Any device that detects or measures human activity or environmental conditions and sends data regarding its measurement to a processor.

service provider — A company that provides data transmission service or other utility services to consumers.

storage device — A computer peripheral that can record and retrieve digital data on magnetic or other media.

subsystem — A group of hardware components and software set up to perform a specific task or function within a larger, multiple-function HTI system.

switch — An electrical device that completes (turns on) or opens (turns off) a circuit.

telecommunications — The general name for all communication and data functions carried on telephone lines or radio signals, or performed by telephone hardware and software.

translator — Another term for a decoder that converts encrypted data into a readable form for display by an output device.

transmission — The movement of data from one location to another. The data can be digital or analog and the locations close together or distant.

video — A digital display of pictures such as television programs or computer screens.

virus — A self-propagating program that is sent to a computer, remains resident in its storage, and can interfere with or disable its operation.

wireless technology — Any of several methods of communicating digital data by means of radio waves without the need for any wires connecting the sender and receiver.

World Wide Web (WWW) — The global system of interconnected networks over which users can share data through the use of common protocols.

X10 — A data-transmitting technology that uses the existing wiring of a home or building as a carrier for its signals.

REVIEW QUESTIONS

1. What does the abbreviation HTI stand for?

2. What are the major components found in an HTI system?

3. What are some of the areas of home automation that can be addressed by an HTI system?

4. Which of the following would not be purchased by a consumer from a service provider, as discussed in this chapter?

   a. electric service

   b. gas service

   c. a computer

   d. a DSL

   e. a decoder

5. What groups of people can benefit particularly from HTI's automation features?

6. What are the six main areas of the home environment that HTI systems provide, manage, or control?

7. What is the function of a sensor?

8. What device is usually used to connect a home network to the Internet?

9. What is one limitation of wireless technology in a home environment?

10. What is one advantage of wireless technology in an HTI system installed in an existing home?

11. What is HVAC?

12. How can HTI reduce home utility costs?

13. What does a satellite television hookup require for each television set connected to it?

14. What is CompTIA, and what is its involvement in HTI?

15. Why is a central HTI processor usually better than independent processors in subsystems?

16. When installing infrastructure wiring, why is it usually better to install more than just the required capacity?

17. All of the following can be detected by a sensor except:

   a. heat

   b. smoke

   c. time

   d. motion

   e. pressure

18. What is a firewall in a computer system?

19. Can a computer virus reside in a sensor?

20. If the outside temperature dropped suddenly to freezing, what actions might a complete HTI system take in response?

HANDS-ON PROJECTS

Project 1-1: Research HTI Products on the Internet

In this project you find several sources of HTI hardware and locate specific items you want. Save the results of this project for future use. To complete the project you should have a computer with access to the Internet and a functioning Web browser. Be sure your research includes a visit to at least one of these sites: *www.smarthome.com/*, *www.homeauto.com/*, or *www.hometoys.com/*.

1. Open your Web browser and connect to the Internet.

2. Use your browser's search function or connect to another search engine that you prefer, and then do an Internet search for the phrase **home technology integration**.

3. Browse the results of your search, and find at least three companies that sell home technology integration products. Note each company's site so that you can return to it.

4. On each of the vendor sites you found, find a device that remotely turns a lamp or other electrical device on or off as directed by a remote control.

5. Print out the information for each device and compare the cost and features of each device. Determine which you would buy if you were installing your own HTI system.

6. Record the results of your research in your lab book or journal for future reference.

Project 1-2: Find Components for a Control System on the Internet

In this project you find what other components are required to make the control devices you found in Project 1-1 functional. You also determine what the total cost for these additional components is and which of the three original devices now represents the best buy. You may wish to save the results of this project for future use. To complete the project you need a computer with access to the Internet and a functioning Web browser.

1. Open your Web browser and connect to the Internet.

2. Return to each of the three sites you noted in Project 1-1. Find the items you priced to control an electrical appliance and determine what additional components are needed to make the device fully functional.

3. Make a list of the needed items for each device and their prices. Print out the information on the subsystem parts if possible.

4. Add up the subsystem prices for each of the three devices. Would you change your mind about which to buy for your own HTI system? Why or why not?

Project 1-3: Design a Whole-house Lighting Control System

One of the advantages of HTI is its ability to get multiple uses from many components. In this project you explore a Web site and design a full HTI light control subsystem. You may wish to save the results of this project for future use. To complete the project you should have a computer with access to the Internet and a functioning Web browser.

1. Open your Web browser and connect to the Internet.

2. Return to one of the three sites you noted in Project 1-1. Explore this site to find the components for a complete home lighting control subsystem. Print out information on each component and determine how they can connect together.

3. Also determine how the components can interface with the home lighting. Be sure you plan for the necessary central control station and the wiring or wireless technology needed to connect it with the control devices on the home's lights.

4. Price your system as fully as you can.

5. Estimate the number of hours of your labor that will be needed to install the system. Determine the cost of your labor at $20.00 per hour.

6. Add your materials and components cost to your labor cost to determine what the completed lighting control subsystem costs.

Project 1-4: Review the Requirements for Certification as an HTI+ Professional

In this project you will review the subjects that are covered in the examinations that you must pass to become an HTI+ Professional. To complete the project you need a computer with access to the Internet and a functioning Web browser.

1. Open your Web browser and connect to the Internet.

2. Go to the Web site **www.comptia.org/**.

3. From the home page, click the **I'm interested in** list box, and then click **CompTIA HTI+**.

4. On the HTI+ page, click **About HTI+ Exam** and **HTI+ Objectives** to learn about how you can become a certified HTI+ Professional after completing study of this book.

Project 1-5: Determine the Availability and Cost of Internet Service in Your Area

In this project you will determine the availability and cost of Internet service from providers in your area. To complete the project, you need a computer with access to the Internet and a functioning Web browser.

1. Using your browser's search engine, search for the phrase **"Internet service provider"**. You will probably receive more than a million responses.

2. Refine your search by adding the state and town where you live to the search. For example: **"Internet service provider" +Nebraska +Lincoln**. (Note that the syntax given may work on some search engines, but not on others, because each search engine has its own rules for how to phrase searches.)

3. Note several of the Internet service providers (ISPs) for your area. Try to find two nationwide providers who offer service throughout the country, and two local providers who only offer service in a smaller area.

4. Visit the Web sites of the ISPs you selected or contact them by telephone to determine whether they can connect to your home and what they charge for their service.

5. Compare the features offered by each service in relation to their cost. Determine which you think offers the best Internet service for your needs.

CASE PROJECTS

CASE PROJECTS

Case Project 1-1: Report on Benefits of HTI for a Physically Restricted Client

You work for High Tech Home Tech, Inc. as an HTI system designer and installer. A client calls you and requests information on what HTI can do for her home environment. She tells you that she lives in an apartment on the fourth floor that is accessed by elevator and stairway. The home has two entrances, but she must use the elevator because she uses a wheelchair for mobility. She has full use of her hands and upper body and has no sensory limitations. She prefers to live alone, but wants to have some additional safety and security as well as convenience added to her home. Write a brief report summarizing what HTI can do for this client's lifestyle. Divide your recommendations into categories that include safety devices, security devices, convenience devices, and entertainment systems.

2

HOME TECHNOLOGY NETWORK BASICS

After reading this chapter, you will be able to:

♦ Describe what a local area network (LAN) is and how it functions

♦ Describe the network architecture and data control mechanisms of Ethernet, token ring, wireless, and FDDI LANs

♦ Describe how data flows and is directed on the Internet by routers, switches, bridges, and hubs

♦ Identify the major components of a home network and describe how each of them functions

In the first chapter you learned what HTI is and about some of the data services, security, automation, and other benefits an integrated home network can provide. In this chapter, you learn what a **local area network (LAN)** is and how it functions. You also learn about the two basic types of network architecture, **Ethernet** and **token ring**, and how a LAN receives and sends information on the **Internet**. You will understand how a LAN connects to external information sources through the Internet and how internal information is transmitted within the LAN. Finally, you learn about the different hardware that can be connected as **nodes** in a LAN, some of the data services these devices provide, and how output devices, such as **monitors**, **flat panel screens**, and printers, work.

WHAT IS A LAN AND HOW DOES IT WORK?

A local area network (LAN) is a specifically designed configuration of computers and other devices, located within a confined area such as a home or office building, and connected by wires or radio waves that permit the devices to communicate with one another to share data and services. Computers and other devices connected on a LAN can send and receive information from one another without confusion. The network directs the communications passing through it and acts as a sort of electronic traffic cop to prevent collisions or mixing of data. The LAN can also be connected to the Internet and the World Wide Web, either through a direct cable connection or by a telephone link through a modem, so that workstations on the LAN have access to all the networks and sites linked to the global Web.

A LAN's connection to the Internet is sometimes accomplished by having one of the LAN's nodes connected as a node on a wide area network (WAN). A WAN is a network that extends over a larger geographic area than a LAN, and it is connected through one or more of its nodes directly to the Internet. Data from the LAN travels through its connecting node to the WAN and through the WAN's connecting nodes to the Internet. Data coming from the Internet first travels through the WAN and then to the LAN.

The OSI Model

The Open Systems Interconnect model (OSI model) is a standard means of describing a network operating system by defining it as a series of layers, each with specific input and output. The OSI model was developed by the International Standards Organization (ISO) and has seven layers that are numbered in order from the bottom layer (Layer 1) to the top layer (Layer 7). The names of the various layers, starting from the top layer, are as follows:

- *Layer 7*—Application layer (top layer), the layer in which applications on a network node (computer) access network services such as file transfers, electronic mail, and database access.

- *Layer 6*—Presentation layer, the layer that translates application layer data to an intermediate form that provides security, encryption, and compression for the data.

- *Layer 5*—Session layer, the layer that establishes and controls data communication between applications operating on two different computers, regulating when each can send data and how much.

- *Layer 4*—Transport layer, the layer that divides long communications into smaller data packages, handles error recognition and correction, and acknowledges the correct receipt of data.

- *Layer 3*—Network layer, the layer that addresses data messages, translates logical addresses into actual physical addresses, and routes data to addresses on the network.

    ■ *Layer 2*—Data Link layer, the layer that packages bits of data from the Physical layer into frames (logical, structured data packets), transfers them from one computer to another, and receives acknowledgement from the addressed computer.

    ■ *Layer 1*—Physical layer (bottom layer), the layer that transmits bits (binary digits) from one computer to another and regulates the transmission stream over a medium (wire, fiber optics, or radio waves).

All parts of network operating systems discussed in this book function in one of these seven layers. If you can visualize the layer in which an operating system functions, you will have a clearer understanding of how it relates to the rest of the network operating system.

Data Packets

To maintain order and avoid loss of data through misdirection or collisions, all data that moves on a LAN is sent in **packets**. A packet consists of a small piece of data with information about what type of data it is, where it came from, and where it's going, attached at the beginning of the packet as a **header** and at the end of the packet as a **trailer**. Figure 2-1 shows the structure of a typical Ethernet data packet with header and trailer.

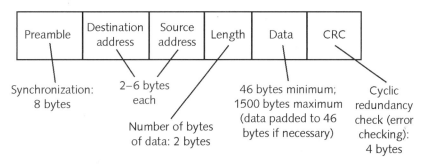

Figure 2-1   Diagram of a typical Ethernet data packet

Each individual packet contains a small amount of data. The maximum amount of data a packet can contain depends on the type of network. Each network type has a **protocol**, a set of formatting guidelines and rules that allows information sent by one computer or device to be accurately received and understood by another on the network. The protocol specifies how the data being sent is divided into packets of suitable size to travel on the network and adds the identifying information to each packet before it is transmitted on the network. Some protocols also determine if each data packet is correctly sent and then received by the destination device. If necessary, the protocol can resend a data packet that failed to arrive or arrived corrupted.

Sending the information on the network in packets provides several critical advantages. First among these advantages is that the information in each packet can easily be checked to be certain none is missing or corrupted. The receiving computer's **network interface card (NIC)**, the device that connects the computer to the network, uses a system called **checksum** to verify the integrity of data it receives. Checksum compares a value that is sent with the packet to a value calculated by the NIC using the data received in the packet.

If the two values match, the data is deemed to be uncorrupted. If they don't match, the packet is assumed to be corrupted and must be sent again. Only the corrupted packet must be repeated, however, not the entire data stream. Using packets minimizes the amount of data that goes astray or is corrupted and must be repeated.

A second advantage to data packets is that sending information in these small pieces permits more data to quickly travel from many sources to many destinations than would be possible if the data were sent in large blocks. A large data block would fill the network's wires, preventing any other traffic from moving until the entire block was transmitted, checked, and its receipt confirmed. Data packets are small and are quickly delivered, checked, and confirmed to the sender. As soon as one packet is off the network, another can move onto it, either from the same sender to the same receiver or over a different network path. Data packets can be kept constantly moving on the network and the aggregate of data they can contain is greater than what could be moved and verified in larger blocks.

The third advantage is that data packets make the information flow in a network easier to control by means of **routers**, **switches**, **bridges**, and other devices. Small packets are easily and quickly directed and they don't tie up the network for long at any critical point. Unlike large data blocks, packets can travel by multiple routes and be reassembled into their correct order after arriving at their destination. A delay or malfunction on one part of the network doesn't slow packets down much: they are simply directed to another open route to their destinations.

Each computer on a LAN must have a protocol installed on it for the computer to communicate with other computers on the network. **Network BIOS Extended User Interface (NetBEUI)** was until recently the most commonly used protocol. It is a proprietary Microsoft suite that can be run only on computers using a Microsoft Windows operating system. NetBEUI cannot be used with computers running Linux or with Macintosh computers. NetBEUI also cannot be used as an Internet protocol because it is not **routable**. TCP/IP protocol, which is routable and therefore can be used on the Internet, has now replaced NetBEUI as the dominant protocol for LANs.

Network Architecture

A network's architecture consists of the design of its wiring or radio wave connections, the configuration of its other physical components, its software (programming), and the protocols by which it operates. All of these parts must be tightly organized into a physical structure with consistent operating methodology to establish a smoothly working communication system among all the devices connected to the network.

Each device connected to a network is called a node or **host**. A node can be a computer, a router, a printer, a sensing device, a video camera, a controller, or any number of other electronic devices. A host is always a computer.

The four common types of network architecture used today are Ethernet, token ring, FDDI, and wireless. Each has advantages and limitations, which you'll examine in some detail in the following sections.

Ethernet

Ethernet is the most popular form of LAN in use today. Three types of Ethernet architecture are available now. Each is distinguished primarily by the speed at which it operates. Each version can be set up using different types of wire or cable, but the different speeds of the versions and the different conditions in which they operate may dictate what type of connecting wires are used. Remember that most current Ethernet installations use shielded twisted-pair cable, unshielded twisted-pair cable, or **fiber-optic cable**. Older Ethernet installations used either 50-ohm RG58/U coaxial cable, also known as thin Ethernet, or 50-ohm RG8/U coaxial, known as thick Ethernet, but these are both obsolete now.

10-Mbps Ethernet operates at a speed of 10 megabits per second (Mbps) of data. It was the first Ethernet version and was developed by the Xerox Corporation in the 1970s. It later became known as Ethernet IEEE 802.3. There are several variations of the 10-Mbps Ethernet, distinguished mainly by the type of cable and connectors used.

100-Mbps Ethernet or Fast Ethernet operates at a speed of 100 Mbps. It can also handle data at 10 Mbps, and this feature allows devices running at the slower speed to operate on the same network along with those operating at 100 Mbps. As with 10-Mbps Ethernet, there are variations of 100-Mbps Ethernet distinguished by the cable used to create them. 100BaseTX, for example, uses two pairs of wire in a CAT5 twisted-pair cable that contains eight wires, while 100BaseFX uses fiber-optic cable.

1000-Mbps Ethernet or Gigabit Ethernet operates at a speed of 1000 Mbps (1 gigabit per second). It is the newest version of Ethernet and is intended for large, high-speed LANs and heavy-traffic **server** connections. Few, if any, home networks require Gigabit Ethernet.

Ethernets can be physically arranged in either of two configurations: a **bus topology** or a **star topology**. These configurations refer to how the nodes (devices) are connected into the Ethernet. In a bus configuration, each node is connected to the next by a direct line so that the Ethernet forms a continuous line. There is no central point in this arrangement. Each node is simply connected to the next one on either side of it. When the end of the line is reached and there are no further nodes to be connected, the Ethernet is closed off with a **terminator** device specific to the infrastructure used, i.e. some use 50 ohm and some 92 ohm. See Figure 2-2 for a diagram showing both a bus and star design Ethernet configurations. Note that the bus design connects nodes directly while the star design uses a **hub**.

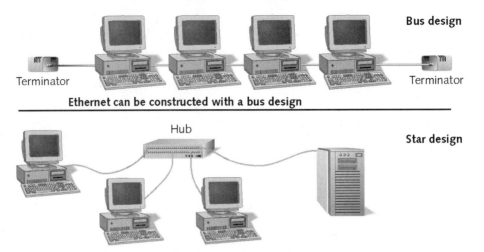

Figure 2-2   Bus and star design Ethernet configurations

In a star configuration, the Ethernet is set up with each node connected to a central hub, which serves as a distribution device. It passes all the information packets it receives from any device to every other device on the network. The hub doesn't use or even evaluate any data; it simply broadcasts all data it receives to every other device on the network.

A star Ethernet may be slower than a bus Ethernet, especially if there are many nodes on the network. This happens because the hub generates a lot of data traffic that isn't used. Because it replicates all the data it receives from any source and sends it to every node, the amount of data being sent increases for every node added to the network, even though most of the data sent to each node is not intended for that node and is discarded on arrival. As the amount of data sent increases, more and more data packets from different nodes competing for **bandwidth** on the LAN collide with one another. The network detects these collisions and resends the data packets involved, but the collisions and replication of data transmissions slow down the network.

In a bus Ethernet, data is sent on the network line in both directions from the source node. The data passes from one node to the next until it reaches the terminator at the end of the network. The terminator simply cancels the data signal, discarding the data so that it can't echo back on the network line and head back to the node it just came from. All information on the network passes through each node, but only once. There is no replication and broadcasting of data as in a star configuration. Each node determines if data it receives is addressed to it. If it is, the data is read and receipt is confirmed. If it isn't, the packet is passed on to the next node.

A large LAN might use a combination star and bus design with nodes connected to several hubs and the hubs connected in a bus configuration. This design is useful for constructing large networks with a minimum of wiring, but because all the hubs must still broadcast their data to the nodes, it tends to slow down as the amount of data flowing in it multiplies. Figure 2-3 shows a combined bus and star Ethernet design.

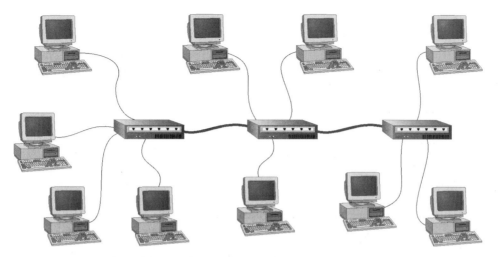

Figure 2-3   Combined bus and star Ethernet design

Thin Ethernet designs, wired with RG58/U coaxial cable, are limited by the attenuation (weakening due to distance traveled) of signals in the cable and can only support network segments up to 185 meters long. Thick Ethernet designs, wired with 50-ohm RG8/U coaxial, are more resistant to attenuation and can span up to 500 meters. Neither of these are being widely used now because more advanced cable types can span distances up to 1,000 meters with less attenuation of network signals.

Ethernet Data Control

Ethernet networks are passive designs, which means that they do not take any active role in controlling the movement of data on them. They just provide a means for data to move along the connecting wire. The nodes that receive and send the data must have some arrangement for controlling the flow. The protocol on an Ethernet causes any computer or device that is trying to send data on the network to first listen for silence. If the computer hears nothing on the network, it transmits a data packet, listening as it does so for any other data being transmitted at the same time. If it hears anything other than its own transmission, it stops transmitting and sends a collision signal indicating that two computers have attempted to send data at the same time. Each computer then waits a short, but random, amount of time and sends its data again.

This protocol ensures that two data packets are not sent at the same time, or if they are, that transmission is stopped and they are sent again. This type of network technology is called a contention-based system because each node on the network must contend for space on the network. This arrangement is known as the **Carrier Sense Multiple Access/Collision Detection (CSMA/CD)** method of data transmission. Another, but somewhat slower, method is called **Carrier Sense Multiple Access/Collision Avoidance (CSMA/CA)**, in which each node signals its intention to transmit data and waits to see if the line is clear before doing so. The AppleTalk protocol, used on networks with Macintosh computer nodes, uses CSMA/CA.

Data signals traveling in a wire get weaker over distance. If an Ethernet extends over a certain distance (which varies according to its structure and the type of cable used), amplification of the data signals on the network is required. This is done with an amplifier **repeater** placed as a node on the network that amplifies the signal, including any noise or static it may have acquired, and sends it on. Another type of repeater, called a signal-regenerating repeater, can also be used. This type of repeater reads the incoming signal and creates a full-strength duplicate of it, which it then sends on the network in place of the original weakened signal. A signal-regenerating repeater not only strengthens the signal, but also eliminates noise and static that may have come into it. Figure 2-4 shows how a repeater is placed in a network to strengthen and clarify the signal.

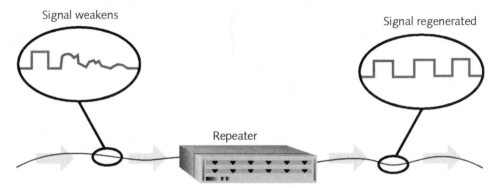

Figure 2-4   A repeater strengthens network signals

A hub in a star Ethernet design can, if so designed, also act as a signal-regenerating repeater, which is sometimes a reason to use this configuration even though it's slower than the bus design. Even when they use repeaters, Ethernet LANs must be limited in size because the Ethernet protocol limits the length of time a signal can take on the network to reach its destination. Networks that traverse long distances and contain many repeaters have problems with this limitation because each repeater that the signal traverses adds a small amount of time to the transmission.

An Ethernet protocol rule known as the 5-4-3 rule requires that between any two nodes on a bus topology there can be no more than five segments, connected through four repeaters, and only three of the segments can include user nodes. Another rule, known as the 5-4 rule, limits the length of cable and number of hubs that can separate nodes on a 10-Mbps Ethernet. Somewhat different rules apply to Fast Ethernet and 10-Mbps Ethernet configurations wired with newer cable types. Only very large home LANs will approach these limitations on overall size and cable length, but you should be aware that they exist and examine them in more detail when working on a LAN that extends over more than a 500-foot-diameter circle.

Token Ring

Token ring LAN technology was developed by IBM Corporation. It operates at slower speeds than Ethernet, but it's physically arranged in a star topology, one of the designs also used by Ethernet. Token ring LANs are so named because their protocol for data control uses a token, a small packet of data, to determine which node on the network can transmit data, and because all data actually travels in a circle or ring on the network.

In a token ring star design, each node is connected to a central device, referred to as a **Multistation Access Unit (MAU)**, by two wires. The token packet is always present somewhere on the network. It travels from the MAU up one connecting wire to a node and back to the MAU through the other wire, then up one wire to the next node and back through the other. It passes through the MAU after each node and, after passing through all of them and returning to the MAU, it travels back to its starting point at the other end of the MAU through the token ring's main ring cable. The token thus travels in a circle or ring on the network even though the nodes are arranged as a star. For this reason, the token ring topology is sometimes called a star ring. Figure 2-5 shows how a token ring network connects nodes through a MAU.

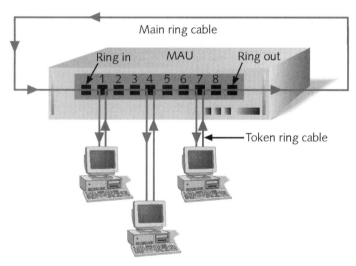

Figure 2-5   A token ring network

Data control in the token ring is maintained by the simple rule that data can travel on the network only if it's attached to the one token on the network. If the token is busy (already has data attached to it) when it reaches a node, the node cannot attach more data, and the token moves on until it reaches the node for which its attached information is intended. The receiving node reads the information from the token and attaches a code confirming receipt of the data. The token then travels back to the sending node, which reads the confirmation code and detaches the data it sent from the token, leaving it free for new data to be attached. If the node has more data it wants to communicate, it attaches that data to the token and sends it on. If not, the token moves to the next node that does have information to communicate, which attaches it to the token and sends it on. In this manner, the token continually circles the ring picking up and dropping off information as requested by the various nodes. The token method of data control is also used by some other LAN designs.

The MAU in a token ring can also serve as a repeater to boost and clean up the data signal if necessary. Token ring networks operate at a speed of either 4 Mbps or 16 Mbps. A token ring can theoretically have any number of nodes, but because data can travel only with the token, the efficiency of the network declines when the token must pass through many nodes and through the MAU many times for each packet of data communicated.

Token rings use either UTP or **STP cable** that contains four wires (two twisted pairs) to connect the nodes with the MAU and for the main ring cable. In Chapter 4, wiring and connectors are discussed in detail.

Wireless Networks

As their name suggests, wireless LANs don't use wires to connect the nodes of the network. The nodes are not physically connected at all to one another or to a central device. They communicate with an **access point** or **wireless hub** using a wireless network interface card (NIC) which includes a transceiver and an antenna. The **wireless NIC** allows the node to communicate over relatively short distances using radio waves, which it sends to the nearest hub and receives from the hub. Figure 2-6 shows how nodes on a wireless LAN connect by radio waves to access points or hubs that are wired to the network.

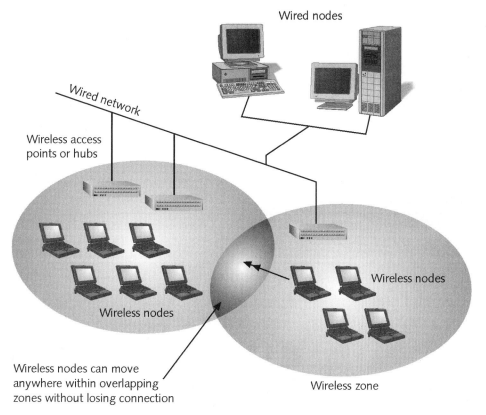

Wired nodes

Wired network

Wireless access
points or hubs

Wireless nodes

Wireless nodes

Wireless nodes

Wireless nodes can move
anywhere within overlapping
zones without losing connection

Wireless zone

Figure 2-6   A wireless network design

Wireless connections can be made from a node to a hub through walls and other obstructions because radio waves pass through solid obstructions fairly easily. This ability makes wireless LANs very useful and cost effective in already finished buildings where retrofitting wiring is both difficult and expensive. It's also an advantage where hardwiring a network may be impossible, such as on the beach at a summer home, or to a boat tied up at a private dock. Wireless LANs are limited, however, both by the low transmitting power of their NICs and hubs and by the fact that dense metals, especially ferrous metals, as well as heavy layers of concrete, stone, brick, or dirt, absorb radio waves. These factors restrict the distance over which a wireless network can be extended and may require more hubs than anticipated to obtain full-area coverage.

Hubs or access points must be placed so that the wireless NICs of nodes can access at least one of them from any location within the LAN's defined area. Wireless networked nodes communicate with one another only through a hub rather than directly node to node as in a bus Ethernet. Hubs must be wired together or connected by wireless technology into a network that allows all hubs to communicate with one another and transmit the data they receive from their wireless nodes. A wireless LAN is thus not entirely free of wired connections. It is usually connected to a cable network by its hubs, which constitute nodes on a wired LAN.

Wireless LANs don't have tokens and their NICs have no way to detect whether collisions of data have occurred in the transmission process. For this reason, wireless LANs must use collision avoidance technology (CSMA/CA) in communicating from node to hub and back. Collision avoidance communication requires confirmation from the recipient that each packet of data was received accurately. This process slows down communication and makes wireless LANs less efficient, especially when multiple nodes are trying to communicate on them simultaneously. Figure 2-7 illustrates why wireless LANs are easily accessible to hackers and require strong internal security to protect their data.

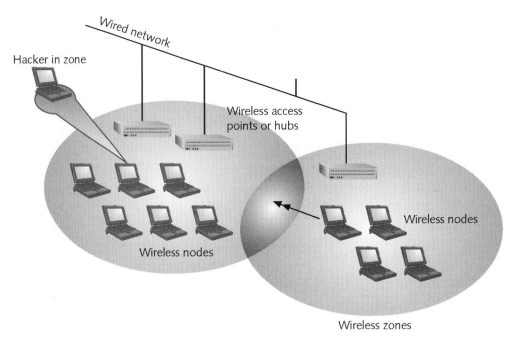

Figure 2-7   Wireless LANs are open to unauthorized users

Wireless LANs are inherently less secure than hardwired LANs because data sent on a wireless LAN is broadcast as radio waves, which can be received by anyone tuned to the proper frequency and close enough to pick up its transmissions. The broadcast range of a wireless LAN is normally short, but it invariably extends out into some public space where unauthorized receivers can eavesdrop on the data being sent. Because all wireless network communication goes through the hubs, a single intercept receiver, properly placed, can eavesdrop on all the traffic traveling on the LAN. A laptop computer in a car parked at curbside near a home with a wireless LAN can almost always pick up the wireless transmissions. For this reason, wireless LANs require strong internal security to prevent their data from being read by unauthorized users who may receive it.

Fiber-optic Cable Networks

Fiber Distributed Data Interface (FDDI) networks are large, fast networks that almost exclusively use fiber-optic cable to communicate data at speeds of 100 Mbps. Because of their high speed and the expense of their components, they're almost never used in home network installations. Most FDDI networks are installed in large commercial buildings and are sometimes used as a backbone to join smaller LANs into an integrated system.

RECEIVING AND SENDING EXTERNAL INFORMATION ON A LAN

Outside information comes into a home network from the Internet. Information that originates in the LAN can also be sent out to other locations on the Internet. This outside data exchange is in addition to the data being sent and received among the various nodes on the LAN.

Communication between networks requires that they use a common protocol and that each computer or other device attached to each network have a unique address. The most common protocol currently used on LANs and to connect networks is **Transmission Control Protocol/Internet Protocol (TCP/IP)**. This protocol is used throughout the Internet. TCP/IP addresses each node on a LAN by a unique Internet Protocol address (**IP address**), which consists of four numbers separated by periods. Each of the four numbers in an IP address must consist of no more than eight bits of binary data, which means that each number cannot be higher than 256. This keeps the addresses short and standardized for consistency.

How Data Travels on the Internet

The Internet is really a vast collection of WANs, all interconnected to one another and able to communicate with each other. Data going from a node on a home LAN to a node on a distant network reaches its destination by traveling through the communication lines of other networks located between the originating point and the destination. There are usually many possible routes the data can take. Some are long and require more time for the data to arrive than others, but since all the WANs that make up the entire Internet are connected, it is possible to send data from a node on any LAN to a node on any other, provided the IP address of the destination is known and the data is directed toward that address by the Internet's data management devices, or routers. Figure 2-8 shows the Internet as a web of interconnected, but independent, networks over which data travels from source to destination by various routes.

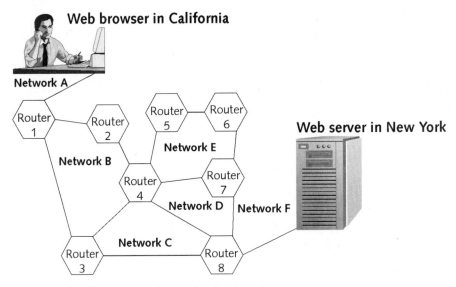

Figure 2-8   The Internet is a web of networks

The Role of Routers

Routers are the hardware units responsible for directing data traffic between interconnected networks. They function as intelligent switches that have the ability to make decisions based on preprogrammed instructions and implement those decisions by directing electronic data along specific routes. They read the IP addresses of each packet of data that comes to them, decide which is the most efficient path for the data to take to reach its destination quickly, and then switch the data packet onto that path.

A router is connected as a node in a network, but there is a significant difference between a router and any other node on a network. The router is always connected as a node in at least two networks and it may be connected as a node in many networks. For each network that it is connected to, the router has a separate, unique IP address. Data from a node on network A to which a router is connected can be routed directly to any node on network B, to which the router is also connected, simply by switching the data packet from one network to the other so that the addressee node can receive it on its network.

For data that is addressed to a node on a network to which the router is not directly connected, the router can only transmit the data to the remote network if the data packet was produced using a routable protocol such as TCP/IP or **Internetwork Packet Exchange/Sequenced Packet Exchange(IPX/SPX)**, which is the protocol used by Novell NetWare networks. The protocol used to produce data packets transmitted between nodes of a single LAN, NetBEUI, is not a routable protocol and data packets produced using it cannot pass outside the LAN through a router. This is a useful feature of NetBEUI, as you'll see when other LAN components are discussed later in this chapter.

When a router receives a routable data packet, it reads the IP address on the packet and decides which of the other networks that it is connected to should receive that data packet. It then switches the data packet to that network where another router receives it, reads the

IP address, and passes it on to another network closer to its destination. The process continues, perhaps through many networks and routers, until the data packet reaches the LAN on which its addressee node resides.

A router uses the IP address of a data packet and conditions existing on the network to determine how to route the packet. The route it chooses may not be the shortest, but is probably the fastest at the time the packet is transmitted. As routers send data packets, they "learn" the best (fastest) routes and remember them. If the first data packet sent to an IP address is slow to arrive, the next one to that address may be sent by a different route. When the router finds an efficient path to an address (not necessarily the absolute fastest route, but an acceptable one), it uses that path whenever data is sent to the same IP address, unless other conditions on the Internet slow the data down and require the router to seek a new route.

Connecting a Home Network to the Internet

Most home networks connect to the Internet through an **Internet service provider (ISP)** by means of an ordinary telephone line using a modem. The modem converts the binary **digital data** of a computer into **analog data** (frequency modulation or FM) signals that can be communicated over a telephone line.

The amount of data that can travel over a communication line or wireless connection in a given length of time is called bandwidth or **line speed**. The greater the bandwidth the faster communication can be because more data can move through the communication line in a given time. For digital data transmission, bandwidth is measured by the number of data bits per second (bps) that can be communicated over a given line or connection. One thousand bits per second is noted as one kilobit (Kbps), and one million bits per second is noted as one megabit (Mbps).

Home network Internet connections can have varying bandwidths, depending on the service provided by the ISP and the physical connection. It is important to remember that the useable bandwidth of any communication line is determined by the smallest link in the line. If the home's central computer is connected to an ISP via a 384 Kbps DSL, but the modem in the computer has a capacity of 128 Kbps, then the connection has a maximum capacity of 128 Kbps, the smallest link in the system.

The most common methods of connecting a home LAN to an ISP are the following:

- The slowest, but least expensive, Internet connection to an ISP is affectionately known as **Plain Old Telephone Service (POTS)**. This is the most common method of home connection and uses a dial-up system each time the connection to the ISP is made over the telephone line. The connection is not continuous, and when the line is not connected to an ISP, it can be used for regular telephone service, or any other telecommunications function. Data speed on a regular telephone line is a maximum of 56 Kbps.

- **Integrated Services Digital Network (ISDN)** technology also uses a telephone line to transmit data, but unlike POTS, the data is not converted to analog form. An ISDN line is digital and consists of two phone circuits, both carried on one pair of wires along with a slower, third circuit used for control signals. Each data circuit can transmit data at up to 64 Kbps and the two circuits can be combined to move data at a speed of 128 Kbps. This configuration of an ISDN line is known as the Basic Rate Interface (BRI) and is intended for home and small-business users. Another higher-cost ISDN level of service is called Primary Service Interface and is intended for larger users. It has 23 data channels and a control channel.

- A **Digital Subscriber Line (DSL)** is a high-speed data and voice transmission line that still uses telephone wires for data transmission, but carries the digital data at frequencies well above those used for voice transmission. This makes possible the transmission of voice and digital data on the same line at the same time. The regular voice telephone line must be dialed for each use, but the DSL part of the line is always connected to the computer. A DSL can transmit data at speeds up to 1.5 Mbps in both directions, or it can be set up as an asymmetric line (ADSL), which can transmit up to 640 Kbps upstream (to the ISP) and 7.1 Mbps downstream (from the ISP).

- A **cable modem** connects to the cable television line that is already installed or available in most homes. With a cable modem, digital data is converted to analog signals and placed on the cable at the same time as the incoming television signal. Incoming analog data signals are converted to digital for the computer by the modem. The data frequencies differ from the television signal frequencies, and the two signals do not interfere with one another on the cable. Depending on the individual configuration, a cable modem can transmit data at speeds from 500 Kbps up to 5 Mbps.

- A **satellite link** Internet connection to an ISP is now available nationwide. It is especially attractive in rural areas where telephone-based services may be limited and cable is sometimes not available. A satellite communication link uses a dish similar to a satellite television dish mounted on the home to communicate with a stationary satellite in orbit. The home's central computer is connected to the dish antenna. Incoming Internet data travels from the ISP to the satellite in orbit, then down to the home-mounted dish and into the central computer of the home LAN. The speed of the connection varies according to the ISP, but can go up to 1.5 Mbps. The uplink connection from the LAN to the ISP is usually by a telephone line/modem connection and is not as fast as the satellite downlink. A digital radio signal from the LAN up to the satellite, which in turn sends the signal to the ISP is also available, but at a much higher cost than the telephone connection, which is usually adequate for sent data. Figure 2-9 illustrates how a satellite ISP sends data at high speed to home LANs via a stationary satellite and receives data from the LAN over a slower telephone/modem line.

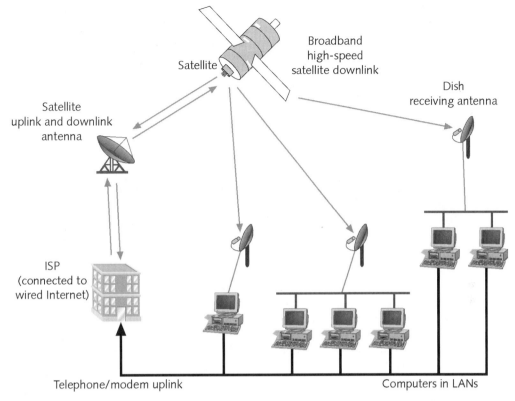

Figure 2-9   Satellite ISP configuration

- Wireless access using radio signals, infrared transmission, or beamed signals is possible in many areas, but hasn't proved very popular for two principle reasons. First, it is usually more expensive to install and use than other readily available technologies. Second, it is often subject to interference from other radio signal sources such as cell phones, radio transmitters, pagers, electric grids, large motors, and other devices. Wireless networks may themselves interfere with some devices such as pacemakers, aircraft control systems, and other sensitive electronic equipment. A wireless Internet connection works well for a LAN where the required range of transmission is short (100 yards or less), but for more distant Internet connections through an ISP, wireless has not yet proved as economical or efficient as other methods.

Table 2-1 compares a number of communication bandwidth technologies, their common uses, and their speeds.

Table 2-1 Bandwidth technologies

Technology	Maximum Throughput Speed	Common Uses
POTS	Up to 56 Kbps	Home and small-business access to an ISP using a modem
ISDN	64 Kbps to 128 Kbps	Medium-level home and business access to an ISP
ISDN Digital Subscriber Line (IDSL)	128 Kbps	Home and business access to an ISP
DSL Lite or G.Lite	Up to 384 Kbps upstream; up to 6 Mbps downstream	Less-expensive version of DSL for home and business
Asymmetric Digital Subscriber Line (ADSL)	640 Kbps upstream; up to 6.1 Mbps downstream	Home/business access with most bandwidth from ISP to user
Symmetric DSL (SDSL)	1.544 Mbps	Home/business access; equal bandwidth in both directions
High-bit-rate DSL (HDSL)	Up to 3 Mbps	Home/business access; equal bandwidth in both directions
Cable modem	512 Kbps to 5 Mbps	Home/business access to ISP
802.11b wireless	5.5 Mbps or 11 Mbps	Home/business LANs
802.11a wireless	Up to 54 Mbps	Home/business access, in development
Ethernet	10 Mbps or 100 Mbps	Home/business LANs
Token ring	4 Mbps or 16 Mbps	Home/business LANs
T1	1.544 Mbps	Business access to an ISP
FDDI	100 Mbps	Network backbones

Transmitting Internal Information on a LAN

Each node on a LAN can communicate with all the other nodes on the network. Depending on the LAN's architecture, each node may "talk" directly to another node (as in a bus Ethernet) or through a hub or intermediate device (as in a star Ethernet).

Every node has access to information stored on hard drives and other storage devices contained in each computer. This access may be limited by password protection or other security measures, but if it isn't, then any node on the LAN can search the other nodes for information and retrieve the information off of any storage device in any computer on the LAN. A node can also receive information from sensors and other devices that are connected to the LAN and programmed to send their data on it.

In the same manner, any node can send information over the LAN to be stored on any storage device available on the system, or to any output device (printer, display monitor, etc.) that is connected to the LAN. A node can also send operating instructions and programs to control devices instructing them to take certain actions or perform certain functions.

Making all the information stored on every node of a LAN available to every other node isn't always desirable. Control over which nodes have access, how much access they have, and which particular users of a node have that access is the responsibility of the LAN's administrator. This person determines each node's access and function using network management software installed on the LANs and programmed to send data to a central computer.

The network administrator also needs to control access to the LAN from the outside. This security control permits the administrator to prevent certain types or categories of information from reaching any node on the LAN by blocking it from entering the system. It also prevents unauthorized users outside the LAN from retrieving information stored on nodes in the LAN.

A LAN is usually insulated and partially isolated from the Internet to which it is connected by means of a **firewall**. This is a software program (sometimes augmented by hardware devices) that controls information passing in either direction: from the Internet onto the LAN or from the LAN onto the Internet. A firewall can be set up to block all information from some IP addresses, block information containing certain key words, require a password before allowing certain information to pass, or perform a variety of other restrictions. A firewall can also filter out viruses and data requests from unauthorized or unknown users. It can also prevent some or all data being sent from the LAN to any outside user.

Major Hardware Components of a Home Network

A home LAN can have any number of nodes connected to it using one of the designs discussed. These nodes can consist of several types of hardware devices, each with a separate function or set of functions to perform in the system. In this section you'll examine pieces of hardware likely to be found in a home network.

Computers

The heart of a home network is the central computer. This computer probably functions as a workstation and is multitasked to perform many other functions on the home network. In most designs the central computer is also the access point for the home network's Internet connection, regardless of the type of connection used. The central computer is also a node on the home network and as such, is able to communicate with other network nodes. Data coming into the home network from the Internet, which is addressed to other computers on the home network, is sent to them via the network from the central computer.

The central computer's keyboard, mouse, microphone, and other input devices are set up to function as with any workstation, but additional software may permit the central computer to take control of other computers and devices on the network, as well as use its input devices to function as if they were attached directly to the controlled device. The same is true for some output devices such as a monitor, disk drive, or speakers: all can be programmed to function as if attached to another controlled device on the network.

The central computer may have a number of other tasks assigned to it in addition to its workstation and Internet data transmission functions. The central computer can direct the operation of other subsystems on the network including the home security system, the utility control system and the appliance control system, among others. Any of these functions may also be assigned to other workstations on the network.

Besides the central computer, a home network can include any number of other computers, either used as general workstations or having specialized functions. Some of these computers may have their own input and output devices, which function only for the computer to which they're attached. Others may receive data only from other devices on the network and output data only to other nodes on the network, which will be received and acted upon by other nodes. One or more of these additional computers may be programmed to function in the same manner as the central computer, either because of its convenient location in the system or to serve as a backup in case of a system failure in the central computer.

Monitors

A monitor is always connected to a computer, and the video display controller in the computer drives its display. The computer can be programmed to display on its monitor the data sent from any node on the network, including other computers, sensors, or control devices. Because a monitor lacks data-processing capability and can only display video data as directed by a video controller card in the computer, a monitor is never connected to a network as a separate node.

Most monitors are **cathode ray tubes (CRTs)**, which display images on the flat front face of a glass cathode tube. This display is created by a beam of electrons shooting from the back of the cathode tube toward its front screen face. Plates on the top, bottom, and sides of the tube control the direction of the beam and direct it to continuously "paint" lines from left to right, top to bottom, across the screen. A grid placed in front of the filaments that generate the electron beam controls the intensity and color of the beam as it paints an electron stream across each line on the screen. Phosphor dots on the inside face of the screen light up when struck by the beam and produce dots of color on the display face. These dots of color are visible on the outside of the tube. The beam's color is controlled by the grid and can cause any combination of red, green, and blue phosphors on the screen to light at the appropriate level to produce the desired color for that area of the screen image. Figure 2-10 shows how a cathode ray tube (CRT) monitor works.

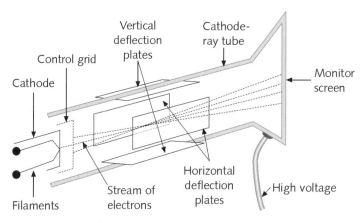

Figure 2-10   The operation of a cathode ray tube (CRT)

Monitors come in many sizes, from 8-inch screens (screen size is always measured diagonally from one upper corner to the opposite lower corner) to 24-inch screens for computers and up to 42 inches for television displays. Screen size measures the actual surface of the screen. The image displayed on the screen is usually about two inches smaller than the measured size of the screen.

The **refresh rate** or **scan rate** is the number of times per second that the electron beam in the tube repaints the entire screen. The higher the refresh rate, the less flicker is apparent in the screen display and the more steady it appears to the viewer. Most monitors being sold today are set to refresh at a rate of 60 Hz which means the screen is completely repainted 60 times each second. This is adequate to prevent almost all flicker unless the display on the screen has an extreme amount of very rapid movement. In that case, the refresh rate can be set higher to eliminate the problem. The refresh rate of a PC monitor can be adjusted from the control panel in Windows.

Flicker in a monitor is also affected by whether the refresh method is **interlaced** or **non-interlaced** (progressive). Interlaced monitors paint their screens in two passes; they draw the odd-numbered lines on the first pass and the even-numbered lines on the second. This has the effect of changing only half the screen at a time and tends to minimize any flicker when the refresh rate is slow. Noninterlaced monitors paint their screens completely in one pass. When the refresh rate is high (60 Hz or more) they appear steadier and have less flicker than an interlaced display. Noninterlaced (progressive) monitors also appear to cause less eyestrain when viewed for long periods, though why this occurs is unclear. Computer monitors are noninterlaced.

Television monitors are nearly always interlaced and nearly always have a refresh rate of 30 Hz. This slow refresh rate plus their limited **resolution**, makes television monitors unsuitable for use as computer displays and very few are used as such today.

High-definition TV monitors have the same **dot pitch**, refresh rate, and interlaced method of refreshing as standard monitors. Their higher resolution and improved picture quality come from increasing the number of lines painted on the screen and changing the aspect ratio of the display from the 4:3 ratio (width to height) found in standard television and computer monitors to a 16:9 width-to-height ratio.

The dot pitch is the distance between the color phosphor dots on the monitor screen. The closer the color dots are to one another, the sharper is the displayed image. Each location on the screen actually contains three dots, one for each color: red, green, and blue. The three dots are called a **triad**, and dot pitch is the distance between a color dot in one triad and the same color dot in an adjacent triad. Monitors with a dot pitch of .28 mm or .25 mm give the sharpest images, but are also more expensive than those with larger dot pitches of .35 mm or more. The larger dot pitch means fewer actual color dots for screens of the same size, and hence, lower resolution and sharpness for the monitor. On very large monitors, a larger dot pitch may be acceptable because the physical size of such monitors means they have a sufficient number of screen dots to display any available screen resolution sharply.

Monitors also have several levels of resolution, which is a measure of the amount of detail that can be discerned on the screen. For a computer monitor, resolution is measured by the number of small square areas called pixels (a shortened expression of picture elements) on the screen that can be individually addressed by software and controlled by the computer's video card. The more pixels that appear on the screen, the finer the detail that can be seen clearly in the image. Resolution is controlled by the computer and doesn't depend on the number of dot triads that exist on the screen. A small monitor may use only a few triads to form each pixel. A large one can use many. Table 2-2 shows some of the common resolutions for computer monitors. The number of pixels noted for each resolution level is the same regardless of the size of the monitor.

Table 2-2   Monitor resolutions

Resolution	Horizontal Pixels	Vertical Pixels
VGA	640	480
NTSC TV	720	525
SVGA	800	600
XGA/SVGA2	1024	768
XGA+/SVGA3	1268	1024

Most monitors can display both analog and digital signals and some computers have television signal tuners built into them. This allows the monitors to display standard television programs. If the resolution of the monitor is set to a higher level than 640 by 480 pixels, then the computer either resets the resolution to that level or the television display utilizes only part of the screen. Table 2–3 defines some of the characteristics of monitors.

Table 2-3   Characteristics of monitors

Characteristic	Description
Screen size	Diagonal (top left to bottom right) width of screen surface
Refresh rate	The number of times per second an electron beam fills a video screen with lines from top to bottom
Scan rate	The number of times per second an electron beam moves from top to bottom of a video screen; equal to refresh rate in progressive screens, and to ½ refresh rate in interlaced screens
Interlaced	Screens in which the electron beam draws every other line with each top-to-bottom pass to reduce flicker from slow refresh rate
Progressive	Screens in which the electron beam draws every line with each top-to-bottom pass
Dot pitch	The distance between adjacent same-color dots on the screen
Resolution	The number of pixels (picture elements) that can be addressed on a screen by software
Multiscan	A monitor that supports a variety of refresh rates and resolutions so that it can function with a variety of input devices
Green monitor	A monitor that uses minimal electricity and thus supports the EPA Energy Star program

Flat panel monitors, while still more expensive than CRT monitors, are becoming more common and less costly. They are now available in sizes comparable to CRT monitors, and they have the advantages of being much lighter, more compact in size, and consuming less electricity than CRTs. Flat panel monitors are known as **liquid crystal display (LCD)** panels, and they form images by activating pixel-sized areas in a layer of liquid material sandwiched between two arrays of electrodes, one arranged in columns behind the liquid layer, and the other arranged in rows in front of it. By activating the electrodes on either side of the liquid layer, the controller allows a particular color of light to pass through the layer at each pixel location. The lighted pixels produce an image on the panel. Figure 2-11 illustrates how a flat panel (LCD) monitor works.

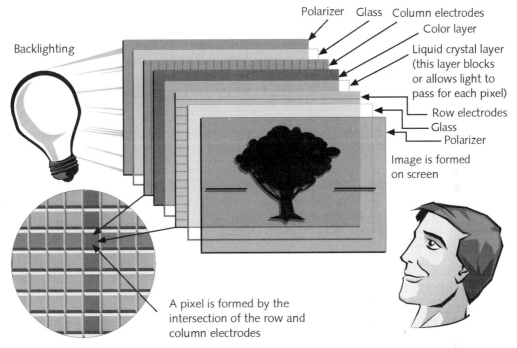

Figure 2-11   How a flat panel screen works

Early LCD panels were dim compared to CRT monitors. Dual-scan, passive matrix displays improved performance by adding a second set of vertical electrodes to the sandwich, but these monitors still were not as bright as CRTs. Most new LCD panels are active matrix displays in which a transistor is added to enhance the brightness and color of each pixel. Active matrix displays can be used in lighted rooms and compare favorably with CRT monitors for brightness and resolution.

LCD panels can display only digital data. They can be used for analog (television) displays only if the data signal is first converted to digital form. High-definition LCD panel television screens up to 60 inches in size (16:9 aspect ratio) are becoming more common in home theaters.

Printers

Printers are devices that output digital information on paper in text and graphic form. There are several types of printers, each using different technologies to produce printed images. Some printers print only black-and-white images while others can print in color including full-color photographs and other graphic images. The three major types of printers are impact printers, **laser printers**, and ink jet printers. Impact printers print only black and white, while the other two types can print in color or black and white.

Impact Printers

Early impact printers were almost like automated typewriters. They had individual metal character keys, or a multiple-key daisy wheel, which struck the paper in the printer through a ribbon placed between the key face and the paper. Because its keys actually struck the paper, an impact printer could print multiple copies and forms using carbon paper or carbonless treated paper to create the copies. Where multiple-copy forms are still needed, some of these printers are still in use, but most impact printers today are **dot matrix printers**.

Dot matrix printers still strike the paper through a ribbon, but they use a matrix of small pins (nine pins in early models, twenty-four in later ones), which are used in combinations, to form characters. One matrix of pins forms all text characters and can also be directed to create graphics images one line a time. The print quality is only fair and deteriorates as the ribbon continually wears out or is depleted of ink. Dot matrix printers are relatively slow because they print only one character at a time and for this reason are sometimes referred to as "character printers."

Laser Printers

Laser printers are page printers. They form an image in much the same way as a photocopier and then print the entire page at one time. Laser printers have become so advanced and are now produced in such mass quantities that they are available at very reasonable cost and are very reliable. A small home-use laser printer can be purchased for about $200. Laser printers are the most economical type of printer due to the relatively low cost of the toner cartridges they use and the large number of pages (2000 or more) that can be printed from a single cartridge.

Larger and heavier-duty laser models cost more and are intended to do a larger volume of printing over a period of time. A medium-range laser printer costs around $400 and is easily capable of printing several thousand pages a month for several years without needing repair or service other than replacement of the toner (ink) cartridge.

Laser printers work by picking up toner on a charged image on the surface of a rotating drum. The charged image is created on the drum by laser light reflected off mirrors and onto the drum in a pattern controlled by data coming into the printer from the computer. Wherever the reflected laser light shines on the drum, it reduces or neutralizes the electrical charge of the drum in that area. The image is created a full page at a time without regard to whether it contains text, graphics, or both. The printer simply reduces the charge on areas of the drum according to its controlled instructions and these of reduced charge areas form the image.

The areas with a reduced charge pick up toner from the cartridge as the drum rotates. The toner adheres only to the reduced charge areas on the drum because it is also negatively charged at a voltage below the white areas on the drum but above the image areas. The toner is thus negatively charged in relation to the white areas of the drum and is repelled from them (because like charges repel one another), but positively charged in relation to the dark image areas and is attracted to them (because opposite charges attract one another). As the drum surface rotates through the toner cavity in the cartridge, a toner image is deposited on its surface as formatted on the drum by the computer instructions the printer received.

Paper is moved through the printer at the same speed as the image drum rotates. The paper is also given a positive charge relative to the toner adhering to the drum. The toner is attracted to the paper as the paper passes near the drum. This transfers the toner image to the paper where it sits as loose bits of material until it is fused to the paper by hot rollers squeezing it onto the surface. The printed sheet then rolls out of the printer and into a tray. Figure 2-12 shows how a black-and-white laser printer works.

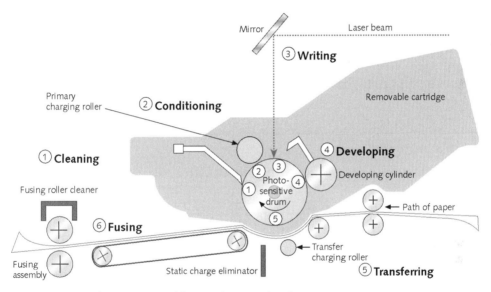

Figure 2-12   The six steps of laser printer technology

The preceding description explains how a black-and-white laser printer produces single-color printed pages. Color laser printing is done in a similar way except that the image-writing process is repeated four times, one for each color toner needed for full-color printing (cyan, magenta, yellow, and black). A color laser printer must contain four separate writing, developing, and transferring systems that must be synchronized to work together and to print their separate images in register (in the exact same position relative to one another). For this reason, it is a much more complex and expensive machine than a single-color printer.

In a color laser printer, the various colors of toner are deposited on the paper one after the other and then fused in place. The fusing process also turns the colors of toner somewhat transparent and blends them together in varying amounts to form the many colors possible. In color printing, digital instructions from the computer must not only specify the shape and size of images, but also the color of each dot in them. This can be done by identifying a specific color for an image area, or by having the computer separate the colors in a photograph or color graphic and send each of them to the printer to recreate the color image.

In a black-and-white laser printer and some color lasers, the removable toner cartridge contains not only toner, but also the most wear-prone moving parts of the printer. These include the photosensitive drum, developing cylinder, and primary charging roller. When a depleted toner cartridge is replaced, these parts are also replaced, thus keeping the printer in peak operating condition and eliminating the need for most common repairs caused by worn parts.

Some color laser printers do not combine any moving parts into the toner cartridges and these printers require periodic replacement of the photosensitive drum and part or all of the fuser assembly to maintain high-quality printing. This maintenance involves expensive parts and makes color laser printers still more costly to use for high-quality printing.

Laser printers provide an excellent quality of printing with high resolution and good color control. Medium-quality printing for a laser printer is 300 dots per inch, about the same as the best dot matrix printer can achieve, but with much better ink coverage and much greater speed. High-quality laser printing is done at 600 or 1200 dots per inch. Single-color printers run at speeds of eight pages or more per minute and color laser printers can often do four.

Ink Jet Printers

Ink jet printers are similar to dot matrix printers in that they print one line at a time using a print head that moves across the page. Both types of printer place ink on the paper using a matrix of small dots, but the ink jet printer uses smaller dots and more of them. It is not an impact printer. It squirts or jets ink onto the paper from the print head, which never actually touches the sheet.

Because they print line by line, ink jet printers are slower than laser printers, but they are becoming ever more popular for home use due to three factors: their printing is high quality, they can print in color inexpensively, and their initial cost is lower than a comparable-quality color laser printer.

Most ink jet printers work by heating ink in the tiny tubes of their print head until it boils. Tiny bubbles of ink form at the ends of the tubes and are ejected onto the paper. The droplets are charged (ionized) so that they're attracted to the paper and magnetic plates in the print head direct the ink placement to form characters and other shapes. Typical ink jet printers use 64 ink nozzles or 128, all of which can squirt ink according to instructions from the computer as the print head moves across the page.

Most ink jet printers have two print heads, one with a black ink cartridge for single-color printing and another with cyan, magenta, and yellow ink for color printing. This feature allows the black cartridge to be used independently of the color one, which conserves ink on single-color printing and produces brighter, cleaner black areas in color printing than is possible by simply combining the three primary colors.

Early ink jet printers printed 300 dots per inch, but newer ones typically print up to 1500 dots per inch and can produce color prints of photographic quality, especially on coated, high-quality paper that holds the ink, but that does not allow it to soak into the surface or bleed. A page from an ink jet printer is often somewhat wet when it emerges from the printer, especially if the print is in color and the ink coverage is heavy. Fast-drying inks reduce the time needed for ink jet prints to achieve full stability.

A printer can be connected directly to an individual computer and serve as its dedicated printer, but the same printer can also be connected to the LAN as a node with its own IP address. When connected to a network, a printer can receive data from any node in the network or even from a node in another network and print output for all of the computer workstations that have access to it. Such printers are designated as **network printers**, or shared printers, because the network connection allows several computers to share the output of a single printer. This greatly increases the amount of output a single printer can produce and often eliminates the need for dedicated printers at each workstation.

To function on a network, a printer requires a NIC and an IP address that identifies its location to other users who may wish to send it data for printing. The NIC is usually an internal component of the printer, but it can also be contained in an external box and connected to the printer through a USB or parallel port.

Network Interface Card (NIC)

A network interface card (NIC) is an electronic board that plugs into one of the expansion slots that all PCs have on their motherboards or attaches to the computer through an external port. The NIC has one or more ports built into it that are used to connect the NIC and its computer to a network using a cable that plugs into the port. A NIC can support Ethernet, token ring, or FDDI network architecture, but only one of the three. It may have ports that can accept more than one type of cable connection.

The function of the NIC is to send and receive information from the system bus in parallel and to send and receive information from the network in series. The NIC also converts the data which it receives from the system into a signal that is appropriate to the network. For an Ethernet card, this means converting the data from the 5-volt signal used on the computer's motherboard into the voltage used by twisted-pair cables. The component on the NIC that makes this conversion is called a transceiver (transmitter/receiver). An Ethernet card may have more than one transceiver to convert data into the appropriate voltage for different types of cable connectors, which are wired into the NIC. Such cards are called combo cards. Figure 2-13 shows some examples of NICs.

FDDI

Token ring

Ethernet

Figure 2-13   Types of NICs

NICs have built-in identifying addresses coded into them by the manufacturer, which are used by the network to identify the computer (node) using the card. These addresses are called Media Access Control (MAC) addresses, physical or adapter addresses, or Ethernet addresses. They consist of 6-byte (48-bit) hexadecimal codes, which are unique for each card. Part of the address contains the manufacturer identifier and the rest is a unique number. No two NICs have the same identifying code.

When selecting a NIC, it is critical to match it with the network architecture to which it will connect, the specific type of cable connection it will use, and the type of slot in the computer (PCI or ISA) in which it will be installed.

2

Server

A server is simply a computer or device on a network that provides services or manages network resources. For example, a file server is a computer and storage device dedicated to storing files. Any user on the network can store files on the server. A print server is a computer that manages one or more printers, and a network server is a computer that manages network traffic. A database server is a computer system that processes database queries.

In large networks, servers are often dedicated, meaning that they perform no other tasks besides their server tasks. In a home network, however, a single, central computer can execute several programs at once, including server functions. A server in this case generally refers to the software program that is managing resources rather than the entire computer, which may be performing other functions as well.

As its name suggests, a server is something like a waiter or food server. A client (node on the network) asks it for something—a file—and the server gets the file from storage and sends it to the client. In most cases the server does not read or otherwise process this file, but simply hands it off to the client that asks for it.

The client may also request a service, printing for example, and a server, which manages network-printing functions provides that service to the requesting client. As stated earlier, in many networks, servers are highly specialized and often dedicated to a single function or service, but in a home LAN, a single server is likely to be multifunctional and sufficient for all required services.

Among the types of server that a home network is likely to use are the following:

- Print server to control printer functions

- File server to store and retrieve files

- Video server to store and send video files to playing devices

- Audio server to store and send sound files to playing devices

- Backup server to keep backup copies of critical files updated on a scheduled basis

- Remote Access Server (RAS), which allows clients using Microsoft dial-up networking and some others to dial into the server from outside the LAN

Router

A router is an intelligent switch, that is, a device that can make decisions according to preprogrammed instructions about the best routes for electronic data packets to travel, and direct the packets accordingly. Routers are the hardware units responsible for directing data traffic between interconnected networks. They read the IP address of each packet of data that comes to them, decide what is the most efficient path for the data to take to reach its destination quickly, and then switch the data packet onto that path.

A router is always connected as a node in at least two networks and may be connected as a node in many networks. For each network to which it is connected, the router has a separate, unique IP address. A router routes the data packets it receives from one LAN onto another LAN, which contains the data packet's destination node or is connected to another router closer to its destination node.

A home network won't require a router as one of its nodes unless it is connected by cable directly to another network. Most home networks connect to the Internet using a modem to dial an ISP link. A router isn't necessary for sending data to the Internet by this method. Once the data reaches the ISP and is transmitted onto the Internet, routers in the system direct the data to its destination by choosing the most efficient path to send it, but the home user's connection to the Internet is solely through the telephone modem link and only one choice is available for transmitting the data.

Switches and Bridges

A switch or a bridge can sometimes be useful in a home network to reduce traffic and thereby make the system more efficient. Both switches and bridges function only in a local network, and both make decisions about allowing data traffic to pass. These decisions are based on their address tables and the MAC address contained in each data packet that identifies the packet's destination address. Because bridges and switches do not send data to the Internet, but transmit it only within the LAN, the tables they maintain contain only local area addresses (as distinct from the Internet-routable addresses used by routers). The tables themselves are referred to as bridge tables, forwarding tables, or content addressable memory (CAM) tables, depending on the type of device.

When a hub receives data from a node in a LAN, it broadcasts the data to every other node in the LAN. Because the data is addressed to one node only, all the other nodes that receive a packet not addressed to them discard it. Each node receives all the data addressed to every other node, but discards everything except its own data. This means that the majority of data packet traffic on the LAN is discarded, but in a small network the volume of traffic isn't great enough to warrant any improvement in this broadcast technique. The broadcast hub works fine.

On a larger or busier LAN, data packet traffic may be sufficient to justify using a switch or a bridge. Which to use depends on how traffic flows on the LAN and where it is heaviest.

If heavy traffic flows between two nodes on a LAN and the other nodes have only lesser amounts, then a bridge may be called for. A bridge is a device that acts like a hub joining several segments of a LAN. Unlike a hub, however, a bridge doesn't broadcast the data it receives unless certain conditions are met. When the bridge receives a data packet from a segment of the LAN, it checks its routing table to see whether the destination node is located in the same segment of the network from which the packet arrived. If it is, the bridge refuses (discards) the packet because it can reach its destination by another route within the segment. If the destination address is not in the routing table for the source segment of the network, the bridge broadcasts the packet to all sections of the LAN to which it's connected, just like a hub.

Bridges work well in LANs where there is heavy traffic between nodes within segments of the network and not much traffic between nodes in different segments. They don't work well where traffic is more evenly distributed among nodes in different segments of the LAN. In this case, the bridge acts mostly like a hub and broadcasts too much unnecessary traffic on the network. The traditional 80/20 rule suggests that 80% of a node's data traffic is to another node within its own network segment. While this may hold true in some business LANs, the reverse is more likely to be the case in a home LAN. The majority of data traffic is coming from and going to locations outside the LAN in the form of e-mail, Internet data transfers, and similar data services. Only a relatively small portion of a home LAN's data traffic is likely to be directed to other nodes on the LAN.

Figure 2-14 shows how a bridge or switch connects two or more segments of a network in the same manner that a router connects two or more LANs. A device can function as either a bridge or a switch depending on how it is programmed to process the data packets it receives. A hub, by contrast, makes no data decisions, but merely broadcasts all data packets it receives.

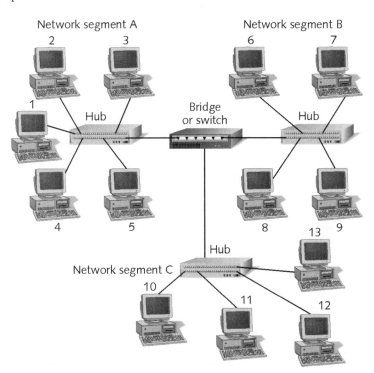

Figure 2-14   Bridge in a LAN

A switch, however, is useful to limit unnecessary traffic on a LAN, no matter where the traffic occurs within the network. Like a bridge, a switch has a routing table of MAC addresses for all the devices connected to it on the network. Also like a bridge, it refuses any packet it receives which is addressed to a node within its own segment because such a packet is received by another route on the network. If the address of the packet is not in the routing table of the switch's network segment, it doesn't broadcast the data as a hub or bridge would. It sends the packet only to that segment of the LAN where its addressed node is located. A switch connecting four segments of a network, each having an equal volume of traffic to the others, reduces network traffic by half over what would occur if the segments were connected by a hub or a bridge.

Wireless Access Hub

In a wireless network, an access hub receives data packets from all the nodes within its operating **zone**. The nodes may vary in identity and number because they are mobile and frequently move from the zone of one hub to that of another. The wireless hub doesn't know what nodes are within its range until each node's wireless NIC contacts the hub and associates with it by identifying itself and "signing on" to the hub. The hub broadcasts all the data packets it receives for all the nodes that are associated with it. The hub continues broadcasting data for each associated node until a node becomes associated with another hub. In a home LAN, only one wireless hub may be operating and all wireless nodes receive their data through that one hub. However, the same wireless node that operates on the home LAN may at times connect to a wireless hub at an office or other LAN outside the home.

 NOTE The fact that any wireless node can associate with and receive data from any wireless hub broadcasting on its frequency means that every wireless network is potentially open to unauthorized users and should be made secure before any private information is sent on the network.

Wireless hubs are also connected to a wired network to which they also send all the data packets they receive. All data sent to a wireless hub from other networks and the Internet is usually sent via a wired connection. The hub then broadcasts these data packets to wireless receivers who are associated with it. A node on a wireless network can receive data only from other nodes on the network or from the Internet after the node has associated with a wireless hub on the network and by so doing announced its location. Until a wireless node associates with a hub and reveals its location, no other node on the network or the Internet can know where to send data intended for it.

Firewalls

The Internet now has more than 150 million users with more going online each day. Among that vast throng are many who use the Internet for malicious, immoral, unethical, or illegal purposes. A firewall prevents such users from sending inappropriate data to or accessing data on a home LAN. Placed at the connection point of the network with the Internet, a firewall can be a software program, hardware device, or combination of both. A firewall function module enhances the security of networks by filtering incoming and outgoing traffic, thus protecting against unauthorized access to any node or stored data on the LAN and blocking unwanted data from entering the LAN.

An effective firewall acts in both incoming and outgoing directions. It can be programmed to grant Internet access to the network only to selected "trusted" locations, or public access can be limited to selected "safe" services. On the other hand, outgoing traffic can also be filtered to ensure that valuable data is sent only to approved locations. Figure 2-15 shows a LAN with firewall protection on its central computer and an unprotected computer set up for Internet access to cleared data.

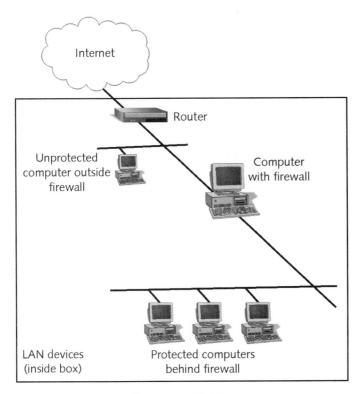

Figure 2-15　　Firewall-protected LAN

A firewall with full ingress/egress packet filtering can support dynamic packet processing for all of these filtering parameters:

- Internet Protocol—TCP, UDP, ICMP, and others

- Source IP address

- Destination IP address

- Source TCP/UDP port

- Destination TCP/UDP port

- SYN packet filtering

The firewall module should also provide an alerting, logging, and reporting system, which permits easy inspection of firewall activity as well as timely warnings for suspicious traffic activity.

Firewalls also protect against virus programs, which can be sent to a node via the Internet and reside in its storage indefinitely. Such programs may harm a computer's data or permit access by a hacker. Because new and more sophisticated virus programs are continually being created, it is important that firewalls and other security devices be upgraded frequently to incorporate defenses against the newest attacks.

Firewall software is often purchased as a "fit-and-forget" antihacking program that can be easily installed and offers straightforward LAN protection. Most systems can also be customized to control which programs may access the Internet. In addition, they may have an IP-filtering tool that the user can set to specify which IP addresses can connect inwards or outwards. If, for example, a rogue program hidden within an unspecified e-mail attempts to connect to the network, the firewall can detect it and prevent it from being allowed to connect.

CHAPTER SUMMARY

- ❑ A local area network (LAN) is a specifically designed configuration of computers and other devices, located within a confined area such as a home or office building, and connected by wires or radio waves that permit them to communicate with one another to share data and services. A wide area network (WAN) covers a large geographic area and is connected to the Internet.

- ❑ All data on a LAN is sent as packets, which consist of a small piece of data with information about what type of data it is, where it came from, and where it is going.

- ❑ The four common types of network architecture used today are Ethernet, token ring, FDDI, and wireless. Ethernet is the most common and can be physically arranged in either a bus topology or a star topology.

- ❑ Wireless LAN nodes are not physically connected at all to one another or to a central device. They communicate with an access point or wireless hub using a wireless network interface card (NIC) which includes a transceiver and an antenna.

- ❑ The Internet is a collection of LANs and WANs, all interconnected to one another and able to communicate with each other. Data going from a node on a home LAN to a node on a distant network reaches its destination by traveling though the communication lines of other networks located between the originating point and the destination.

- ❑ Most home networks connect to the Internet through an Internet service provider (ISP) by means of an ordinary telephone line using a modem. Connections with higher speeds and capacities are available through an ISDN line, a DSL, a cable connection, or a satellite connection.

- ❑ The heart of a home network is the central computer, which performs multiple functions. Each device connected to a network is called a node, or host. A node can be a computer, router, printer, sensing device, video camera, controller, or any number of other electronic devices. A host is always a computer.

- ❑ Monitors are CRTs that display images on the flat front face of a glass cathode tube or flat panel LCD. Their defining characteristics include screen size, refresh rate, dot pitch, resolution, and interlaced or progressive scanning.

2

❑ The three main types of printers in use on networks today are dot matrix printers that strike the paper through a ribbon using a matrix of small pins; laser printers that are similar to a photocopier; and ink jet printers that squirt or jet ink onto the paper from the print head.

❑ A NIC is an electronic board that is mounted on a computer's motherboard, plugged into a PC expansion slot, or connected through an external port. The NIC connects the computer to a network using a cable that plugs into a port on the NIC.

❑ Hubs, routers, switches, and bridges are all devices that are used for transmitting or directing data traffic between interconnected networks and nodes. A server provides network services and manages network resources.

❑ A firewall is a software program, hardware device, or combination of both that filters incoming and outgoing traffic, thus protecting against unauthorized access to any node or stored data on the LAN and blocking unwanted data from entering the LAN.

KEY TERMS

access point — A wireless hub or device through which a wireless node can connect to a LAN.

analog data — Data in nonnumeric form such as radio waves, sound waves, etc.

bandwidth — The amount of data which can travel over a communication line or wireless connection in a given length of time.

bridge — An intelligent switch that limits data flow on a LAN.

bus topology — One form of network architecture for Ethernet.

cable modem — A device that converts digital data to analog signals and connects a LAN to an ISP via the cable television connection.

Carrier Sense Multiple Access/Collision Avoidance (CSMA/CA) — A method of data transmission in which nodes avoid data packet collisions through use of a token or other device controlling the movement of data.

Carrier Sense Multiple Access/Collision Detection (CSMA/CD) — A method of data transmission in which data packets contend for space on the network, and nodes sense packet collisions that require resending.

cathode ray tube (CRT) — A monitor or TV screen.

checksum — A mathematical method for a receiver to determine if a data packet has been corrupted.

digital data — Data in the form of binary numeric code or a derivative of binary.

Digital Subscriber Line (DSL) — An advanced form of ISDN line that makes possible the transmission of voice and high-speed digital data on the same line at the same time.

dot matrix printer — A printer that prints using a matrix of small pins that strike the paper through a ribbon and combine to form characters.

dot pitch — The distance between the colored phosphor dots in a color monitor that determine the sharpness of its image.

Ethernet — The most common form of LAN architecture. It uses bus or star topology and employs CSMA/CD to manage the flow of data on the network.

Fiber Distributed Data Interface (FDDI) — Large, fast networks that are constructed almost entirely using fiber-optic cable.

fiber-optic cable — A very high-speed means of transmitting data using light beams through glass or plastic threads or fibers.

firewall — A software program or hardware device that controls information passing from the Internet onto a LAN and from a LAN onto the Internet.

flat panel screen — An LCD monitor or television. *See* liquid crystal display (LCD).

header — Data at the beginning of a data packet identifying its source and destination.

high-definition TV — New television standard with higher resolution, improved picture quality, and a 16:9 width-to-height ratio.

host — Another name for a computer on a LAN.

hub — A device that connects nodes on a LAN and broadcasts data received from any node to all other nodes.

Integrated Services Digital Network (ISDN) — A technology that uses a telephone line to transmit digital data at high speed.

interlaced — A type of CRT on which the screen is refreshed alternately on its odd and even lines.

Internet — A worldwide web of interconnected, but independent, networks over which data travels from source to destination by various routes.

Internet service provider (ISP) — A company that provides Internet connections to home and business LANs.

Internetwork Packet Exchange/Sequenced Packet Exchange (IPX/SPX) — The protocol used by Novell NetWare networks.

IP address — An Internet Protocol address is a unique node address that consists of four numbers separated by periods.

laser printer — A printer which works by picking up toner on a charged image on the surface of a rotating drum and depositing it on paper where the image is fused in place.

line speed — The amount of data that can travel over a communication line or wireless connection in a given length of time.

liquid crystal display (LCD) — A thin, lightweight type of video display that uses liquid crystal material sandwiched between two layers of electrodes to create a color image.

local area network (LAN) — A regionally confined network consisting of computers that communicate and share data and services.

monitor — A screen output display for a computer or TV signal. Can be CRT or LCD.

Multistation Access Unit (MAU) — Device used in a token ring star design to which all nodes are connected.

Network BIOS Extended User Interface (NetBEUI) — A Microsoft proprietary protocol commonly used for LANs.

network interface card (NIC) — A device for connecting a node to a LAN.

network printer — A printer of any type connected to a LAN as a node with its own IP address.

node — A computer or other device connected to a LAN by a NIC.

noninterlaced — A type of screen refresh that renews each line of the screen in order. This method of refreshing is also called progressive.

packet — A small segment into which data is divided and packaged with a header and trailer for transmission on a network.

Plain Old Telephone Service (POTS) — The most common method of home Internet connection.

protocol — A set of rules and standards that a network uses to communicate among its nodes.

refresh rate — The number of times per second that the electron beam in a CRT repaints the entire screen.

repeater — A device in a LAN which receives and strengthens the data signal to offset its attenuation over distance.

resolution — The number of pixels on a monitor that are individually addressable by software.

routable — A protocol that allows data to be sent to interconnected networks on the Internet.

router — A device that connects two or more networks and directs the data traffic passing between them.

satellite link — An Internet connection to an ISP via a satellite through a receiver dish antenna.

scan rate — The number of times per second that the electron beam in a CRT repaints the screen from top to bottom. Same as refresh rate in progressive screens, equal to twice refresh rate in interlaced screens.

server — A computer or device on a network that provides network services or manages network resources.

star topology — One type of network topology in which nodes are arranged in a star pattern.

STP cable — Shielded twisted-pair cable used for LANs.

switch — A device used in a LAN to direct data traffic among the nodes.

terminator — A device on an Ethernet that ends the data flow in a bus topology.

token ring — A type of network in which data flows in a circular pattern and is controlled by a token.

trailer — Data attached to the end of a data packet.

Transmission Control Protocol/Internet Protocol (TCP/IP) — The most common protocol used to connect networks.

triad — A set of three dots in a color monitor which in combination can produce all colors.

wireless hub — A device to which nodes in a wireless LAN can connect using radio waves.

wireless NIC — A device in a wireless node that connects it to a hub using radio waves.

zone — The area around a wireless hub which its transmission reaches and from which it can receive data from wireless nodes.

REVIEW QUESTIONS

1. What are three types of Ethernet and what distinguishes them from one another?

2. The device on a LAN that broadcasts the information it receives is called a _____.

   a. switch

   b. router

   c. bridge

   d. repeater

3. What is the difference between a switch and a bridge?

4. The header of a data packet contains a destination address. True or False?

5. How does a token ring network differ from an Ethernet network?

6. CSMA/CA is a protocol procedure for _____.

   a. detecting data packet collisions

   b. detecting a line fault

   c. avoiding data packet collisions

   d. avoiding line interference

7. A device that strengthens the data signal on a network and also amplifies any noise on the line is called a(n) _____.

8. Describe how the token controls the flow of data on a token ring.

9. A wireless NIC connects to an RJ45 port. True or False?

10. An inkjet printer uses powdered toner to print. True or False?

11. The term CRT in a computer monitor refers to _____.

   a. certified receiving terminal

   b. central route tray

   c. cathode ray tube

   d. cyan, red, turquoise (colors)

12. An interlaced display differs from a noninterlaced display because it scans (refreshes) its screen in a progressive manner. True or False?

13. How does a router function in networks?

14. An IP address is used on the Internet to direct _____ to their destination.

15. What is the function of a firewall on a network?

16. The abbreviation "Mbps" stands for _____ and refers to the speed at which data travels on a network.

17. A Multistation Access Unit (MAU) is used on a _____ network.

18. Can a wireless node outside the zones of all access points still connect to a wireless LAN? Why or why not?

19. A wireless LAN is inherently less secure than wired LANs. True or False?

20. In a home LAN, an Internet service provider (ISP) provides a connection for the LAN to the _____.

21. What is a DSL line, and does it carry digital or analog data?

22. In most satellite ISP connections, data is sent from the LAN to the ISP by _____.

23. The aspect ratio of most computer monitors, television screens, and high-definition television monitors is 16:9 high. True or False?

24. What does a laser printer toner cartridge typically contain besides toner?

25. If a router receives data from a node that is using only the NetBEUI protocol, it discards the data packet. True or False?

HANDS-ON PROJECTS

**HANDS-ON
PROJECTS**

Project 2-1: Research Installation of a DSL

In this project you will research the possibility of installing a DSL in a home. For this project you need access to a computer connected to the Internet or a telephone yellow pages directory. You will also need access to a local telephone.

1. Find out what companies can provide DSL service in your area and the specific neighborhoods they cover. You can find this information in either of two ways:

   a. Look in your local telephone directory under the heading "Internet service providers."

   b. On the Internet, do a search for the phrase **"Internet service prvoiders"** plus the name of your city and state.

2. Select three companies whose phone directory advertisements or Web sites indicate that they can provide DSL service.

3. Determine from the Web site or call the company to determine if the target home can be served with a DSL line. If it can, continue with the project as if it were for your own home. If it can't be served, select an address (such as for your school) that can be served and continue the project as if for that address.

4. Contact each provider by phone and determine the following information:

   a. What is the cost for DSL service from each provider?

   b. What additional services does each offer?

   c. Are you required to use the same company that provides the DSL line as your ISP? If not, what other ISPs are available?

   d. What equipment are you required to buy or lease to use the service?

   e. What is the installation cost for a DSL line?

   f. What is the monthly cost?

5. Write a short report noting the answers to the above questions for each of the three providers. Indicate which of the three you would choose as a DSL line provider. If you choose one other than the lowest cost provider, tell why you selected it over the others.

Project 2-2: Compare Cable Modem and Satellite ISPs

In this project you compare the cost and availability of cable modem and satellite service to your home. For this project you will need access to a computer connected to the Internet or a telephone directory. You will also need access to a local telephone.

1. Find out what companies can provide cable modem and/or satellite service in your area and the specific neighborhoods they cover. You can do find this information in one of these ways:

    a. Look in the yellow pages listings of your local telephone directory under the heading "Internet service providers."

    b. On the Internet, do a search for the phrase **"satellite Internet service providers"** plus the name of your city and state.

    c. Do another search for the phrase **"cable Internet service providers"** plus the name of your city and state.

    d. There may be only one service provider for each type of service in your area. If there's more than one, select one provider of each type of service and continue the project with those providers.

2. Determine from the Web site or call the company to determine if your home is within their service area. If it is, continue with the project as if it were for your own home. If it isn't, select an address (such as for your school) that is within the service area and continue the project as if for that address.

3. Contact each provider by phone and determine the following information:

    a. Is the firm's service two way or downstream only?

    b. If the service is one way, how can you obtain an upstream connection to go with it?

    c. What are the startup costs for each service?

    d. What is the monthly fee?

    e. What services are included?

    f. Do you have any choice of ISP other than the cable or satellite provider?

    g. Does the service require a long-term contract or other unusual conditions?

4. Write a short report comparing these two services and the DSL line provider you selected in Project 2-1. Note which service you would choose and your reasons for doing so.

Project 2-3: Show How Bridges, Switches, and Routers Work

In this project you use Figure 2-16 to answer the subsequent questions about functions and effects of network devices.

1. If a data packet is sent from Computer 3 to Computer 12, what routes does it travel if Device A is a router, Device E is a switch, and all other connecting devices are hubs?

2. If a data packet is sent from Computer 3 to Computer 12, what routes does it travel if Device A is a router, Device E is a bridge, and all other connecting devices are hubs?

3. If a data packet is sent from Computer 9 to Computer 6, what routes does it travel if Device A is a router, Device E is a switch, and all other connecting devices are hubs?

4. If a data packet is sent from Computer 9 to Computer 6, what routes does it travel if Device A is a router, Device E is a router, and all other connecting devices are hubs?

5. If a data packet is sent from Computer 10 to Computer 1, what routes does it travel if Device A is a switch and all other connecting devices are hubs?

HANDS-ON PROJECTS

Project 2-4: Find a Firewall Protection System

In this project you find a suitable firewall software package for use on your own LAN. For this project you need access to a computer connected to the Internet. The information that you obtain in this project could be useful in the future should you ever need to make a related purchase.

1. Open your Web browser and connect to the Internet.

2. Connect to a search engine that you prefer, or go to **www.yahoo.com**.

3. Do an Internet search for **"firewall software protection"** or another phrase that you think will locate firewall programs available on the Internet.

4. Browse the results of your search and find at least three companies that sell firewall software. Bookmark each company's site so that you can return to it.

5. Evaluate each firewall product for the protection features it offers, how easy (or complex) its installation process is, what additional hardware, if any, it requires, and its cost.

6. Select the firewall product you prefer. Write a short report noting why you selected it over competitors.

HANDS-ON PROJECTS

Project 2-5: Determine the Resolution of a Computer Monitor

In this project you will use the Windows operating system of a computer to determine the resolution of its monitor.

1. Press the Windows key on your computer keyboard, or click the **Start** button in the lower-left corner of the screen.

2. From the Start menu, point to **Settings**, and click **Control Panel**.

3. On the Control Panel window, double-click **Display**.

4. In the Display window, click the **Settings** tab at the top of the window.

5. In the Settings screen, find the display resolution of the monitor.

6. Click the resolution setting and try to move it to a lower resolution. Do not attempt to increase the resolution to a higher level. The computer's video card or monitor may not be able to display a higher resolution.

7. If you can reset the resolution lower, see how the detail visible on the screen decreases. When you have observed the lower resolution, reset the display to its normal resolution.

HANDS-ON PROJECTS

Project 2-6: Change the Toner or Liquid Ink Cartridge in a Printer

In this project you will change the black toner cartridge in a laser printer or the black liquid ink cartridge in an ink jet printer. Because the old cartridge will probably not be empty when you remove it, you will insert the same cartridge back into the printer as if it were a new one.

1. Find the user manual of the printer you plan to work on and review the instructions for changing its black toner or ink cartridge. If the printer is only one color, black is the only cartridge it contains. If it is a color printer, be sure you are changing the black cartridge and not one of the color ones.

2. Follow the instructions in the user manual to remove the old toner or ink cartridge from the printer. Most printers do not have to be turned off to change their cartridges, but it is a good idea to do so, especially if the printer is connected to a network or another computer that you don't control. If it is, someone could attempt to use the printer while you're working on it, so turning off the power is the safe procedure.

3. Perform any cleaning or other maintenance called for in the user manual, even though the cartridge may not be empty yet.

4. Return the cartridge to the printer as if it were a new one. Be sure the cartridge is seated correctly in the printer and that you have closed any moving parts that were opened in removing it.

5. Turn the printer on again, and print a test page to be sure that the cartridge is functioning correctly.

CASE PROJECTS

CASE PROJECTS

Case Project 2-1: Design a Two-family LAN

Two families who live next door to one another, in houses whose sidewalls are only 30 feet apart, each plan to install LANs in their home. They would like the two LANs to be connected to one another so they can share data easily and so the two families can share the use and cost of a high-speed Internet connection. Write a short report or draw a diagram showing how you would set up these two LANs so that they are connected directly to one another and can share an Internet connection.

CASE PROJECTS

Case Project 2-2: Recommend a Simple Network Design

A client asks you to recommend a network topology for her home LAN. She has only three computers and one printer to network. One computer has an Internet connection, which the others need to share. She might want to expand the LAN in the future, but for now she wants to get it working with a minimum of expense and new equipment. Write a short recommendation about the topology you recommend as being least costly to install, but expandable later. Give the reasons why you chose it over other topologies.

CASE PROJECTS

Case Project 2-3: Research a Printer to Meet a Client's Needs

A client wants to purchase a new printer for home LAN use. All members of the family will use the printer. Most of the printing they do will be color photographs taken by their digital cameras and downloaded onto a computer. They also want to print their own color holiday cards. They'll print some school reports with color illustrations as well as some business reports with graphs and diagrams, also in color. Finally, they'll print letters, reports, and other documents in black and white, but these probably won't amount to more than 10% of their total printing output. Research at least three brands of printers and recommend a cost-effective, quality printer for the type of printing the client will be doing. Specify the type of printer (dot matrix, laser, or ink jet) and the model you choose. Give a first, second, and third choice. (Three large printer manufacturers are Hewlett Packard at *www.hp.com*; Epson at *www.epson.com*; and Canon USA at *www.canon.com*. You can find printer information at these sites, but you may need to check retail dealers for prices.)

CASE PROJECTS

Case Project 2-4: Research a Display for a Visually Impaired Client

A client who suffers from glaucoma, a condition that severely impairs sight, asks you to recommend a display for his computer that can enable him to read the screen accurately. To do this he needs the ability to display the screen at least three times as large as a 17-inch monitor. Four times as large would be even better. He doesn't need greater resolution than 1024 wide by 768 high, because he can't see fine detail, but he does need the large-size display. Research what type of display he should buy. Can you find a monitor or flat screen display three times as large as a 17-inch screen? What about an LCD projector? (Start your search at *www.canon.com* and *www.proxima.com*.) Don't forget to check on a video magnifier (Aladdin Genie Pro Video Magnifier at *www.optelec.com/Catalog.asp*). Write a short report on what is available and the cost of several solutions.

3

HOME NETWORK DESIGN AND CONFIGURATION

After reading this chapter, you will be able to:

♦ Describe home information distribution requirements

♦ Describe wired network types

♦ Describe the various wireless protocols and standards that can be used in constructing all or part of a home LAN

♦ Understand network configuration and settings

In the previous chapter you learned how networks are structured, how data is transmitted on a network, and the various protocols used to assure the uncorrupted movement of information. In this chapter you learn the varied information needs and installation requirements of home LANs and about other networking technologies that use power lines or telephone lines already installed in a home to carry data. You also learn about several types of wireless technology that can create a home LAN without any wiring at all. Lastly, you learn about the network configurations and settings for a simple network.

HOME INFORMATION DISTRIBUTION REQUIREMENTS

The definition of a home network is rapidly broadening with advances in technology. Initially, the definition of a home network was limited to home automation (automatic control of home appliances, security, lighting, temperature, etc.), but the growing number of homes with multiple PCs and peripherals, the advent of networking technologies efficiently connecting these devices, and the exponential growth of high-speed Internet subscribers (DSL, cable modem, etc.) has greatly expanded the definition of the home network. Today's home LAN is a network design providing intelligent communication and mutual data transfer between computers and peripherals, digital home appliances, automated utilities, security systems, and other devices, as well as supplying a gateway and access to the Internet.

The home network can be a hardwired system, wireless, or a combination of both, but it must provide a far greater degree of compatibility and adaptability to individual components and systems operating on different protocols and standards than is usually required in business systems.

Home technology systems are usually engineered to give adequate performance in specific consumer applications at minimum cost. This design standard makes such systems affordable for the average homeowner, but often requires some limitations in the hardware, protocols, or other design parameters as compared to business-oriented networks.

WIRED NETWORK TYPES

Chapter 2 examined the structure of Ethernet and token ring networks that are mainly designed for business use. While these designs can be set up on a scale using hundreds of nodes, they can also be used for much smaller networks, including home LANs. The cost of wiring and installing Ethernet or token ring may be high for some homeowners. Much of that cost centers around the expense of installing new wiring dedicated to the network. To reduce or entirely avoid this expense, several technologies have been developed that use wires to transmit data, but require no new wires to be installed in the home. Still other technologies don't use wires at all, but rely on radio waves to transmit network data. This chapter looks at several of these "no new wires" and wireless technologies in the subsections that follow. But first, the text takes a look at what's required to physically wire an Ethernet or token ring network in a home.

Wiring an Ethernet or Token Ring Network

Both Ethernet and token ring topologies use UTP or STP wiring for all the connections in the network. They can use coaxial cable or even fiber-optic cable, but both of these are more expensive than UTP or STP cable and also use more costly plugs and jacks or other connectors which further increases their cost differential. The vast majority of home LANs using Ethernet or token ring topology are wired with UTP or STP or an improved version of UTP called Category 5 cable. Figure 3-1 shows the composition of UTP and STP cable as well as that of coaxial cable and fiber-optic cable. Table 3-1 compares how the different cables are used in the various Ethernet configurations and the maximum length the cables can extend.

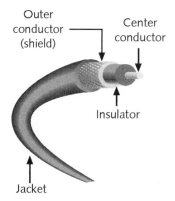

a) Coaxial cable

b) Unshielded twisted-pair (UTP)

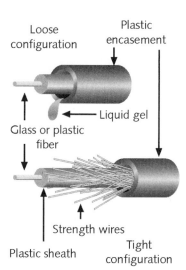

c) Fiber-optic cables with tight and loose sheaths

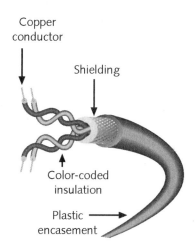

d) Shielded twisted-pair (STP)

Figure 3-1   Networking cables

Table 3-1 Variations of Ethernet and Ethernet cabling

Cable System	Speed	Cables and Connectors	Maximum Cable Length
10Base2 (ThinNet)	10 Mbps	Coaxial uses a BNC connector	185 meters or 607 feet
10Base5 (ThickNet)	10 Mbps	Coaxial uses an AUI 15-pin, D-shaped connector	500 meters or 1,640 feet
10BaseT and 100BaseT (twisted-pair)	10 to 100 Mbps	UTP or STP uses an RJ-45 connector	100 meters or 328 feet
10BaseF, 10BaseFL, 100BaseFL, 100BaseFX, or 1000BaseFX (fiber-optic)	10 Mbps up to 1 Gbps	Fiber-optic cable uses an ST or SC fiber-optic connector	500 meters up to 2 kilometers (6,562 feet)

In many newer homes, UTP or STP wiring is installed during construction so that every room in the home is wired for network service in much the same manner as it is wired for electrical service. The contractor rarely installs the network equipment, but simply puts the wiring in place, adds standard connectors, and finishes the connecting point boxes in the walls with cover plates. When the homeowner is ready to install a network, he or she can refer to the wiring diagram provided by the contractor and connect the network components directly into the wall-mounted points without the need to install any wiring except the patch cables from the wall connectors to the nodes. Figure 3-2 shows a home network with both wired and wireless segments.

3

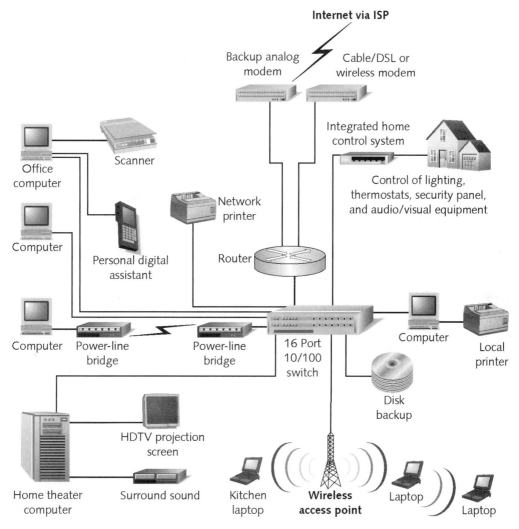

Figure 3-2 A home LAN may have wired and wireless segments

If a home has installed UTP or STP wiring, it's definitely the best option to use for a network. All the other wired and wireless network technologies have some potential drawbacks (limited capacity, potential for **interference**, slower speeds, etc.) that make them poorer choices for network infrastructure even under ideal conditions.

Most home LANs, however, aren't installed under ideal conditions. Network wiring as a built-in feature has only been around for a few years, and not all the homes constructed even during the last decade have it. It is estimated that less than five percent of current U.S. homes have UTP or STP wiring put in at the time of construction. For all the rest, installation of wiring after the home is completed is more difficult and more expensive. For many of them, other alternatives may be preferable.

In existing homes, network wiring must be installed by running or pulling it through the walls from access opening to access opening in order to provide connecting points in all the rooms where network service is desired. Pulling wires through existing walls often means taking the easiest route for running the wires, rather than the shortest. This tends to increase the amount of cable used over the amount used in a comparable new home where the wiring can be run more economically via the shortest routes.

Pulling wire for an installation in an existing home nearly always uses more wire, takes more time, and does some damage to the home (holes in the walls, moldings removed, etc.) that must be repaired. As a general rule, the older the home is and the more often it has been renovated in the past, the more difficult and expensive it is to wire it for a network. Heavy construction (brick, concrete block, plaster over wood lathe, or heavy sheetrock) is more difficult to work with than lighter construction (wood siding, stucco, or plasterboard interior walls).

As you consider whether to install new wiring for a home LAN, carefully evaluate how long the job will take and how much damage will require repairing. Substantial homes built before the 1960s may well be exceedingly difficult to retrofit with new wiring. And some built before the 1930s may be virtually impossible without literally destroying a substantial part of the structure.

As the potential cost and difficulty of retrofit wiring increase, the use of other wired or wireless technologies for a home network becomes more attractive. Several of these technologies are less expensive to begin with than dedicated network wiring. If the cost differential mounts in a particular application, it won't be difficult for the network designer to see that another choice of technology is best for the job.

HomePNA or Phone-line Network

Phone-line networking is a technology based on sending network data over the same wires which carry voice telephone conversations in the home. The Home Phone Networking Alliance (HPNA), a group of networking technology companies, developed the specifications for this technology. The phone-line data transmission standard that HPNA developed is commonly referred to as **HomePNA**. The first version of the standard was designated HPNA 1.0 and transmitted data at up to 1 Mbps. **HPNA 2.0**, the current specification, can transmit data at speeds up to 10 Mbps, and is based on technology developed by Broadcom. An even faster specification, designated HPNA 3.0, is currently being tested at speeds up to 128 Mbps, but products using it are not yet available to consumers.

As a network technology for home LANs, HomePNA offers some attractive features, particularly for installations in homes that are already extensively wired for telephone service. Consider the following:

- The system can be installed one unit at a time wherever a telephone line connection is available. The cost of individual transmission units is low.

- A large variety of networking devices are available from many manufacturers, all compatible with one another and all operating on the same HomePNA standard.

- HomePNA can accommodate both PCs and Macs on the network.

- The network functions as a peer-to-peer system that requires no hubs or routers. All data is sent to all nodes. Each node reads only what is addressed to it.

- The HomePNA standard transmits data at frequencies that don't interfere with analog voice traffic, so the telephone lines can also be used for voice transmission while the network is operating.

- The HomePNA 2.0 standard is fast enough that it can meet almost all home network requirements including video transmission. An even faster HomePNA version is under development.

- As many as 25 devices can be networked using HomePNA, and the HomePNA system can also be connected as a segment to an Ethernet LAN.

The limitations of a HomePNA system mostly derive from limitations of the telephone wire system over which it operates:

- Each device must connect to the network through a telephone jack. The network is limited in scope by the number of available connection points. New jacks can be added, but wiring these is as difficult as wiring new jacks for an Ethernet.

- The system has some physical size limits. The maximum length of wiring between all devices on the network is 1000 feet, and the area encompassed by the network cannot be more than 10,000 square feet, which is slightly less than the area of a quarter-acre lot.

- There are some large homes, with old and extended telephone wiring, on which HomePNA won't work.

- Once installed, HomePNA systems sometimes increase noise levels or cause distortion on the voice side of the telephone lines. This problem can often be solved with filtering devices, but doing so adds to the cost of the network.

How HomePNA Works

To transmit digital data over wires that are simultaneously carrying voice conversations, the HomePNA technology uses frequency-division multiplexing (FDM). FDM uses different frequencies from those used for voice transmission and sends each type of signal over the wire in its own separate channel or segment of bandwidth. By dividing the available bandwidth on a telephone line into uniform segments and sending data on each segment at a distinct frequency, FDM can actually increase the data capacity of a telephone line so that it can simultaneously handle analog voice transmission, a high-speed DSL modem, and the 10-Mbps data transmission of a HomePNA network. Figure 3-3 diagrams how network devices and voice telephones might be combined on a HomePNA network and used at the same time.

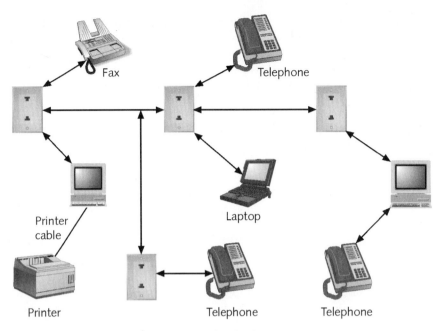

Figure 3-3   HomePNA network with telephones

To begin a HomePNA network, which can be expanded by adding new devices later, requires only a starter kit available for about $100. These kits typically include HomePNA cards for two computers, the cables needed to connect them to the telephone line, and an installation CD. There are now two versions of HomePNA adapters: an internal Peripheral Component Interconnect (PCI) card or an external **Universal Serial Bus (USB)** adapter, which connects through a USB port.

Additional individual PCI cards or USB adapters can be purchased to increase the number of nodes on the network. No other hardware is required. Laptop computers can't accommodate the internal PCI cards, but work well with USB adapters. If the computer doesn't have a USB port, it can still be connected using a USB-to-PCMCIA adapter or USB-to-parallel port adapter.

The HomePNA architecture includes two chips. The smaller 4100 chip is actually a transceiver which translates the analog data signals traveling over the telephone wires into digital data and sends it to a second chip, the 4210, to be interpreted. Conversely, the smaller 4100 chip translates digital data received from the 4210 chip into analog signals and sends them out on the network telephone lines. The chip's signal is strong enough to carry up to 1000 feet on a typical phone line. The translator chip doesn't process the data it receives or sends; it only converts it from analog to digital form, or the reverse, and sends it on to the network or the controller chip.

The controller chip receives data in digital form from the translator and filters it to remove noise that may have been picked up during transmission on the network phone line. The filtered data is then sent to the computer or other device where it is processed. For each packet of data received, the computer sends an acknowledgement back to the sender noting that the data was received. The computer processes all the data it receives, but only acknowledges the data packets that are addressed to it. Everything else is discarded. On a network with many nodes, this peer-to-peer arrangement means most data is not used, but because the computers communicate at a maximum speed of 10 Mbps on the LAN, the transfer of data is still fast enough for almost every application.

The two electronic chips that are the heart of devices using the HomePNA standard were both developed by Broadcom, but many companies now manufacture devices for HomePNA networks. These include 3Com, D-Link, Diamond, Intel, Linksys, and SMC.

3

Installing HomePNA

Installing a HomePNA network in a home where telephone jacks are in place next to or near each node is simple. Kits containing the necessary adapters, cables, and software for a two-computer system are readily available and additional nodes can be added using either PCI or USB adapters, each for $75 or less. When each node's hardware is in place, the cables are connected to a phone jack, and the software is installed on the computers; then the network is operational.

More than one device can be connected through a single jack if the connection point is fitted with a splitter such as those used for supplying multiple phone extensions in a room. Be sure to buy high-quality fittings to avoid imperfect connections that can introduce noise or interference on the line.

The signals transmitted over the phone lines by a HomePNA network are analog and not digital, and they are subject to degradation by noise on the line. Many of the analog devices that send data over phone lines (lines which are shared by the HomePNA network) introduce noise on the line along with their signal. The noise level is usually very low and it doesn't affect the relatively slow signals of telephones, fax machines, or most other telephone line devices. Because HomePNA sends data at high speed and low power, noise can seriously disrupt the signals.

A slow rate of data transfer on a HomePNA network, or complete failure to communicate, is most often caused by noise from other equipment operating on the line. The noise corrupts some of the data packet transmissions, requiring them to be resent and slowing down the network, or it blocks so much of the data that the system can't function at all. The solution to such noise problems is to remove the offending device from the network lines or place a low-pass filter between the device and the jack so that its signals must pass through the filter. The filter blocks noise coming from the device, but still permits its legitimate signals to pass. Filters only operate one way: from the device to the line. A filter placed on the line from one device has no effect on noise originating in other devices. This means that a filter must be inserted between each noise-producing device and the telephone line to which it is connected.

Some fax machines, cordless phones, and other AC-powered communications devices also can produce another type of signal noise which must be filtered out of the AC power line to prevent it from affecting the telephone line network. To accomplish this, a different type of low-pass filter is placed between the AC wall outlet and the power cord connecting the device to it.

Because there's some resistance in wire to the passage of electrical signals through it, all signals lose some of their energy and get weaker as they travel over long distances in the wire. This weakening process is called attenuation, and it affects all signals, both digital and analog. HomePNA signals are low power to begin with and are generally limited to travel of 1000 feet in phone lines. This is adequate for the vast majority of homes, but not all. A few homes have wire runs that exceed this limit between two or more nodes on the network, and they won't be able to communicate with one another. HomePNA is a peer-to-peer system, so most nodes can function normally on the network, even though the two or three most distant from one another cannot. There's no cure for this problem except to relocate the nodes closer to one another or rewire them so that the connection is more direct and shorter. The latter option may be so expensive that a wireless network or another technology is a better option.

AC Power-line networks

Like HomePNA, a **power-line network** uses existing wiring to carry data on the network. Instead of using telephone wires, however, this technology achieves the "no new wires" objective by transmitting signals on the regular AC electric wiring that also provides power throughout the home.

There are two competing power-line network technologies. The original technology is called **Passport**, and is manufactured by a company named Intelogis. The HomePlug Alliance, an industry group established by companies that manufacture products for the power-line networking technology, has selected a newer technology called **PowerPacket** as the standard for power-line networking. Intellon developed this technology, and several companies are now producing products based on it.

Power-line networks offer many of the same advantages of HomePNA networks because both use existing wiring rather than requiring new installation. Among the features that power-line technologies offer are the following:

- The system can be installed one unit at a time wherever an electric outlet is available. Because power outlets are usually more numerous and more widely distributed in a home than telephone jacks, power-line networks can often reach areas where HomePNA doesn't go.

- Many manufacturers are now producing PowerPacket-compatible devices, all of which operate on the same standard. The older Passport standard has fewer manufacturers.

- Power-line networks can accommodate both PCs and Macs.

- Like HomePNA, power-line networks function as peer-to-peer systems, which require no hubs or routers. All data is sent to all nodes. Each node reads only what is addressed to it and discards the rest.

- Power-line technology transmits data at frequencies that don't interfere with the low-frequency AC electric current flowing in the same wire. The network can function without regard to whether electric current is flowing or how much.

- Power-line technology allows data transmission at rates up to 14 Mbps, somewhat faster than Ethernet or HomePNA and easily able to meet all home network requirements.

- Unlike HomePNA technology, power-line systems don't require a card to be installed in the computer (although there are companies working on PCI-based systems).

Most of the disadvantages of networking through power lines apply only to the older Passport technology, which is now being phased out. The disadvantages are as follows:

- The network speed is much slower, about 50 Kbps to 350 Kbps.

- Performance can be reduced, or in some cases entirely blocked, by increased home power usage and older wiring.

- Passport works only with Windows-based computers and limits printing features.

- The access devices used in electrical outlets are rather large and unsightly.

Products based on PowerPacket technology have overcome most of these problems, but networks built with them may still be subject to interference from other electrical devices on the power lines. As with HomePNA, this problem can be solved with filters on the offending devices.

PowerPacket Network

PowerPacket technology is derived from the same FDM technology used for phone-line networking. The range of frequencies available for use on the electrical subsystem (4.3 MHz to 20.9 MHz) is divided into 84 separate carriers by a system called orthogonal frequency-division multiplexing (OFDM) which is similar to the technology used in DSL modems. These OFDM-generated frequencies can all be used for data transmission without interference from AC power running on the same lines. Figure 3-4 illustrates how a power-line network connects nodes through the home's AC power lines.

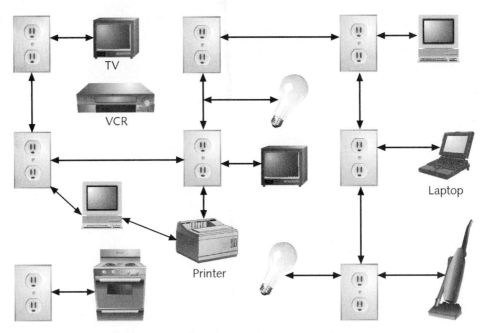

Figure 3-4   Power-line network connects through AC wires

OFDM sends packets of data simultaneously along several of the carrier frequencies, which allows the network to operate at high speed. If noise or a surge in power usage corrupts a data packet being sent on one frequency, the chip in the NIC that sent the data detects the problem and resends the packet on another frequency. This multiple frequency design, in which only some frequencies are used at any given time, allows PowerPacket to switch data packets onto clear frequencies as often as necessary to maintain an Ethernet-speed connection without losing any data.

Installing a PowerPacket Network

A small wall adapter, which fits in the electrical outlet supplying the computer's power, connects the device on a PowerPacket network by means of a USB or Ethernet cord. Manufacturers are now developing power cords with PowerPacket technology built in so that in the future, the only connection needed will be the power cord.

Software available with the PowerPacket adapters automatically detects all nodes (computers and printers) on the network and configures each device for the presence of all the others on the network. Like HomePNA, PowerPacket is a peer-to-peer network system in which all data is sent to all nodes, but individual data packets are accepted only by the device to which they're addressed. Other nodes simply discard packets not intended for them.

The network's Internet connection can be by cable modem, DSL, or normal modem. In each case, the proxy server software included with the system allows all computers to share the Internet connection.

Computers can be added to the network by simply plugging in a new outlet adapter, connecting the computer to it, and installing the software on the new node. Existing nodes detect the presence of the additional node and configure for it. Additional printers can be added using the printer plug-in adapter. File and printer sharing is done through Windows.

PowerPacket technology can function as a complete network or as a segment of an Ethernet-based LAN. Because it is compatible with both wireless and HomePNA technologies, this version of power-line networking can also serve as the backbone for a multitechnology home network.

The cost of power-line network technology is significantly less than 802.11 wireless solutions, but comparable to HomePNA equipment.

Passport Network

Passport, the older power-line technology, uses frequency-shift keying (FSK) to send data over the electrical wires. FSK uses only two frequencies, one for 1's and the other for 0's, to transmit digital information between the computers on the network. Unlike PowerPacket, which leaves some of its multiple frequencies unused most of the time, both the Passport frequencies are used continuously. The frequencies are in a narrow band just above the level where most line noise occurs, which makes the technology vulnerable to noise interference. Anything that impairs data flow on either frequency requires the transmitting computer to resend the lost data over the same frequency. If the noise level hasn't abated, the data still won't get through and the network is slowed down even more.

Heavy use of electricity in the house, such as the air-conditioning compressor, washer, or dryer, may increase noise levels and slow the network down. Line-conditioning power strips must be inserted between the wall outlets and computer equipment to reduce electrical line noise, but these can only filter out the noise as data is received. They don't eliminate the noise from the network wiring. If the noise level rises too high from loaded electric motors or other sources, the filters may not be able to eliminate it sufficiently for the data signals to be read. In this case, the network can't function until some power usage is ended and the noise level drops.

To install a Passport power-line network, each computer is connected by a parallel cable to a wall device that is plugged into an electrical outlet. The cable is connected to the parallel port of the computer. The power-line network connection must be the last item connected to the parallel port. If a scanner or Zip drive is connected to the parallel port, it must have a pass-through for the parallel port available.

Unless the computer has a second parallel port, the printer must be connected to the network through a separate wall device of its own. Passport power-line networks do not support bidirectional printing. "Bidirectional" means that data is sent in both directions, allowing the printer to send status information back to the computer. Lack of this feedback data does not keep the printer from working, but the return data from the printer is lost.

The network created by the Passport technology is a client/server topology rather than a peer-to-peer system such as HomePNA. When the software is installed on a computer, that first installation becomes the application server. As new devices are added to the network, the application server detects their locations and directs the flow of information to and from them.

X10

The X10 technology started as a simple remote control system and has been expanded to perform other functions as well. Like Passport, it uses the AC wiring in a home to transmit signals for home automation. X10 is older than the other power-line technologies and, though equipment for it was originally produced by only one company, many firms now manufacture and market **X10**-compatible equipment, including GE, Radio Shack, Sears, Stanley, IBM, Zenith, and others.

Basic X10 equipment consists of modules, which are plugged into electrical outlets and *receive* data, and control panels, which are also plugged into outlet receptacles but *send* data. Data packets are sent only in one direction, from control panels (transmitters) to modules (receivers). Each module has a unit number by which it identifies data being sent to it. Control panels need no identifying number as they don't receive data, but only send it.

The X10 protocol begins a data packet with a destination address consisting of a house code and a unit number of a module, or a group of destination unit numbers if the same command is to be sent to all of the modules. A command follows the unit numbers that is received by all the addressed modules. Modules not addressed also receive the data packet, but discard it.

To control a lamp, for example, using an X10 module, the lamp is plugged into a module, which has a preset unit number, and the module is plugged into a wall outlet. The lamp's switch is then turned on and left on because the lamp can now be controlled from an X10 control panel located anywhere in the house. Figure 3-5 shows an extensive X10 network with connections to lighting and appliances and various control panels (wired, telephone, wireless, and infrared remote) located throughout the home.

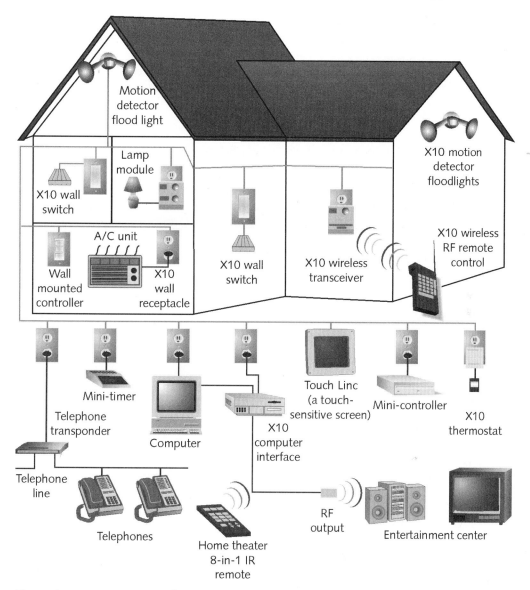

Figure 3-5   An X10 network

A control panel is connected through the AC wiring to every module in the home's X10 network simply by being plugged into an outlet. Additional control panels can be added wherever they're needed. Each control panel is an independent unit and functions without regard for what any of the others may be doing. A control panel requires no address or unit number because the modules which receive data from it don't need to know where the commands come from, only that they are addressed to the module.

The only control panel that is active on the network at a given time is the one that sends a command signal. Commands travel only one way: from a control device into the AC wiring and thence to all modules on the network. Each signal is sent throughout the home's wiring and is eventually received by the addressee for which it is intended. The system is very flexible. Several modules can be assigned the same unit number, and they will always respond to the same commands. Several unit numbers can be sent one command.

X10 technology distinguishes between lamp modules and appliance modules, which are capable of handling larger AC power loads. Lamp modules can be turned on and off or dimmed and are limited to loads of 300 watts or less. Appliance modules simply turn on and off, but can handle up to 1000 watts of power. To remotely turn on your coffee maker in the morning using an X10 network requires that it be connected through an appliance module.

Because X10 signals travel on power lines, they can travel outside the home where the control panel is installed and into other homes which share a common AC power grid. For this reason, X10 includes in its protocol a house code, represented as the letters A through P. X10 modules respond only to control signals that carry the correct house code. The X10 protocol allows for 16 house codes and 16 unit codes (module numbers). More than one module can share a unit code. If 16 unit codes are not enough, even with sharing unit codes, a second or even third house code can be used for one network.

After the success of the original control devices, manufacturers of X10 hardware added new products to the technology along with new commands and bidirectional communication capability for some devices. Radio-based X10 devices and computer interfaces have also been developed to permit automated home lighting and appliance control in place of the former manual remote control. An X10-compatible telephone answering machine allows control of the system by calling in commands, and timers can send preset X10 signals as programmed. The line of X10-compatible equipment is growing continuously.

Compared to wireless, HomePNA, or power-line technologies, X10 is old, primitive, and slow, but it still has many uses and is particularly wellsuited to automated or remote lighting and appliance control. In addition to now being capable of radio or telephone control, X10 devices are also available that can interface with Ethernet, thus allowing X10 networks to be computer controlled. For managing such automation tasks as lighting and appliance control, activating mechanical functions, and managing simple control sequences, X10 technology offers one of the most cost effective and easy to install network systems available. Despite some limitations, it continues to be viable in the face of heavy competition from newer and more sophisticated network technologies. Part of the system's appeal is that its components are less expensive than any other networking solution. Another plus is that, in simple configurations, it requires very little technical knowledge to install.

The weaknesses of X10 as a home network system are mainly the result of the same simplicity that makes it an attractive automation choice. The most significant of X10's shortcomings is that the protocol has no signal verification. If a sent command isn't received, the control panel that sent it doesn't know that. Moreover, X10 is slow, which makes its lack of signal verification worse. It takes about a second to send an X10 command. While that command is being sent, another can't be sent, or both data packets (commands) will collide and be lost. Data packets may fail to arrive because most houses are wired with two separate 110-volt circuit legs. X10 signals sent from a control panel connected to one leg may not reach a module connected to the other. A signal bridge can correct this problem.

X10 data packets can be blocked by other carrier-current devices, including wireless intercoms. They can also be blocked by power-conditioning equipment such as power strips, computer power supplies, and other devices. An X10 device called a "choke" can overcome this problem, but finding where to place the choke can be difficult. Interference from an outside source is also a potential problem for X10 signals. An expensive signal block may be required to filter such outside signals. Signal block installation is also costly and must be done at the main service panel by a professional electrician. Finally, appliances in the home can generate interference or block X10 signals entirely. Such devices require noise filters to correct the problem.

3

WIRELESS PROTOCOLS AND STANDARDS

Wireless technology is becoming increasingly popular for home LANs, especially those installed in existing structures. The primary reason for this popularity is that wireless requires no new wires to be installed. The corollary reason is that, because it requires no new wires to be installed, wireless technology is usually less expensive than hardwired systems.

Wireless popularity has also been enhanced by the appearance of numerous wireless products that offer data transmission speeds and reliability levels comparable to hardwired systems. Many of these products are custom-designed specifically for home LAN applications and, for the trade-off of more limited application, offer easier installation, quicker configuration, and lower cost than hardwired devices adapted from business LANs.

In a wired network, each node's network interface card sends digital data down a cable by changing the voltage on the wires from +5 volts to -5 volts using a prearranged protocol. Wi-Fi, HomeRF, and other wireless technologies simply replace the cable transmissions with short-range broadcasts of the data from small, low-powered, two-way radios. Instead of changing voltage on a wire, the wireless NIC encodes the zeros and ones by laying an alternating radio signal over a constant existing carrier signal, again using a prearranged protocol. The alternating signal encodes zeros and ones on the radio waves. Figure 3-6 shows a network configuration with several wireless segments. Wireless access points can be connected directly to the wired network or connected through a wireless bridge to another wireless access point.

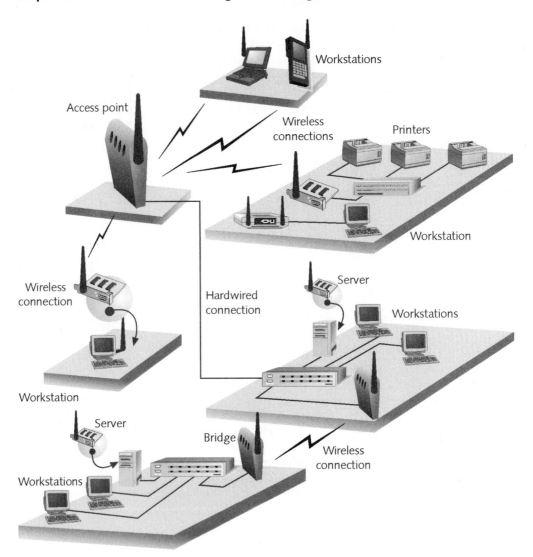

Figure 3-6   Wired network with wireless segments

There are at least four major wireless protocols:

- **Wi-Fi (Wireless Fidelity)** is the most widely used wireless technology at present. It is an **IEEE 802.11b** wireless standard and can transmit data at up to 11 Mbps.

- **HomeRF (Home Radio Frequency)** is a wireless technology that was developed for the home market. It uses the Shared Wireless Access Protocol (SWAP) to transmit data on multiple frequencies in the 2.4 GHz radio band at rates up to 5.4 Mbps.

- **Bluetooth** is a short-range wireless technology limited to transmission distances of about 100 meters or less, which generally confines it to connecting nodes within a single room, or adjacent rooms.

- **WiFi5** is an improved version of the original Wi-Fi technology and is also based on the same IEEE 802 standard. It is designated as IEEE 802a and can transmit data at speeds up to 54 Mbps. Products using the WiFi5 standard are just becoming available to consumers.

Each of these technologies is discussed in more detail later in this chapter; this current section won't do more than mention several other currently minor ones, any one of which could (and probably will) become a major player in the future home LAN market.

These current, less popular Home LAN technologies include wired and wireless standards and the following:

- **IEEE 1394**, which is a standard known mostly by its brand names, FireWire (Apple) and i.LINK (Sony). It is now used widely in the video production and graphics industry to connect digital video cameras and graphics peripherals to computers. Consumer use in the same areas is becoming common, and IEEE 1394 has recently been used for networking some devices, particularly video systems. IEEE 1394 is a fast serial protocol that can transmit data at speeds from 100 to 400 Mbps—and up to 800 Mbps in the next version.

- **IEEE 802.11g** is another version of the IEEE 802 standard that has a fast transmission speed of 54 Mbps. Unlike WiFi5, it is compatible with older and slower 802.11b hardware.

- USB (Universal Serial Bus) is a bidirectional serial interface that is widely used to connect peripheral devices such as game controllers, cameras, scanners, and other input devices to computers. USB connections can be made while the equipment is running and its high speed (USB 1.1 transmits data at 1 to 12 Mbps, and USB 2.0, which is just coming to market, transmits at up to 480 Mbps) makes it a convenient method of downloading large files. USB connections are now being used in some networks, particularly with Home Plug systems.

Unlicensed Shared Use of Wireless Frequencies

All the major home LAN wireless technologies operate in the range of radio frequencies for which no transmitting license is required by the Federal Communications Commission (FCC) in the United States or by a similar agency in any foreign country.

The 2.4 GHz industrial, scientific, and medical (ISM) radio band is 83 MHz wide. This ISM band is used by all the main wireless networking technologies, cordless analog and digital phones, microwave ovens, and some medical equipment. As is the case with most unlicensed radio bands, no one owns or has exclusive use rights to any particular frequency in the band, so all users must share the radio spectrum.

Interference Potential

Because there are hundreds of thousands (and eventually there could be millions) of users broadcasting wireless transmissions on the ISM band, the potential for interference of any one signal by others is great. This potential is reduced by the requirement that the transmitting power of an ISM device remain low and its broadcast range limited.

But even with limited range, wireless broadcasts are virtually certain to encounter some interference. The Federal Communications Commission (FCC) has rules that define how the ISM band can be used. They contain two key provisions that make spectrum sharing possible by reducing and mitigating interference. The first provision requires that all ISM devices must include some type of interference mitigation so that when interference does occur, the equipment automatically adjusts itself to reduce the effects of the interference.

The second provision requires that ISM devices must employ some sort of **spread spectrum** radio technology. Unlike conventional radio signals (broadcast AM or FM stations, for example) that occupy a fixed spot in the radio spectrum, spread spectrum transmitters constantly change the frequency at which they broadcast. This process is known as "hopping," and it significantly reduces the amount of power needed to broadcast a wideband radio signal through the air. This power reduction also minimizes any potential radiation hazard from the signals.

There are two basic types of spread spectrum: **Frequency Hopping Spread Spectrum (FHSS)**, which is used by Bluetooth and the HomeRF wireless networking system, and **Direct Sequence Spread Spectrum (DSSS)**, which is used by 802.11b. As their names imply, FHSS systems hop around the radio band in a pseudorandom fashion, while DSSS systems step through a range of frequencies in a sequential order. DSSS provides higher data throughput than FHSS, but it is also more susceptible to interference.

Wi-Fi (Wireless Fidelity)

Wi-Fi(Wireless Fidelity) is the marketing name for an 802.11b wireless Ethernet specification. The Wi-Fi specification is still a young technology. It was introduced in 1999 by Apple Computer in its AirPort components. New equipment using the specification is continually being developed. 802.11b is an extension of the Ethernet protocol to wireless communication. It can handle many kinds of data. It is primarily used for TCP/IP, but can also handle other forms of networking traffic, such as AppleTalk or PC file-sharing standards.

The 802.11b standard was originally designed to enable high-performance radio to support roaming devices in large offices or business campus environments. It has now been expanded to use in LANs and is the most widely used wireless LAN technology.

The 802.11b specification allows for the wireless transmission of data over the 2.4 GHz unlicensed band. Up to 11 Mbps of data can be sent over distances ranging up to several hundred feet. The range of any specific transmitter depends on what type of obstructions its signal encounters and a clear line of sight between transmitter and receiver.

Each Wi-Fi transceiver can connect, with appropriate software, to any other similarly equipped device for computer-to-computer (peer-to-peer) transmission, but this is not the usual configuration. Most Wi-Fi LANs (and other wireless networks) use one or more access points or hubs, which are dedicated stand-alone hardware units with more powerful antennae than are found on any wireless NIC. The Wi-Fi access point often includes routing to the Internet, a **Dynamic Host Configuration Protocol (DHCP)** server, NAT, and other features necessary for a home network that includes a residential business operation. Residential gateways are a new class of device that offer features similar to access points, but without the advanced management required for corporate networks or high-traffic installations.

The Wi-Fi standard is backwards compatible to earlier specifications, which are known as 802.11. This flexibility allows data to move at speeds of 1, 2, 5.5, and 11 Mbps to and from the transceivers. Several new, incompatible protocols are in the process of being released, including 802.11a (54 Mbps over the 5 GHz band), 802.11g (54 Mbps over 2.4 GHz), and Texas Instruments' PBCC 22 Mbps standard. Several new 802.11a/b chipsets have recently been released, which may make these two standard compatible with one another.

An industry group known as the Wireless Ethernet Compatibility Alliance (WECA) certifies its members' equipment as conforming to the 802.11b standard and allows approved hardware to be stamped Wi-Fi compatible. The Wi-Fi seal of approval is an attempt to guarantee compatibility between hundreds of vendors and thousands of devices. (The IEEE does not have such a mechanism, as it only promulgates standards.)

Wi-Fi is the only wireless standard now being used for public short-range wireless networks, such as those found at airports, schools, hotels, conference centers, coffee shops, and restaurants. Several companies currently offer hourly, monthly, session-based, or unlimited paid access via these networks around the U.S. and internationally. The Wi-Fi standard's wide acceptance has already made it the dominant wireless protocol for business, although in the home network arena, competition is still very strong among several protocols.

Home Radio Frequency

Home Radio frequency (HomeRF) is a localized wireless technology designed for home LAN use. It operates in the 2.4 GHz band and uses a digital frequency hopping spread spectrum radio transmission technique called Shared Wireless Access Protocol (SWAP). This protocol can carry both voice and data traffic and can interoperate with the **Public Switched Telephone Network (PSTN)** and the Internet. It was originally designed to provide data networking and dial tones between devices, such as PCs, cordless phones, Web Tablets, and a broadband cable or DSL modem.

HomeRF is capable of transmitting 1 Mbps (using 2-frequency shift keying or 2FSK modulation) and 2 Mbps (using 4FSK modulation). A SWAP network can have a maximum of 127 nodes and can cover a range of the standard home environment.

The Home Radio Frequency Working Group, composed of companies interested in producing HomeRF-compliant products, developed the SWAP specification in 1998 for use in a broad range of consumer devices. SWAP is an open industry specification that can connect to most of the existing PC industry infrastructure, as well as the Internet, and Ethernet. SWAP technology supports both a Time Division Multiple Access (TDMA) service to provide delivery of interactive voice, and a CSMA/CA service for delivery of high-speed data packets. A standard is also available in HomeRF, which allows connection to the PSTN for voice telephony.

Many HomeRF, SWAP-compliant products are already available. Future specifications of SWAP are currently being researched and developed. These future specifications are planned to offer increased security and higher data transmission rates. Thirteen companies originally committed to build products based on SWAP, including Compaq, HP, IBM, Intel, Microsoft, Motorola, and Samsung. Many others, including National Semiconductor, Siemens, and Proxim, have since entered the market with HomeRF devices.

Bluetooth

Bluetooth technology is based on short-range radio transmitters and receivers that are built into individual devices and that broadcast signals in the 2.0 to 2.4 MHz radio frequency band. The transmitters and receivers are application specific integrated circuits (ASICs) and can transmit data at rates as high as 721 Kbps with up to three voice channels also available. The data rate and additional voice channels are achieved through a very high rate of frequency hopping (1,600 hops per second as compared to the 50 hops per second used by HomeRF).

The range of the original technology is only about 10 meters, however, making it practical for use only in small areas. Bluetooth technology allows wireless connections between computers, printers, fax machines, and other peripherals, but doesn't have the range to serve as a wireless connection between an access point and laptops dispersed throughout a home and yard. Some vendors have developed Bluetooth devices with higher transmitting power, which increases the range of the technology up to 100 meters, but these higher-power devices haven't yet gained wide acceptance.

Bluetooth technology is presently most effective when used in wireless personal area networks (WPANs) that consist of electronic devices in a single room or in otherwise close proximity to one another. If increased power in new Bluetooth devices gives them the range to encompass a full home and yard area, this technology may well become a first choice in home networking. It is supported by many large companies that are already producing the lower-power devices for it. Bluetooth advocates are also encouraging its use by waiving payments for rights to use the technology.

WiFi5

WiFi5 is a wireless networking successor to Wi-Fi (802.11b). What is the really significant difference in this alphabet soup of designations? Speed. Wi-Fi transmits at speeds of 11 Mbps, while WiFi5 rams data through the airwaves at up to 54 Mbps. If its higher cost is acceptable, WiFi5 could be an option for a wireless home LAN easily capable of broadcasting high-definition DVD movies to TVs located throughout the house without worrying about bandwidth or cables.

Before adopting WiFi5 as a protocol, remember that its extreme high speed is attained by using a wider bandwidth in the radio spectrum and its sequence hopping is incompatible with other Wi-Fi products. This means that no previous generation Wi-Fi devices can use the WiFi5 protocol. If you adopt this protocol, or either of the other new high-speed 802.11b protocols being introduced, you must use only equipment designed specifically for the protocol you choose.

Which Wireless Technology Is Best?

The simple answer is this: all of them. Each has its strong points of application and each has some limitations. Which one should be used in a particular home network design depends on the design, its physical location, what objectives it is trying to accomplish, and cost. In many cases a combination of wireless technologies, which utilizes the advantages of each, and a wired technology may be the best solution.

Here are a few general statements about wireless technologies. Remember that, like all generalizations, they have exceptions in certain situations.

- Wi-Fi and HomeRF provide data transfer rates about equal to Ethernet and ten times faster than Bluetooth.

- Wi-Fi consumes more power than Home RF and much more than Bluetooth. This is only important where network devices are battery-powered and must be recharged more often when power consumption is high.

- Wi-Fi and HomeRF devices provide a longer broadcast range and a larger coverage area than Bluetooth devices.

- Wi-Fi can be used to connect to the Internet, network computers, and PDAs, as well as a wide range of home appliances and devices. It doesn't connect to voice lines.

- HomeRF can connect to all the devices that Wi-Fi can and also connect to voice telephone lines.

- Bluetooth can connect even more types of devices such as: telephones, PDAs, computers, printers, headsets, GPS devices, storage devices, etc., but only if they're physically close to one another.

- Wi-Fi devices are more expensive than HomeRF, although devices in both technologies have come down in price.

- Bluetooth devices are more expensive than Wi-Fi, although Bluetooth devices have come down in price.

- Not all Bluetooth devices support the same profiles, and each network using this technology must be designed with products that have a common profile.

- It is easier to configure Wi-Fi and HomeRF equipment than Bluetooth equipment.

- Wi-Fi and HomeRF are in direct competition. Bluetooth is not in direct competition with either.

There is a lot of overlap in the capabilities of the wireless technologies, and they might compete in the future, but today, each technology has weaknesses. Where these weaknesses exist, another technology fills the gap. Some advocates of each technology are so enthusiastic about their cause that they can't see the benefits of the other alternatives, but each wireless protocol has a valid place in the home LAN arena.

NETWORK CONFIGURATION AND SETTINGS FOR A HOME NETWORK

Creating a home LAN begins with setting up the central components or computer which will serve as a node on the network, as well as perhaps fulfilling other functions such as a gateway to the Internet, automation control console, etc. Whether the home LAN is hardwired or wireless, the basic requirements are the same. Only the data transmission method differs. The hardwired network requires wiring to be installed in the home and connected to each node through its NIC. A wireless network requires the installation of one or more wireless access points or hubs, which sends and receives data to and from the nodes, and a wireless NIC in each node, which sends and receives data to and from the hub.

The installation process is very similar for computers running Windows 9x or Linux operating systems. Installation and configuration of a wireless NIC is also similar. For detailed instructions on setup using these systems, refer to the following sources.

- *Windows 9x Installation: A+ Guide to Hardware*, 2002 edition, by Jean Andrews, PhD.

- *Linux NIC Installation: Guide to Linux Installation and Administration,* 2003 edition, by Nicholas Wells

TCP/IP Addressing

Transmission Control Protocol/Internet Protocol (TCP/IP) is the primary protocol used on the Internet. A PC must have TCP/IP loaded in order to access the Internet, and even most networks that don't connect to the Internet still use TCP/IP. It is important to understand the basis of TCP/IP so you can accurately set up a home LAN to use it correctly.

In a TCP/IP network, nodes don't have names; they have IP addresses that consist of four sets of eight-bit numbers separated by periods. As was noted earlier, the eight-bit limitation on the size of each number means that no **IP address** number set can be higher than 255, which is the maximum number that can be expressed in binary using eight bits (11111111). TCP/IP rules forbid the use of some combinations of numbers and reserve others for special functions.

The total number of IP addresses available using four eight-bit numbers is less than 3.3 billion and the Internet has now grown so large that a serious shortage of available IP addresses has developed. (Three billion Internet-connected computers in the world aren't enough! What to do?) This shortage of IP addresses has now resulted in the creation of a means to share IP addresses, which is discussed a little later in this chapter.

The TCP/IP protocol supports file sharing and printer sharing and a number of other services that are also available in different protocols. TCP/IP also has some functions, which are grouped under the umbrella term TCP/IP services, which are unique and not available in other protocols. The most important of these are Hypertext Transfer Protocol (HTTP), TELNET, PING, IPCONFIG, and TRACERT.

- Hypertext Transfer Protocol (HTTP) is the protocol of the World Wide Web. Web sites are constructed using Hypertext Markup Language (HTML), which HTTP can read and interpret.

- **TELNET** allows a user with a computer in one location to access a computer in a remote location as if the user were physically sitting in front of the remote machine, looking at its screen and entering data on its keyboard.

- **PING** is a utility that enables a user at one computer on a network to determine if that node can communicate with another node also connected to a network. **PATHPING**, an improved version of PING, displays the route followed by an inquiry through every IP address to the destination of the queried computer and back.

- **IPCONFIG** is a utility that displays the computer's adapter address, IP address, subnet mask, and default gateway, and allows the DHCP lease to be renewed or released by the user. **WINIPCFG** is the Windows 9x utility for this function.

- **TRACERT** shows the complete path that data packets are taking from the computer to reach any given destination.

The function of TCP/IP is to link together a whole array of LANs to form a wide area network (WAN) which is, in turn, linked via telephone line, cable, satellite, or other means, to all the other WANS around the world. This linked array of WANs is what we know as the Internet.

To make data transmission on the Web fast and efficient, TCP/IP is designed to use the high-speed, expensive transmission links as little as possible, leaving them free to transmit long-distance traffic quickly. As discussed in the last chapter, routers are special network devices that direct data packets to specific IP addresses. Only packets with an IP address are passed by a router onto the WAN and perhaps the Web. All non–IP-addressed packets travel only in the LAN. Routers are by far most commonly used in TCP/IP protocol networks, although they can be used by some other protocols, such as IPX/SPX.

A computer using TCP/IP has a number of settings that must be correctly configured for it to operate on the network. TCP/IP settings can be set for both dial-up connections (modems) and direct (NIC) connections. Windows 2000 makes the configuration easy to access if the user right-clicks My Network Places, and then clicks Properties. Simply select the type of connection you want to configure, then set its TCP/IP properties.

A node in a LAN that wants to send data to another node located in another LAN via the Internet addresses the data packet to the IP address of the computer with which it is trying to communicate. The only IP address it can send the packet to, however, is the default gateway in its LAN, which is the computer node that is connected to the WAN. This machine serves as a router and, like all routers, is connected to at least two networks, in this case, the LAN where the node desiring to communicate is located, and the WAN, which is part of the Internet. The router sends the data packet to the WAN where another router will pass it on to its destination.

Domain Names

Domain names were developed as a means of making IP addresses more friendly to users. On the Internet, special computers called **Domain Name Service (DNS)** servers keep databases of IP addresses and their corresponding domain names. A node seeking data from another node with the domain name of *new-horizons-college.edu* can query a **DNS server** and obtain the IP address of *new-horizons-college.edu*. It can then use that address to find the correct node.

Because they are user-friendly and easily identified with commercial and other Web sites (imagine trying to remember or even look up an IP address for every Web site you want to visit!), Internet domain names are highly regulated by the **Internet Corporation for Assigned Names and Numbers (ICANN)**. Those who want a DNS name that can be accessed on the Internet must register the unique name with an ICANN-accredited registrar and pay a yearly fee.

DNS names used to end with one of these seven domain name qualifiers:

- .com for general business

- .org for nonprofit organizations

- .edu for educational organizations

- .gov for government organizations

- .mil for military organizations

- .net for an Internet organizations

- .int for international

However, this is no longer true. As more countries joined the Internet, new endings were added for each country. A few examples of these two letter (digraph) endings are in the following list, and a complete list can be found at *www.iana.org/cctld/cctld-whois.htm*:

- .ar for Argentina

- .be for Belgium

- .ca for Canada

- .de for Germany

- .cn for China

3

- .ve for Venezuela

Recently, ICANN announced the creation of several new domain endings to keep pace with the demands of the growing Internet. These include:

- .biz for businesses

- .name for individuals

- .museum for museums

- .pro for professionals

- .aero for aviation

- .coop for cooperatives

- .info for general information

Dynamic Host Configuration Protocol

Dynamic Host Configuration Protocol (DHCP) enables a computer to create a pool of IP addresses that are given to other nodes on a LAN when they need them and then taken back into the pool when no longer required. The group of addresses is called a DHCP scope, and when a node is assigned one address, the duration of the use is called a lease. Leases from the DHCP pool can also include the names of the LAN's gateway and the DNS server, which helps speed data transmissions for the leasing node.

Most home LANs are not large enough to need this feature, but it is a good idea to set it up in case future expansion creates a need. It is especially useful where several LAN nodes use a dial-up Internet connection, but each machine is only on the network for short periods. When each is on line, it needs an IP address; the rest of the time, it doesn't. If you accept the automatic TCP/IP settings for Windows 2000 (or Windows 98), these systems will use DHCP.

Dial-up connections to the Internet use a different hardware protocol called Point-to-Point Protocol (PPP). This is a streaming protocol developed to permit access over a telephone line. Windows simply regards the dial-up modem as a specialized NIC that has its own configuration in the network settings. PPP is required in addition to, not in place of, TCP/IP, which the network must still use for Internet traffic. PPP is only used for the telephone line portion of the connection; as soon as the data reaches the Internet through the ISP, it must use TCP/IP to find its destination.

Network Addressing Translation

The Internet has grown larger than anyone ever imagined. Although the exact size is unknown, the current estimate is that there are over 100 million hosts and more than 450 million users actively on the Internet. That is more than the entire population of North America! In fact, the rate of growth has been such that the Internet is effectively doubling in size each year.

When IP addressing first came out, the system was designed to provide enough available addresses to cover any need. Theoretically, there are 4,294,967,296 unique IP addresses (2^{32}). The actual number of usable addresses is smaller (somewhere between 3.2 and 3.3 billion) because of the way that the addresses are separated into classes, and because some addresses are set aside for multicasting, testing, or other special uses.

With the exponential expansion of the Internet and the huge increase in home networks and business networks, the number of available IP addresses is now simply not enough. The obvious solution is to redesign the IP address format to allow for more possible addresses. This is being done (in a development called IPv6), but the new system will take several years to implement because it requires modification of the entire infrastructure of the Internet.

Network Address Translation (NAT) is a temporary interim solution to the IP address shortage. NAT allows a single device, such as a router, to act as an agent between the Internet (or "public network") and an entire LAN. This means that only a single, unique IP address, the one assigned to the agent router, can represent all the nodes on the LAN to which the router is connected.

When a LAN connects to the Internet through an agent device, the connected LAN is called a stub domain. The data traffic on a stub domain is mainly local, within the domain itself, and isn't addressed to any node outside the LAN. A stub domain can use both registered and unregistered IP addresses within the LAN for addressing local traffic. A registered IP address is one that is registered through an ICANN-approved registrar to only one node on the Internet. An unregistered IP address cannot be used on the Internet at all because it may conflict with a registered IP address assigned to another node. Unregistered addresses are locally assigned by a network device and can be used only within a LAN for locally addressed traffic. If a node with an unregistered IP address needs to communicate on the Internet, it must use NAT to do so.

The agent device (**firewall**, router, or computer) that connects the LAN to the rest of the network world uses NAT. NAT has different forms, which work in varied ways:

- Static NAT maps an unregistered IP address to a registered IP address on a one-to-one basis. It is used when a node on the LAN needs to be accessible from outside the local network.

- Dynamic NAT maps an unregistered IP address to a registered IP address from a group of registered IP addresses.

- Overloading maps multiple unregistered IP addresses to a single registered IP address by using different ports. This is known also as PAT (Port Address Translation), single address NAT, or port-level multiplexed NAT.

- Overlapping occurs when the IP addresses used on a stub domain LAN are registered IP addresses already in use on another network. The agent router must maintain a lookup table of these addresses so that it can intercept them and replace them with registered unique IP addresses. The NAT agent router translates the "internal" addresses to registered unique addresses, and translates the "external" registered addresses to addresses that are unique to the stub domain LAN.

Security Firewall Configuration and Filtering

The network security concerns of a home LAN are smaller in scale, but otherwise much the same in content as those which occur on larger business networks. The influx of offensive material and the potential for theft of data or damage to the LAN are the main dangers against which a firewall protects. The word "firewall" for these hardware devices or software programs is derived from their function as a barrier. A firewall in a building prevents fire in a high-risk area from spreading to the rest of the structure. A network firewall performs the same function: it prevents unwanted data and unauthorized persons on the Internet from gaining access to the LAN.

A network firewall doesn't block all access to the Internet, but it filters incoming data and access requests that arrive through the outside connection. Any packet of data that doesn't meet the standards set in the firewall's filter configuration isn't permitted to pass through to the LAN.

Without a firewall in place, all of the nodes on a home LAN are directly accessible to anyone on the Internet. A skilled hacker can probe these computers, try to make FTP or TELNET connections to them, or alter data in any number of ways. If only one user on a LAN leaves a computer unprotected, hackers can gain access to that machine, exploit its lack of security, and perhaps attack the entire network.

Threats to Home LANs Security

There are many creative ways that are used by hackers and outright criminals to access or abuse unprotected networks and individual computers:

- Application backdoors are used in some commercial programs. These backdoors contain code that allows for remote access by the developer of the program. Others contain bugs that inadvertently provide a backdoor or hidden access, enabling an outside person to take control of the program.

- Denial of service occurs when a hacker sends a request to a server to connect to it. When the server responds with an acknowledgment and tries to establish communication, it cannot find the system that made the request. By flooding a server with these unanswerable communication requests, a hacker overloads the server until it slows down or crashes.

- E-mail bombs happen when someone sends the same e-mail to a recipient hundreds or thousands of times until the receiving e-mail system fills up with messages and cannot accept any more.

- Many applications allow the creation of a sequence of commands that the application can run as a set. These sequences are called macros. Hackers can sometimes break into a program and create macros that, depending on the application, can destroy data or crash the computer.

- Like application software, some operating systems have backdoors. Others provide remote access with insufficient security controls or have bugs that an experienced hacker can use to take control of the system and use or damage it.

- Hackers change (redirect) the path that information takes by sending it to a different router. These are known as redirect bombs. This is one way that a denial-of-service attack can be launched with information requests redirected to a computer that can't answer them because it can't identify their origin.

- Remote login occurs when an outside person is able to connect to a computer and control it in some form. This can include viewing or accessing files, storing illegal data, or actually running programs on the computer.

- SMTP is the most common method of sending e-mail over the Internet. A hacker with access to a list of e-mail addresses can send thousands of unsolicited junk e-mail (spam) to users. The source of the spam is disguised by redirecting the e-mail through the SMTP server of an unsuspecting host who may then be blamed for the attack. This is known as SMTP session hijacking.

- In most cases, the path a packet travels over the Internet (or any other network) is determined by routers along that path. But the source providing the packet can arbitrarily specify the route that the packet travels. Hackers manipulate the source routing to make their disinformation appear to come from a trusted source or even from inside the LAN.

- Usually harmless, but always annoying, spam is the electronic equivalent of junk mail. It may contain Web links or attachments which, if activated, provide the sender a backdoor access to the receiving computer.

- A virus is probably the most common threat to a computer or a LAN. A virus is a small program that can copy itself to other computers. By doing so, it can spread quickly from one system to the next. The actions of a virus range from harmless messages to erasing a computer's hard drive or disabling its operating system.

A firewall on the LAN can greatly reduce or entirely eliminate all of these threats. The firewall implements a set of security rules set up by the LAN administrator. These rules closely control what information comes into the LAN from any source outside, and controls what information goes outside to the Internet from any node on the LAN.

A software firewall is a program installed on the computer in the home LAN that has an Internet connection. This computer then functions as a gateway because all access between the home network and the Internet must pass through it and its firewall software.

A hardware firewall itself functions as the LAN gateway. It is wired directly to the modem or other Internet connection, and all data coming from the Internet or moving from the LAN to the Internet passes through it. The firewall has a built-in Ethernet card and hub. Nodes on the home network connect to the firewall/router, which provides their only access to the Internet. The firewall is configured via a Web-based interface reached through the browser on one of the computer nodes of the LAN.

Hardware firewalls are extremely secure and not very expensive. Home LAN versions that include a router, firewall, and Ethernet hub for broadband connections can be found for under $100.

Software and hardware firewalls use one or more of three methods to control traffic flowing in and out of the network:

- *Packet filtering*—Packets of data are analyzed against a set of filters that define what information is acceptable. Packets that make it through the filters are sent to the requesting system and all others are discarded.

- *Proxy service*—Requested information coming from the Internet is received by the firewall, analyzed, and then sent to the requesting system, if it is acceptable. Outgoing information requested by an outside node is similarly sent to the firewall, analyzed, and sent on to the Internet, if its release is permissible. The firewall serves as a proxy to receive and transmit incoming and outgoing information, thus preventing direct data transfer between the Internet and the LAN until the information has been validated.

- *Stateful inspection*—This method uses a state table to compare certain key parts of each data packet to a database of trusted information. Information from inside the firewall going to the outside is monitored for specific defining characteristics. Incoming information is then compared to these characteristics. If the comparison shows a reasonable match, the information is allowed through. Otherwise, it is discarded.

Firewalls can be customized for the individual LAN. This means that the user can add or remove filters based on several conditions. Some of these are:

- *IP addresses*—Specified IP addresses can be blocked from access by nodes on the LAN as can a range of IP addresses. Similarly, if certain IP addresses outside the LAN are seeking access to information inside the LAN, the firewall can block all traffic to or from those IP addresses.

- *Domain names*—The firewall can block access to certain domain names or domain names containing specific words or letters. Some firewalls can also be set to allow access only to those domain names specified by an administrator.

- *Protocols*—The firewall can be set to accept or exclude information sent via a certain protocol. These restrictions can be very specific, allowing some nodes on the LAN access to a protocol while denying it to others. Protocols for which firewall filters can be set include:

  - *Internet Protocol (IP)*—This is usually done for a specific address rather than the entire protocol because IP is the main information delivery system for the Internet. Blocking the entire protocol eliminates almost all Internet access.

  - *Hypertext Transfer Protocol (HTTP)*—This protocol is used for Web pages, and all or parts of it can be restricted to limit access on the Web.

- *File Transfer Protocol (FTP)*—This protocol can be restricted to be used only by a proxy server on the LAN or by one node so that access to LAN files is limited.

- *User Datagram Protocol (UDP)*—This protocol is used to send data that requires no response from the receiver, such as streaming audio and video, which some LANs may want to limit.

- *Simple Mail Transport Protocol (SMTP)*—A protocol used to send text-based information (e-mail) on which many restrictions may be appropriate.

- *Simple Network Management Protocol (SNMP)*—A protocol used to collect system information from a remote computer. It would not be needed by most LAN nodes unless the user is trying to hack another system.

- *TELNET*—Since this protocol is used to perform commands on a remote computer, it too is often restricted to prevent hacking into or out of the LAN.

NOTE   A home LAN firewall might set up only one machine on the network to handle a specific protocol and ban that protocol on all other machines.

- *Ports*—All servers makes their services available to the Internet using numbered ports, one for each service that is available on the server. A firewall can open or close any of these ports to grant or restrict access.

- *Specific words and phrases*—The firewall can search through each packet of information for an exact match of any text listed in the filter. It could, for example, block any packet with the word "sex" in it, or any other string of characters. Any number of strings can be set, but the filter only blocks those packets with strings that exactly match the ones specified.

The level of security a firewall establishes determines how many threats can be stopped. The highest level of security is to simply block everything, but that defeats the purpose of having an Internet connection. The most secure method of determining access is to first block everything, then select what types of traffic to allow. Making selections singly is time consuming, however, and it may be more restrictive than intended because the administrator forgets to allow some desired data to be accepted. For most home LANs, it is best to start with the default settings provided by the firewall developer and change them only if there is a specific reason to do so.

Firewalls offer the best available protection against unauthorized entry into a home LAN. No firewall offers perfect security, and some of the items in the list above are hard, if not impossible, to filter entirely. While some firewalls offer virus protection, it is worth the investment to also install antivirus software on each LAN computer. Some spam is likely to get through even the best firewall, if it accepts e-mail. Spam can contain a virus, and so the individual machine protection is useful.

Proxy Server

A function that is often combined with a firewall is a proxy server. A home LAN may have some data that the owner wants to make available to others on the Internet. The most secure way to do this is by using a proxy server. When an outside computer requests data, it is retrieved from the LAN node by the proxy server and then sent to the requesting outside computer. This isolates the home LAN from the Internet while still allowing access in both directions. Only the proxy server can retrieve data from nodes on the home LAN, and requests for data go only to the proxy server, never directly to other nodes on the LAN.

3

Proxy servers can also make the home LAN's Internet access work more securely and more efficiently. If a page is requested on a Web site by a LAN node, it is cached (stored) on the proxy server, from where it can be accessed by the requesting node. No data entering the home LAN from outside can be stored anywhere but on the proxy server. This prevents any contaminated data from infecting any node on the LAN except the proxy server. It also allows frequently accessed pages to be kept on the proxy server rather than retrieved from a remote Web site for each use.

CHAPTER SUMMARY

- A home LAN is a network design enabling intelligent communication and mutual data transfer between computers and peripherals, digital home appliances, automated utilities, security systems, and other devices, as well as providing a gateway and access to the Internet.

- If a home has installed UTP or STP wiring, that's the best option to use for a network. For homes without installed wiring, installation of wiring is more difficult and more expensive. For many of these, other alternatives may be preferable.

- HomePNA uses frequency-division multiplexing (FDM) to put computer data on a voice phone line using separate frequencies from the voice signals being carried by the line.

- Power-line networking technology uses a form of orthogonal frequency-division multiplexing (OFDM), similar to the technology found in DSL modems, to put computer data on AC power lines at the same time as the high-voltage power.

- Wi-Fi (Wireless Fidelity) is an IEEE 802.11b wireless technology standard that can transmit data at a rate of 11 Mbps. It is presently the most popular wireless standard.

- Home Radio frequency (HomeRF) is a wireless technology that uses Shared Wireless Access Protocol (SWAP) and operates in the 2.4 GHz band at data transmission rates up to 5.4 Mbps.

- Bluetooth is a short-range (100 meters) wireless technology which uses high-speed frequency hopping to transmit data at speeds up to 742 Kbps.

- WiFi5 is a version of the IEEE 802 standard which allows for fast, 54 Mbps data transfer speeds through 802.11a-capable hardware, but is not compatible with earlier, slower 802.11 technologies.

❏ Installing and configuring a NIC in a computer under Windows 2000 is an easy process. After a NIC is physically installed, Windows 2000 automatically detects the card and guides the user through the process.

❏ TCP/IP is the primary protocol used on the Internet. Any PC must have TCP/IP loaded in order to access the Internet, and even most networks that don't connect to the Internet still use TCP/IP.

❏ The most important TCP/IP services and functions are Hypertext Transfer Protocol (HTTP), TELNET, PING, IPCONFIG, and TRACERT.

❏ Domain names were developed as a means of making IP addresses more friendly to users. They are always linked to an IP address.

❏ Dynamic Host Configuration Protocol (DHCP) enables a computer to create a pool of IP addresses that are given to other nodes on a LAN when they need them, and then taken back into the pool when no longer required.

❏ NAT is a temporary solution to the IP address shortage. NAT allows a single device, such as a router, to act as an agent between the Internet (or "public network") and a LAN, so that the LAN uses only a single IP address.

❏ A firewall is a program or a hardware device that filters the information coming from the Internet connection into a private network or computer system.

KEY TERMS

Bluetooth — A short-range (100 meters) wireless connection technology now being used for networking.

Dynamic Host Configuration Protocol (DHCP) — A method of automatically assigning IP addresses to nodes on a LAN.

Domain Name Service (DNS) — A part of the TCP/IP protocol that translates domain names into their corresponding IP addresses.

DNS server — Special computers on the Internet that keep databases of IP addresses and their corresponding domain names.

domain name — A unique name assigned to a network and registered with ICANN.

Direct Sequence Spread Spectrum (DSSS) — A method of signal hopping or rapidly changing frequencies in a specified sequence to transfer data at high speed.

Frequency Hopping Spread Spectrum (FHSS) — A method of signal hopping or rapidly changing frequencies in a random sequence to transfer data at high speed.

firewall — A program or a hardware device that filters the information coming from the Internet connection into a private network or computer system.

HomePNA — Dominant standard of HomePNA technology currently in use for networks using telephone lines for connectivity.

HomeRF (Home Radio Frequency) — A wireless network technology for home LANs.

HPNA 2.0 — Network standard currently in use for HPNA networks.

Internet Corporation for Assigned Names and Numbers (ICANN) — The group that assigns and regulates domain names and IP addresses through accredited registrars.

IEEE 1394 — A fast serial protocol running from 100 to 400 Mbps.

IEEE 802.11b — Wi-Fi version of the IEEE 802.11 wireless network standard.

IEEE 802.11g — New and extremely fast version of IEEE 802.11 standard not yet in use.

interference — Noise and conflicting signals that can occur in transmissions in unlicensed radio bands such as the ISM band.

IP address — Internet Protocol address, a 32-bit address consisting of four numbers separated by periods, used to uniquely identify a device on a network.

IPCONFIG — TCP/IP utility which displays the computer's adapter address, IP address, subnet mask, and default gateway, and allows the DHCP to be renewed or released by the user.

Passport — Older and slower type of power-line technology for networking.

PATHPING — An improved version of PING.

PING — A TCP/IP utility that enables a user at one computer to determine if that node can communicate with another computer connected to a network.

power-line network — Network technology that transmits data over a home's AC power lines at the same time high-voltage power is running on the lines at a different frequency.

PowerPacket — High-speed power-line technology for networking.

Public Switched Telephone Network (PSTN) — The network of voice and data telephone wires.

spread spectrum — Spread spectrum signals constantly change frequency, a process known as hopping, to reduce the power requirements for transmission.

TELNET — A TCP/IP utility that allows a user in one location to access a computer in a remote location as if the user were physically sitting in front of the remote machine.

TRACERT — A TCP/IP utility that shows the complete path that data packets are taking from the computer to reach any given destination.

Universal Serial Bus (USB) — A bidirectional, isochronous, dynamically attachable serial interface for adding devices on a single bus.

WiFi5 — IEEE 802.11a was designated by its promoters as WiFi5, a very high-speed wireless technology.

WINIPCFG — Windows 9x version of IPCONFIG, a utility for displaying a computer's adapter address, IP address, subnet mask, and default gateway and renewing or releasing its DHCP.

Wi-Fi (Wireless Fidelity) — IEEE 802.11b wireless standard with an 11 Mbps transmission rate. It is presently the most popular wireless standard.

X10 — A wired technology that transmits data on existing high-voltage AC power lines in the home, and thus requires no new wires for installation.

REVIEW QUESTIONS

1. Which of the following is not a wireless protocol for home LANs derived from the IEEE 802.11 standard?

   a. Wi-Fi

   b. HomePNA

   c. HomeRF

   d. Bluetooth

2. How does X10 technology work?

3. How does home power-line technology differ from X10?

4. Which of the following is not a service offered by TCP/IP?

   a. HTTP

   b. PING

   c. TELNET

   d. ICANN

5. The two main types of cable used by Ethernet are _____ and _____.

6. What is a network firewall and what is its function?

7. Wi-Fi stands for _____ _____ and is a technology that uses signal _____ to achieve high-speed data transmission.

8. HomePNA technology uses _____ lines to transmit data and _____ information.

9. The long range of Bluetooth technology makes it ideal for linking wireless laptops. True or False?

10. Which of the following is probably not valid domain name?

    a. yahoo.com

    b. wireless.org

    c. home.lan

    d. Bluetooth.net

11. An IP address always consists of _____ 8-bit numbers separated by _____.

12. Network Address Translation (NAT) is a method of temporarily assigning a registered IP address to a(n) _____ _____.

13. The acronym WAN stands for _____ _____ _____ and forms part of the _____.

3

14. TELNET is a utility that allows a user in one location to access a computer in a remote location as if the user were physically sitting in front of the remote machine. True or False?

15. FHSS stands for File Head Sharing System and is used to store information on a disk. True or False?

16. What is a denial-of-service attack?

17. FTP stands for _____ _____ _____ and is a protocol used to transmit _____.

18. If a domain name ends in .edu, what kind of organization does it belong to? _____ How about .org? _____

19. X10 technology is less expensive than a Wi-Fi system, but has equal capacity because X10 is wireless and Wi-Fi is wired. True or False?

20. Power-line technologies connect network devices by using _____ wiring.

21. The ISM band is a shared use, unlicensed radio frequency. Explain what this means.

22. Interference in wireless data transmission is usually dealt with by the use of _____.

23. Which wireless technologies can be combined with Ethernet in a single LAN?

    a. Wi-Fi

    b. HomeRF

    c. Bluetooth

    d. all of the above

24. What is NetBEUI?

25. If using X10 technology when nearby homes are also using it, a(n) _____ _____ must be used with X10 commands to prevent commands from other systems from entering the home.

HANDS-ON PROJECTS

Project 3-1: Build a Simple Network

In this project you will build a simple network using NICs and a Microsoft network protocol. For this project you will need access to two computers. One should have Windows 2000 and the other should have Windows 9x or 2000. If the computers do not have network cards installed, you will also need to acquire two NICs that can be installed in the computers. You will also need a crossover cable.

1. Check the two computers to see if they have NICs installed. If they do, go to Step 2. If they don't, follow these instructions to physically install the card:

   a. Unplug the computer from its power source.

   b. Remove the computer's casing or a side panel to gain assess to the interior of the machine.

   c. Remove one of the small cover plates that cover the card slot openings on the back of the computer so that the NIC can fit into the opening.

   d. Install the NIC in the slot designed for it on the motherboard.

   e. Attach the NIC to the back of the computer frame with the screws or other fasteners that formerly held the plate.

   f. Replace the casing or side panel.

   g. Plug the computer into its power source.

   h. Repeat these steps to install the NIC in the second computer, if necessary.

2. Connect both computers using the crossover cable. Insert a cable end into the jack on each NIC.

3. Start both computers.

4. On the Windows 2000 computer, the system detects the NIC automatically, and an installation window appears with instructions to guide you through the process.

5. When installation is completed, you can verify that the card is correctly installed by clicking **Start**, and then clicking **Control Panel**. Double-click **Network and Dial-up Connections**.

6. When the dialog box opens, right-click **Local Area Connections**, and then click **Properties** to view the card's properties.

7. From the Properties window, install the NetBEUI protocol.

8. On the Windows 2000 desktop, right-click **My Computer**, and select **Properties** from the shortcut menu. Click the **Computer Name** tab, type a name for the computer, and click **OK**.

9. Close the System Properties window and My Computer.

10. Repeat Steps 4 through 9 to complete the installation of the NIC in the other computer, if necessary.

11. Click the **My Network Places** icon on one of the computers, and double-click **Computers Near Me**. You are able to view both networked computers.

Project 3-2: Wire an X10 Control Network and Troubleshoot It

You can follow these instructions to install and troubleshoot a simple two-node network using X10 devices.

1. Obtain an X10 lamp module and a control unit.

2. Plug the lamp module into a wall outlet in a classroom or home. Plug a lamp into the lamp module.

3. Plug the control module into a wall outlet in another part of the classroom or home.

4. Turn the lamp on and off with the control module.

5. Relocate your X10 lamp module and control module so that they are separated as far as possible in the classroom or home. Plug both units into wall outlets.

6. Test the network to see if it still works correctly.

7. If the lamp doesn't control properly, troubleshoot the network to see if you can get it working again at the greatest possible distance.

   ▪ Check for interference, mismatched power legs, and attenuation.

   ▪ If necessary, install a noise filter, bridge, or repeater.

8. If you have a friendly neighbor, place the lamp module in another classroom or home and see if you can control it with the control module in yours.

Project 3-3: Trace Data from a Government Web Site

In this project you will use TRACERT or the Windows 9*x* equivalent utility to trace data packets from your computer to a Web site located outside your local area. For this project you will need access to a computer running Windows 2000.

1. Log on to the Internet.

2. To open the command prompt, click **Start** at the lower-left corner of your computer screen.

3. Point to **Programs**, and click **MS DOS** prompt.

4. In the command prompt window, type **tracert www.nasa.gov**. This shows the path to the National Aeronautics and Space Administration Web site.

5. In the command prompt window, type **tracert www.royal.gov.uk**. This shows the path to Queen of England's Web site.

6. Try to determine from the display what other countries the data may have passed through on its way to its destination. At the end of the trace, the words "trace complete" should appear if the complete route was traced. If the words "timed out" appear, the trace took too long and was cancelled before completion.

HANDS-ON PROJECTS

Project 3-4: Configure a NIC or Review the Configuration of a NIC

In this project you will configure an installed NIC or review the configuration of a NIC using Windows 2000. Configuring a NIC in a computer under Windows 2000 is an automated process.

1. After a NIC is physically installed, turn the computer on and wait while Windows 2000 loads and detects the NIC.

2. Follow the instructions that appear on the screen in sequence to install the necessary drivers.

3. After the installation, verify that the card is installed with no errors by using Device Manager. To activate Device Manager, click **Start**, point to **Settings**, and then click **Control Panel**. Double-click **System**. On the Hardware tab, click **Device Manager**.

4. In Device Manager, the network card should be listed under Network adapters. Right-click the card, and select **Properties** to view the card's properties.

5. Another way to access the NIC Properties window in Windows 2000 is to use the Network and Dial-up Connections applet in Control Panel. Open Control Panel and double-click **Network and Dial-up Connections**.

6. When the dialog box opens, right-click **Local Area Connection**.

7. From the shortcut menu, select **Properties** to view the Local Area Connection Properties window.

CASE PROJECTS

CASE
PROJECTS

Case Project 3-1: Connect to a Public Wireless Network

3

For this project you need to obtain the use of a wireless laptop computer for a short period. Find an area in your school or at another location that is equipped for wireless data transmission. Your task is to determine how well and at what range the laptop functions as a wireless node in the area set up for it. To do this, you must first connect to the network through a wireless access point and log onto the Internet. Once you've brought up an Internet site, move to a different location within the wireless LAN area and log onto a different Web site. Move to some other locations within the wireless access point's range and see if your laptop remains connected. If it loses its connection, make note of where you were when the connection was lost. If the laptop doesn't lose its connection in the access area, move outside that area and see how far you can get from the access point before the connection fails.

CASE
PROJECTS

Case Project 3-2: Research a Home LAN

A client has asked you to research a LAN design for her 1200-square-foot, three-bedroom apartment. The apartment is only a year or two old and is wired for a telephone outlet in every room. It has standard electrical wiring, and the service panel for each apartment is located within the unit. The apartment owners will not permit new wires to be pulled within the apartment's walls, but they will allow wiring to be installed in raceways on the walls surfaces. The client has to pay for the installation and for its removal when she moves from the apartment. The client wants to network a computer in each bedroom and another in the kitchen. She also needs to connect a color printer and a black-and-white printer so that all the computers can use them. Finally, she wants a lighting control system for the apartment and a security alarm on its two entrances and three windows that she can monitor from her bedroom or from the kitchen. Based on this information, recommend the network technology or technologies you would use for this installation and the basic design for the system.

CASE
PROJECTS

Case Project 3-3: Research a Home Wireless Personal Area Network (WPAN)

A client operates his business from his home. In his home office he has two workstation computers and a server. He also has two printers and a laptop computer that he uses when making calls out of his office. All of his computer equipment is in one room and he wants a secure network linking it and allowing him occasional access to the Internet. Cost is not as important a factor to this client as is a secure, reliable network. Write a short report recommending what technology he should use and how his network should be configured. Note how you would connect his laptop to the network, and how you would interface this WPAN with the Internet. Give reasons why you chose the technology you did and why you rejected others.

Case Project 3-4: Link Two Computers with a Home Network Technology

Place two computer workstations in a room. Set up both computers so that they are operational, but not connected to any network. Choose one of the home network technologies discussed in this chapter (HomePNA, Home PowerPlug, Wi-Fi, HomeRF, or Bluetooth) and connect the two computers using one of these technologies. Obtain and install the NICs, wiring, and other devices and connectors you need to complete the connection between just the two computers. Keep the cost of networking the two stations as low as you can and still get a data transfer rate of at least 500 Kbps over the network. When you have the computers networked, time the transfer time for a 500 K file across the network and compare this time to what is required to transfer the file manually using disks or whatever output devices the computers have.

4

INSTALLING CENTRAL COMPONENTS AND LOW-VOLTAGE WIRING

After reading this chapter, you will be able to:

♦ Plan a home LAN

♦ Understand the basic central LAN components

♦ Install concealed and surface wiring for a LAN

♦ Configure hardware and cables of a LAN into a working system

Now that you're familiar with the various network designs and the components that make up a network, you're ready to plan and physically construct a home LAN. In this chapter, you'll learn how to evaluate the location where a LAN is to be built, determine how many nodes the LAN should have and where each should be positioned, map a wiring or wireless connection path to each node, and develop a written diagram of the complete LAN on a floor plan of the home. You'll also learn how to pull cables in both new construction and existing buildings, how to position central components and nodes, and how to connect the cables, connectors, and components and integrate them through a patch panel into a working LAN. Finally, you'll learn how to install a home run cable to connect the LAN more directly with its ISP.

PLANNING A HOME NETWORK

As you prepare to install a home network, some planning at the beginning means less work in completing the project and better performance of the network. To design an efficient home network, you need to ask six basic questions, and then use the knowledge you've acquired about the different types of networks, network infrastructure, and hardware devices to answer them for the network installation project on which you're working. Each home network is different, both in its setting and in what it is designed to accomplish. For this reason, you need to individually plan each networking project to provide the most effective solution for the client.

The questions for planning a network installation are as follows:

1. Where will the network be built?

2. What nodes will be in the network?

3. Where will each node be located?

4. How will each node be connected?

5. Do I have a proposed diagram of the home LAN?

6. Is my proposed diagram correctly labeled?

At first the answers to these questions seem obvious, but as with so many apparently easy questions, the problem is in the details. Examine each question closely to find the answers that can make any networking project run more smoothly and turn out better.

Note that planning a home network is as much an art as a science, because the answers to each of the four questions above influence or even determine the answer to some of the others. The type of construction of the home where the network is to be installed, for example, may determine how some or all of the nodes are connected. (Old, heavy brick construction, twice remodeled, suggests a wireless LAN for most nodes.) The data requirements of some nodes may determine how they must be connected in order to get the required transmission speeds. (Multiple high-definition television nodes and extensive audio nodes in the network may require a wired Fast Ethernet.)

The following sections discuss some details of each of these questions. Keep in mind that a good network plan requires that you evaluate each factor according to its importance in the particular situation in which you're working. Your job is to envision the home network as a whole entity, then create an integrated plan that fits the home LAN to the needs and wishes of the client, the house in which it is placed, and the technology available to do the job based on the available budget. That's what home technology integration really is.

Where Will the Network Be Built?

The "where" for a network is not so much the geographical location as the physical construction of the building where it will be installed. The type of network chosen and the technology used to connect the nodes is heavily influenced by whether the network is installed in new construction where wiring is easy, or in an existing structure which must be retrofitted with greater difficulty.

Prewired New Construction

4

Examine the building site in detail. If it is new construction, is network wiring being installed? If it is not in the plans, can it be added so the contractor can include it with the other wiring already planned? If that can't be done, can you do the network wiring while the house is under construction? Almost any way to install the network wiring while the home is under construction is easier than installing it after the house is finished.

This also applies to remodeling. If a basement is being finished or an addition put on the house, and a network is planned as part of the project, get the wiring in place before any of the finish work is done. Use the area being added or finished to run as much of the network wiring as possible, even if doing so means longer wire runs to some of the network nodes. Plan each wire run so that it extends from the node's connection point toward the **patch panel** or central hub, but in a manner that gets it quickly from the finished area where it must be concealed to unfinished areas where it can be run exposed. The exposed wiring is later covered by the finished surfaces installed as part of the home's construction or remodeling.

If the new or remodeled home has any network wiring installed, be sure you get a schematic drawing of the existing wiring before creating the plan for the LAN. When you have the schematic, examine the home itself and locate all the connecting points that are supposed to be there. Some may have been inadvertently covered over by plaster or paint and you may need to locate them from the drawing. Sometimes the wiring technician moved a connection because he or she encountered a problem placing it where the plans specified. It is far better to note these changes or possible omissions before creating the network plan than to discover later that a needed connection isn't there.

You want to make use of as much of the existing wiring as possible, even if it is not all placed in exactly the locations you'd have chosen. Good planning can make the most of a general wiring installation done before the design of the LAN was completed. For example, if the LAN has several nodes (computers, printers, file server) located in one room, but only a single wiring connection is available in that room, you may still be able to use the existing wiring by segmenting the network nodes in the room and connecting them via an internetworking device to the rest of the network.

Retrofitting Existing Structures

If the network is going into a home that's already built, what wiring is already installed that can be used as part of the LAN? The newer a home is, the more likely it is to have some wiring installed beyond the minimum required for its original utilities. There may be additional telephone jacks installed, cable television connections, or even a basic network cable system. None of these are likely to be found in a home more than 15 years old, and the closer a home is to that age, the less future-oriented wiring it has.

The same general rule applies to wiring an existing home as to one being remodeled: install the wiring so that it runs from each node's connection point in a finished area to an unfinished area in as short a distance as possible. In an existing home, the unfinished areas are usually the basement or the attic. In these situations, cables should be fished inside the finished wall of the room to the basement below or the attic above and then run in the unfinished space to the central hub or patch panel.

Carefully plan the wiring run for each node in an existing home. You can't run wiring inside brick walls. If the home is brick construction, all the outside walls (and maybe some interior walls) aren't available for wiring. This may not apply if the construction is brick veneer (a facing of brick over wood frame outer walls), but all outer walls are more difficult to run wiring inside than interior walls. Exterior walls are nearly always filled with insulation and have obstructions at the top and bottom that are hard to drill through for wiring. Pulling wire up or down an exterior wall is at best a frustrating and time-consuming experience.

Plan the network so that you can use interior walls for wiring wherever possible. In a multistory home, don't plan on running any wires from one floor to another inside a wall. Homes are constructed so that the floor extends across the entire area inside the foundation or walls and is covered with one or more layers of subflooring. The walls of each story are then built on the floor and attached to it. Holes are drilled through the floor for any pipes or wiring that extend between floors or into the basement. A wall may appear to be continuous through two or more floors, but the floor will usually interrupt the open space inside the wall, preventing wiring from being fished between floors after the wall is finished.

What Nodes Will Be on the Network?

What does the client want to include in the home network? What is he or she likely to want added to it later? Even if the home's builder didn't plan for the future, you should do so when designing the home network. Plan for every network node you can think of and how you will wire it into the system. You may not actually install everything you plan for, but the network will have a better design, and the installation of future nodes will be easier if you plan for them in the beginning.

More than 25 million U.S. homes currently have two or more PCs. The vast majority of these households will install a home network to share Internet access among the PCs and new Internet appliances, and avoid paying for two or more monthly Internet services. The number of homes equipped with multiple PCs will probably double over the next 10 years with an even larger number acquiring other networking devices and automation systems.

At a minimum, a home network should connect all the computers in the home and give each of them access to the Internet. Start your network plan with that core. Decide if the existing computers should be connected through a central computer or through a hub. How will you set up a firewall to protect the home network from abuse? How will additional computers be added, and where will they be located? Where are the printers, and how are they connected? Scanners? File servers? Other input or output devices? Is wireless access needed in some or all parts of the home? In the yard? Don't forget the garage.

Beyond the basic computer network, does the client want television and audio entertainment systems connected? What about a security system? A lighting control system? A water control system? A heating and air-conditioning control system?

Plan for how each of these systems will be connected to the network, even if they won't be installed immediately. Build in enough excess capacity to the core network nodes and the wiring or wireless connections you install so that the network can be expanded later without the need to completely rewire it. Try to think beyond what you see in current home networks to what might become common in the near future.

4

It is possible, even probable, that not all the home network will be a wired Ethernet. Specialized network functions operating on different standards can be designed into the LAN and connected to it as network segments through a compatible device. In this manner any number of segments using standards such as HomePNA, HomePlug, Bluetooth, and others can be incorporated into the total LAN design.

Wireless hubs can be installed to give laptop access throughout the home and in the yard. Each access point can be set up as a node on the Ethernet or all of them can be wired as a separate segment and then connected to the network through a bridge. The latter method reduces wireless traffic on the main network, but this is only an important consideration if wireless traffic is likely to be heavy, such as multiple laptop users playing video games or streaming music and video.

A lighting control system can be installed using HomePlug or X10 technology to set up all the controls. The system can then be connected to the network through an Ethernet-compatible device that translates commands into the auxiliary technology. This setup allows overall control of the lighting system from the network's central computer while still permitting remote lighting control from other locations set up with HomePlug or X10 devices. Further information on how these technologies can interface with an Ethernet LAN is available at *www.homeplug.org* and *www.x10.org*.

Utility management systems such as sprinkler controls, heating and air-conditioning controls, de-icing systems, and timed electrical functions such as outdoor lighting, pumps, ventilators, and other devices can all be set up as network segments. All use the most efficient technology available for their individual control modules, and connect to the network through an Ethernet-compatible hub or other device. Again, this segmentation minimizes traffic on the main network while allowing monitoring and overall control of each system to be exercised from the central computer.

The home security system can be set up as a network segment, connected to the main network for monitoring and central control, but isolated from other network segments and from the Internet to prevent any tampering with, or disabling of, its functions. Good security practice requires that monitoring of sensors and video surveillance nodes be separated from control of security devices such as door locks and alarms. This can be accomplished by setting up each part of the security system as a separate segment, both linked to the main network, but neither accessible to the other or to anyone except an authorized user.

Where Will Each Node Be Located?

Which rooms in a home will have nodes located in them is generally apparent from the needs of the client, but the specific location of each node within the room can often be adjusted to make installation easier and minimize wiring requirements. If nodes are to be set up in adjacent rooms, for example, a double wire can often be fished in the wall between them and outlet **jacks** installed on either side of the wall to accommodate both nodes.

If the node is a computer, printer, or other device that must be easily accessible to a user for long periods of time, then it needs to be positioned conveniently at a desk or table with its connection wiring out of the way of rolling chairs or people's feet. Nodes where devices require **AC power** connections should have their network connections near enough to power outlets so that extension cords don't have to be strung long distances to reach them.

If other technologies are being used for segments of the network, then an access hub, bridge, or other device should be planned where each of these segments connect to the main network. These access devices for network segments each need to be connected to the LAN with a wired connection to the patch panel. The connecting devices should be located where most convenient for running a cable from them to the patch panel and also connecting the network segments running on alternate technology to them. For HomePlug or X10 hubs, this can be wherever there is a power outlet, often right next to the patch panel and allowing a direct connection to it. For HomePNA hubs, it can be any convenient telephone jack near which an Ethernet jack can also be installed. Figure 4-1 shows a conceptualized diagram of a multiple technology LAN in which the computers, printer, and modem are connected in an Ethernet topology, and other home appliances are connected in a power-line network such as HomePlug. The network segments are interfaced through the central computer, which is a node on both segments.

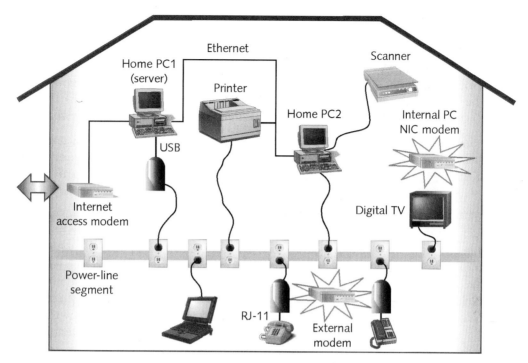

Figure 4-1   Conceptualized multiple technology network

Wireless hubs should be sited in locations where they offer the most effective coverage of the desired range, but that criterion can usually be met while still placing them in a convenient spot for wiring into the network. In some cases a wireless hub may need to connect to another wireless hub or bridge to get its wireless data transmission close enough to the LAN's wired segment so that the bridge can be connected as a node to the patch panel.

How Will Each Node Be Connected?

Until recently, the easy (and usually correct) decision has been to connect the computers in a home network through an Ethernet using UTP or STP cable. Standard UTP and STP telephone wire can handle current high-speed Internet traffic, but with access speeds steadily increasing, its 10-Mbps transmission capacity (which is several times faster than the 1.5 Mbps "high speed" Internet traffic of just a few years ago) is all but certain to be outmoded within a short time. Most electrical contractors now wiring new homes are no longer installing this wire, but are specifying **Category 5 (Cat5) cable**, an enhanced form of UTP telephone wire that can simultaneously handle up to 100 Mbps of high-speed data.

Cat5 is considerably more expensive than other categories of UTP or STP cable, but is still a bargain considering the transmission speeds it offers and the fact that installing it is only slightly more difficult than installing the cheaper wire. When using Cat5 wire, extra care is needed to avoid pulling the wire too hard, bending it too sharply (kinking), or forcing it through too tight an opening. All of these errors can alter the way Cat5 wires are twisted inside their plastic jacket and thereby reduce the cable's performance. Each network node jack also needs its own separate **cable run** from the patch panel or central gateway. Cat5 cable can't be spliced along the way, nor can it run closely alongside AC electrical wires because the **electromagnetic fields** that high-voltage wires generate when in use can interfere with the relatively weak digital signals in the cable. Keeping the two types of lines at least a foot apart protects against such interference.

Because it is the labor, not the cost of cable, that is the main expense in any home LAN wiring job, it makes sense to install the highest quality and capacity cable, even if it won't be immediately used to full measure, to ensure against future obsolescence. To be doubly sure of meeting future needs, some wiring specialists put in parallel runs of coaxial cable (for TV and satellite reception) and even fiber-optic cable. These are both low-voltage cables, which can run alongside Cat5 cabling without any of the lines producing interference in the others.

Cat5 cable is the current quality standard for wiring home LANs. For the best wiring value and expansion capability, use composite cable which combines Cat5 and other transmission cables within a single PVC jacket. It makes multiple-wire installation easier and saves on the cost of future wiring. Some of these cables contain two Cat5 wires (for the network) and two shielded RG-6 coaxial cables for cable and satellite television. The top-of-the-line, "future-proof" version of this type of cable contains Cat5 and RG-6 wires, as well as a fiber-optic line, the fastest available transmission medium. Figure 4-2 shows some of these cable types.

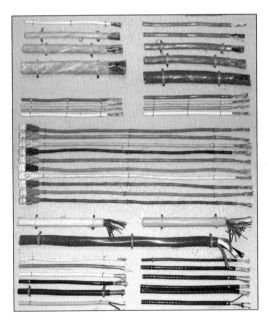

Figure 4-2   Cable types

Fiber-optic lines, which carry light-based data through strands of glass no thicker than a human hair, are the fastest and the most expensive transmission media yet devised. Few home LAN users currently want to purchase the costly conversion equipment required to change electrical impulses into photons, but the future price of these devices is virtually certain to decline. This makes their widespread use in the future more likely. At present, however, there is no practical way for homeowners to use fiber optics, which explains why a network jack accepts **plugs** only for co-ax and Cat5 cable connections.

Do I Have a Diagram of the Home LAN?

Before starting installation, it is a good idea to diagram the home LAN noting the location of all node connecting points, wiring runs, wiring closets and pipe chases, the range areas of wireless hubs, and all the specific components that are included in the LAN. The diagram can be best drawn as an overlay on a schematic diagram of the home and surrounding yard that shows the location of existing electrical wiring and other circuitry as well as the basic construction of the home. A typical diagram of a home LAN is shown in Figure 4-3.

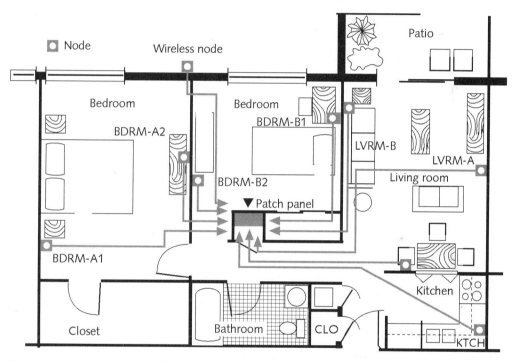

Figure 4-3 A LAN design for a small home with a wireless node for the yard

As shown in Figure 4-3, note the location of all the network nodes and, very specifically, the location of each of the wall jacks by which they connect to the network. If you plan to have part of the network running on technologies other than Ethernet, also note where the devices for these technologies are located and, if they require AC power, how they connect to it. If you use wireless, HomePNA, HomePlug, or X10 segments in the network, you want to connect them at some point to the Ethernet. The most convenient place to do this is usually near the patch panel and gateway setup, so plan to place those devices where you also have enough room for additional devices linking non-Ethernet segments into the main LAN.

The first priority is to select a location for the patch panel and other equipment in an unfinished area of the home, if at all possible. All the wiring for the network comes into the patch panel and fishing all of them through finished walls enormously increases the labor of installing the network. It is far better to work in an unfinished area (which can be finished after the network is completed, if desired).

The second priority for the location of the patch panel is to find the (unfinished) place in the home which is most conveniently situated for pulling wire from all the other areas of the home where nodes will be placed. This likely won't be a distant corner of the building, but someplace more centrally located. Under stairs, in a utility (furnace) room, or in a centrally-positioned closet are all good possibilities. All of these are likely to have good access to the basement or attic, both places through which much of the wiring can easily run. In a two-story home, these are also the areas most likely to provide access from the lower floor to the upper. If these areas don't have access already, holes to provide it can be cut or drilled in the unfinished floor beneath and ceiling above. These access points can later be covered with finished wallboard or cabinetry when the wiring infrastructure is in place.

If the network includes a new line to the **Network Interface Device (NID)**, the data line connection point on an outside wall of the home, a cable line to a modem, or a satellite dish antenna connection to the outside, you must also determine how these cables will run from the patch panel to their exterior terminals. If the home has an attic or basement, these lines can probably run in one or the other to a point near the outside terminus, then pass through a wall or roof to the outside. If the LAN is being installed in an apartment, locating the patch panel at or near an outside wall may be necessary because cables cannot be run through the walls to reach an outside location.

If you choose a utility room for the patch panel, be sure to position it as far as possible from electric motors and other devices that could interfere with the network. If you do find interference from other electrical appliances in the network, you may need to replace or filter the offending devices.

Once you have the patch panel location set, note it on the diagram, and then plan where the cables will run from each jack to the patch panel. The diagram is two-dimensional, but you have to think in three. Each cable run has to reach its destination within the length and breadth of the home, but also run up and down in the vertical dimension so that it remains concealed either within the building's structure or surface mounted on the walls. **Retrofit** wiring requires more cable than wiring in new construction, and there is also more waste because cable segments often have to be cut long in order to be pulled into place and then trimmed off later.

Is My Diagram Correctly Labeled?

When your diagram for the network is complete, label everything on it with a short, unique designation. Start with the rooms: living room equals LVRM, master bedroom equals BRM1, and so on. The jacks in each room can take their names from the room: LVRM-A, LVRM-B, and so on. If each jack has only one cable running to it, then the cable ends can be labeled with the name of the jack. If the jack has multiple ports for data, telephone, or video, then each port must have a separate name: LVRM-A2, LVRM-A3, and so on, and the cable running to each must be correspondingly identified.

Labels are among the most critical items in the network installation process. Nothing saves more labor than accurate and complete labeling of every port and cable end. Nothing causes more frustration and makes troubleshooting more difficult than cables you can't identify running you know not where. Label everything, and use labels that stick fast and won't come off when the cable is handled and pulled through narrow openings.

4

BASIC CENTRAL LAN COMPONENTS

Some components of a network serve the entire system rather than only a single node. These components are those which connect the network nodes into a linked whole and those which connect it to the Internet. Carefully setting up the gateway, patch panel, cables, and home run results in a smoothly functioning network that can be easily upgraded or expanded over time.

Patch Panel

A patch panel is essentially a group of RJ-45 jacks mounted in a row or block. They are installed in a convenient location, and each cable line in the home is run from its **outlet box** to terminate at one of the RJ-45 jacks on the patch panel. An Internet gateway or a hub (or combination) is typically located close to the patch panel, and patch cables are used to connect each cable outlet in the house to a port on the gateway. Figure 4-4 gives an idea of how these elements are connected. It shows a patch panel switch and firewall installed in a small rack.

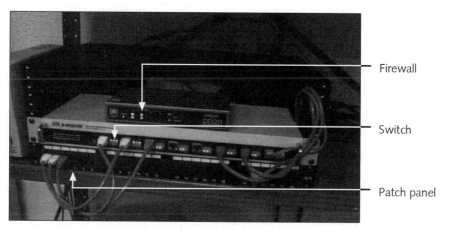

Figure 4-4 Network components installed in a rack

A patch panel is important for several reasons. The outlets to which nodes connect on the network are fixed in place permanently. They are part of the home's infrastructure, as is the cable that runs through a building to connect the outlets to a router, switch, or hub.

The devices that connect to the outlets are not permanent. They're equipment that can, and will be, replaced or upgraded periodically. The same is true of the router, switch, or hub at the other end of the cable line. These are all replaceable devices, and it is better to connect them through a patch panel to the permanent wiring so they can be easily detached for repair or replacement.

By running cable between fixed outlets and a permanent patch panel, you avoid any strain on the cable or its connections that might impair the network's function. You also make all network devices easily removable from the network if the need arises. The patch panel allows for network connections to be changed and updated quickly, making the network more flexible and open to expansion as new additions are made.

Patch panels add some cost to a home network, but they also add a lot of flexibility and allow the network to be more easily upgraded and expanded. They are well worth their cost and the amount of extra effort needed to wire cable lines into them. Most patch panels that you buy off the shelf are designed to fit in 19-inch wide equipment racks. These can be bought in many sizes from miniversions that are 10 inches high (a suitable scale for most home LANs) to 6-foot-high stand-alone units. The patch panels have holes on the ends for screws to mount them in the rack, but they can also easily mount in a wall panel box, in a cabinet, or between wall studs.

Straight-through and Crossover Cables

The cables that connect the network (and the patch cables that connect the devices to the jack and the ports on the patch panel) are **straight-through cables**, which means that pin 1 of the plug on one end of the cable is connected to pin 1 of the plug on the other end.

Crossover cables are crossed end to end; patch cables are not. Figure 4-5 shows the wiring at both ends of a straight-through or patch cable on the left, a crossover cable in the center, and a rollover cable on the right. A rollover cable is used on certain routers, but rarely has an application in a home LAN. It is not the same as a straight-through cable and cannot be used in place of one.

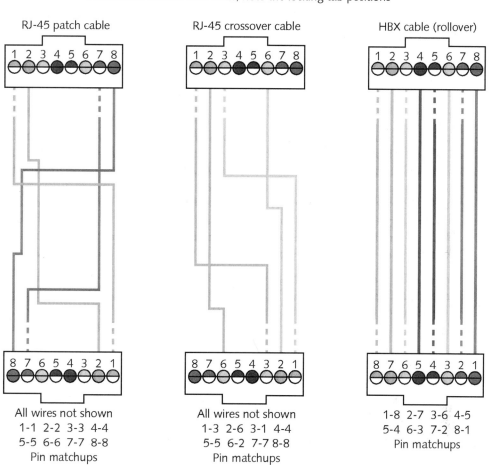

Figure 4-5 Network cable connector wiring

The only time connections are crossed over is when two Ethernet devices are directly connected together without a hub. This connection can be between two computers connected without a hub, or between two hubs connected via standard Ethernet ports in the hubs. In either case, a crossover cable, which crosses the transmit and receive pairs (the orange and green pairs in normal wiring), is required. In a crossover cable, one end is normal, and the other end has the crossover configuration. If a crossover cable is used, it should be labeled so that it won't be used as a "normal" patch cable in the future.

Remember that only two computers can be networked together with Cat5 cable. To add extra PCs to the network requires a bus topology or a hub.

NOTE

Residential Gateway

If the LAN has only one or two computers, one of them can be wired as the network's gateway to the Internet and the other can receive its Internet data through the gateway computer. If the LAN includes multiple computers, or might in the future, a separate **residential gateway** is a good idea. It adds $100 or more to the network's cost, but like the patch panel, it also allows for more flexibility, easier expansion, and greater capacity for the network.

A residential gateway connects the home's local area network (LAN) to the Internet. A hardware device similar in function to a router, the residential gateway provides a unique combination of features. By definition, a gateway joins two networks together. In the home network setting, this means joining the home LAN with a WAN that forms part of the Internet.

As home networking continues to grow in popularity and capability, vendors are working to make home networks easier to build and use. Many elements of a home network, such as IP addressing, present unnecessary complexity to the user and are being simplified and automated in emerging gateway products. Gateway hardware exists in multiple forms including general-purpose servers with multiple network adapters (also known as multi-homed computers) and routers.

Home or residential gateways vary significantly in their capabilities, so that no one typical home gateway exists. However, most residential gateways have some basic features:

- POTS and DSL cable service connectivity

- Internet connection sharing

- Firewall security

The rising popularity of broadband networking has also stimulated the improvement and flexibility of home gateways. Broadband brings a new realm of Web-based applications into the home, including real-time, high-quality audio and video streaming and online gaming. A central device such as a residential gateway is best able to support this new generation of Web technologies.

Because residential gateway products are relatively new, their technical specifications continue to evolve. Home networks may include segments using several technologies. Any or all of these systems, each using a different networking technology, might be included in a single LAN:

- Ethernet home network

- Wireless home network

- HomePNA network

- PowerPlug Network

- Bluetooth Network

Residential gateways are now available that provide connectivity for all of these network technologies as well as Home Audio Video interoperability (HAVi) and Open Services Gateway initiative (OSGi), two additional technologies discussed in Chapter 7. If the home LAN you're installing uses more than one technology, a residential gateway with multiple capabilities is the ideal solution for connecting the various network segments.

The D-Link DI-804 is a residential gateway with four switched Fast Ethernet ports. It allows multiple computers to share a cable or DSL Internet connection. It provides security as a firewall between a local network and the Internet. The DI-804 allows multiple computers to simultaneously connect to the Internet through the same ISP account. It employs Dynamic Host Configuration Protocol (DHCP) that provides dynamic allocation of IP addresses for up to 253 clients on the network. The DI-804 connects to any Ethernet device and multiple types of machines and operating systems. The unit sells for about $125. Figure 4-6 shows a picture of this device.

Figure 4-6   D-Link DI-804 gateway

The UGate-3200 gateway also acts as a DHCP server for multiple computers. It provides dynamic allocation of IP addresses for up to 253 clients. It has more capacity than the DI-804 and supports 11 Mbps wireless and 10/100 wired connections for PC or Mac computers. It has a built-in print server as well as Dynamic DNS and NAT firewall security. It sells for about $250.

The Cisco Internet Home Gateway (iHG) connects computers, telephones, and fax machines to a single broadband connection. Designed to be mounted on a wall, the iHG is about the size of a VCR.

WIRING A HOME LAN

Wiring is the backbone of a network. It is also the part most vulnerable to performance problems caused by poor installation practices. Wiring in new construction is generally a straightforward process, but it needs to be carefully and precisely done if the wiring is to perform at capacity and endure for years. Wiring in existing structures, whether done within the walls or on the surface, can be a frustrating experience, but this type of wiring needs to be as professionally installed as that in new construction. Forcing cables around corners and through openings too small to accept them may enable an installer to get a connection made, but it rarely performs up to standard. No network is better than the quality of the wiring on which it runs.

Wiring in New Construction

If you are lucky enough to get the network installation job while the house is under construction, take a few minutes to celebrate your good fortune. You should wait until the **rough-in** for the electrical, plumbing, and HVAC systems are installed in the home before doing the rough-in for the network wiring. Letting these other pros do their work first means you won't have to worry about them cutting through any of the cables you install. You'll also be able to keep your cable runs well away from any infrastructure that might cause interference in the network.

Install the boxes for the jacks in the walls first. You can use plastic or metal outlet boxes commonly used for AC wiring, and these are easily obtained at any building supply. Place the boxes as near as possible to the locations specified in your wiring diagram. Move them only to avoid obstructions already in place or that are likely to block the run of the cable to the box. Also be sure that neither the cables nor the jacks are too close to other electrical lines or equipment in the locations you chose. Put the boxes at the same height from the floor as the AC outlet boxes installed by the electrician (a stick cut to the correct height for the bottom of the box saves measuring each one) so that the **face plates** match when installed.

When all the boxes are in place, drill the holes in the wall studs, floor **joists**, and ceiling **trusses** that are necessary to make the cable runs on your diagram. Cat5 cable is just shy of 1/4-inch in diameter. For single cable runs, a 3/8-inch hole is plenty large. Two Cat5 cables together, however, will bind when being pulled through a 1/2-inch hole. For these double cable runs, use a 5/8-inch hole. This size can also accommodate three Cat5 cables in a bundle. If you are pulling any other wires which are larger in diameter (RG-6 video wire, for example), you should try a set of all the cables that are in a run to see what size hole they can easily pull through without binding.

Drill the holes for cable runs as aligned with one another as you can to make pulling the cable easier. Wherever possible, drill the holes in the same direction you'll pull the cable. Clear splinters from the backsides of the holes. Adjust hole locations to make turns in the cable as gradual as possible to avoid altering the twist structure inside the cable and reducing its performance. Keep the cable holes centered in the middle of the wall **studs** and far enough from the edges of joists and trusses that the cables won't be in danger from wallboard fasteners or molding nails driven into the wall later.

Run Cat5 cables as required from each box to the patch panel location. Leave at least a foot of cable protruding from each box and a full loop (two or more feet) at the panel end for each run. Run the cable loosely, and avoid bending it sharply around corners. Be gentle with the cable to avoid damaging it as you pull.

Pulling cable is a lot easier and faster with two people working, one to pull the cable and the other to feed it in from the starting point. If a second person isn't available, he or she can be partially replaced by a cable reel (to pay out the cable as it is pulled) and some pull cords and rods.

Tips for Working with Concealed Wiring

CAUTION When drilling or cutting into any existing wall, the AC power should always be shut off for the area in which you are working. This cannot be stressed enough. In addition, before drilling or cutting, carefully check that you will not be hitting an AC power line with your tool(s).

Working with **concealed wiring** has its tricks. For example, for cable runs that are concealed inside an existing wall, start with an outlet box that is designed to be installed into the wallboard. To place the box, cut a rectangle into the **drywall** in the correct location, slide the box in, and tighten up the binding screws. Tightening the screws pulls some plastic tabs tight against the backside of the drywall to secure the box in place.

Cut the opening for the box, and then pull the cable for it before placing the box. If the opening is located near the floor, you may be able to slip a small power drill inside the wall and drill a **pilot hole** for the cable down through the floor plate and subflooring into the basement or crawl space. This pilot hole guides you in drilling a larger hole with a drill up from below.

The pilot hole should be no more than 1/8-inch in diameter, just big enough to shine a penlight through and locate the position from beneath. The final hole should be large enough for the cable to pass through easily without binding: 5/8 or even 3/4-inch.

If you can't drill a pilot hole to locate the correct position of a cable wire hole from above, measure the position from a heat vent, pipe, or other construction feature that passes through the floor. Measure the exact distance from the outlet box to the feature (in two directions, making sure you determine both at right angles to one another and aligned with the direction of the wall itself). Then, measure from the feature in the basement to locate the hole position, making sure the directions of each measurement are the same as above.

Try to place outlet boxes midway between wall studs. Doing so helps reduce the risk of later drilling wiring holes up from below inside the wall, but on the wrong side of a stud. Also remember that most interior walls have **fire-stops** (cross pieces of wood that block off the interior space between studs) about halfway up the wall. If you wire from the attic down to an outlet near floor level, you probably have to go through a fire-stop in the wall. There's almost never an easy way to do this. It generally requires cutting an access hole in the wall, drilling through the fire-stop and then patching the hole after the wire is in place. Accessing the outlet box from below is always the better option, if available. Figure 4-7 shows typical wood construction in older homes and where the fire-stops are placed.

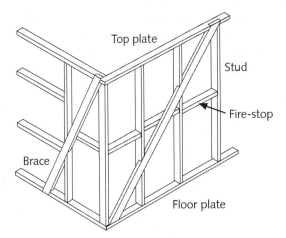

Figure 4-7   Wooden frame construction showing fire-stops

Taping the end of a cable to a 1/4-inch dowel can be helpful in pushing the cable through an opening that you can't reach directly. You can also sometimes pull a cable through an inaccessible area by dropping a weighted string through from above, then attaching the string to the cable end and pulling it back.

When pulling cable in existing construction, especially Cat5 or multiple-wire cable, leave plenty of slack in the line. A full loop of extra wire inside the wall at an outlet box allows the box to be easily connected before it is placed in the wall and secured. This also allows you to easily pull the outlet box out should you ever need to work on it in the future. You can also afford to cut off the cable end should a new jack be required.

When cutting openings for outlet boxes, fit one box in place with the jack inside and the face plate over it to see if the face plate lays flush against the wall surface. Some boxes require that their lip be mortised (fitted into a notch cut around the edge of the opening) into the wall surface before the face plate becomes flush. If this is necessary, it should carefully be done for each outlet box after the cable is pulled to avoid breaking away the edges of the opening too far while getting the cable in place.

When securing cable in unfinished areas (to walls, floor joists, etc.), don't use staples or nails that must be hammered in. You are almost sure to hit the cable or drive a staple too deep and damage the cable. Use small clamps on the cable and secure them with small Phillips-head screws. The clamps can be removed if changes in the cabling are needed, and a cordless screwdriver is far less likely to damage the cable.

Tips for Surface Wiring

Using **surface wiring** takes some planning. When there is no way to get behind the finished walls in a room where a node outlet is required, the alternative is to run the cable on the surface in a **raceway** or under molding. When using a raceway, a little advance planning makes for an easier installation and a better finished appearance.

- Mark out the exact route of the raceway, and be sure you get fittings that can adapt to all of it, leaving no uncovered parts.

- Be sure that the raceway you select is deep enough to accommodate the cable you're using. Test a piece with the cable inside and the cap in place before you purchase the raceway. If the raceway mounts with screws, make your test with the screws also in place.

- Buy all the raceway fittings and the outlet boxes that attach to them from one manufacturer. Don't try to fit one company's boxes to another's fittings. They usually won't mate perfectly and won't look good when forced together.

- If the walls (especially the corners) of a room are not flat and true, don't use raceway that attaches with an adhesive backing. If there is tension on the raceway after it is fitted in place, the adhesive may stick for a time, but will eventually come off. For these situations, use raceway that attaches with screws or add screws to adhesive-backed raceway wherever it can't adhere properly.

- Raceway looks best if run near (but not at) the bottom of the wall, just above the baseboard molding. When painted the same color as the molding, it blends in and is hardly noticeable. If you want the surface-mounted outlet boxes a little further up the wall, use a T-junction in the raceway, and run a short vertical piece up to the level you want the box to be.

- Try to avoid running raceway around door casings and window openings. It is almost impossible to fit it perfectly, and anything less looks tacky. Wherever possible bring the cable into the room at a point from which it can reach the outlet box without passing a doorway. If an opening can't be avoided, run the raceway to the casing, then remove the casing and cut a channel in the back of it in which to run the cable around the door. The raceway can be continued on the opposite side of the door.

- Leave some slack in the cable as it enters the raceway. This is useful if adjustments are necessary later and also avoids unnecessary pull strain on the cable as the temperature changes.

If the cable needs to run near the ceiling, it is best to run it a few inches below the top of the room. Adding a geometric-patterned wallpaper border under the raceway may help camouflage its appearance. Alternatively, a ceiling-level cable can be run inside **crown molding** which has adequate space behind it to easily hold a cable. From the crown molding, a cable can be dropped vertically to the outlet box in the room either inside the wall or in a surface raceway. Crown molding is more expensive than raceway, both for the materials and installation, but it results in a fully concealed installation and a much cleaner finished appearance. Figure 4–8 shows a section of crown molding and a diagram of the space behind it in which cable can run.

Figure 4-8   Crown molding can conceal cables

Cable can also be run inside baseboard moldings and chair rails, but because both of these are installed flat against the wall, they present an additional challenge. A groove must be cut into the molding or the wallboard under it to accommodate the cable. This makes installation more time consuming and expensive. Neither base molding nor chair rail can pass cable around a doorway, so they are only suitable covers for short cable runs within a room.

Working with Wiring Connectors and Terminating Jacks

Once cables are installed for the network, the next important step is terminating the cables with jacks at the node end and terminating them with connector plugs at the patch panel end. Stripping the cable ends and installing connectors requires great care. Stripping dimensions must be observed and the wires and insulation must not be damaged, particularly in high-speed Ethernet connections in which the connectors must have the same transmission characteristics as the cable.

Cable Connector Standards

RJ-45 connectors look a lot like the regular RJ-11 snap-in telephone connectors except they are a little larger. The RJ-45 connects eight wires as opposed to six in the RJ-11. The jacks with which the two types of connectors mate have corresponding conductor counts and different sizes. An RJ-45 connector won't fit into an RJ-11 jack.

The "RJ" in the jack's designation simply means "Registered Jack," and the "45" refers to the specific wiring pattern used for the jacks and connectors. The EIA/TIA-568-A standard defines two wiring patterns for Ethernet CatX cabling: T568A and T568B. These standard specify the pattern in which the color-coded wires in the cable are connected to the pins of the RJ-45 connector or the jack.

If you hold an RJ-45 connector in your hand with the tab side down and the cable opening towards you, the pins are numbered from left to right: 1 through 8. The pin numbers connect to the following colored wires in the cable for T568A and T568B. Table 4-1 shows how the colors are usually designated in wiring diagrams and instructions.

Table 4-1 Wiring standards for RJ-45 connectors

Pin	T568A Standard	T568B Standard
1	Green/White	Orange/White
2	Green	Orange
3	Orange/White	Green/White
4	Blue	Blue
5	Blue/White	Blue/White
6	Orange	Green
7	Brown/White	Brown/White
8	Brown	Brown

T568A standard is preferred for residential applications and T568B for commercial applications. Both, however, are electrically identical as long as you use the same color pattern to connect both ends of a given cable. If you are consistent in this, pin 1 at one end of a cable is always connected to pin 1 at the other end, and pin 2 on one end is connected to pin 2 on the other end, etc., regardless of which of the two color patterns you use.

For the network you're working on, pick one standard and use it for all the wiring. It doesn't matter which you choose. If you were to buy a premade Cat5 patch cable that has been made to the other standard, it still works on the network because both ends of the cable are wired to the same standard.

Terminating Cable to an RJ-45 Plug

To terminate an RJ-45 plug on the end of a Cat5 cable, use a **CatX cable stripper** tool to remove about 1/2-inch of the cable jacket. Next, untwist the **twisted-pair wires** and arrange them in the order (left to right as you hold the cable pointing up in your hand) of the color pattern you've selected to use. Press the eight wires flat on a hard surface or between your thumb and index finger so they can slide into the RJ-45 connector. When you have the wires in the right order and flat, cut the ends so the flattened portions are all 1/2-inch long, if necessary.

Insert the flattened wires into the RJ-45 connector and use an **RJ-45 crimping tool** to crimp the connector in place on the cable. You must push the cable into the connector until the jacketed portion of the cable goes all the way up into the plug because the crimping tool presses down on a hinged tab that grips the cable's outer jacket to hold the connector in place on the cable without pulling on the wire connections. The crimping tool also presses the connector's electrical contacts down until they pierce the insulation of the wires and make contact with the copper conductors.

Follow the directions for using the crimping tool carefully. Practice two or three connecting operations on a scrap piece of cable until you feel comfortable doing the job correctly. Then you can start on the network cables. Figure 4-9 shows the combination CategoryX cable stripper/crimper and the steps described in this section for terminating cable to an RJ-45 plug using the tool.

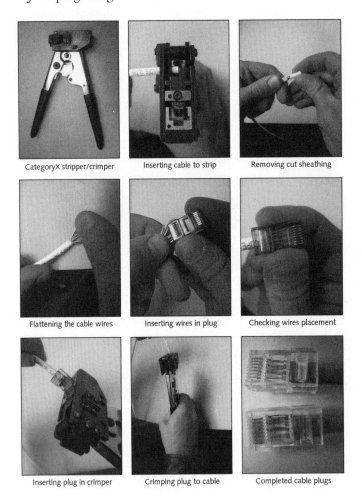

Figure 4-9   Terminating cable to an RJ-45 plug

Terminating CatX to RJ-45 Jacks

To terminate Cat5 or similar cable to an **RJ-45 jack** you must use an **RJ-45 punchdown tool**, which can be purchased in a wide range of qualities and prices from $10 to $90. The more expensive versions use a compression spring hammering action to drive the cable into position. The spring-loaded impact is like that of a staple gun and strikes with a consistent force to produce a uniform connection every time. These tools also have replaceable bits to extend their service life. The cheaper models use only hand pressure to set the cable and are not serviceable for a large volume of wiring.

Both RJ-45 and RJ-11 jacks use type 110 IDC terminals, and to terminate them requires the use of a type 110 bit in the punchdown tool to both cut and terminate the wires. To begin the termination process, remove about 1-1/2 inches of jacket from the cable. Untwist the full length of the exposed wire pairs. Place the cable end onto the jack and arrange the wires into the IDC slots on the jack using the color code printed on the side of the jack. As with attaching an RJ-45 connector, the jacketed portion of the cable must go all the way up into the jack. Don't leave any of the twisted wires in the cable exposed without a jacket covering them.

Using the punchdown tool, press the tool's bit down onto the terminal with the side of the bit that cuts the wire pointed to the outside of the jack. Press down on the tool to compress the spring until the tool hammers down the wire into the terminals slot. At the same time the hammer action drives down the cutting edge of the bit to terminate and cut the wires. Snap on the protective cover that is included in the RJ-45 and RJ-11 jack to cover the area where the IDC contacts are, and the job is complete.

Installing a Home Run Cable

If the home LAN's connection to the Internet is an ADSL, a telephone line which transmits both high-speed data packets and voice signals, a **home run cable** running directly from the LAN's patch panel or from a new inside jack to the ADSL service hookup is a good investment. This can make the LAN's operation as trouble-free as possible. The home run cable, which bypasses all the home's internal telephone wiring, and is isolated from it by an **ADSL splitter** at the service connection point, carries data directly to the LAN without any possibility of interference or noise from other parts of the home's telephone system.

Planning and Preparing a Home Run Cable Route

A home run cable installed in combination with an ADSL splitter ensures a clean path for the ADSL signal from the splitter to the patch panel and then to the ADSL modem. The splitter, as its name suggests, splits the ADSL signal into voice and data segments and isolates all of the existing telephone wiring in the home and any equipment operating on it from the data signal. The data signal (and the separated voice signal if desired) is sent directly to the patch panel via the home run cable, and the splitter blocks any interference to these signals caused by problems with old wiring or malfunctioning equipment on the existing voice side of the line inside the home.

Installing a home run and splitter combination is a somewhat more involved job than installing inside wiring because it requires a cable run through an exterior wall and perhaps around the outside of the home, but it is worth the effort and expense to know the LAN has a clean data signal.

For a home run cable installation, you need an ADSL splitter, a roll of Cat5 cable long enough to do the job, and some mounting hardware. You also need a jack and mounting box if that is what the home run cable connects to inside. If it is going to the patch panel, then an RJ-45 connector for the inside end is required.

Before starting installation, plan where the home run will go. The inside end of the cable connects either to the LAN patch panel or, if there is no patch panel, to a wall-mounted jack to which the modem is connected. First determine where the inside end will be located, and then map a route to the **Network Interface Device (NID)** on the outside of the home.

The NID is a device installed by the telephone company that connects the home's inside telephone wiring to the outside telephone network. It is a gray box mounted on the outside of the house, usually near the electrical meter. In addition to connecting the home's phone lines to the outside, the NID contains a modular plug that allows the homeowner to test whether the local telephone exchange network is working. The NID has two sides, one accessed by the telephone company and one accessible by the homeowner. All of the wiring for a home run is connected on the customer side of the NID. Some older homes may not have an NID, but have a "protector block," a small box where the line coming out of the house connects to the telephone company's incoming cable.

As with other retrofit wiring, the route that the home run takes is based on the most reasonable path for installing it between the NID and the patch panel or jack. Many factors may influence that path, including overall distance, obstructions along the route, and appearance requirements for the finished line.

There are three main ways to get a home run from the NID to the patch panel:

- Run the cable through a wall, and attach it to the outside of the home from the exit point to the NID.

- Run the cable through the attic to an inside point near the NID, then run it through the wall and down the outer wall to connect to the NID.

- Run the cable through the basement or in a crawl space under the home, then out through a wall and to the NID.

Before starting the work, survey the interior and exterior walls of the home to determine exactly how and where you are going to run the cable from the NID to the desired jack or patch panel location. If aesthetics are of concern, try to run as much of the cable as possible inside the house. Run the outside portion along the sides and back of the home, away from the street. Once you've decided on the route the home run will take inside the home, the point where it exits the house through a wall, and the path from there to the NID, you can begin the installation.

Running the line through the attic or basement is similar to running the other patch panel-to-jack cables for the network. Getting the cable through an outside wall and connected to the NID requires a little more care and a few specialized tools.

Mark the point at which to drill a hole through the exterior wall for the cable. If the cable connects to an ADSL jack on the inside of the wall, the hole should be in the center of the square where the jack mounting box is located on the wall. Mark the box position on the wall and the center point in the square. If the cable is coming from a basement or attic run, mark the most convenient point to drill a hole through the wall to the outside.

Use a 3/8-inch drill bit (masonry or wood, as appropriate) to drill a hole from where the wall is marked to the outside. Drill from inside the house outward, but be careful to avoid hazards such as water, sewer and gas pipes, electrical wires and conduit, and cable TV lines when drilling. The hole should be drilled at a 15-degree tilt downward toward the outside of the wall. This prevents water from running inside the home along the bottom of the cable.

On the outside of the house, the cable mounts in **drive rings** for a cable run to the NID. These can be installed under the **eaves** on the building's wall or under the eaves next to the fascia board. Installing the drive rings under the eaves next to the fascia board hides the cable better and allows it to go around corners in two 45-degree bends.

Starting six inches to a foot to the NID side of the wall hole, drive rings should be installed every three feet on straight runs and no more than a foot on each side of a corner. They should be nailed through the eave into the roof trusses, which can be seen through the attic vents or located by the nails in the eave. If the drive rings are installed against the fascia board, use two rings, spaced six to twelve inches from each side of a corner to go around it. Don't install a ring at the corner. The two rings allow the cable to make two 45-degree bends instead of one 90-degree bend. If the drive rings are installed on the wall, apply two layers of friction tape or six layers of electrical tape to the cable where it contacts the corner of the building. A short section of plastic tubing can also be used to ease the bend and provide the same protection.

Running the Cable

If the cable terminates at a jack just inside the hole in the outside wall, it is most efficient to pull in the cable working from the NID back to the jack location as you install the drive rings. If most of the cable run is inside the house going through the attic or basement, work the other way from the jack or patch panel toward the NID. Either way, run the cable to the hole, and fish the end through the wall. Pull sufficient cable through to complete the run outside to the NID or inside to the jack.

When running it outside on the building's wall, keep the cable behind other cables and pipes, if possible, but don't pinch it. Inside and outside, don't run it parallel to PVC (plastic) electrical conduit or AC wiring. To avoid possible interference, maintain at least 12 inches of clearance from other wiring, and don't fasten the cable to any type of electrical wiring or fixture.

Allow plenty of slack, at least two feet at either end. The excess can be cut off at the connected ends, but the cable can't be spliced if it is short. If the cable runs for some distance inside the house, leave at least a full loop of slack at the patch panel or the jack located on an interior wall. If the cable is going to the patch panel, secure it to the inside of the wall above the hole so it can't pull outward. If the cable is going to a jack that is on the exterior wall and the cable goes directly outside from the back of the mounting box, follow the instructions in the next paragraph to wire the jack before completing the cable run on the outside of the house.

For a jack connection, fasten the back box or mounting ring in place on the inside of the wall. The mounting procedure varies depending on whether the wall is brick, block, brick veneer, siding, or stucco. Strip off eight inches of the cable's jacket. Separate the four pairs, but leave the individual wires that make up the pairs twisted. Follow the instructions supplied with the jack to connect the jack to the cable. You only use one or two pairs from the cable, so wrap the other pairs back around the jacket to prevent any shorts. When all wires are connected, carefully push the excess cable into the outer areas of the back box or into the hollow space between the drywall and the outside wall of the home. Place the jack on the mounting ring and fasten it in place.

For a patch cord connection, attach an RJ-45 connector to the cable, following the instructions in the "Terminating Cable to an RJ-45 Plug" section of this chapter. This completes the inside part of the cable run.

For the outside run, start from where the cable exits the wall and extend it up to the top of the wall where it can run horizontally to the NID. The vertical part of the cable run is fastened to the wall with galvanized straps. Place the first strap an inch to the side and two inches below the hole where the cable exits the wall to form a drip loop. Place the next strap level with the hole and two inches to the side of it. This strap is the bottom one in the vertical run. Keep the cable vertical and put another strap at the top of the wall about six inches below the level at which the cable turns for the horizontal run. With the cable secured at the top and bottom, install additional straps every three feet to hold it in position. Seal the hole around the cable with caulking to keep out water and insects. Loop the cable into the drive rings, working from the vertical run back to a point above the NID.

Install the Splitter

Install the ADSL splitter adjacent to the NID, but not so close that the cover of either one blocks the other when they are open. Use screws to secure the splitter to the wall. Run the home run cable to the splitter using straps as you did going up the wall from the exit hole.

Wire the Splitter

Open the NID and locate the wiring for the ADSL line. After you have identified the correct wiring, unplug all of the modular connectors from the Entrance Bridge Network (EBN) demarcation point in the NID. This disconnects all the incoming lines and prevents shocks.

Make notes of where each wire is connected to the EBN so you can reconnect them exactly the same way. Note the colors, but also keep those on the right and left or top and bottom together. When you are sure you have notes of how the wiring is connected, disconnect all the wires from the EBN of the ADSL line. Figure 4-10 shows the NID as it appears closed on the left, then opened in the center, and a close view of the wiring terminals on the right.

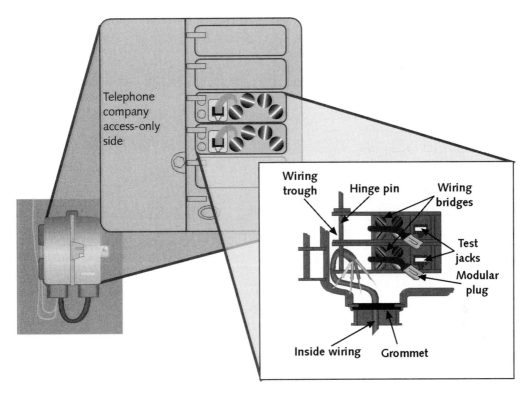

4

Figure 4-10   Network Interface Device wiring

Run a length of cable between the NID and the splitter. Secure the cable where it enters the NID, leaving a foot or so inside the NID. Strip off about nine inches of jacket and connect the white/blue and blue wires to the binding posts that the existing inside telephone cable was on. If the existing cable was connected to more than two binding posts, tighten down the unused posts to prevent static.

Using connectors, connect the white/orange and orange wires of the cable from the splitter to the existing inside telephone cable going color for color or using the following color code: white/orange = green or black, and orange = red or yellow. Wrap any remaining conductors of the cable running from the NID to the splitter around the jacket.

Run the other end of the cable from the NID and the home run cable into the splitter and secure them. Cut the cables, leaving about nine inches inside the splitter. Strip off the insulation on both cables as before. Working with the cable to the NID, connect the white/blue and blue wires to the network binding posts in the splitter, and the white/orange and orange to the voice binding posts. If you are installing a two-port jack on the home run, connect the white/orange and orange wires of the home run to these terminals also. Connect the white/blue and blue wires of the home run cable to the data terminals to complete the splitter wiring. Close the splitter. Reinsert the modular plugs into the EBN(s) according to your notes, and close the NID. The home run cable is complete.

CONFIGURING THE HARDWARE AND CABLES

With all the cables in place and connected to the jacks, and the central hardware components waiting with the patch panel, the network is ready to be configured. How everything connects depends on the size and complexity of the network you've created. Some network setups are illustrated in the figures below. Figure 4-11 shows a basic network with an ADSL connection, a gateway, and one hub or switch.

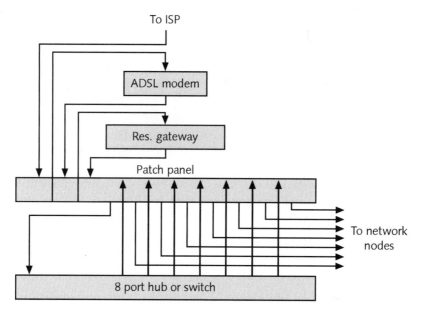

Figure 4-11   Basic network configuration

In this simple network configuration, all components connect through the patch panel. The ADSL line comes into the panel and connects through it to the modem. The modem connects back to the patch panel and out to the hub. The hub's ports connect back to the patch panel and through it out to the nodes. For most home LANs, this setup is sufficient, at least at the beginning. It has plenty of excess capacity and can readily be expanded later with additional Ethernet components or network segments using other technologies.

Figure 4-12 shows a larger network with an ADSL, gateway, and two hubs or switches. This is a larger but still basic configuration. The second hub, again connected through the patch panel, gives you more ports, but the rest of the configuration is the same.

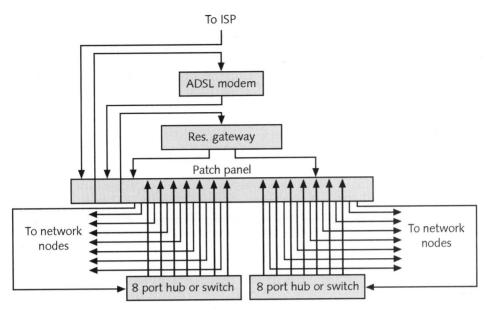

To ISP

ADSL modem

Res. gateway

Patch panel

To network nodes

To network nodes

8 port hub or switch   8 port hub or switch

Figure 4-12   A larger network configuration

CHAPTER SUMMARY

- Planning for a home network should answer questions about where the network will be built, what nodes it will include, where each will be located, and how each will be connected. The plan should be diagrammed and labeled in detail.

- The plan for a home LAN should be diagramed on a floor plan of the house and should show the location of the central patch panel and other main components, the location of each node connection point, and the cable runs that will connect them.

- Network cable runs and connection points should be kept clear of other electrical circuits and equipment that could introduce interference into the network.

- Installing network wiring while the home is under construction is always easier than installation after it's finished.

- If a new or remodeled home has any wiring installed, you should make use of as much of the existing wiring as possible, even if it is not all well placed. Good planning can make effective use of a general wiring installation done before the design of the LAN was completed.

- Most home LANs are wired as Ethernet topologies, but specialized functions operating on different standards, such as HomePNA, HomePlug, Bluetooth, and others, can be designed into the LAN and connected to it as network segments through bridges or other Ethernet-compatible devices.

- When diagramming and installing a network, label everything, including each room, each node access point, each cable run, and all components with a short, unique designation.

❑ Rough-in network wiring in a house under construction should be done after rough-in work for the electrical, plumbing, and HVAC systems is installed in order to avoid cable damage from the other systems and to enable the network wiring to be kept away from any wires or devices that might cause interference in the network.

❑ In existing homes, network wiring should be run wherever possible inside finished walls to unfinished areas and then to the central patch panel. Where inside wiring is not possible, wires can be run on wall surfaces in raceways or wireless access points can be set up which can provide coverage in the inaccessible areas.

❑ Cat5 cable is connected by means of RJ-45 connector plugs, which connect eight wires in a standard pattern and plug into RJ-45 wall-mounted jacks, which are also connected to Cat5 cable using the same standard color pattern.

❑ A patch panel is a group of RJ-45 jacks mounted in a row or block and installed in a convenient location, to which each cable line in the home network connects from its outlet box.

❑ Cables that connect the network and patch cables that connect the devices to the jack and the ports on the patch panel are straight-through cables. Crossover cables are crossed end to end so that two wire pairs are reversed on opposite ends of the cable.

❑ A residential gateway is a hardware device similar in appearance to a router, which connects a home LAN to the Internet by joining the home LAN with a WAN which forms part of the Internet.

❑ A home run cable installed in combination with an ADSL splitter ensures a clean path for the ADSL signal from the splitter to the patch panel and then to the ADSL modem, and blocks any possible interference which might originate in other existing wiring in the home.

KEY TERMS

AC power — Alternating current electric power; the standard electric service in homes.

ADSL splitter — A device attached to the NID, which splits an incoming ADSL data line, isolates other telephone lines and equipment, and allows a home run to be installed to the modem.

cable run — A cable installed between two connecting points such as a patch panel and jack.

Category 5 (Cat5) cable — A high-speed eight wire UTP data cable for Ethernet.

CatX cable stripper — A tool for cutting and removing the outer jacket from Category 5 and other similar types of cable.

concealed wiring — Retrofitted wiring installed within the finished walls of a structure.

crown molding — Angled decorative slats installed at the junction of interior walls and ceiling. It can conceal cable.

drive ring — A metal ring that can be hammered into walls to carry cable on the exterior of buildings.

4

drywall — The paper-covered gypsum board that is fastened to studs to finish the walls in most homes.

eave — The underside of a roof that overlaps the outer walls of a building.

electromagnetic field — Force field of electrons generated by high-voltage equipment and wires.

face plate — The decorative cover on wall boxes that contain data jacks or AC power outlets.

fire-stop — A wooden crosspiece set between studs in interior walls to retard fire.

home run cable — A data cable running direct from an ADSL splitter to the network modem assuring a clean incoming signal.

jack — A connecting device terminating a cable into which a plug is mated to connect a node.

joist — A horizontal support beam in a floor.

Network Interface Device (NID) — A device that connects the ISP service line to a home's inside telephone and data wiring.

outlet box — A wall fixture containing a data jack or AC power receptacle.

patch panel — A device consisting of a row or block of jacks, used for connecting all components of a network.

pilot hole — A small hole drilled to locate a position or guide a larger drill bit.

plug — A terminator on the end of a cable that mates with a jack to make a connection.

pulling cable — The process of drawing a cable through an existing structure from one connector to another.

raceway — An enclosed track in which to run cable; the track is attached to the surface of walls.

residential gateway — A device that connects a LAN with a WAN that is part of the Internet; the gateway controls the data coming into or going out of the LAN.

retrofit — To add new wiring or other infrastructure to an existing building.

RJ-45 crimping tool — A tool used to attach an RJ-45 plug as a terminator on the end of a cable.

RJ-45 jack — A terminator device on a cable into which a plug is mated to make a network connection.

RJ-45 punchdown tool — A tool used to attach an RJ-45 jack as a terminator on the end of a cable.

rough-in — To install the outlet boxes and cable runs for a network.

straight-through cables — Cable wiring that is connected to the same terminator pins at both ends of the cable.

studs — The 2 x 4 or 2 x 6 wood uprights in the walls of homes.

surface wiring — Wiring run along the outside of a wall, usually in a raceway, although it can be bare.

truss — The triangular structures that support a roof.

twisted-pair wires — A set of two wires twisted around one another in a specific manner to improve data transmission in a high-speed cable.

REVIEW QUESTIONS

1. What questions should be answered when planning a home LAN?

2. When diagramming a network, three dimensions must be considered to allow for the network connections extending up and down in the home as well as over its floor plan. True or False?

3. Network cables and connecting points should be kept away from electrical equipment because it can cause _____ in the network.

4. If network wiring is being installed in a home under construction, the rough-in wiring should be done before the electrical and HVAC rough-in is done. True or False?

5. In network wiring, "fishing" a cable means _____.

    a. wetting it before using it

    b. pulling it through an inside wall

    c. lubricating it with fish oil

    d. bending it into a fishhook shape

6. Why can't cables be run as easily in exterior walls as interior walls?

7. Why is it important to label each part of a network design and each physical component with a unique label?

8. The currently preferred cable for wiring an Ethernet network is _____.

9. Why should Cat5 cable be installed gently without sharp angles or deforming of the wire?

10. What is a home run cable?

11. A residential gateway controls a home LAN's access to the _____.

12. A patch panel contains a number of _____ into which RJ-45 plugs are mated to connect the network.

13. A combination stripping/crimping tool is used for attaching RJ-45 plugs to cable. True or False?

14. Cat5 cable contains how many pairs of wires?

   a. one

   b. two

   c. three

   d. four

15. In a crossover cable, which two pairs of wires are reversed when connecting the two ends to RJ-45 plugs?

   a. 2 and 6, 1 and 3

   b. 2 and 4, 1 and 5

   c. 4 and 6, 5 and 8

   d. 5 and 6, 7 and 8

16. The device that terminates a cable run from the patch panel to a node on an Ethernet network is a _____.

17. A crossover cable is used to connect two _____ in an Ethernet without a hub.

18. When running concealed cable in an existing home, why is it better to run the cable to the basement rather than up to the attic?

19. What is a raceway and what is its function in network wiring?

20. The diameter of Cat5 cable is _____ and the diameter hole that should be drilled to accommodate two Cat5 cables going through it is _____.

21. The most convenient place for a HomePlug segment to be connected into the network is at or near the _____.

22. What are two configurations for setting up three wireless access points in a LAN?

23. Why should staples, nails, and similar fasteners not be used to secure Cat5 cable?

24. A punchdown tool is used to connect RJ-45 plugs to cables. True or False?

25. The term NID stands for _____ _____ _____, and it is the connecting point from the network to the _____.

HANDS-ON PROJECTS

Project 4-1: Diagram a Network of the Floor Plan of a Building

In this project you draw a diagram for a network using a scale floor plan of a building as the basis for your design. In the network diagram, include a node in each room, a central patch panel, and a home run to the NID.

1. Obtain a floor plan from a home design magazine or an architectural floor plan drawing.

2. Assume the building is under construction and the network wiring can be installed while building is in progress.

3. Diagram the network on the floor plan as closely to scale as you can.

4. Estimate the amount of cable that is required to complete the network. Use the scale of the floor plan (usually 1/4-inch per foot) to determine the approximate length of the network cable runs and add 30% to the total to allow for vertical segments and slack.

5. Count the number of jacks, RJ-45 plugs, outlet boxes, and face plates the network requires. Add 10% to each total to allow for breakage and spoiled installation. Round each count up to the nearest whole item.

6. If cable is $.22 per foot, outlet boxes are $1.45, jacks are $.59, face plates are $.49, and plugs are $.28, how much do the materials for the network cost?

Project 4-2: Terminate a Cat5 cable with an RJ-45 Jack

In this project you terminate one end of a four-foot cable to a jack. The cable length will also be used in Project 4-3 and so should not be shorter than four feet.

1. Use a CatX cable stripper to strip the cable jacket 1-1/2 inches.

2. Place the stripped end of the cable in the jack and arrange the wires in the correct pattern. Be sure the stripped wires are pulled as far into the jack as the sleaving allows so that the excess stripped wire is cut off when the wires are set.

3. Use an RJ-45 punchdown tool to set the cable, connect it, and cut the wires.

4. Cut off the jack from the cable end, leaving a three-foot piece of cable that can be used for Project 4-3.

Project 4-3: Make a Patch Cable

In this project you terminate both ends of a three-foot Cat5 cable with RJ-45 plugs.

1. Use a CatX cable stripper to strip the cable jacket 1/2-inch.

2. Untwist and flatten the wire pairs in the correct pattern for a straight-through cable.

3. Cut the stripped wires to a maximum 1/2-inch length, if necessary.

4. Place the plug on the cable end with the flattened wires in the correct position. Be sure the wires are fully inserted in the plug.

5. Use an RJ-45 crimping tool to crimp the plug in place.

6. Repeat the above steps to terminate the other end of the cable with an RJ-45 plug. Use the same wire pattern so that the patch cable is a straight-through cable.

4

Project 4-4: Rough-in an Outlet Box and Cable Run in an Open Stud Wall

In this project you rough-in an outlet box in a wall under construction. The wall can be a practice wall set up in a classroom or an actual wall in a residence.

1. On an open stud wall, attach an outlet box one foot above the floor at the far-right end of the wall.

2. Attach a second outlet box one foot from the floor at the far-left end of the wall.

3. Drill 1/2-inch holes in the studs for the cable run between the outlet boxes.

4. Run Cat5 cable between the boxes.

5. Tie back the cable ends in the boxes so they won't be damaged by the drywall installation.

Project 4-5: Install an Outlet Box and Cable Run in an Existing Wall

In this project you install an outlet box in a finished wall. The wall can be a practice unit set up in a classroom or an actual wall in a residence.

1. In an existing interior finished wall, cut a hole for an outlet box one foot above the floor.

2. Create a path for a cable run from the opening down to the basement or up to the attic. Depending on the wall's construction, this may require you to drill up from beneath the wall or down from above it. If the wall is a classroom practice unit, assume an attic exists above it and run the cable up into it.

3. Fish a cable from the basement or attic to the outlet box inside the wall.

4. Secure the outlet box to the wall face and bring the cable through an opening into it.

Project 4-6: Run a Cable in a Raceway

In this project you run a cable inside a raceway on the surface of a wall. If possible, use the same outlet box for this project that you used for Project 4-5. The wall can be a practice unit set up in a classroom or an actual wall in a residence.

1. Install an outlet box in an existing wall one foot above the floor.

2. Attach raceway to the wall one inch above the baseboard or six inches above the floor if there is no baseboard.

3. Using a corner angle, run the raceway around at least one corner of the room and over to the box. Run an elbow extension up to the outlet box.

4. Run cable in the raceway around the corner and up into the box.

5. Put the raceway covers in place so that the installation has a finished appearance. Finish the installation so that the cable is completely concealed from the point where it enters the raceway to the box.

CASE PROJECTS

Case Project 4-1: Select Technology and Design for a LAN

A client for whom you're designing a home LAN lives in an apartment constructed in the 1950s of brick exterior walls with wood and plasterboard interior walls. The apartment has multiple-line telephone service, with a jack in each room of the apartment, and regular electrical service, but the owners will not permit any cables to be installed through the outside walls or on the inside of any interior walls. The home LAN needs an Internet connection and at least one node in each room of the apartment. In this situation, what networking technology do you recommend to the client in order to install the LAN without damage to the apartment? How would you connect the network to the Internet, and where would you try to place the gateway?

Case Project 4-2: Troubleshoot a Network Connection

You are helping a friend determine the cause of a failure in one of his network nodes. Everything is working on his newly installed LAN except the computer in his daughter's bedroom, which the network does not recognize as a node. The LAN's owner says that the cable from the patch panel to the daughter's bedroom has been tested and is working correctly. You check the connecting cable from the jack to the computer and the cable from the hub to the patch panel plug connected to the daughter's bedroom. Both appear to be wired correctly, although their outer sheathings are different colors. Suggest some possible reasons why the bedroom computer isn't receiving data from the network. How would you determine if your diagnosis is right? How would you correct the problem?

Case Project 4-3: Find a Solution to a Node Placement Problem

A LAN you are designing needs a network node located near the center of a 20-foot-long wall in the family room of a residence. The home is a large and expensive modern design and the owner wants all the network wiring concealed so as not to detract from its interior decoration. This presents a problem for the node because the 20-foot wall is made of solid brick. The home has cathedral ceilings so there is no attic space in which to run cables. It has wood floors with a small crawl space underneath. The network patch panel is located in a closet on the opposite side of the family room and at least 20 feet from the brick wall. Suggest two ways in which you could connect a network node located along the brick wall without using a raceway or having any exposed wiring.

4

Case Project 4-4: Recommend a Trouble-free Network Technology

The person who has hired you to install a home LAN lives in a condominium development in which each building contains twelve residential units. She tells you she wants a wireless network so the installation won't damage her condominium. She says that eight other condominiums in her building already have wireless networks and she wants the same kind. She also says she wants her network to be as fast as possible with as much power in the equipment as you can buy because some of her neighbors' networks seem to operate very slowly. Would you recommend a wireless network for this installation? Could another wireless network operate faster than those already installed in the building? If not wireless, what other technology could you recommend that might meet the client's needs? Why might it be better than wireless?

5

HIGH-VOLTAGE WIRING

After reading this chapter, you will be able to:

◆ Define electrical safety hazards and describe good practices in performing high-voltage wiring

◆ Describe how to determine load requirements, install new circuit breakers in a service panel, and connect them to the electric service

◆ Pull high-voltage AC cable in existing walls and install and wire electrical outlet boxes and devices in new circuits

◆ Describe how to install ground wires, surge and spike suppressors, and interference filters in AC circuits

In this chapter, you will learn how to identify high-voltage electrical safety hazards and how to eliminate them by upgrading and improving home wiring according to current code standards. You will learn how to evaluate a home's AC wiring infrastructure and determine whether it will adversely affect a home LAN, either by failing to provide adequate, clean, and consistent electric power for the network's nodes or by introducing noise and **interference**, which reduces the network's speed and efficiency. You'll also learn how to add new AC **circuits** to a home wiring system in order to supplement the existing circuits or to provide a more interference-free source of power for the network. Finally, you'll learn how to minimize or eliminate the high-voltage phenomena that can affect the performance of low-voltage networks: static electricity, electromagnetic induction, and interference.

HIGH-VOLTAGE ELECTRICAL SAFETY STANDARDS

Before working with high-voltage electrical wiring, you must be certain that you meet the required knowledge and licensing requirements for the state and local area in which you are working. You should also know what inspection procedure, if any, your work has to pass before going into service. Specific state requirements are in "State Electrical Regulations: Guide to Electrical Codes, Enforcement and Licensing (2002)," which is at http://*www.necanet.org/store/index.cfm?fuseaction=search_results&index_number=5060*.

Only qualified electricians should perform high-voltage wiring and electrical circuit installation. Many states have laws requiring that commercial and residential wiring be performed only by licensed electricians. Some states' laws allow others to do electrical work, but require that it be approved by a qualified inspector before it is put into service.

The information in this chapter is provided only to enhance your knowledge. Do not attempt to install or work on high-voltage wiring unless you are a licensed electrician or are working directly with or under the supervision of someone who is.

Organizations that Develop Electrical Standards

Electrical wiring and installation requirements also vary from state to state. Some state laws subscribe entirely to the **National Electrical Code (NEC)** which is a safety standard developed by the **National Fire Protection Association (NFPA)**. Other states subscribe in part to the NEC, but amend or add to it as their individual state legislatures decide.

The NEC standard is revised every few years, and it is called NFPA Code #70. The current edition is from 2002; the next planned edition is 2004. It defines minimum requirements for the wiring and installation of "electric conductors and equipment installed within or on public and private buildings or other structures, including mobile homes and recreational vehicles, floating buildings; and other premises such as yards, carnivals, parking and other lots and industrial substations; conductors that connect the installations to a supply of electricity; and other outside conductors and equipment on the premises." Note that the code covers all electrical installations in buildings of any type, as well as the electric power grid which supplies electricity to those end users. Any wiring you do in an individual home becomes an integrated part of a much larger electrical system. Your work must meet the same installation and safety standards as the rest of the system or it puts not only the home where it is installed at risk, but also other parts of the system.

The primary intent of the NEC is to promote safety in the installation and use of electrical wiring and equipment. The code has been developed and refined over many years and represents the combined experience and judgment of literally thousands of electricians and other experts in the field. Its standards and requirements are taken very seriously by state building inspection and permit departments nationwide.

Other organizations also develop electricity-related standards. The Electronic Industries Alliance (EIA) and the Telecommunication Industry Association (TIA) provide forums for industries working in the electrical field to develop standards and publications in several major technical areas: electronic components, consumer electronics, electronic information, telecommunications, and Internet security. TIA oversees the telecommunications sector, and EIA oversees the others. The electrical standards developed by these organizations primarily deal with low-voltage products and processes. They have not produced any standards for high-voltage wiring, either in homes or in commercial buildings, but they do have standards for many electronic products and components which are powered by high-voltage AC circuits. These products include many of those used in computer networks, audio systems, video systems, and home automation systems of several types. You can learn more about the various EIA and TIA standards at their respective Web sites: *www.eia.org* and *www.tiaonline.org*.

The Institute of Electrical and Electronics Engineers (IEEE) is a professional association of individuals who work in the electrical and electronics areas. IEEE (the acronym is pronounced eye-triple-e) has over 375,000 members in 150 countries and is a nonprofit organization that publishes many professional papers and standards. Its standards in areas such as telecommunications, electric power, consumer electronics, and computer engineering do not have the force of government regulation, but are consensus-based and accepted in the various fields because of the technical authority that IEEE represents. You can learn more about IEEE standards (established and under development) at *http://standards.ieee.org*.

Underwriters Laboratories, Inc. (UL) was founded in 1894 as a product testing facility. It is an independent, nonprofit organization not affiliated with the government or any manufacturer. Its technicians perform product safety testing and certification of products that meet its standards for many companies world-wide. Companies submit their products to UL for safety testing, and if they are judged to be safe for consumer use, the manufacturer of the product can attach a UL-approved sticker to each unit as an indication to the public that it has met UL safety standards. Very few electronic or electrical products sold in the U.S., whether manufactured in this country or abroad, do not have a UL sticker attached. The UL listing has come to be the minimum accepted safety standard for all consumer products. You can learn more about UL and its safety testing procedures at *www.ul.com*.

Avoiding Electrical Safety Hazards

Electrical safety hazards in a home environment consist mainly of two types: fire and **shock**. Both can be avoided by correct wiring and installation practices; both are virtually certain to occur if good practices are ignored. Many potential errors may put you at personal risk; many others may leave behind an electrical problem that can cause serious harm years later. As a participant in the HTI field, your career depends on performing safe, reliable electrical installations that stand up to immediate inspection as well as the test of time.

All electrical circuits produce heat. The **resistance** to the flow of electricity in the wires of a circuit and in the electrical equipment connected to a circuit transforms some of the electrical **current** into heat. The higher the resistance within the circuit, or the larger the current flow, the more heat is generated. The NEC specifies wire sizes and other standards for electrical installation in order to prevent heat from building up in the circuit to the ignition point. A large number of home fires are caused each year by overheated electrical circuits: too much current flow forced through wires too small to carry it adequately. When this happens, the wiring accumulates heat over time until the insulation on the wire ignites or melts away, allowing the hot wires to touch something else flammable and causing a fire. Most home electrical fires aren't caused by a short circuit; they're heat-produced fires caused by overloaded wiring.

A short circuit is caused when the circuit doesn't have enough resistance to limit the flow of current passing through it. Touching a **"hot"** wire to a **"ground"** wire produces a short circuit because there's nothing in the circuit to resist the flow of current and too much electricity flows instantly. The amount of current flowing produces a lot of heat, which can quickly cause a fire. The current can also cause sparks at any point along the circuit where some of the current can arc or jump to another conductor and bleed off from the overloaded circuit. These sparks are like miniature lightning bolts, and they're almost as hot. An electrical spark can ignite wood instantly or fuse metals like a welding torch, creating the potential for even more current flow and a worse fire danger.

Short circuits can also cause severe shock to anyone touching the circuit or near enough for the current to jump to his or her body. Depending on how much current then flows through the person's body and the path it takes, an electrical shock can result in a stab of pain, a serious burn, or death.

Whether you are working on a client's home or your own, if you perform any high-voltage wiring work, always be sure you follow the requirements of the electrical code applicable in the area where the home is located. Adhering to the code ensures that your wiring functions properly and won't turn into a liability in the future.

CAUTION The information in this chapter is provided only to enhance your knowledge. Do not attempt to install or work on high-voltage wiring unless you are a licensed electrician or are working directly with or under the supervision of someone who is.

CALCULATING AC LOAD REQUIREMENTS

Alternating current (AC) is the type of current that almost all homes receive from the electric utility company. AC is so named because the electric flow reverses direction in the wires several times each second. 60 cycle (60Hz) AC, the U.S. standard, reverses 60 times each second. The reversing nature of AC enables it to be sent longer distances over wires than the other type of current, which is called DC, or direct current. The reversing nature of AC is also used to control the speed of motors and for other purposes. DC, the type of current that comes from batteries and is used for low-voltage circuits such as networks and electronic devices, functions much better in transistors and other electronic parts than AC.

Load requirements refers to the amount of electric power a home, or a circuit within the home, must have to meet the maximum needs of all the electrical devices in the home or wired to the circuit. To effectively participate in the HTI industry, you need to understand how load requirements can affect the function of home networks.

This section begins by discussing the factors involved in bringing electricity to the home, and then it discusses how to calculate loads for modern dwellings.

Electrical Use in the Home

Residential electrical service is delivered to a house in two "legs" of electricity with a total **potential** of 240 **volts**. Some appliances in a home, such as the stove, oven, electric clothes dryer, and air conditioner, run on 240-volt power. These appliances are connected to both legs of the residential service. The balance of the home's electrical needs are usually 110-120 volts, and all of these circuits are connected to only one leg of the 240-volt service, thus cutting the voltage by half.

You'll recall from your knowledge of basic electricity how **Ohm's Law** describes the relationship among **amperes** (amps), or the amount of current flowing, volts, which is the electrical potential between the two ends of a circuit, and ohms resistance within the circuit to the flow of current:

Ohm's Law: V = IR or Volts = Amperes × Ohms

Electric power used is usually expressed in **watts**, which are commonly calculated in a circuit by multiplying the volts by the amps. Using this formula, a light bulb in a 110-volt circuit through which .9 amps of current flow can be said to consume about 100 watts of power. This simplified calculation doesn't allow for resistance in the circuit, but it gives results accurate enough to calculate load requirements in a home system.

Most average-size homes constructed before 1950 were typically wired for **electric service** of 60 to 100 amps, usually divided into five or six circuits of 15 amps (at 110 volts) or 30 amps (at 240-volts) each. Such a home could have an electric stove (the 30 amp, 240-volt circuit), 20 or 30 electric lights (up to 100 watts each) and still have plenty of capacity for electric radios, toasters, coffee makers, furnace motors, phonographs, and the new black-and-white television sets that were then sweeping the country. Electric dryers and air conditioners were uncommon.

In the third quarter of the twentieth century, typical home electric service began to rise to around 150 amps as the use of electrical appliances, lights, and some electronic devices expanded. By the end of the century, most average homes were being wired for 200 amps, and larger ones for more. A power company research group calculated in the 1990s that the average home had 86 electric motors running at various times within it. Electronic devices, particularly computers and peripherals, became fixtures in most homes, and video systems (television sets and video recorders) and high-powered audio systems increased exponentially in both size and number.

One result of the dramatically increased use of electric power has been that the electrical devices in many homes exceed the capacity of the home's wiring. Many older homes have been rewired to increase their service ceiling, but many others haven't. Some of those that have been rewired were done in a manner not meeting code requirements, and still others had one or two circuits added, but still come up short of what is needed to meet the demand for electricity in the post-2000 home.

5

Calculating the Load

The average power consumption of a home can be calculated from the electric bill or as a percentage of the available maximum service, but **average use** isn't a good method of determining whether a home needs more electrical service capacity and additional wiring. Average home power use has been found by numerous tests to be only about five percent of **peak use**.

Peak use is when everything electric in the home is operating. Think of a hot summer evening when the air conditioning is running, the lights are on, the entertainment center is in use, dinner is cooking in the oven, someone is doing laundry, kids are playing games on every available network node, and the refrigerator and freezer have to work hard to overcome the heat. That is peak use, and if the wiring and electric service in the home can't meet that demand for a few hours each day, an upgrade may be needed.

A home LAN doesn't require a great deal of electric power. A computer won't often use more than 200 watts. Printers that have heating elements use more, but only for short periods. Network hardware such as gateways, routers, **switches**, and similar devices, mostly measure their power consumption under 100 watts. Consequently, if a home is currently powering one computer and a printer, adding a couple more and wiring them into a network probably won't **overload** the electrical service.

Nevertheless, calculating the current and likely future load requirements for a home in which you plan to install a network is a good idea for several reasons. Among them:

- Computers, peripherals, and network hardware all work best on **clean power** that is at or very close to the recommended voltage. The closer a home's power consumption approaches to its capacity, the more vulnerable the power supply becomes to voltage drops, spikes, power surges, and outright blackouts.

- Even though the total power consumption in the home is well within normal limits, individual circuits may be at or above their rated capacity. If any of these circuits are running electric motors or electronic equipment, their performance may be affected and they may generate interference, which can find its way into the network.

In AC circuits operating at a constant frequency (60 cycles per second in the United States), the speed of most electric motors (furnace blowers, air conditioners, etc.) is determined by the current frequency and is nearly always an even multiple of it. Most AC motors run at 3600 rpm or at 7200 or 1800. If the frequency remains constant, so does the motor's speed. If the voltage drops, however, the motor consumes more power in order to maintain its speed. As it consumes more power, it runs hotter and the wires supplying it get hotter, too. A serious voltage drop can burn out the motor, cause a fire in the wiring, or blow the circuit **breaker** or fuse. It is not good to have computer equipment running on the same circuit (or in the same house) if this happens.

- A network that includes wireless segments or any of the technologies that rely on data transmitted over existing wires (HomePlug, X10, or HomePNA) is much less likely to have radio frequency (RF) interference if the home's existing wiring isn't straining (and overheating) to meet demand. This type of interference is much easier to eliminate by replacing or supplementing old or inadequate wiring than by filtering it out after it has entered the network.

For all these reasons, you should check the electric load requirements in the home before you install a home network. If all the circuits are operating well under capacity, then you know you can proceed with confidence in the existing wiring. If additional circuits are needed, they can be installed before you begin the network installation, and outlets for the new circuit can usually be placed so that the network's equipment runs only on them. This setup can help isolate the network from any interference generated in older wiring or equipment.

Checks for Inadequate Home Wiring

A couple of easy checks can help determine if the home in which you're planning to install a network has adequate wiring to provide the new equipment with consistent, clean power, while still meeting the needs of the rest of the home's electrical system.

Start your check by turning on all the lights in the house and all the electric appliances that normally stay in operation for considerable periods of time (radios, TVs, etc.). If lights flicker or dim before you finish activating everything that could normally be running, the home definitely needs additional circuits. If a breaker trips or a fuse blows during this part of the check, the house wiring is probably unsafe and needs to be upgraded to reduce the risk of fire as well as to provide adequate electrical service.

If all the lights and regular appliances can operate at the same time, leave them on for a few minutes and try these additional checks.

- Turn on two burners on the electric stove, and watch for lights dimming or breakers tripping. If either happens, upgrading is needed. An electric stove is connected on a separate circuit in a home. If its operation causes problems in the rest of the circuits, all are probably inadequate, not just the stove circuit.

- Start each of the large appliances that run periodically in various rooms of the house: the refrigerator, the clothes dryer, the microwave, the dishwasher, the furnace blower, and the air-conditioning compressor. As each starts up, watch for lights dimming or breakers tripping. Electric motors draw more current when starting than they do when operating at normal speed. For this reason, dimming or circuit overload is more likely to be observed when a motor in an appliance is starting than when it is running at regular operating speed.

- Take a vacuum cleaner into each room of the home, plug it in to a wall outlet, and turn it on. Watch for lights dimming or circuit breakers tripping. Again, this is most likely to happen as the vacuum cleaner starts up.

- In the kitchen, turn the electric stove on and start both the dishwasher and the microwave. Both these devices have heating elements that draw significant power. If both run without tripping a breaker, while other appliances and electric lights are also operating, the home's wiring is probably adequate.

If any of these tests causes observable dimming, blown fuses, or tripped breakers, then some upgrade to the home wiring is called for. If only one or two circuits continually shows symptoms of overload, then the solution may be as simple as moving some of the devices on those circuits to another existing circuit or to a new one that you install. If the symptoms show up randomly throughout the home, then additional circuits need to be installed and the overall electrical load in the home redistributed.

Installing new circuits in a home doesn't mean the whole house has to be rewired. That can be done, if there's reason to believe that the original wiring, even if used at its intended load level, is a fire or safety danger, but in most cases it isn't. Adding some new circuits that take a portion of the load off the old ones almost always solves an overload problem. You may also want to replace some switches and other fixtures, either for improved performance or an updated appearance, but the wiring generally performs acceptably, if it is not pushed beyond capacity.

You'll want to install new circuits where they can take over as much of the home's electrical load as possible, but require the least amount of new wiring. Before planning or installing any new electrical circuits, find out what is operating on the ones already in place. To do this, turn on all the lights and appliances again and trip one circuit breaker at a time to find out what goes off. As each breaker is turned off, check the unused outlets in the area to see if they are connected to the disconnected circuit. Circuits aren't usually wired to outlets on more than one floor, but you should check to be sure, especially if the basement or a top floor was finished some time after the original house.

PLANNING AND INSTALLING NEW AC CIRCUITS

Once you've determined that some new circuits are needed for the home, the next step is determining exactly where they are needed and how near to these areas you can actually install them. Before cutting any holes in walls for new outlets, you want to make sure that you can connect an outlet at that location to the **service panel** on a new circuit. Not all areas in a finished home are accessible for installing new wires and outlets easily. The location of new circuits in most cases is a compromise of where you would like them and where you can place them.

Plan the Electrical System Upgrade

When you've mapped the circuits in the home, decide where you can install new ones to take over some of the heavy electrical load. If the laundry room isn't already on a separate circuit, it is often a good place to start because the washer and dryer can be put on a circuit with one duplex outlet. Even if the dryer is gas heated, it has an electric motor to spin the load, and a new circuit can take the load of both washer and dryer off the old wiring. The existing circuit can then easily handle the remaining load still wired to it.

Other places for new circuits are the kitchen, where several appliances can be conveniently grouped on a new breaker, and the furnace or utility room. The latter is often a good location for the network's central components and an easy place to wire into because it is generally unfinished (all or part of the walls aren't covered with wallboard, the ceiling is completely or partially open to the joists or rafters above, and the floor may have open communication with the basement below). If you are lucky, the service panel for the home's electrical system will also be there, making the installation of additional circuits even easier.

A new circuit installed exclusively for the home network gives plenty of capacity for hardware components and the probability of cleaner power for the system. If all the main devices of the network are on one circuit, they won't be affected by other tripped breakers, and you can put an uninterruptible power supply (UPS) for all the network components on the network-only breaker.

If you're installing additional circuits to increase the home's total electrical service, in addition to wiring one for the network, keep a general rule in mind. A 15-amp circuit should have a maximum of five outlet **receptacles** on it, and a 20-amp circuit not more than seven outlets. This allows an average of 300 watts usage for each outlet if all are in use simultaneously. That probably won't happen, but some outlets often have loads greater than the average, so the five or seven outlet limits are reasonable. If lights are included on a circuit, a two- or three-light fixture is equivalent to one outlet receptacle in calculating the circuit load.

In an existing home, you need to plan not only where the new circuits will be, but how to run **AC cable** to them. Take some time to calculate the best routes for running the wiring. Plot the route of each wire by observation to be sure the paths you select can be followed all the way from service panel to outlets with no insurmountable obstacles in between. Careful route planning can save you the lost time and frustration of literally running into a brick wall or other obstacle that you can't get a cable through.

Install Outlet and Switch Boxes

Mount receptacles at the same height as the existing wall outlets in the home, which is usually about 12 inches above the floor. In a kitchen, utility room, or closet, you may want to mount the **outlet boxes** at about a three-foot height for easier access, but before doing so be certain you can get wiring to them in that location.

In most rooms, a receptacle should be placed on each wall and a second one on walls with 12 or more feet of usable space (open area without windows or doors). Walls with less than three feet of space don't need an outlet. These are guidelines, but there is no maximum number of outlets, and it is better to have too many than too few.

If switches are to be added on some circuits, boxes for them should be mounted on the inside of rooms near the doorway and opposite to the hinge side of the door. Place switches close to the door opening and at the same height as existing switches in the home. In old homes, the switches may be mounted lower than seems preferable now, but it is better to maintain a consistent appearance throughout.

Outlet boxes mounted in finished walls must be the type that can be secured in the wall by means of flanges that tighten against both sides of the wallboard. Don't try to use the stud-mounted boxes that are intended for new construction. You won't often find a stud located near the hole you cut in the wall for the box and even if you do, it is almost impossible to attach the box to the stud with only the small wall opening to work through.

Wall-mounted outlet boxes work well, but should be permanently installed only after the cable going to them has been pulled into place. Remember also, boxes that mount flush in the wall and accept a hidden cable from behind are different from boxes that mount on the wall or protrude from it and accept cable from a surface raceway. Figure 5-1 shows three types of boxes: on the left is a standard stud-mounted metal box for use in unfinished walls, in the center is a wallboard-mounted box (with grip tab extended) for use in finished walls, and at the right is a surface-mounted box with mounting plate for use on wall surfaces with a raceway.

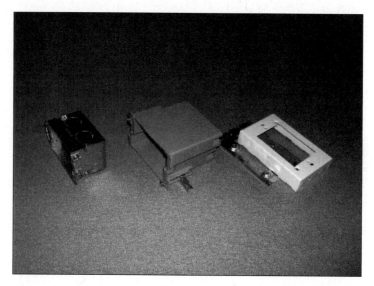

Figure 5-1   Three types of outlet boxes for electrical outlets

In unfinished areas, stud-mounted boxes or boxes with mounting brackets attached can be used and secured in place with nails or screws. Mount the outlet box on a stud, flush to the stud's outer edge if the wall won't be finished later, protruding from the stud edge the thickness of the wallboard used in the home (3/8 inch to 5/8 inch) if it will.

Drill cable holes in the studs from the unfinished area outlet boxes in as direct a path as possible to the service panel. Also drill holes for cable going to finished areas through unfinished routes. Then, after the openings for outlet receptacles and switches are cut and holes for cables are drilled, it is time to pull the cable for the new circuits.

Install AC Wiring

Circuits in a home are wired with cable made up of three or more copper wires in a casing. Each copper wire consists of a single copper strand in the smaller sizes or multiple copper strands in the larger sizes. The conductor wires (one black, which is the hot wire, and one white, which is neutral) are insulated with plastic and are encased together with an uninsulated third wire in a plastic sheathing to form the cable.

The standard by which wire size is measured is the **American Wire Gage (AWG)**. Small wire sizes have higher numbers such as #20, which is a small wire indeed. As the number decreases, the wire size increases, which means that #14 wire is smaller than #12, and #4 wire is larger than both. The size of wire determines how much current it can safely carry. Table 5-1 shows wire sizes, current ratings, and breaker sizes for the most common sizes of wire.

Table 5-1 Wire sizes and current capacities

Wire Size	Current Capacity (Amps)	Breaker Size (Amps)
14	15	15
12	20	20
10	30	30
8	45	40
6	65	60
3	105	100

The most commonly used wire size is **2-conductor wire** (plus ground) #14, which is used in most home circuits to wire outlet receptacles, switches, and lights. Use 3-conductor #14 wire for 2-way switches and split outlet receptacles. Use 3-conductor #12 wire for equipment that may require AC power up to 20 amps, such as heaters and air-conditioning compressors. Larger wires are used for 240-volt circuits that can carry up to 40 amps of current, such as for electric stoves and dryers.

Nonmetallic Sheathed (NM) Cable

Nonmetallic sheathed (NM) cable (often referred to as Romex) consists of several insulated wires and a ground wire encased in a plastic or composite sheath. The cable can have two insulated wires, three, or four, along with the obligatory ground wire. **NM cable** is the most widely used type of cable for AC wiring in homes. The NEC allows this type of cable to be installed exposed in the building or contained in a sleeve or raceway for physical protection. If it is installed exposed, the cable must not be in an area where it may be damaged or subjected to any physical abuse.

The cable can be installed exposed in a residential garage or in an attic or basement. In an unfinished basement, an NM cable must be installed through bored holes in the framing members. In attics, it can be installed in holes through the frames or laid on top of them, if doing so won't subject the cable to damage. In walls, the cable can be dropped from overhead or brought up from the basement without any sleeve requirements. It can also be run through holes in wall studs as long as it is protected inside the finished wall. Cable run on the outside surface of finished walls, or in other exposed situations where it could be damaged must be run in a raceway that covers and protects it.

In addition to inside wiring, NM cable is often used outside the home to provide power for devices on the exterior of the building. Where the NM cable may be exposed outside to physical damage, the NEC requires that it be protected by installing it in conduit, electrical metallic tubing (EMT), polyvinyl chloride (PVC) pipe, or surface metal or nonmetallic raceways. Floodlights on exterior eaves, for example, are often powered using NM cable that has been sleeved to protect it from physical damage and from deterioration from the outside elements, such as dampness or sunlight.

Either metal or plastic outlet boxes can be used when wiring circuits with NM cable. If metal boxes are used, the cable should be secured in them with snap-in plastic connectors. If plastic boxes are used, the connectors aren't required as long as the cable is secured with staples close to the box. When this isn't possible in an existing wall installation, connectors should be used.

Metal Clad (MC) Cable and Armored Cable (AC)

Some local electrical codes require the use of Metal Clad (MC) cable or armored cable (AC) for interior wiring in homes. AC cable was historically referred to as BX. Both of these types of cable contain insulated wires covered with a flexible metal outer casing which protects the interior wires from damage. Both MC and AC cable can be obtained with different numbers of insulated wires. The significant difference between them is in their grounding technique. **MC cable** has a green, insulated ground wire inside the cable, while AC cable has no grounding wire, but uses the outside metal casing as the ground. AC cable now also has a bonding strip on the inside of the cable armor, which improves its ground continuity.

Both MC and AC cable require the use of metal boxes and connectors. With MC cable, the boxes must be insulated from the metal cladding of the cable by using a plastic antishort bushing at every point where a box connects to the cable. Both AC and MC cost more than NM cable and both are more time consuming to install because of the increased connector and grounding requirements. MC and AC cable can be purchased with a plastic or rubber outer covering for use in damp areas, but without such protection, neither of these cables should be used for wiring in wet conditions. Figure 5-2 shows an example of NM cable at the top, MC cables at the bottom left, and AC cables at the bottom right.

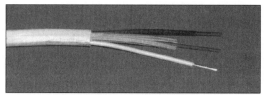

2-conductor NM cable
with copper ground wire

MC cable with
ground wire

AC cable with
aluminum bond wire

Figure 5-2　NM, MC, and AC cables can have from two to four connector wires

Wiring New Circuits

Each new circuit should be wired using the correct size two or three-wire insulated cable (#12 or #14, depending on code requirements in the area). The cable must be pulled from the service panel box to the new outlet boxes in much the same manner as Cat5 cable is pulled for the network. NM (Romex) cable need not be handled with as much care as Cat5, because it is not carrying data, and AC electric current isn't affected by sharp turns or twists in the cable.

Run each cable through unfinished areas as near as possible to the outlet box, then fish the cable inside the wall or run it in a raceway on the wall surface to the outlet box. After the cable is in place, run it through an appropriate knockout opening in the box, and mount the box in the wall. Check wall-mounted boxes with an outlet and faceplate in place to see if the faceplate rests flush against the wall. If it doesn't, you have to mortise the box into the wall slightly to get a flush fit. This requires cutting a shallow notch around the face edge of the outlet opening so that the flange on the front of the outlet box recesses into the wall far enough to let the face plate mount flush with the wall surface.

For boxes mounted in unfinished areas, run the cable into the box and secure it in place with the holding plate in the box. Leave half a foot or so of slack outside the box and at least eight inches inside the box.

Follow the instructions that come with the outlet receptacles to wire them in the boxes. Buy good-quality outlets for your wiring. The main difference between low-quality outlets and good ones is that the cheaper ones lose their ability to grip a plug firmly. After a period of use, they become loose and allow a plug to fall out. Even when the plug stays in place in a loose outlet, it often makes a poor connection to the current and generates interference in the wiring. Spend a few cents more and purchase outlets that last.

Be sure each outlet is correctly connected to all three wires in the cable: black to the hot side (usually brass colored), white to the neutral side (usually silver), and bare wire to ground. Always connect the ground wire first. Even though it isn't grounded at the service panel yet, it is a good practice to follow this rule so that if you are ever working with hot wires, the habit is established. Mount the outlet in the box, and attach a faceplate to cover it.

Multiple outlets wired to one circuit must always be wired in parallel, never in series. This means that all the wires from all the outlets on a circuit must connect directly to the circuit breaker. Wires from multiple outlets are either brought together in a junction box or connected in a line from one outlet to the next. The outlet at one end of the line or the cable in the junction box is then connected to a cable running to the breaker for the circuit. An outlet box can also serve as a junction box for cables from only one other outlet on a circuit, but cables cannot be spliced outside a junction box inside a wall. Figure 5-3 shows a parallel-wired circuit.

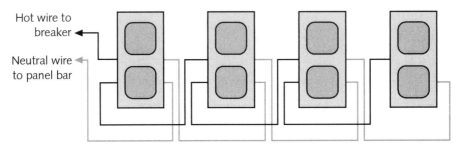

Hot wire to breaker

Neutral wire to panel bar

Figure 5-3   A parallel-wired circuit connects all the outlet receptacles directly to the service panel

High-voltage Electrical Components

A new circuit wired in a home may contain different kinds of electrical devices. The most common are electrical outlets into which network devices and other appliances can be plugged, but there are several others that may be included, either to balance the electrical load on the home's circuits more evenly or to provide additional electrical service and convenience along with power for the network.

The following sections discuss in detail the different kinds of electrical devices.

AC Outlets (Controlled and Uncontrolled)

AC power outlets are the standard source of AC power for appliances, electronic equipment, and other devices in the home. Up to four outlets can be wired in a single circuit, but the number and placement of outlets should be planned so that their combined average usage does not exceed the 15 or 20-amp capacity of the circuit.

Outlets can be wired in an "always on" configuration directly to the service panel as shown in Figure 5-4a. This is the most common arrangement, but at least two others are possible. In Figure 5-4b, the outlet is wired through a switch so that the switch controls power to it. This allows a lamp plugged into the outlet to be controlled by the wall switch, but it also makes the outlet unsuitable for any device which needs continuous power, such as a clock or refrigerator. Fig 5-4c shows a third alternative called a "split" outlet in which the top side of the duplex outlet is wired to the switch while the bottom side is wired directly. This allows the outlet to be used as a continuous power source or as a controlled source governed by the switch.

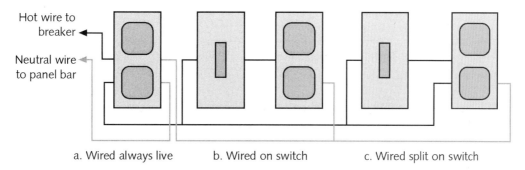

Hot wire to breaker

Neutral wire to panel bar

a. Wired always live   b. Wired on switch   c. Wired split on switch

Figure 5-4   Alternative methods of wiring an outlet receptacle

Switches

Switches are installed in circuits to control lights or outlets. They can be wired in several configurations, but the most common is as a single switch controlling a light or outlet, as shown in Figure 5-5a. Another wiring configuration is shown in Figure 5-5b. It shows how two switches can control a single device such as a light fixture or outlet. This allows convenient access from opposite sides of a room, the top or bottom of a stairway, or the inside or outside of the home. This arrangement uses double-pole, double-throw switches and is known as a **3-way switch**.

A third configuration, shown in Figure 5-5c, also provides for a 3-way switch, but gives one of them ultimate control (either on or off). With this arrangement, switch 1 can turn the light on and it remains on regardless of the position of switch 2. If switch 1 is in the off position, switch 2 can turn the light on or off, but only so long as switch 1 remains in the off position. This last configuration is more useful in an automated system than with a strictly manual one, as you'll see later in this book.

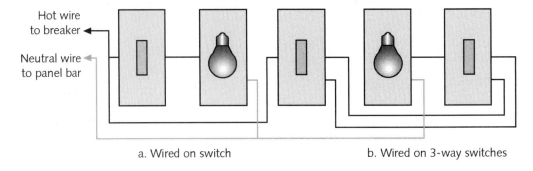

a. Wired on switch   b. Wired on 3-way switches

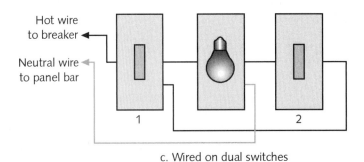

c. Wired on dual switches

Figure 5-5   Options for wiring switches

Dimming Modules

Dimming modules that can dim a single room light or several lights wired together are now common in automated homes. Manual dimming modules can be incorporated into any wall switch and used to control the lights connected to the switch. These modules can now be controlled with either X10 technology or RadioRA wireless technology in order to automate the lighting system completely. Both X10 and wireless lighting controls can be connected to the home LAN through an Ethernet-compatible device. We'll discuss automated home lighting controls later in this book, but any needed additional or upgraded AC wiring should be in place before the automation is installed. X10 and RadioRA controlled dimmer modules can be manually operated from the switch. They can be installed and used before the automated system is activated.

Dimmer modules are wired in the same manner as regular switches and can be configured as single-pole switches, single-pole, double-throw switches, or double-pole, double-throw switches, without affecting the dimming component.

Fixtures

Light fixtures are wired in the same manner as outlet receptacles, either directly to the service panel so that power to them is always on, or through a switch so that power can be controlled from the room in which the fixture is located.

Service Panels

New circuits in the home will probably mean that a new service panel is required to hold the additional breakers. This must be done because electricians rarely leave excess capacity in the original box. In some areas, a second service panel can be installed and wired from the first, but in many areas of the country, a second service box isn't permitted, and a larger one must be put in to contain the original and the additional breakers.

Additional circuits that increase the home's total electrical load capacity may also require new wiring to connect to the power grid outside. The utility company can bring new wires to the original connection point. You have to connect them from that point to the new service panel.

Adding a new 100-amp service to a home requires #4 stranded copper, three-wire cable from the outside connection point to the main breaker in the service panel. But this is only if the new line runs parallel to the original and is installed in addition to it, not in place of it. If the original wiring to the service panel is replaced, the wire size must be sufficient to carry the total number of amps now coming into the home. A 150-amp service requires #1 stranded copper wire and a 200-amp service requires #2/0 stranded wire. Figure 5-6 shows a service panel with main **service lines** (two legs of 120 volts) connected at the top and circuit breakers wired down both sides of the central panel.

5

Figure 5-6   Service panel with cover removed to show wiring in place

The wiring from the outside connection point to the service panel usually runs in a conduit. If the wiring must be replaced, the old wire can usually be used as a pull cable to get the new wiring through the conduit. This can only be done when the conduit is large enough to accommodate the new wire and it may require that part of the conduit be cut or disassembled to eliminate curves and angles that heavy wire can't be pulled through.

The incoming service line exits the conduit (which is attached to the service panel box) inside the box. It is then connected to the two main circuit breakers (one for each leg of the 240-volt service or a two-leg breaker double the size), which may also have to be replaced with units of larger capacity. A 150-amp service needs 75-amp main breakers on each leg. A 200-amp service needs 100-amp breakers.

The main breakers in the service panel connect to the branch circuit breakers, as shown in Figure 5-6. Each circuit is wired through the breaker that controls it. Only the hot side of the circuit goes through the breaker. The neutral side is always connected to main neutral (which is a grounded bar in the service panel), and no breaker can interrupt it. From the breakers, the home wiring extends out to the individual devices and fixtures in the home.

If you're not licensed as required and absolutely certain that you can correctly install the service panel wiring, get someone who is fully qualified to help. There is no room for error in wiring a service panel and the circuit breakers that go in it.

CIRCUIT PROTECTION

Circuit protection is a form of insurance for a network and the data on it. This section discusses the factors involved.

Ground Connections

The first level of protection for a network is to carefully ground all the devices on it. All the AC circuits in a home must be grounded either through a grounding rod or water pipe passing deep into the earth. The rod or pipe is connected to a ground bar or plate in the service panel box, and the ground wire of each circuit in the home is connected to that ground bar.

Because grounding is a part of the NEC and the wiring requirements of every state code, all circuits in a home are grounded at each outlet. When a network is connected to an outlet by a three-wire power cord, the device is grounded through the power cord. No further action is needed. If the device connects to the outlet with a two-wire power cord, it should be grounded by connecting a ground wire from the metal frame of the device to a ground connector in a wall outlet or to a metal pipe. Ground wires should not be connected to other metal objects in the home (metal studs, rails, etc.) as these frequently do not connect to ground in a complete circuit.

Grounding is a safety precaution in case a short circuit should develop in a device, but its more important function for network devices is to eliminate static charges and other noise-producing electric impulses before they reach the network and interfere with data transmission.

Surges and Spikes

An electrical **surge** is a sudden momentary increase in the rate of current flow or the voltage in a circuit. Surges can be produced by power equipment starting up or shutting down either inside the home or at a more distant location, or by lightning strikes or other atmospheric electrical disturbances. Another name for a power surge is a **spike**, although some people define a spike as having a shorter duration and a higher voltage than a surge.

Both surges and spikes mean that for a short period of time there is too much electricity in a circuit. These electrical excesses may last only a few millionths of a second or they may persist for many times that long. In either case, they can do serious damage to electronic equipment.

The electric potential forced into the circuit by a surge may discharge by arcing from wiring to a ground connection. The heat of such an arc can fuse components or burn them out just as a light bulb filament shatters when subjected to excess power. Even relatively small surges, repeated over time, reduce the life of low-voltage electronic parts by subjecting them to momentary current flow and resulting heat far above their designed maximums.

Devices are available to protect against surges and spikes. These can be installed at the point where network devices connect to the AC power or at the point where potential carriers of surges, such as AC power lines, telephone lines, and television cables, enter the home. Because surges can originate from within a home or from outside, protection from both sources is necessary to prevent damage to home LAN equipment. This dual protection is particularly important when part or all or the network's data transmission wiring is shared with or connected to television cables, telephone lines, or outside antennae.

Surge **suppressors** that can be installed at electric outlets vary widely in price and quality. The primary consideration for a surge protector is how fast it acts when a surge occurs. If suppression starts only after .1 seconds of increased voltage, for example, most surges will have come and gone, doing whatever damage they're capable of, before the suppressor even begins to respond. Such devices are useless for protecting against surge damage.

Devices that can suppress only a few thousand surge amps are also useless. The most damaging surges often attain up to 50,000 surge amps for a few millionths of a second, during which time they can burn through low-capacity suppressors and wreak havoc among low-voltage electronic circuits.

Home LAN equipment should be protected by grounded surge suppressors that are rated to act within a few picoseconds and suppress at least 50,000 surge amps. These industrial-grade suppressors are available in the same one, two, four, and six socket configurations as the less effective "power strip" models, and they look much alike. The high-quality units can be distinguished by two factors: they have their response time and suppression strength ratings printed on them (low-rated suppressors rarely publish their numbers), and they cost more than unrated units. Expect to pay between $50 and $100 each for these suppressors, depending on their configuration and amperage.

Combination surge suppressors and noise **filters** are available for installation on telephone lines, cable television lines, and satellite antenna lines. In all cases these suppressors should be placed in the lines before they connect to any network equipment. The vast majority of their effect on the home network is improved performance from noise and interference reduction, but the few times they intercept a surge or spike prevent far more damage than their cost, which is about the same per unit as a good AC suppressor.

Surge protection on the main AC power lines coming into the home usually takes the form of a circuit interrupter that cuts off the electric current when the voltage rises above a preset maximum or drops below a preset minimum. Either condition can damage electric equipment, although electronics are more vulnerable to high voltage than low. Electric motors, such as those on furnace fans, air-conditioning compressors, refrigerators, and freezers, can overheat and burn out if the voltage drops too low over a period of time.

Main line interrupters are expensive and are probably only warranted in areas where the danger of surges originating outside the home is fairly high. A little research into the weather history of a location and a check of whether any large-capacity commercial or industrial electrical equipment is operating nearby can help determine whether a power line interrupter should be installed in a home system. A middle course of protection may be to install smaller interrupters on individual circuits that power expensive equipment.

Minimizing High-voltage Interference

High-voltage interference in a home LAN can originate from a number of sources and affect several parts of the network.

Outside interference can be caused by lightning and the atmospheric conditions that produce it. Wind can also generate static electricity, either by the friction of air moving over stationary objects or by the motion that wind pressure produces in everything from tree leaves and flags to tumbleweeds and windmill blades. Other sources of interference from outside the home include radio stations, citizens band, and police radios, and inside the home, sources include household appliances and fluorescent lights.

Inside interference is mainly produced by differences in electrical potential between different parts of the home or between objects in the home. These differences cause electric currents to flow for very short periods of time between some of the points with differing potential. The brief electrical flows tend to neutralize the potential between the different points, but the current flow often passes through wires, metal component parts, and other conductors that form part of the network structure. When this happens, the high voltage of the flow disrupts the low-voltage flow of data in the network, or may even entirely obliterate it for a time.

Interference can also be caused by operating pieces of electrical equipment that create electromagnetic fields around themselves. Imperfectly wired electrical connections can produce tiny current arcs. These arcs result in interference being generated around the circuit.

Finally, almost any movement of an object through the air or while in contact with another object can generate a static electric charge on the object which when discharged produces interference. This can mean anything from feet walking on a nylon carpet (and discharging with a painful spark when the walker touches a metal object) to clothes tumbling in the drum of an automatic dryer.

Static electric discharge, correctly termed electrostatic discharge (ESD) occurs whenever the static charge on two objects is dissimilar. If the two objects touch, electricity from the one with the higher voltage charge flows to the one with a lower voltage charge until the two charges are equalized. Static discharges can attain very high voltages. If you touch a metal object and feel an electric discharge, the static charge (voltage difference between you and the object) was 3,000 volts or more. If you saw a spark when the discharge occurred, the voltage difference was at least 8,000 volts.

Such voltage discharges can produce high levels of interference and also damage or destroy low-voltage electrical circuits and parts that normally function in a voltage range of five volts or less. Even a mild static discharge can wipe out a data packet running in a low-voltage wire, or completely fry a milivolt-rated capacitor or other electronic part.

Static charges can also be produced by high-voltage devices. All cathode ray tubes (computer monitors, television screens) contain high-voltage electron beams and create static on the face of their screen and also on surrounding objects. Laser printers, copiers, and power supplies in computers and many types of electronic equipment all produce static charges as part of their normal functions. These static charges can remain for long periods on the equipment even after power to it is shut off. The charge can also transfer to other objects or people, creating interference as it does so and forming a new voltage difference on the object or person that can then create more interference when it discharges again.

Finally, fluorescent lights produce interference through a phenomenon called electromagnetic induction (EMI). The high-voltage transformer, called a ballast, in a fluorescent light causes an electromagnetic field to be generated around the transformer by the current passing through it. This field is what causes a fluorescent light to glow. It induces a current to flow through the fluorescent tube, causing the phosphorus inside the tube to emit light. The electromagnetic field can also induce a similar current in other nearby objects, including network cables and electronic equipment. This is why network cables (and other low-voltage wiring) must never pass close to fluorescent lights or other high-voltage devices. Induction currents in the network wiring can destroy data and can damage equipment if the discharge reaches it.

How much the interference generated in and around a home affects a home LAN depends on climatic conditions in the area (dry, windy conditions produce more static electricity and hence more interference), its location (proximity to radio stations, power lines, industrial plants), and how well the home is constructed to deal with the causes of interference. Most interference can't be prevented, but it can be minimized and its danger to the functioning of the home LAN almost entirely eliminated by careful wiring, good grounding, and perhaps a few filters.

The first defense against interference is to create as little of it as possible. Clean, securely connected wires and adequate separation of low-voltage lines from high-voltage equipment and circuits reduce interference. So does good maintenance of electrical equipment. Devices with electrically connected moving parts such as motors, relays, switches, solenoids, and sensors all produce interference if their parts are worn or dirty. Keeping all the home's electrical systems, not just the network-connected devices, in top working order minimizes the interference that must be dealt with after the fact.

The next step to zero interference is to ground everything electrical. Again, this applies to all the electrical devices in the home, not just those connected to the network. It may even apply to a few nonelectrical objects, if you suspect that static charges are being generated on their surfaces. A carefully installed ground wire won't harm any object and may reduce interference on the network by eliminating a source that can't easily be filtered because it is not part of a circuit.

Floor surfaces, furniture, and glass don't ground well, but they all take a static charge quite readily. If these surfaces are near network wiring or devices, they can bleed interference into the network. Antistatic sprays, grounding mats, and removal, where possible, are all methods of eliminating this type of interference. You must determine on a case-by-case basis whether it is easier to eliminate a source of interference or filter it out after it is created.

For the interference that remains in a home after as many sources as possible have been removed, two other defenses remain: shielding and filtering.

Shielding

Shielding applies primarily to the network's cables and is actually a refined form of grounding. The data-carrying wires in a shielded cable are surrounded for the full length of the cable by a webbing of metal wires. Interference entering the cable through its insulation is intercepted by the web of shielding wires and grounded before it can reach the data-carrying wires in the cable. If shielded cable is used in the network, it is important that the connectors are all properly attached so that the shielding is grounded and can discharge any electrical interference it intercepts. If the shielding isn't grounded, it can accumulate an electrical charge and eventually discharge part of it into the data line.

Twisted-pair cable also helps eliminate electromagnetic interference induced in the cable by proximity to AC power lines or equipment. This isn't as big a problem for most home LANs as it is in commercial networks, but wherever network wiring comes near AC wires or devices, shielded twisted-pair (STP) cable is a must.

Filtering

Filters are electronic devices designed to permit the normal function of a device, but block or suppress any other signal coming from it. Filters can be placed on either the source of interference (the preferable location, if it can be found) or on the recipient of the interference. The latter is the usual practice because the sources of interference are often impossible to locate.

AC power-line filters are often built into high-quality surge and spike suppressors. They allow the AC current powering a device to pass, but block any other frequency of signal. They are designed to be placed on equipment that might produce power-line interference or network devices that may be the recipient of the interference. One multiple outlet filter/suppressor can protect up to half a dozen devices for a reasonable cost.

Radio frequency interference (RFI) generally originates outside the home, and enters the LAN through a telephone or cable modem. An RFI and electrical noise filter placed on the incoming connection cable in front of the modem (so the incoming signal passes through the filter before reaching the modem) can eliminate this type of interference. These filters cost around $100, but can greatly speed up a modem connection with serious interference by eliminating the need to resend many data packets corrupted by interference. The filter can also reduce lost connections to the ISP caused by interference.

An interference filter can also be wired into the network itself. These filters (which also often function as surge and spike suppressors) operate by eliminating high voltage from the network lines. Since network data is transmitted at plus or minus 5 volts, the filter simply suppresses any voltage significantly above that level and thereby eliminates interference. The key to good suppression is speed, and a quality network filter should act within a couple of picoseconds in order to block interference effectively. Network filters cost about $50.

CHAPTER SUMMARY

- Electrical wiring and installation requirements are mainly based on the National Electrical Code (NEC), which is a safety standard developed by the National Fire Protection Association (NFPA). Most states codes subscribe to all or part of the NEC.

- The main electrical safety hazards in a home environment are fire and shock. Both can be avoided by correct wiring and installation practices.

- A short circuit occurs when too much current flows because the circuit doesn't have enough resistance to limit the amount of electricity passing through it.

- Ohm's law states that Volts = Amperes × Resistance and describes the relationship among amperes (amps), or the amount of current flowing, volts, which is the electrical potential between the two ends of a circuit, and resistance within the circuit to the flow of current.

- Most homes need to be wired for 200 amps of electrical service, but many older homes are insufficiently wired and do not meet current electrical needs.

- If additional circuits are to be installed in a home, it is a good practice to put most or all of the home LAN equipment on a new circuit in order to isolate the network from any interference generated in older wiring or equipment.

- A home in which a LAN is to be installed should be checked for inadequate wiring and electrical service, both in the home as a whole and in its individual circuits.

- New AC circuits added in an existing home should be placed to take some load off existing circuits and allow sensitive electronic equipment to run on the new circuits as much as possible.

- Wiring for new circuits should be installed using NM cable of an appropriate size. MC and AC cable should only be used if local codes require them because they are more expensive and more difficult to install than NM.

- Wire sizes are measured by AWG numbers, a system in which larger wire sizes are given smaller numbers. Circuits with 15-amp breakers should be wired with a minimum of #14 wire. Circuits with 20-amp breakers should be wired with a minimum of #12 wire.

- All outlet boxes, switches, and fixtures in a circuit must be grounded by a separate wire from the conductor wires.

- Manual dimming modules can be incorporated into any wall switch and used to control the lights connected to the switch. These modules can also be controlled with either X10 or wireless technology in order to automate the lighting system.

- An electrical surge is a sudden momentary increase in the rate of current flow or the voltage in a circuit caused by power equipment starting up or shutting down, or by lightning strikes and other atmospheric disturbances.

❏ Interference is any signal which blocks or corrupts data flow on a network. It is caused by lighting, radio transmitters, operating electrical equipment, and differences in electrical potential between different parts of the home or between objects in the home.

❏ Networks and the electrical circuits to which they are connected must be protected from surges, spikes, and interference by grounding the equipment, reducing interference sources, and installing filters and suppressors.

KEY TERMS

2-conductor wire — A high-voltage cable containing a hot wire, a neutral wire, and a ground, which is not counted as a conductor.

3-way switch — An arrangement by which either of two switches can control power to a device.

alternating current (AC) — The type of power that almost all homes receive from the electric utility company.

AC cable — Armored cable; type of cable sheathed in metal. Also, any cable used for AC wiring.

amperes — The unit used to measure electric current flow.

average use — The amount of electricity used in a home over a period of time, usually a day.

American Wire Gage (AWG) — The standard for electrical wire sizes.

breaker — A safety device which is wired into a circuit to cut off current flow if the circuit becomes overloaded.

circuit — A conducting "circle" in which electricity flows from a source to a device, through the device, and back to the source.

clean power — AC current which does not contain noise, interference, surges, or spikes.

current — Flow of electricity, measured in amps.

electric service — Electric power purchased from a utility, also the cable bringing the electricity to a home from the utility.

filter — A device to remove interference from an electric circuit.

ground — A wire which connects an electric device to the earth so that excess current can flow to the ground rather than elsewhere.

hot wire — The wire in a cable which is connected to the source of electric potential, usually colored black.

interference — Any signal which corrupts or blocks a data signal.

load — The amount of current flowing in a circuit, measured in amps or watts.

MC cable — Metal clad cable used for AC wiring.

National Electric Code (NEC) — A safety standard for electrical wiring and installation developed by the NFPA.

National Fire Protection Association (NFPA) — Publisher of the NEC.

NM cable — Nonmetallic cable used for AC wiring.

Ohm's Law — Describes the relationship among amperes (amps), or the amount of current flowing, volts, which is the electrical potential between the two ends of a circuit, and resistance within the circuit to the flow of current.

outlet box — A metal or plastic wall box into which an outlet receptacle is wired.

overload — Current flow greater than a circuit can carry without danger of burning out.

peak use — The maximum load of electrical consumption in a home.

potential — The flow force of electric current, measured in volts.

receptacle — A device into which AC-powered appliances can be plugged to obtain power.

resistance — The force inhibiting the flow of electricity in a circuit, measured in ohms.

service line — The cable which brings electric power into a home from the utility.

service panel — The wall box containing a home's circuit breakers to which the service line is connected.

shielding — Metal webbing around a data line which grounds noise and interference before it can reach the data line.

shock — Electric current flowing through a person.

spike — A large but very brief increase in voltage or current flow in a circuit.

suppressor — A device for blocking surges and spikes in a circuit.

surge — A brief increase in voltage or current flow in a circuit.

switch — A device for controlling the flow of electricity in a circuit.

volts — The unit used to measure electric potential or flow pressure.

watts — The unit of electric power, often calculated for a circuit by multiplying the number of volts by the number of amps.

REVIEW QUESTIONS

1. NEC stands for _____ _____ _____ and was developed by the _____.

2. What is the primary objective of the NEC?

5

3. The two main hazards of AC electrical circuits in a home are fire and shock. True or False?

4. What is Ohm's Law and how is it used in designing electrical circuits?

5. What is the voltage of one leg of a 240-volt electric service in a home?

   a. 60 volts

   b. 120 volts

   c. 240 volts

   d. 480 volts

6. Can 12 light bulbs each drawing 100 watts of power be safely wired in a single 15-amp circuit?

   a. yes

   b. yes, but only 10 can be on at one time

   c. yes, but only six can be on at one time

   d. no

7. If the average power use in a home is 1200 watts and this is five percent of the peak usage in the home, how many amps of electric service should the home have?

   a. 100 amps

   b. 150 amps

   c. 200 amps

   d. 250 amps

8. What can cause lights to dim momentarily in a home when an air conditioner or furnace blower turns on? Why don't the lights remain dim?

9. The most common speeds of electric motors running on AC power in the United States are 7200 rpm, 3600 rpm, and 1750 rpm. True or False?

10. If the voltage going to an AC electric motor drops, what happens to the motor?

    a. It stops.

    b. It runs faster and uses less power.

    c. It uses more power and runs hotter.

    d. It doesn't change at all.

11. Give some reasons why network equipment may function better on a new circuit in a home rather than an old one.

12. If a breaker frequently trips when most of the equipment powered through it is running, what does this indicate?

13. What is the difference between NM cable and MC cable, both of which are used to wire home AC circuits?

14. Which of the following have to be grounded: outlet boxes, outlet receptacles, switches, or light fixtures?

    a. outlet boxes and switches

    b. outlet boxes and receptacles

    c. none of them

    d. all of them

15. In a 2-conductor NM cable, the hot wire is _____, the neutral wire is _____, and the ground wire is _____.

16. Three-conductor #14 NM cable can carry more current than 2-conductor #12 MC cable. True or False?

17. If NM cable is likely to be damaged after it is installed, how must the installation be changed?

18. On an outlet receptacle, the hot connector is colored _____ and the neutral connector is colored _____.

19. What is a split outlet receptacle, and how is it wired?

20. Why should ground wires not be connected to metal wall studs or fasteners?

    a. They may not be grounded.

    b. They don't conduct electricity.

    c. They don't have water in them.

    d. They may be connected to electrical fixtures.

21. What is a surge in an electric circuit and what can cause it?

22. When buying a surge or spike suppressor, the two most important specifications to look for are _____ and _____.

23. What is interference and what are some of its causes?

24. How does a filter on a low-voltage data line act to eliminate interference?

25. How does shielding in a cable act to suppress interference?

HANDS-ON PROJECTS

HANDS-ON PROJECTS

Project 5-1: Licensing and Electric Code Standards in Your State

You can download the State Electrical Regulations file of the National Electrical Installation Standards (NEIS) by following these steps. Note that you will need to provide a credit card number to complete the download. Although the credit card number is needed to complete the transaction, there is ultimately no charge for the download.

1. Get on the Internet, and go to the Web site *www.neca-neis.org/catalog/*.

2. Click **Other Code and Technical Publications**.

3. Click the **State Electrical Regulations** price box (it's free), and then click the **Add to Cart** button.

4. Complete the required name and address information, and then follow the instructions you receive for a free download of the booklet.

5. Look up the state where you will be working to find out what the licensing and electrical code standards are. If the text notes that there are local government regulations in addition to the state's, find out what these are for the area where you will be working.

HANDS-ON PROJECTS

Project 5-2 Map the Circuits in a Home

Use your own home or a comparable building where you can spend some time evaluating the electrical system, and follow these steps to map the electrical circuits.

1. Draw a floor plan of the home as accurately as you can. Scale the drawing at ¼ inch to the foot so it is large enough to note the information you need.

2. Mark all electrical fixtures, outlets, switches, and appliances in their correct locations in each room of the home.

3. Turn on all the lights, electrical fixtures, and appliances in the home.

4. Turn off the first breaker in the home's service panel and observe what electrical devices go off. Test unused outlets with a tester or portable device to see if they are working.

5. Note each electrical device that is off by marking a number 1 near it to indicate that it is connected to the first circuit.

6. Repeat Steps 4 and 5, turning off each circuit in the home service panel in succession and noting what devices go off with each. Complete your home electrical map.

Project 5-3: Install an Outlet Box and Two Switch Boxes and Rough Wire Them

Complete this project on an unfinished wall section in a home or on a classroom test wall where a new electrical circuit can be installed.

1. On the lower-right end of the wall, use screws to install an outlet box on a stud 12 inches above the floor. (You could use nails to attach the box, but the screws allow it to be removed so other students can repeat this exercise.)

2. Install another box above the first one and 44 inches above the floor. Install a third box at the same height on the left end of the wall.

3. Drill ½-inch holes in the studs in a line from the high box on one end of the wall to the high box at the other end.

4. Rough-wire a cable between the two high boxes and another from the right high box to the outlet box below it. Run the cables out of a knockout hole in one box, through the holes between the boxes and into a knockout hole in the other box. Leave the cable slack between the boxes with at least six inches of cable protruding from each box.

5. Run another short length of cable out of the left switch box to represent the cable to the service panel.

6. Clamp the cables in the boxes with six inches protruding from each box.

Project 5-4: Connect a Switch to an Outlet or Light

Use the rough-wired wall section and boxes you completed in Project 5-3 to complete this project. Use a standard outlet receptacle and a single-pole, single-throw switch.

1. Connect the cable in the outlet box to an outlet receptacle, starting with the ground wire (green or copper), then the neutral wire (white), and then the hot wire (black).

2. Install the receptacle in the outlet box with the two mounting screws in its face tabs.

3. In the switch box above the receptacle box, connect the ground wires to ground. Connect the white wire from the outlet box to the white wire of the cable going to the other switch box. Twist the wires together clockwise, and use a screw-on connector to secure the pigtail splice.

4. Connect the black wire from the outlet box to one side of the switch. Connect the black wire in the cable from the other switch box to the opposite side of the switch.

5. Mount the switch in the box using the two screws in its face tabs.

6. If you have a low-voltage source of current available, connect it to the cable in the second switch box, and test your wired circuit by plugging an electrical device in the receptacle and turning the switch on and off.

7. Disassemble the switch and outlet so you can use the same wall section for Project 5-5.

Project 5-5: Connect a 3-way Switch Circuit to an Outlet or Light

Use the rough-wired wall section and boxes you completed in Project 5-3 to complete this project. Use a standard outlet receptacle and two double-pole, double-throw switches for this project. Replace the 2-connector wire between the switch boxes with a 3-connector cable.

1. Connect the cable in the outlet box to an outlet receptacle, starting with the ground wire, then the neutral wire, and then the hot wire.

2. Install the receptacle in the outlet box.

3. Follow the wiring diagram in Figure 5-7 in this step and the following steps. In the switch box above the receptacle box, connect the ground wires to ground. Connect the white wire from the outlet box to the white wire of the cable going to the other switch box. Twist the wires together clockwise, and use a screw-on connector to secure the splice.

4. Connect the black wire from the outlet box to the side of the switch that has only one connecting screw.

5. Connect the black wire and the other colored wire from the 3-connector cable to the two screws on the opposite side of the switch. These are called traveler wires.

6. Mount the switch in the box.

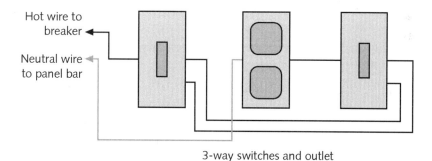

3-way switches and outlet

Figure 5-7   3-way switch wiring

7. In the left switch box, connect the ground wires to ground. Connect the white wires from the two cables in the box together with a screw-on connector.

8. Connect the two traveler wires from the right switch to the two-screw side of the left-side switch. Connect the black wire from the short cable (to the service panel) to the single screw side of the left-side switch.

9. Mount the switch in the box.

10. If you have a low-voltage source of current available, connect it to the short cable from the second switch box, and test your wired circuit by plugging an electrical device in the receptacle and turning the switches on and off.

11. Disassemble the switches and outlet.

**HANDS-ON
PROJECTS**

Project 5-6: Identify a Surge Suppressor and Filter Suitable for Use on a Home LAN

In this project you search on the Internet for an AC power line surge suppressor and filter to use for a home LAN. Try to find a suppressor that can act in two picoseconds and can suppress at least 50,000 surge amps, and a filter that suppresses as much signal noise and interference as possible in AC wiring.

1. Get on the Internet and go to a search engine such as Google or Yahoo. You can use any search engine with which you feel comfortable.

2. Search for the phrase "AC surge suppressor" and examine the responses you receive to find a suitable suppressor.

3. You may want to refine your search by adding additional qualifying words, such as "surge amps" or "filter" to find the exact type of product you want.

   (*Hint*: If your search engine has an image search mode, using it lets you see pictures of the suppressors and more easily identify them.)

4. Find at least three suppressors, and compare their features and price. Choose the one you would use for a home LAN.

CASE PROJECTS

**CASE
PROJECTS**

Case Project 5-1: Recommend a Wiring Solution

A client has asked you to recommend a solution to an electrical problem and a related network problem. He wants to install a home LAN, but his house is more than 100 years old, constructed of solid brick, and has been remodeled many times. The home is inadequately wired, but installing new circuits would be almost impossible without doing great damage to the historic building. The only unfinished room in the house is the main floor furnace room in the center of the house, which also contains the electric service panel. Write a short proposal telling how you would get at least one new circuit into the house, what you would use it for, and what technology you recommend for a home network in this house with old and inadequate wiring.

**CASE
PROJECTS**

Case Project 5-2: Wire a Room for Switched Power

You're installing new wiring in an older home. You have the design complete except for the two children's bedrooms. In these rooms, the client wants an outlet on each wall of the room, except the doorway wall. On that wall he wants a switch that turns off all power in the room, except to the electric clock plugged into an outlet on one wall, which must remain on. Draw a diagram of how you could wire the room so that every outlet and light is controlled by a switch except one half of one duplex outlet.

Case Project 5-3: Find and Install a Wallboard-mounted Outlet Box

For a wiring job you are completing, you need to install a new outlet box in the center of a finished plasterboard wall. You haven't done this installation before and want to practice a bit before cutting a hole in the client's wall. Mount a piece of plasterboard between two studs or other uprights at least a foot apart. You can mount the board with nails, screws or clamps. Purchase a wall-mounted box at a building supply store (*Hint:* they are often called "remodel boxes" and they cost less than a dollar.) Follow the instructions that come with the box to cut a correctly sized hole in the mounted wallboard, and mount the box securely in the hole. The instructions will vary depending on the type of box you get. After mounting the box, decide if the box you selected was a good choice for ease of mounting. Would you buy the same type again, or do you want to find another type that might be easier to install?

Case Project 5-4: Find Sources of Static Electricity and Interference

You've installed a network for a client, and it works well, except that there seems to be a lot of interference that occasionally slows down data flow. You think it is caused by something electric operating at intervals and producing the interference. Obtain a portable, battery operated AM-FM radio that you can use for a short while. Take it outside and tune to a place on the FM dial where you can hear no station at all. Find the quietest place on the dial when the volume is turned up high. Now walk into a building with the radio still tuned to the quiet frequency. Hold the radio very close to each piece of operating electrical equipment you can find. Can you hear static on the radio when it is near some equipment? If so, what you are hearing is radio frequency interference (RFI) produced by the equipment. Note which pieces of equipment produce the most RFI and which produce the least. What do you think makes the difference? How would you silence the static producers and stop the network interference?

CHAPTER 6

VIDEO AND AUDIO FUNDAMENTALS

After reading this chapter, you will be able to:

- Describe the difference between analog signals and digital signals and how each is created
- Describe how analog radio broadcasting and recording is accomplished and how analog audio signals are transformed to digital files of various formats and compressions
- Describe how analog television functions and how television images are converted to digital form in a variety of formats and compressions
- Identify the sources of audio and television signals and describe how each reaches the home user
- Define the various types of digital video available on the Internet and the features and limitations of each
- Describe the system design issues surrounding the connection of audio and video

In this chapter you'll learn about how sounds and visual images are changed into analog signals that can be broadcast on radio and television or recorded. You'll learn how analog audio signals are converted into digital data that provides higher quality for broadcasting and recording of sound. You'll also learn how television began as an analog picture that was converted into electronic signals for broadcasting and recording, then was later transformed into digital formats that are higher in picture and sound quality and easier to transmit over broadcast systems, cable, the Internet, or satellite systems. You'll learn how digital audio and video files have multiplied into a multitude of sizes, compression formats, aspect ratios, and file types so that they can be transmitted, stored, and used in a variety of ways. Finally, you'll learn how digital versions of both audio and video signals are transmitted and played on the Internet and over home networks.

FROM ANALOG RECORDING TO DIGITAL TRANSMISSION

When Guglielmo Marconi developed the first method of wireless or radio communication (patented 1900) and Philo T. Farnsworth developed the first television transmitter (1927), both used analog technology. Some years previously (1876), a gentleman by the name of Alexander Graham Bell had also used **analog** technology when he invented a device by which one person could speak to another over a wired connection called a telephone.

The term "analog" is derived from the word "analogous". When something is analogous, it has a similar or related pattern to something else. An analog device converts a pattern such as light from an image or a sequence of sounds into an analogous pattern of electromagnetic waves. An example of an analog device is a video recorder, which converts the light and sound patterns of a scene into electrical signals with similar patterns. Analog is simply a form of data transmission that is created using a continuously varying electromagnetic signal, which can then be stored (recorded) or sent to a distant destination where it can be converted back into the original sounds or pictures.

Sound is created by the rapid vibration of objects that produces waves in the air surrounding the objects. The vibrating object can be a guitar string, human vocal chords, a bell, or anything else that can move in two opposite directions rapidly to create a wave pattern in the air. Just how rapidly the object vibrates determines the pitch of the sound it makes. The sound of middle C on a piano keyboard is made by wires in the piano vibrating at 262 cycles per second. The frequency of middle C is 262 cycles. Higher pitched sounds have higher frequencies; lower pitched sounds have lower frequencies. Sound waves can be transformed into analog electromagnetic waves of the same frequency or a multiple of the frequency. These electromagnetic waves can then be transmitted to a distant location and changed back into sound waves of the original frequency. This is the process that radio uses to broadcast audio programs.

Visual images are also created by waves, light waves that are reflected from objects and strike the retinas of our eyes producing a visual image. Each color of light is a different frequency and the human eye can distinguish about a million different colors. The frequencies of the visible light spectrum are hundreds of millions of times higher than the frequencies of sounds, but these frequencies can still be converted into **radio frequency (RF)** analog electromagnetic signals and transmitted to a distant location. The signals are then converted back into light patterns on the screen of a television or other visual display on which we can see a reproduced image of the original scene. The process of converting light waves into analog signals is more complex than the process for converting sound, but the result is still an analog: a continuously varying signal that reproduces a visual image on a screen.

Digital technology, which was developed after analog, isn't based on a continuously varying signal, but on discrete bits of data which are precisely defined. These bits consist of various combinations of only two numbers (digits), 0 and 1. Using this binary numerical system, analog data can be encoded into digital form.

Analog signals such as sound waves or visual images are converted to digital form by taking samples of the characteristics of the sound waves and light images at regular intervals. The more often the samples are taken (up to thousands or even millions of times per second), the more digital data can be recorded and the more closely the digital representation resembles the original analog signals.

Figure 6-1 shows an analog sound wave and how a digital representation can be made of the same sound wave by using the **sampling** technique. The more frequent the samples taken, the more accurate the digital representation of the analog wave becomes.

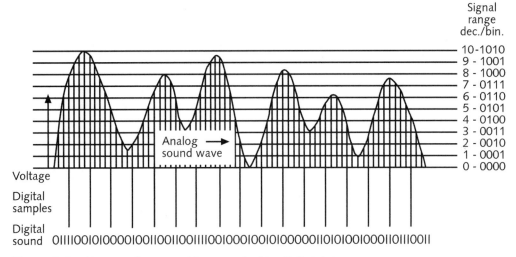

Figure 6-1   How analog sound is converted to digital data

Both sounds (voices, music, etc.) and visual images (motion pictures and television) were transmitted for years as various types of analog signals. Today audio and video data is mainly recorded, stored, and transmitted in digital form.

There are several advantages which digital data has over analog that have made it the preferred choice of most listeners and viewers, as well as most professionals in the business of creating and distributing audio and video data:

- Copies of an original digital audio or video recording can be made without any loss of quality. Unlike copies of analog recordings, which lose some quality as they become further removed from the original, a copy of a copy of a copy of a digital recording contains exactly the same numerical data as the original; the numerical data is, of course, the binary number combinations that were created by sampling the analog signals made from the original sounds of voices or music.

- Digital data recordings are virtually unaffected by noise or interference because digital sampling techniques record data only about the sound or visual image, not the background noise or interference around it.

- Transmitting digital data doesn't degrade its quality as it does an analog signal, which can pick up noise and interference on the way to its destination or even after arrival. The numerical data of digital signals arrives unchanged.

- An error correction algorithm is usually included in digital recording systems that reconstructs areas of lost signal using similar adjacent data. A "hole" in a digital image can be filled in with numbers taken from areas around it. This type of correction isn't possible with analog signals.

- Computers can only record, interpret, and output digital sounds and images. They cannot handle analog signals at all because computers are completely digital devices. The ability of computers to manipulate digital data enables them to enhance, modify, edit, copy, store, and otherwise use audio and **video images** in many ways that are impossible with analog signals.

The first method of recording and transmitting both sound waves and visual images was to create analog signals from the original sound and light patterns. These analog signals were then stored on media or broadcast as RF signals to receivers in homes where they reproduced the original sounds and images. Analog audio and video signals had some limitations, but are still widely used today. Digital sound and visual recording was developed after the analog processes. Digital recording uses sampling techniques to encode continuous wave analog signals into binary numerical data which can also be recorded and transmitted using RF signals. Digital audio and video signals can be transmitted and stored more easily and in more ways than analog signals. They can also reproduce higher-quality audio and video images than are possible with analog signals.

AUDIO RECORDING AND BROADCASTING

We perceive sound by means of continuous sound waves in the air striking our eardrums. These waves cause the eardrums and the mechanisms behind them to vibrate and send messages to our brains that we hear as sound. The highest point of a sound wave is called the peak and the lowest point the trough. The wave is composed of a continuous sequence of peaks followed by troughs. The shape of sound waves (as well as all electromagnetic waves including radio waves, light waves, and even x-ray waves) is a sine wave. This shape is set by the trigonometric ratio of the same name and is shown in Figure 6-1. The frequency of a sound is defined as the number of wave peaks which pass a given point in a second. The loudness (amplitude) of a sound is determined by the size of the wave, that is, by the height of its peaks and the depth of its troughs. The higher the peaks and deeper the troughs, the louder the sound is. But it has the same pitch as long as its frequency remains unchanged. In sound, frequency equals pitch and amplitude equals loudness.

The pioneers of audio technology sought some means of preserving sound waves so they could be reproduced artificially and then transmitted over distance. Once they learned enough about sound to record it, a method of transmitting sound, first over a wire and then by wireless broadcasting, soon followed. Improved methods of storing and transmitting sound are still being developed today, even though many of the old ones are still in use.

Home technology uses several methods of audio and video recording and transmission and will probably continue to do so for years. Technicians need to be familiar with each of these technologies and how to compatibly fit them into an integrated system.

Audio Recording

Thomas Edison first recorded the human voice in 1877 and by 1900 at least three competing styles of **phonograph** cylinders and discs were being manufactured and sold. Discs or **records**, as they came to be called, eventually won the competitive battle for recording sound, but proved to be a somewhat limited medium because of the short length of their recordings. Making the grooves in the record smaller and closer together and reducing the speed at which records turned from 78 rpm to 45 rpm and then 33 1/3 rpm increased the playing length to a maximum of about 30 minutes, but the development of magnetic tape recording began to overshadow records after World War II.

Magnetic recording on steel wire was patented by Valdemar Poulsen in Denmark in 1898 and in the United States in 1903. Magnetic recording (still using wire) was developed in Europe and somewhat in America during the first half of the 20th century, but never seriously competed with records because it offered no extended length of recording. This was not true of **magnetic tape**, however, which was developed in the late 1940s and had the ability to record 40 minutes of material on a 1000-meter reel of tape. Later improvements in tape and recording machines allowed the recording speed to be reduced until a reel of tape could record several hours of voice or music at high quality. The same intense competition that characterized the first century of audio recording and broadcasting continues today. Reel tape recording was challenged by cassette tapes, which are now being replaced by CDs. All three systems are sometimes still included in new audio systems such as those HTI technicians install. Some users may even want a phonograph (turntable) for records wired into an audio system.

Magnetic recording of analog sound is accomplished by recording an "image" of the sound waves on tape, which is coated with metal particles that can be arranged in patterns by passing the tape over a magnetic recording head. Sound waves from a microphone are fed into the recorder head, which then magnetizes an analog pattern of the sound waves on the magnetic tape as it passes over the recording head. As with records, the analog magnetic recording doesn't reproduce the sound perfectly. Noise and interference can occur in magnetic recording and, in addition, magnetic tape has a unique type of noise called hiss. This is a high frequency, narrow band noise that occurs in all tape recording. It can be reduced but never entirely eliminated in analog recordings.

Figure 6-2 shows how a sound wave signal is recorded in analog form on magnetic tape. The figure shows the tape divided into two tracks, or channels, which can each record separate sound information. The separate tracks allow sound to be recorded in both directions on the tape or stereo sound to be recorded using one track for each side.

6

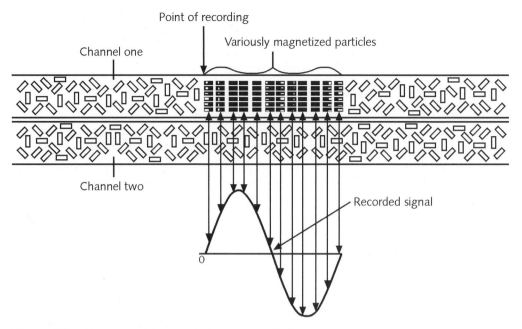

Figure 6-2   How sound is recorded on magnetic tape

AM Radio Broadcasting

The first radio broadcasts sent a simple sine wave from the transmitter to the receivers. This worked well, but was very limited in the amount of information that could be sent on the wave. Since the wave was a signal of constant strength and frequency, no information of a varying nature could be sent on it. The only way to transmit data was by patterns of starts and stops in the signal transmission. This was why early radio used the same Morse code as the telegraph (sets of short signal pulses — dots, and long ones — dashes) to send messages. Information had to be sent one letter at a time in this "manual digital" format by a radio operator who could never exceed a speed of 50 words per minute. The message had to be decoded at the receiving end before it could be read, so early radio couldn't have a wide audience. Only those who could decipher Morse code could understand a transmitted message.

To transmit voice and music by radio, a way had to be found to attach this information to the sine wave of a given frequency that a radio station transmitted. The method used is called **amplitude modulation (AM)** and it was an adaptation of the original Morse code radio. Instead of simply turning the transmitted signal on and off to get the dots and dashes of code, radio engineers developed a means of varying the strength of the wave from low to high in a pattern that matched the sound waves of voices or music. The frequency of the radio wave (called the carrier wave) remained constant; only its strength or amplitude changed. The result was that the carrier wave could now carry analog voice and music signals. Figure 6-3 shows a music or voice sound wave at the top, a constant frequency, unmodulated carrier wave in the center, and an analog AM radio wave (carrier wave modulated by the sound wave) at the bottom.

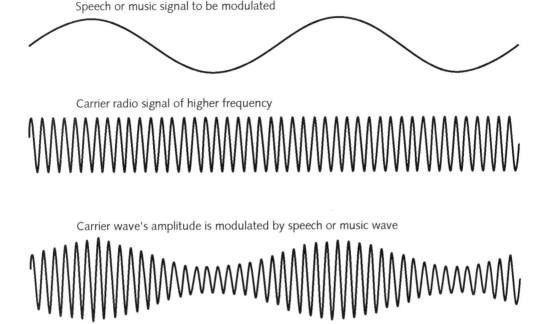

Figure 6-3   How AM radio waves carry sound waves

All the early radio stations used AM transmissions for their broadcasts, and its success made radio the first truly mass method of communication around the world. AM was not, however, the perfect form of radio transmission. Its main drawback was the fact that most natural and man-made radio noise (interference) occurs in the frequency range used by AM. This noise interferes with AM signals and reduces the quality of their voice and music transmissions. AM is also restricted in the distances it can travel by the strength of its signals. Since amplitude modulation means that, by definition, a low-frequency voice or music sound has a lower power (weaker) signal than a high frequency sound, AM signals tend to break down before they've traveled many miles from their source. Increasing the power of the transmitter and building receivers that filtered some noise and compensated for signal strength variations helped AM radio increase its popularity around the world, but radio engineers were still looking for a better form of radio transmission.

FM Radio

The man who found a better way was Edwin H. Armstrong. Instead of modulating the amplitude of a radio carrier wave (AM), Armstrong modulated the frequency of the carrier wave. The result was **frequency modulation (FM)** radio, which had a signal of constant strength (amplitude) but could still carry voice and music data. The peaks of a sound wave were transmitted as higher frequencies and the valleys as lower frequencies. By this method, the frequency of the sound wave could be represented almost perfectly in the analog FM radio signal. Figure 6-4 shows how this representation was created. An unmodulated carrier wave is shown at the top, a sound wave in the center, and a frequency modulated (FM) wave at the bottom in which the sound wave is incorporated in the varying frequency of the carrier wave.

Unmodulated carrier signal

Speech or voice wave

FM modulated carrier signal

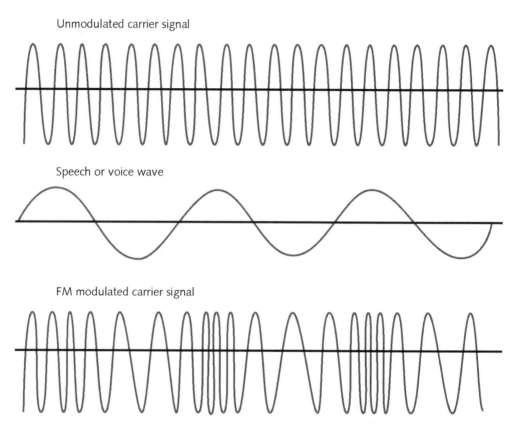

Figure 6-4   How FM carrier wave is modulated to carry sound waves

FM also operates at different, more noise-free frequencies than AM. It has become the standard of radio transmission today, although many AM stations still operate efficiently in local markets and a few as long range, clear channel stations (those which have exclusive right to a frequency nationwide) with up to 50,000 watts of transmitting power.

Digital Radio

Although some other nations have adopted digital radio transmission for both AM and FM stations, commercial stations in the United States have only recently begun to seriously consider adopting this technology. Various methods have been proposed. A system called In-Band On-Channel (IBOC) digital radio broadcasting received the endorsement of the National Radio Systems Committee for full-time use on FM radio stations, but only daytime use on AM radio stations because of nighttime skywave interference issues. Station WOR in New York City became a test station for IBOC digital AM radio in 2003. IBOC digital offers AM stations FM stereo audio quality. WOR's participation in the testing of IBOC transmission will be instrumental to the commercial launch of the technology throughout the United States.

While U.S. commercial stations have been slow to adopt digital technology for their commercial broadcasts, hundreds of them have launched Web sites for streaming digital radio signals over the Internet. Thousands of other schools, colleges, hobbyists, and others have also started Web-based radio streaming sites that offer a tremendous variety of listening options. New laws, just passed or under current consideration by Congress, are intended to allow these digital stations to expand their online audiences while paying modest royalties for the music they broadcast. These laws, along with the development of relatively inexpensive streaming equipment and software, will ensure that the home LAN user has an almost infinite choice of online listening options available through an Internet connection.

6

The extensive availability of online digital radio programming may reduce or even eliminate the need for most home LANs to also have broadcast AM or FM radio reception (analog or digital) included among their incoming data options. Many cable and satellite music channels are also available as part of the typical packages of channels offered to consumers by each of these services. This source of music data combined with Internet services further reduces the need for broadcast radio reception. Many LAN users may choose to entirely forego traditional broadcast radio reception, particularly if the stations in their local area don't soon switch to digital broadcasting.

Digital Audio Recording

Audio sounds can be digitally recorded on magnetic tape using the same **sampling** technique described at the beginning of this chapter. The sound wave is sampled at a high rate of speed and its amplitude in digital form is recorded on the tape. To get a high-quality recording, the rate of sampling must be at least twice the frequency of the highest sound the human ear can detect. The range of sound which most people can hear are frequencies from a low of 20 cycles per second, to a high of 20,000 cycles per second. Consequently, digital sound recording techniques sample the sound waves being recorded at a rate of at least 40,000 times per second (40 KHz). The sampling process produces a steady stream of signal–waveform values 1/40,000 of a second (25 microseconds) apart. The actual standard sampling rates for digital recording are 44.1 and 48 KHz, both somewhat higher than the 40 KHz example given.

An **analog-to-digital converter (ADC)** performs the sampling process and expresses the values as binary numbers (0s and 1s only). It is this digital information, rather than the analog waveform itself, which is recorded. Because there is a lot of digital information to record, and it must be recorded rapidly in order to keep up with the playing music or speaking voices, **digital audio tape (DAT)** is not recorded in straight tracks running down the length of the tape as shown with analog recording in Figure 6-2.

Digital sound is recorded by a rotating head that very rapidly "swipes" short tracks of recorded data across the tape at an angle as the tape moves forward on the reels. The tape head is rotating at 2000 rpm and so can record the large amount of data required for high-fidelity digital sound. Digital tapes cannot be cut or spliced, however, because the dense, angular recording method is disrupted by any break in the tape. Figure 6-5 shows how digital audio tape (DAT) is recorded with angled tracks. As the measurements on the figure indicate, the recording tracks must be very precisely placed and can be read only by a digital tape player configured in exactly the same manner as the recording machine.

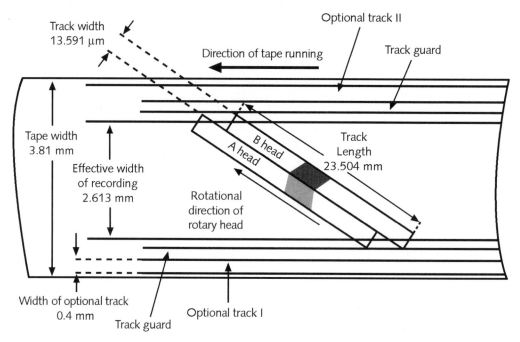

Figure 6-5   Digital sound is recorded on angled tracks across the tape

Digital sound can also be recorded on other **magnetic media** such as computer disks and hard drives, although usually not in the same format as on magnetic tape. Digital audio intended for storage on disks or hard drives must also be organized in named files so that the computer can locate the desired selection of music or voice clip among many that may be stored randomly on the disk.

CD Audio Recording

Compact discs (CDs) are the most common form of recorded music today. They also offer the highest quality of music or voice recording. This is because CDs use a recording system called **pulse code modulation (PCM)** to convert analog sounds into digital form and store them on a CD. The PCM process produces very high–fidelity sound quality, but also requires a large amount of storage space. There is a direct relationship, as we have seen in other analog to digital conversion standards, between the rate of sampling the analog sounds and the amount of storage space required to store the digital data derived from the sampling. The CD is a high example of this relationship. A single CD recorded in CD audio format can hold 600 million characters of text, but only 74 minutes of uncompressed music. Five seconds of recorded music require as much storage space as 135,000 words of text, enough to write a complete novel. Only the large storage capacity of a CD makes the CD audio format practical for high-fidelity music recording.

CD audio format samples the analog sound 44,100 times per second, which enables it to record sounds up to 20,000 cycles per second, the limit of human hearing. As it records, the system must deal with the errors between the sampled discrete values and the actual continuous sound. This is referred to as the **signal-to-noise (S/N) ratio**, and in recording it's the ratio between the difference of the highest and lowest frequencies and the average background noise level. The higher the S/N ratio, the better the sound. S/N ratios must be greater than 70 **decibels (dB)** or the background noise becomes audible. CD audio format achieves S/N ratios in the low 90 dB range which gives it a very low noise level while maintaining a high quality of sound reproduction.

CD-ROM drives in computers can nearly all play CD audio format music recorded on a CD, but computers rarely store music in this format on any other type of storage device because doing so requires too much space. For any type of magnetic disk or hard drive storage, a magnetic media format, such as those described in the next section of this chapter, is generally used because they compress the data into smaller file sizes. While this results in some loss of quality compared to CD audio, the loss is not detectable in most sound recordings, and the savings in storage space justify it for any but the most high-fidelity recordings heard by discriminating listeners.

Computer Audio Recording

Computer audio files must also be recorded in a compatible format, which the computer can read using software that is contained in its memory or stored on its disks. While digital audio is recorded on tape in a continuous stream using a specified format, such full-length recordings are usually too large to be conveniently stored on a disk or hard drive. For this reason computer-based audio storage formats nearly all compress the full-size audio files into smaller size files, which the computer can more easily store and handle. Among the formats used for digital sound recordings, which can be played back on a computer, are the following:

- **WAV files** are virtually the same quality as data on audio CDs, and therefore offer the best sound reproduction available. The files are very large, however, about 10 MB per minute of recorded sound, and so require storage devices of large capacity.

- **MP3 files** are the most popular audio standard since WAV. The German company Fraunhofer patented it, and users must pay royalties for compressing files with it. With MP3 compression, computer users can compress the content of a music CD to one tenth of its original size. This allows up to 20 hours of music to be stored in one gigabyte of storage space. MP3 files are also streamable. This means that a computer can begin playing an MP3 file when only the first part of it is loaded in the computer's memory. It also allows an MP3 file to be sent over the Internet and played on the receiver's computer as soon as the head of the file arrives, while the rest of the file is still being transmitted.

- **Windows Media Audio(WMA)** is part of the Windows Media software package that is patented by Microsoft. It is an integrated part of the Microsoft Windows Media Player, which can also play video files. WMA files are about a third the size of CD files, but are still larger than MP3 files. WMA files can also be streamed over the Internet and, unlike MP3 files, they contain a built-in protection against the copying of copyrighted music. This is the primary reason why many music and entertainment companies publish only in WMA format and not in MP3.

- **Ogg Vorbis (OGG)** audio format is also known as "Squish." OGG is an open source format and hence is free of any patents. It was designed as a substitute for MP3 and WMA and is almost as popular and well known as MP3. The algorithm is still being developed, but the files are backwards compatible so that older recordings can be played with newer versions of the software. OGG also supports multi-channel compression (stereo or surround files) and is streamable.

- **MP3PRO** is the next generation of MP3 and has only been available for a short time. MP3PRO offers the same quality as MP3, but requires files only half as large. MP3PRO will likely replace MP3 over the next few years. Like WMA and OGG, MP3PRO is backwards compatible, so that MP3PRO files can be played with older MP3 players. It also offers copyright protection for published music and streaming capability for the Internet.

TELEVISION RECORDING AND BROADCASTING

The most common analog television format in the United States is the **National Television Standards Committee (NTSC)** standard which has 525 horizontal scan lines in its picture and runs at the speed of about 30 frames per second. This standard has been in place for more than 50 years and is now badly outdated. The improved standard, digital television with high definition, has not yet been widely adopted and the equipment to receive it is still expensive. The vast majority of HTI systems installed during the next few years, if they include any television component, will include NTSC television. Many will also include the newer and better digital standards, but analog television is so much a part of American life that its demise in favor of new technology is occurring very slowly.

Most analog television broadcast stations transmit a picture that contains 480 horizontal interlaced lines with approximately 340 **pixels** per line. Europe and some other parts of the world have adopted the **PAL** or **SECAM** formats for television, which both have a practical resolution of about 720 pixels (picture elements) wide by 576 high (625 scan lines high counting overscan). These formats operate at 25 frames per second to more easily function on the European standard power grid which is 50 cycle AC current at 240 volts. Even though the PAL/SECAM formats have higher resolution than NTSC, they're not updated (refreshed) as often and so their picture quality is comparable.

Because analog television remains a part of most home technology systems, it's important to know how it is created, how it is recorded, and how it is broadcast. It's also important to know how analog television differs from digital television, which is slowly replacing it, and how the two systems can be integrated into the same home technology system.

Analog Television

To broadcast analog television as a **radio frequency (RF)** signal, the television image seen by an analog camera, and its accompanying sound, must be broken down into elements that can be transmitted on radio waves. When the signal is received by a television receiver, it must be interpreted by the electronics of the receiver and reassembled into picture elements that the **cathode ray tube (CRT)** display in the television can scan onto its screen. This process has to be repeated 30 times each second for picture and sound. A standard NTSC screen includes 525 lines of picture data and stations broadcast at 15 frames per second (30 **interlaced scans**). That means that a tremendous amount of data must be squeezed into the 6 MHz bandwidth of a television channel. The crowded bandwidth of television channels means that any improvement in analog transmission (more raster lines or faster scanning) is difficult or impossible.

Analog video is turned into a broadcast signal by first breaking it down into rasters. A **raster** is one scan line of a television image. Each raster is recorded along its full width of pixels by the camera in terms of its color and luminosity (brightness). To the raster content signal is added two additional signal elements, the horizontal sync and vertical sync, which together specify precisely where each raster was scanned by the camera and, when received, where it is to be scanned onto the CRT screen display. All this information (263 rasters of color and luminosity, with horizontal and vertical sync signals for each raster) are broadcast 30 times per second on an analog television signal. They're received and interpreted by the receiver to produce a color television picture. In addition, on the same frequency band, the sound portion of the signal is broadcast as an FM radio signal.

Because analog television signals are large and complex, they're extremely subject to noise, interference, and attenuation with distance. Nearly all analog television sets display some of these signal problems in such effects as snow, static lines, color shifts, ghosts, dropout lines, or just overall poor picture quality. Sound is usually not badly affected because it's an FM signal and stays strong through the full distance that the picture signal can be received. Analog television arrives at the receiver through an antenna as RF (radio frequency) signals, which also include stereo sound, all through one wire. The system has worked well for more than 50 years, but it has long since reached its maximum potential for quality transmission. The demand for better television resulted first in recorded video programs that didn't suffer from the same defects as broadcast television, then in the digital television revolution.

Analog Video Recording

When television broadcasting began, the only way to record a television program was to photograph a television set that was receiving the show using a synchronized motion picture camera. This process was known as kinescope recording and a number of early television shows were recorded in this manner, even though the quality of the image was poor and the filmed recording of a television program couldn't be used to transmit the program electronically. If the program was to be rebroadcast, the kinescope film had to be projected into a television camera using a device called a film chain to synchronize the two machines. The quality of the second (and all subsequent) broadcasts was even lower than the original kinescope recording.

Magnetic recording of digital video programs proved even more difficult than digital recording of sound because of the large amount of information contained in each digital image. The changing data in each of those 525 scan lines in each frame of an NTSC video picture had to be recorded in real time. The first attempt to do this with a linear recording system was made in 1955 and required a tape recorder that operated at a speed of 200 inches of tape per second. It wasn't practical for recording programs more than a few minutes in length and an improved system was soon developed.

Angling the recorder's recording head relative to the tape's direction of travel proved to be the solution for video recording as it later would for digital audio. The angled heads rotated and recorded the video information in a series of short tracks running at an angle across the tape. Even with four recording heads on the drum recording information simultaneously on magnetic tape that was two inches wide, the early video recorders still had to run at fairly high speed to record the amount of information required for video. Later improvements in video technology allowed reductions in the speed of the tape and its width, first to the one-inch wide C type, then to 3/4 inch, and finally to the ½-inch VHS standard used in consumer cassettes today. The smaller tape size caused some quality loss, but was far more economical for consumer use. Figure 6-6 shows how analog video is recorded on the tape. Note that the tape is wider than that used for audio recording, which allows more information to be placed on it, and the recorder has four recording heads mounted on the rotating drum, each of which records a portion of video data each time the drum revolves.

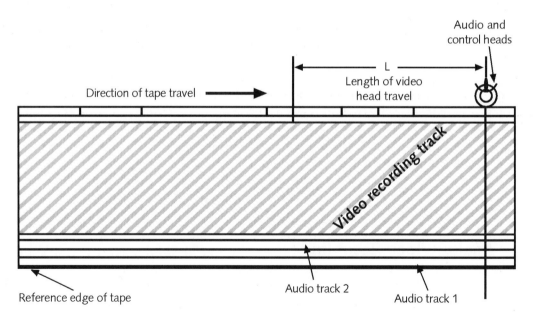

Figure 6-6 Analog video is recorded with a slanted rotating 4-head drum

Digital Video

Storing and transmitting a video picture in digital form is actually a more direct process than storing sound in digital form. Rather than sampling an analog sound wave and then recreating it based on the samples, video images can be converted to digital form using complete picture data that reproduces the scanned image perfectly. This absolute conversion is possible because video images are all made up of the small individual rectangles called **pixels** (picture elements). Not all of the NTSC standard screen's 525 pixels high by 720 pixels wide can be seen on the screen. Some scan lines at the top and bottom are used to convey other information and, in addition, the NTSC standard calls for some "overscan" on all sides of the video picture. The lines used for other data and the overscan reduce the visible pixels to about 480 from top to bottom of the picture and about 640 from one side to the other. Despite the fact that the other pixels aren't visible on screen, they're still part of the NTSC standard and must be included in digital video conversions of that standard.

Another factor also affects NTSC television displays. In television screens, the pixels are not square but rectangular in shape with a height slightly greater than their width. This means that an array 480 pixels high and 720 wide has an **aspect ratio** (width to height) of 3 to 2. When the pixels are displayed, however, their rectangular shape makes the actual screen size show an aspect ratio of 4 to 3. This 4 to 3 ratio is the same for all television screens using the NTSC standard, and the fact that the pixels are not square simply means that more of them must be stored for each video image in order to maintain the 4 to 3 aspect ratio of the picture.

Digital video is created by assigning a numerical value to every pixel that makes up a video image. This is done either by a digital video camera which converts the image seen through its lens directly into digital data, or by a scanning process in which a digital video scanner converts the frames (individual pictures) of an analog video program or a motion picture film to digital form. The numerical value assigned to each pixel describes its position on the screen, its color, and its luminance (brightness). Since there are more than 375,000 pixels on an NTSC screen, and millions of possible colors for each, the amount of data to be stored for each video image is many times greater than a sound file which samples a sound wave a mere 44,000 times per second.

For each second of digital video, 30 frames of picture data must be recorded, but in **NTSC format** this actually requires a total of only 15 complete images because the pictures are **interlaced**. This means that each time the screen image is refreshed, only one half of it is actually scanned with new digital information. This half-screen scanning is not detectable to the viewer because it is accomplished by scanning every other line on the screen. In one **frame** all the even-numbered lines are refreshed and in the next frame all the odd-numbered lines. Only half as much data is thus required for each interlaced frame as would be necessary for a complete screen refresh. Consequently, an interlaced program requires much less storage space than a noninterlaced or **progressive**-scanned program in which every frame is completely refreshed. Figure 6-7 shows how one half of an interlaced screen is refreshed each time the screen is scanned. The illustration shows only the part of the screen scanned in each **field**. In an actual television picture the white lines of each interlaced field would be filled by picture data from the preceding field. A complete interlaced frame is shown below the two fields.

Digital television is a significant improvement over analog, even when the NTSC format remains unchanged. As with digital sound recording, digital television removes nearly all of the noise and interference from the recorded images and defines the picture information much more precisely. When digital television is displayed, the picture and sound are almost flawless. Reception doesn't deteriorate with distance as analog signals do. If the digital signal is received, the picture display will be near perfect. The "if" regarding reception is because of a characteristic of digital transmission, called the **cliff effect**. Unlike analog transmissions, which get progressively weaker and decline in quality as the distance from the transmitter increases, digital signals retain their quality to the end of their transmission range, but then just suddenly stop, as though they've fallen off a cliff. This can mean that a house in one block will get excellent reception, while a house a block further from the transmitter will get no reception at all.

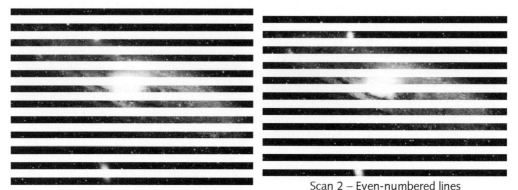

Scan 1 – Odd-numbered lines   Scan 2 – Even-numbered lines

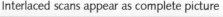

Interlaced scans appear as complete picture

Figure 6-7   Two interlaced fields make up a complete NTSC television frame

Digital Television Compression

Digital television is even more data intensive than analog television and would require even more bandwidth for broadcasting, except for the fact that digital data can be compressed. Nearly all digital video is compressed before being recorded or broadcast. There are two types of video **compression: lossless** and **lossy**.

Lossless compression, as the name implies, means that after compressing the video, and then decompressing it, the restored video has all the exact same data as the original. Lossless has the advantage that no matter how many times it is compressed and decoded, none of the original data is lost. The decompressed video has all the quality of the original. The limitation of lossless compression is that it can't save nearly as much space as lossy compression algorithms. Consequently, lossless video **codecs** (codec is an acronym for compression/decompression) such as **Huffyuv** and Lossless MJPEG are not used nearly as much as lossy codecs which compress further, and thus save more storage space.

Lossy compression is the form of video compression that 95% of all video codecs use. This means that when they compress video and then decompress it, the decompressed video does not still have all the data of the original. Lossy codecs include **MPEG-1**, **MPEG-2**, **MPEG-4**, **Quicktime**, DV, Digital-S, **RealVideo**, Sorenson, Indeo, and Cinepak. Each of these loses some data when it compresses video. The objective of lossy compression is to not lose any data which will be observable on the screen as a deteriorated image. None of the codecs achieves this standard, but some come close to it.

The two main methods of lossy compression are called intra-frame and inter-frame compression. Intra-frame means that each frame of video data is compressed independently without regard to what is contained in any other frame. MPEG is an intra-frame compression method that uses the familiar JPEG graphic compression found in computer graphics and on the Internet to compress each frame. This type of compression results in very little loss of quality in the picture, but is limited in the amount of compression possible.

Inter-frame compression exploits the fact that most of a television image is not moving all the time. Inter-frame codecs look at the preceding frame (and sometimes the following frame) to see what's changed in the frame they're compressing. They then compress only the changed part of the new frame and repeat the unchanged part of the preceding frame to get a complete picture for the next frame. Figure 6-8 shows a simplified example of how this is done. The numbered list that follows the figure explains what's happening in each frame of the figure.

6

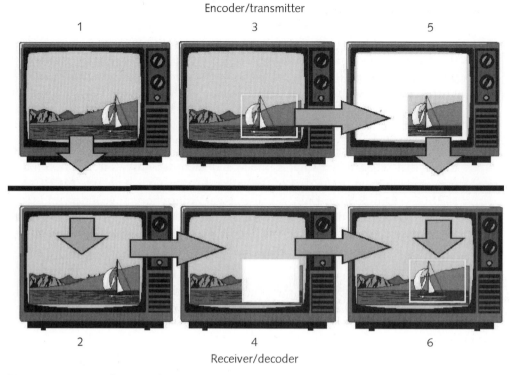

Figure 6-8   Inter-frame video compression

1. Frame 1 of a new scene is compressed by the video encoder in digital format and transmitted. The encoder retains the data from Frame 1 for comparison with later frames.

2. Frame 1 is received by the receiver, which displays it on screen and retains the data from the frame for use in other frames, if needed.

3. The video encoder compares Frame 1 of the scene with Frame 2 and compresses only the part of Frame 2 that is different from Frame 1.

4. The receiver is instructed to repeat the unchanged part of Frame 1 to use as part of Frame 2.

5. The transmitter sends the changed part of Frame 2 to the receiver.

6. The receiver combines the unchanged part of Frame 2 that it retained from Frame 1 with the changed part that it receives from the transmitter to create a complete Frame 2. Frame 2 requires only one quarter as much data transmission as Frame 1.

All digital video broadcasting is done in compressed format in order to squeeze the required quantity of information into the available bandwidth. Using digital compression enables a broadcaster to send five channels of standard definition television (digital television with a 4:3 aspect ratio) in the same bandwidth as a single channel of analog television. Compression also enables the much more data intensive high definition television (digital television with a 16:9 aspect ratio) to be squeezed into the same bandwidth as an analog channel.

Changing Video Formats

NTSC has been the format for television in the United States since commercial broadcasting began in the middle of the last century, but new and more advanced television formats are now slowly making their way into the market. Computer monitors also display video images in several formats, which are different from NTSC or from the new formats used for television. Finally, cable and satellite television transmission, as well as video streaming on the Internet, have brought international television broadcasts within range of American receivers, and many of these programs arrive in formats different from NTSC.

Currently, there are nearly 250 million television sets in the United States. As digital television (DTV) gradually replaces analog broadcasting on the NTSC standard, the change will not make all of these sets obsolete, because converter boxes will allow consumers to display digital programming on their current analog TVs. Owners of analog TVs will be able to receive digital programs by connecting the TV's antenna through a set-top box that converts the digital signal for analog display. Since the TV was designed for NTSC quality, however, it won't display the increased sharpness and resolution of the digital transmission. The reception will be free of snow and other distortions of analog transmissions, which will be a great improvement for many viewers.

Standard Definition Television

When the United States decided to make the transition from analog television to **digital television (DTV)**, the Federal Communications Commission agreed to let broadcasters decide whether to broadcast **standard definition television (SDTV)** or **high definition television (HDTV)** programs. Most have decided to broadcast SDTV programs in the daytime and to broadcast HDTV programs during prime time in the evening. Both SDTV and HDTV are supported by the Digital Video Broadcasting (DVB) and Advanced Television Systems Committee (ATSC) set of standards.

SDTV is a digital television (DTV) format that provides a picture quality similar to that recorded on digital video disc (DVD). SDTV and HDTV are the two categories of display formats for digital television (DTV) transmissions, which are becoming the standard in the United States. SDTV has a range of resolutions and no precisely defined aspect ratio although most stations broadcasting SDTV send a signal with approximately the same number of scan lines (vertical pixels) as NTSC and about 720 horizontal pixels. New digital-receiving television sets will be either HDTV-capable or SDTV-capable, with receivers that can convert the received signal to their native display format. SDTV and HDTV both use the **MPEG-2 file compression** method.

HDTV provides a higher-quality display than SDTV, with a vertical resolution display from 720 lines progressive to 1080 lines interlaced or higher and 1920 horizontal pixels per line, making the resolution much better. The HDTV aspect ratio (width to height ratio of the screen) is 16 to 9, about the same as a movie. HDTV, in common with SDTV, uses the MPEG-2 file compression method. Table 6–1 shows a comparison of several television formats with popular computer screen resolutions, photo print sizes, and digital camera formats. It also shows the number of pixels required to create one frame of data in each of these formats.

Table 6-1 Digital image resolutions and data sizes

Format & Other Info	Aspect Ratio (H:V)	Horizontal Pixels	Vertical Pixels	Total Pixels
3x5 photo scanned at 100 dpi	5:3	500	300	150,000
SVGA computer screen	4:3	640	480	307,200
Standard MPEG-2	16:9	724	408	295,392
NTSC television standard	4:3	720	525	378,000
SDTV	4:3	720	525	378,000
Anamorphic DVD	16:9	960	540	518,400
8x10 photo scanned at 100 dpi	5:4	1000	800	800,000
XGA computer screen	4:3	1,024	768	786,432
1.3 Megapixel digital camera	4:3	1,280	960	1,228,800
HDTV	16:9	1,920	1,080	2,073,600
2.35:1 HDTV	2.35:1	2,538	1080	2,741,040
3.3 Megapixel digital camera	4:3	2,048	1,536	3,145,728

SOURCES OF AUDIO AND VIDEO SERVICES

A home network can receive its audio and video data from any of several sources. Which of these sources is chosen will, to some extent, determine how the LAN will be set up to distribute the audio and video data throughout the home.

Broadcast Radio and Television

The most widespread source of audio and video programs, and the least costly, is commercial broadcast stations. Every large American city has television and radio stations, as do most mid-size and smaller ones. Rural areas are served by repeaters and translators, which extend the range of commercial stations into areas beyond the reach of the primary transmitters. Commercial television and radio are free and require only an antenna (usually built in to current television and radio receivers) to receive the broadcast signal.

Neither television nor radio stations have been swift to convert their broadcasts to digital format, but both are moving slowly in that direction. Digital broadcasting will improve reception in those areas where the signal can be received because digital broadcasts don't suffer from interference as do analog signals. Some areas now served by analog broadcasters may lose that service in the switch to digital because of the "cliff effect" of digital transmission. If digital signals don't reach an area, translators to extend their reach will probably be a long time coming due to their expense and the limited return of investment they would bring.

The government is trying to hasten the conversion to all-digital television broadcasting and, since market forces don't seem to be driving that process very fast, has set a nominal deadline of 2007 for the end of analog broadcasting. The deadline isn't absolute and has many conditions that may allow extensions, but it has had some effect on speeding up the conversion process. Whether it will actually be met remains to be seen.

Those homeowners who are satisfied with broadcast television service probably won't want to link that service to a home LAN because it's much easier to simply receive the signal through the antenna in each television in the home. The same is true for AM and FM radio broadcasts. When commercial stations make the change to digital broadcasting, listeners and viewers will need to have digital-capable receivers in order to hear or see the programming.

Analog television sets can display digital programs with the help of a digital **decoder**. These are available as set-top boxes for those who want to continue using older televisions. The incoming digital signal first goes to the box, much like a cable feed, where it is decoded into analog form and sent to the television for display. Alternatively, consumers will need to buy new digital decoder-equipped television sets.

The converted digital picture on an analog television is an improvement on analog reception in all cases. Picture quality equal to playing a DVD on an analog set will be the norm because an analog television is capable of displaying a better picture than it gets from a conventional broadcast signal; however it can't display the picture of a high-definition digital broadcast. For that, an SDTV or HDTV receiver is required.

6

At present some "digital" televisions come with a built-in digital tuner while others have only an analog tuner but are "digital-ready," which means they can display a digital picture, but only if they receive the proper signal from a decoder. There's no way to tell whether a television has a digital decoder by looking at it. When buying any new set today, the product sheet should be checked to see if it has a decoder. If it does and can display digital signals, don't be concerned about also receiving current analog programs. Every television made for the next several years will have an analog tuner, regardless of whether it also has a digital tuner.

Digital radio broadcasts also require a digital receiver. Because the conversion of radio to digital broadcasting has been slow in this country, digital radios aren't readily available here, although they are common on the international market and are manufactured by such companies as Hitachi, Panasonic, and Sanyo. As digital broadcasting in America increases, so will the availability of receivers through retail outlets.

Cable Television

Most of the cable television reception in the United States today is analog and not digital. That's because as recently as 2001 when more than 25 million television sets were sold in this country, only about 150,000 of them were digital ready, less than one percent. Consequently, even though cable companies send their television signals to homes in digital format, the set-top boxes in most homes not only determine which cable channels are received, they also convert the digital cable signal to analog so the consumer's television can display it. Cable television companies at present transmit in digital format because doing so enables them to compress the signal and provide more channels in the available bandwidth, rather than because of consumer demand for the digital display.

While a converter box allows viewers to see a program that has been broadcast in digital format, it doesn't display the visual clarity and CD-quality sound that a digital set provides. The reception may be a considerable improvement over ordinary analog, but its quality is defined by the limits of the analog set that's displaying it. Only with a digital television set can the full capability of digital television be displayed. Figure 6-9 shows some of the differences between an NTSC image and an SDTV image.

Figure 6-9   An SDTV picture (right) is sharper and clearer than NTSC (left)

Television sets with digital decoders for cable or broadcast reception are still expensive and uncommon in the United States. The FCC has adopted labeling rules for such sets specifying three levels of **digital cable ready** television receivers:

Digital Cable Ready 1: A consumer electronics TV receiving device capable of receiving analog basic, digital basic and digital premium cable television programming by direct connection to a cable system providing digital programming. There is no 1394 digital connector or other digital interface. This device does not have two-way capability using cable facilities.

Digital Cable Ready 2: A consumer electronics TV receiving device that in addition to the features of the Digital Cable Ready 1 sets also includes the 1394 digital interface connector that may be used for attaching the receiving device to various other consumer appliances.

Digital Cable Ready 3: A consumer electronics TV receiving device that in addition to the features of the Digital Cable Ready 1 sets is capable of receiving advanced and interactive digital services by direct connection to a cable system providing such service.

- FCC Media Release, 14 September 2000

Television sets in category 2 can be attached through the 1394 connector to a video recorder or to a computer so that the digital video signal can be transmitted over a LAN (with sufficient bandwidth capacity). It's important to remember, however, that the decoding device is only capable of decoding one channel of digital television at a time, and the channel to be decoded must be selected by the decoding device. This means that if the decoded signal is transmitted on the network, every display that receives it shows the same channel. A change of channel can only be made by the decoding device, not the individual displays, and any change made affects all displays.

Cable companies will offer or are now offering SDTV to their customers, but the existing cable network infrastructure doesn't have enough bandwidth to transmit HDTV. Only by replacing the cable network with high-speed, fiber-optic cables would enough bandwidth be available for HDTV via cable. No plans exist at present to make this conversion, but if digital cable attracts enough customers in the next few years, the expense of the cable upgrade may be warranted.

Digital Satellite Television

All satellite television broadcasting is digital. This technology was developed after digital television was already beginning to overtake analog in ground-based broadcasting and so was designed from its beginning to take advantage of digital technology. Satellite television broadcasting differs from ground-based television broadcasting primarily in the location of the transmitter and the power of its transmission.

Satellite signals are first transmitted from a transmitting facility on the ground to a satellite orbiting the earth. Television transmission satellites are placed in geosynchronous orbits. This means that the satellite stays locked in a stationary specific location above the earth. In effect, it is "parked" 22,300 miles above the earth. It orbits with the earth so that its position above the surface does not change. Unlike most satellites, which rotate in orbit, television satellites do not. They hold a constant, steady orientation in space with their solar power panels facing toward the sun 24 hours a day and their signal receiving and broadcast antennas pointing steadily toward earth at all times. Because the satellite is stationary in space relative to the ground, transmission signals can be aimed at it very precisely. Receiving stations can also be aligned accurately to receive the strongest signal from it.

Once the signal reaches the satellite, it is rebroadcast to customers on the ground. Satellite transmitters don't have the power of ground-based television transmitters, but they don't need to because their signals are received by **dish antennas** which are precisely aimed at the satellite. These aimed antennas concentrate the received signal at a point in front of the dish and send it to the decoder. The decoder converts the signal into a digital display and sends it to the television.

Satellite systems can broadcast 150 digital television channels from a single satellite, but all satellite companies have more than one satellite in orbit in order to have backup capability and multiple coverage over all areas of the country. The satellites broadcast all 150 channels to all customers. The decoder selects which channel it decodes for display based on instructions it receives from the satellite and selections made by the customer. The decoder can only process one channel at a time, so if the decoded signal is sent to more than one television, all must show the same decoded channel. If more than one channel at a time is to be available for separate television sets, a splitter is required on the **dish antenna** to send the signal to independent decoders attached to each set. Up to four separate decoders can operate off of a single dish antenna equipped with splitters.

As with cable television systems, most of the television receivers linked to satellite antennas and decoders now are displaying analog pictures, superior to broadcast analog reception, but still not equal in quality to SDTV, let alone HDTV. The decoders in these systems convert the digital transmission to analog so that a standard television can display it. A satellite system can only display a digital picture (STV or HDTV) if it is equipped with a digital decoder similar to (but not compatible with) those used for digital cable television. Relatively few of these are currently in operation, but the numbers are beginning to increase significantly as the amount of digital broadcasting, especially in HDTV, increases.

Unlike cable systems, satellite broadcasters have plenty of bandwidth to broadcast HDTV and most of the HDTV being offered today arrives over satellite systems. Digital **converters**, whether set-top boxes or built in to the television cost between $500 and $800, but their price is falling as sales increase and manufacturers remain confident that about 40% of the 250 million U.S. television sets will convert to digital reception by the time most commercial stations change over fully to digital broadcasting in 2007. The remaining 60% will still be able to view digital programming on analog sets using a converter, but all new television sets are expected to be digitally compatible by that time.

Video Storage Files and Formats

Video is stored on media (magnetic tape, magnetic disks, DVDs) in many different formats. Because computers are digital devices and computer networks also handle only digital data, all video formats used on the Internet or by computers to store and transmit video data are digital formats. Television programs are still mostly analog, although the proportion of digital television is growing. Consequently, television programs are stored as both analog programs (files) and digital files in several formats. Analog video programs can't be compressed. Digital video files almost always are compressed to save storage space.

Internet Video

Four prominent formats of video files are available on the Internet. Each is compressed using a lossy algorithm and consequently exhibit some loss of quality from the original (uncompressed) video format. Internet video files are typically short, a few minutes in length rather than a full-length movie or even a half-hour program, although many of the latter shows are available for those who have the patience to download them over a home connection.

- MPEG-1 files offer very good quality in an aspect ratio of 4 to 3 and image size 320 pixels wide and 240 pixels high. This size is one quarter of a 640 by 480 pixel television screen and is large enough to be viewed easily on most computer monitors. MPEG-1 files cannot be streamed over the Internet, which means that the entire file of a video clip must be downloaded before the file can be played by the receiving computer. This lack of ability to play while completing a download makes MPEG-1 less popular than the other formats which do not have this limitation.

- QuickTime files are played using the QuickTime player and are compressed using any of the supported codecs. They have better quality than MPEG-1 video files and they are streamable. This means the file can begin playing as soon as the first part of it has been downloaded. The video program plays smoothly as long as the speed of downloading new data in the file stays ahead of the player. If the player overtakes the download, the video display stops until additional data has been loaded. QuickTime is made by Apple Computers Inc. and was originally a Macintosh-only video format. Later versions can also be used on PCs. QuickTime is a very well-supported format and is often used in video editing, as well as for distribution over the Internet.

- Windows Media Player uses the MPEG-4 compression system and can stream video files. Windows Media is a relatively new format, but is growing fast in popularity. It provides very good quality video and is manufactured by Microsoft. It is included as a standard feature in all new Microsoft operating systems (Windows 9X, Windows 2000, Windows XP). Media Player can stream video.

- Real Player offers somewhat lower quality in video, but the Real media format was the first to deal with streaming video and has the widest user base. Its maker provides authoring tools for creating streaming video files. The current version of the software, RealOne Player, also supports full-screen (640 by 480 pixels) video playback over a connection fast enough to maintain the download while playing.

Most video files available on the Internet can be downloaded in at least two of the common formats. Generally, one of the available formats is of lower quality but also smaller in size so that it can be conveniently downloaded over a 56K modem connection. The other format is often higher in quality with larger files and intended for use by those who have a high-speed connection of 128K or more.

Stored Video Media

Analog **Video Home Standard (VHS)** video tape cassettes have been until recently by far the most common means of duplicating and distributing analog video movies and other programs. Millions of these cassettes are still being manufactured and more than 80% of American homes have a video cassette recorder/player (VCR).

VHS cassettes are analog only, so neither SDTV nor HDTV programming can be recorded on them or played on them. For this reason, their popularity is declining and being rapidly overtaken by **digital video discs (DVDs)**, which are digital recording media only and which provide higher quality video.

DVD technology offers crystal-clear pictures, superb multidirectional sound, massive data storage for computers and a host of interactive features such as selectable camera angles and a choice of movie endings. A majority of U.S. homes will soon have DVD players which convert the digital data recorded on a DVD to analog video which a nondigital television can display. These DVD player converters are now available for about $100, a price which assures that their popularity will continue to grow and that DVDs will rapidly replace VHS cassettes as the core of most home video libraries. DVDs are recorded in the MPEG-2 compressed format which allows up to four hours of digital video to be placed on a single DVD. Quality is excellent, even though the playback for most users is still analog, and DVDs have now become the standard against which any other video compression format and display is measured for both picture and sound quality.

DVD movies are anamorphically encoded, which means that when a movie filmed in a wide-screen format is transferred to a DVD for home video viewing, the black bars that appear at the top and bottom of the NTSC (or SDTV) screen are encoded along with the movie. If the user has, or later gets, an HDTV digital receiver with a 16:9 aspect ratio, that television receiver can play the movie from the same DVD, but display the picture stretched out to fill the wide screen and eliminate the top and bottom bars. This ability of DVD technology to be forward compatible so that it can provide improved viewing on existing analog television equipment and still be compatible with more advanced digital technology added later by the consumer, is one of the most appealing features of DVDs. It is made still more attractive by the fact that a DVD movie never wears out like VHS cassette tapes do after frequent viewing.

CONNECTED AUDIO/VIDEO SYSTEM DESIGN

The ideal networked video system might be one that allows the users to simultaneously view HDTV programs or movies on any of several screens located throughout the home, or to play graphics-intensive, three-dimensional action games across the LAN and with other players on the Internet. In addition, the ideal system would allow users to video conference with others around the world while still monitoring their home security systems, children's play areas, summer vacation home, and sailboat. Unfortunately, while such a system is possible, it isn't easy to accomplish technologically, and it isn't cheap.

Networked entertainment video taxes the capacity of most LANs because quality video, even when compressed by the most sophisticated codecs (coder/decoder algorithms), still requires the fast transmission of huge amounts of data and the fast processing of that data in order to render it viewable on screen in real time. Both the bandwidth of the LAN and the processing power of its nodes must be not just momentarily rapid, but consistently so for as long as the video stream is running. Any significant drop in transmission rates or processing speed can result in dropouts in the video display, jumps in the action, unintended freeze frames, and even audio distortion. None of these are acceptable when watching a movie or playing an action game, and they're equally annoying when participating in a video conference, watching a downloaded video clip, or scanning the yard for any sign of intruders. Some unpleasant truths about networks make these problems more likely to occur than most system vendors want to acknowledge.

The first of these truths is that most network technologies don't operate consistently at their maximum rated speeds. Tests have suggested that some, like HomePlug, and Wi-Fi, average only about half their rated maximums. Since these are both rated at speeds above 10 Mbps, even an average data transmission speed of 5 Mbps is more than adequate for most network functions, but not always for video.

The reason for this becomes evident when we consider how the average network speed is attained. An easy analogy illustrates the problem: if a person sits down with one half of his backside resting on a hot stove and the other half on a block of ice, on average, he's comfortable. But not really, because the average "comfortable" temperature doesn't exist anywhere on his seat and the deviations from that average are too extreme to tolerate. The same thing happens on many networks: sometimes they operate at maximum speed, sometimes a momentary run of interference or noise will slow transmission to a tenth of maximum or even stop it altogether. When the slow periods and fast ones are averaged, there's plenty of bandwidth for most transmissions because the data is simply being stored at the receiving end until the file is complete and can be displayed or otherwise used.

Compressed video, however, can't easily tolerate the slowdowns or the stops because it is a data stream in which each frame is interrelated. A slowdown or momentary break in the data stream leaves the processor unable to decode a frame on time. When the data starts up or speeds up, the processor has to relocate where it was in decoding the stream, perhaps decode a couple of previous frames again because parts of succeeding frames depend on the data content of earlier ones, and then proceed forward. Buffering the video stream at the receiving end can mitigate some of the effects of slowdowns in data transmission, but to transmit a smooth, uninterrupted video stream, a LAN must be able to function consistently for long periods at high speed with very few slowdowns in its transmission rate.

Few of the most popular home LAN technologies can meet this performance standard and, hence, are not good choices for networking full-screen, real-time video. This includes HomePlug, Wi-Fi, HomeRF, HomePNA, and X10 in their present versions. The advocates of each of these technologies have introduced an upgraded (faster) version or are developing one which may answer the need for video networking, but none have yet been proven in actual operation to be consistently able to do so.

10Mbps Ethernet and 100Mbps Ethernet can both network video with consistently high quality, provided that the cabling and connectors of the system are professionally installed so as to not degrade the performance of the LAN. A network's speed is only as fast as the slowest link in its infrastructure, so the quality of work done by the installing technician is critical, if video is to be carried on the LAN. Ethernet networks can also be slowed by heavy traffic, which makes smooth video tranmission impossible.

If video programs of any length are to be downloaded from the Internet, or games played with players on other networks, a high-speed Internet connection is a must. Video programs can be downloaded with a 56K modem, but the user needs to start the download in the evening and plan to play the program the following morning. Modems don't always connect with the ISP at their full-rated speeds. Large providers often limit their low-speed connections to 20K or 25K, especially during peak hours of usage, in order to still have adequate bandwidth available for high speed customers who are paying for that service specifically. A recent test of a Microsoft video tutorial download using a 56K modem revealed a speed of only 4.5K in the connection. A 9MB video file required 23 minutes to download. Real-time video games are virtually impossible unless the Internet connection is at least 128K and performance improves proportionally if the ISP connection is raised to the DSL level.

Entertainment video, whether it comes into the home as an analog or a digital signal from a broadcast antenna, a cable connection, or a satellite dish, should probably be distributed separately from the home LAN. At present there simply are no convenient ways to link these transmission systems to the LAN so as to make video distribution on the network easy and routine. A DVD can be played on any computer with player software and a drive, but there's no easy way to distribute the show across the network, nor to access a DVD located at one node remotely from another node. As SDTV and HDTV become more prominent, distribution systems that allow programs to be sent to more than one location in the home are certain to be developed, but at the moment, there are few of these and each requires a decoder for the satellite or cable signal at every receiver.

Video programs that display in formats less than a full screen (MPEG-1 for example, at 320 pixels by 240) can be networked quite easily by any of the home LAN technologies as well as Ethernet. This type of video includes most Internet downloads and video conference programs. Likewise, most security system videos can be networked, even if they display full-screen because they typically transmit no more that two or three frames per second, often in black and white, and thus are not nearly as data intensive as entertainment video.

Audio files can also be networked on any reasonably fast system. Audio formats that download completely before playing generally present no difficulty with dropouts or interference and have excellent quality. Those that are streamable, such as MP3, are subject to the same potential problems as afflict streamed video programs. The decoder for such files often has difficulty recovering bits of data lost due to interference or noise on the network, and the lost bits translate into dropouts and sound distortions in the playing file.

Chapter Summary

- Analog audio and video signals are radio frequency (RF) transmissions, which have patterns that are related to the sounds or images they represent and can be interpreted and displayed by radio and television receivers.

- Digital audio and video signals are conversions of the analog signals into numerical form, which can also be transmitted and received as RF signals or over wires. Rapidly sampling the analog data and assigning numerical values to each sample create digital audio and video signals.

- Compact discs (CDs) are the most common form of digital audio recording. A CD can contain over an hour of audio and has a response range from 20 to 20,000 cycles per second, equal to the total range of human hearing.

- Audio files can be recorded on computers using any of several formats such as WAV (Windows Audio), MP3 (MPEG Audio Layer 3), WMA (Windows Media Audio), OGG (Ogg Vorbis), and MP3PRO (Motion Picture Professional).

- Analog television is still the most common type in the United States and is always in NTSC 4:3 format. Digital television can be in SDTV 4:3 format or in HDTV 16:9 format.

Digital television broadcasts are usually converted to analog for display on nondigital sets, but digital sets which display a true digital image are becoming more common.

◻ Digital video discs (DVDs) are the most common form of digital video-recording media. They are recorded using the MPEG-2 compression format and can contain up to four hours of video.

◻ Digital video is always transmitted in compressed form because of the large amount of data involved. Lossless compression (Huffyuv) is the best type because it loses no data, but 95% of compression is done in lossy formats (MPEG-2, Quicktime) which lose some data, but can compress the video files to much smaller sizes.

◻ Analog television is transmitted over RF frequencies and received by an antenna, which is connected through a tuner to the television display. Cable transmission of analog television is also common, though declining.

◻ Digital television is transmitted by broadcast to antenna-equipped receivers (this method is just getting started in the United States), by cable networks, and by satellite broadcasts to aimed receiver dishes. Digital signals are not affected by noise or interference as analog are, but do terminate their range suddenly in the "cliff effect."

◻ Digital video is transmitted over the Internet and on LANs using any of four formats: MPEG-1, QuickTime, MPEG-4 (Windows Media Player), and RealOne Player. All except the last display pictures smaller than full-screen size (640 by 480 pixels) and all use lossy compression technology to reduce the size of transmitted files.

◻ The data transmission requirements for entertainment video (speed and quantity) make it impractical for most home LAN technologies. DVDs can be played over home networks, but must be controlled at the node where the DVD is physically located.

KEY TERMS

amplitude modulation (AM) — A method of converting sound waves to radio signals by varying the amplitude (strength) of the signal, but not its frequency.

analog — Sound or video signals which are analogous to (have patterns similar to) the actual sounds or images.

aspect ratio — The ratio of a video screen's width to its height. NTSC screens have a 4:3 ratio, HDTV screens a 16:9 ratio.

cathode ray tube (CRT) — The display tube in a television set on which the picture appears.

cliff effect — A description of the sudden termination of the range of digital video transmissions which can end as if they "fell off a cliff."

codec — Coding/decoding: a software program or hardware device which encodes and/or decodes digital transmissions.

compact discs (CD) — A plastic disc on which audio files are encoded using the pulse code modulation method.

compression — Any technique which uses math algorithms to reduce the size of digital files for storage or transmission.

converter — A device which changes digital signals into analog, or vice versa.

decibel (dB) — A unit for measuring sound level. Used in audio engineering.

decoder — A device which changes digital video or audio files to signals which can be displayed or heard on audio visual systems.

digital — Any kind of data which is recorded in numerical (discrete) form rather than analog (continuously varying).

digital audio tape (DAT) — Standard for recording uncompressed digital audio on tape at the same quality level as a CD.

digital cable ready — A government designation for television sets denoting their capability to play digital cable programs.

digital television (DTV) — Television signals which are in numerical format and create a picture in pixels rather than rasters as does analog TV.

digital video discs (DVDs) — Media for recording digital video.

dish antenna — A parabolic-shaped antenna that receives satellite broadcasts.

field — One scan of an interlaced television frame which refreshes one half the frame.

frame — One complete refresh of a television screen, which can be two scans (fields) if interlaced, one scan if progressive.

frequency modulation (FM) — A method of broadcasting sound be varying the frequency of the carrier wave, but not its strength.

high definition television (HDTV) — Digital television format with a 16:9 aspect ratio and high resolution.

Huffyuv — A lossless codec for digital video compression.

interlaced — Method of refreshing a video screen in which only odd-numbered lines are scanned on one pass and even-numbered lines on the next.

lossless — Type of video compression in which no data is lost. Huffyuv is an example.

lossy — Type of video compression in which some data is lost, but files can be made smaller than with lossless compression.

magnetic media — Any media with a ferrous coating capable of storing analog or digital data recorded on it by a magnetic head.

magnetic recording — Any analog or digital data recorded on magnetic media.

magnetic tape — Plastic tape coated with ferrous material for recording data.

MP3 file — A file created with an audio compression algorithm with the same name.

MP3PRO — A file created with an audio compression algorithm with the same name; higher compression than MP3, but equal in quality.

MPEG-1 — A file created with a video compression algorithm with the same name.

MPEG-2 — Video compression algorithm used for DVD video recording.

NTSC format — Standard analog U.S TV format with 525 scan lines and 4:3 aspect ratio.

Ogg Vorbis (OGG) — An open source video compression format and hence free of any patents.

PAL format — European analog TV standard equivalent to U.S. NTSC standard.

phonograph — A machine that plays analog recordings from a plastic disc embossed with grooves bearing the sound wave impressions.

pixel — A picture element in digital television; the unit of color and brightness that forms the picture in digital television.

progressive — Method of refreshing a video screen in which all lines are scanned in sequence.

pulse code modulation (PCM) — The method used to record compact discs using MP-2 compression. Not a magnetic process. Uses light diffraction to record data.

Quicktime — An Internet and computer video file format which uses compression and is widely used by PC and Apple computers.

radio frequency (RF) — Any electronic wave with a frequency in the radio band of the electromagnetic spectrum. Includes all radio and TV frequencies.

raster — One scan line on an analog television screen.

RealVideo — A computer and Internet video compression algorithm.

record — A plastic disc with grooves bearing sound wave impressions that can be played on a phonograph.

sampling — A technique for converting analog signals into digital form by taking quantified samples of the analog data.

SECAM — A French-created European equivalent of NTSC analog standard.

signal-to-noise ratio (S/N ratio) — The difference in sound level between the recorded audio and the background noise on any type of audio recording.

standard definition television (SDTV) — The approved format for U.S. digital television with a 4:3 aspect ratio and a 525 by 720 pixel screen.

Video Home Standard (VHS) — The U.S. standard analog video recording format used in video cassettes.

video image — Any image, analog or digital, displayed on a CRT or other type of screen.

WAVE file — A compression algorithm for sound files.

Windows Media Audio (WMA) — An MPEG–4 audio compressed file.

REVIEW QUESTIONS

1. Analog sound signals can be converted to digital form using a _____ technique.

2. Lossy is a form of _____.

    a. video compression

    b. audio compression

    c. analog-to-digital conversion

    d. recording

3. NTSC is a digital television standard with an aspect ratio of 4:3 and 480 scan lines. True or False?

4. Most radio stations in the United States have been broadcasting in digital format since 1992. True or False?

5. Frequency modulation is used to broadcast high-quality _____ _____.

6. HDTV has a 16:9 aspect ratio and 1080 interlaced scan lines. True or False?

7. Hertz (Hz) is a unit of measurement for the frequency of all _____ _____.

8. DVD stands for _____.

    a. direct video display

    b. directional vane dominance

    c. digital video display

    d. digital video disc

9. What is the difference between an interlaced screen display and a progressive one?

10. DVDs are recorded using what form of compression?

    a. OGG

    b. WAV

    c. MPEG-2

    d. Huffyuv

11. For a television to display digital television images it must have a digital to analog converter. True or False?

12. What is the difference between interframe and intraframe video compression?

13. Satellite TV broadcasts originate on the ground and are broadcast to the satellite which then rebroadcasts the signal to customers on the ground. True or False?

14. Why are there so few digital radio receivers in the United States?

15. A dish antenna is used to _____.

    a. receive analog audio broadcasts

    b. receive analog TV broadcasts

    c. receive digital TV broadcasts

    d. download cable signals

16. SDTV has 525 vertical pixels and 720 horizontal pixels giving it an aspect ration of _____.

    a. 4:3

    b. 3:4

    c. 9:16

    d. 5:3

17. The "cliff effect" applies to _____.

    a. analog TV signals

    b. all TV and radio signals

    c. digital TV signals

    d. audio recording

18. Why are digital television images always compressed before being broadcast?

19. If television satellites orbit the earth, how do customers receive their signals when the satellite is on the other side of the world?

20. A raster is _____.

    a. a device for mounting a dish antenna

    b. a single scan line on an analog TV screen

    c. a security program for video

    d. a connector cable

21. The most significant difference between pixels on a computer screen and those on a television screen is _____.

    a. the TV pixels have more colors

    b. the computer has more pixels

    c. the TV pixels are not square but rectangular

    d. the TV pixels invert the colors

22. Why isn't analog television broadcast from satellites which could allow one station to cover the entire country?

23. MPEG and QuickTime video files can be transmitted on the Internet because they compress the video data and because they display a screen that is _____ than a digital television broadcast.

24. The LAN technology best suited to transmit video at present is _____.

25. To stream video on the Internet or download streamed video, a LAN should have at least a _____ ISP connection.

Hands-on Projects

**HANDS-ON
PROJECTS**

Project 6-1: Download the QuickTime Player

In this project you will download a video player program from the Internet. You will need access to a computer that is connected to the Internet. If the computer you are using already has the QuickTime Player loaded on it, download another video player such as RealPlayer or Windows Media Player

1. Log onto the Internet and go to **www.apple.com/quicktime/download/**.

2. Select the operating system the computer is using and register your name if you wish. If not, click off the news group subscription, and click download. The QuickTime file downloads automatically.

3. When the security warning displays, click **Yes** and proceed with the download of the installer program.

4. When the installer program has downloaded, it launches the download for QuickTime. Follow the screen instructions to start the download of the program which is about 5 MB in size.

5. After the program has downloaded, it installs automatically. Select the default choices at the various screen prompts unless you have specific reasons for changing them.

6. When the program completes installation, close the installer. Return to the Internet, and check the installation page to be sure the program installed correctly. If there are any problems noted, select the appropriate prompts to correct them.

7. You can test your download by playing one or more of the movie trailers that are listed on this site. Compare the time it takes to download and play a trailer at low resolution and high resolution.

Project 6-2: Download an Animation Video from the Internet

In this project you will download and play an animation video from the Internet. You will need the use of a computer, which has access to the Internet.

1. Log onto the Internet and go to **http://mars.jpl.nasa.gov/**.

2. Click the picture captioned "Mars Exploration Rover makes Progress."

3. Under the gallery heading on the left side of the screen, click videos.

4. Click the "Animation" picture in the center of the screen.

5. Click the QuickTime movie for the "MER Launch and Cruise 2002" animation.

6. Select Save from the window that appears, and select a directory on the computer in which to save the file. (If your computer has a QuickTime browser installed, the file will play immediately, and you can save it afterward.)

7. Download the file. It's about 3.1 MB. See how long it takes the computer to download it. Do you have a slow or fast Internet connection?

8. When the file has downloaded, close the window and play the file using the player you downloaded in Project 1.

Project 6-3: Download an Audio File and Play It from the Computer

For this project you will need access to a computer that has a CD-ROM drive. You will also need access to a music CD and the Internet.

1. Insert a music CD into the CD-ROM drive and close it. Windows 2000 or Windows XP will open the CD player. If the player doesn't open automatically, open it in Windows 2000 by clicking **Start**, **Programs**, **Accessories**, **Entertainment**, and **Windows Media Player**. In Windows XP, you can open it by clicking **Start**, pointing to **All Programs**, and then clicking **Windows Media Player**.

2. Select a music track to play and listen to it as played from the CD.

3. When you've listened to the selection, click Stop, and then click the Copy from CD selection on the left side of the Media Player screen.

4. When the selections on the CD appear, check only the one you want to copy to the left of its title. All the other check boxes should be blank. If they're not, click them off.

5. Click the Copy Music button at the top of the Media Player screen.

6. Click OK to leave the copy protection on if the work is copyrighted (as almost all are). If it isn't, click the **Add Copy Protection** button and follow the screen instructions to continue making the copy.

7. The copy is recorded on the computer in the default directory listed at the bottom of the Media Player screen.

8. When the file has completed loading, close the Media Player and remove the CD from the player.

9. Click the Start button, and then click My Music or go to the alternate directory where you saved the music file.

10. Right-click the file and choose to play the music.

11. Listen to the music again. Can you hear any difference in the quality of the music?

Project 6-4: Explore Available Media on the Internet

In this project, you will learn media types.

1. If you are using Windows XP, click the **Start** button, point to **All Programs**, and then click **Windows Media Player**. For Windows 2000, click **Start**, **Programs**, **Accessories**, **Entertainment**, and then **Windows Media Player**.

2. When the player opens, click **Media Guide** at the left side of the window.

3. Explore the video downloads available at this site. Select and download one of the 300 KB video clips and play it. How does its quality compare with the 3 MB file you downloaded in Project 6-1?

4. Select one of the movie Web sites listed in the media guide and visit it. Download the highest-quality movie trailer you can find. If you're using a computer with a 56 K modem, limit your search to files that are 5 MB or less. If you have a high speed connection, you can download larger files.

5. Play the large high-quality video on your computer. Does it play in Windows Media Player or QuickTime? If not, what player is required? How can you get it? What is the cost?

6. How does this video compare to the video you downloaded in Project 6-1?

Project 6-5: Record Analog Television from a Broadcast Source

For this project you will need access to a television set capable of receiving broadcast (antenna reception) television stations and a VCR that can be connected to the television. You will also need a recordable video cassette.

1. Connect the VCR to the television so that it can record a program playing on the television. Plug one end of two RCA cables into the TV's video out and audio out jacks. (These are usually found on the back of the TV, but may be on the front in some models.)

2. Plug the video out cable into the VCR's video in jack. Plug the audio out cable into the VCR's audio in jack.

3. Tune the television set to a channel which is broadcasting television in your area.

4. Place a blank recordable video cassette in the VCR and begin recording the program that is playing on the television. Press the record button on the VCR to begin recording. (Some VCRs require you to press the Record and the Play button together.)

5. After you've recorded about five minutes of programming, stop the VCR and rewind the recorded cassette to the beginning.

6. Change the cables connecting the TV and VCR. Connect one cable to the VCR's video out jack and the TV's video in Jack. Connect the other cable to the VCR's audio out jack and the TV's audio in jack.

7. Set the TV's tuner to channel 3 or the input channel, if it has one. Play the recorded material on video cassette through the TV. Observe how it appears. Is the recording as clear and well focused as the broadcast program? If the original broadcast program had ghosts or lines in it, do they appear in the recording?

8. Switch back and forth between the recorded program and the broadcast program. See if you can detect differences in quality between them. This is one of the problems of analog television recording. The recorded image always loses some quality compared to the original. The recorded image also records all the defects of the original program. If the original had ghosts or dropout lines, so will the recording, even though the original broadcast from the station did not.

9. Play a commercially recorded video cassette in the VCR and compare its quality to the recording you made. Do you see a difference? The commercial video cassette was recorded from a hardwired connection to the original camera image or video recording, so it doesn't have any of the defects that appear in broadcast signals sent over distances.

HANDS-ON PROJECTS

Project 6-6: Compare Monaural and Stereo Playing of a Music Selection

For this project you will need access to a stereo audio system set up to play with left and right speakers. The audio receiver must have a monaural select button on it so that it can be set to play in single track format. You will also need a stereo recording (cassette tape or CD) that can be played on the audio system.

1. Place the audio recording into a suitable player and turn the system on.

6

2. Start the recording and play a selection through in stereo format. Listen for the balance of the instruments or voices on the recording. You should be able to discern them separately as if each were standing in a different location in front of you and playing at that spot. The more widely spaced the speakers of the audio system are, the more widely spaced the players of the music should sound.

3. Switch the stereo audio system to monaural. This causes the system to play both tracks of music through both speakers, effectively combining the two tracks into only one.

4. Play the same selection of music again. Does it sound the same? To which version would you prefer to listen? Can you describe why the stereo version sounds better?

5. Switch the audio system back to stereo and play the music selection a third time. For this playing keep your hand tightly pressed over one of your ears. Does the stereo playing sound better than the monaural with only one ear to listen? Why?

CASE PROJECTS

CASE
PROJECTS

Case Project 6-1: Research a Service Provider for HDTV

A client has asked you to recommend a service provider for HDTV service as well as SDTV and as wide a selection of channels as can be obtained. He lives in your area. Find out what television services are available in your area and how the client can best obtain the level of service he wants. Be sure to check on what channels are actually broadcasting HDTV programming in the area rather than just which services offer HDTV. Don't overlook pay-per-view channels, but be sure to note the costs of these services. Write a short summary of what's available in the local area and how much it will cost monthly for the service.

CASE
PROJECTS

Case Project 6-2: Determine When Local Television Stations Will Go Digital

Visit the Web sites of the television stations in your area. Find out if any or all of them have plans in place for commencing digital broadcasting. If they do, note what the startup dates are for each station and what programming hours they plan to broadcast in digital format. If the Web sites don't have this information, contact the stations directly and see if they have made any announcements or have a plan in place. Write down your findings and give your opinion about whether you feel the purchase of a digital television set is justified by the amount of digital programming that is (or will be) available in your area on broadcast stations.

Case Project 6-3: Test a Network for Streaming Video Files

Visit a local supplier of home LAN hardware in one or more technologies. Ask if the vendor can demonstrate the ability of the technology being offered to stream video from one node of a LAN to another. If the vendor has no demonstration network set up, ask if he knows of anyone who has a network using the technology that is streaming video files over it. Try to find at least one technology that can successfully demonstrate video streaming in a working LAN using a home LAN technology.

Case Project 6-4: Compare a Large Screen HDTV to an LCD Projection System for HDTV

Visit an electronics dealer who handles large-screen entertainment centers. Get information on television sets, rear projection television sets, and LCD projection systems that provide a screen size at least 50-inches wide and display HDTV images as well as SDTV images, along with analog video. Write a short report comparing the prices of each system, their sizes, and the quality of images they provide. Note any special requirements they may have that might influence a buyer, such as large space requirements, room darkening, etc. Give an opinion on which system you would recommend to a client if price was not a consideration, and tell why you chose it.

AUDIO AND VIDEO INSTALLATION AND SETUP

After reading this chapter, you will be able to:

♦ Identify the major components of audio and video systems and describe the function of each

♦ Install and set up an audio or video system as part of a home network

♦ Configure an audio or video system for receiving and displaying external programming

♦ Configure an audio or video system so that it can receive and display internal and streamed programming

♦ Perform preventive maintenance for audio and video systems

In the previous chapter you learned about how analog and digital audio and video programs are created, broadcast, received, and displayed. In this chapter you'll learn about the specific components that make up audio and video systems. You'll also learn how to install these components into working systems, and how to configure the systems for peak performance, both for displaying external programs received from commercial providers and for receiving streamed audio and video programs from the Internet or from the home LAN. Finally, you'll learn how to maintain audio and video systems to prevent high-repair costs and preserve performance standards.

AUDIO AND VIDEO SYSTEM COMPONENTS

The audio and video systems we enjoy today are the culmination of many years of development. They are still evolving today as new and more advanced technologies provide the means of still higher-quality audio and video programming than what has been available previously. As new technologies are adopted, older ones fall into disuse and are gradually abandoned, but this is a slow process. The investment people have made in their existing entertainment systems, plus the often higher cost of purchasing a newer technology, makes many content to stay with their tried-and-true systems, as long as they continue to function normally. Hence, millions of people are still listening to audio cassette tapes and analog radio broadcasts many years after CDs and digital broadcasting have raised quality standards tremendously. Millions more are still watching analog NTSC television and VHS cassettes when HDTV and DVD movies could greatly enhance their viewing experience.

This tendency to retain old technology is increased by the fact that neither the equipment nor the storage media of obsolete systems are compatible with newer ones. A record or tape collection can't move up to CD audio quality, even if the music recorded on them is rerecorded to the newer media. The same limitation applies to VHS cassettes: they can't be turned into DVDs with anywhere near the higher quality of the newer medium. Each time a new technology is adopted, a new media collection must begin for the consumer. Figure 7-1 shows some of the development of video and audio media from early forms (at the bottom part of the picture) to current forms (at the top part of the picture). None of these audio and video media are forward compatible.

Figure 7-1   Some outdated and current audio and video media

This part of the chapter discusses some components of audio and video systems that are older than the current digital technology because many home LAN users want to include some of these devices in their home entertainment systems. Most home users probably also want to continue using their existing entertainment collections until they acquire new versions in the current media. Retaining older equipment as a subset of a new audio or video system costs very little and allows the transition to CDs and DVDs to be more gradual and easier on the budget.

Audio System Components

Nearly all audio broadcasting and recording, except AM radio, is done in **stereo** or multiple sound tracks. Stereo recording creates two separate soundtracks, one recorded from the left side of a performer and the other from the right side. Stereo recording is accomplished with multiple microphones placed around the performers being recorded so as to record sound from multiple angles as it would actually be heard in the room. The sound is recorded on multiple tracks and broadcast as a stereo signal. The tracks are **synchronized** together when recorded and played back. All current audio equipment plays in stereo and many systems are capable of playing four or more tracks.

All the components described below function in stereo audio systems although some of them are **monaural** (single track) devices. To maintain high quality in an audio system, the stereo source signal is divided into its separate tracks when it is output from the tuner or player. From that point on, the two (or more) tracks of sound signal pass through separate pre-amplifiers, amplifiers, and speakers, all of which are monaural devices. For the highest quality of sound reproduction, it is important that the two separate tracks be configured and wired identically so that synchronization of the separate stereo tracks is not lost.

Audio programs can be brought into the home through commercial radio stations, satellite music broadcasts, cable music channels, and the Internet. All of these audio signals can be converted back into audible sound by a set of the same basic components that were used to receive early radio broadcasts. By adding player components to these, music and voice programs stored on CDs, cassette tapes, and records can also be played over the same audio system.

An analog radio receiver requires only four basic components to function: an antenna, a **tuner**, a speaker, and a ground. A digital receiver requires these plus a fifth component, a **converter** (or decoder), which renders digital data back into audio waves. Everything else in the modern radio set are refinements. When you think of a radio receiver, you usually think of an integrated device that contains all of these components. That's an accurate view of most radios, but in high-quality sound reproduction systems the major components are almost always separated into individual units, often produced by different, highly specialized manufacturers. These systems usually include additional components which supplement the basic ones found in the radio receiver, or provide additional sound quality, volume, or distribution.

Figure 7-2 shows the basic configuration of an analog radio receiver at the top and a digital radio receiver at the bottom. The main difference between them is the **decoder** which the digital radio requires to convert its numerical signal into an analog format which can be amplified and sent to the speaker for playing. These components are essential for a radio, whether they are housed in a single box or are widely spaced from one another.

7

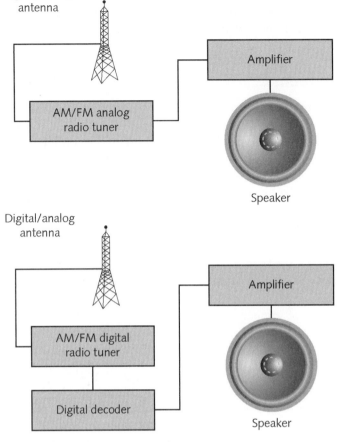

Figure 7-2 Basic analog and digital radios

Antennas

Most AM and FM radios now have a built-in **antenna** that is part of the radio itself. They don't need an outside antenna connected to the radio by a wire. In rural areas distant from broadcast transmitters, an external antenna, sometimes called an aerial, can improve radio reception by bringing in a stronger signal. The stronger signal requires less amplification and therefore contains less noise and interference. This means better quality sound and a better signal to noise ratio for the system.

For digital radios an outside antenna may make reception possible at distances greater than would otherwise be possible. Digital radio broadcasts are just beginning in this country, but their signals suffer from the same "cliff effect" as digital television signals that were discussed in Chapter 6. The signal has to be received perfectly or it isn't received at all. Because an outside antenna brings in a stronger signal, a digital radio may be able to read the enhanced signal and play the radio station even though it is to do so with only its built-in antenna.

When an antenna is used for an audio system, it should be mounted on a roof or other structure as high as possible in order to have the best chance of picking up **attenuated** signals. It should be connected to the receiver by a shielded wire (in order to prevent noise and interference from corrupting the signal on its way from the antenna to the receiver) and it must be grounded, both for safety from lightning and other electrical phenomena and to complete the signal-carrying circuit to the receiver, which is also grounded.

Tuners

A radio tuner is a device which enables the radio to receive only the selected frequency of the station which the user wants to hear and to reject all others. The tuner is variable so that all stations can be received, one at a time, by simply tuning to the correct frequency for each. The quality of a tuner is measured by how precisely it can tune to a selected frequency and how completely it can block all other frequencies, thereby reducing noise and interference.

Analog tuners process the continuous signal they receive into a continuous output wave that is sent to the amplifier to be strengthened, and then to the speakers. Digital tuners are actually decoders which convert the digital data samples of an audio program (discussed in Chapter 6) into a very close approximation of the original continuous signal and send that approximation to the amplifier. If the digital audio signal is in the format used for CDs or another very rapid sampling technique that uses very little compression, the sound quality is actually better than a comparable analog signal and has less noise. If the digital signal uses a less frequently sampled format, or more compressed so that some of the data is lost, the reconstituted audio sound is lower in quality, but still equal to almost any analog signal.

Tuners are often combined with an **amplifier** in a radio. The amplifier increases the power output of the signal received from the broadcast station so it can drive speakers at a higher volume. Strictly speaking, an amplifier isn't a required component of a radio, but without it, the output volume of the speaker is barely audible to the listener.

Amplifiers

Amplifiers come in many sizes and qualities, but only in two basic categories: **pre-amplifier**s (pre-amps) and power amplifiers (amps). Pre-amplifiers amplify the source signal coming from one of the audio system's tuners or players. A pre-amplifier typically receives a source signal of perhaps 5 millivolts (5/1000 of a volt) from the tuner or player. It boosts (increases) this signal strength several thousand times to a strength of up to 5 volts and sends the strengthened signal on to the power amplifier.

The power amplifier must increase the output strength of the signal several more times in order to drive the speakers that actually produce the sound in the audio system. The size of power amplifiers is measured by the output wattage of the signal coming from the amplifier. This power is what drives the speaker or speakers and it can range from only 20 or 30 watts of output to several hundred watts or even more in amplifiers designed to power huge speaker systems. More power is required to produce low notes on the sound scale than high ones, so much of any amplifier's output power is only used when it is producing low-frequency sounds. These low-frequency notes are what give reproduced music from a radio or recorded source the full tonal qualities that otherwise can be heard only in a live performance. High-quality sound reproduction requires these sounds and hence, powerful amplifiers are usually a part of any good sound system.

The quality of both pre-amplifiers and power amplifiers is measured by how cleanly they amplify sound frequencies without adding any noise or interference and without **distortion** in their output signal so that it sounds different than the original input signal. Signal-to-noise ratio is as important for an amplifier as for a tuner. Both must produce clean output signals in order to give good sound quality.

Speakers

Speakers are the audio system components that render electronic signals audible to the ear. They are electromagnetic devices through which a varying frequency current is passed. Speakers convert this electrical energy into sound waves. Figure 7–3 shows a diagram of a speaker and its internal working parts.

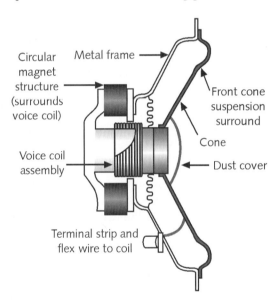

Circular magnet structure (surrounds voice coil)

Metal frame

Front cone suspension surround

Cone

Voice coil assembly

Dust cover

Terminal strip and flex wire to coil

Figure 7-3   A speaker produces sound through a vibrating electromagnet and cone

Electrical current from an amplifier travels through the speaker's flex wire to the voice coil. Current flowing through the voice coil turns it into an **electromagnet**. The magnetic field created by the voice coil causes the coil to be attracted to or repelled from one pole of the magnet structure, depending on whether the current in the voice coil is positive or negative.

As the current in the coil varies in both positive and negative directions in a pattern analogous to the original sound wave signal, the voice coil acts like a piston, moving rapidly back and forth as it is attracted to or repelled from the magnet structure. Since the voice coil is connected to the **cone**, they both move as a single unit. The cone vibrates in the air, alternately compressing and evacuating the air immediately around it, thus producing sound. The vibrating cone produces sound waves that match those which originally were converted into an electric signal when the sound was recorded.

As the above description suggests, speakers are extremely inefficient. They convert only one or two percent of the power fed into them into sound. All the rest of the energy is lost as heat. This heat radiates from the voice coil and circuits inside of the speaker. If a speaker's voice coil overheats, the speaker is destroyed by the distortion caused from intense vibration combined with the heat. The speaker is then said to be "blown."

The output sound of good-quality speakers closely matches the frequencies of the current fed into them without distortion or addition of noise or hum (a low-frequency sound similar to tape hiss, but produced by a different cause). Although the human ear can perceive sounds at frequencies ranging from 20 to 20,000 cycles per second (cps) or Hertz (Hz), no single speaker is capable of responding accurately to that broad a range. For this reason, several speakers (each responsive to a range of frequencies less than the range of hearing) are nearly always connected to an amplifier through a **crossover network** of wires and electronic circuitry in high-fidelity sound systems. The crossover network divides the sound signal coming from the amplifier so that the high-frequency portion is sent to speakers designed for high-frequency response (these speakers are called "tweeters" for the obvious reason), the middle frequencies are sent to mid-range speakers that are responsive to them, and the lower frequencies are sent to low-frequency responsive speakers (called "woofers," again for the obvious reason).

The power of the sound signal that is sent to a speaker or group of speakers must not exceed the capacity of the magnetic circuit of the speaker to carry it. If it does, the speaker overheats and eventually burns out. When a speaker is overdriven (too much power is sent to it), its sound output also distorts because the speaker cone cannot vibrate far enough and fast enough to utilize all the power available to it. The result is that the cone simply stops each vibration at the limit of its movement capability and the resulting sound has its peaks suppressed.

Small, single-speaker audio systems have electronic circuits built into them that limit the power output and the frequency response of the tuner and amplifier. The single speaker may, for example, have response limits of 60 to 10,000 Hz and a maximum of 10 watts input power. This means it can't move fast enough or slow enough to reproduce frequencies above or below its limits, and it overheats if more than 10 watts of power is applied to it. The output signal to the speaker is limited by the system's electronics so that its maximums don't exceed the capacity of the speaker. The frequencies of sound below 60 and above 10,000 are simply cut off and not reproduced by the speaker at all. At average voice volume, fewer than one person in every hundred can hear any difference between a sound track that includes only the mid-range (60 to 10,000 Hz) frequencies and one that covers the whole hearing range.

Equalizers

One other nonessential, but often desirable, component that is often found in audio systems is an **equalizer**. This device allows the user to increase or decrease the volume of various bands of sound frequencies in the output of the system. This is often valuable in adjusting sound for maximum listening pleasure according to the acoustics (sound reflection and absorption qualities) of the particular room where the sound system is located. An equalizer divides the range of audible sounds into three or more bands of frequencies and allows the user to adjust the volume level of each band independent of all the others. If high frequencies tend to be absorbed by the furniture and carpet in the room, the level can be increased to compensate for the loss. If the soprano's high notes threaten to break the windows, they can be reduced to a more pleasant level.

There are many types of equalizer circuits, and digital equalizers operate differently than analog, but all are intended to allow the listener to adjust the sound output to his or her preferred taste. Equalizers are used extensively when recording voice and music media in order to produce a recorded sound that is as close as possible to what the performer intended. For most listeners, the artist's rendition may be perfect, but if it's not, the listener also has the option to change it.

Audio Players

Audio that doesn't come into the home through broadcast signals, cable channels, or the Internet almost always arrives stored on some form of **media**: CD, cassette tape, or record, with perhaps an occasional floppy or Zip disk on which is recorded a rare piece that a friend has, or a personal performance. All of these media can be played on the same audio system that plays radio broadcasts, provided a player unit is substituted for the antenna and tuner that receive the broadcast signals.

CD Player

A **CD player** is now found in many, if not most, home audio systems, and a CD-ROM drive, which can also play CDs, is part of nearly all new computers. Many CD-ROM drives are also **CD burners**; that is, they can record CDs as well as play them. CD drives that can record CDs (designated CDR-R for recordable format or CD-RW for rewritable format) enable users to record voice or music from the Internet. These recorded CDs can be played over a home LAN from the CD drive or played on the audio system's CD player.

Computers provide the most convenient platform for creating CDs, not only to record **digital audio files** from the Internet and other sources, but also to encode analog music selections and standard **MIDI (Musical Instrument Digital Interface) files**. Encoding hardware is now available to the consumer for converting analog music to digital format for storage on CD. An **encoder** allows the user to convert both records and audio cassette tapes to digital format. Consumer digital audio encoders are priced above $700, but for serious music enthusiasts or people with large record or cassette tape collections that they want to convert to digital format, they are a good investment. A CD drive in a home network computer can play or send audio files to any other node. It can also play to an audio system, provided that system is also connected to the network.

Audio Cassette Player

Very few new music recordings are being made on audio cassettes, but many voice recordings (books, educational programs) still use this format. Millions, if not billions of audio cassettes, which could be converted to digital format and played on a digital audio system, still languish in private collections around the country. Either of these continuing uses provides a strong enough reason for anyone who already owns a cassette player to keep it connected to their audio system. New cassette players now cost less than $50 and that price may justify adding one to a system, if the owner wants to convert any significant quantity of cassettes.

A digital encoder is required to convert cassettes to digital format. Because the encoder is most likely at a computer node on the network, that may be the best location for the cassette player as well. Analog sound from the player can then be fed into the computer's sound card input and converted to digital form. It can then be recorded on a hard drive or on a CD, or transmitted over the network to other nodes.

7

Phonographic Record Player

A phonograph (also called a record player or turntable) is now an antique. The main reason to have one in a current audio system is to play records featuring music that can't be obtained on other media, or to play records so their content can be converted to digital format and stored on new media. If conversion is the objective, locate the record player near the encoding computer so its output can feed through an amplifier into the computer sound card input. If playing the records is still the principal pleasure, locate the player with the audio system, and connect it to the audio amplifier. If a digital receiver with analog-to-digital encoding capability is part of the audio system, the record player's output can be digitized like any other analog signal and played or recorded on digital equipment.

Television System Components

Like audio systems, television systems require only a few basic components to function. Some of these components are very similar to those used in audio systems. Others are much more complex because they must process and display more complex signals than those which are required for sound reproduction.

The sound portion of television signals, whether analog or digital, are broadcast as radio signals and television sets have a separate radio tuner, amplifier, and speaker to reproduce sound along with the picture.

Antennas

Analog television antennas are usually built into the television set, but these antennas are not as efficient in picking up a television signal as set-top models or roof antennas. Because the quality of analog television reception is directly related to the strength of the incoming signal received, an efficient antenna, correctly adjusted for maximum signal strength, can make a very significant difference in the clarity and interference level of the picture.

Television antenna reception can be affected by the electrical fields that exist in city areas where consumption of power is high. It can also be affected by weakening of the broadcast signal due to obstructions such as densely concentrated buildings, land masses, and foliage, or by interference from RF signals and television signals reflected from the ground or from layers in the atmosphere.

The effect called "ghosting," which appears on a television screen as multiple shadows of the image, is caused by reception of the main signal and reflections of it that arrive at a slightly different time. Ghosting may appear on one channel and not another because the transmitters of the two channels are located in different places and their signals reflect differently toward an individual receiving antenna. Adjusting the antenna's position or orientation may correct ghosting on one channel, but not on others. Antennas should be kept away from structures that create ghosting by reflecting broadcast signals. These include tall buildings, metal utility towers, high-voltage power lines, and water towers. Smaller versions of these objects such as wooden utility poles, other antennas, and local power lines rarely cause ghosting.

The quality of digital television signals is not affected by any of the reception problems that can degrade an analog picture, but these problems can affect whether or not a digital television signal is received at all. Because a digital television signal is encoded and compressed, all of the digital data in the signal must be received in order for the signal to be decoded and displayed. If some of the data is lost in transmission, the loss doesn't degrade the picture quality; it prevents the decoder from converting the signal into a picture at all. This is the "cliff effect" of digital transmission, which was discussed in Chapter 6. The abrupt cutoff of digital transmission can be caused by interference as well as distance from the transmitter. Adjusting a digital antenna, or moving it to a better location may be all that's needed to obtain reception. If reception is obtained, the picture is nearly flawless. With digital television, it's all or nothing.

Satellite or dish antennas can suffer from a weak signal and interference, but not the same type as broadcast antennas. Because these antennas are aimed directly at the single transmission source, the geosynchronous-orbiting satellite, the only interference that can affect their reception is that which comes from the same direction as the satellite to which they're pointed. Interference from the sky is almost entirely caused by electrical storms in the Earth's atmosphere and electromagnetic storms on the sun's surface which produce corresponding disturbances in the Earth's atmosphere that can disrupt satellite broadcasts. In addition, the relatively weak signal strength of satellite broadcasts can be attenuated by heavy rain or snow occurring between the satellite and the dish antenna. A blizzard or a summer downpour can temporarily block satellite TV reception.

Television Tuners

It was noted in Chapter 6 that the vast majority of television tuners now in use are analog receivers that cannot process digital signals. It was also noted that this ratio of analog to digital sets is changing as more digital broadcasting becomes available and more recorded digital programs on **DVD**s appear to take the place of analog VHS cassettes.

SDTV is the new standard for digital broadcasting and HDTV is the premium television standard. The signals of these two formats are not compatible with one another and each requires its own tuner/decoder to render a signal which a monitor can display as a picture on the screen. The new descriptions for digital television formats put out by the **Advanced Television Systems Committee (ATSC)**, the television industry and government people who determined the standards for the new digital system, now clearly differentiate between a digital television and a digital tuner or receiver.

An **SDTV tuner** is defined as an RF receiver that receives ATSC terrestrial (transmitted from the ground) digital transmissions and decodes all ATSC Table 3 video formats. Its output can be in the form of an NTSC signal so that it can be played on an analog TV, but nearly all such tuners also output an SDTV signal in a 704 by 525 pixel format for display on a digital **Enhanced Definition Television (EDTV)** monitor. The EDTV monitor, which presumably doesn't have a tuner built in, has active vertical scanning lines to meet the 480 progressive (480p) format or higher, but does not have a specified picture aspect ratio. The tuner must also receive, decode, or pass through for decoding Dolby Digital audio. Table 7–1 shows the ATSC approved television compression and format and the specific characteristics they can have. As the table clearly indicates, the television industry is still far from standardization in the area of formats.

Table 7-1   Digital television format constraints

Vertical Size (pixels)	Horizontal Size (pixels)	Aspect Ratios	Frame Rates	Scan Sequence
1080	1920	1:1, 16:9	24, 30	Progressive
1080	1920	1:1, 16:9	30	Interlaced
720	1280	1:1. 16:9	24, 30, 60	Progressive
480	704	4:3, 16:9	24, 30, 60	Progressive
480	704	4:3, 16:9	30	Interlaced
480	640	1:1. 4:3	24, 30, 60	Progressive
480	640	1:1. 4:3	30	Interlaced

An **SDTV television** is a fully integrated television receiver that receives all ATSC terrestrial digital transmissions and decodes all ATSC Table 3 video formats to, in the words of the Consumer Electronics Association's Video Division Board, "produce a useable picture." It can have active vertical scanning lines less than EDTV quality. No aspect ratio is specified for it, but it must also receive some form of useable audio signal.

SDTV tuners appear likely to become the standard for the next generation (the first digital generation) of television systems because the new standards specify they can play to NTSC televisions or monitors, but also play to those EDTV digital monitors that have a 4:3 aspect ratio. An SDTV tuner can thus bridge the conversion period from analog to digital broadcasting by playing on both types of screen and conforming to the higher digital standard when the conversion is complete. A digital television system based on this standard should also be able to play downloaded video from computers and the Internet with a suitable decoder program.

HDTV tuners and televisions, with their 16:9 aspect ratio and high resolution, are much more difficult to connect to a home network, either to send video to a computer or to receive a video program from the network. Manufacturers have so far not produced any products which enable the two systems to exchange data.

Television Displays

Television displays come in the three main forms that are also used for computer screen displays: cathode ray tubes (CRTs), flat panel displays, and LCD projection systems. The technology of each of these has been discussed in Chapter 2 and Chapter 6.

Analog television displays differ from digital television and computer screens only in two important particulars: they create their images in **rasters** (scan lines) rather than pixels (square or rectangular picture elements) and they have somewhat lower resolution than the digital displays. Because the analog signal that paints the picture is continuous, the raster lines of an analog TV screen are also continuous, rather than being divided into individual pixels set in rows across the screen as digital screens are. The color and brightness of each raster varies continuously across its full width, in contrast to pixels, each of which has only one color and one brightness level set by its digital designation.

The pixels of a television screen are rectangular (slightly higher than they are wide) where those of a computer screen are square. This difference makes computer images difficult to display without distortion on a television screen and vice versa. The fact that television screens (analog and digital) also come in many different sizes, aspect ratios, and resolutions, as opposed to relatively few for computers, makes the conversion of images from one format to the other still more difficult.

The truth is that computer-based graphic images don't play well on television screens. And television images don't play much better on computer screens. Both transitions can be accomplished, but both take a lot of compromise and usually result in some loss of picture quality in order to force a video program created in one format to play in a different technology.

Because both digital television tuners and digital television displays don't adapt well to a networked environment, the question naturally arises: how can a television system be connected as part of a home LAN so that television reception and computer/Internet images can be played throughout the home? The answer is that it can't, at least not with presently available equipment. If a home LAN owner really wants television distribution throughout the home, it needs to be wired separately from the network as a video distribution system with perhaps an SDTV tuner connected as a node to the network so that compatible programs can be transmitted to and from the network. Video distribution networks are discussed in the next section.

Video Recorder/Players

The price of a VHS video cassette recorder/player (VCR) has now fallen to around $50 in discount stores across the country. This is a sure indication that DVDs are rapidly taking over as the medium of choice for viewing recorded motion pictures and other video programs. Nevertheless, the multitudes of VHS cassettes sold over the last two decades won't be replaced overnight and so a VCR should continue to be a component of most home video systems for the next few years.

VCRs, which play VHS cassettes, are analog only and so cannot play to an HDTV display which is digital only. They can, however, play on an SDTV display which, though digital, also has the capability to display an NTSC analog image. Most SDTVs will probably play analog NTSC, but this may not be true of those adhering to the newer EDTV standard. Because EDTV displays are only required to display the digital screen formats specified by the ATSC, with nothing mentioned about analog or NTSC images, you should check carefully when purchasing a set built to this standard, to be sure it can play an NTSC-format image.

The variety and range of quality available in VCRs has been enormous, but is now diminishing as their market share is being taken over by DVD players. Price ranges for VCRs still range from the low-end $50 models, which can be expected to last no more than a year to machines costing $1,000 or more and built to last a lifetime. If a VCR is being purchased today, with its end of useful life clearly visible not more than a few years in the future, it's probably best to opt for a mid-range machine with good playing specifications and a fair degree of durability, rather than shop at either end of the price spectrum.

A good VCR should have at least four playing heads, full tracking adjustment, fast forward and reverse, pause, single frame advance, blue screen off mode, and remote control. All of these features in a major brand, high-quality player are available. Also available are **multisystem VCRs**. These machines can play video cassettes recorded using any of the broadcast standards (NTSC, PAL, or SECAM) on any analog television set. This flexibility allows the user to play a PAL cassette tape on an NTSC television screen, but with some compromise in quality. As an archival system to play the occasional video cassette that will never be available in DVD format, one of these machines may be a good investment.

DVD Players

DVD players are available in an even more bewildering variety than VCRs were a few years previously. A DVD player at the high end of this price range is the Denon DVD-9000, which offers just about every feature that can be found on a DVD player and has heavy-grade construction for durability. Among its standard features are the ability to play CD, **CD-R (CD-Recordable format)**, **CD-RW (CD-Rewritable format)**, DVD-R/RW (DVD-Recordable and Rewritable formats), and CDs that contain JPEG-format graphic files. It also has a deinterlacer that allows it to convert interlaced format discs to play in progressive format, an MP3 decoder for playing encoded CD-R/RW discs, a 2 MB memory buffer to decrease pauses and pickup dropouts, 6-channel DVD-A playback, PCM, DD, DTS-compatible optical and coaxial digital outputs, and component, S-video, and composite video outputs. Figure 7-4 shows front and back panel views of this unit. A more complete description of it can be found at *www.usa.denon.com*.

Figure 7-4   Denon DVD-9000 Player, front and back views

INSTALLATION AND SETUP OF AUDIO AND VISUAL SYSTEMS

Whether they connect directly to the home network or are wired independently as separate networks, audio and video systems can use the same wiring and wiring techniques that are used for connecting an Ethernet network. Coaxial cable is generally used for wiring an audio or video network. It has the data-transmission capacity to handle audio and video streams without difficulty. If the audio and video networks are to be separate from the rest of the home LAN, the cables for these independent segments should be installed at the same time as the other network wiring.

There's no need to worry about running audio and video cables close to network transmission cables. Because all the cables are carrying low voltage signals (plus or minus five volts), none of the cables has sufficient electromagnetic field to induce interference in the others. Like network lines, however, video and audio lines should not be run near high-voltage AC power lines or equipment because these definitely can introduce interference into the data circuits. In new construction installations, this means that the audio and video wiring should be installed after the electrical rough-in is completed so the two wiring systems can be kept well separated. In retrofitted installations, it means locating audio and video components away from existing electrical equipment and, as far as possible, running the cables on routes that won't be close to high-voltage wiring. If audio or video cables must cross over or under AC power lines, they should do so at right angles (90°) to the AC lines. As with network wiring, it's also important to handle Cat5 cable gently so as not to disturb the internal twisting of the wires that enable it to carry data at high capacity.

Termination points

Audio and video systems use different connectors than those typically found in computer networks. Audio and video cables are similar to patch cables in that they have plugs at both ends, but they use different types of cable. When audio and video cables are installed as structural wiring, each cable is terminated in a jack which then becomes the connecting point for one end of a two-plug cable. The other end of the cable is connected to another jack in the audio or video device. Table 7-2 shows the common audio and video connector plugs and the main uses for them. Each of these plugs mates to a corresponding jack in the equipment.

Table 7-2 Common audio and video connectors

Connector	Connector Name	Common Uses
	¼-inch phono	Speakers and headphones
	3.5 mm sub mini	Computers, speakers, microphones, headphones
	Coaxial cable	Cable TV, satellite TV
	USB cable	Video-to-computer connections
	FireWire cable	Video equipment
	RCA cables	All audio and video equipment
	BNC 75-Ohm cable	Television, VCR
	S-video and SVHS cables	Audio and video equipment

Connector	Connector Name	Common Uses
	Splitter or Y cables	Multiple audio and video equipment
	XLR microphone and instrument cables	Microphone

The cables to which these plugs are connected are usually made in set lengths with connectors attached at both ends. When specifying cables for an installation, it is necessary to state the length of the cable as well as the connector at each end. Some combinations of connectors won't be available as a premade cable, but the necessary connection can nearly always be made by using one or more **adaptors**.

Adaptors are connector devices that convert one type of connector that is already attached to a cable into another type of connector needed to plug into a jack in a piece of equipment. Figure 7-5 shows four examples of adaptors that split single connections into dual connections, and that sometimes change the gender of the connector as well.

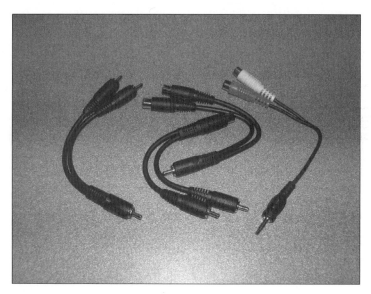

Figure 7-5   Four examples of adaptors for audio and video connectors

As with low-voltage cables run inside walls, the connector cables that attach audio and video units together or link them to wall jacks should be kept away from power cables for the devices to which they attach. The same potential for induced interference exists from high-voltage wires that are free standing as from those in walls. Low-voltage lines need a foot of clearance from the equipment power line to avoid interference. Most equipment is wired with the power cord at one end and low-voltage connectors at the other end to preserve this separation. The installer should be sure that the lines don't converge anywhere along their lengths.

Many connectors and the jacks to which they connect have gold-plated surfaces where the connectors make electrical contact with one another. The purpose of this plating is to help make the connection better and longer lasting, particularly if it's outside. Gold is not only a good electrical conductor, but it is also inert to all forms of corrosion. Plating a connector ensures that there will be no oxidizing of metal to diminish the electrical flow. Because the plating is only a few millionths of an inch thick, electricity quickly passes through it to the metal beneath it.

Receiving Components

Audio and video components receiving outside broadcast signals or cable input must be connected to their antennas or incoming cable in such a manner as to avoid any loss of signal strength. Broadcast signals in particular typically reach the antenna at a strength of a few millivolts (thousandths of a volt) and must be boosted by a factor of thousands before being sent to the output speaker or display. Careful antenna wiring can help keep the signal as strong and as clean (interference free) as possible so that there is less chance of data loss during processing.

Use shielded coaxial cable for antenna-to-receiver connections in both audio and video systems. This recommendation applies whether the system is analog or digital and whether the antenna is for receiving ground-based transmissions or satellite transmissions. Shielded cable can protect the incoming signal from interference, which can be severe in outdoor areas. Video antenna connections to a television, tuner, or VCR use a standard coaxial single wire BNC connector which locks or screws into place on the jack. Most new audio tuners use the same connector, but some older ones may have a bare wire connection. In this case, an adaptor should be used on the wire screws so that the coaxial connector can be plugged into the adaptor from the antenna.

Audio Components

Audio and video components connect to one another using one or more of the cable types shown in Table 7-2. Cables and adaptors with appropriate ends are available at electronic supply shops. Because the cable ends are already attached, you must be certain to get the correct minimum length needed for the hookup. Cables that are longer than necessary can still be used to link components, but the excess length should be coiled out of the way and kept distant from any source of interference or power induction.

Most audio and video cables are not shielded and don't need to be if they are short (6 feet or less) and are kept clear of induction-producing power cords to the components. The signals coming from player components are stronger than antenna signals, and in most cases, have already been boosted to a level where interference is less of a problem. Still, if a cable run to a component is long, or the home highly infected with interference, a shielded cable might be warranted. These can be purchased in most end configurations, but at greater cost than the unshielded versions.

Audio connections are all one way: that is, the audio signal is traveling into the device or out of the device, but never both ways in the same wire. A typical route for an audio signal to travel, for example, is out of a CD player (where the signal originated by being played from a CD) and into an amplifier, out of the amplifier, and into speakers. The signal travels into the amplifier in one set of wires and out of the amplifier in a different set. Because nearly all audio devices are stereo or multitrack, two or more wires are required to bring the signal into a device and two or more different wires to bring it out. Most connections between audio devices are made with RCA connector cables, usually color coded to help identify the correct connection. Some audio connections are made with BNC connectors, standard and mini phone plugs, and even bare wires (the last usually only for speaker connections). Figure 7-6 shows the back of a stereo audio amplifier with a number of input jacks available and a number of outputs.

Figure 7-6   Audio amplifier showing input and output connections

Output devices such as CD players and phonograph turntables have only output jacks because they don't receive input. They create signals and output them to other devices. On the left side of Figure 7-6 are the audio input connections (left stereo side is white at the top, right stereo side is red at the bottom) for these devices. This amplifier has connections for a phonograph, a CD player, a radio tuner, a DVD player, and an auxiliary input. To connect any of these devices to the amplifier, a pair of RCA connector wires is run from the output jacks on the device to the appropriate input jacks on the amplifier.

In the center part of Figure 7-6 are input and output jacks for devices which can have both input and output. These are devices such as tape recorders which can both play a tape and record one. This amplifier has side-by-side stereo input (left) and output (right) jacks for a tape recorder, a VCR, and a second tape recorder, VCR, or other device. To connect a tape recorder to this amplifier, four RCA connector wires are required. Two of these must run from the left and right output jacks of the tape recorder to the corresponding left (top) and right (bottom) input jacks of the amplifier. The other two must connect the output jacks on the amplifier with the input jacks on the tape recorder.

Any other input and output device requires the same connectors: two from the output of the device to the input of the amplifier and two from the output of the amplifier to the input of the device. Notice how audio connectors always connect output to input. Input never connects to input and output never connects to output. The audio signal is always traveling from one device (output) to the other device (input).

On the right side of Figure 7-6 are four sets of speaker connections. These are output connections that allow the amplifier to power two pairs (left and right) of speakers. This amplifier uses bare wire connections for speakers. They are connected by attaching wires to red and black terminals on the amplifier and then attaching them to corresponding connector terminals on each speaker. It doesn't matter which way the speaker wires are connected because the current passing through them to drive the speaker is an alternating current. All speakers must be connected with the same polarity, however, so that their output will be in phase. There must be two wires connecting each speaker, so four speakers require a total of eight wires leading from the amplifier. Although bare wire connectors are used on this amplifier, most speaker connections are made with mini-phone plugs or RCA plugs.

All audio components should be carefully grounded to reduce the risk of interference. This is especially important if shielded connector cables are used as connectors because the shielding grounds to the frame of the component. If the frame isn't grounded, the shielding can't perform its function correctly. Instead of grounding interference, it simply transfers it into the component frame where it may be picked up by other parts and still do harm to the system. The ground connection for the amplifier in Figure 7-6 is the single screw clamp on the far left side of the unit. A bare wire connected from this clamp to ground can ground the device.

Video Components

Video signals, like audio, travel only one way: from an output connection to an input connection. Video devices that are strictly output, such as a DVD player, have no input jacks because they don't receive any input. Devices that send output signals and also receive input, such as a VCR, have separate connectors for input and output. The two signals never run in the same wire.

Analog television components are usually connected with RCA connector cables. These connectors are the standard for composite video signals and their accompanying audio signals. Composite video signals consist of three color elements (red, green, and blue) all combined into a single channel signal and delivered on one wire. A second wire carries monaural audio signals, or two additional wires carry stereo sound. Figure 7-7 shows the backs of a set of video components that includes a satellite decoder at the top, a VCR in the center, and a DVD player on the bottom.

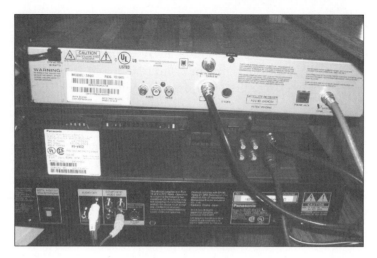

Figure 7-7 Video components connected by coaxial and RCA cables

On the right side of the satellite decoder in Figure 7-7, you can see the coaxial cable input that brings the satellite signal into the decoder. In the center of the decoder is another coaxial connection which is the output from the decoder to the television set. In this setup, the television is an analog unit, and so the output of the decoder is sent as a composite analog signal to the VCR located just below it. The signal goes into the input jack of the VCR, and an output connection (again a coaxial cable) runs from the VCR to the television, which is not visible in the photo.

In this arrangement the VCR, which is an input and output device, receives its input from the satellite decoder. It can record the input signal on a video cassette or it can output the signal to the television or do both. The VCR also has RCA input and output jacks (monaural audio and composite video) just to the left of the coaxial cable connectors, but these are not used in this setup.

Just to the right of the coaxial connector output on the satellite decoder is an S-video output jack. S-video (separated video) is another type of video connection which does not combine the entire video output into a single signal, but leaves it as separate brightness and color elements which are sent by separate wires (along with separate audio wires) in the output connection. S-video is also an analog video output, like composite output, but it provides better quality than the composite signal. On the left side of the decoder the composite video output RCA jacks (white and red stereo audio and yellow video) can also be seen. These are not used in this setup to connect the decoder to the television.

The DVD player in Figure 7-7 (the device at the bottom of the picture) is wired directly to the television. The DVD player is an output-only device and has no need of any input connection. It is wired using three RCA connectors (white and red audio and yellow video) which go to corresponding RCA connectors on the television. This connection provides stereo sound and composite analog video from the DVD player to the television. An S-video output jack is located to the right of the yellow RCA composite video connector, and three component video RCA jacks are located just to the right and above the composite connector, but neither of these are used in this setup.

Component video connectors use three RCA connectors to send a brightness signal and two color signals. The three connectors are labeled red, green, and blue. Together they provide a higher-quality signal to the television than can be obtained with either a composite or S-video signal. Component video connections sometimes use BNC connectors or the VGA-type connector used for component connections on computers, but both of these are unusual on television connections. All component video connections use separate wires for audio in addition to the three video signals.

The separate RCA connection of the DVD player allows it to play on the "input" channel of the television (channel 1). The VCR and TV, as wired in this setup, play on channel 3 of the television, and the individual channels are selected from the decoder using its IR remote. As with all satellite connections, only the channel selected on the decoder can be recorded on the VCR or played on the TV.

All analog video devices connect in much the same manner as the three illustrated in Figure 7-7. The connectors can be BNC type, but these are rare in newer components. Video components can be wired as easily as audio components by remembering the same basic rule. Connectors always go from output jacks to input jacks, never to the same type jacks (output to output or input to input) on different devices.

HDTV devices also connect from output to input jacks; but they frequently use different types of connectors. The two reasons for the different connectors are to get a higher quality signal and to prevent unlicensed copying of HDTV movies on home devices. HDTV devices with standard RCA connector jacks can easily be wired to DVD burners with similar connections. This enables broadcast HDTV movies or rented DVDs to be illegally copied by anyone with the equipment to do so. To prevent this and provide a better signal for displaying the HDTV programs, several new connector types have been introduced which can connect to output devices, but not to input devices, thus blocking illegal copying. Among these connectors are:

- RGB+H/V (component video plus horizontal and vertical sync) is a 5-connector video signal method which provides the red, green, and blue signals, but also separate horizontal and vertical synchronization signals that tell the receiver how to display the colors. The five connectors are bundled in a single cable except at the ends where they separate into individual BNC connectors. No recording devices have this connection so it effectively prevents copying. The 5-element signal is asserted to be better than regular 3-element component video, but some consumers doubt this and feel the only reason for the new system is to prevent copying.

- Digital Video Interface (DVI) connectors are 18-pin single cable connectors with D-shaped ends. A DVI connection transmits digital video in completely uncompressed format which no consumer device can record so it also effectively prevents all copying. DVI connections also include a copy protection scheme called High-bandwidth Digital Content Protection which prevents transmission to any unlicensed device (one without the copy protection).

- FireWire connectors are small connection plugs that have been used for transmitting video and graphic images from video cameras to computers for several years, but have recently begun to appear on HDTV devices as well. FireWire connectors are unique in the HDTV field because they are two way connections which can send data through the cable in either direction. This connector can also be found on many computers with DVD burners and so would appear to permit an HDTV program to be conveniently recorded. FireWire connections on HDTVs and other video devices, however, include Digital Transmission Content Protection (DTCP) which allows codes to be transmitted with a program that prevent it being copied.

Control Components

Handheld wireless remote controllers for audio and video systems and other electronic equipment are **infrared (IR) devices**. They operate as transmitters, but the signal they send is on a frequency far above that of any radio band. It's just below the frequency of visible light and has nearly all the characteristics of light except that it's not visible to human eyes. Like other light colors, infrared won't pass through most solid objects, and the transmitter that produces it also produces heat. The amount of heat infrared transmissions produce means that the signals have to be kept short to avoid causing damage to the transmitter or the receiver due to heat buildup.

The **carrier frequency** of such infrared signals is around 36 KHz. The digital control codes from the controller are sent in serial format by turning the carrier signal on and off (in the same manner as the original Marconi radio, but much faster than a human code clerk). The data transmission rate is actually quite slow, only around 1 KHz per second. There are many different coding systems in use, and different manufacturers can use different codes and different data rates for transmission. Many remote controls are interchangeable, however, because the technology is quite flexible and not very sensitive to either frequency accuracy or data transmission rate. Most receivers respond to data sent at anywhere near their designed parameters.

Television remote controls send commands only one way, to the TV in a low-speed burst for distances of up to 30 feet. They use directed IR produced by **light-emitting diodes (LEDs)**. The transmitted infrared signal spreads out from the front of the controller so that it doesn't have to be aimed precisely at the receiver, only pointed in the general direction. Any solid obstruction between transmitter and receiver can block the signal, however.

IR control systems are inexpensive and are generally reliable, although interference from other IR sources can be a minor problem. The problem can originate with other remote controls or other IR sources such as fluorescent lights. One way to limit interference is to use higher IR carrier frequencies for the control transmissions. Some IR systems now use carrier frequencies in the megahertz range. IR controllers do not cause interference in radio or television transmissions because their carrier signals are too low and the infrared light frequency much too high to be a concern to any radio or television band. If, on the other hand, IR interference from multiple remotes or other sources is evident, the solution may be to purchase a universal remote (a unit capable of "learning" the IR signals of all the audio and video equipment in the system) that operates on a high-carrier frequency that is not as susceptible to interference. Such a remote should be tested with all equipment to be sure it can respond to the higher frequency signals. Some devices, especially older ones, won't accept high-frequency IR signals and their IR receivers are not adjustable.

CONFIGURATION AND SETTINGS FOR EXTERNAL AUDIO AND VIDEO

Audio and video systems should be designed as segments of a home network or as independent networks that are internally linked but operate entirely outside the computer-based network. Audio systems can connect fairly easily to an Ethernet topology, a wireless network, or even one of the power-line or phone-line systems. This section describes how the connection can be made using various network technologies.

Television systems won't link well to any of the network technologies because the data flow requirements for television distribution are high and the technology of picture creation, transmission, and storage in television is just different enough from the same technology in computers to make integration of the two systems difficult. Consequently, most television systems do not connect easily, if at all, to a home network. A video distribution system must be wired and connected separately from the home network.

7

Audio Systems

All the components of an audio system connect to one another through their input and output jacks. The output signal of one device is the input signal for the next device in the configuration. This input/output process continues until the audio signal is transmitted onto the network (and passes out of the audio system entirely) or until it is sent to the speakers. The speakers' output is audible sound which is input for human ears, but not for any other device in the audio system. There are literally hundreds of audio system components which can be configured in thousands of combinations. Figure 7-8 shows a diagram of an audio system. Major components and how they connect to one another are shown.

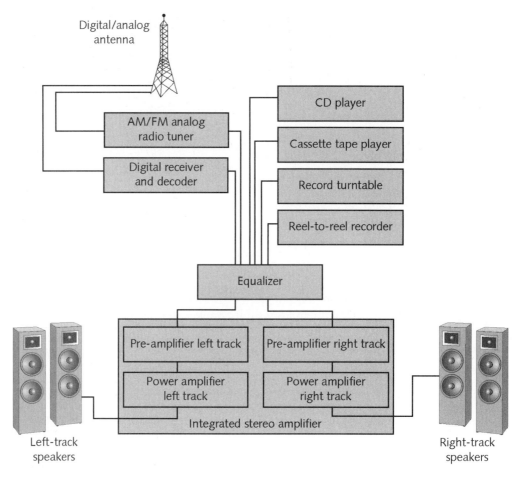

Figure 7-8   Audio system diagram

The best way to connect an audio system to an Ethernet network is by placing a digital audio receiver as a node on the network. The receiver's Ethernet port connects directly to the network and its audio connections allow a large number of digital and analog players and other input sources to be connected to it. All of these sources can be converted to digital format, if necessary, and transmitted to other network nodes or even out onto the Internet.

The Onkyo TXNR900 7 Channel Receiver with Ethernet Connection, shown in Figure 7-9, is an example of such a receiver. It provides not only an Ethernet connection, but also analog-to-digital and digital-to-analog audio conversion, plus decoders for both THX and Dolby Digital theater five-track sound systems. These can be interconnected to a DVD player, an SDTV receiver, or an HDTV receiver to receive the most complete available multitrack digital sound with video programs and recorded movies. The receiver also has multiple inputs (analog, digital, S-video) and outputs and audio amplifier output of 110 watts on each of its five tracks. This receiver isn't for the price conscious ($2,500), but it does provide state-of-the-art digital audio and a hardwired network connection to facilitate distribution of audio both to and from the network.

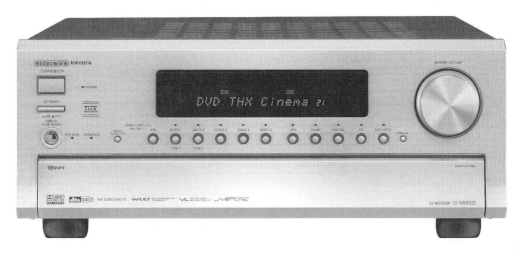

Figure 7-9   Digital 7 channel audio receiver

Other network-to-audio system connections are available with less features, but considerably lower price tags. **Wireless audio transmitter**s can transmit a stereo audio signal up to 300 feet. These devices typically include a transmitter, which is located near and connected to the audio system amplifier, and a receiver which is connected to, or actually installed in, a network computer. The transmitter connects to the audio system with standard RCA line-level input and output jacks. The transmitter sends audio signals to the receiver at the computer, which provides the network connection for the system. Wireless audio devices provide an easier and less expensive (about $150) solution for connecting an audio system to a network, but they also have limitations. The connection is one way, from the audio system to the network. To send data requires a second transmitter and receiver with their locations reversed. Data traveling in either direction on a wireless connection is much more prone to interference than are other types of connections.

An audio system can also be directly cabled to a computer. Like a wireless transmitter, this connection is technically outside the network, but it has the same result of connecting the audio system through the computer, which is a networked node. Direct cable connection requires a separate cable run from the audio system to the computer. The cable type used needs to conform to the type of connection that is made at either end. This connection can be through a USB port, if both the computer and the audio amplifier have one, or through the computer's sound card and the input/output jacks on the audio system. Mini jacks, standard 1/4-inch jacks, and RCA connectors can all be accommodated with appropriate adaptors.

Television Systems

At least eleven different companies manufacture **video distribution system**s that can send video and audio signals throughout a home suitably wired for the system. Not one of these systems, however, can interconnect with an Ethernet topology or any of the other home networking technologies. Each is based on a **digital video/audio switcher** that can distribute from three to sixteen separate video sources (cable channels, DVD, analog broadcasts) simultaneously to as many as 22 separate locations throughout the house. These systems rely on a wired pathway for distributing video and audio signals to multiple displays. Because the distribution system transmits data in one direction only, from the video sources to the video displays, it isn't really a data-sharing network in which each node communicates with all the others. It's a video and audio signal-sharing system that transmits programming from source to display. Figure 7–10 shows a video distribution system with multiple displays in one room. Additional displays are located throughout the home.

Figure 7-10   Multiple displays in a video distribution system

Most video distribution systems are modular so that they can be started with display units in two or three rooms and expanded later as the owner can afford to do so. Wiring for the system, however, must be installed during construction of the home or retrofitted in a finished residence the same as for a home LAN. In either case, the structural wiring is better done as a complete project with connections to every room where they might be wanted, even if some cables have to wait unused for a time.

Connectors for video/audio distribution systems are often a mixture of those used for single-room, home entertainment setups and those used for home networks. The equipment manufacturer chosen for the system determines how the various components are connected. Each of the companies now making video distribution systems has come into this area of home technology integration from another specialization. Some were primarily audio component manufacturers, others control specialists, and still others automation experts. Each has adapted some of the technologies they have previously used to video and audio distribution. The result is working systems, but very little standardization. Figure 7-11 shows a video distribution based on Leviton components.

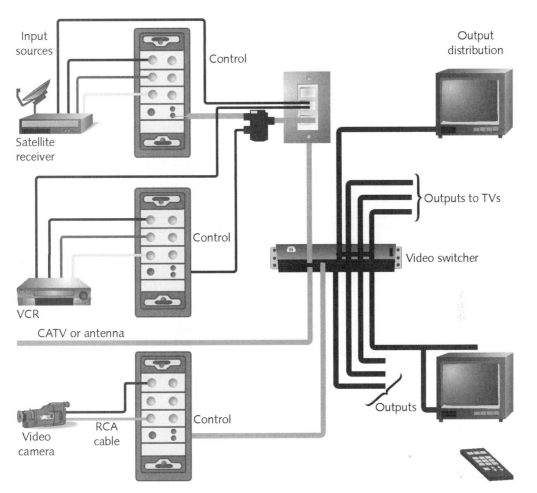

Figure 7-11   Video distribution system with multiple sources

Most video distribution systems can include **wall-mounted controllers** (keypads) or free-standing infrared remotes that can direct the video and audio components in the room (and sometimes the entire system). The wall-mounted controls are hardwired and may include a video display that allows the user to see the status of every component, source, and receiver, connected to the system.

Like audio systems, a video distribution system can be linked to a computer which is also a node on the home network. The link is most easily accomplished by connecting the video system switch to the computer's video output jack. This setup allows the computer to send any video program playing on its monitor to the video system as a source signal. From the switcher, the signal can be directed to any video display in the home. This is again a strictly one-way data transfer, from the computer to the video system. The display seen on the remote screens is subject to the limitations of the computer's video display.

CONFIGURATION FOR INTERNAL VIDEO/AUDIO

Any audio or video program that can be streamed from the Internet to a computer on the home network can also be distributed to other nodes on the network or to a video distribution system linked to the computer's output. No additional processing of the program is required to distribute it. If the television display is digital, the computer can output a direct digital signal to it, although the television image might have some distortion due to the difference in pixel shapes between the video and computer images. If the television display is analog, the computer output must be processed through a scan converter in order to be displayed on an NTSC screen.

High-quality, low-priced digital video cameras and video editing systems have now made it possible for everyone to create video programs and stream them on their own home network or out onto the Internet. Producing and streaming digital video involves several key steps. Some of these require only software additions to a home computer. A few require additional hardware components.

The first requirement for creating video is a camera to record original footage. There are now a number of high-quality digital cameras available for less than $1,000 and many others priced above that figure. As with most hardware, you generally get what you pay for, but the lower-priced cameras produce video of high enough quality to satisfy most viewers. The camera should have a **FireWire** connection or USB port so that its video can be downloaded to the computer without the need for a digital playback machine capable of playing the **miniDV cassettes** on which most cameras record. If a user plans to record and download a large quantity of video, a playback/download device may be a good addition to the computer system, but for most home video systems it isn't necessary. With the download port, recorded cassettes can be played back in the camera and their content downloaded directly to the computer's hard drive.

Once captured (transferred from the video camera to a computer storage system), the next hardware need of a home network video streaming system quickly becomes evident. About five minutes of uncompressed video footage occupies a gigabyte of storage space. If the computer has a 60-gigabyte hard drive, it will be completely filled by less than five hours of video footage. This heavy storage requirement suggests the need for a **video server** with multiple high-capacity drives that can hold all the user's **uncompressed original video footage**, as well as edited shows and compressed video that is ready for streaming.

A video server can be set up as a network node so that all nodes can request data from it and can store video on it, whether downloaded from a camera, or from the Internet, or from another digital video player connected to the network. A video server should have enough storage capacity to meet the user's likely needs for at least a year or two, and the capability of being upgraded with more storage in the future. It should have a fast processor and fast hard drives so that it can respond quickly to video data requests and keep up with the requirements of streaming video data.

Stored video can be edited on any computer node equipped with editing software and sufficient processing capacity to handle the large files. Once a video program is edited it needs to be compressed for streaming either on the home network or on the Internet.

Video shouldn't be compressed prior to editing because all the common compression techniques use lossy compression algorithms and some of the data in the original video is lost. If compression is done before editing, the editing process may cause further data loss and a corresponding loss in quality in the edited video. Waiting to compress video until after it is edited requires more storage space for the raw (unedited) footage, but results in higher quality of the finished product.

Video compression is a software function that, like editing, can be accomplished on any computer with sufficient processing power and access to the stored footage. Not all compression systems allow streaming of the compressed program, but if the video is to be downloaded from the Internet, it should be compressed into a format that does permit streaming. Even compressed video files are large and time consuming to download completely before playing. Streaming allows the viewer to watch the front end of the program while the back portion continues to download, and many viewers find this a preferable option.

Compressed video programs, whether produced in the home or downloaded from the outside, can be sent to any network node on request and viewed on the computer's screen. They can also be broadcast on the home's video distribution system, if it is linked to the network. As noted earlier in this chapter, most video system links to the network are through the video output of a computer node rather than a direct connection to the network. The video output link to a video distribution system permits any video playing on the computer node to be distributed through the system. When direct network connections to video distribution systems become common, as they surely will within a few years, the video system will be able to access video programs directly from the video server without the need to pass them through another network node.

7

MONITORING AND MAINTAINING VIDEO/AUDIO SYSTEMS

Video and audio systems are combinations of electronic and mechanical components and as such are subject to the same wear and environmental problems that afflict other similar devices. Because video and audio systems must continually operate at peak performance levels in order to produce quality output, even small maintenance problems can cause a serious degradation in their output. Electronic systems are adversely affected by three main factors: heat, water, and electric power variations. Mechanical systems are also adversely affected by these three and a fourth: dirt.

Video and audio systems produce heat which needs to be dissipated or it will build up in components until they burn out. Many components contain **heat sinks** to help prevent heat build-up, and most systems provide for cooling with ventilating fans that carry heat away from the components. These work well if not obstructed by placement of the system in an enclosure where air circulation is restricted. Components should not be stacked on top of one another or enclosed so that the cooling fans in components can't circulate air freely. Likewise, components shouldn't be placed where they are subject to additional heat from outside sources such as heating fixtures, fireplaces, and space heaters. Keep the system in as cool an environment as possible, and its own cooling components will maintain a good working temperature inside.

Water problems for video and audio systems usually occur in the form of condensation of moisture from the air on internal components. This usually happens when the system is turned off and warm parts cool down, picking up condensate from the air as they do so. If the system is again turned on before the condensed moisture has had time to evaporate, short circuits or other damage to electronic parts can result. The key to avoiding condensation in a system is the same as for avoiding heat buildup: keep good air circulation within the components. The less heat buildup in the system, the less danger of condensation when it cools down. Likewise, the more air circulating in the system, the less chance for moisture to accumulate. This is another reason to keep systems out of areas or enclosures where slow-moving, moisture-laden air can create condensation.

Power fluctuations are the surest way to damage a video or audio system, just as they can damage computer systems. High-quality, fast-acting surge suppressors are a must for video and audio systems. Voltage drops should also be avoided. This may mean connecting the system on an independent circuit and making sure that the home's power load requirement doesn't periodically pull down the voltage as equipment starts up.

Finally, dirt, usually in the form of dust particles, is to be avoided in all mechanical systems. It increases wear on moving parts and can sometimes bring them to a halt. Video recorder/player heads rotate at over 1000 rpm. So do CD players, DVD players, and hard drives. All of these are motor driven and rotate on shafts set in precision bearings. Even small quantities of dust can shorten the life of these parts. A component's internal parts can't be cleaned of dirt. The most that can be done is to keep dirt away from the equipment and out of the air that circulates through it. The more dust free the interior of the home can be kept, the longer its electronic systems (and perhaps its occupants) will last.

CHAPTER SUMMARY

- Video and audio system in the United States are changing from analog to digital formats, but at present many users still primarily have analog equipment and media that they wish to retain until the digital conversion process is more advanced.

- Digital audio systems consist of five basic components: an antenna to receive broadcast signals, a tuner to select frequencies, an amplifier to strengthen the received signal, a speaker to convert the signal back into audible sound, and a ground connection to complete the broadcast circuit.

- Audio recordings are distributed mostly on CDs (for music) because this medium provides the highest-quality digital reproduction of sound. Cassette tapes are often used for voice recording and millions of recordings on plastic records still exist and are being converted to digital format.

- With one addition, digital television systems require the same basic components as audio systems in order to receive and display digital television transmissions: an antenna, a tuner, an amplifier, a speaker and display monitor, and a ground.

- SDTV tuners and television sets, HDTV tuners and television sets, and EDTV television sets are all approved digital television standards under the ATSC Table 3 definitions. There are a total of 18 digital television formats approved by the ATSC and U.S. digital components must process and/or display all of them.

❏ Digital video programs are recorded on DVDs which are played on DVD players and displayed on digital or analog television sets. Analog VHS cassettes are still widely used for television recording, but are slowly being replaced as digital television becomes the new standard.

❏ Audio and digital components always connect from the output jacks of one device to the input jacks of another device. Audio and video signals travel in one direction only. No connection on these systems can be both input and output.

❏ Audio systems can be connected directly to an Ethernet topology for data transmission on the network. They can also be connected through a computer node's sound inputs.

❏ Video systems, both analog and digital, are not easily connected to a network because of the differences in the technologies of both systems. Video can be downloaded from a network to a video distribution system, but the reverse transfer of data to the network hasn't been perfected.

❏ Both video and audio programs in digital format can be produced by the home network user and streamed on the home network or out onto the Internet.

❏ Maintaining audio and video systems requires controlling heat buildup, keeping away moisture and condensation, suppressing electrical current fluctuations, and preventing dirt from entering mechanical assemblies.

7

KEY TERMS

adaptors — Devices which change audio and video connectors from one form to another, including gender changes.

Advanced Television Systems Committee (ATSC) — The government-run and industry-influenced group that sets standards for the television industry.

amplifier — A device which strengthens the power of an RF signal it receives from an antenna or pre-amplifier.

antenna — The component of a radio or television receiver which receives a broadcast signal from a distant transmitter.

attenuated — Weakened by distance from the source; resistance; used to describe radio and television signals.

carrier frequency — In radio transmission, a signal at high frequency on which a signal of lower frequency is carried.

CD burner — A device for recording compact discs (CDs). A CD burner can also play a CD, but CD players are not always burners.

CD player — A device for playing recorded compact discs.

CD-R (CD-Recordable format) — A compact disc which can be recorded once on a CD burner, but is then a permanently fixed recording that cannot be changed.

CD-RW (CD-Rewritable format) — A CD which can be recorded multiple times with succeeding recordings added to or replacing older ones on the disc.

cone — The part of a speaker that vibrates in the air producing sound.

converter — A device which renders digital data into analog signals in audio and video systems. *See* decoder.

crossover network — A wiring circuit in speaker systems that permits several speakers of different ranges to function seamlessly together.

decoder — A device which renders digital data into analog signals or vice versa in audio and video systems. *See* converter.

digital audio file — A recorded music or voice audio segment stored on a computer hard drive or other similar media.

digital video/audio switcher — A device which receives digital signals from multiple sources and routes them as instructed to multiple outputs.

distortion — Changes in reproduced sound waves caused by excessive power or other interference in the recording and playback processes.

DVD — Digital Video Disc. A small plastic record on which digital video programs are recorded using a laser process.

electromagnet — A magnet created by passing a current through a coil of wire. Used in audio speakers and many other devices.

encoder — A device or software program for changing analog audio or video signals into digital format. Video versions are also called coders.

Enhanced Definition Television (EDTV) — An ATSC-defined television which can play both analog and SDTV digital programs.

equalizer — An audio device for balancing the levels at which sound frequencies are recorded or played back.

FireWire — A 1394 standard data connection for transmitting digital data at high speed between two devices or nodes on a network.

HDTV tuner — A digital television tuner which receives full resolution HDTV signals in 16:9 format.

heat sink — A relatively large piece of metal or other material placed near a heat source to absorb heat from it and dissipate it into the surrounding air.

infrared (IR) devices — Devices which function as controllers by sending command signals using infrared light which is invisible to human eyes.

light-emitting diode (LED) — An electronic device, similar to a vacuum tube, which emits red light or infrared radiation.

media — Any means of storing or recording audio or video information: magnetic tape, CD, DVD, phonograph record are examples.

MIDI (Musical Instrument Digital Interface) file — A type of digital music recording in which the file stores an actual musical score. MIDI files can be played on any electronic instrument or software-equipped computer.

miniDV cassettes — A small-format recording medium used in many digital video cameras.

monaural — Having only one track or sequence; not stereo. Used to describe single-track audio recording.

multisystem VCR — A video player capable of playing NTSC, PAL, or SECAM video cassettes on any analog television.

pre-amplifier — A device which strengthens an original signal from an antenna or other source before it goes to an amplifier.

rasters — The individual horizontal scan lines which make up an analog television picture.

SDTV television — A television which receives and displays all ATSC digital formats, but not necessarily at full high resolution.

SDTV tuner — An RF receiver that receives ATSC terrestrial digital television signals and decodes all Table 3 video formats.

stereo — Two soundtracks recorded from the left and right side of a musical performance to give balance and depth to the recording.

synchronized — Operating or playing together at the same rate. Stereo sound tracks are synchronized as are the picture and sound of a video program.

tuner — The device in a radio or television that sets the one station frequency to be received and excludes all others.

uncompressed original video footage — Digital video recorded without use of any algorithm to reduce file size. Produces large files which contain all digital data in sequential format.

video distribution system — A wired system for distributing video programs from multiple sources to multiple viewing sites in the home.

video server — A computer set up as a storage location for video programming on a network, from which the video footage can be requested by other network nodes.

wall-mounted controllers — In video and audio systems, a device for controlling distributed programming in a room or for the whole system.

wireless audio transmitter — A wireless transmitter that sends analog or digital audio signals to a computer.

REVIEW QUESTIONS

1. A VHS video cassette tape can contain either an analog or a digital television program. True or False?

2. FM radio is broadcast with two audio tracks and is called a _____ transmission. AM radio is broadcast with only one track and is called a _____ transmission

3. What is the function of an audio tuner?

4. A converter renders a digital audio or video signal into analog format. True or False?

5. Signals from an antenna are usually sent first to _____.

   a. the speaker

   b. the equalizer

   c. the tuner

   d. ground

6. The function of an amplifier is to _____.

   a. filter noise from the signal

   b. increase the strength of the signal it receives

   c. tune out unwanted frequencies

   d. none of the above

7. Another name for a converter is a _____

8. Distortion of audio output is caused by overdriving the speaker. True or False?

9. The part of a speaker which actually vibrates the air to produce sound is called a _____.

   a. shield

   b. voice coil

   c. frame

   d. cone

10. The range of human hearing is about 20 cycles to 20,000 cycles per second. True or False?

11. What is the function of a crossover network?

12. An equalizer cannot change the signal coming from the antenna or the pre-amp. True or False?

13. The function of an encoder is to change _____ signals to _____ signals.

14. What is "ghosting" and where does it occur?

15. Two phenomena that can cause interference with digital satellite transmissions are _____ and _____.

16. Computer graphic images look a little distorted on a digital television screen because _____.

    a. the two systems use different shaped pixels

    b. one is a digital image and the other analog

    c. signals traveling between them are distorted

    d. the television screen has a different aspect ratio

7

17. CD-RW stands for CD _____ and means that the CD can be _____ several times.

18. The most common type of connector for analog video and audio devices is _____.

19. DVD stands for _____ _____ _____.

20. An audio system can connect directly to an Ethernet topology, but a television distribution system can't. True or False?

21. What is an adapter and how is it used?

22. Cables running from an antenna to a tuner or pre-amp should be what type? _____

23. Remote control devices use _____ signals to send commands to components.

24. A wireless audio transmitter is used to _____.

    a. send audio signals to a tuner

    b. send audio signals to a computer

    c. convert audio signals to analog

    d. strengthen audio signals

25. When video is "captured" it is transferred from a(n) _____ to storage on a(n) _____.

HANDS-ON PROJECTS

HANDS-ON PROJECTS

Project 7-1: Compare Analog and Digital Audio Sources

In this project you will compare the quality of sound played over an audio system from a CD to that played over the same system from a radio tuned to an FM radio station. To complete this project you need access to an audio system which includes a CD player and an FM tuner.

1. Obtain the use of a CD containing music that you enjoy listening to. Play the CD on the audio system and listen for the following characteristics:

   ■ Signal to noise ratio: Can you hear any background noise or hiss at all?

   ■ Interference: Can you hear any sounds that do not appear to be an intended part of the recording?

   ■ Sound quality and balance: Does all the music sound clear and precise, as if you were actually in the presence of the performers? Are the high and low notes distorted?

2. Tune to an FM radio station of your choice at a volume that is comfortable for you. Listen to it for a while and evaluate the sound quality on the basis of the same three criteria as the CD.

3. Turn the volume of the FM radio station lower and listen to some more music. Then, turn the volume of the CD player lower and listen to some more music. Does the lower volume change the relative quality of the two sources?

4. Turn the volume of the FM radio station higher than it was in Step 2, and listen to some more music. Then, turn the volume of the CD player higher than it was in Step 1, and listen to some more music. Does the higher volume change the relative quality of the two sources?

5. Write a short evaluation of this sound comparison. Which do you think is better for music listening? Why? If volume levels made a difference in the comparison, why do you think they did?

HANDS-ON PROJECTS

Project 7-2: Compare Analog Digital Sources

In this project you will compare three different sources of analog television to see which provides the best picture. For this project you will need access to an analog television set, a VCR, a DVD player, and the cables to connect them.

1. Turn the television on and select a local channel that has reasonably good reception in your area. Evaluate the picture you see for the following items:

   - Are there ghosts in the image? Snow? Lines, moving or static?

   - Is the picture clear and sharp, or does it appear fuzzy around edges?

   - Are the colors well defined and clear, or do they appear muddy?

   - Is the sound clear and crisp with no noise, and is it synchronized with the picture?

2. Play a video cassette with the output going to the television, and evaluate the picture and sound on the same points as in Step 1. Is the analog video cassette picture better, worse, or the same as the broadcast image?

3. Play a DVD with the output going to the television and evaluate the picture and sound on the same points as in Step 1. Is the digital DVD (playing in analog format) picture better, worse, or the same as the broadcast image?

4. Write a short report noting which picture you considered best of the three you saw, and why you think it was. Give any reasons you can think of for the lack of quality in any of the three pictures.

**HANDS-ON
PROJECTS**

Project 7-3: Record a Digital Audio Selection

In this project you will record a voice or music selection on the computer and store it to a hard drive. For this project you will need access to a computer with a sound card and a connected microphone operating on Windows 2000.

1. To check the microphone and sound recording hardware, click **Start**, point to **Settings**, click **Control Panel**, double-click **Sounds and Multimedia**, click **Audio**, and then check to see that the microphone is functioning correctly.

2. To open Sound Recorder, click **Start**, point to **Programs**, point to **Accessories**, point to **Entertainment**, and then click **Sound Recorder**.

3. Set the microphone in a convenient position for recording and prepare the material you want to record so you can read it easily.

4. When you are ready to record, click the **Circle** (Record) button on the Sound Recorder and begin speaking. When you finish speaking, click the **Rectangle** (Stop) button.

5. Click the **Right Arrow** (Play) button to play back your recorded voice. If you want to rerecord any portion, stop playing the recording where you want to make the change, and repeat Step 4 to record from that point to the end of the recording again.

6. Click **File** and then **Save** to save your recording to the hard drive. The default folder for saving the file is My Documents, but you can change to another folder if you want to. When you have the folder you want open, enter a name for the file and press **Enter** to save it.

HANDS-ON PROJECTS

Project 7-4: Record a CD and Play it on a CD Player

In this project you will record music on a CD and play the CD on a CD player connected to an audio system. For the project you will need access to a computer with an Internet connection and a CD burner/player. You will also need music selections that you want to record on your CD.

1. Open the CD drive door, place a CD that you want to record from in the drive, and close the door. When the Audio CD window opens and asks what you want to do, click **Play Audio CD**, and then click **OK**.

2. When the Windows Media Player opens, click **Copy from CD** on the left side of the window.

3. Click to check the boxes on the left side of the titles of selections you want to record. When you have all desired selections checked, click **Copy Music** at the top of the window and wait until the computer finishes copying. The music file is stored in the **My Music** folder.

4. Repeat Steps 1 – 3 to record all the music selections you want on your CD. Remember a typical CD can store up to 650 megabytes of data, so you can put up to 15 selections or more on a CD.

5. Insert a blank recordable CD into the CD recording drive.

6. Click **Start** and click the **My Music** folder. Click the files you want to copy to the CD. After the clicking the first file, hold down the Ctrl key while you click each of the others. (*Note*: You must select at least two files before you can proceed to Step 7.)

7. Under **File and Folder Tasks**, click **Copy the selected items**.

8. In the **Copy Items** dialog box, click the CD recording drive, and then click **Copy**.

9. In **My Computer**, double-click the **CD recording drive**. Windows displays a temporary area where the files are held before they are copied to the CD. Verify that the files you want to copy appear under **Files Ready to be Written to the CD**.

10. Under **CD Writing Tasks**, click **Write these files to CD**. Windows displays the CD Writing Wizard. Follow the instructions in the wizard.

11. When the process is finished, close the wizard and remove the recorded CD from the drive.

12. Place the CD in the audio system CD player, and press the **Play** button. Listen to your CD on the audio system.

Project 7-5: Connect an Audio System

In this project you will connect several audio devices into a working audio system. For this project you will need access to a CD player or other audio output device, an amplifier, a cassette recorder or other input device, and two speakers. You will also need 10 RCA connector cables or cables of the appropriate type if the devices use different connectors.

1. Place the equipment on a table with each device close enough to the others that the RCA connectors you are using can easily reach from one device to the others. Don't stack the devices on one another if they have vent louvers or access doors on top. Don't stack the amplifier on any other device.

2. Using two RCA connector cables, one for the left stereo track and one for the right track, connect the output jacks of the CD player to the input CD jacks of the amplifier. If the amplifier doesn't have a specific set of CD jacks, connect to the Auxiliary jacks.

3. Using two RCA connector cables, one for the left stereo track and one for the right track, connect the output jacks of the cassette recorder to the input Tape 1 jacks of the amplifier. Use two more RCA connectors to connect the Tape 1 output jacks to the cassette recorder's input jacks.

4. Use two RCA connectors to connect the left speaker to the left output jacks of the amplifier. Use two more connectors to connect the right speaker in the same manner. Connect both speakers' wires in the same order so that their polarity will match.

5. Connect the AC power plugs of the CD player, amplifier, and cassette recorder to an AC power strip or multiple outlet.

6. Turn the amplifier and CD player on. Switch the amplifier to the CD input (or other input jacks that you used for this device).

7. Play a CD to test that the audio system is working. If you don't hear the music, check all the connections to be sure you have output wired to input and each speaker connected by two wires to the speaker output jacks on the amplifier output panel. Test again.

8. Put a blank cassette in the cassette player. Play another music selection on the CD and record it on the cassette player while the music is also playing over the speakers. Did your system function correctly? Troubleshoot any problem until you can record a cassette from the CD while playing the music at the same time.

9. Play back the recorded sound from the cassette through the amplifier and speakers. Can this sound be recorded on the CD player? Why not?

7

Project 7-6: Connect a Video System

In this project you will connect several video devices into a working video system. For this project you will need access to a DVD player or other video output device, a VCR or other video input device, and a television set. You will also need eight RCA connector cables or cables of the appropriate type if the devices use different connectors.

1. Place the equipment on a table with each device close enough to the others that the RCA connectors you are using can easily reach from one device to the others. Don't stack the devices on one another if they have vent louvers or access doors on top.

2. Using two RCA connector cables, one for the left stereo track and one for the right track, connect the audio output jacks of the DVD player to the audio input jacks of the television. Use another connector to connect the DVD player's composite video output jack to the television set's composite video input jack.

3. Plug the television set and DVD player into AC power outlets and turn them on. Put a DVD in the player and play it to the TV.

4. Use three more RCA connectors to connect the VCR's output jacks to the TV. Don't disconnect the DVD player to make this connection. If the TV doesn't have enough input jacks to allow both devices to connect to it, then connect the output of the DVD player to the input of the VCR and the output of the VCR to the TV.

5. Use three more connectors to connect the output of the TV to the input of the VCR. If you've already connected the DVD to the VCR's input and the VCR doesn't have enough input jacks to also accept the TV output, skip this step for now.

6. Plug the VCR into an AC outlet. Put a tape in and play it to the TV. Start the DVD player and play it to the TV also. Can you switch between the devices while both are playing, or does one block the other?

7. How can you connect the VCR and DVD player so both can play simultaneously on the TV and you can choose between them by just switching channels from Channel 3 to Input (Channel 1)?

8. Experiment to see if you can get both devices playing at the same time. Remember, output jacks must always connect to input jacks. Can another type of connector such as an S-video cable or a coaxial cable help make this setup possible?

CASE PROJECTS

Case Project 7-1: Research a Video System

A client wants to have a new television system installed as part of his home technology. He wants the new system to play NTSC broadcasts and VHS cassette tapes, but also play DVDs in HDTV format and digital satellite broadcasts in SDTV format. Your job is to research on the Internet or at a large electronics store what compatible components are required for this system in order to meet all the requested output formats. Note the components and their prices, and compile a list for the client. What does the total system cost, including the required cables to link the components to one another?

Case Project 7-2: Evaluate a Conversion Proposal

CASE
PROJECTS

A friend tells you that he's planning to purchase a DVD burner to add to his computer. He then plans to connect his analog VCR to the computer and copy each of his VHS video cassettes onto a DVD. He can then discard the video cassettes and have digital quality DVDs of his movie collection. Write a short response to this plan. Can it be done in the manner your friend suggests? Will it work? Will he really be able to get high-quality DVDs in this manner?

Case Project 7-3: Connect Video Components

CASE
PROJECTS

You're setting up a video system for a home entertainment center. You need to connect a DVD player and a VCR to the television so that both devices can play to the TV. The VCR also needs to be connected so it can record from the television or from the DVD player. On checking the equipment, you find that the TV has only one set of video input jacks and one set of video output jacks. The VCR also has one set of video input jacks and one set of video output jacks and the DVD player has only video output jacks. Using RCA cables and adaptors, describe or diagram how you would connect these devices to accomplish the desired setup. (*Hint*: Check this chapter for an adapter that allows splitting an output or an input.)

Case Project 7-4: Advise a Client About Digital TV

CASE
PROJECTS

A client asks your advice about installing digital television in her home. The reception of analog TV signals is poor in her area. Several local channels are now broadcasting digital programming, but the digital programs don't look any better on her analog TV than the regular broadcasts. She's concerned that digital broadcasts seen on a digital TV will be no better. Is she right? What would you advise her about putting in digital television so far as the quality of the reception she's likely to get?

SECURITY AND ACCESS SYSTEM FUNDAMENTALS

After reading this chapter, you will be able to:

♦ Define the factors which go into designing security systems and integrating them into a home technology system

♦ Describe the various types of home security systems and the differences between them

♦ Identify the factors which determine the locations of various security equipment

♦ Describe the characteristics of the system components used in security systems

Security systems form a unique part of home technology. In this chapter you will learn about the factors of a security system and how one is designed to protect the home environment and the people who live in it. You'll learn the significant differences between the types of security system, and when each is best used. You'll also learn how to identify effective locations for security equipment and what factors should be considered in setting it up. Finally you'll learn the function of each of the many system components that are used in security systems.

SECURITY DESIGN AND INSTALLATION FACTORS

Home security has been a concern of homeowners since long before the age of technology. People have tried to ensure their personal safety and protect their property in almost every society since the Egyptian kingdoms of 5,000 years ago. The technology available for home security systems today permits a greater assurance of protection than ever before, but it also requires some security decisions that weren't really necessary even a generation ago.

In former times, people often bought all the physical security they could find, or at least all they could afford. Cost is still a consideration in security systems now, but it shouldn't be the only determining factor. Among the questions to ask when designing a security system for a home are the following:

- What or who is the security system mainly going to protect?

- What are the major threats that must be protected against?

- What is the level of risk for which protection must be provided?

- What factors external to the home environment affect the risk assessment?

The three traditional objectives of home security are protecting people, premises, and property. Everyone has a right to be personally safe in their own home and for members of their family and guests visiting their home to also be safe. Consequently, protecting the home's occupants is usually the first priority of a home security system. After personal safety, and often connected to it, comes protecting the premises of the home, first from persons who might try to enter and harm the occupants, and secondly, from fire, flood, or other dangers that could damage or destroy the house and also pose a hazard to those inside. Last, and again often connected to personal safety, is the protection of property inside the home from theft or destruction.

The amount of threat to the people in the home, the home itself, or property within it, is partially a constant and partially a variable influenced by individual circumstances. The constant part of the risk is from inanimate disasters: mainly fire, but also flood in some locations, gas or other poisons from the home's systems or the surrounding environment, and weather related factors such as severe storms and lightning. Wherever any of these exist (remembering that the danger of a fire is omnipresent), they should also be guarded against by a home security system.

The variable part of risk is much harder to evaluate. Wherever wealth is stored, theft is a threat. The more wealth, the more threat, especially if the wealth is unprotected. Threats to property often turn into threats to premises as thieves try to break into where the goods are kept. Sometimes threats to property turn into threats against people who may be in the way of a successful robbery, or the homeowners themselves may be a target of kidnapping. Every homeowner should evaluate how much his or her personal safety and possessions are likely to be at risk in the area where they live. If the risk appears significant, then maximum home security precautions are the surest way to peace of mind for the family.

Outside factors can influence risk. A home's isolation from help or observation by others may be a reason to increase its fire protection as well as its personal protection security system. It may also warrant perimeter security in the yard to give more timely warning for people to seek safety in a secure area if danger threatens.

All these factors, as well as cost, weigh in the decision of how much home security to include in an HTI system. This chapter discusses maximum protection features and systems. Most homeowners will want less than everything, but knowing about the highest levels of home security can help them and you make that judgment on a factual basis. All of the following factors should be considered in the design of home security and its integration with the rest of the home's technology system.

Existing Home and New Construction Environments

As with other areas of home technology, whether the home security system is installed in a new home under construction or retrofitted into one already completed has a large influence on what type of system is used. Hardwired systems can be easily installed in new construction, but are much more difficult to retrofit in existing homes. Wiring can also be better concealed in new construction than when retrofitted. Building the wiring into the walls makes it much more difficult to cut or bypass than if it's tucked under a molding or inside a raceway. Like other home technology system wiring, security cables should be roughed in by the HTI technician on new construction projects after the home's utilities are installed.

The main reason for installing security lines after the utilities are in is to avoid having them cut or damaged by the other utility workers. Being the last to install also allows the security technician to be sure the system's lines are located where they don't provide any easy access points for intruders to cut or **bypass** them. Alone among home technology systems, security lines and hardware must be considered at risk not only from normal age and use, but from intentional sabotage by intelligent persons. Consequently, they always need to be installed with an eye toward preventing deliberate damage by persons trying to get past the security system's protective screen.

Wireless security systems are usually the preferred choice for retrofitted installations as well as many new homes. Remote sensors with wireless transmitters don't require a lot of electricity to operate and can be battery powered at nominal expense. Wireless **sensors** can be placed almost anywhere and still send their signals to a central **security panel** without the need for any physical power or data connection. Many also transmit the state of their batteries so that the homeowner can tell from the central control device when the batteries of any sensor need replacement.

Concealed wireless sensors may offer better security than wired ones too. Because they have no wires to bypass and sensor failure triggers an alarm, they are more difficult to evade than some wired units.

8

Security Zone Layout

Security systems are organized in zones so that their protection devices can be easily monitored and the origin of any security breach quickly located. A **security zone** can be any area of a home or yard. It can consist of a single room or multiple rooms and can include outside and inside areas. The limits of a zone are really the number of devices that the security system's central control panel can monitor for a zone. Typically a zone can include four devices to be monitored from the central control. Some systems allow up to six devices, but more than that calls for the area to be divided into two or more zones, each with their own group of devices to monitor.

Determining how a home should be segmented into zones should take into account how homes are usually entered by burglars or other unauthorized persons. The strongest protection (and perhaps **redundant protection** to detect any intruder who manages to disable or evade one device) should be placed in those areas most often targeted for illegal entry.

Using a variety of **detection devices** and sensors in the most vulnerable areas helps assure than any attempt to break into the home immediately sounds an alarm and summons assistance. Figure 8-1 identifies the common entry points in homes where break-in attempts are made. Statistics shown in Table 8-1 are from ADT Security Systems and indicate the percentages of burglary attempts that are made for each entry point.

Figure 8-1   Common entry points for burglary attempts

Table 8-1   Break-in entry points and percentages

Rank	% of Break-in Attempts	Location
1	34	Front door
2	23	First-floor window
3	22	Back door
4	9	Garage
5	4	Basement
6	2	Second-floor entry
7	6	Unlocked entrance and storage areas (not shown in Figure 8-1)

Standard security systems usually allow for up to eight zones, and large scale systems allow up to sixteen. Any system can have a number less than the maximum by simply not connecting devices to some zone monitoring circuits. Figure 8-2 shows a home floor plan divided into zones for a security system and possible locations for sensor devices within each zone.

8

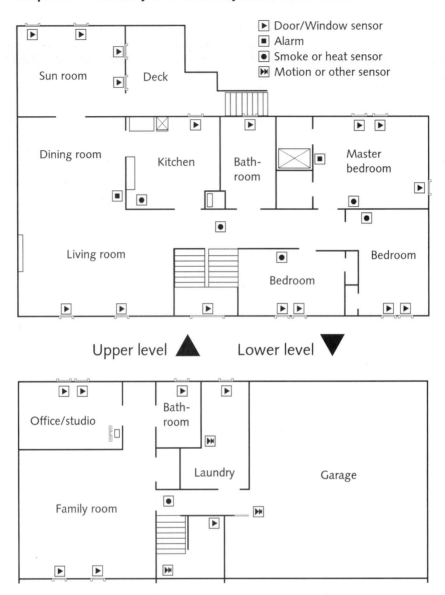

Figure 8-2   Home security system plan

Home Utility Specifications and Capacity

One or more of the zones in a home security system may be devoted to the home's utilities by the use of sensors to monitor whether they are functioning correctly, or at all. Electrical system monitoring is especially important because, if it fails, the home's occupants could be left in a dark building trying to find their way out in the face of an intruder or a smoky fire. A sensor on the electrical service line can let the homeowner know if power is out to the entire house. The security system can also be set up to activate emergency, battery-powered lighting in the event of a power failure and to contact the utility with a service failure notification. Individual circuits within the home can also be monitored, but this would only be warranted if a power failure in the circuit might jeopardize the safety of the home in some manner. Circuits where a power sensor might be worthwhile include those to furnace and air-conditioning motors, those to pumps needed to keep the home dry, and those to freezers containing perishable food.

Homes that have natural gas service for heating can monitor that service by means of a pilot light sensor connected to the security system. The pilot light monitor can be either a **light sensor** or a **thermocouple**. In gas heating systems without continuous pilot lights, a **pressure sensor** on the gas line can be used to confirm that gas is still available for use. Another useful sensor in the area of a gas furnace or water heater, as well as a gas dryer or stove, is a **gas detector** which can warn of a leak in the gas system. The vast majority of gas leaks result from an appliance inadvertently left on, or from a crack or burn-through in the gas-fired heating element of the appliance. A gas sensor placed in the room where these appliances are located can quickly alert the security system of a problem.

Water sensors are of two types, both of which can be very helpful in avoiding water damage in the home. The first is a **flow meter** placed in the main water line to the home. This device can monitor the flow of water in the home's pipes and sound a warning if the flow is excessive or if water is flowing at all in the hours when it shouldn't be. By checking the flow meter for the early morning hours, say from 2 until 4 a.m. when no water would normally be flowing in most homes, even fairly small leaks in bathroom fixtures can be found and corrected. A flow meter is very helpful in detecting water loss in leaking sprinkling systems as well.

The other type of water system sensor is simply a device that detects the presence of water where there shouldn't be any. Water sensors placed in dry areas or a basement can warn of a broken pipe or leaking appliance before serious damage is done. If the home is in an area where ground water is a problem, a basement sensor can alert the home owner to incoming water as soon as it appears. If the problem is pervasive enough that the home has a sump pump, which is a self-starting pump installed in a pit below floor level to keep ground water out, then a water sensor is a necessity as a backup for the pump in case it fails mechanically or from lack of power.

Security System Integration with Home Utility Systems

Which utility system sensors a home security system includes, if any, depends on the degree to which any of them is at risk of failure. Most areas of the country can experience the occasional short duration power failure, caused by lightning storms or equipment failure at power stations. That risk may justify a **power failure warning sensor** in case the problem occurs at night when it wouldn't otherwise be noticed, or in case it occurs through the deliberate effort of someone trying to circumvent the home security system. Other than these two situations, most power systems don't fail often enough to need additional security warnings.

Gas and water leaks are rarer than power failures, but they're also less likely to be noticed before doing serious harm. In areas subject to earthquake, catastrophic storm, or heavy flooding, these warnings may be a valuable addition to a home security system. Utility sensors are most easily installed during home construction, but they can be added later, either as hardwired components or as wireless devices.

Safety and Code Regulations

All utility systems are installed according to local codes and regulations. Security systems should supplement the built-in safety devices in utility systems, but never replace or circumvent them. Electrical wiring installed and maintained according to the National Electric Code (NEC) and local regulations ensures home safety by preventing electrical hazards. Security devices can detect a system breakdown only after it has happened. Prevention of a utility problem is preferable to detection and response after the fact.

Gas and water utilities also have installation and maintenance codes that should be diligently followed. The best security for utility systems is careful construction and good maintenance. You should be aware of the requirements for utility installation and maintenance in your area, and adhere to local ordinance requirements when working on them or installing security systems that monitor them.

There are many local regulations governing minimum safety standards and security in homes. You should be aware of the requirements for home safety and security in your area so that the systems you install conform to local ordinances.

Doors and windows and means of securing them in residences are among the items most frequently addressed by local ordinances. Some communities, for example, prohibit barring lower story windows or permanently locking them closed because doing so presents a hazard to people inside who may be fleeing a fire. Other communities recommend barred windows as a crime prevention measure. Some ordinances require double-keyed locks on exterior doors (locks which require a key to open from the inside as well as the outside). Others ban these locks and require a twist-knob opening on the inside as a safety measure in case of fire. Electric and remotely operated door locks (and in some cases window locks) are regulated by many local ordinances. You should be sure that your security system designs conform to the local ordinances of your community.

SECURITY SYSTEM TYPES

Security systems, like home networks, transmit data between devices or nodes. Security systems differ from high-speed data networks in that their data is usually low volume and moves relatively slowly in comparison to say, an Ethernet. Most of the data flows only one way: from the security system's input sensors and devices to the central control module that monitors the entire system. The only output from the control module in some systems is the sounding of a siren or alarm bell and the possible automated summoning of outside emergency assistance (police, fire, or medical aid) in certain instances. Other more sophisticated systems may have additional built-in emergency responses such as activating sprinkler systems, shutting off utilities, or locking down entrances to prevent a break-in, but even in these systems, the vast majority of data flows from the sensors and monitors in the home to the central control with only an occasional instruction going the other way to an output device.

Hardwired Security Systems

Hardwired security systems, like hardwired networks, are easiest to install during new construction. Security system wiring is low voltage and so can be retrofitted in existing buildings, but with the same difficulty and additional expense that is encountered wiring an Ethernet or a video distribution system. The wired security system may actually be a little more difficult to install than other networked systems because it tends to be concentrated on outside walls where wiring is hardest to pull. Window and door sensors, as well as outside monitors and sensors, are all mounted on exterior walls that, depending on their construction, pose a real challenge for wiring installation.

Hardwired systems, although they've been used longer than the wireless types, offer no inherent advantages over them. Wired systems can be bypassed or disabled by a determined intruder, but this is also true of most wireless systems. Professionally installed security systems connected to central monitoring stations outside the home were formerly all wired systems, but this is no longer the case. All the major monitoring services now offer wireless installations, and some appear to be moving away from the older wired technology and adopting the less expensive wireless systems.

The most convenient wired security systems are those that use existing home AC or telephone wiring rather than requiring the installation of new cables. HomePlug manufacturers and X10 suppliers both offer extensive lines of home security devices that can be plugged into wall sockets and thereby interconnected. Both technologies can also interface their security systems with the home network so that the security system can be PC-monitored and controlled by the system's central computer. Figure 8-3 shows the basic components of an X10-based system. You can add components to it that expand the system up to 16 zones and permit a variety of sensing devices in each.

Figure 8-3   Basic X10 security system components

HomePNA is the telephone-line network technology discussed in Chapter 3. These manufacturers have not yet targeted home security as a focus of their development efforts, but this technology is adaptable for security system use. Some of the HomePNA controller devices now on the market can easily be set up to control security sensors and to feed security system data into an Ethernet network for PC control.

Wireless Security Systems

Wireless systems are less expensive to install than wired ones and offer the same security features for the most part. Wireless transmissions can be disrupted by interference produced accidentally or deliberately, so the wireless security systems are no more secure against tampering than the wired ones, although they do have more flexibility and economy than their wired counterparts.

Wireless sensors and other components can be installed almost anywhere with no need to be concerned about how to get wires to them. This is a big advantage when placement of a sensor or other device may be critical to its function. The fact that most security input and monitoring devices don't need two-way communication with the central control unit of the system means that only a transmitter is required in the sensor or monitor. No receiver is necessary, which reduces costs for these devices.

At least six companies manufacture wireless home security systems ranging from starter kits at $149.00 up to 16-zone, add-on systems that can cost $1,000 or more. None of these, however, can connect to a PC through any existing technology, and none operate on the standard wireless networking technologies. Despite the fact that wireless home security systems offer considerable advantages and a large potential market, neither of the major wireless technologies in the home networking market, WiFi and HomeRF, have security systems available at present.

Remote Access Systems

Remote access or monitored security systems have been a standard for businesses and homes for many years. Both ADT and Brinks, the two largest firms offering this service, have programs through which the company installs a home security system for a nominal charge (or at times, during promotional specials, without charge) and the customer is charged a monthly service fee for the monitoring of the system by the company's personnel over a telephone line. Monitoring service contracts can range from two to five years in duration after which they are renewable for as long as the customer desires to maintain the service.

Monitoring companies install either wired or wireless security systems and the extent of coverage within the home and outside is a matter for individual negotiation and pricing. Some monitoring contracts specify that the installed security equipment is leased and will be reclaimed and removed by the company at the expiration or termination of the monitoring contract. Other arrangements allow the customer to either retain the installed equipment at the end of the monitoring contract or to buy it at a reduced amount.

Monitoring services offer professional installation of security equipment and 24-hour monitoring. They also maintain the equipment they install. Many professional installers work for firms associated with ADT, Brinks, or one of the other monitoring services.

SECURITY SYSTEM EQUIPMENT LOCATIONS

A security system's components may well be the most spread out of any home technology installation. Home security devices are designed to monitor the perimeter of a home environment against intruders as well as the interior against fire and other hazards. Consequently, the system usually has sensors and other input devices outside the home directed toward the farthest corners of the yard, and other devices inside the home monitoring conditions there. A control unit, located centrally in the home and probably near the network gateway or central computer, receives the input data from all the sensors. The central location of the control unit allows it direct and easy access to telephone lines and other communications links that may be needed to summon assistance in the event of an emergency. A central location also places the control unit well away from any outside intruder who might attempt to disable it or shut it down.

Lock and Keypad Locations

Keypads should be located near the doors they serve, but also in plain sight so anyone using them will be visible to passersby. Wireless keypads can be mounted directly on the door above the doorknob. Hardwired units need to be placed on a wall with access to power. Most wired keypads and some wireless ones operate on either 9-16 volts or 20-26 volts. The power can usually be either AC or DC and is stepped down (reduced) from the 120-volt current in the home's electrical system by a **transformer**.

Some wireless keypads are battery operated, as are the locks they control. These units require at least an annual battery change, more frequent if use is heavy or if the unit is located where it is subjected to a lot of heating from sunlight. (Heat increases the chemical reaction of batteries, depleting their power more rapidly.)

Battery-operated keypads are usually 6-9 volt units, while the locks often use 12 or more volts. The expense of battery replacement may eventually outweigh the convenience of wireless installation for these keypads and locks. Nonetheless, they offer security protection as good as the hardwired units for considerably less initial expense. Figure 8–4 shows on the left a battery-powered keypad lock, which is self-contained and functions somewhat like a combination padlock or safe. On the right is a typical front door area keypad location.

Figure 8-4 A self-contained keypad lock (left) and a wall-mounted keypad for a lock

Keypads and other access devices such as **swipe slots** for **magnetic keys** and identifier pads for fingerprint impressions should be located high enough from the ground that small children won't be tempted to play with them, but low enough so that the homes's occupants can easily access them for input. Between four and five feet from ground level is the usual height for these devices and this height may mean that they need some protection from sun and weather if the door is in an unsheltered position. This may consist of a protective cover or similar shield. Such covers should open to the side, not toward the top, so that they will remain open without being held and only one hand is required to access the keypad or identifier unit inside.

Sensor Locations

Sensors can be located throughout a home and yard and connected to one of the zones defined on the security system's main control panel. The type of sensor used determines to a large degree where it can be located to function efficiently, but some general rules apply to placing these devices.

Sensors should be located where they won't be disturbed by curious (or malicious) people. This usually means locating them high enough to be out of reach without the use of a ladder. Most types of sensors can function well when placed at least 7 or 8 feet above ground level. When a sensor can't be located high up, either because there's no suitable mounting location or because it won't function in a high position, then the alternative is a low location with good concealment of the device or strong protection for it against tampering.

Outdoor sensors need some protection from strong sunlight or heavy weather. This may mean mounting them under roof eaves or in other sheltered places, or it may require that some type of screen or cover be added to protect the sensor. Constant sunlight and water can eventually damage even most weatherproof hardware, so a protected location or some type of weather cover is always a good investment.

Sensors also need to be placed where they can't be easily blocked from functioning. Motion sensors shouldn't have any large objects in front of them that would mask an intruder's approach. They also shouldn't be placed where a shield can be placed in front of them from the side. Placing such a shield may trigger the sensor once, but if the shielding remains in place, the sensor thereafter regards it as the normal setting of the area and any movement taking place behind it goes undetected.

All wired sensors should be located where their wiring cannot be easily cut or bypassed. Many security systems sound an alarm if a sensor is cut out of the system, but not all do. Making the wiring as difficult to access as possible helps prevent tampering.

Sensors need to be placed where false reports won't be triggered by events or conditions which are not security threats. Motion sensors shouldn't be placed where the normal wanderings of family pets can trigger an alarm. Heat sensors, whether inside or outside, should never be placed where direct sunlight falls on them during any part of the day at any time of the year. They also shouldn't be placed where unusual heat from a fireplace or cooking appliance can reach them. Smoke detectors shouldn't be placed directly above a stove or oven where the occasional smoke or steam from normal cooking may trigger them. Placing such fire-warning devices a little distance away from heat and smoke particle sources can prevent constant false alarms, but still give adequate protection from a genuine fire.

NOTE NFPA standards call for at least one fire and smoke detector to be located on every floor and outside each sleeping area. Additional units can be placed near hazards such as kitchens, fireplaces, furnaces, and any open flame.

Camera Locations

Video cameras allow the home and its yard to be monitored remotely. A good design has all outside areas covered by two cameras, if possible. This requires placing the cameras high up, away from visual obstructions, and using cameras that can pan (move from left to right and back) by remote control. A panning camera under the eaves of a home can often cover 270 degrees of the surrounding yard. With a camera on each corner of the home, all areas of the yard are at least double-covered and some more. Double coverage of yard areas eliminates any blind spots that a single camera might have because of visual obstructions such as trees and other landscaping in the yard.

If cameras are also placed inside the home, double coverage usually isn't necessary, but the camera needs to be placed out of the way of visual obstructions. Inside cameras should also be concealed if at all possible. Their obvious presence makes many people nervous and may cause a definite chill in the home's social atmosphere. Placing inside cameras in concealed locations within the home's decor lets them function without the drawback of making guests, or even the home's usual occupants, uncomfortable. Miniature cameras are now available that can be placed in books, ceramic pieces, picture frames, or other home furnishings. These devices can be easily relocated if the occasion requires, and they eliminate the need for any hole in the wall such as was once necessary to conceal a camera behind a one-way mirror.

Cameras, like most electronic equipment, don't like heat or water. This means that they should be kept away from direct sunlight, inclement weather, and sprinklers. Cameras can also be blinded by light sources shining directly into the lens. They should be located, as much as possible, so as to avoid this problem. Yard lights can usually be relocated or redirected so they don't shine into the camera lens. The direction of sunlight can't be changed, however, and may require careful positioning of the camera so that sunlight doesn't hit the camera lens during any part of the day. Remember that the sun's angle in the sky changes with the seasons. A camera safely in the shade of the eaves during July and August may be exposed by the lower angle of light in December and January. This phenomenon is significantly more pronounced in the country's northern latitudes (and is extreme in Alaska where the summer sun circles around the horizon), but it affects all areas to some degree. Reflected light coming off of a nearby window or the surface of a swimming pool can also blind a camera. So can car headlights entering the driveway or sometimes passing by on a curved street. All of these possibilities should be checked, and to the extent possible, eliminated when placing video cameras.

SECURITY SYSTEM COMPONENTS

A number of individual components make up the typical security system. Not all of these are used in any given system, but you should be aware of their functions so that you can specify the most effective pieces of hardware for each system you design. Some systems include many of a single type of sensor and none of another. The overall size of the system is determined by the size of the home and yard and the degree of security protection desired. Each of the following devices may find application in a security system you design.

Access Devices

The ideal access formula for any security system is that it allows the home's family and their guests to enter with minimum effort, and prevents everyone else from entering at all, unless specifically cleared to do so by the homeowner. The problem with implementing this formula, of course, is providing a means for the home security system to determine who is welcome and, by elimination, who isn't. Access devices are the methods used to do this. They identify those authorized to enter the home and allow them to mechanically or electronically unlock an entrance door. Access to a home through its security system can be governed in different ways. How restrictive these methods are is determined by the homeowner.

Keypads and Identifiers

Almost all home security systems include electrically operated door locks and garage door openers. These can be activated with a remote signal from a key-ring transmitter, but most also include a keypad or another form of access control near the door for use by those who don't have a remote unit.

A keypad is a device with numerical keys in the same pattern as a telephone that allows the user to manually enter the numeric code that opens a **cipher lock**. Keypads can be battery-operated or hardwired to a low-voltage electrical connection. Entering a preset four- to six-digit number on the keypad activates the electric lock mechanism so that the door can be opened.

Most doors equipped with keypad-activated locks have no key lock mechanism at all. The door can be opened manually from the inside, but there is no keyhole on the outside for a burglar to attack. Only the correct number combination entered on the keypad activates the lock. Many of these systems also have a **lock-down feature** that allows the outside keypads to be deactivated at night or while the homeowner is away. When deactivated, the keypad does not open the lock even if the right number combination is entered. Only the remote unit can open the door from the outside, although it can still be opened manually from the inside. Even with plenty of time to guess number combinations, a would-be burglar won't get the door open.

8

Passwords

Passwords are alphanumeric combinations that the security system recognizes. They can be composed of any number or letter combination that can be easily remembered, but not easily guessed by an unauthorized person. The password is entered on a keypad and, when it's recognized by the security system, the door lock is opened to admit the person. If the password is a name or letter combination, it's entered on the keypad using numbers for letters in the same manner as the letters of the alphabet are listed on a telephone keypad. Michael, for example, is 6424235 and Monique is 6664783.

Passwords are good access devices and provide strong security for the home, as long as they are used correctly. To remain effective, passwords can't be shared with other people (who may share them with others until everyone has them), nor written down, used or otherwise divulged in a manner that allows unauthorized persons to find out what they are. Giving a password to a friend seems innocuous, but it's really giving the friend the key to your house, and the right to duplicate it (by passing the password to others) as often as he or she decides. Passwords are only as safe as the authorized users keep them. For this reason other access restrictions are sometimes added to the home security system.

Keys

Keys are the original method of opening locks and they are still effective for access control. Keys have been stolen and duplicated for hundreds of years and the locks they fit have been picked and forced for an equal length of time, but a well-designed mechanical lock with a closely fitted key offers a good measure of protection for a home, even today.

The security potential of keys has also been enhanced by new technology in recent years. Keys can be used alone to open a lock, or used in combination with a password so that both are required to gain entrance. In this case, entering the password tells the security system that the person has the right to use the key, so when the key turns the lock, the door opens. Without the password, the door won't open, even with the key. The two devices work independently of one another and neither alone can open the door.

New types of keys and locks have also been developed. Some of these are electronic and connect directly to the home security system. Instead of having the traditional cuts and ridges found on most keys, which fit moving tumblers in standard locks, these new keys are fitted with a numerical combination recorded on the magnetic strip of a plastic card, or imbedded as a code on a metal key.

Figure 8-5 shows a standard double-cut mechanical key on the left, a metal Marlock key with a numeric password encoded on it in the center, and a plastic magnetic-stripe key on the right. Both of the encoded keys work electronically. They have a numeric combination recorded on them that can be unique to every key, and is read by the security system when the key is inserted in the lock or passed through a reader. If the numeric code is recognized, the lock opens.

Figure 8-5   A mechanical key (left) and two encoded electronic keys

Electronic keys have the additional security advantages of being very difficult to duplicate and being recordable every time they are used. Being difficult to duplicate prevents a would-be intruder from copying the key and also prevents the rightful owner from inadvertently or deliberately giving away the password on it. Neither the owner nor anyone else can read the password or see it input, so it remains secure no matter how the key is used. If the key is lost or stolen, the password on it can simply be blocked on the security system. No other keys are affected and no change of locks or other devices is required to maintain security.

Recording the use of electronic keys allows the homeowner to monitor who is using them and when. Each time a key is inserted in a home lock, the security system records its password and the time it was used. All entries into the home are thus recorded and, if any security problem later develops, the users of the keys can be traced through the file in the security system.

Time Coding

Electronic keys and locks can also be time coded so that the lock either does not open during set times of the day, or automatically sends a notification if it is opened during those times. In home security systems, such times might be set for the late hours of the night and during the day when parents are at work and children at school. Setting the lock to notify a monitor during certain hours still allows an authorized person entry, but also signals that the door has been opened, thus alerting the homeowner to check on who has arrived.

Biometric Identification

Biometric identification systems are presently not used much in home security systems, but may become more common in the future. They simply take the password concept to another level by identifying authorized persons according to something unique in their physical makeup.

Biometric identifiers include a fingerprint (usually a single thumb print impressed on a sensitive pad and scanned into the security system), a retinal scan, or a photographic image of a person measured for uniquely distinguishing features by the security system. All these identifiers are unique to every individual and so offer an absolutely secure means of identifying the person who is authorized to enter a secured area. Since these identifiers form part of the individual's body, they can't be loaned out, duplicated, or stolen.

At present, all of the identifying programs used for these body identifiers are so expensive that they simply can't be justified for a home security system. As such systems come into more common commercial use, however, their cost may eventually become low enough that some home systems will use them as well.

Cameras and Recorders

Video cameras located at strategic points around the exterior of a home and at the entrances provide a means of visually checking the area in view of the camera. This allows the homeowner to identify visitors personally and also spot any potential intruders. If the cameras are connected to video recorders so that their views are intermittently recorded on tape, then any event which occurs at the home can be reviewed on the video tape later. This record of events, with the time recorded on the tape, is very helpful to police investigating a crime that occurred in the owner's absence and may even be instrumental in solving the crime. If nothing unusual is recorded on a tape, it can simply be reused.

Surveillance video cameras need not be expensive. Good, quality units are available for under $200, and the addition of an automatic/remote motor that pans the camera left to right and back again at a set speed, won't add more than another $75 to a station. It's more important that the cameras function well in low-light levels than that they view in color. A black-and-white camera with high-light gathering capacity provides better images for identifying people and details than most color cameras, especially at night.

If a video camera does have a **panning motor** attached, it needs to be hardwired to a power source as the motor will consume too much power for long-term, battery-powered use. A stationary video camera can be battery powered, but will still require frequent battery changes or recharges, especially if the batteries are exposed to high heat in an outdoor location, which tends to discharge them more quickly. Figure 8-6 shows a miniature surveillance video camera on the right and its wireless receiver on the left. This camera is less than four inches high. It is intended for interior use and is not weatherproof.

Figure 8-6   A wireless video surveillance camera (right) and its receiver

The recorder for a video surveillance system should be a high-quality unit capable of recording all the resolution picked up by the camera. It should also have durable recording heads that are serviced frequently as it will be in constant use recording images, most of which won't be of any value, but a few of which may be very important. These few will need to be as clear as possible in order to reveal valuable details; hence the need for a recorder that records everything that the camera sees.

The best recording unit is the type that records only one frame per second from the camera. This conserves video tape, allows the frames that are recorded to be of the highest quality, and permits up to a continuous week of surveillance to be recorded on a single tape. Alternatively, the recorder can be an extended time type that records 24 frames per second, but runs the recording tape more slowly so that up to 10 hours of surveillance can be recorded on each tape. This type does not record at the same resolution as the single frame per second unit, and its tapes have to be changed daily.

Monitors

A security system with video surveillance cameras doesn't have to have a monitor if the camera images are being recorded. They can be played back later from the tape if the only need is for information on a recorded event. A video monitor is a good idea, however, if the cameras are to be used to visually monitor the yard or entrances to the home at any time. Generally, one large-screen monitor that can be switched to display any of the camera images is preferable to an array of small monitors constantly displaying each camera's image. The larger display can reveal details better, and there's almost never a need to have more than one camera image on display at a time.

Any good television set can serve as a monitor for a security system. None of the video cameras used for security has resolution higher than the NTSC standard, and a television set can display that format adequately. Higher-quality monitors may last longer, but they won't produce a better image because the original camera images aren't of a high enough definition to begin with.

Sensors

8

Sensors are the devices that provide input to a security system. They tell whether conditions are normal, usually by reporting nothing except that they are still functioning. If conditions do change, then the sensor reports the altered state of whatever condition it's designed to monitor. At a minimum it reports only that the condition is not normal. If the device is more sophisticated, it may report the exact degree of change or how much it has altered from the normal state, but the basic purpose of a sensor is to report that the condition it is monitoring has changed out of the normal range. There are many types of sensors.

Break Switch and Make Switch Sensors

These are switch sensors that signal when they are either turned on or turned off. One state is defined as the normal condition, the other is the changed condition. As long as the normal condition is maintained, the switch sends no signal except to confirm that it is functioning. If the condition changes to the abnormal state, the sensor signals the change.

Break switches are normally closed so that a current or magnetic force flows through them constantly. They are the type of sensor placed on window casings and doors. The switch is placed on the door or window casing and the plate which completes the circuit in the switch is placed on the window or door. As long as the window or door remains closed, the switch plate keeps the circuit closed and the sensor remains quiet. If the window or door is opened, the plate is pulled away from the switch thus breaking the circuit. The sensor then sends a signal indicating that its circuit has been broken by the opening of the window or door.

Break sensors can be attached to any fixture where movement of one part opens the switch by separating the plate from it. Besides outside doors and windows, these sensors can protect cabinets containing valuables, rooms that shouldn't be entered, and objects that shouldn't be moved.

Make switches are sensors in which the normal state is open and the changed state is closed. These are most often found as **pressure pads** which signal an alert if weight is placed on them forcing the switch closed and completing the circuit. Pressure pads can be found in driveways where they signal a car or other vehicle moving over them. They can also signal the approach of a person stepping on them. In either of these cases the pressure pad might not signal any alarm because of the movement. It might simply trigger the opening of a gate or start a video camera to record the arrival or departure of a person. Note that a pressure pad doesn't tell direction of movement unless two are placed in line and successively tripped. Pressure pads are sometimes more useful as initiator devices than light beams or motion sensors because their normal range can be set to exclude some weight but respond to anything over a set amount. Thus the family dog or cat walking on the pad won't open the gate or door, but the weight of a person will. Likewise, the children can play on the driveway without opening the outer gate because half the weight of a car is required to set it in motion.

Light Beam Sensors

Light beam sensors consist of two pieces, a sender and a receiver. The sender sends a beam of **laser light** toward the receiver which receives it constantly. Receiving the light is the normal state. If something moves between the sender unit and the receiver, cutting off the light beam from the latter, the sensor sends a signal that the light beam has been interrupted, the abnormal state.

Light beams are used to sense movement, usually in places where there should be no movement. A beam can be sent across an entry way, a section of yard, a driveway, a room in the house, or any other place where the beam should not be broken during specified times. If the beam is broken, an alarm can be sounded or assistance summoned.

Light beams are limited as security devices by the fact that they can be tripped by anything that breaks the beam, and not everything that does so is an intruder. Light beams don't work well where pets roam or animals (belonging to neighbors, or living in nearby wilderness) are likely to break them. They can also be tripped by falling leaves, drifting snow, or windblown newspapers and other debris. They work best when set close to the ground (so an intruder can't slip under them), but that's also the position where they're most likely to be set off by nonthreatening events. Figure 8-7 shows a light beam transmitter on the left and its receiver on the right. These units send a beam across the front of a three-car garage to signal any person or vehicle entering or leaving through the doors.

Figure 8-7   Light beam transmitter (left) and receiver

Under normal conditions, a light beam is invisible, so it's hard to detect or disable. Indoors, a light beam can be set high off the floor, where it's less likely to be tampered with or obstructed accidentally, and still function well. It can be placed so that opening doors or cabinets break the beam as well as an intruder walking in front of it. An inside beam can also be reflected in two or even more directions to increase its range. Note that the presence of a visible mirror suggests that something is being reflected and may indicate the presence of an otherwise undetectable light beam.

Heat/Motion Sensors

Most home security system **motion sensors** are actually **infrared devices** that detect changes in heat (infrared) radiation within their ranges. These devices sense a given amount of radiation coming from surrounding objects within their detecting range, usually about 50 feet. They then regard that amount of radiation as the normal state of their environment and don't react to it. Whenever any object which radiates heat, such as a human body or a warm car engine, enters the device's range, it radiates additional heat toward the device thus moving the amount of radiation received out of the normal range and causing the sensor to signal that something has moved into its range. It's actually the change in heat that has been sensed rather than the motion, but the response is the same.

Infrared sensors are very good at sensing heat changes as large as a human body, but can be set so that they don't react to a smaller change such as that made by the presence of a cat, small dog, or other animal of similar size. Once an infrared sensor has been triggered by a heat change, it usually resets itself so that the current heat pattern becomes the normal, including the intruding person if he or she is still present within the device's range. The sensor won't trigger again unless the heat level changes again so the intruder can stay undetected within the range of the sensor. It does trigger again, however, when he or she leaves the range because again the heat level is changed, this time downward.

Infrared sensors don't work well in high heat. As the ambient air temperature approaches 98 degrees, the temperature of the human body, the movement of a person into the sensor's range no longer alters the radiant heat pattern greatly. The person is radiating about the same amount of heat as the air and surrounding objects so the sensor doesn't signal any change. It doesn't "see" the intruder as a difference in heat. For this reason, infrared sensors shouldn't be used outdoors in areas where the temperature may often reach the high 90s. Figure 8-8 shows an X10-type infrared motion sensor on the right and its wireless transmitter on the left.

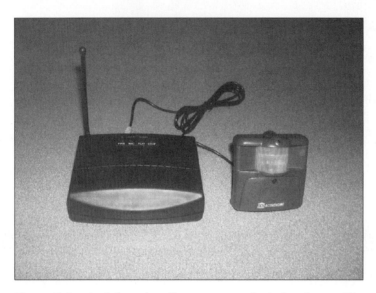

Figure 8-8   An infrared motion sensor and wireless transmitter

Temperature Sensors

Temperature sensors can be used to signal either high heat or cold. They measure the temperature of the air around them and they have a normal range to which they don't react. If the air temperature rises above (or falls below) the normal range, the sensor signals the changed state. Some temperature sensors can record temperature changes degree by degree so that actions may be taken when certain levels are reached, but most are simply switches that signal only when the temperature moves outside their normal range. Most are set to signal a temperature drop or a temperature rise, but not both.

High-temperature sensors are used as fire alarms. They're usually mounted high in a room and signal a temperature change when air temperature at ceiling level reaches about 140 degrees. Since heat rises in a room, a fire burning at floor level will quickly raise the temperature at the ceiling to this critical level. Heat from a stove or other warming device won't get the air up to critical temperature unless these appliances are left on too long and become a fire danger. Temperature sensors don't react to smoke, only to heat, so they make good fire detectors in areas where some occasional smoke is common and smoke detectors can't be used.

Low-temperature sensors are mostly used for freezing protection. Their normal range may go down to the mid 30s, but as the temperature drops to near freezing (32 degrees) they signal a temperature change. The security system may then be programmed to shut off outside water systems to prevent pipes freezing. It may also activate de-icing systems on driveways, roofs, and rain gutters. When the temperature rises again, these latter systems are shut down, although the sprinkler system may remain off until a programmed length of normal temperature time has elapsed. Low-temperature sensors can also be useful in outbuildings where they can signal danger to animals or machinery when the temperature falls too low because of failed heaters, windows or doors left open, or other mishap.

Water Sensors

Water sensors are switches that react to the presence of water. Their normal state is dry. If they detect water, a circuit is completed and a signal sent to the central control. They are used to warn of water where it shouldn't be. The cause of such water can be leaking or broken pipes, seeping groundwater, excessive lawn watering, or any number of other causes. If the water is in the home's basement, it will likely cause damage. The water sensor can prevent that with a timely signal. A water sensor should be placed at the lowest point in the drainage area it is protecting. This will allow the first water entering the area to trigger the sensor. The signal may start a pump working or merely send a warning alarm that something is amiss.

Fire/Smoke Detectors

Smoke detectors are sensors that constantly measure the purity of the surrounding air. Whenever the air becomes polluted with smoke particles, the smoke detector signals an alarm and usually an audible warning. Smoke detectors are the preferred means of fire detection because they cost less than heat detectors and thus can be more economically placed throughout the home, but they do have some limitations. They're often set off falsely in homes where people smoke or where fireplaces or cooking smoke exist to any significant extent. When this happens frequently, the smoke detector is likely to be left off to stop the false alarms and it thus becomes useless for its intended purpose. Smoke detectors don't react to heat, only to smoke, so a fire burning with relatively little smoke won't trigger them for a while.

Smoke detectors, like heat detectors, can be connected to a security system and trigger a call for the fire department when they go off, but this setup should only be created if false alarms are very rare. The fire detection system least vulnerable to false alarms may be one with smoke detectors in bedrooms, family rooms, and living rooms, and heat detectors in kitchens, furnace rooms, and wherever open fireplaces or barbecue grills are located.

Security Panels

Security panels are the central control devices for security systems. Each of the sensors set up in the security system is wired to or wirelessly connected to the security panel and reports its status to the panel. If a security breach is signaled from any of the sensors, the panel can be programmed to take appropriate action in response. This may be to sound an audible alarm to notify the homeowner of the problem, or to automatically call and summon emergency assistance, as in the case of a fire alert.

The monitoring functions of a security panel are divided into zones so that the location of any security breach signal can be easily located. Some panels can connect to a PC, either as a node on a network or directly through a USB port. This connection enables security status to be displayed on the PC and its display monitor to serve as a monitor for the security system's surveillance cameras.

Some security panels can record the time of any security breach anywhere in the system and make other responses as well. These responses may include turning on lights in the home to aid the occupants in getting out, starting video cameras and recorders photographing in real time, sounding an outside alarm intended to summon assistance from neighbors, or shutting off gas lines. The panel doesn't perform any of these actions, but sends signals activating response devices in appropriate locations.

Alarms

An alarm is a response device that sounds an audible or sometimes a visual warning of a security system breach. The alarm is connected to the security system's control panel or, in some systems, may be built in as part of the panel. When the panel receives an alert signal from a remote sensor, it directs the alarm to sound the appropriate warning. Different alarm sounds can be programmed in an alarm as responses to different warning signals from sensors. A siren sound might signal fire danger while a repeating bell might be programmed as response to an unauthorized entry attempt. Both signals are intended to alert people in the home to the security breach, and the latter one may also scare off a potential intruder by letting him or her know clearly that his or her presence has been noticed.

Alarms are usually low-voltage powered (12 or 24 volts) and should have back-up battery power in case house current is interrupted. They should always be loud enough that their sound reaches all areas of the home. They should also be impossible to sleep through. Because they're loud and sound a high pitched noise, alarms can be very annoying if they continue to sound once their alert has been delivered. For this reason, alarms should be placed where they can be easily turned off in case of a false alert. (If the alert is genuine, it's intended that the intense sound will literally drive people out of the house and to safety to get away from it.) Alarms generally don't do more than sound an audible warning, but they are often connected to calling devices which summon emergency assistance automatically.

Call-in Devices

Call-in devices are essentially automatic telephones programmed to call one or more numbers and deliver a preprogrammed message. The simplest call-in devices dial a number and begin repeating their message. They don't detect any response at the other end of the call they've placed. More sophisticated call-in devices dial a number, wait for a pickup response at the other end, and then deliver their recorded message. If a busy signal is noted on the line, the call-in device goes into a recall mode, waiting a specified length of time and then redialing the number. It may also call a second number and deliver its message. Some devices can call up to four numbers in succession to be certain that someone at one of them hears the intended emergency message. Call-in devices are also powered by low-voltage current and should have a battery back-up power source in case the AC current in the house is shut off.

CHAPTER SUMMARY

- When designing a security system for a home, these factors should be considered: what or who the security system is going to protect, what major threats must be protected against, what level of risk exists, and what factors external to the home environment affect the risk assessment.

- Security systems can be wired, wireless, or a combination. Hardwired systems can be easily installed in new construction, but are much more difficult to retrofit in existing homes. Wireless security systems are usually the preferred choice for retrofitted installations as well as many new homes.

- Remotely accessed or monitored security systems have been offered by commercial security firms for years. For a monthly fee, the company installs a security system and monitors its sensors over a telephone line.

- Security systems are organized in zones so that their protection devices can be easily monitored and the origin of any security breach quickly located. A security zone can be any area of a home or yard. The limits of a zone are really the number of devices that the security system's central control can monitor for a zone.

- A home security system should be integrated as much as possible with other technology systems in the home. It should conform to local code and ordinance requirements and provide monitoring of utility systems against failure or breakdown.

- Security devices, especially sensors, need to be placed where they can't be easily blocked from functioning. They need to be placed where false reports won't be triggered by events or conditions which are not security threats, where they won't be disturbed by curious (or malicious) people, and where they are protected from weather and other hazards as much as possible.

- Access devices in security systems include electronic locks which are accessed by keypads or encoded keys. Other access controls include timed locks, passwords, and biometric identifiers, but the last of these is expensive and rarely used in home systems.

- Video cameras located around the exterior of a home and at the entrances provide a means of visually checking the area in view of the camera. The camera images can be monitored from inside the home on a television screen and recorded on tape for later review of significant events.

- Sensors are the devices that provide input to a security system. They tell whether conditions are normal, and if conditions change, they report the altered state of whatever conditions they are designed to monitor.

- There are many types of sensors including break and make switches, motion detectors, heat sensors, smoke detectors, light beam sensors, temperature sensors, water detectors, and electric current monitors.

- Security panels are the central control devices for security systems. Each of the sensors set up in the security system reports its status to the security panel. If a security breach is signaled from any of the sensors, the panel can be programmed to take appropriate action in response.

KEY TERMS

Biometric identifiers — Unique distinguishing physical features of an individual that can be used as means of identification. They include fingerprints, eye retinas, voice prints, and facial characteristics.

break switch — A sensor which monitors a closed switch and signals if the switch is opened and the circuit broken. Used on doors, windows, and containers that should remain closed as their normal state.

bypass — Any means of evading a security device by making it appear to be functioning in a normal state when, in fact, conditions have changed. A window sensor, for example could be bypassed by slipping a loose plate onto its contact points to make the switch continue to signal normal (closed) even when the window is opened.

cipher lock — An electronic lock which is opened by entering a preset numerical code. Some locks can have many access codes, some only one.

detection devices — Sensors which discern changes in conditions that indicate the presence or passage of a person or persons.

flow meter — A device which measures the amount of water flowing in a pipe and signals its measurement to a recording device. Used to detect leaks or breaks in pipes or sprinkling systems.

gas detector — A device which senses the presence of natural gas, carbon monoxide, or other poisonous gas.

infrared devices — A device which functions by detecting heat (infrared-wavelength energy) or changes in the heat level of its surroundings.

keypad — A numeric pad similar to a telephone dial pad which is used to input passwords to cipher locks and other security devices.

laser light — Coherent light waves transmitted in parallel beams so that they maintain their intensity over long distances. Used in light beam sensors and many other devices.

light beam sensor — A device in two pieces, one of which transmits a beam of light to the other across a distance. If the light beam is obstructed, the sensor signals its failure to arrive.

light sensor — A device which senses the presence of light and signals it or senses the absence of the light and signals it.

lock-down feature — A program in some security systems which allows all door locks to be deactivated during specified times so that they can't be opened from the outside at all, even with a valid access code.

magnetic key — A key similar to a plastic credit card with its access information coded on a magnetic stripe which can be read by an access device.

make switch — A sensor which monitors a switch that should remain open and signals if it is closed. Most commonly used as pressure pads which are closed by weight passing over them.

motion sensor — A device which detects any object which radiates heat moving into its range and signals the change in its surroundings.

panning motor — An accessory device for a surveillance video camera. The panning motor slowly swings the camera right and left allowing it to cover more area than a stationary camera could.

power failure warning sensor — A device which detects the presence of voltage (electrical pressure) in a circuit and signals its absence to a monitor.

pressure pads — A make switch which is closed when a set weight is placed on it. The sensor then signals its changed state.

8

pressure sensor — A device which monitors gas or liquid pressure in a pipe or tank. If pressure drops too low (or, in a steam pipe, rises too high) the sensor signals the change.

redundant protection — In a security system, having two or more sensors or detectors monitoring one area or entrance. Provides additional security to high-risk areas.

remote access — Security system monitored by an outside commercial firm through a telephone or radio connection to the home control panel.

security panel — The control center of a security system to which all of the system's sensors and surveillance devices report their status. The panel may also direct responses, record data, and sound alarms.

security zone — An area in a home or its yard that is monitored by a specific group of sensors in the security system. Zones are set up with defined monitoring devices so that the location and nature of any security breach can be quickly identified.

sensors — Devices which monitor an object (door, window, floor area) or condition in or around the home and signal the security panel if its status varies significantly from normal.

smoke detector — A device which signals the presence of smoke in the air around it. It does not react to heat or flame, only to the presence of smoke particles.

surveillance video camera — A small video camera used in a home security system to monitor a yard or part of the home's interior. The camera's output can be displayed or recorded or both.

swipe slots — An input device for plastic magnetic-striped keys. The plastic key is passed (swiped) through the slot in the device which reads the key code and grants access.

temperature sensor — A device which measures the ambient air temperature and signals it to a security system monitor that can compare it to programmed instructions and take appropriate action.

thermocouple — A device which transforms heat into an electrical current. Used in gas appliances to monitor the pilot light. If the light goes out, the thermocouple stops generating electricity, thereby signaling a problem.

transformer — An electrical device for stepping voltage in a circuit up or down with an inverse increase or decrease in amperage.

water sensor — A device which senses the presence of water and signals it to a security monitor or panel.

REVIEW QUESTIONS

1. The three traditional objectives of home security are protecting _____, _____, and _____.

2. Most security system data lines don't carry large amounts of data in comparison to network cables. True or False?

3. Why are wireless security systems usually the preferred choice for retrofitted installations?

4. Security systems are organized in _____ so that their protection devices can be easily _____ and the origin of any security breach quickly located.

5. Statistics show that most burglary attempts are made at what three entry points: _____, _____, _____.

6. The most convenient wired security systems are those which use existing home AC or telephone wiring rather than requiring the installation of new cables. True or False?

7. The two largest firms offering remote access service in which the company installs a security system for a nominal charge and the customer pays a monthly service fee for monitoring are _____ and _____ .

8. Keypads on or near doors are used to enter _____ .

9. Motion sensors' locations should take into account what factors?

10. Why is double coverage of video cameras in a yard a good security practice?

11. An encoded key contains a _____ _____ recorded on it, which opens an electronic lock.

12. Using a telephone keypad, what is the numeric code for the password "Nicholas"?

    a. 54145616

    b. 64246527

    c. 74173637

    d. 10726685

13. How can a time-coded electronic lock with keypads deactivated from midnight to 6 a.m. be opened at 2 a.m.?

14. Any good television set can serve as a monitor for a security system. True or False?

15. The normal state of a break switch sensor is _____.

16. A make switch sensor is used for turning off lights. True or False?

17. A light beam is usually used as a _____.

    a. water detector

    b. motion detector

    c. fire alarm

    d. none of the above

18. The normal condition of a water detector is _____.

19. A smoke detector signals when the temperature reaches 140 degrees. True or False?

20. A motion detector actually senses changes in _____.

    a. infrared radiation

    b. air pressure

    c. moisture content

    d. weight

21. A low-temperature sensor is usually used to protect against _____.

    a. open door

    b. water heater failure

    c. frozen pipes

    d. power failure

22. The central control device for security systems is the _____ _____.

23. If a security breach is signaled by sensors, the respective security panel can be programmed to take appropriate action in response. True or False?

24. What function do call-in devices perform?

25. An alarm device is most often used to warn the home's occupants of
_____ .

HANDS-ON PROJECTS

Project 8-1: Find Specifications for a Freeze Sensor

In this project you will search the Internet to find a low-temperature sensor called a freeze sensor that signals when the temperature around it drops to the freezing point of water. You will determine the specifications of this device and what other hardware items are required for it to perform its function. For this project you will need access to a computer that can be connected to the Internet.

1. Log onto the computer and connect to the Internet.

2. Use your browser to go to a search engine you prefer and start your search.

3. Search for the term **"freeze sensor"**.

4. In the results the search engine returns, find a freeze sensor that sends a signal when the air temperature falls to near freezing.

5. Carefully note the specifications of the freeze sensor you select. Is it wired or wireless? What signal does it send, and what does it send the signal to?

6. Determine what additional hardware and wiring items you would need to have to install this freeze sensor and be able to monitor its signal. Does it require a control panel to receive the signal? Could the signal go directly to an audible alarm?

7. If the purpose of the freeze sensor is to protect a sprinkling system from freeze damage, can the sensor connect directly to the sprinkler system? If not, what additional devices are needed to shut down the sprinkler system?

8. Try to diagram a complete sprinkler protection system using the information you've found. Include all the items that are required to get a freeze warning signal from the sensor and activate a device to shut off the sprinkling system.

9. Identify what parts of the sprinkler protection system could be used for other security functions. What are those functions?

Project 8-2: Set up a Motion Detector

In this project you will connect an infrared motion detector to a control module so that its signal can be monitored. You will test the range of the detector in a classroom or other test area. For this project you will need access to an X10 wireless motion sensor and transmitter and an X10 security control panel.

1. Connect the security control panel to its power supply, and plug the power supply into an outlet. Follow the instructions that come with the unit to set it up. Do not use any power supply other than the one which comes with the panel.

2. Set up the motion sensor and connect it to its wireless transmitter. If the transmitter is battery powered, be sure it has good batteries. If it has a power supply, plug the power supply into an outlet in the room.

3. Position the sensor in a corner of the room opposite the entrance door. Aim the sensor at the door.

4. Turn on the sensor, its transmitter, and the security control panel.

5. Walk in front of the sensor a few feet away from it. You should get a signal at the security panel. If you don't, check the setup of both the panel and the sensor. Be sure both are powered and that the transmitter antenna is pointed toward the security panel. Test the system again, if necessary, until you get a signal from walking in front of the sensor.

6. Once you have the sensor working, test its range in the room. Try to find the edges of the area where it signals motion. Work outward from the sensor and observe how the range area fans out in a broad arc.

7. Have someone enter the room through the door. Does the sensor immediately signal motion? If it does, can a person move slowly into the room without setting off the sensor? Can a person move along the walls and not be detected in motion?

8. Find a large sheet of cardboard to use as a shield. Walk into the room with the shield held between you and the sensor. Does it signal motion? How close can you approach the sensor before it signals.

9. Slowly place the shield a foot or so in front of the sensor. Does it signal motion? With the shield in front of it, does the sensor still function as it did before? Why doesn't the sensor respond to motion of the shield as it does to motion of a person?

HANDS-ON PROJECTS

Project 8-3: Set up a Wireless Heat Sensor

In this project you will connect a wireless heat sensor to a control module so that its signal can be monitored. You will test the detector in a classroom or other test area. Most heat sensors provide only an audible alarm when they detect heat, but in order to alert the security panel so it can summon emergency assistance, the sensor must transmit a detection signal to the panel. For this project you will need access to an X10 wireless heat sensor and transmitter and an X10 security control panel. You will also need an electric hair dryer.

1. Mount the wireless sensor on a wall about 4 feet above the floor. Before doing so, be certain that it has batteries. Follow the mounting and setup instructions furnished with the unit.

2. Set up the control panel as you did in Project 8-2.

8

3. If the sensor has a test button, use it to test whether the security panel can receive the sensor's wireless signal. If the test button sends the signal, proceed to the next step. If the signal isn't sent and received, check the setup of the sensor and the security panel and try the test again.

4. When the sensor tests correctly with the test button, test it again with heat. Turn the hair dryer on high heat and point it at the sensor from a distance of about 1 foot away. Keep the dryer pointed at the sensor until it sends a high-heat signal to the security panel.

5. Turn off the dryer and wait until the sensor cools and resets itself.

6. Turn the dryer on again and repeat the test. Do you think the heat sensor is a reliable indicator of fire danger? Why or why not?

HANDS-ON PROJECTS

Project 8-4: Diagram a Security System for a Home

In this project you will draw a diagram for a home security system using a scale floor plan of a residence as the basis for your design. Use a floor plan from a home design magazine or an architectural floor plan drawing. Assume the home is already built and that you will use a wireless security system for your design.

1. Diagram the security system on the floor plan as accurately as you can.

2. Designate areas of the home as zones. Assume you can have a maximum of four devices in each zone and a maximum of eight zones.

3. Include protection for all windows and doors. Include fire protection devices in the kitchen and at least two other rooms. Include motion detectors outside the home to cover both the front and back door areas. Include any other protective devices you feel appropriate that can be accommodated within the limits of the system.

4. When your diagram is complete, total the number of devices of each type that you've included. Make a complete list of hardware required for the system.

5. Visit an X10 Web site such as *www.smarthome.com* or *www.x10.com* and price the items you need for your security system. Try to price some items together in package deals to save money.

6. Calculate the total cost of the hardware for the security system you designed.

HANDS-ON PROJECTS

Project 8-5: Research the Cost of a Remotely Monitored Security System

In this project you will research how much a security system installed by a commercial company will cost, including the monthly service fee. For this project you will need access to a computer connected to the Internet.

1. Log onto the computer and connect to the Internet.

2. Use your browser or go to a search engine you prefer to start your search.

3. Search for the term **monitored security system**.

4. In the results the search engine returns, find a company Web site for a firm that provides monitored security service in your area. You may want to check several firms and decide which one you like best before pricing the service.

5. For the firm you choose, note the cost of installing a basic security system and what is included in the base figure. How does the hardware list compare to the system you designed in Project 8-4?

6. Note the cost of any additional hardware items you would want added to the system if it were going into the home for which you designed a system in Project 8-4.

7. Note the monthly fee for monitoring and the minimum length of the required contract for monitoring. Multiply the number of months in the minimum contract by the monthly fee to get the total cost of the monitoring service. Add that amount to the installation cost and any extra items you've determined are needed.

8. Total all the costs to get the amount of the monitoring service. How does this figure compare with the hardware costs for the system you designed?

8

HANDS-ON PROJECTS

Project 8-6: Research the Marlock Lock and Key System

In this project you will learn more about one type of electronic lock and key system. In Figure 8-3 of this chapter, a Marlock system key is displayed. This key is metal, but it is also electronic and has a number encoded on it rather than cuts and ridges as the traditional key beside it in the picture does. For this project you will need access to a computer connected to the Internet.

1. Log onto the computer and connect to the Internet.

2. Go to a search engine you prefer to start your search.

3. Search for the term **Marlock system** or just **Marlock**.

4. In the results the search engine returns, try to find the site of the company that makes this lock system. If you can't locate the manufacturer, find several companies that sell it and learn as much about it from their sites as you can.

5. Try to answer all of these questions about the Marlock system:

    a. How are the keys encoded?

    b. Does every key have a unique number?

    c. What information can a Marlock lock record?

    d. What features does the lock have that a traditional key lock doesn't?

    e. How much does a Marlock lock cost?

    f. How much are the keys?

    g. How can key codes be changed or new keys obtained?

    h. Do you think this lock system offers better security than a traditional key lock?

CASE PROJECTS

CASE PROJECTS

Case Project 8-1: Research the Need for Security Systems in Your Area

You're planning to offer security systems as part of the HTI products you install. To sell these systems, you need to know what benefits you can offer customers for installing a security system. On the Internet or at your local library, find out the following information about your area. Research your city, county, or state, whichever you can find the statistics for.

1. How many home fires occurred in the past year?

2. How many home burglaries?

3. How many home break-ins when people were at home and at risk of personal harm?

4. How do these numbers compare with national figures for the same events?

CASE PROJECTS

Case Project 8-2: Prepare a Sales Presentation for a Security System

Two clients ask you about installing a security system as part of their home technology. They've never had a home burglary, but they travel a lot and are concerned about their children being in the home alone at night. They would like some protection and some peace of mind about their children's safety when they're away. Based on the information you learned in Case Project 8-1 and the concerns the clients have expressed, write a brief presentation about what a security system could do to reduce real risk to this family and calm perceived fears.

Case Project 8-3: Prepare a Sales Presentation for a Security System

The typical home fire takes only a few minutes to spread rapidly and do enormous damage to a house and its contents. The more rapidly firefighters arrive at a home fire, the more quickly they can put out the fire and minimize damage. Contact the fire department in your area and find out what their average response time to a fire is after an alarm is received. Ask what the minimum and maximum time is, and whether they have any records of which home fires were in buildings equipped with call-in security systems. If this information is available, find out how the homes equipped with security systems compare with others in damage from the fires they had. How much do you think a client would spend on a security system that might reduce fire damage to his home by $10,000? By $20,000?

Case Project 8-4: Research Insurance Rates for Homes Equipped with Security Systems

Contact several insurance companies in your area that write casualty insurance (home owners insurance). Ask each of them if they offer reduced premiums for insurance on homes with security systems. If they do, find out exactly what protection the system must include to earn the discount in insurance. Ask each company what information caused them to offer such a discount (insurance companies always determine premiums on the basis of hard financial data, although they may not always be willing to share that data with you). Write a brief report on what you find and your conclusion about whether a security system can save money on insurance premiums.

SECURITY SYSTEM INSTALLATION AND SETUP

After reading this chapter, you will be able to:

♦ Describe how hardwired, wireless, and combination security system infrastructure should be installed

♦ Install various types of sensors and other components in a security system

♦ Install various accessory devices

♦ Program a security system with appropriate settings and parameters

♦ Describe the procedures for monitoring, maintaining, and servicing a security system

In the last chapter you learned about the various types of security systems and the large variety of components that these systems can include. In this chapter, you will learn how to install the infrastructure needed for a security system. You'll also learn how to install and set up the appropriate components to create an effective home protection system. You'll learn how accessory devices can enhance the function of a security system, and you'll be able to describe how to program a security panel, keypad, and call-in device. After you understand how the system is set up and operated, you'll learn how to maintain it and how to service components so that their operation remains flawless.

SECURITY SYSTEM INSTALLATION

Many manufacturers offer components for security systems, both wired and wireless. Some offer complete lines of products from which a full security system can be assembled. Those whose product lines are this extensive generally also offer preselected packages of components ranging from so-called "starter kits," consisting of a security panel and two or three sensors, to entire house security systems with a dozen or more varied components. Remote access companies, who usually install the security systems they monitor, also offer security component packages of various sizes from which their customers can select, along with several levels of monitoring service.

The level of standardization in security products isn't high, particularly among wireless components. Buyers shouldn't assume that any two components, especially if they are made by different companies, are compatible with one another unless the packaging and instructions clearly indicate that they are. For this reason, buying a preassembled package of security components to use in a home security system makes sense. Components sold as a package will work together and are offered by those manufacturers whose product lines in the security area are the most extensive. Both considerations are important in assuring that all elements of the security system are compatible with one another and that a range of additional products are available from the same company that can work with the package system, if needed.

Not all security systems are capable of being integrated with a home network. Some definitely are, but this fact should never be assumed any more than compatibility among manufacturers. The ability to integrate with a home network, or even a single computer, is a valuable feature and is always advertised as such. If a security panel's packaging and instructions don't clearly state that it can connect to a PC and has the necessary software included to do so, you should assume that it can't.

In this chapter, you'll learn about the installation of a wired security system and a wireless one. Each is representative of a type of system, but not all similar systems include all the features described here. Some may also include features not covered. As with other home technology products and systems, the user should become familiar with the range of products available and choose the system and manufacturer that best meets his or her needs.

Low-voltage Wiring

As was noted in the last chapter, the amount of data sent over most wired security system lines is minuscule when compared with the multi-megabit data capacities needed for an active home LAN. Lines from sensors to a security panel operate at a similar low voltage as do network systems, but they rarely carry a megabit of data in a month, and so there is no need for them to be installed using Cat5 cable or even standard UTP or STP cable. Wire that is less expensive and smaller in size is preferable for security system use.

Category 2 telephone wire, containing two pairs of wires, is adequate for most security component wiring. Only one pair of wires is needed for a sensor, so two sensors can actually be wired from a single run of Category 2 wire. If multiple sensors are to be wired to windows and doors in a room, a run of Category 2 or **Category 3 wire** containing four or six pairs of wires can be used. This eliminates multiple wire runs and provides individual home run wiring for each sensor.

Neither Category 2 nor 3 wire is armored or in any way resistant to being cut, but this is not a requirement for security system use. All monitored security system sensors regularly report their status to the security panel. The frequency of reporting varies with the system and is a feature that should be evaluated when selecting a system: the more frequently status is reported, the sooner any security breach creates an alert. Failure of a sensor to report its normal status is regarded by the security panel as a breach, the same as if the sensor had been activated by an opening window or other break-in. Consequently, cutting a sensor's wires has the same effect as opening a secured door: a **security breach** is noted by the security panel. Sensors can be **bypassed** (made to appear normal when dysfunctional by a device wired into the sensor circuit), but only by a sophisticated signal generator that can match the timing and duration of the sensor's own signal and be wired into the circuit between the sensor and the security panel without triggering an alarm. This is an occurrence so rare, except in movies, as to not justify armored wiring.

Unlike high-speed data lines, telephone wire can be spliced. A single 4- or 6-pair line can be run to a junction box and the pairs in the line spliced to individual Category 2 lines running to sensors in different parts of a security zone. Because the signals from security components are low power to start with and attenuate with distance traveled on the wire, any splices should be carefully made and soldered or clamped under screws to assure a good connection.

Many security (and telephone) installations using Category 2 wire have been made by running the wire on the surface of walls, usually on or just above the baseboard, and holding it in place with small staples. Category 2 wire is only a little more than 1/8 inch in diameter, smaller than Category 5, and is less obtrusive when run on the surface. Its data-carrying capacity, being much lower, is also not impaired from being squeezed by the staples as Category 5 or other high speed cables are.

Surface runs of security wire are still acceptable in many cases and may be necessary at the ends of runs to get wires close enough to window and door sensors so they can be connected. But concealed wiring looks better in the home and should be used wherever reasonably possible for a more professional appearance and usually a more satisfied customer. If surface runs are necessary, it's better to do them with the wire alone rather than use raceways, which are too large for the Category 2 or 3 wire and detract more from a room's appearance than the exposed wire. Category 2 wire can be bent sharply without damage and so can be made to follow irregular contours of moldings or other obstructions closely. If the installer runs the wire so that it blends with wall surface features (along grooves in baseboards and moldings, up the sides of door casings, under window sill overhangs) as much as possible, an almost invisible finished appearance can usually be achieved.

If a house or room has wall-to-wall carpeting, Category 2 wire can be run along the inside edge (the edge away from the wall) of the tack strip that holds the edges of the carpeting, and then stapled to the floor. The tack strip prevents damage to the wire, but wire should not be run under carpet across the middle of a room as furniture or constant foot traffic is almost sure to damage it.

9

In large security systems, 4- or 6-pair wires should be used wherever needed to avoid multiple wire runs on wall surfaces. More than a single wire on a wall never looks good and will look worse over time as lint and dust becomes trapped between the parallel running wires. Avoid two wires next to one another wherever possible, even if it means running a single wire around opposite sides of a room to reach two window sensors.

Another solution to wiring closely spaced sensors (on two windows on one wall or on French doors in a room) is to wire them in series (not in parallel) on a single wire run. This eliminates one wire run to the security panel while still allowing both sensors to be fully active. If wired in series, both sensors are on the same connection at the security panel and there is no means of determining which sensor is tripped in case of a break-in, but this really doesn't matter. Through which of two windows or doors in a room a burglar makes his or her entrance isn't important as long as his or her attempt is signaled to the security panel. Figure 9-1 shows how two sensors can be wired in series so that if either sensor (**break switch**) is opened, the security panel is alerted.

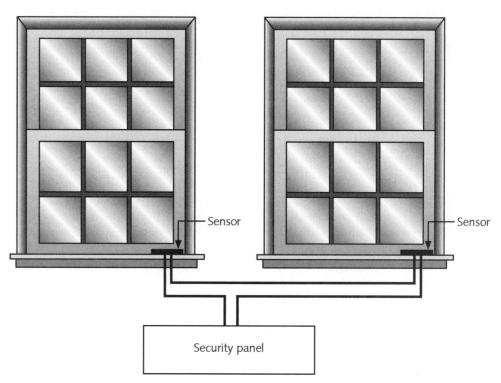

Figure 9-1   Window sensors wired in series

Many security panels are constructed with zones that have four (or sometimes six) sensor connections in each zone. These systems can often be wired by running a single Category 2 or 3 wire (4-pair or 6-pair) to a central point in the zone and then splitting the wire pairs into individual runs from the central point to sensors in the zone using smaller wire. This reduces wire runs to the security panel and still allows each sensor to be individually connected and **monitored**.

Sensors can all be wired with Category 2 wire, as can all **response devices** such as emergency call-in devices, remotely activated locks, electronic valves, automated appliances, utility controls, and intercom speakers. The only notable exceptions to this wiring standard in security systems are video surveillance cameras. These require standard composite analog video cables with RCA connectors at each end. Only one cable is required for each camera because security cameras don't have any audio output as does a regular TV camera.

Video camera cables connect into a monitor or a **switcher** that can switch the monitor from one camera to another. Other than the different wire and connectors used, wiring for video cameras is similar to wiring for other security sensors and input devices. The video cables can be run on the surface of walls or concealed. There's no restriction on sharp bends in the cable, but it does need to be kept clear of high-voltage, AC wiring and equipment, which can introduce interference in the signal just as it can with cables to other video devices.

Wireless Security Systems

Wireless sensors don't require any wires either to transmit their signals or for power to the unit. Transmission of data is handled by a transmitter and both the sensor unit and the transmitter are battery powered. Good, quality sensors and other wireless devices also monitor their batteries and signal when battery power is getting low. This feature enables the user to change the batteries in a timely manner without waiting until the sensor goes dead or by changing the batteries too soon and losing a large portion of the batteries' life.

Power Usage of Wireless Systems

Wireless sensors and their transmitters consume little power and their batteries often last a year or more, but the batteries used are typically 9- or 12-volt alkaline type and are three or four times the price of 1.5-volt C or D batteries. Action response devices such as audible alarms, emergency call-in devices, video cameras, utility controls, and intercom speakers can also be battery powered, but are more usually wired to an AC power outlet either directly or through a step-down transformer, which is a device that lowers AC voltage to the level required by the equipment. It's easier to power these devices with AC current because they're nearly always located near a power outlet (appliance controls, lamp modules, and utility controls) or can be located near one (audible alarms and emergency call-in devices). Some response devices also require quite a bit of power to perform their functions and battery power would be expensive to provide for these.

Some AC-powered devices do have battery back-up power in case the AC connection is lost or the power in the home is cut off. These are primarily warning devices such as alarms and emergency call-ins that absolutely must function properly in life-and-death situations. Back-up power for these devices is critical.

Signal Transmission

Wireless sensors can transmit their signals to a security panel through walls and other obstructions within reasonable limits. The transmitters are low power and their signals are degraded by distance. This means that their transmission range is limited to a few hundred feet. Heavy obstructions such as concrete walls, metal structures, and other dense materials can absorb some of the signal and further reduce its range. For this reason, all sensors in a wireless security system should be tested after the sensors are mounted and the security panel is positioned where it will be permanently located. Testing assures that the system is working under the actual range and obstruction conditions of the home. If either a sensor or the security panel is relocated, the testing should be done again (if it is the security panel that's moved, all sensors should be retested) to be sure that all transmissions can still be received.

Wireless video cameras are also available for home security systems, but most of the wireless transmitters on these units can only work across a direct **line of sight**. This allows the camera to be located in a good surveillance position without the need to be hardwired. It can then broadcast its images to a wireless receiver located in a position from which it can be wired to the monitor by standard video cable. Wireless video cameras can be battery-operated or connected to AC power through a transformer, if an outlet is available. To conserve battery power, wireless video cameras usually do not operate continuously, but only on a timed schedule or when signaled from the monitoring station to turn on.

Standards Organizations and Related Technologies

Any discussion of home security systems based on either the HomePlug or HomePNA standards must of necessity be short. Despite the development expertise and power of the companies promoting these technologies through the alliances organized for that purpose, no viable home security systems have yet emerged operating on either standard. The same can be said of both the HomeRF and WiFi wireless standards: no company or consortium has introduced any significant home security products despite the fact that home security systems are one of the two most sought after applications of home technology integration. One WiFi manufacturer does offer a wireless video camera that can be set up as part of a home security system, but so far the company has made no discernable effort to market the camera in the home security context.

The wireless security systems manufactured by SkyLink, Honeywell, and others all operate on RF standards not related to any of the networking technologies. They also have no means of interfacing with any of the networking technologies, wired or wireless, except Ethernet. Not all security systems can interface with Ethernet, but you'll examine a couple that do and see how the network connection enhances the security function of both.

X10 Security Systems

Alone among the power-line technologies, X10 manufacturers have developed and marketed a wide array of security components and systems. These include sensors and security panels that operate on the traditional X10 technology of data transmission over AC power lines, but also a range of wireless devices that have greatly expanded the X10 system's capability and enabled it to interface with networks through an Ethernet port built into X10 components.

With power-line wired and wireless components, X10 security systems are actually hybrids that utilize both technologies to advantage in providing extensive, well-placed security protection and easily installed monitoring devices at convenient locations. Lighting control modules, the original automation devices for which the X10 technology was developed, can readily be incorporated as action response devices to any security alarm received. Appliance modules and other specialized devices can also be activated in response to a security signal or on a timed schedule as part of a monitoring routine.

COMPONENT INSTALLATION AND SETUP

Setting up the components of a home security system can be either the easiest part of the installation process, or the most difficult, depending on the type of system selected. In a wired system, pulling the necessary wiring is the labor-intensive part of the job and, once it's completed, components can be mounted and connected quickly. In a wireless system, no wire pulling is necessary (except for power connections to some devices), but the sensors and other devices must be positioned, mounted, and tested with the security panel to be certain that reception is good from every location.

The variety of components provided and available as options with each type of security system make every installation a custom design job, although common elements will be present in all of them. The three examples discussed in the following sections give a clear idea of what is involved in installing security system components.

9

Wired System Components

A basic security hardwired system, such as the one described in the following example and offered by a large offsite-monitoring security firm, includes some devices as standard requirements and offers others as options. The standard items include:

- One multizone security control panel (to which all sensors and response devices are wired)

- Three door sensors (to detect outside doors opening)

- One motion detector (for inside or outside use)

- Two emergency buttons (installed at convenient locations to summon emergency assistance)

- One digital keypad (to **arm** and **disarm** the system)

- One interior siren (to sound alarm in case of security breach)

- One back-up battery

- One yard sign and several window decals (noting monitored protection)

- One telephone connection link to **monitoring service**

- Around-the-clock monitoring service

All of the sensors and emergency buttons are wired to the security panel to warn of an intruder. If a security breach is detected, the siren is directed to sound and the monitoring service is automatically contacted. The service, in turn, contacts the homeowner, sends its own personnel to check on the breach, or summons **emergency response** from community services, according to the service contract instructions.

NOTE

The yard sign and window decals may seem minor pieces in the security system, but they actually contribute greatly to the accomplishment of its purpose. Most burglars "case" a home before attempting a break-in, either days before the crime or a few moments before starting it. A sign or decal noting that the premises have a security system is often enough to dissuade them from attacking. This is especially true if there are other equally attractive targets nearby that don't advertise the presence of a security system. By advertising the presence of the security system, the signs enhance the system's effectiveness by deterring burglary attempts rather than sounding an alarm when they occur. Many security systems offer these signs, and they should always be used.

In addition to the basic package, the following additional wired items can be added to this security system:

- *Glassbreak detector*—A wired device that detects when a window is broken. Not the same as a window sensor, which detects a window being opened

- *Smoke detector*—An alarm from this device causes the fire department to be notified immediately by the monitoring service

- *Pet-immune motion sensor*—An adjustable motion sensor that can be set to ignore infrared radiation changes caused by small animals, but still respond to any person intruding its range

- *Wireless key*—An RF device, similar to the keyless entry devices on cars, which can arm or disarm the security system with the push of a button from outside the home, thus eliminating the need to use keypad codes

Video surveillance is not available from the company that offers the just-described system and usually isn't included with monitored service contracts because of the cost of connecting a video signal to the monitoring station. Video cameras could be added with monitoring done inside the home by the homeowner who could summon assistance, if needed, through the monitored system's emergency buttons when any **intruders** were detected.

The installation of this system, as is the case with most monitored security systems, is done entirely by the monitoring company, which maintains a staff of professional installers to do the work. The installed equipment is leased, but after the expiration of a three-year monitoring contract, it becomes the property of the homeowner. The homeowner can then continue the service contract for monitoring at a lower rate, or drop the service and keep the equipment. Original cost for this system is about $900, including installation, but this amount is normally included as part of the monthly monitoring fee for the first three years of service. The monthly fee is about $48.

To install this system, the technician first determines the best locations for the control panel, the keypad, the motion detector, the door sensors, and the telephone connection point. Such a system doesn't include window sensors, but they could be added, if the technician determined they were necessary for the system to give adequate protection. Once component locations are identified, wiring for each of them is run.

Security wiring can be run on the surface of walls in the same manner as telephone wire (which it actually is), but the installation detracts less from the home's appearance if as much of the wiring as possible is concealed. Concealed wires are pulled through unfinished spaces (mainly attic and basement) and within walls to a point near the location of the security device, then brought to the surface through a small hole so that the wires can be connected to the device. Because many security devices are mounted on exterior doors and windows, it's often not possible to run their wiring within the walls, which often are solid masonry or insulation filled. In these situations, the wire should be run through the basement, if possible, to a floor hole at the base of the wall and directly below the location of the device. The wire is then pulled up through the hole and run on the wall surface up to the security sensor. Telephone wire staples or contact adhesive hold the wire in place on the wall surface.

You then label the control panel end of each wire as it is installed. Label the sensor end as well with a label that's identical to the one on the control panel end. For a better appearance, you can remove the labels from the sensor ends after (and only after) the wires are connected and the system is tested and working properly.

There's often a little more flexibility in the location of motion sensors, light beams, emergency buttons, and similar devices than there is with door and window sensors, which must be placed on the openings they secure. It's best to pull concealed wiring for all components before actually fastening them in place. By doing this, the locations can often be altered to better accommodate the run of the wiring. A few inches movement one way or the other won't usually make any difference in a sensor's function, but could be a great help in getting wiring to it through a convenient path.

Concealed wiring can be run in any unfinished spaces through holes drilled in the wood framing members. Wiring can also be run on top of attic truss plates (the bottom part of the roof trusses to which the ceiling wallboard is fastened), or stapled to the bottom of floor joists in the basement. If there's any danger of damage to the wire, it should be covered or run through holes drilled in the wood framing. Security wire can also be run through conduits installed for the home's AC wiring and through heating and air-conditioning ducts. In the latter case, the NEC requires that the wire be protected from damage, and be, according to NEC Supplemental Electrical Safety Standards 3.1.1, "plenum cables that pass the NFPA262/UL 910 Fire and Smoke Test." Points where the wire enters or exits the ducts must be sealed so as to prevent smoke from leaking from them.

Surface wiring should not be run in raceways unless multiple wires must be used because a single strand of exposed wire is less obtrusive than a raceway. Wiring can be run along the top of baseboards or the bottom of crown molding. It can also be run next to door and window casings and along the bottom of chair rail or similar decorative molding in the center area of a wall. Staples are the easiest method of fastening it, but adhesive makes a smoother appearance. Unlike Cat5 cable, telephone wire can be tightly bent to conform to shapes around which it is run. This is a useful characteristic when wiring in window casings and around doorjambs where the wire must often be tucked into corners and other tight areas.

Once the system wiring is in place, the components are mounted in place and connected to it. Security components generally connect with clamp screws that the wire ends are wrapped around. The screws are then tightened to make a secure connection. When wiring for networks, some slack in the cables is a good thing, but this isn't true with security wiring. All wire should be trimmed as short as possible before connecting so that it is flush with the windowsill or door frame on which the sensor is mounted. The less excess wire there is, the more professional the installation appears.

Door sensors should mount on the top part of the door casing on the opposite side from which it hinges so that any movement of the door inward opens the sensor switch. Window sensors can mount anywhere on the casing as long as the plate mounted on the window can be positioned so that any movement opens the circuit and signals a security breach.

Emergency buttons, which are intended to be pressed by the home's occupants in case of a problem, should be conveniently located where they can be reached easily, but won't be accidentally pressed by someone leaning against them. Most people want the buttons placed out of sight, such as under a counter, so they can be pressed unobserved. This is fine as long as the homeowner can remember easily where the button is and get to it easily in an emergency. For elderly persons or those with disabilities, a fully-visible location is often better.

Motion detectors and other sensors must be located so that they function according to design and are not triggered accidentally. This often requires a compromise between the ideal placement (the location that is safe from false alarms) and the easiest wiring spot.

The opposite ends of the wires are connected to the control panel according to the labels on each wire. If the security system plan calls for zones, connect the wires to make up the zones on the security panel for which you planned. If the plan doesn't have zones, connect the sensors in a linear fashion and leave the labels attached to each wire. Connect the telephone wire to the telephone system and hook up the alarm. Last, connect the keypad arming/disarming device to the control. When all components are wired, turn the system on, arm it, and test each sensor to be certain that it's working.

Wireless System Components

Some homeowners are willing to invest in the cost of hardwiring a security system, especially if the wiring can be installed as part of the home's original construction. For others, a wireless system is a better choice, both because of its lower initial cost and its comparative ease of installation. A typical basic wireless security system is offered by SkyLink Home Security and contains the following:

- One multizone security control panel

- Two door/window sensors

- One motion detector

- One keychain transmitter (for arming and disarming the system)

- One emergency dialer

- One backup set of batteries

An alarm siren is not included as a separate item in this system, but is a built-in feature of the security panel, which also activates the automatic dialer to summon assistance in case an alarm is triggered. Because calls for assistance don't go to a monitoring service, but to private telephone numbers designated by the user, up to nine numbers can be dialed in succession and the same **recorded emergency message** played to each when the line is answered. Cost for this basic system is about $300.

The security panel in this system can accommodate up to 24 different sensors. In addition to the door/window sensors and motion detectors included in the basic package, the following sensors and response devices are available and are compatible with the system:

- Smoke detectors

- Heat detectors

- Flood (water) detectors

- Light beam detectors

- Freeze detectors

- Light control modules

All of these are wireless and battery powered. They also signal their operational and battery status to the security panel. The security panel, dialer numbers, and recorded message are programmed by a coded process using the panel's keypad, but the system can also be connected to a PC and programmed from the computer screen using software provided. The monitoring function of the security panel can also be duplicated from the PC.

No video surveillance is included with such a wireless system, but wireless video cameras and transmitters, such as the one shown in Chapter 8, are available at reasonable cost for use with wireless security systems. Unlike the wireless sensors, however, the wireless transmission of video signals is usually confined to direct line of sight, and the receiver must then be wired to a monitor.

No wiring is necessary for the described system. Installation consists of placing and testing the components. All the sensors are battery powered, so no power lines are required for them. The security panel and call-in dialer are both AC powered and must be placed near an outlet. The security panel needs to be centrally located within the home because all the sensors broadcast to it and must be within its receiving range. Because no wiring other than AC power is needed, the control panel can be placed on a bedroom dresser or a kitchen counter. After the panel is located and the sensors tested for transmission to it, it shouldn't be moved significantly unless the wireless devices are tested again to be sure the new location is workable.

9

The call-in dialer can be connected to a telephone line through a splitter so that the same telephone jack can also connect a telephone extension. The call-in dialer has a 6-foot AC cord and therefore must be fairly close to an AC outlet, but the telephone connection line can be up to 25 feet long in order to reach a jack. No wired connection is necessary between the control panel and the call-in dialer. The panel communicates with it wirelessly if a call-in is required, and the dialer is programmed independently for the numbers to call and the message to play.

Sensors are placed on windows and doors in the same positions as wired units. Other types of sensors are placed so that they can function effectively, but no consideration needs to be given to their connections since all send wireless signals to the control panel.

When all sensors and the control panel are in place and equipped with batteries, the sensors should all be tested to be sure their signals reach the control panel correctly. In this type of wireless system, the sensors all broadcast on one frequency, but are equipped with individual unit numbers. This allows an alarm or low-battery signal to be identified to the sensor sending it so that appropriate action can be taken. The control panel is not set up for a zone system, but only to identify the responses of each unit. The testing should be done before the call-in dialer is connected so that accidental alarm signals won't trigger a call.

When the sensors are confirmed to be working correctly, the call-in dialer can be connected to the telephone line and programmed with the numbers it is to call and the message to be recited. The call-in dialer can be tested by programming it with the telephone number of another line to the home or to the home of a friend who can be made aware of the test beforehand. With only the one call number programmed, test the system by triggering an alarm from one of the sensors to see if the call-in dialer performs as intended. If it does, the test number can be deleted and replaced with the permanent call-in numbers the system is to use.

X10 Power-line System Components

X10 security systems are hybrid wired and wireless systems. The wired portions of an X10 system utilize the home's AC wiring, and components are connected by being plugged into an AC outlet or wired into a wall switch. No new wiring needs to be installed for an X10 system. The security panel of the system requires AC power to function and so must also have a battery back-up power source in case of power failure. The components that use the AC wiring for data transmission are battery powered and signal the state of their batteries so that no back-up power is required. The data transmission of an X10 system is not affected by whether or not AC current is flowing in the wiring: the systems sensors function with or without AC power.

The wireless components of X10 systems are also battery powered and can be installed without regard to a power source. Some broadcast directly to the system's security panel, but others (notably the video surveillance cameras) may broadcast only on a direct line of sight to a receiver some distance away. The receiver must then be wired into the security system in order for the broadcast signal to complete its journey. For video cameras, this means wiring the receiver with a video cable to a monitor or switch panel. For sensors that broadcast to a remote receiver, the receiver can be connected to the AC wiring through an outlet, and the signal received from the wireless unit is relayed from the wireless receiver over the AC power line to the security panel.

There are many X10 security system packages available on the market. Most include only the basic components that are required in almost every home security system. These can be augmented with an enormous array of additional devices to customize and complete each individual system. Figure 9-2 shows a typical basic system offered by SmartHome, a large supplier of X10 systems. The system includes the following items:

- One PRO2000™ security control panel (including alarm siren and call-in function)

- One motion sensor

- One handheld remote

- One keychain remote

- One X10 lamp module (for controlling lighting)

- Two window/door sensors

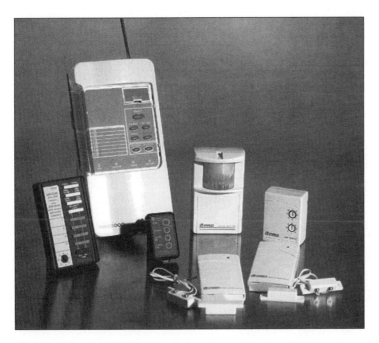

Figure 9-2   Basic X10 security system components

To install the X10 security system, the security panel is connected to the AC power through an outlet (the unit's AC cord also connects it for data transmission). The remote AC units (light modules and some sensors) are similarly connected by being plugged into wall outlets in appropriate locations. The wireless components function like any wireless system and are installed where needed. All sensors and lamp modules must be set with a house code and unit number so that their transmissions can be identified by the control panel. These numbers are set with selector wheels mounted on the units or by programming buttons located under the battery covers.

Wireless sensors should all be tested to be certain that they are within range of the receiver in the security panel. If any are not, an auxiliary receiver can be installed at a wall outlet within range of the wireless units. The auxiliary receiver can then relay the wireless transmissions via the AC wiring to which it is connected.

In addition to the basic system components, literally dozens of other devices are available to address every possible security need. Among these are:

- AC-current detector
- Appliance control modules
- Carbon monoxide sensor
- Electric deadbolts
- Electric door locks
- Freeze detector
- Glassbreak sensors
- Humidity sensor
- Keypads
- Light control modules
- Light sensor
- Listening devices and intercoms
- Outside alarms
- Pressure pads
- Proximity access sensor
- Smoke detectors
- Temperature sensors
- Video surveillance cameras
- Water detectors

In addition to all these sensor and response components, X10 systems have many control options available, including touch screens, telephone links, remote wireless controls, and computer links with software so that a system can be controlled and monitored on a PC.

ACCESSORY SECURITY COMPONENTS

In addition to the sensor and emergency response security systems described in earlier sections of this chapter, several accessory devices may be installed in both wired and wireless systems. These won't be wanted by all users, but they are regarded as essential by some.

Outside Alarms

Inside alarms alert the home's occupants to danger from intruders, fire, or other problems. Outside alarms alert the neighbors to the same dangers. Not all home security systems should have an outside alarm, but they're helpful in some cases. If the security system includes an emergency response notification device, that may be sufficient in summoning professional emergency help. Most call-in devices can include multiple numbers, so some neighbors, as well as the authorities, can be notified of trouble.

In homes that have an elderly or disabled resident, an outside alarm may help summon nearby assistance to get people out of the home quickly. An outside alarm can also have some deterrent effect on a burglar, both seeing it mounted on the home and hearing it if he or she decides to attempt a break-in anyway.

Outside alarms can be wireless or wired. They require AC power or a large battery to produce a high-volume sound. Batteries are quickly drained, so most use rechargeable units. Wireless alarms are usually battery powered, and wired ones use AC current from the home. Both types are connected in the same manner as an inside alarm on the system (and can be connected to the same circuit so that both alarms sound together). Wires that run through the outside wall of a home should be sealed to prevent heat loss and insect penetration.

A good feature to have on an alarm is a timed shutoff. Ten or fifteen minutes of sound is adequate to bring a response and, especially if it is a false alarm, that is all most people want to hear. If the alarm can be shut off only from the inside security panel, it's likely to fray nerves.

Controlled Access Components

Controlled access components (exterior door locks and garage door openers) can be installed independently of the home security system or as an integrated part of it. Independently installed locks and openers can be activated from outside the home by a keypad or other numeric code device mounted near the door or by a wireless access transmitter usually carried by the user. The doors can be accessed from inside only by manually unlocking and opening them.

Door access devices integrated into the security system can be accessed in the same manner as independent doors, but they can also be remotely locked down or opened from the security panel. In addition, their status (locked or unlocked) can be monitored in the same manner as the door itself can be monitored (open or closed) from the panel. This feature allows the homeowner to identify visitors via an intercom or video surveillance camera before unlocking a door. It also allows all access to the home from outside to be cut off during night hours or at other times when the occupants are away.

Independently installed access devices are most conveniently installed with the keypad or access device on the door itself next to the lock. This eliminates the need for any extensive wiring from the keypad to the lock. Most of these locks are integrated units with the keypad and lock combined in one box. These require a little custom fitting in standard doors, but no external wiring. Most are electric and require battery power (accessible from inside the door only), but a few are mechanical and work much like a combination lock with no electric power necessary. The mechanical type can't use a remote opener, but also don't require any battery replacement and are pretty much service free.

Electronic locks, which are operated by a solenoid in the lock mechanism, can have the keypad located on the door or on the wall beside the door. The keypad can either be wired to the door lock or open it by transmitting a wireless signal. The latter method is now more common and also allows the lock to be remotely activated by a keychain remote. The remote eliminates the need for entering any numeric code. It opens the lock at the push of a button. The keypad is still necessary, however, for persons who visit the home and don't have a remote key.

Almost all garage door openers are activated wirelessly by remotes normally carried in the family cars. They can also include a keypad access mounted at the side of the door and this unit can be either wireless or hard wired. Wiring a keypad from the side of the door to the opener doesn't require the same amount of concealment of the wires as would be necessary in the home's interior. The pad can usually be wired along with the **obstruction detector** that all powered garage doors have (or should have) as a safety precaution against the door being lowered on a person or object under it. Wireless keypads transmit to the same receiver that the remotes transmit to and are no more expensive than buying another remote. A plain remote should never be used as a mounted outside access device, however, because it offers no security against unauthorized use. The keypad assures that only those with the access code can open the door.

Gate Controls

Gate openers and locks are access devices much like garage door openers and door locks, but simply installed on devices at the yard perimeter. Driveway gate openers can be the rollback type that retracts a gate along the fence or wall on wheels or bearings, or the swing type that draws the gate open or closed on hinges in the traditional way. Both types are powered by AC electric motors (or motors attached to hydraulic units) and so must be wired to the home's electric service. Fence and wall gate wiring usually runs underground and so should be armored cable or similar wiring as the local electric code may require.

Any of the remote access devices that are used on doors can be also be used on a gate. The placement of the opening device is usually more remote from the entrance so that it can be used from a car window, but the access device can be wired or wireless. A keypad for visitors and keyless remote units for family members are often the preferred methods of controlling gate access. The family's remote units can often be programmed to also function as garage door openers, thus eliminating the need for two remotes.

Because they open and close slowly and are considerably larger than a car's width, security gates on driveways don't offer much security against unauthorized entrance. Someone can easily walk through a gate while it is open to admit a car entering or leaving the home. If security is needed at such gates, a video surveillance camera should be included to monitor anyone entering while the gate is open.

Fence and wall gates other than those on driveways rarely warrant openers. They're not used often enough, but if high security in the home's yard is important, they can be fitted with door/window sensors to monitor if they're opened.

UNINTERRUPTIBLE POWER SUPPLY

Many home security systems have back-up battery power, which can be used in case of power failure, or some type of fail-safe system that warns if power is low or sends an emergency signal in the event of power failure. This backup power method is sufficient for most systems, but if the home network has an uninterruptible power supply (UPS) for use in maintaining all or part of the LAN's operational ability during a power failure, this power backup can easily be configured to include the home security system. Security panels don't require a lot of power and so won't put a heavy drain on a UPS designed to supply and protect the network.

9

A 12- or 24-volt security panel powered by an AC adaptor can simply be plugged into one of the UPS outlets and the unit is supplied through the UPS. Wired sensors that are powered from the security panel are also powered by the UPS through the adaptor hookup. Wireless devices that are battery powered can't be connected to a UPS, but they also aren't affected by a power failure and shouldn't need back-up power. Their low-battery warnings should always be heeded so that they don't lose battery power in an emergency situation.

Home UPS systems are battery powered and have limited operating times under load. They're not designed to keep large systems running, only to give enough time for orderly shutdown so that no data is lost. The home security system won't tax a UPS nearly as much as the LAN, but when other devices deplete the UPS batteries, the security system shuts down as well. In the event of power failure, the operating limits of the UPS should be noted and the homeowner should be aware that the security system ceases functioning when the battery power runs low.

BACKUPS AND FAIL-SAFE SYSTEMS

Commercial security systems generally hold to the rule of **double protection** wherever possible so that if one level of security is evaded or fails, a second still picks up the emergency and sounds a warning. Home security isn't usually as deep as the commercial type because the risk of home fire and crime isn't usually as great. There are exceptions to that generalization, however, and some home situations may justify multiple levels of protection.

No system of security is absolutely **fail-safe**. The level of protection is increased by how many separate warning systems are in place and operating on the premises. If two detection systems are present and the chance of either failing is 1 in 1000, then the chance of both failing at the same time is 1 in 1,000,000. To get that 1 in 1,000,000 failure rate, both systems must operate entirely independently of one another so that the failure of one doesn't have any effect on the other.

Most home security systems don't have two independent warning systems, but they can have dual elements that substantially increase the protection level. Window and door sensors combined with inside motion detectors are one example of dual protection against intruders. Smoke detectors combined with heat detectors are a dual fire protection. If all sensors connect to one security panel, then the system as a whole isn't stronger than the security panel. But security panels, especially with back-up power, almost never fail and are almost never compromised by intruders, fire, or other hazards they protect against. Dual sensor protection may be justified for some homes, but one good panel is enough security for any system.

Other back-up features commonly available in home security systems, such as multiple call-in numbers, low-battery warnings, double-function locks, and others make even the average system virtually certain to detect danger and warn the home's occupants of it.

Security System Programming and Settings

The main items that need configuration in a security system are the security panel and the response devices it controls. All the sensors in a security system are normally set to signal any alert that they detect to the security panel. When the panel receives an alert signal, it then directs the response of various devices. If the security system includes other devices, these may need to be programmed individually.

Programming may be needed for keypad access devices, security panels, and timers and notification devices. Each must be programmed so that it makes the correct response to the input it receives. This chapter discusses these items next.

Keypad Access Devices

A keypad access device needs to be programmed for the codes that open it. Most systems allow for multiple codes to be used and, if this option is available, it's good to program a separate code for each family member. If one person's code is compromised, only that person has to learn a new one. One code can be reserved for visitors who need temporary access to the home. That code can then be changed whenever necessary without impacting the codes of any other family members.

Some access devices allow for a **duress code** (a code to be used in the event the person is accosted or threatened at the door) that opens the door, but also summons help. This is normally a single code that everyone with access can use and should be an easily remembered combination (12345, for example, or 77777) because it is used very rarely and may be forgotten, especially when under duress.

Some access devices can also be scheduled for times of day. Electronic keys as well as keypad systems often have this function. For some times of the day or night, the access device can be set to deny outside access to everyone or to allow it only to one master code number.

This feature can provide better security when the home is unoccupied and also when the occupants are sleeping. If the homeowner is away from the home for an extended period, the lockout times can be extended to cover around the clock and allow no one inside, or they can be customized to allow a house sitter in at specified times to feed pets and water plants.

Security Panel Programming

The main programming of a security panel is for the outside and inside arming of the security system.

Outside arming activates all security sensors to function while the home is unoccupied. The outside armed state is usually set by entering a command code on a keypad near the home's entrance when the occupants leave. The code can also be entered on the security panel itself. In either case, after entry of the code, a delay follows during which the occupants leave the home and secure the entrances. When the delay expires, the security system activates all sensors inside and outside the home, and sounds a chirp or bell to confirm that it is functioning.

When the home's occupants return and open a door to enter the home, another delay is activated during which the security system must be disarmed so that it won't interpret the homeowner's return as an intrusion. Typically, a 30-second delay is sufficient to disarm the system. During the delay, most systems sound an intermittent beep to remind the entering person that an alarm will be triggered if the system isn't disarmed. Exit codes, exit delays, and entrance delays can all be varied to suit the needs of the owner.

Inside arming activates perimeter devices in the security system and may activate some interior devices, but usually not all. Inside armed is the normal status for the security system at night while the family is asleep. All window and door sensors and any sensors and detectors in the yard are active. Some inside motion detectors, such as those that guard doors, might also be activated, but motion sensors covering broad areas of the home's interior are left inactive. These provide additional protection when the house is empty (outside armed), but create too high a risk of false alarms to use with inside arming because anyone moving in the home at night could set them off.

Inside arming is done from the security panel and involves no delays, when either arming or disarming the system, because the home's occupants can still move about freely with the security system functioning in this mode. Many systems allow inside arming to be set by a timer so that it activates every night at, for example, midnight and disarms automatically each morning at 6 a.m. Timing the system eliminates forgetting to arm it (or disarm it), and the schedule can be overridden manually with different settings when necessary.

If a sensor signals an attempt to enter the home, the usual programmed response from the security panel is to sound an alarm siren inside the home, and direct the call-in device to telephone for emergency assistance. This response is made whether or not anyone is present in the home. The panel is normally programmed to summon the police, but many police departments won't respond to automated alarm calls because so many of them turn out to be false alarms. If the police in an area won't respond to a security system call, the security panel can be programmed to call a family member or friend who is willing to receive the call and summon assistance or take other appropriate action. A fire sensor signal triggers an audible warning (which could be the same as the intruder alarm or different) and a call-in response to the fire department.

Fire and intruders are the two most common sensor signals for which a security system is programmed, but others may also be needed, depending on the other sensor devices the system includes. Water sensors and freeze sensors may require only an audible warning if the homeowner is available to correct the problem. If not, an automated response such as shutting off a water line or starting a heater may be programmed into the security system. Other responses that can be programmed into security systems include turning lights on in the home or the yard (or flashing them repeatedly as a warning), turning on speakers with recorded messages, turning on sprinkler systems, or shutting down utilities.

Some security systems have access devices with a **latchkey function**. This function programs the call-in device to notify a set telephone number (or two numbers) when a specific door of the home is opened during set hours. This feature can notify working parents that children have arrived home from school or that service personnel have arrived or left the home.

Time and Notification Settings

Security systems should always be set to the correct time of day so that timed functions occur at the hours specified. Many systems record the time of sensor alarms and notifications and the accuracy of these recorded events may be important in later investigations or insurance claims.

Call numbers programmed into call-in devices should be thought through carefully. A 911 emergency call is normally the first entry, if the jurisdiction where the home is located permits automated calls. Other call numbers should include relatives or friends who can respond appropriately. Call messages should give the address of the home, even if the call is going to someone who knows it. There's no need to give the telephone number, however, since emergency services record all incoming calls and the numbers from which they originate.

MAINTENANCE, SERVICING, AND RECOVERY

Security systems rarely break down. Their reliability is partly a function of good initial construction to meet the durability requirements of a quality system, and partly due to the fact that their components have few moving parts and a very low level of activity. They simply observe and occasionally signal conditions around them. Security system components almost never wear out. Most service and maintenance for these systems centers around their aging rather than mechanical or electronic breakdowns.

System Service and Maintenance

Security sensors are self-monitoring, sending a signal to the security panel periodically to confirm their functioning status. They also monitor their batteries and signal when power begins to drop off. Finally, if the condition that a sensor is monitoring changes, or something happens to the sensor to impede its monitoring of that condition, it signals an alarm. With this degree of self-monitoring, little external monitoring of sensors is ever needed. As long as their batteries are changed when signaled as low, sensors can function almost indefinitely without service.

Security panels also require little in the way of service or maintenance. They are generally AC powered and have back-up batteries that age over time. These should be changed every two to three years, even if never used. Like all electronic equipment, security panels can be damaged by power surges and spikes and should be protected by a surge suppressor on the AC circuit.

The response devices in a security system are the most vulnerable to maintenance problems and should be tested annually to see that they are still functioning well. Electronic speaker alarms rarely malfunction, but mechanical bells do and should be activated to confirm that they are working. The same is true of any mechanical response device that functions only if an alarm is signaled. Electric solenoids, motor driven actuators, and especially valves, left unused for a year or more, can corrode and become frozen in their static position. They should all be activated periodically to be sure that they can activate when signaled to do so by the security panel.

As is the case with all electronic systems, the enemies of electronic security systems are heat, dirt, power spikes, and water. Wherever any of these can attack a part of the system, it should be protected as much as possible and regularly monitored for possible failure. Among the specific points in a security system that should be checked are:

- Wireless window detectors (for heat damage to the transmitters from sunlight coming through the glass)

- Outside motion sensors (for dirt or obstructions that may block all or part of their fields)

- Inside motion sensors (for dust and spider webs blocking their fields)

- Outside wireless sensors (for weather damage)

- Break switches on window and door sensors (to detect anything inserted in the switch to prevent its opening)

- Make switches on pressure pads or similar devices (to detect anything inserted in the switch to prevent its closing)

- Locks (to be sure they don't stick open)

System Recovery

If a security system signals a fire through one of its sensors, that sensor should always be replaced when the system is brought back into service after the fire. Fire and smoke sufficient to set off an alarm should always be assumed to be sufficient to damage the sensor so that it won't function as well in the future. These sensors are not expensive and the safe practice is to replace the possibly damaged sensor with a new one.

Fire damage to other parts of the security system, especially a wired one, should be carefully checked and, if necessary, repaired. Heavy smoke can damage some sensors even if fire doesn't reach them. Water damage is also a real possibility, particularly for wireless transmitters on sensors and the security panel.

Other sensors in a security system are rarely damaged by being activated. They can usually just be reset and used again. The possible exception is a water sensor, which may be affected if submerged for a long period of time. Again this is not an expensive sensor, and to assure that it functions well, replacement may be the best policy.

If a security system is breached by an intruder, all of its sensors should be checked afterward to be certain that no attempt was made to evade or disable them. The fact that the system worked to signal an intrusion doesn't preclude the possibility that efforts were made to get around it in some other way.

False alarms can sometimes be very troublesome in security systems. Whenever they occur, they indicate the need for a service evaluation of the system. Eliminating the causes of false alarms makes the system more reliable and also makes the homeowner and emergency services more willing to rely on it.

False alarms can be partially prevented by careful wiring and installation so that signal failures don't occur as a result of poor connections. False alarms can also be generated from a number of innocent sources that are difficult to entirely eliminate. Outside motion sensors may be triggered by debris blowing in a high wind. Light beam sensors can be broken by a wandering cat or a sleepwalking child. Window and door sensors can sometimes be tripped by strong winds flexing the door or window inward slightly, thus breaking the sensor switch.

There's no sure way to entirely prevent false alarms, but they can certainly be minimized by noting the conditions under which they occur and carefully trying to trace the cause. Adjusting or repositioning a sensor may be all that's needed to correct the problem. If not, changing to a different type of sensor may be an answer or simply eliminating one troublesome sensor and covering the area with other devices in different locations. If false alarms happen only at night or only with sensors that can't be easily observed by those inside the home, the possibility that someone is deliberately testing the security system's effectiveness shouldn't be dismissed. False alarms shouldn't be used as a reason to turn off a security system.

CHAPTER SUMMARY

- ❏ Security systems are manufactured by many companies and are not standardized to any great degree. Systems bought as groups of components are most likely to function well together.

- ❏ Wired security systems have low data transmission speeds and can be wired with Category 2 (2-pair) wire or category 3 (4- or 6-pair) wire. This wire is smaller than high-speed network cable and can be concealed or run on the surface of walls without the need to use raceways.

- Wireless security system sensors are generally battery operated and require no data or power wiring. The security panels of wireless systems are AC powered, but can always be located near a power outlet and connected to it. They may include both a wireless receiver and a transmitter.

- Wireless security systems do not operate on the same frequencies used by wireless networks and none of the wireless network technologies or the power-line network technologies have developed security systems or products except the X10 system.

- Most security systems, both wired and wireless, are marketed as packaged sets of compatible products to which accessory devices can be added according to need.

- X10 technology offers the most extensive array of security-related products in both power-line wired devices and wireless systems. All X10 devices in both technologies are compatible with one another.

- Accessory security components that can be added to basic systems include alarms, access devices, gate controls, uninterruptible power supplies, and backup devices.

- Installed security systems must be programmed for access control, arming (outside and inside), disarming, timing, and notification schedules.

- Security systems are low-maintenance systems with few moving parts and low activity rates. Their components should be tested periodically to be certain that they can work if activated, and their power supplies should be regularly maintained.

- If a security system is breached either for a fire or a break-in, all its components should be carefully checked for damage before being placed back in service.

9

KEY TERMS

arm — Activate a security system so that its sensors are functioning.

break switch — A type of sensor that consists of a switch whose normal state is closed. If the switch opens (breaks), a security breach is signaled.

bypassed — In security systems, a situation where a sensor is made to appear in normal status, but in reality is not.

Category 2 telephone wire — A low speed data wire containing two pairs of solid core insulated wires. Named for its widespread use in wiring analog telephone lines.

Category 3 wire — Low speed data wire with the same composition as Category 2 wire but having either four or six pairs of wires.

disarm — Deactivate a security system so its sensors are not functioning.

double protection — In security systems, at least two devices monitoring a means of entry into a home so that if one is disabled or fails, the other still detects any intruder.

duress code — An access code (to be used in the event a person is accosted or threatened at the door) that opens the door, but also summons help.

emergency response — Any assistance delivered as a result of a security system call-in. Fire department, police department, and medical teams are all emergency responses.

fail-safe — A theoretical term for a security system that can't be disabled or bypassed. Not possible to achieve in actual systems.

false alarms — Any security breach not produced by a genuine security threat.

inside arming — Code or command that activates perimeter devices in the security system and may activate some interior devices, but usually not all. Inside armed is the normal status for the security system at night while the family is asleep.

intruders — Any unauthorized person trying to enter a secured home or yard.

latchkey function — A command or code that programs the call-in device to notify a set telephone number when a specific door of the home is opened during set hours.

line of sight — A term used to describe the location of wireless transmitters and receivers. It means that the receiver must be visible when viewed from the transmitter for the signal to be received.

monitored — In security systems, watched either by a person at a control console or by the electronic security panel itself, so that any change in status can be responded to.

monitoring service — A commercial service in which a company's staff continually watches a home security system via a telephone line linked to the home.

obstruction detector — A safety device that detects anything unusual under a descending garage door and stops the door's downward movement.

outside arming — A code or command that activates all security sensors to function while the home is unoccupied.

recorded emergency message — A message recorded on a security system call-in device; it plays after a device calls a preset telephone number and gets a connection. Some systems dial multiple numbers in succession and some can play multiple messages.

response devices — Security devices that can perform an action when commanded to do so by the security panel. They may sound alarms, call for assistance, activate systems, or perform other tasks.

security breach — An event that occurs any time a sensor signals a change of status to a security panel.

switcher — A multiple video input panel with a single output to a monitor and a switch that allows the monitor to display any video input selected.

REVIEW QUESTIONS

1. Companies that provide remote access service with a security system usually provide 24-hour-a-day _____ of the home security system.

2. Security systems can be wired with what type of wire?

    a. Category 2

    b. Category 5

    c. Category 6

    d. Category 7

3. Category 3 wire is like Category 2 wire except it contains _____ or _____ pairs of wires instead of two.

4. Bypassing a sensor means making it appear to be working normally when in fact it isn't. True or False?

5. Security system wiring can be bent sharply, stapled to the surface of walls and spliced, but network data lines can't. Why aren't the security system wires as fragile as network data lines?

6. Two window or door sensors can be wired together to one security panel connection provided they are wired in _____.

7. What is a zone in a security system?

8. A video camera in a security system is wired to a monitor or switch panel using what type of cable and connector?

    a. Category 2 with RJ-45 connectors

    b. composite video cable with RCA connectors

    c. Category 5 with RJ-45 connectors

    d. MIDI cable with USB connectors

9. Wireless sensors can transmit through walls and obstructions to a security panel, but wireless video transmitters usually must transmit on a _____ to their receivers.

10. Wireless security systems work on which of these technologies?

    a. HomeRF

    b. WiFi

    c. Bluetooth

    d. none of the above

11. What does arming a security system for outside or away status mean?

9

12. Wired security systems work on which of these technologies?

    a. HomePlug

    b. HomePNA

    c. X10

    d. all of the above

13. Why isn't back-up battery power needed for sensors?

14. A duress code is _____.

    a. a back-up access code to be used if you forget the main one

    b. an access code that reads the same in either direction

    c. an access code that opens the door and summons emergency help

    d. an access code for visitors so that they don't learn the main one

15. Timed access devices may exclude some or all persons with valid access codes during certain hours. True or False?

16. An exit delay on a security system allows the user to _____ before the security system arms.

17. Inside arming of the security system is used when people are not inside the home. True or False?

18. When a security panel receives a breach signal from a sensor, what does it normally do?

19. What is a latchkey function on an access device?

20. To prevent damage from electrical surges and spikes, a security panel should be powered through an_____ _____.

21. If a fire sensor detects a fire, what should be done with it when the system is reset?

    a. The homeowner resets the sensor.

    b. The homeowner relocates the sensor.

    c. The homeowner replaces the sensor with a new one.

    d. The homeowner replaces the sensor's battery.

22. X10 security systems are usually hybrid systems. What does this mean?

23. Raceways are not usually used in wiring security systems because
_____.

    a. they are too large for security system wires

    b. they interfere with the security system's transmissions

    c. they are too small for the security system's wires

    d. they can't be installed on windows

24. Security system wiring isn't armored because the risk of it being cut is very low. True or False?

25. An independent access device may use a keypad, but it is not connected to the _____ _____.

HANDS-ON PROJECTS

HANDS-ON PROJECTS

Project 9-1: Set up a Motion Sensor

In this project you will set up a wireless motion sensor and connect it to a lamp so that when the motion detector signals motion, the lamp turns on. For this project you will need access to an X10 MS14A or MS 13A Motion Sensor, an X10 RF transceiver (model RR501 or TM751), an X10 lamp module (any model), and a lamp.

1. Set the X10 lamp module to house code A and the unit code to 1.

2. At one end of a classroom or other large room, plug the X10 lamp module into an AC outlet.

3. Plug the lamp into the module.

4. Plug the RF transceiver into an AC outlet at the opposite end of the room.

5. Remove the holding screw from the battery cover of the X10 motion sensor and remove the battery cover. If the sensor doesn't have batteries installed, put two AAA batteries in it, but don't replace the battery cover.

6. The sensor's default setting is A1, so it doesn't need to be reset. Test the sensor by pressing the House button once. The unit transmits "device on" and the red light on it flashes. Press the Unit button once. The unit transmits "device off" and the red light flashes.

7. Place the motion sensor in a position at least six feet from the floor and facing out into the room.

8. Stand aside from the sensor for a full minute to let it arm itself and set a heat pattern.

9. Walk past the sensor and observe the lamp at the opposite end of the room. It will turn on and remain on for one minute (the default setting on the sensor).

10. Walk in front of the sensor again and watch the light come on. Stand as still as you can for one minute and see if the light goes off with you still in front of the sensor, but not moving.

11. If the light goes off, move again and see how quickly it comes back on as the sensor detects movement.

HANDS-ON PROJECTS

Project 9-2: Change the House and Unit Codes and Light Delay on a Motion Sensor

In this project you will use the same equipment as in Project 9-1 but will change the house code and unit code to which the sensor broadcasts, and the length of time it transmits.

1. Unplug the lamp from the X10 module and the module from the AC outlet.

2. Set the house code on the lamp module to D and the Unit Code to 3.

3. Plug the module back into the outlet and the lamp into the module.

4. On the motion sensor, press and hold the House button until the red light flashes and then blinks the current setting (A = 1 blink).

5. Immediately release the button and then press it four times to set the house code to D. On the last press, hold the button down for three seconds. The red light blinks the number of the house code you set. Release the button.

6. Press and hold the Unit button until the red light flashes and then blinks the current setting (1 = 1 blink).

7. Immediately release the button and then press it three times to set the unit code to 3. On the last press, hold the button down for three seconds. The red light blinks the number of the unit code you set. Release the button.

8. Set the delay on the sensor for two minutes. To do this, press the House button once. The red light flashes. Immediately press the Unit button and hold it until the green light turns on. After three seconds, the red light blinks the current delay setting (one blink for one minute).

9. Immediately release the Unit button and press it twice to set the delay to two minutes. On the last press, hold the button down for three seconds. The red light blinks twice showing the delay is set at two minutes.

10. Follow Steps 7 through 11 in Project 9-1 again to test the sensor and determine if it turns the lamp on using the new house and unit codes, and whether the lamp stays on for two minutes.

HANDS-ON PROJECTS

Project 9-3: Set up a Wireless Video Receiver with a TV

For this project you will need access to a television set with a video input jack (on the front or back of the television), and an X10 wireless camera system (Model VR36A or equal) which contains a wireless video camera and a wireless receiver, both with power supplies.

1. Set the television up in one end of a classroom or other large room. Plug it into an AC outlet.

2. On the bottom of the wireless receiver, find the channel switch and set it to C.

3. Connect the receiver's power supply to the jack in the back of the receiver. Set the receiver on top of the television.

4. Plug the power supply in an AC outlet.

5. Connect the receiver to the television using a video cable with RCA connectors at both ends. Plug one end of the cable into the receiver and the other into the video jack of the television.

6. Turn the receiver on with the switch on the side of the unit.

7. Raise the antenna panel and turn it so that the receiver side faces toward the opposite end of the room where the camera is placed.

8. Turn the television on and select video input.

9. Adjust the antenna of the receiver, if necessary, to get the least interference on the screen. You will know that the interference is decreasing when the picture quality is more pleasing to the eye.

9

Project 9-4: Set up a Wireless Video Camera

For this project you will need access to an X10 wireless camera system (Model VR36A or equal) which contains a wireless video camera and a wireless receiver, both with power supplies.

1. Set up the camera tripod on a table or other support at one end of a classroom or other large area. Mount the camera on the tripod using the screw mount on the bottom of the camera base.

2. Plug the power supply jack into the adapter cable attached to the camera. Plug the power supply into an AC outlet.

3. Carefully remove the rubber plug on the base of the camera. Set the channel switch under the plug to C using a pen point or other pointed object. The switch position at the bottom of the base (where the cord exits) is A. The position at the top is D.

4. Adjust the camera antenna so its broadcast side is toward the opposite end of the room where the receiver is.

5. Point the camera where you want its image to be. The camera is now transmitting.

6. Check the television and receiver you set up in Project 9-3. Is the television showing a picture from the camera? If it is, adjust the antennas to get the best quality picture you can.

7. If there's no picture, check the settings for the camera and receiver to be sure they match and check all connections to be sure they are secure. Check the television to be sure it's set on the input channel. Troubleshoot the system using the instructions provided with the equipment until you get a clear picture on the television screen.

Project 9-5: Configure a Motion Detector to Trigger an Alarm

In this project you will set up a wireless motion sensor and connect it to a control panel so that when the motion detector signals motion, the control panel signals an alarm. For this project you will need access to an X10 MS14A or MS13A Motion Sensor and an X10 Wireless Security Console (Model PS561 or similar).

1. Check to be sure the control panel has a backup battery (9 volt) installed. Connect the panel to an AC power outlet that is always on. Extend the unit's antenna fully and place it on a table or desk.

2. Set the panel's house code dial to C.

3. Set the slide switch on the upper right of the panel to Install.

4. Press the House button on the motion detector once. The unit transmits "device on" and the red light on it flashes. The control panel's first available zone indicator light goes on, and the panel sounds a tone. This indicates that the panel has received the signal from the motion detector and assigned the detector to a zone.

5. Set the panel's slide switch to run.

6. Place the motion sensor in a position at least six feet from the floor and facing out into the room. Face it away from the control panel.

7. Stand aside from the sensor for a full minute to let it arm itself and set a heat pattern.

8. Walk past the sensor and listen for the control panel. It will chime a tone indicating that the motion sensor has detected motion. You can repeat the test after a minute. The sensor has a built-in delay so that it won't transmit an additional motion signal for about 20 seconds. This helps extend the unit's battery life.

9. Stand away from the motion detector for a minute. Press the Arm button on the control panel to arm the system.

10. Walk in front of the motion detector again. The alarm will trip and sound.

11. Press the Disarm (bypass) button on the control panel to shut off the alarm.

Project 9-6: Configure a Call-in Dialer to Make a Programmed Call

In this project you will configure a call-in dialer to call a phone number in response to an alarm warning triggered by the wireless motion sensor and control panel you set up in Project 9-5. For this project you will need access to an X10 MS14A or MS 13A Motion Sensor, an X10 Wireless Security Console (Model PS561 or similar), and a telephone line with RJ-11 plugs on both ends.

1. Check to be sure the control panel has a back-up battery (9 volt) installed. Connect the panel to an AC power outlet that is always on. Extend the unit's antenna fully and place it on a table or desk.

2. Connect an RJ-11 phone line plug into the back of the control panel. Connect the other end of the line to a live telephone jack. If the only jack available already has a phone connected to it, use a splitter to divide the jack connection so that both the phone and the control panel can be connected to the same line.

3. Set the slide switch on the upper right of the panel to Install.

4. Press the Prog (program) button on the panel. Enter the telephone number you want the dialer to call on the keypad at the lower left of the panel. When you've entered the 7-digit number, press the Mem (memory) button, then press the 1 button on the keypad to store the number in the first call position.

5. If you want to enter a second number, press the Program button again and follow the procedure in Step 4. When the number is entered, press the memory button followed by the 2 button to store the second number. (Caution: Only program a phone number if the owner is aware that you're doing so and expects to receive the called message. Do not program a police or other emergency number.)

6. Connect an earphone to the control panel's earphone jack on the side of the unit. Keep the slide switch set to Install.

7. Press the panel's Record button and watch for the Record light at the bottom of the panel to come on. When the light comes on, record the message you want the dial-in caller to give when it dials the phone number. For this test, the message might be, "This is a test of the Smith's security system. Please call back 555-1234 to confirm that you received this call."

8. Set the control panel slide switch to Run. The message you recorded plays back. If you need to rerecord it, repeat Steps 6 and 7 to do so.

9. Press the Arm button on the control panel. Wait a full minute for the system to arm itself.

10. Walk in front of the motion detector. The alarm sounds and the call-in dialer calls the number you entered and delivers its message when the phone is answered.

11. Disarm the system and wait for the person you called to call you back with confirmation that he or she received the security message.

9

CASE PROJECTS

Case Project 9-1: Design a Security Response for a Hearing-impaired Person

You've been asked to install a security system in a home occupied by a family with a child who is severely hearing impaired. The child has her own bedroom on the second floor of the home. The security system is configured to warn of fire and intruders with a warning alarm and emergency response call-in, but this child probably wouldn't hear the warning alarm. Research what other visible warning device could be installed in her room or in other parts of the home that would give her warning of an emergency. Describe in a short report what you would do to set up such a warning response.

Case Project 9-2: Diagram a Video Surveillance System

In the Hands-on Projects, you set up a motion sensor and a video camera. These devices can work together. If you were installing a security system with a video surveillance camera, describe or diagram how you could connect the motion sensor, X10 wireless receiver, X10 module, video camera, video receiver, and television so that the video camera would turn on only when someone walked in front of the motion sensor. Would any additional equipment be needed or could the video system be set up with only the items noted?

Case Project 9-3: Use a Security System to Identify an Intruder

A client with an installed security system contacts you with a problem. He believes that someone is entering his home while the security system is activated, turning off the system, and searching for confidential information in his home office. The intruder then resets the security system and leaves the home. This could only be done by someone who knows the arming and disarming codes to the security system. Describe what could be done to the programming of the security system to prevent such an intrusion from happening again. Also describe what could be done to identify the intruder without permitting him to actually enter the home again.

Case Project 9-4: Design a Swimming Pool Security System

You've installed a security system for a client who has a swimming pool. The home owner is often away leaving the home and pool unattended. Many small children live in the neighborhood and often ask to swim in the pool. When he's home, the home owner allows this, but he fears that one of the children could come while he's away and drown in the pool. Standard motion sensor alarms don't work well around the pool because heat reflected from the water causes continual false alarms. What type of device can you recommend installing in or around the pool that could warn of someone about to enter the pool?

10

TELECOMMUNICATIONS FUNDAMENTALS AND INSTALLATION

After reading this chapter, you will be able to:

- Describe the characteristics of analog and digital telephone communication systems and the differences between them
- Define the characteristics of the various local telephone systems
- Identify the components of telephone systems and describe their functions
- Describe the installation of wiring and components of various telephone systems
- Define external services offered through local and central telephone systems

Telecommunications systems are both an independent voice communication system in the home and a data transmission system that forms an integral part of the overall home technology network. In this chapter you will learn about analog and digital telephone communications and the capacities of each. You will understand the various types of local telephone systems and how they are integrated with home networks. You will learn about the basic components from which telecommunications systems are assembled and how these devices function. You will also learn how to install telephone systems and set up their operation for maximum efficiency. Finally, you will learn how to configure the services that are offered by local and central telephone systems.

TELECOMMUNICATIONS SYSTEM TYPES AND CHARACTERISTICS

Telecommunications began with an analog device which quickly developed into a world-wide analog system. The telephone was invented in 1876 for the transmission of speech over wires. Speech is analog sound and calls on telephone lines were exclusively analog signals from the 1870s until the 1960s.

Telephones were the first means of transmitting voice messages over wires. They became the first mass communication system, quickly surpassing the first digital communication system, the telegraph, which never achieved wide consumer use because of the complexity of its Morse code. Telephone use grew until the demand for ever greater voice transmission began to exceed the capacity of analog lines. By that time, digital transmission of voice and other data had been developed to a point where it could provide the additional capacity needed in the telephone transmission system. Digital telecommunications systems now have taken over much of the transmission load for both voice and data, but analog systems continue to function in many areas.

Analog Telephone Communication Systems

What we know as Plain Old Telephone Service (POTS) is an analog system of phone lines and equipment. Even today, some forty or more years after the introduction of digital voice transmission, most home telephones are still analog devices that are connected to analog phone lines. Once the phone line reaches from the home to the nearest telephone exchange, it likely connects to a digital transmission line, but the local "last mile" of phone line from the telephone exchange to the typical residence is still analog.

As the need for more and faster communication accelerated in recent decades, the analog phone system was taxed to provide the necessary service. Analog signals move relatively slowly when carried in physical media such as copper wire and cable. Telephone voice transmission signals travel at speeds from about 300 Hertz (cycles per second) to 3300 Hertz. Although this might seem relatively fast when compared with, for example, the speed of an electric motor, it's downright snail-paced when compared with digital data speeds over a network that are measured in millions of Hertz (MHz) or wireless data transmissions that are measured in billions (GHz).

Analog voice communication signals are also subject to weakening due to resistance in the wires on which they travel, and to interference (noise) caused by electrical equipment, power lines, and even some electric lights. In a telephone conversation, this noise is heard as **static** on the line. The weakened signal of an analog transmission must be strengthened periodically by an amplifier. Unfortunately, an amplifier cannot separate the noise from the voice part of the signal and it consequently amplifies both. Voice conversations that have been amplified several times usually can still be understood because the human hearing system is very adept at extracting the correct meaning of spoken words from background sounds. Data transmissions sent over analog lines don't always fare as well because the data is interpreted by machines who don't "hear" as well as people. The result is that noise in analog data transmissions frequently causes errors.

Data transmission using analog modems is limited to about 56,000 bits per second when receiving and about 33,000 bits per second when sending data. The analog public switched telephone network operates at 2400 baud. A **baud** is one complete cycle or wave in a transmission signal. A baud starts at zero voltage, goes up to maximum positive voltage, comes back to zero, goes to maximum negative voltage, and finally returns to zero voltage. A 2400 baud line carries current that completes 2400 of these wave cycles each second. The baud rate refers only to the frequency of the current. It doesn't indicate the amount of data that is transmitted on the line. A 56,000 bit modem uses technology that allows it to put 24 bits of data on each wave of a 2400 baud line (56,000 divided by 2400 = 24). The line current is still running at 2400 baud even though 56,000 bits of data per second are being transmitted on it. That is about the limit for an analog data line, however. To send more than 56 Kbps of data requires a shift to digital transmission technology.

Voice and data can both be sent on an analog line at rates up to the limits that analog lines can transmit. Within a home the requirements for voice communication by telephone will almost never exceed the limits of analog technology. **Frequency division multiplexing** even allows analog lines to carry multiple conversations or data streams simultaneously. This is accomplished by dividing the available analog frequencies on a line and sharing them among different voice and data transmissions. Thus, one voice data stream might be running on a line at 2400 baud while a second was running at a higher baud rate and a third at a still higher rate. Multiplexing allows multiple telephone lines to be installed in homes and businesses without the need to install additional wiring from the telephone company office to the home.

If voice links were all that were required of phone lines, analog alone would probably be sufficient, at least within the home. But most homes now also require data transmission over the same telephone lines that handle conversations on the telephones. If the phone lines are even occasionally filled by analog voice transmissions, which can't be delayed or interrupted without interrupting or garbling a real time conversation, they can't meet data transmission requirements in addition.

To have enough capacity for the system to handle both voice and data needs, additional lines must be installed or the capacity of the existing lines must be increased by transmitting digital data on them. Not only must the data be sent digitally, but the voice transmissions must be sent digitally as well. If either were left in analog form and sent with that technology, they would consume so much of the line's capacity that there would be insufficient capacity left for the digital transmissions.

Changing both voice and data transmission to digital format gives a huge increase in capacity for a telephone line. The majority of homes are still using analog lines for telephone voice transmission and for data lines which connect analog 56 Kbps modems to ISPs, but the shift to digital transmission lines which can carry anywhere from three times to dozens of times the data of an analog line is accelerating. The demand for increased data transmission rather than additional voice lines is driving this transition.

10

Digital Telephone Communication Systems

Digital data transmission over telecommunications wires has several advantages over analog, the two largest being that it is much faster and much less error prone. As it does on a network, digital data on a telephone line travels in packets. It follows the rules of established protocols so that it can be controlled and sent to the correct address and interpreted when it arrives there. Voice data and other analog sounds are converted to digital form by sampling techniques similar to those used for digital sound recording. The coded audio signals are sent as digital data and decoded at the receiving end so that they can be "played" through a speaker as sound. Data sent by digital transmission (whether it is digital audio data, text data, or video data) travels far faster and with far fewer errors than it would as analog data.

As with analog signals, digital transmissions also weaken and pick up noise as they travel, but the amplification process used to strengthen digital signals is different than that used for analog. An analog amplifier must strengthen an existing signal including the data tones, variations, pauses, and noise that occur in it. The amplifier can't change the data signal or any corruption that's come into it; it can only amplify it and send it on. The distance that analog signals can travel is limited by the amount of noise that the signal picks up. Eventually the noise level becomes so high that the analog voice or data signal can no longer be understood.

Digital signals consist only of zeros and ones (binary numbers) which are very simple to read and to duplicate. A digital amplifier in a data transmission line is called a **regenerator**. Instead of amplifying the existing signal, the regenerator simply reads the signal and generates a duplicate signal of all the data in it, but none of the noise. The clean duplicate signal is then sent on the line in place of the weakened one. Digital signals thus move more cleanly with less chance of error than analog signals because they can be regenerated periodically without any noise being present in the regenerated signal.

Capacity in telecommunications is described as **bandwidth**. Analog transmission or POTS, whether voice or data, is **narrow band**, each line being limited to one voice channel or one data channel at a maximum speed of 56 Kbps. By contrast, a BRI ISDN line, though still narrow band in the digital data transmission scale, provides for two voice or data channels, each capable of carrying 64 Kbps and a third channel for control signals that can carry up to 16 Kbps. A **T-1 line**, which can be carried on two pairs of wires such as Cat5 or similar cable, can carry up to 1.54 Mbps of digital data. This means that it can simultaneously transmit 24 data or voice conversations, each containing 64 Kbps of data. T-3 lines and other broadband technologies, transmitted over fiber-optic cables or radio frequencies, can reach capacities ranging from 44.7 Mbps to 13.22 Gbps.

For most home telephone users, a Digital Subscriber Line (DSL) which provides digital data capacity from 128 Kbps to 7 Mbps or even more is adequate for both voice and network data requirements. Cost for a DSL line is usually less than for a T-1 connection, and DSL service is becoming available in ever wider areas as telephone companies install additional lines. Where DSL service is not available, users generally retain their analog telephone service and obtain digital data service through a cable company or a satellite hookup. Both cable and satellite services are more widely distributed than DSL because neither is subject to the distance restrictions from a central telephone exchange that limit Digital Subscriber Lines.

There are several varieties of DSL, not all of which are available in some areas. Rural areas are unlikely to have DSL service available because of their distance from a central exchange. Distance of the user from the telephone company central office is a determining factor in the availability of all DSL lines. Table 10-1 shows different DSL line types and the varying distance limits, typical speeds, and characteristics that each has. Users should check carefully on the type and speed of service they will receive when purchasing a DSL line.

Table 10-1 DSL types and characteristics

DSL Service	Data Rate Upstream/Downstream	Central Office Distance Limit	Voice	Comments
Asymmetric DSL (ADSL)	1.76/1.54 Kbps 640 Kbps/7.1Mbps	18,000 ft. 12,000 ft.	Yes	Uses one wire pair
DSL Lite	384 Kbps/1 Mbps	18,000 ft.	Yes	Uses one wire pair
G.SHDSL	192/192 Kbps 2.3/2.3 Mbps 4.62/4.62 Mbps	40,000 ft. 6,500 ft. 6,500 ft.		Uses one or two wire pairs
High-bit-rate DSL (HDSL)	1.54/1.54 Mbps	12,000 ft.	No	Uses two wire pairs
HDSL2	1.54/1.54 Mbps	12,000 ft.	No	Uses one wire pair
Symmetric DSL (SDSL)	1.1/1.1 Mbps	24,000 ft.	No	Uses one wire pair

10

LOCAL TELEPHONE SYSTEMS

The first telephones were wired to each other so that a conversation could be transmitted between them. A few telephones could be wired in this manner, but the cost and labor of wiring every telephone user to every other user quickly became excessive. By the year after the telephone was invented, **switchboards** had begun to appear. Individual telephones weren't wired to one another any longer, but only to the central switchboard. An operator there answered every call and connected the requesting party to another telephone subscriber through the switchboard. By 1891 automatic switching gear was patented which could automatically connect calls through relays according to the number dialed on the rotary phone. No operator was required.

This section describes the various local telephone systems that were developed to provide local area switching services. At first this switching service was provided by the telephone company, but competing systems now provide most local switching.

Centrex Systems

The central switching exchange or **Centrex** was the forerunner of **private branch exchange (PBX)** telephone systems located on site at many businesses. While switching was done at the telephone company's central exchange, every telephone line coming into a home had to connect to that exchange. A line could have several **extensions**, but a call could be placed on only one of them at a time because all extensions had only one line connecting to the exchange where it could be switched to the number called. PBX systems have become very common in business establishments and have taken over much of the local switching once done by Centrex systems. In turn, PBX systems now face strong competition from another control method known as a **key system**.

Centrex service, which uses telephone company-supplied and maintained switching equipment, is still used on 10% to 15% of U.S. telephone lines. Centrex switching has some advantages, especially for large organizations with facilities spread out over a wide area. None of the Centrex equipment needs to be located on the customer's premises, although some of it can be if there's a cost or efficiency advantage in doing so. All switching can be done from the telephone company's central exchange. This allows incoming calls to be routed directly to individual extensions without passing through an operator or receptionist. Likewise, outgoing calls can be placed directly without an operator or need to dial for an outside line. All outgoing calls are also identified and billed to the extension that made them. There are no "common line" calls.

Centrex systems are best used by organizations that have many telephones in many locations. The telephone company can provide the wiring infrastructure to connect separate locations without any need to install private lines. It can set up the organization's service so that internal calls are routed to other extensions using an internal dialing sequence and outside calls are routed correctly using the public telephone number system. Local governments, hospitals, large educational institutions, and businesses with multiple locations or divisions are among the types of organizations who find Centrex systems the most efficient and economical for their needs. Smaller users favor PBX systems for the same reasons.

PBX Systems

A PBX is a private on-site switching system that routes calls within a single entity in the same manner as a central exchange routes calls on the public telephone system. The site for a PBX can be an entire organization such as a business or educational institution occupying one building or several. It can also be a small business occupying only a suite of offices or an individual home.

A PBX system controls telephone lines and switching from the **demarcation point** or demarc, the place where the incoming lines from the telephone company connect to the internal wiring of the home, to extensions and other devices throughout the house. Figure 10-1 shows the inside (user side only) of a demarc with three incoming telephone lines wired in it. The lower two lines are voice lines and are wired with old style, single-strand wire (see the section on connecting telephone equipment in this chapter for details about old and new style wiring). The top line is a data line and is wired with new style wire.

Figure 10-1   An open three-line demarc box on a residence

Telephones are connected to the PBX rather than directly to outgoing telephone lines. The telephone lines leading out of the home to the demarc point are also connected to the PBX. Calls from one telephone to another in the home are connected through the PBX and calls going out to the public telephone system are connected to an outside line through the PBX. Incoming calls on any line can be routed to any extension telephone within the home, again through the PBX.

Mid-size businesses and other organizations find PBX switching meets their needs more effectively and economically than Centrex. Calls going out of the PBX are carried on **trunk lines** to the central exchange where they are routed on to their destination. Incoming calls travel on the same trunk lines. Most organizations with a PBX use a T-1 line for their trunk. A T-1 line can carry up to 24 voice or data lines simultaneously. Those 24 lines can be shared by 100 or more voice users (only a few of whom would be making calls simultaneously) and still provide data connections for the business as well.

PBXs are **ground start systems**. This means that when a telephone receiver connected to the PBX is lifted to make a call, the PBX responds by sending a **dial tone** to the phone and also by requesting that an outside trunk line from the PBX to the central station be reserved or "seized" for the call. If the extension dials an access code (usually 9) for an outside line, it is connected to the seized trunk line, the caller hears another dial tone provided by the telephone company over the trunk line, and the call can be dialed. If the call is to an internal extension on the PBX system, it is routed directly to the called number and the seized outside line is released. Incoming calls are also sent over a "grounded" line seized by the central exchange when it receives the incoming call destined for the PBX.

Few homes have enough telephones or enough user demand to warrant installation of a PBX, even a small one. A large home having one or more offices with multiple lines and several additional home lines might want a PBX that could monitor outgoing calls from the business extensions in order to track expenses for tax purposes. Trunk-line service of less than a T-1 line, however, would hardly ever justify a home PBX, especially when another type of switching system is available for smaller users. Figure 10-2 shows the back (connection panel) side of a "home-size" PBX system with a voice mail attachment on top of it. This system, made by DataLabsUSA, allows for three incoming trunk lines and up to eight residential extensions. It provides all standard PBX features including fax detection which routes incoming fax calls to a designated extension.

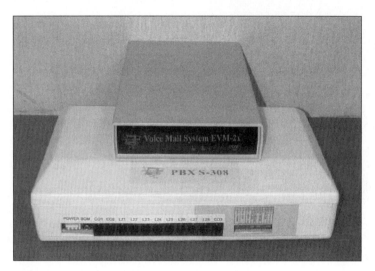

Figure 10-2   Small PBX and voice mail system suitable for home use

Key Systems

Key systems are designed for smaller organizations with fewer users than a mid-size business. Key systems began when the old AT&T company began installing individual telephones connected to multiple lines. These phones had buttons or keys which could connect them to any one of the several lines and a hold button which kept a line that was in use connected while another line was used by the same telephone extension. The line buttons each had lights to show when their line was in use so that another extension user wouldn't push a button for a busy line, unless of course, he or she wanted to listen in on that conversation.

On these early key systems, all the extensions could connect to all the lines simply by pushing a connect button to access the line. No access code for an outside line was required because there was no PBX to request that an outside line be seized for a call. Key systems are **loop start systems** rather than ground start as a PBX is. This is the major difference between the two systems.

In a loop start system, when a telephone receiver is lifted to make a call a dial tone is sent from the central office to show that a path is open for the call, but the line is not seized until the call is actually placed. Likewise, an incoming call is sent to the destination number by any available path with no line being seized from the central station to the receiver in advance. This means that it's possible, though unlikely, that a user on a key system could pick up a telephone to make a call and find someone already on the line calling her or him, even though the telephone hadn't rung. The incoming call simply arrived over the available path slightly before the outgoing call could be placed. The loop path was filled first by the incoming call which would have to end before the outgoing call could be completed.

Key systems with multiple loop start lines are well suited for small business users and homes with more than one line. All phones have access to all lines and can use any available line for outgoing or incoming calls. Key systems have an **intercom** button that allows them to make internal calls to other extensions without accessing an outside line. The internal call simply goes to the called extension over inside wires.

Hybrid Systems

Newer key systems have most of the features of a PBX system and in fact may be hybrid systems that offer multiple-line buttons with holding feature as well as the grounded trunk lines with a dialed outside access code used in PBX systems. These hybrid systems also offer many convenient features including:

- Hold buttons for keeping a line open

- Speed dial and redial buttons for rapid dialing of frequently called numbers

- Voice mail alert lights

- Caller identification screens

- Cordless telephone sets

These features and the multiple-line capacity of key systems and hybrids make them ideal for home use where multiple-line service is desired.

Both PBX systems and key systems carry voice calls over **circuit-switched lines**. This means that all the data in a call follows the same path on the telephone network and the line over which it travels is held open for that data for the full duration of the call. Telephone systems have now converged with computer networks over which data is sent in packets that travel by different routes to the same destination. Manufacturers of PBX systems and key systems have now equipped their products with data transmitting capabilities using Internet Protocol. The result is **Voice over Internet Protocol (VoIP)** telephone service.

Voice over IP (VoIP)

Data moving on a LAN or other network travels in packets which adhere mainly to the Internet Protocol (IP). Voice data packets can also travel on the same networks, provided they follow the same protocol.

VoIP systems must perform a number of tasks rapidly and flawlessly in order for voice telephone conversations to be sent over a network. When a voice call is made over IP, the sending system must encode the analog voice signal into digital form, compress the digital data to reduce its size, assemble the compressed data into packets with appropriate headers and trailers, and transmit the data onto the LAN. At the receiving end, the data packets must be received on the LAN, reassembled into the order they were sent in, decoded (decompressed and converted from digital to analog voice), and sent to a speaker (in a telephone or in a computer). All of this must be done as nearly as possible in real time because the telephone conversation is a two-way process and any appreciable delay in sending or receiving the transmissions results in periods of silence between every statement of the two speakers.

Data packets sent over a network don't need to arrive in sequence and can easily be sent again if a collision causes one to be lost. Voice data packets, however, are made up of parts of a real-time conversation and need to be reassembled at the receiving end in proper sequence and in real time. A lost packet or delayed transmission often causes the reconstructed voice to sound choppy or "clipped" and is difficult to understand. The biggest challenge for VoIP telephone transmission is to prevent the telephone conversations from being degraded significantly below the quality of analog voice transmissions.

To avoid significant degradation of VoIP transmissions, the network must have sufficient capacity so that only a small part of its data packets suffer collisions and must be sent again. The voice data packets must also be sufficiently compressed (uncompressed sound files are large) so that they can be sent and converted back into sound in real time, despite the delay caused by any lost packets. Providers of VoIP equipment are continually working on these two requirements in order to improve the quality of VoIP transmissions. New electronic chips that more efficiently compress audio and put it into packets for network transmission are being developed. Some of these new systems for VoIP also provide a means for voice data packets to have priority over other data packets so that the continuity of transmissions can be better maintained when traffic on the network is heavy.

Most home network users with IP-based phone systems still make the majority of their calls over the **public switched telephone network (PSTN)**. Intercom calls between nodes on the LAN are made over the network and long-distance calls can be made to a receiver node on another LAN that has appropriate software for decoding the data into voice. The installed number of such IP-telephone-equipped LAN nodes is not yet large, but interest in the technology is high because of its potentially low cost for long-distance phone service and its ability to make greater use of network infrastructure in place of new telephone wiring. The reliability of VoIP telephone systems is not yet as high as PBX or key systems, which don't crash anywhere near as frequently as the typical computer system. Manufacturers are working on this problem, and the use of VoIP in business and in home LANs is slowly increasing.

Remote Access Methods, Standards, and Protocols

VoIP systems can deliver telephone service to standard analog telephones, to PBX- or key system-connected multifeatured phones, or to softphones built into a computer with software. **Softphones** are software programs that display phone features (hold button, caller ID, message waiting) on the computer screen and route the calls through a handset or an earphone and microphone wired to the computer. In addition to enabling VoIP phone capability with a minimum of new equipment (softphone programs work with standard PC peripheral audio components), softphones also can provide remote phone access. If the computer is a wireless laptop, then the softphone system can go with it anywhere within the range of wireless reception. For the home user, this extends the telephone system to the full limits of the wireless hubs on the LAN without the need to install cordless phones or carry any additional equipment.

Another means of extending telephone service to all parts of a home or yard is through the use of limited range **cordless phones**. These phones are transceivers (transmitters and receivers) which operate on radio frequencies in the 900 MHz band and 2.4 GHz band. Calls on these phones are relayed back and forth between the wireless handset and the base unit in a two-way radio broadcast. The handsets are battery powered, but many base units require AC power through a low-voltage transformer in addition to the line voltage in the telephone system.

Neither cordless phones nor wireless VoIP softphones are secure from eavesdropping by significantly interested parties. Calls on both types of phones can be received by anyone within range who has suitable equipment. The home user of wireless telephone equipment should be as careful as the business user not to give personal information, identification numbers, or any other nonpublic data over a wireless phone call.

TELEPHONE COMPONENTS AND FEATURES

The telephone is a fairly simple electronic device, especially when compared to modern computers, audio systems, and other devices that are used in communications. Telephone service, however, is one of the most universally available communications systems on Earth and its widespread use has resulted in many refinements in the basic unit over the years. Many pieces of peripheral telephone equipment providing enhanced telephone service or adding additional features to its basic communication function have also been developed. The basic telephone's design and some of the important improvements made in telephone service and equipment since its invention are described in this section.

10

Telephone Fundamentals

A telephone delivers (plays) audible sound derived from electronic signals received over wires and also converts audible sound into electronic signals that are then sent over the same wires to another telephone. Figure 10-3 shows the main parts of a modern telephone, which are still fundamentally similar to those that would be found in an early telephone. In fact, most antique telephones from the 1900 era, if plugged into a present-day analog telephone circuit, would still work.

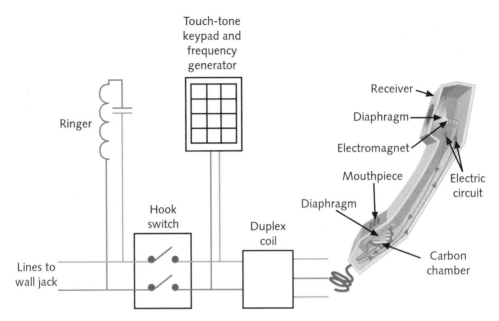

Figure 10-3   Telephone working parts

The handset of a telephone contains a diaphragm attached to an electromagnet at its upper end. Together they form a speaker which reproduces sound from the signals coming to it on the electric circuit in the handset. At the bottom of the handset another diaphragm set in a carbon-filled chamber acts as a microphone to convert sound waves into analog electric signals which travel to the base circuitry of the telephone.

The base of the telephone contains a duplex coil through which the wires containing both the incoming and outgoing speech signals pass. This device blocks outgoing speech signals from feeding back into the receiving speaker so the telephone user won't hear his or her own voice echoing in the phone's speaker when talking. Other devices inside the telephone base are the hook switch, which disconnects the telephone from the outgoing line when the handset is hung up on it; the ringer, which remains connected to the outgoing line and rings when an incoming current (call) on the line activates it; and the touch-tone keypad and frequency generator, which generates the tone signals to dial numbers as its keys are pressed.

Many telephones have additional features added to them for enhanced service, but all telephones have the basic components described above and all work in the same manner. Telephones are analog devices only. If their voice signals are sent in digital form over networks, they must be encoded (converted) into digital form after leaving the analog telephone at the sending end of the call, and decoded (reconverted) into analog signals again at the receiving end of the call before the signals are delivered to the receiving phone.

Extension Dialing

When telephones were all switched through Centrex systems and each telephone was connected to an outside line, extensions could be added so that one line was connected to several phones simultaneously, but conversations between extensions on the same line were not possible. There was no way to switch one extension to connect directly with another without also being connected to the outside line. Since both were already connected to the same line, if two people picked up extensions on a line, all either would hear was the dial tone sent from the Centrex denoting that it was ready for them to make a call.

PBX systems, which are connected to all the extensions in a home, allow any extension to be connected to any other without the need of also being connected to an outside line. The PBX simply switches the two extensions together as an internal phone call. Each extension has its own internal number that can be used only by another extension on the system. Outside calls come from the PSTN using the assigned number of the telephone. Internal calls use the extension number (usually one or two digits in a home system) to connect one extension to another.

Phone-line Extensions and Splitters

Extension phones can also be added on a single line in a home by using splitters. **Splitters** are devices which allow two (or even three) telephones to be connected to a single wall jack. In this arrangement, both extensions ring when a call is received and either or both can answer it and hear the incoming call since they are connected to the same line. Only one splitter extension at a time can make an outgoing call, however, because there's only one outgoing line on which it can travel. The other extension can listen in on the outgoing call, but can't make another until the first is completed and disconnected.

In addition to phone extensions, a splitter also allows a line to be connected to a phone and a peripheral device such as a fax machine. In this arrangement, all incoming calls are answered first by the fax machine, which must be equipped to determine which calls are fax messages. If the incoming call is not a fax message but a voice call, the fax machine allows it to ring through to the phone. Outgoing fax messages are also sent over the line from the fax machine. The extension phone is only used for outgoing calls when the fax machine is not in use.

Another peripheral that can be attached as a splitter extension is a computer, giving it a primary or backup connection to an ISP or allowing it to receive and record voice mail and fax messages on its hard drive. In the former use, the computer only accesses the phone line when an ISP connection is needed. At all other times the line is available for use as a regular phone extension for placing and receiving calls. Such a computer extension hookup might also be used for an emergency assistance call by the computer as part of the home's security system. An emergency link would rarely be used, but needs to have constant availability of a phone line in case a distress call is required.

10

If the computer is used for messages (voice mail or fax), then incoming calls are answered by the computer so that it can process messages. When the computer is on the line, the other extension should not be picked up or it will interfere with data transmission to the computer. A line-in-use light should be placed on the phone line in this arrangement so that users can avoid interrupting data transmissions.

Key systems are like the early Centrex systems in that they can't connect one extension to another directly because all the internal lines in a key system are also connected to outside lines. If a caller on an extension pushes a line button, he or she gets the dial tone from the Centrex. The caller can then call another extension by calling through another outside line to the extension. This amounts to placing an outside call to the Centrex and then having it routed back to the home on a second line as an incoming call. Such calls require relatively long travel for the signal and tie up two phone lines to make one extension call; it's not a very efficient way to talk to someone at the other end of the house. A more effective solution was clearly needed.

Intercom

To get around the problem of Centrex-routed extension-to-extension calls, all key systems have intercom capability. An intercom link is simply an internal method of connecting two telephones in a home without connecting either to an outside line. If there are four incoming lines to a home with a key system, each phone has four line buttons so that it can connect directly to any of the incoming lines. It also has a fifth button for intercom calls. This button doesn't connect to an outside line, but to a switch panel that is also connected to each of the other intercom buttons on the other telephones in the home. As with the PBX system, each extension has a number and any other extension can dial it directly, but only on the intercom line. If an outside line button is pressed for an intercom call, it can't connect because those buttons only connect the phone to an outside line, not to the inside switch that links all extensions.

Intercom service is very useful in letting users in different areas of the home talk to one another without either person moving to the other's location. Some systems allow conference intercom calls (three or more participants) and many include a paging feature.

Paging allows one extension to call another and talk over a speaker on the called extension before the extension handset is picked up by anyone. A person looking for someone can thus page them at various extensions around the house and yard (some paging features allow all extensions to be dialed for a page simultaneously) without having to shout their name or conduct a physical search for them.

Caller-line Identification

The rise of telemarketing and other unsolicited (and unwanted) telephone calls has made caller line identification (caller ID) a high-demand feature of home telephone service. **Caller ID** is a feature made possible by a signal sent by the telephone company with an incoming call which identifies the calling number and its registered owner. Telephones with electronics capable of reading this signal display the caller ID information on a small LCD screen. The called party can then decide whether to accept the call or not.

Call Conferencing

PBX and key systems both permit conference calls between three or more persons. Both systems accomplish this feature in similar ways. In either system, by connecting the two outgoing lines to one another the three parties are all joined on the same circuit and can talk to one another. Conference calls involving more than three persons simply repeat the steps needed to add another line and caller, using the PBX or key system to connect the new individual into the call.

Video Conferencing

Video conferencing, sending full-motion picture images with a telephone call, requires a lot of bandwidth, high-level compression of the video data, and **multiplexing** (combining different types of data from multiple sources on a single transmission path). Video conference software has to transmit data at rates of 128 Kbps up to 768 Kbps in order to provide acceptable quality video reproduction at the receiving end. The compressed video in conferencing systems still isn't equal to the quality found in broadcast systems. It travels at a slower pace and runs at slower speeds (fewer frames per second) than commercial video. The audio portion of a video conference is also compressed by using slower sampling techniques, skipping silent times, and predicting future sounds based on previous ones. These improvements in compression techniques and the use of slower video make video conferencing practical using software that requires transmission speeds of only 128 Kbps to 384 Kbps.

10

Videoconferencing is now available to home network users who have adequate bandwidth to support the software. All those participating in a video conference must have common software and be able to connect to one another on the Internet or via telephone lines. The high-speed data rates of video conferencing require multiplexing the voice and video portions on the same transmission line in order to maintain the synchronization and timing of audio and video portions. Multiplexing is done with both analog and digital data, but the compression and speeds necessary for video conferencing require both the audio and video to be digital.

Call Restriction

Most PBX and key systems provide **call restriction** options for outgoing calls, and some can also block specified incoming calls. Outgoing restrictions can be applied to any or all of the phones internally connected to the system. Incoming call restrictions are nearly always universal (blocked from entering the phone system, hence not available to any extension). A few systems allow specified incoming calls to automatically route to a specified number in the system. Among the outgoing call restrictions available are:

- Total restriction (no outgoing calls permitted)

- Long-distance calls restricted (all calls out of the local area code are restricted or only specified codes permitted)

- Call-time restrictions (outgoing calls permitted only during specified hours)

- International calls restricted

- Specific telephone numbers restricted

Those systems that can restrict incoming calls usually do so with a recorded message such as "This telephone subscriber does not accept calls from . . ." or similar wording. For the restriction message to be played, the call must be connected to the PBX or key system. On long-distance calls, this results in a minimum charge to the calling party, even though the call did not actually reach the called party. Among the call-in restrictions that some systems can invoke are:

- Total restrictions (no incoming calls accepted for specified extensions)

- Calls without caller ID (or on which the ID has been deactivated or blocked)

- Long-distance calls (or calls from specific area codes)

- Calls from specified telephone numbers

Voice Mail

As with call restriction features, **voice mail** functions were originally offered by the central phone company. All digitally processed and stored voice mail systems trace their beginning to the VMX Corporation's original system first installed in 1980. All current manufacturers of Centrex, PBX, and key systems with voice mail still license their software from the successors of the first patent holder.

Voice mail is usually compressed in order to conserve storage space on the hard drive. Messages are indexed in sequential fashion for playback, but the data is stored randomly as files on the hard drive. If the drive fills, no more messages can be stored until space is cleared by erasing some of the older ones.

PBX and key systems performed voice mail functions as a stand-alone telephone system feature until recently. Now voice mail is changing from an independent telephone feature to **unified messaging** in which storage is located on a PC's hard drive and the messages include not only voice mail but also fax and e-mail. Cisco System's Active Voice messaging software is a unified system that operates on Microsoft Exchange. Other manufacturers are developing or have announced unified messaging software. The convenience and efficiency of unified messaging allows the home user to review all messages at one time. The systems can perform several levels of sorting to bring up the most time-sensitive messages or the most important first.

Most new PBX and key systems now offer unified messaging as an option, if not a standard feature, and use a PC as a storage and display console. Unified systems store calls as voice files, faxes as graphic files, and e-mail as text files. The voice mails can be played on the PC's sound system and the faxes and e-mail displayed on the computer screen and then printed, if necessary.

Fax Machine Communications

Fax machines are digital devices that operate on analog telephone lines. The analog telephone line's capacity limits the speed of a fax machine to about 54,000 bits of data per second, and at this speed, some errors in data transmission are likely. However, the top speed of current machines is 33.6 Kbps.

A fax machine views a page of printed material (text or pictures or both) as a bit-mapped graphic. It divides the page into tiny dots (about 300 dots per inch) arranged in rows across the page. It scans the page to determine whether each dot on its surface is white or black (there are no grays or other colors in fax transmissions), then compresses the digital data it derives and sends it over the telephone line to another fax machine. The receiving machine reverses the process: it decodes the digital data back into white or black dots on the page and then prints the black ones in their correct positions on the bit-mapped graphic, thus reproducing the original printed page.

All fax machines scan documents in the same manner, but some have memory chips which enable them to store the scanned data before sending it. These machines can scan documents more quickly than those which don't have memory chips because they aren't limited by the speed at which the data can be compressed and sent over the telephone line. The scanned information is simply stored in memory, and later sent on the telephone line as rapidly as the line can carry it. Fax machines can have memory capacity for a single-page document or for many pages. The larger the machine's memory capacity, the faster it can scan a document and store the data, but the speed of the fax transmission is still limited to the capacity of the analog telephone line over which it's being sent.

Fax machines print the documents they receive in different ways. The least expensive printing process is called thermal printing. It uses a heat-sensitive paper on which the fax machine prints by using a row of heated elements across the width of the paper. The heating elements do not actually touch the thermal paper, but they pass very close to it and the heat transfer is sufficient to print on the paper. Plain paper fax machines use the same printing technology found in laser printers or ink jet printers. Instead of receiving printing data from a computer, the fax machine receives its data over the telephone line and with it creates the image for the laser printing module or ink jet technology to print.

When sending or receiving a document, a fax machine uses the full capacity of a telephone line. No simultaneous voice transmission is possible. But fax machines don't operate constantly, especially in home environments, and this means they can usually share a telephone line that is used for voice calls when not occupied by a fax transmission.

Many fax machines are designed for this type of line sharing. They have built-in circuitry that determines whether an incoming call is a fax transmission or a voice call. If it's a fax message, the machine activates to receive and print it. If not, it allows the call to ring the attached telephone so that the voice call can be answered. In many fax machines a voice telephone is also built in so that incoming calls that are not fax transmissions can be answered on it and outgoing calls can be made. Fax machines that don't have a built-in telephone can still share a telephone line by being connected to a telephone jack through a splitter which also has a telephone attached.

10

Telephone Installation and Configuration

Since telephone service began, the equipment used has continually increased in complexity and capacity to meet the demands of users. Looking back, it's easy to see with perfect hindsight that early wiring and infrastructure didn't provide for nearly enough future expansion. This is especially true in residential telephone service where single line analog telephone service wired with two wire telephone line is the norm. Wiring and installation of telephone systems today should benefit from past experience and provide not only for more capacity than is currently needed, but more than current technology levels suggest will ever be needed. Experience has shown that the use of data transmission systems (telephone, network, radio, and television) has continually increased at a pace that far exceeded the most optimistic predictions. There's no reason to think that home telephone service ten years from now won't need a hundred times the capacity it needs now.

Telephone equipment is wired and installed in much the same manner as network and other electronic equipment. The same care should be taken in wiring to use adequate cabling and install it to standards, make data-secure connections, and test systems carefully to be certain that they function correctly.

There are literally thousands of devices available for use in home telephone networks. This section discusses only a few of the basic installation procedures that you need to know for all home systems. The installation instructions for any telephone system device should always be studied and followed precisely to ensure that the individual requirements of the equipment are met.

Connecting Telephone Equipment

Analog telephones have long been wired with cable consisting of two or four copper wires. The wires were single strand and were not twisted into pairs. A single telephone line requires only two wires and so a four-wire cable could connect two lines. Because the wires were not twisted, cross talk interference was common. Persons speaking on one telephone line could often hear a low-volume background conversation, which was usually someone talking on the other line. Figure 10-4 shows an old-style wiring block wired for two lines with single strand wire. The round four-wire cable, secured with staples, can be seen coming in from the right side of the photo. The individual wires lead out to an extension phone above the block, but not visible in the picture.

Figure 10-4 An old-style telephone block wired for two lines

This old-style wire has a color code that is slowly disappearing in favor of the color coding used for twisted pair cables that connect high-speed data networks. Table 10-2 shows this older wiring color scheme for a four-wire or a six-wire cable. This color code is still important to know as you will likely encounter many existing telephone systems wired with it.

Table 10-2 Old-style wire colors for telephone lines

Wire Pair	Wire 1 Color	Tip/Ring	Polarity	Wire 2 Color	Tip/Ring	Polarity
1	Green	Tip	Positive	Red	Ring	Negative
2	Black	Tip	Positive	Yellow	Ring	Negative
3 (6 wire only)	White	Tip	Positive	Blue	Ring	Negative

The designations "tip wire" and "ring wire" come from the old 1/4 inch phone plugs (see Table 10-2) that were used to connect phone lines in operator-run PBX boards. Each jack connected a phone line and so had two wires running from it. The tip wire was the positive wire and was connected to the tip of the plug. The ring wire was the negative wire and was connected to the ring or side of the plug. This traditional designation has remained in use even though its original meaning no longer applies.

The old color code is now being replaced by one easier to remember. It is shown in Table 10-3.

Table 10-3 New-style wire colors for telephone lines

Wire Pair	Wire 1 Color	Tip/Ring	Polarity	Wire 2 Color	Tip/Ring	Polarity
1	Blue/white	Tip	Positive	Blue	Ring	Negative
2	Orange/white	Tip	Positive	Orange	Ring	Negative
3	Green/white	Tip	Positive	Green	Ring	Negative
4	Brown/white	Tip	Positive	Brown	Ring	Negative
5	Slate/white	Tip	Positive	Slate	Ring	Negative

There are additional pair colors for this color code, as there were for the older one, but home telephone systems aren't likely to use cables with more than five pairs of wires.

Today telephone wiring is installed using twisted pair cable. Category 3 cable is adequate for analog telephone lines and contains at least two pairs of wires which can be used to wire multiple telephone lines. In keeping with the practice of installing excess capacity, new telephone wiring, especially if it is to carry any digital transmissions, is usually done with Cat5 cable. Basic telephone wiring is not difficult, but should be performed carefully to ensure good connections and that lines will meet their data transmission requirements.

Pulling Cat5 or similar cable for telephone connections should be done using the same techniques and following the same cautions as cable pulled for a network. Even though the data transmission requirements for the telephone lines may not be as high as for the data lines, installing the cable with the same (maximum) adherence to standards ensures that it performs with peak efficiency and can be used in upgraded systems with higher data requirements later.

RJ-11 Connections

The Bell System telephone company developed the Universal Service Ordering Codes (USOC) specifying the wiring configurations for the series of Registered Jack (RJ) types used to connect residential telephone equipment to the public network. Figure 10-5 shows these wiring configurations for one line, two lines, three lines, and four lines. An **RJ-11 jack** is the standard single line telephone connector. An **RJ-14 jack** is the standard 2-line connector.

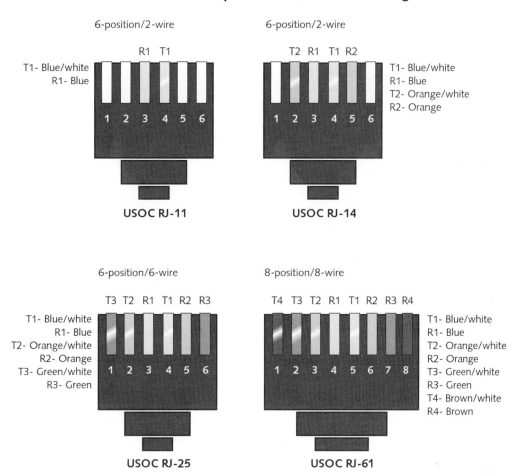

Figure 10-5   Telephone plug and jack wiring standards

These color codes for telephone wiring differ from those used for RJ-45 jacks and plugs, but the procedures for terminating cables to jacks and plugs are the same. Wires must be set in the plug according to the color pattern shown in Figure 10-5, but all the other steps in the terminating process are the same. Wires not used in a multiple-pair cable when terminating it to a jack or plug should be cut off at the plug or jack entrance so that they do not interfere with connected wires or produce short circuits in the cabling. Figure 10-6 shows some of the major parts used for wiring telephone lines. Moving clockwise from the upper left, the photo shows an RJ-11 plug, 4-pair wire, a splitter for doubling extensions from an RJ-11 plug, and an RJ-14 4-wire jack with its cover removed.

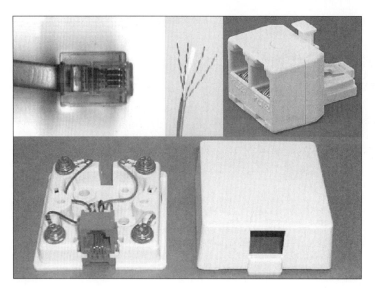

Figure 10-6   Telephone wiring components

If wiring is being installed for a network and for telephone lines, a single Cat5 or similar cable can be used to accomplish both connections. Only two of the Cat5 cable's four pairs of wires are used for network connections. The remaining two pairs can each be used to wire a telephone line in a combination jack. If one cable is used for both types of connections, the RJ-45 jack must be wired using only the two pairs of wires actually needed for the data connection. The other two pairs are not included in the jack connection, but are left free to be wired to an RJ-11 or RJ-14 jack as telephone connections.

The colors of the pairs that must be used for the telephone lines will not follow the USOC standard, but will be one or both of the twisted pairs not used for the 2-pair data connection. You must keep careful track of which pair is used for each telephone line, and connect the lines identically at both terminations.

Connection Blocks

Multiple telephone lines can be connected to a centrally located **punchdown block** or patch panel that is connected by a trunk cable to the telephone company's lines at the demarc point, which is usually located on the outside of the home.

Punchdown blocks are the usual means of centrally terminating telephone lines and connecting them to the trunk lines, but these blocks are used primarily for commercial installations which have many lines. Figure 10-7 shows a large 110-type punchdown block with connections for 100 pairs of wires, as well as a 110C-4-4 block designed for four wire pairs and a 110C-5-5 block designed for five pairs. The smaller two are the ones likely to be used in home installations.

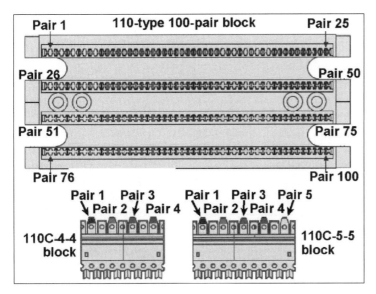

Figure 10-7 Large and small punchdown locks for telephone connections

For home installations which usually won't exceed three or four lines, a patch panel termination may be preferable to a connection block. Patch panels provide for easy reconfiguration of the wiring, and because they are connected through RJ-11, RJ-14, or similar jacks, also assure good connections for the multiple stranded wires found in Cat5 or other multiple-pair cables. Punchdown blocks connect by insulation deformation when each wire is punched down into the block. They work best with single-strand wire which is strong enough to accept this type of connection without damage to the conductors.

EXTERNAL SERVICES

Some telephone services that are available on PBX or key systems still require some participation by the telephone service provider. For homes that don't have a local phone system, the central telephone company may provide the entire service. Telephone companies charge a monthly fee for each of these services, so obtaining all of them can eventually cost more than purchasing a local system that has the features built-in. This is especially true if the home has multiple incoming telephone lines because, unlike a local telephone system that can apply its features to all the home's telephone lines, the outside telephone provider charges a fee for each line that subscribes to these services.

Caller ID

Caller ID is always provided in part by the telephone service company because it's the only entity that can supply the caller information on incoming calls. Local equipment must have the necessary electronics to read and display the caller ID signals. If a local system has caller restrictions on incoming calls, the incoming lines must have caller ID signals on them because these signals are the means which the local system uses to determine if a call should be allowed through or blocked.

Call Blocking

Central telephone company call blocking is limited to an inserted message that states which calls are not accepted by the subscriber. The law requires that callers who are included in a blocked group hang up when they hear the blocking message, but if they don't, the call goes through and the subscriber has to pursue the violation through a complaint to the service provider. A local system also receives blocked calls, even after playing a recorded message that they're not accepted. But a user won't ever actually receive one of these blocked calls because the local system simply doesn't put them through to any phone extension where they could be answered. The calling party will hear a ring signal on his phone, but no ring sounds in the home. The local system either disconnects the call or holds it until the caller hangs up.

Three-way Calling

Three-way calling provided by the telephone company has the advantage of only using one line from the home that originates the call. If a three-way conference call is set up by a local system (PBX or key), it uses two lines to bring both of the called parties to its home connection. If more than three parties are included in a call, a local system must have a new line available to add each one to the call. The telephone company has no such limitations. Through its central switching facilities, it already has a line connected to every phone and can connect any number of these lines into a single call.

Call Waiting

Call waiting on a single telephone line can only be provided by the telephone company. The company can keep both lines open to their station until the user disconnects them, but only one conversation at a time can reach the destination phone. Voice mail service is also available from the phone company on both lines of a call-waiting setup. Because the telephone company's voice mail system is located in the central office, it doesn't need to route a waiting call to the home; it simply redirects it to the subscriber's voice mail located in its offices.

Emergency Response System

A home with a security system that has an emergency response function should always have an available outside line on which an emergency call can be sent. Whether the call goes to a commercial security service or to a family member or friend, the security system must always be able to get a clear line to make the call or calls immediately. In rare cases, this may mean that the local telephone system needs to disconnect another call in order to free a line for an emergency.

Since some incoming calls can't be immediately disconnected by the receiver (the line is seized by the originator of the call and won't be released until he or she hangs up), the safest line to put emergency call-in equipment on is one that is used exclusively for that purpose and no other. If keeping an open telephone line for only one possible call in years seems a needless expense (as it will to most), the next safest line for a call-in response is one on which only outgoing calls are made. If the home has a separate line for the home LAN

ISP connection, that's the line to also put the emergency call-in device on as well. It's possible that an emergency call might interrupt a data transmission one time, but that small risk is more than offset by having a line that can be instantly cleared when the emergency response call is activated.

If an independent line or an outgoing-only line isn't available, emergency response devices can be connected to any other line coming into the home. The only security risk in using a regular voice line is that an incoming call, which the emergency response device can't override, might be on the line and delay an emergency call for a time. A few cases have even been reported in which burglars called into a home in order to occupy the phone lines so that an emergency call-in couldn't get through, but criminals this clever are rare.

CHAPTER SUMMARY

- POTS is an analog voice telephone system which has been built as a worldwide network over a period of about 130 years. Its lines can also transmit data at a maximum speed of 56 Kbps.
- Digital telephone transmission of voice and data began in the 1960s and vastly expanded the data-handling capacity of POTS. Digital transmission of data, including voice, text, and video, can now be achieved at speeds ranging from 128 Kbps to 7 Mbps or more.
- The Public Switched Telephone Network (PSTN) provided central exchange or Centrex services to connect telephone calls nationwide. Centrex handled all switching until local systems were developed to provide organizations with internal switching.
- Local PBX and key systems now handle 85% of telephone switching. PBX connects all local phones through a switchboard to trunk lines that go to the central exchange. Key systems connect multiple lines directly to Centrex and also provide intercom service.
- Digital telephone transmission is now expanding over the Internet as VoIP that provides fast and economical service to customers who have suitable transmitting and receiving software. Some users have integrated softphones on their PCs and receive all telephone service by computer.
- Telephones are analog voice devices with a microphone, speaker, and digital keypad for tone dialing. In addition to basic calling service, other functions offered on telephones include intercom, call waiting, caller ID, split lines and extensions, conference calling, call restrictions, voice mail, and video conferencing.
- Fax machines are digital devices that operate on analog telephone lines. They send printed pages containing text and graphics at speeds up to 54 Kbps.
- Telephones are wired with two wires per line and do not require a high-speed data cable. Most telephone wiring now being installed uses high-speed cable because digital transmissions do require it and telephone systems are becoming more digital and high speed.
- RJ-11 and RJ-14 jacks and plugs are the standard terminators for telephone cables. They are wired according to a color code which is not the same as that used for network cables and RJ-45 jacks.

10

❑ Some telephone services are still provided wholly or partially by the central telephone system. These include caller ID, call blocking, three-way calling, call waiting, and emergency response call-in.

KEY TERMS

bandwidth — In telecommunications, the amount of data transmission capacity in a line.

baud — One complete cycle or wave in an analog transmission signal. A baud starts at zero voltage, goes up to maximum positive voltage, comes back to zero, goes to maximum negative voltage, and finally returns to zero voltage.

call restriction — A telephone system feature that allows certain calls to be blocked from incoming or outgoing lines.

Caller ID — A system in which a signal sent by the telephone company with an incoming call identifies the calling number and its registered owner. Telephones with electronics capable of reading this signal display the caller ID information on a small LCD screen.

Centrex — Central exchange, the main switching point in the telephone company where calls are connected by switching them to the line called.

circuit-switched lines — The normal method of completing an analog call in which the calling line is physically connected to the called line by a defined path, and the path is kept open for the duration of the call.

cordless phones — Phones with transceivers (transmitters and receivers) that operate on radio frequencies. They have a limited range from the base unit, which contains another transceiver.

demarcation point — The physical place where the incoming telephone lines from the telephone company connect to the internal wiring of the home; also known as demarc.

dial tone — A continuous tone sent on a telephone line by the PBX or the central exchange to indicate that it is available for a call.

extensions — In telephone systems, an additional phone wired in parallel into a single line.

fax machines — A digital device that operates on an analog telephone line. It sends and receives printed documents by transmitting them as bit-mapped images.

frequency division multiplexing — An analog technology for carrying multiple data streams, voice or data, on the same wires.

ground start system — Local telephone system that seizes a telephone line as soon as a receiver is lifted so that no other call can transmit on the line.

intercom — A line in key systems that allows any extension to connect to any other for an internal call without accessing an outside line.

key system — A local telephone system in which multiple phones are connected to multiple lines by switching buttons so that any telephone can use any line.

loop start system — Local telephone system in which a Centrex-supplied dial tone indicates when a line is available for a call, but no line is seized until a call is actually placed.

multiplexing — Combining different types of data from multiple sources on a single transmission path.

narrow band — In telecommunications systems, bandwidth of 128 Kbps or less.

private branch exchange (PBX) — A local switching point where phone lines within an organization can be connected to one another or to outside lines.

public switched telephone network (PSTN) — The commercial network of telephone lines and transmission facilities over which most telephone calls are made.

punchdown block — The usual means of centrally terminating telephone lines and connecting them to the trunk lines.

regenerator — A digital data amplifier which reads weakened data signals and recreates them at full strength and without noise on the transmission line.

RJ-11 jack — The standard single line telephone connector wired with two wires.

RJ-14 jack — The standard 2-line telephone connector wired with four wires.

softphones — Software programs that display phone features (hold button, caller ID, message waiting) on the computer screen and route the calls through a handset or an earphone and microphone wired to the computer,

splitters — Devices which allow two or more telephones or peripherals to be connected to a single wall jack.

static — Noise or interference on a telephone line that is typically heard as a background crackling sound.

switchboard — A device to which a number of telephone lines are connected and which can switch any line to connect to any other.

T-1 line — A high-capacity telephone trunk line capable of simultaneously handling up to 24 voice lines or 1.5 Mbps of data.

trunk line — A telephone line from a PBX to the telephone company which can be used by any of the telephones connected to the PBX.

unified messaging — A computer-based system for storing messages from multiple sources. Storage is located on a PC's hard drive and the messages include voice mail, fax, and e-mail.

video conferencing — A technology for sending full-motion picture images with a voice telephone call so that callers can both hear and see one another.

voice mail — A digital system that allows telephone callers to record messages that the system stores, retrieves, and plays on demand.

10

Voice over Internet Protocol (VoIP) — A system whereby analog phone calls are digitized and sent in packets over the Internet. At the destination, the digital data is decoded to analog form and delivered to the receiver.

REVIEW QUESTIONS

1. Plain Old Telephone Service (POTS) is an analog network of telephones and connecting lines. True or False?

2. Data transmission over analog modems is limited to about _____ for receiving information and about _____ for sending information.

3. A complete cycle in the frequency of an analog transmission line is known as a:

   a. bit

   b. baud

   c. byte

   d. bend

4. Give one reason why digital transmissions over long distance are less prone to errors than analog transmissions.

5. In telecommunications, "bandwidth" means _____.

6. What does a regenerator do?

7. A T-1 line can carry data at speeds up to:

   a. 128 Kbps

   b. 256 Kbps

   c. 1 Mbps

   d. 1.54 Mbps

8. What is the unique feature of an ADSL compared to other types of DSL lines?

9. All DSL lines are limited by a maximum _____ from the central exchange.

10. A PBX can connect _____ _____ directly without the need of using any _____ _____.

11. A PBX controls local telephone lines from the _____ _____ to the end user extensions.

12. A trunk line runs from the central exchange to a microwave station. True or False?

13. What is a ground start system?

14. A key system is a local telephone system that doesn't require callers to dial a code for an outside line. True or False?

15. An intercom feature is available on which local system(s)?

    a. PBX

    b. key

    c. PBX and key

    d. neither

16. What is a loop start system?

17. The weakened signal of an analog transmission must be strengthened periodically by an _____.

18. Why is digital voice data more difficult to send over the Internet than ordinary numerical data?

19. A softphone is:

    a. a padded telephone

    b. a wireless telephone

    c. a computer-based telephone

    d. a telephone with no speaker

20. The PSTN includes all the public telephone network up to a home's individual _____ _____ .

21. A splitter is used to divide T-1 lines into multiple trunks. True or False?

22. For a PBX or key system to set up a three-way conference call requires how many outside lines?

    a. one

    b. two

    c. three

    d. four

23. The standard plugs of terminating 1- and 2-line telephone connectors are _____ and _____.

24. In the old-style telephone wire color code, what colors are paired?

    a. Blue/green red/yellow

    b. green/red black/yellow

    c. white/blue black/green

    d. yellow/green black/white

25. Call-waiting service can only be provided by the _____ _____ system.

10

HANDS-ON PROJECTS

Project 10-1: Terminate a 4-wire Telephone Cable with an RJ-14 Jack

In this project you will terminate one end of a 10-foot cable to an RJ-14 jack. The cable length will also be used in Project 10-2 and so should not be shorter than 10 feet. Use 2-pair Category 3 telephone wire for this project. The cable can be round or flat. You will also need an RJ-14 jack, a cable stripper, and a punchdown tool.

1. Use a CatX cable stripper to strip the cable jacket 1½ inches.

2. Place the stripped end of the cable in the jack and arrange the wires in the correct color code for an RJ-14 jack as shown in Figure 10-5. Be sure the stripped wires are pulled as far into the jack as the sleeving allows so that the excess stripped wire can be cut off when the wires are set.

3. Use an RJ-14 punchdown tool to set the cable, connect it, and cut the wires.

4. After your instructor inspects your work, cut off the jack from the cable end, leaving a 9-foot piece of cable that can be used for Project 10-2.

Project 10-2: Make a 9-foot RJ-14 2-line Telephone Cable

In this project you will terminate both ends of a 9-foot telephone cable with RJ-14 plugs. Use the same length of cable you used in Project 10-1 for this project. The cable should be 2-pair Category 3 cable, round or flat. You will also need two RJ-14 plugs and a combination cable stripper and crimping tool.

1. Use a CatX cable stripper to strip the cable jacket ½ inch.

2. Untwist and flatten the wire pairs in the correct color pattern for a 2-line (4-wire) RJ-14 cable.

3. Cut the stripped wires to a maximum ½-inch length, if necessary.

4. Place the plug on the cable end with the flattened wires in the correct position. Be sure the wires are fully inserted in the plug.

5. Use an RJ-14 crimping tool to crimp the plug in place.

6. Repeat the above steps to terminate the other end of the cable with an RJ-14 plug. Use the same wire pattern so that the telephone cable is a straight-through cable.

Project 10-3: Connect a Fax Machine to a Phone Line through a Splitter

In this project you will connect a fax machine and an extension telephone to a single phone line using a splitter. You will then test the line to see if the fax machine can separate fax calls from voice calls. You will need access to a fax machine, a telephone extension, a splitter, and a working telephone line for this project.

1. Find the wall jack where the telephone line you're using connects to the extension telephone. Disconnect the phone extension plug from the jack.

2. Insert the splitter into the wall jack.

3. Connect the phone extension's telephone line into one side of the splitter.

4. Connect the fax machine's telephone line into the other side of the splitter. Plug the fax machine into an AC power outlet and turn it on. Check the fax machine to be sure it has paper in it and shows that it is ready to operate.

5. From another telephone connected to a separate line, call the fax machine telephone number (voice call). Does the telephone extension ring or does the fax machine pick up the voice call?

6. If the fax machine picks up the voice call, check its instruction manual to see if there is any setting on the machine that you can configure so that it does not pick up voice calls, but passes them through to the telephone extension.

7. If you can set the fax machine to separate voice calls, test it again to be sure it actually works that way.

8. If the fax machine can't separate calls, is there any way you can set up the phone extension and the fax on one line so that some voice calls can still be made to the extension? How would you do it? What calls could be made?

Project 10-4: Test the Range of a Cordless Phone

In this project you will test the range of a cordless phone to see how far it extends and what happens to a call when the range is exceeded. You will need access to a cordless telephone set that is connected to a working telephone line.

1. Using the cordless phone, call someone who is willing to assist you with this test. The person doesn't need to be nearby, just willing to stay on the phone until you complete the test.

2. When your call is connected and answered, talk on the phone with the other party while you move away from the base of the cordless phone. Keep moving away until you can no longer hear the other person talking and they can no longer hear you.

3. As soon as you're sure that you're beyond the cordless phone's range, turn around and walk back toward the base unit. As you move closer to it, can you talk to the other person again or has the call been disconnected?

10

4. If you were able to talk to the other person again without placing another call, why do you think the call didn't disconnect when you walked out of range? Where do you think the control for disconnecting a call is located in this phone?

5. If the call did disconnect, where do you think the control for disconnecting a call is located in this phone set?

6. Ask the person who's assisting you to call you at the number of the cordless phone. Repeat your range experiment while talking on the call that was placed to you.

7. When you go out of range on this call, does the line disconnect? Does the system act the same for an incoming call as for an outgoing call? Why do you think it does, or doesn't?

HANDS-ON PROJECTS

Project 10-5: Handwire Two RJ-14 Jacks to One Another

In this project you will wire two telephone jacks together so that a telephone line can be connected through one to the other. For this project you will need two surface-mounted RJ-14 handwired jacks, enough telephone wire (2-pair or more) to connect the jacks, a telephone cable with RJ-14 plugs on both ends, and a telephone that can be used to test the finished line. You will also need a wall area or upright board on which to mount the jacks, a flat-bladed screwdriver, and a wire stripper or knife for stripping wire.

1. Mount the two RJ-14 jacks on the wall a few feet apart and one foot above the floor using the screws that come with the jacks. Both jacks should mount with the plug insert opening facing down toward the floor.

2. Strip the outer jacket from 1½ inches of the length of telephone wire on one end. Don't strip the wires, just the outer jacket.

3. Strip ½ inch of insulation from two pairs of exposed wire in the length of telephone wire. Strip the first two pairs noted in the color codes of Table 10-2 (old style) or Table 10-3 (new style), depending on what type of wire you are using. If the cable contains other pairs besides 1 and 2, don't strip them. Cut them off at the point where the jacket is stripped from the cable.

4. Insert the stripped end of the cable into the left jack through one of the cable channels in its side and bring the wire pairs up through the center of the jack. Pull the cable into the jack until the outer sheathing is at or inside the cable channel.

5. Keep the cable in place with one hand, and place a staple in the wall over the cable to hold it from slipping out of the jack,

6. Connect the four wires to each of the jack's connecting screws. Match the wires color for color with those in the jack or match the correct pair 1 and pair 2 leads by color code to the pair 1 and pair 2 leads, if the color codes are not the same on the jack and the cable.

7. Measure the length of cable needed to reach the other jack and the additional amount needed to connect to it (1½ inches). Cut the cable at that point.

8. Follow Steps 2 through 6 to strip the cable, insert it in the other jack, and wire it to the same color-coded connecting screws. Pull the cable snug between the two jacks so that it forms a straight line between them. Staple the wire in place.

9. Use a double RJ-14 plug patch cord to connect the jacks you've wired to a live phone line. Disconnect the telephone set from the wall jack by pressing the RJ-11 plug's holding tab and pulling the telephone wire and plug out of the jack. Insert one end of the patch cord into the live telephone jack and the other end of the patch cord into the right RJ-14 jack you've just wired.

10. Insert the telephone cord's RJ-11 plug into the left RJ-14 jack you just wired. Pick up the telephone's receiver. You should hear a dial tone and be able to make a call. If you can't, you've wired the jacks incorrectly. Go back and check your work for errors.

11. Keep testing and correcting the jacks' wiring until you can make a call on the telephone.

Project 10-6: Connect Telephone Extensions and Lines to a PBX

In this project you will connect a telephone trunk line and two extension phones to a PBX so that calls can be made and received on the system. For this project you will need access to a PBX (DataLabUSA Model S-308 or similar), two telephone extensions, and three RJ-11 patch cables, each at least eight feet in length. You will also need access to one working telephone line that can be accessed through an RJ-11 jack.

1. Connect the power supply cable to the PBX unit power port. Connect the PBX system's power supply to an AC power outlet.

2. Using an RJ-11 patch cable, connect a telephone extension to the L21 jack on the PBX.

3. Using an RJ-11 patch cable, connect the second telephone extension to the L24 jack on the PBX.

4. Follow the instructions with the PBX to set the dip switches on the unit so that incoming calls from trunk line CO1 rings to extension L21 (operator extension).

5. Using an RJ-11 patch cable, connect the CO1 jack on the PBX to a working telephone-line jack.

6. Pick up an extension telephone receiver and listen for a dial tone. If you hear the dial tone, proceed with testing the unit; if you don't hear a dial tone, check the dip switch settings and connections of the telephone extensions and line hookup.

7. Using extension 24, dial "0" (for Operator). Extension 21 should ring. If it doesn't, check the settings on the unit and change them so that Extension 21 is the operator extension. Test the system again.

8. Using Extension 24, dial "9" for an outside line, and complete a call to an outside telephone number. Ask the party you call to call back using the number of the telephone line you have connected to the PBX.

10

9. When the return call comes in, it should ring on Extension 21 (the operator extension). When it does, answer the call on Extension 21.

10. Press the ★ key to put the incoming call on hold. Dial extension 24 and press the ★ key again to transfer the call. Extension 24 should ring with the call. Answer the call to complete testing the system.

CASE PROJECTS

CASE PROJECTS

Case Project 10-1: Design a Home Telephone System

You've been asked to recommend a telephone system design for a home user. The home contains a business office that includes two computers needing an Internet connection, a fax machine, and two telephone extensions. The rest of the home has eight telephone extensions scattered through it, another phone extension in the back yard, two computers that both need Internet connections, and a security system with an emergency call-in device that must have a phone-line connection. The home is too distant from the telephone company offices to get any type of DSL connection, but the owner wants at least a 1.5 Mbps Internet connection for his business. Write a short report noting what local phone system, what ISP connection, and the number of telephone lines you recommend for this installation. Give your reasoning.

CASE PROJECTS

Case Project 10-2: Recommend Changes in a Home Telephone System

A friend asks you about improving the telephone service in her home. She presently has three telephone lines coming into her home. One is connected to the modem that provides her ISP service, one is connected to a phone in the kitchen, and one has two extensions in the home's two bedrooms. She doesn't use the computer much for Internet connection, but now her son is asking that another (fourth) line be installed so that his computer can have an Internet connection. Even though the expense of another line concerns her, she's about to say yes because it seems whenever she wants to make a call on one of her present phones, her son is on the line. If she uses one of her existing lines for her son's ISP connection, then she'll have even more trouble finding a free phone to make a personal call. What would you recommend? Write a short report noting how this person could get more service out of the phone lines she already has and whether you think she really needs that fourth line.

CASE PROJECTS

Case Project 10-3: Solve a Telephone Traffic Problem

A home with three telephone lines has a continuing problem with their use. Each line has two extensions connected to it in the home. In addition, one line is connected to the home computer's modem, one is connected to a fax machine, and the other to an answering machine and voice mail recording device. The problem with each line occurs when the machine on the line is in use and someone in the home picks up one of the line's extensions to make a call. When this happens, the call can't be made because the line is already in use, but picking up an extension while a line is in use also interrupts the call in progress. If the fax is running or the computer is online, their connections are broken by the pickup. Even the answering machine disconnects from a call when a new extension is picked up. Despite having three phone lines, the family in this home is getting very poor service from its telephones. They don't want to put in more phone lines, but would like some means of improving service on the ones they have. Write a short recommendation of what they could add to their telephone system that would help the interrupted call problem and get more use out of their phone lines.

Case Project 10-4: Troubleshoot a Telephone Extension

CASE PROJECTS

A friend asks you for help with a telephone extension he just installed. He has two telephone lines in his home and wants an extension phone on the second line in his garage where he has a workshop. He installed a 2-wire line to the garage and wired it to the black and yellow wires of the second line coming from his demarc box. The other end he wired to a new RJ-14 jack in the garage, again connecting the wires to the black and yellow connectors in the jack. He bought a used single-line phone and connected it to the new jack, but the phone won't work in the new jack. He tested the telephone on the first line inside the home and it worked all right, so he thinks the new wiring must be wrong. You ask him to look at the plug on the end of the phone cord. He says it's just an ordinary RJ-11 plug with two wire contacts for a single line. Why won't the phone work and how can he easily correct the problem?

10

CHAPTER
11

HOME LIGHTING CONTROL

After reading this chapter, you will be able to:

- ♦ Describe the basics of lighting control design and planning

- ♦ Define the major types of automated home lighting control systems available

- ♦ Describe the major components of an automated lighting system and how they work

- ♦ Describe how to install and set up an automated lighting system in a home

- ♦ Describe how to program an automated lighting system in a home

- ♦ Describe troubleshooting techniques for eliminating problems in lighting systems

In this chapter you learn how data transmission can be used to control the lighting in a home through a system of command modules and control modules linked in a wired or wireless network. An automated lighting control system can enhance the visual impact of a home's architectural design and décor, increase the aesthetic influence of lighting and make the home lighting system more economically efficient. You will learn to define the basic types of home lighting control systems and their characteristics and you will learn about the basic components which make up these systems. You will also learn how to install and set up an automated lighting system and program it to function according to design parameters. Finally, you will learn how to troubleshoot the common problems that can occur in home lighting control systems.

AUTOMATED HOME LIGHTING DESIGN

Every home has lights that provide basic illumination. Some homes have elaborate lighting systems composed of **light scenes** (illuminated rooms or areas within a room) that not only provide light, but also beautify a setting or invoke a mood in those who see the scene or are within it. Whether a home's lighting system is minimal or extensive, it can be significantly enhanced by being automated. Automation enables lighting to respond quickly, and with relatively little effort on the homeowner's part, to changes in natural lighting, specialized illumination needs, social situations, and even the moods of the home's occupants. At the same time the utility of the lighting system is increased, the electrical cost of operating it shouldn't rise and may even decline due to greater efficiency in the timing and use of energy.

In this section you examine the main considerations that go into an **automation** design for a **home lighting system**. This discussion assumes that the lighting system of the home is already installed and working and that the homeowner wants to automate it.

NOTE

Before the automation design process begins, some home owners may want to consider installing additional lighting or changing some of the lighting fixtures already in the home. If lighting is to be upgraded or altered, that should be done before automation is installed. Lighting design and installation is a large field in itself and a subject on which books have been written. This chapter won't discuss lighting design and installation except where it bears directly on our primary focus, the automation of lighting systems.

CAUTION

High-voltage wiring and fixture installation should be performed only by a licensed electrician or under the direct supervision of one. Wiring and fixture replacement descriptions in this chapter are informational only and should only be performed by persons trained and licensed to do so. Always shut off electric power in the area where wiring or other electrical work is being done.

Load Requirements and Grounding

An automated home lighting system, whether it's wired or wireless, won't add any **load** to the home's AC electric wiring, but the adequacy of the in-house wiring should still be confirmed before installing any automation. Both wired and wireless automation controls are subject to interference or "noise," which can be caused or increased by overloaded wiring.

Lights are usually not the cause of **overloading** in a home electric system because they're not the largest consumers of electricity in the system when they are used individually. If acting as a group, such as when an automation system turns all the controlled lights in a home on or off simultaneously, lights can have a significant impact on the power system, but individual lights being turned on or dimmed, won't make much of a difference in the overall power consumption or load. Unlike electric motors, which draw heavy current when starting, lights consume only slightly more electricity when starting than they do when operating, and a decline in line voltage won't cause a light to consume more power either. If line voltage drops, the light simply shines less brightly; that's how dimmers work.

Chapter 5 described in detail how to determine if a home's wiring is inadequate before attempting to install a network. The same evaluation should be made before installing home lighting controls. If new circuits, wiring, or fixtures are needed, they should be installed before the automation or at the same time. New circuits, if necessary, can be used not only to reduce the load on older wiring, but also to connect additional new lighting that might not have been installed at all if the new circuits weren't available. Automation devices like controlled outlets and switches can be installed in new circuits at the beginning, instead of replacing manual units as is necessary in existing circuits.

All these considerations point to the need for a plan for the lighting system itself and for the automation system that will control it. The plan should start with a map of the existing electrical system, which can be researched and drawn according to the instructions in Chapter 5. Make the diagram of existing wiring as complete and accurate as possible on a floor plan of the home. Add any new circuits that are required and design how the wiring for these will be installed. Finally, design the control system noting exactly which lights you plan to control, which lights will be controlled as **zones** (groups of lights controlled as single units), and where the **controllers** will be located. Make the plan as detailed and complete as you can; every item planned before starting the hands-on work enables you to avoid problems during the installation phase.

Label the plan with a unique label for each item. As you later install each device, it should be marked with the label you gave it in your plan. The plan can then serve as a schematic drawing of the completed lighting automation system which you can use in the future to troubleshoot and maintain it. Figure 11-1 shows a plan of the first floor of a large home with all the electrical fixtures noted. Because the plan has been reduced in size for publication in this book, the fixture symbols have been enlarged and only those in the family room are shown labeled. Later, you'll see Figure 11-2, which shows the family room of this plan enlarged with the zones and control devices that will be used in it noted.

11

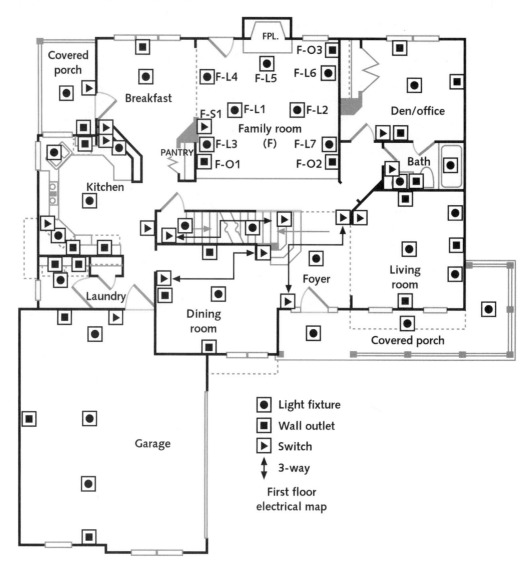

Figure 11-1   Electrical fixtures noted on floor plan with those in one room labeled

All the high-voltage fixtures in the home should be grounded, as should those installed with any new circuits added as part of the automation remodeling. Nongrounded fixtures are almost never found except in old homes constructed before grounding was a code requirement. It's still wise to check that everything is in fact grounded, as a safety measure, and also because any ungrounded circuit is likely to cause interference in the automation system you install. This is true whether it's a wireless system or uses **power-line techno-logy**. **Fluorescent lighting** is especially prone to generate interference in the automated lighting system, as well as in other home technology installations.

Lighting Zones and Scenes

As you develop the lighting automation plan, you need to decide whether each of the lights will be controlled individually or be part of a zone. A lighting zone is simply a group of lights which are related by function (not necessarily by location, although they may be near one another as well). A zone, for example, could consist of all the lighting in the family entertainment room. These lights would nearly always go on or off together or be adjusted for light level as a group to fit the activity (watching a movie, reading, playing games, etc.) that's going on in the room. Each of the lights retain individual manual control, so the occupants can override the automatic controls in case of need, but most of the time, they function together as a zone.

A lighting scene might consist of the lights in a single zone, but can also be any set of lights designed to accomplish a specific lighting objective. A dining scene, for example, might dim the overhead dining room chandelier while turning on small spotlights to illuminate the paintings on the room's walls. Another lighting scene in a family room might dim the overhead lights to eliminate reflections on the glass while turning on backlighting behind the aquarium to make observation of its occupants easy. Still a third scene might turn off floodlights in the back yard garden while illuminating the flowers, fountain, and footpaths with indirect lighting for a romantic effect.

Possible zone and scene configurations for home lighting include:

- Bedrooms

- Dining areas

- Indoor safety lighting (hallways, stairs, entries)

- Emergency lighting (battery-powered lights that activate in a power failure)

- Living room

- Interior decorative lighting areas

- Outside security lighting

- Outside safety lighting (sidewalks, steps, and outside entrances)

- Outside decorative lighting

- Outside special areas (swimming pool, hot tub, game area)

If any of these or other areas fit well with the automation you want for the home, plan the appropriate zone and the controls needed for it. Lights that always function together can be controlled by one device, if they're on the same circuit or can be wired to a single circuit. This is especially true of lamps and other moveable lights, which can often be set up so that multiple lights connect to a single outlet. This allows one module to control all of them, up to the limit of the device's power capacity.

A light can belong to more than one zone, but this requires that it have an individual control, which can be directed for the lighting requirements of each zone. Lights which are part of a room lighting scene, for example, might also be part of a safety lighting zone for the home's interior core. Outside decorative lighting might be also be part of safety lighting that turns on when someone leaves the home late at night, even though the rest of the decorative lighting remains off. Security lighting might override all other zones and turn every exterior light up to full power to give maximum illumination.

Note each zone on the lighting plan and add a zone code to the label of each light that's included in a zone. A light that illuminates a painting hanging in the living room might be labeled LVRM5-Z1 showing that it's the fifth light in the living room and it belongs to Zone 1. A light on a stairway descending to the basement family room might be designated STRS2-Z3-Z7 showing it's a stairway light and belongs to the living room zone (Zone 3) and also to the safety zone (Zone 7). Figure 11-2 shows the electrical fixtures and controls in a family room lighting zone. Each control module is labeled.

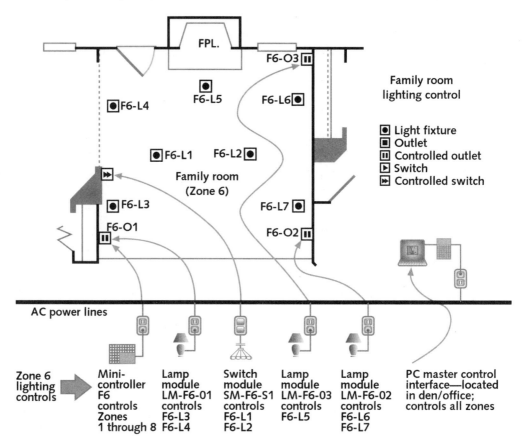

Figure 11-2   A lighting system zone and the controls in it

Home run-connected Lights and Daisy Chains

When a light is connected directly to its power supply, it's said to have a **home run connection**. A lamp plugged into an outlet receptacle is an example of a home run–wired light, as is an overhead light connected to a switch on the wall. The light is wired directly to a power connection (a home run wire) inside the walls. Most, but not all, hard wired lights (those that are wired as part of the home's electrical system) are home run lights. They are connected to the electrical system through a switch which allows them to be turned on and off.

Sometimes a switch controls two or more lights. In this case, not all the lights may be wired to the electrical system directly through the switch. One light may be wired to the switch and the second light is connected to the first light, getting its power from the first light's connection to the electrical system (if there's a third light, it would be connected to the second light). This arrangement of connection is known as **daisy chain wiring** (from the now little-known art of joining daisies by twisting the stem of one around the blossom of the next). Other examples of daisy chain electrical connections are as follows: a series of lamps in which the first is plugged into a wall outlet, the second is plugged into a connection in the first, and perhaps a third into a connection in the second; or a television that is plugged into a wall outlet and a small backlight lamp is connected to the television. Figure 11-3 shows two lamps with home run connections on the left and three lamps connected in a daisy chain on the right.

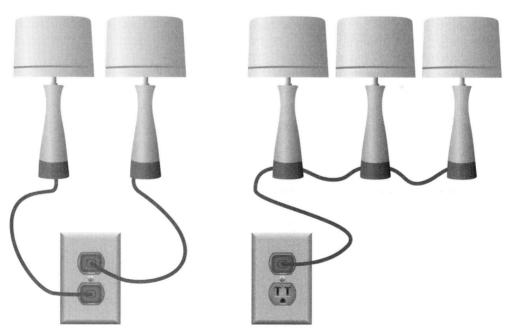

Figure 11-3   Lamps with home run connections (left) and daisy chain connections (right)

Lights with daisy chain connections always work together from a single control device because all the lights in the chain receive their power from one connection. They are wired in parallel, however, not in series, so that if any one light fails, the others in the chain will continue to work. Daisy chained lights are useful because the arrangement permits several lights to be placed in one location without using all the wall outlets. Multiple track lights and indirect fluorescent lights are often connected in daisy chains. Decorative lighting, both indoor and outdoor, is usually in a daisy chain in multiple light segments. Parallel-wired holiday lights are daisy chains, and several strings of them can be connected one to another in an even larger chain. Only one control device can be used on an entire daisy chain, however, because it is all powered from only one controllable point.

Home run-connected lights that are part of the home's electrical system can be controlled individually from the switch that's always wired into their circuit. They can also be controlled from another switch wired into the circuit closer to the light than the first switch, if the first switch is left in the on position. Home run lights plugged into a wall outlet can also be controlled at the outlet or by another switch wired into the light's cord. Because each home run light has its own power connection, it must be controlled by a separate controller. Most plug-in controllers have two or more outlet connections, but all of these are usually controlled by the same commands and so all the lights plugged into the module work together as if they were one. Figure 11-4 shows two lights added in one corner of an underlighted room (a matching pair was placed in the adjacent corner). These lights connect to a wall outlet and have no manual switch on their circuit. They can be controlled, however, by a control module plugged into the outlet and commanded by a controller.

Figure 11-4   Added lights controlled by an automated system

TYPES OF AUTOMATED LIGHTING SYSTEMS

Automated lighting systems are specialized networks that use different protocols, hardware, and frequencies than computer networks or telecommunications networks. Automated lighting networks have very narrowly defined functions. These functions consist of turning lights off and on and adjusting their brightness through a process called dimming. Automated systems can control many lights and be programmed for complex lighting patterns, but the control commands to each light are simple and do not require large amounts of data transmission. Automated lighting systems consist of either power-line control networks or wireless control networks. Each type of control system is discussed in this section.

11

Power-line Control Systems

The most common and extensive method of lighting control and automation uses X10 power-line technology, which was described earlier in Chapter 3. This technology sends signals over the same AC wires that provide power to the lights and other electrical appliances throughout the home. X10 devices were once manufactured by a single company, but the patent on the original technology ran out several years ago and many firms now manufacture and market X10 equipment. With more than 30 years of sales, X10 systems are now installed in an estimated 10 million homes in the United States and other countries, and the basic technology has been greatly expanded and improved. The original company, X10 Limited, and its subsidiaries are still major manufacturers of X10 equipment, but they've now been joined by many other firms who have produced a large array of control devices and controllers to command them.

There are many types of **command modules** for use with an X10 system. All of them connect to an AC outlet and send out signals at a frequency of 120 KHz on the home's electric wiring. This frequency is way above the AC current frequency of 60 Hz and well below radio frequencies (RF) so that neither interfere with the X10 signals on the wiring. Other interference does occur (which is discussed later), but the X10 signal frequency is as well placed in the electromagnetic spectrum as it could be to avoid both high- and low-frequency interference.

All the command signals are sent over all the home's wiring and are received by all the **control modules**. Each module responds only to signals which have its unique address in the header of the packet. X10 control modules in a system are each assigned a letter (house) code and a number (device) code. There are 16 possible letter codes (A through P) and 16 number (unit) codes (1 through 16) for each letter giving a total of 256 possible different control modules in an X10 system (Even more control modules are possible if several are assigned the same codes and function together in a zone.)

Command modules have no code designation because they don't receive commands. They only send them. An X10 system can have several command modules located in different areas of the home, and the control modules respond to commands from any of them so long as the commands are correctly addressed to the module. Table 11-1 shows the six possible commands that basic X10 lighting control systems use. Not all control modules respond to all commands.

Table 11-1   X10 lighting system commands and actions

Number	Command	Action
1	On	Turns on the control module with the code specified
2	Off	Turns off the control module with the code specified
3	All on	Turns on all the control modules in the system
4	All off	Turns off all the control modules in the system
5	Dim	Dims the control module with the code specified
6	Brighten	Brightens the control module with the code specified

X10 control modules come in many varieties. Table 11-2 shows the main ones that are intended for lighting control, the power ratings, the commands to which they respond (as noted in Table 11-1), and the function of each type of module.

Table 11-2 X10 lighting control modules

Control Module	Power Rating	Command Response	Function
110v lamp	300 watts	1, 2, 4, 5, and 6	Plugs into outlet; controls lights plugged into it
110v lamp	600 watts	1, 2, 4, 5, and 6	Plugs into outlet; controls lights plugged into it
110v outlet	600 watts	1, 2, 4, 5, and 6	Replaces outlet; controls lights plugged into it
110v switch	500 watts	1, 2, 3, 4, 5, and 6	Replaces switch; controls lights connected to it.
110v switch (three-way)	500 watts	1, 2, 3, 4, 5, and 6	Replaces switch; controls lights connected to it.
Inductive switch	-	1, 2, 3 ,4, 5, and 6	Controls low-voltage lighting

The following are types of command modules (controllers) that are available for X10 systems. All of them send commands to X10 control modules. The differences between them are mainly how many devices the command module can control and how the command module itself is programmed to perform its work.

- *Mini-controller*—Usually controls up to eight control modules. Works like a hand-held remote with buttons for each control module.

- *Wirelessmini-controller*—Same as mini-controller, but wireless. Sends radio commands to outlet-mounted receiver, which transmits them on AC wiring.

- *Tabletop controller*—Larger than a mini. Manual remote control. Controls up to 16 control modules. Some can control multiple house codes, providing control for up to 256 devices.

- *Programmable controller*—Controls up to 16 modules and can use multiple house codes. Manual remote control or timed sequences of actions.

- *Telephone interface*—Connects to telephone line and AC wiring. Controls up to 16 modules and can use multiple house codes. Manual remote control from any phone.

- *Touch-panel interface*—Controls up to 16 modules and can use multiple house codes. Manual remote control or timed sequences of actions.

- *Computer interface*—Controls up to 16 modules and can use multiple house codes. Manual remote control, timed sequences of actions, or sensor response actions.

11

Standard X10 command modules and control modules use one-way communication only. Signals go from the command module to the control module, but nothing comes back from the control module to the command module. This means that there's no confirmation back to the command module that its instructions were received and carried out. Most of the time they are, but this lack of confirmation signals was the greatest weakness of X10 technology.

One of the best advances in recent X10 products is the development of bidirectional (two-way) X10 modules. These modules confirm receipt and execution of commands and are available (at higher cost) for most X10 devices. They're worth the money, however, because they provide much more reliability in programmed lighting sequences. If a command isn't confirmed, it can be resent and the program kept accurate through its timed sequence. Many of the touch-panel interfaces and nearly all of the computer X10 interfaces use bidirectional modules.

Wireless Lighting Controls

Nearly all the lighting control devices available in X10 technology are also available using wireless technology. The largest wireless product supplier is Lutron, which offers a full range of home lighting control products that use its proprietary **RadioRA** technology. Lutron control modules don't offer the "all on" and "all off" commands that are available in X10 systems, but other than that, just about every feature of X10 control can be duplicated using RadioRA. Because its RF signals are much faster than X10 signals, RadioRA controllers can approach the speed of an X10 "all on" or "all off" command by sending individual signals in sequence to each module.

All RadioRA modules have two-way communication and automatic confirmation of commands from control modules. This wireless system can also be interfaced through an RS232 port to a computer-based control system. RadioRA components are somewhat more expensive than X10 modules, but they offer high quality and reliability and, while still not as widely used as X10 products, are making a definite place for themselves in the market.

X10 and RadioRA are the only full range product lines for home lighting automation presently available. Despite the fact that HomePlug network devices also use AC power-line technology, HomePlug product manufacturers have not marketed any lighting control (or other electrical product control) modules. The same is true of HomePNA technology manufacturers and of all the companies developing products in the wireless networking technologies such as Wi-Fi and HomeRF. None have viewed automation as a significant enough market to warrant any development effort. This dearth of competitors, despite a multimillion home market base already established, somewhat limits the available options for home lighting automation: it's X10 technology or RadioRA with no third choice. Fortunately, both of these technologies are well developed and fully capable of meeting the needs of almost any lighting automation plan.

Wire Runs and Wireless Zones

New wiring should be minimal for an automated lighting system, unless additional circuits are being installed. If that's the case, the new wiring should be integrated as part of a full home upgrade designed to bring the home's electrical system up to current electrical standards for all the technology that will be operating in it. For new circuit wiring, refer to the instructions given in Chapter 5 on high-voltage wiring and be certain that all such work is done only under the supervision of a licensed electrician.

Additional track lighting (lights mounted on metal tracks which contain their wiring and can be attached to the surface of walls or ceilings with screws) and some other fixtures can usually be added to a room without the need for more infrastructure wiring as long as the home's circuits are not overloaded by the increased power requirements. Such fixtures can usually connect to a wall outlet through a power cord run down from the mounted track in a raceway. This gives a permanent finished appearance to the lighting installation without requiring any new wiring within the walls.

Inadequate lighting in a room can often be remedied with new multiple bulb fixtures wired to the original junction box and controlled by the same switch(es). Figure 11-5 shows an example of a single overhead light connection that has been upgraded with multiple lights, which provide improved appearance and better illumination. Figure 11-6 shows a single overhead connection that has been expanded into two chandeliers spaced 10 feet apart without any new structural wiring.

11

Figure 11-5   Multiple lights wired from a single switched connection point

Figure 11-6   Dual chandeliers wired from a single connection point

LIGHTING CONTROL COMPONENTS

Each type of lighting control component is designed for a specific automation function. After completing the lighting automation design, you must determine the minimum number of controllers and control modules you need for the lighting automation system. This section describes the function of each piece of equipment and any specific limitations that you need to be aware of when using it. Whether the lighting automation system uses X10 technology power-line components or wireless RadioRA modules, the various control devices function in much the same manner.

For lights in a single zone, try to connect as many as you can in daisy chains to minimize the number of controllers you need. If a light is in two zones, it must have its own controller (or share one only with other lights in the same zones) that can respond independently to control commands for both zones. For the most professional appearance in a lighting automation system, use modules that are concealed in standard electric fixtures or placed out of sight.

Command Modules and Controllers

The smallest command modules are similar in appearance to a television remote control. They can control up to eight control modules, but are not programmable. Commands for each control module must be entered manually by pressing the appropriate buttons on the command module. An X10 command module must connect to an electrical outlet in order to transmit its signals on the AC wiring.

Wireless X10 command modules are battery operated and send their signals to a separate receiver nearby, which is plugged into an AC outlet. The receiver regenerates the command signal and transmits it on the AC wiring. In homes with more than 2500 square feet of floor space, an X10 signal regenerator may be needed both to strengthen the X10 command signals and to eliminate noise from the signals so that they can be more easily understood by the receiving control modules.

The wireless RadioRA command modules are battery operated and transmit their command signals to a repeater unit located nearby which then repeats the commands in an amplified signal throughout the home. Homes with more than 3500 square feet of floor space may require a second repeater in order to cover the full home.

Command modules and controllers capable of controlling more than eight devices are usually tabletop units or wall mounted. X10 command modules range in size up to those which can control the full 256 devices which this technology is capable of handling. The larger command modules also operate manually so that individual commands are entered by pressing the appropriate buttons on the module to send the desired command to the control module.

Many of these units are also **programmable** with timed sequences of lighting instructions that are sent at preset times to adjust lighting. Several can also store **macros** (sequences of commands in a specified order) in memory, which can then be sent at a programmed time or sent manually by pressing a few recall buttons on the command module.

The most elaborate X10 command modules have touch screens and a graphic interface that allows them to be programmed by touching appropriate entry commands on the touch screen to store the commands in memory.

RadioRA also offers large command modules that can be tabletop units or wall mounted. These can be preprogrammed with macros for specific lighting control sequences, but do not have timed functions unless combined with an astronomic clock interface unit, which allows the command modules to control devices based on regular time-of-day settings or according to sunrise and sunset in the local area.

RadioRA command modules also can be interfaced to a computer using an RS232 interface. Automation control programs on the computer can then control all RadioRA functions based on time-of-day settings, sunrise and sunset times, or on sensor input from light and motion sensors.

X10 command modules also can interface with a computer, and command sequences can be programmed and stored on the computer. As with RadioRA technology, the X10 computer software allows controls to be implemented based on time-of-day settings, on sunrise and sunset times, or on sensor input from lighting sensors or security system components.

Remote-access Controllers

RadioRA technology has wireless remote controllers that can operate the automated lighting system from a television universal infrared remote device, from a car visor remote unit, from a telephone, or from a security system keyless entry device. Several of these controllers are more limited in function than a master control unit, but they are all adequate to command basic lighting sequences when away from the home or approaching it in the dark. The keyless entry control and the car visor unit can also be programmed to control security gates and garage doors.

X10 remote-access control devices are slightly more limited, but still include a telephone interface as well as battery-operated remote controls, keyless entry units, and car visor controls. The latter two, like their RadioRA counterparts, can also control gates and garage doors.

Outlets

Outlet control modules for X10 installations can be obtained either as plug-in units, which are about the size of a small 9-volt power transformer used with many electronic devices, or as replacement outlet receptacles that have the X10 control module built into them and must be wired into the AC wiring in the same manner as an ordinary receptacle. Control module outlet receptacles are identical in appearance to regular outlets and are available with one of the duplex outlets controlled or both. The lights to be controlled are simply plugged into the control module and receive their power through it. Plug-in outlet control modules accept all six X10 commands (on, off, dim, brighten, all on, all off); the wired in outlet control modules accept five of the six X10 commands (on, off, dim, brighten, all off) in keeping with UL safety requirements for this type of device.

The receptacle devices are preferable both for appearance and durability, but are naturally more expensive. The newer X10 two-way communication modules, which confirm receipt and implementation of signals, are presently available only as wired-in receptacles, but will probably soon appear as plug-ins too.

RadioRA outlet control modules are tabletop units that plug into an outlet by means of a six-foot cord. The module's plug has a "piggyback" outlet on its back side and the lamp that the module controls is plugged into this outlet in the module's plug. The module with its manual dimmer switch sits on the table next to the lamp. RadioRA replacement wall outlets are not available at present.

Light Switches and Dimmers

Both X10 and RadioRA lamp control modules are capable of dimming lights as well as turning them on and off. Both technologies also have replacement wall switches available that, in addition to serving as manual dimmer switches, are controlled for automated dimming and brightening. As with controlled outlets, these switches must be wired directly into the AC circuits because they replace the standard manual switches. Both systems have single-pole switches and three-way switches. X10 switches are also available for three-switch locations while RadioRA can go as high as nine switches controlling a single lighting zone. Switch-type control modules accept all six X10 commands (on, off, dim, brighten, all on, all off). RadioRA controlled switches accept on, off, dim, and brighten commands.

Fixtures (Luminaires)

There are some X10 light fixtures and lamps available in which the X10 control module is built into the device rather than attached outside at the wall. These lights must have continuous power supplied from an outlet or a switched circuit in which the power is always left on. The internal X10 control module then turns the light on or off and dims it.

Built in control modules are available with only a very limited selection of lamps and lights, but they do offer additional flexibility in locating controls. They're especially useful for lights that have inconvenient switches, such as basement or garage lights that are turned on by pull strings that are hard to find in the dark.

Built-in control modules are not available in RadioRA technology except as controls on low-voltage lighting sets. The control module can be attached to these and serve as an internal switch and dimmer. X10 systems also have low-voltage control modules.

Automated Window Treatments

RadioRA systems do not provide any window shade control mechanisms, but these devices are available with X10 technology. While not really lighting controls, these modules can be very useful in controlling sunlight through windows, darkening entertainment centers in daylight hours, and other functions. X10 control modules connected to motorized pulls can open shades, blinds, or curtains, close them, or partially open or close them.

Manual remote-operated window coverings are mostly used where the windows are high and are inaccessible for hand pulls. An automated shade or curtain system can be programmed like a lighting system to respond to time-of-day commands, sunrise and sunset macros, or other command sets. Automated window treatments are more fully discussed in Chapter 14.

11

Sensors

Light and motion sensors can be used for lighting control input on both RadioRA and X10 systems that are programmed and controlled through a computer. Among the macros that can be programmed for both systems using sensor input are the following:

- Selected lights turn on when motion is detected by a sensor.

- Selected lights turn off when no motion is detected by sensor for a specified time interval (unoccupied rooms).

- Selected lights turn on or brighten when ambient light level falls.

- Selected lights turn off or dim when ambient light level rises.

- Selected lights turn on when light beam is broken (more selective than motion detector).

■ Selected lights turn off when light beam is broken (closed door or departing vehicle).

SYSTEM INSTALLATION AND SETUP

Once you have the automated lighting system planned and the necessary components on hand, you're ready to install the control modules and the command modules, set up the control program, and test the system. If you do these steps for one lighting zone at a time, even a large automated lighting system can be installed and working in a short time. This section discusses the installation process and how to make it as efficient as possible.

Cautions While Wiring and Connecting Lighting Components

CAUTION

As you go through this part of the chapter, note that high-voltage wiring and fixture installation should be performed only by a licensed electrician or under the direct supervision of one. Wiring and fixture replacement descriptions in this section are informational only and should only be performed by persons trained and licensed to do so. If you're using X10 plug-in modules, these can be installed by someone who isn't an electrician, but the same safety precautions should always be observed when working around high-voltage electrical fixtures.

Before doing any installation, shut off the AC power in the area in which you are working. This usually means shutting off some house circuit breakers while leaving others functioning in nonwork areas. Working in one power-off area at a time minimizes the inconvenience for others of having the AC power cut off and also allows you to run an extension cord from an outlet where the power is still on to the work area so you have light to work with while doing the installation. One final caution: if only some circuits in the house are turned off, don't assume every outlet or fixture you're working on is off. Test each one before doing any work to be sure the power is off. A small two-prong tester or a lamp can tell you whether a fixture is safe to work on.

Installing Interior Lighting Zones

Start with one lighting zone defined on your plan and install all the control modules that are required for controlling its lights. Wired-in outlets and switches should be installed just as if they were standard replacements for the devices already in the circuit. The various ways of wiring outlets and switches must be considered when installing control devices. Some points to remember include:

■ **Always-live duplex outlets** should normally be replaced with matching X10 or RadioRA control modules in which both receptacles are controlled. If one receptacle needs to remain always on, use a control module in which only one is controlled. The other remains always on by default.

■ **Switched duplex outlets** should be replaced with control modules and the switch which controls them left in the on position. UL listing requirements for

RadioRA and X10 wall-mounted control module switches and dimmers state that they be connected only to permanently installed light fixtures and not to lamps or plug-in devices.

- **Split duplex outlets**, in which one receptacle is switched and the other always on, should be treated like switched outlets. If only the switched receptacle is to be controlled, the control module should be placed on the outlet, not on the switch, and the switch left on. If both receptacles need to be controlled, then the outlet should be replaced with a control module and the replacement control module should be wired so that both receptacles are always live. This disables the switch that formerly controlled the receptacle and leaves the control module able to control both.

- **Single-pole switches** should be replaced with single pole control modules wired the same as the original switch.

- **Three-way switches** should be replaced with three-way switch combinations. For both X10 and RadioRA, three-way switch combinations consist of one control module switch and one companion switch which does not have a control module in it, but still allows manual operation of the switch. Both switches must be replaced in a three-way circuit, not just the one that has the control module in it.

- Multiple switch sets above three-way should be replaced with one control module and the other switches as companion switches. X10 can only handle up to four switch combinations, but RadioRA can go to nine.

11

As you install control modules, remember to check loads on each one. RadioRA devices are built for heavier duty than most X10 devices. They can accommodate 500 watts of power on switch modules and lamp modules. Standard X10 devices have 300-watt power load maximums, although units are available with 500-watt capacity and more. Be sure you install control modules with enough current capacity to handle the load you're putting on them.

Also note that control modules shouldn't be placed where a high-current appliance is likely to be plugged into them. Heating appliances like hair dryers, waffle irons, space heaters, and toasters typically use from 800 to 1500 watts of power when operating. This exceeds the load capacity of both RadioRA and X10 control modules and will burn them out in a short time. Plug-in modules can be removed when a high-current appliance is used and then put back into the outlet with no loss of control function. Wired-in control modules can't be taken out, but will definitely burn out if overloaded, so be cautious of where you install them.

Low-voltage light sets require the special low voltage control modules available in both X10 and RadioRA systems. These control modules will normally be wired into the light circuit directly rather than being installed as an outlet or switch replacement.

When the control modules are in place and the lights connected to them, set up the master command module or controller in its assigned location. Program the zone and test it to be sure everything works as you want it to, then proceed to the next zone and continue the installation process.

If the automated lighting system has multiple command modules or controllers, each should be tested with at least one zone of lighting control to be sure it functions correctly in its assigned location. For portable remote controllers, this means testing from several locations to be sure the radio transceiver unit can pick up commands from anywhere in the house. For car visor units and keyless units, it means testing from outside the home to be sure that the wireless transceiver is still within range.

Installing Exterior Lighting Zones

Once you've set up all the interior lighting zones and programmed the light scenes you want for each of them, install the exterior lighting zones. These usually consist of a decorative lighting zone and a security zone. Set up the security lighting zone first as it probably is the larger zone and requires more power. You want to be sure you have enough capacity for controlling all the security lighting before going on to decorative lighting. In the latter, some compromise can be made with bulb sizes and numbers if the load on the electrical system appears to be getting high. In the security system, you want to have all the illumination necessary.

If any new circuits or lights are being added outside, they often need to be wired with armored cable (AC) or metal clad cable (MC). Both these types of cable, along with non-metallic Romex-type cable were described in Chapter 5. Be sure that you follow the NEC requirements as amended by any local or state ordinances when installing outside cable. Also be careful about grounding outside circuits. Don't assume that because the cable is buried in the ground, it doesn't need to be grounded. That's not true. The same rules apply for grounding outside circuits as inside.

Installing Security Lighting Zones

Security lighting is usually programmed with time-of-day settings or to come on and go off at sundown and sunrise. If security lighting control is augmented by sensor input, then these parameters need to be programmed into the system in addition to, rather than in place of, the time settings. Security lighting shouldn't come on during daylight hours, even if a motion sensor detects movement of someone approaching the house. Other security features, such as video surveillance cameras, may activate in daylight from the same sensor input, but the lights should probably stay off unless it was dark.

PROGRAMMING THE AUTOMATED LIGHTING SYSTEM

Automated lighting programs are based on time-of-day schedules, event schedules (sunrise, sundown, etc.), sensor input (motion detected, light level, etc.), or combinations of all three. Every program is a unique sequence developed for the individual home and its occupants. A typical program using time schedules, events, and sensor input is noted in Table 11-3. The programs you develop may include some of these features and many others.

Table 11-3 Automated lighting program

Time/Event	Lighting Action
Sunrise	Outside security light zone off during daylight hours; all shades open
Sunrise +30 min.	East side shades close; south side shades activate close cycle, shutting 20% hourly until full closed
Sunrise +240 min.	West side shades activate close cycle shutting 20% hourly until full closed.
Local noon	East side shades activate open cycle, opening 20% hourly until full open
Sundown	Outside safety light zone on
Sundown +15 min.	All shades close. All inside light zones on (zones do not light unless room is occupied). Family room zone set to activity scene lighting level. Living room zone set to entertainment scene lighting level. Decorative interior lighting on.
Sundown +30 min.	Outside security light zone on. Pool light zone on. Outside decorative light zone on.
8:00 p.m.	Family room zone set to entertainment scene lighting
11:00 p.m.	Pool lights off
11:30 p.m.	Outside safety light zone off (turns on if motion detected); outside decorative light zone off
11:45 p.m.	All inside light zones off (individual zones remain on if room is occupied)

11

Note that lighting control systems timed to events such as sunrise and sundown vary daily by as much as three hours from winter solstice to summer solstice for areas located in the middle latitudes of the continental United States. Northern latitudes vary even more and southern ones somewhat less. These events, as well as local noon, are not affected by time changes (Daylight Savings Time) or by a location's position within a time zone. The data tables from which they are calculated are based on Greenwich Mean Time (GMT) and the geographical location specified.

Time schedules events follow the clock, including changes into and out of Daylight Savings Time. In cases where event programming and time schedule programming are used together, some lighting changes may need to be adjusted during summer or winter time. In Table 11-3, for example, if the home using this program were located in Seattle or Boston, the pool lights would only be on for an hour or so in midsummer because sundown occurs late in these northern cities. For situations like these, a program might include a few time-of-year adjustments to make allowance for longer or shorter days.

In addition to the program in Table 11-3, command controls in rooms throughout the home can also be used to activate lighting scenes and levels for each room. Sensors can control individual lights or zones.

Sensor input to a lighting program and event scheduling of commands both require a computer-based master control system. Time schedule commands can be entered manually on many of the larger command modules in both X10 and RadioRA systems. Complex time schedules are much more easily entered on a graphic interface program such as the X10 touch screens or computer programs.

Another lighting strategy which can be programmed into an automated system is a load reduction strategy. This strategy directs the lighting control system to minimize light use during peak electrical demand hours (usually during warm afternoons) in order to reduce the home's peak use of power. This strategy may be one to consider seriously in areas where utility companies have begun to charge for electric service based on peak demand rather than average use.

TROUBLESHOOTING THE AUTOMATED LIGHTING SYSTEM

Problems with automated lighting systems, both X10 and RadioRA, come mainly from interference or attenuated signals. For X10, the separation of the two legs of the home's electrical system can also be a problem.

AC electrical service to homes arrives as a 220-volt current that is divided into two "legs" of 110 volts each. One of these legs powers each of the home's 110-volt circuits and both power the 220-volt circuits to the stove, clothes dryer, and other 220-volt devices. Both legs of the AC power work together in most homes, but they may not be actually joined in a manner that allows the higher-frequency X10 signals to travel easily on both legs. If the signals can't move freely on both legs, then they're likely to not reach some control modules on one leg or the other, which results in some lighting control commands not being implemented.

The solution to this problem is an X10 bridge installed on the in-house side of the service line, which connects the hot wires of both legs of the house AC current to one another. The bridge can be installed at the electric service box by an electrician, but a new model is now available which can be installed by a homeowner or technician on any 220-volt outlet (such as for a stove or clothes dryer). The bridge, which is available as an X10 accessory from several manufacturers, provides a path for X10 signals to reach control modules on both legs and should eliminate the problem of one leg transmitting no signals or signals too weak to be read by the control modules.

Weak X10 signals can also occur in a home with a large AC electrical system. The signals attenuate with distance and eventually become too weak to be read. A regenerator, placed in an outlet some distance from the command modules but close enough to read their signals clearly, can solve this problem. It reads all command signals on the AC wiring and regenerates them at full strength without any interference or noise they may have picked up in transit. In very large homes, two regenerators, placed some distance apart from one another, may be needed to keep signals strong throughout the house, but in most a single unit is enough.

Even with a bridge and a signal regenerator in place on the AC wiring, some X10 control modules may have trouble receiving commands from controllers. Among the causes of specific problems with individual control modules are the following:

- Reverse-wired outlets with the hot wire connected to the neutral side of the outlet and the neutral wire to the hot side. Correcting the wiring often solves the problem.

- Switched circuits in which the switch is on the neutral wire instead of the hot wire. Again correcting the wiring often solves the problem.

- AC suppresser or filter that blocks signals. Removing the blocking device is the only solution. Lighting circuits usually don't need suppressors or current filters, but if other equipment that does need one or both is on the same circuit, some rearrangement of connections may be necessary.

- Noise from other electrical equipment that interferes with the X10 signals. You can locate noise-producing electrical equipment using a radio tuned to a blank (no station) area of the broadcast band. A filter on the offending equipment often cures this problem, but if not, moving it to another circuit may be necessary.

- General noise that comes from an outside source which can't be eliminated. This type of interference is tough to combat. A filter on the incoming AC service line may help. Sometimes, an extra regenerator to keep the command signals well above the noise level works. If neither solution solves the problem, the only other option is to locate the source of the noise and somehow shield the home's wiring from it.

Wireless RadioRA and X10 systems can also be troubled by noise. RF frequency noise is difficult to filter out. Filtering each wireless receiver is simply too expensive and complex. The only workable answer is to find the source of the noise and filter that device.

Minor noise levels in wireless systems can usually be overcome by simply boosting the wireless signals so that they can be clearly read over the noise level. Both RadioRA and X10 signal regenerators are routinely used in large homes where signals attenuate, but these can also be used in smaller installations where their signal boost may be enough to overcome background noise.

CHAPTER SUMMARY

- Automated lighting systems can be designed to control any number of lighting fixtures according to manual instructions or stored programs. Among the objectives of automated lighting systems are greater convenience in lighting control, more aesthetically pleasing lighting, better energy efficiency, and more effective safety and security for the home.
- Automated lighting systems should be planned in zones according to the function of the lighting as well as its location. Zones can be controlled by a single device or by a number of devices working a unit.

- Lights with home run wiring require individual control modules in order to be automated. Lights which can be wired in daisy chain fashion can all be controlled by a single control device at the head of the chain. Control of multiple lights in a zone is more economical using daisy chains.

- Automated lighting systems use either X10 power-line technology or wireless X10 and RadioRA technologies to communicate on the automation network between command modules and control modules.

- Control modules come in several varieties and respond to signals from command modules to turn lights on or off, or to dim or brighten them. These modules plug into existing outlets or can replace existing outlets and switches in the AC wiring system. Modules hardwired into the AC system should be installed by an electrician. Those connected to existing outlets can be done by an HTI technician.

- Both X10 and RadioRA lighting controls are installed by setting up control modules in separate zones, which can be individually controlled from the command modules in the system.

- Command modules can be small handheld devices that control only a few lights or large computer-based modules that can be programmed to control hundreds of lights and sensors.

- In addition to in-home command modules, both power-line and wireless technologies have wireless remote units and telephone interface units for communicating with the lighting system at a distance.

- Control modules must be installed that interface correctly with the light fixtures and wiring setup they are designed to control. There are several types of outlet control modules and switch control modules, as well as low-voltage modules and relay activators.

- Automated lighting systems can be programmed according to a time-of-day schedule, an event schedule, or a combination of both. It can also be used to reduce peak load on the home's electrical service.

- Attenuation of signals, noise, and RF interference are the main problems encountered in automated lighting systems. All of these can be overcome in most cases.

KEY TERMS

always-live duplex outlets — An AC electrical outlet that is not controlled by a switch and always has current available.

automation — The process of controlling a lighting or other system remotely, either with manual commands from a controller or by a programmed set of instructions from a computer.

command module — An X10 technology controller that sends commands (manually generated or programmed) to control modules that control lights.

control module — In X10 systems, any of the devices that receive lighting control instructions from the controller and implement them by adjusting the lights.

controllers — Lighting control devices that send lighting commands to control modules in an automated lighting system.

daisy chain wiring — Wiring light fixtures in parallel one to another with only the first light being connected directly to a power supply and each of the others receiving power in succession down the chain.

fluorescent lighting — Lighting tubes that contain phosphorescent material and glow when a high-voltage current is passed through them. The tube are made in various lengths up to eight feet.

home lighting system — The entire electrical light configuration in a home including all interior and exterior lights and the controls (manual or automated) that direct them.

home run connection — A wired connection that links a light directly to its power supply without the current to it passing through any other fixture except a switch.

light scenes — Illuminated rooms or areas within a room that not only provide light but beautify a setting or invoke a mood.

load — In electrical systems, the amount of current (amps) flowing in the wiring at a given time.

macros — Sequences of commands in a specified order that a programmable device stores in memory and executes at preset intervals.

overloading — Placing a current demand on an electrical circuit above its capacity to carry safely.

11

power-line technology — Network data transmission method in which data signals are sent on AC wiring using a different frequency and voltage than the regular current flowing in the circuits.

programmable — Capable of storing instruction sets for later execution in sequence.

RadioRA — A proprietary wireless lighting control technology developed by Lutron and used for home lighting control.

single-pole switches — An AC basic switch that opens or closes a circuit to control power to a fixture.

split duplex outlets — An AC electrical outlet in which one receptacle is always live and the other is controlled by a switch.

switched duplex outlets — An AC electrical outlet controlled by a switch that turns current to it on or off.

three-way switches — A type of AC switch that is used in pairs to turn a circuit on or off from two locations.

zone — A group of lights controlled together to provide a specific scene or accomplish a specific task such as security lighting.

REVIEW QUESTIONS

1. A light scene in a home is the same as a lighting zone. True or False?

2. Overloading an electric circuit means:

    a. using wire that is too large for the amount of current being carried

    b. putting more than one circuit breaker in the circuit

    c. connecting more electric devices in the circuit than it can carry current for

    d. grounding the circuit to a lead pipe rather than to a steel rod

3. Power-line networking technology uses _____ to carry its data signals.

4. A lighting zone is a group of lights which are related by _____ and may also be in or near the same _____ .

5. One automated lighting zone that would not be part of the home's AC wiring system are battery-operated _____ lights.

    a. yard

    b. decorative

    c. emergency

    d. security

6. Explain how a single light could belong to more than one zone and what kind of control it would need to have.

7. Home run-connected lights are wired directly to a(n) _____.

    a. outlet

    b. controller

    c. AC circuit

    d. transformer

8. A string of parallel-wired holiday lights is an example of _____ wired lights.

9. The most common automated lighting control technology is _____, which uses AC wiring to transmit control signals.

10. The two wireless technologies for automated lighting are _____ and _____.

11. X10 command modules:

    a. send commands to control lights

    b. receive commands to control lights

    c. strengthen commands that control lights

    d. block commands that control lights

12. X10 systems can use a maximum of _____ house (letter) codes, each of which can have a maximum of _____ unit (number) codes for individual modules.

13. X10 control modules:

    a. send commands to control lights

    b. receive commands to control lights

    c. strengthen commands that control lights

    d. block commands that control lights

14. An X10 or RadioRA three-way control module switch uses what type of additional switch for wiring the three-way circuit?

    a. three-way control module switch

    b. single-pole switch

    c. companion switch

    d. low-voltage switch

15. What does a telephone interface for an automated lighting system do?

16. RadioRA signals differ from standard X10 signals because:

    a. they are wireless rather than power-line signals

    b. they are two-way rather than one-way signals

    c. they are faster than X10 signals

    d. they are all of the above

17. A programmable control module differs from a manually operated controller because it can _____ command sequences for later use.

11

18. An outlet controlled by a switch in an AC circuit should only be replaced with a control module at:

    a. the switch

    b. the outlet

    c. either one

    d. neither one

19. In addition to controlling lights, an automated lighting system may also control:

    a. motion detectors

    b. door locks

    c. window coverings

    d. pool covers

20. In a lighting-controlled room, what two functions could a motion detector serve in controlling the lights?

21. A split duplex outlet has one receptacle _____ and the other controlled by a _____.

22. Outside circuits often must be wired with _____ cable or _____ cable for greater protection from damage.

23. Attenuated (weakened) signals in an automated lighting system can be strengthened by a _____

24. In a RadioRA lighting system, RF interference might be reduced by what means?

25. On July 4, does the sun set later in Houston or Minneapolis? How about on New Year's Day? (*Hint*: Houston is in southern Texas; Minneapolis is in northern Minnesota.)

HANDS-ON PROJECTS

HANDS-ON PROJECTS

Project 11-1: Set Up Two Control Modules That Turn Lights On and Off

In this project you set up and test a basic light control system consisting of a command module and two control modules, each controlling a light. For this project you need access to an X10 wireless remote controller module (Model 4000 remote and base or similar), two plug-in control modules (Model 2000 or similar), two lamps or other plug-in lights, and a room with at least three wall outlets.

> 1. Set the house code and unit code on one control module to A3 using the wheel settings or buttons on the X10 control module you are using.

2. Set the house code and unit code on the other control module to A4.

3. Set the house code on the controller remote and the receiver base to A. Be sure that the remote unit has working batteries.

4. In a room with at least three wall outlets, plug the two control modules into two of the outlets.

5. Plug a lamp or light into each control module. Be sure the lamps are turned on. If you're using control modules with a controlled outlet and an always-on outlet, be sure you plug the lamps into the controlled outlet and not the always-on outlet.

6. Plug the controller receiver module into the third outlet. Turn it on.

7. On the controller, set the lower select switch to the left (modules 1–8 setting)

8. Press the 3 on (left) button to turn the first lamp on. Press the 4 on (left) button to turn the other lamp on.

9. Press the 3 off and 4 off (right) buttons to turn the lamps off.

10. Turn both lamps on again.

11. If your controller has dimmer buttons, press the 3 button followed by the dim (right) button to dim the first lamp.

12. Dim the second lamp with the 4 button and the dim button.

13. Turn both lamps off.

11

HANDS-ON PROJECTS

Project 11-2: Program a Timer Module with a Preset Program

In this project you use the basic light control system you set up in Project 11-1 to run a timed command program from an X10 timer controller. For this project you need access to an X10 mini-timer controller module (Model 1100X or similar), two plug-in control modules (Model 2000 or similar), two lamps or other plug-in lights, and a room with at least three wall outlets.

1. Repeat Steps 1 through 5 in Project 11-1 to set up the control modules and lamps for this project. Set the house and unit codes for the control modules to A3 and A4 as specified in the instructions.

2. Plug the timer controller into the third outlet in the room.

3. Move the upper-left selector switch on the controller to the set clock position, and use the timer arrow buttons to set the time on the controller clock.

4. On the right side of the controller, set the house code wheel to A. Set the selector switch left for unit numbers 1–4.

5. Move the upper-left selector switch to set program.

6. Set the time with the time arrow buttons about 15 minutes ahead of the current time.

7. Press the 3 unit on button. Press the 4 unit on button.

8. Move the time ahead 1 minute.

9. Press the 3 unit on button and then the dim button.

10. Move the time ahead 1 minute.

11. Press the 4 unit off button and then the brighten button.

12. Move the time ahead 1 minute.

13. Press the 3 unit off button. Press the 4 unit off button.

14. Set the upper-left selector switch to run and watch for the program to execute when the time reaches the preset times you entered for turning on the lamps.

HANDS-ON
PROJECTS

Project 11-3: Program Lights to Turn on When Motion Is Detected

In this project you set up and test a basic light control system consisting of a motion sensor and two control modules, each controlling a light. For this project you will need access to an X10 wireless remote controller module (Model 4000 remote and base or similar), an X10 wireless motion sensor (Model MS13A or similar), two plug-in control modules (Model 2000 or similar), two lamps or other plug-in lights, and a room with at least three wall outlets.

1. Repeat Steps 1 through 5 in Project 11-1 to set up the control modules and lamps for this project. Set the house and unit codes for the control modules to A3 and A4 as specified in the instructions.

2. Plug the controller receiver module into the third outlet. Turn it on.

3. On the controller, set the lower select switch to the left (modules 1–8 setting)

4. Check the motion sensor to be sure it has working batteries.

5. The default settings of the motion sensor are house code A and unit 1. Follow the instructions that come with the sensor to reset its code to A3. Put the cover back on the sensor.

6. Test the sensor by pressing the house button once. The sensor sends an on command and the A3 lamp should turn on. Press the unit button once. The sensor sends an off command and the A3 lamp should turn off.

7. Place the motion sensor at least six feet off the ground in one corner of the room in which you're working.

8. Wait a minute or so without moving, then walk in front of the sensor. Lamp A3 should turn on, but lamp A4 should remain off. After 1 minute, lamp A3 should turn off in response to an off command from the sensor because it detected no further motion.

9. Use the command controller to turn both lamps on and wait for a minute without moving. Does lamp A3 turn off in response to an off command from the sensor. Why do you think it did or didn't?

Project 11-4: Program Lights to Turn on When Darkness and Motion Are Detected

In this project you set up and test a basic light control system consisting of a motion sensor and two control modules, each controlling a light. For this project you need access to an X10 wireless remote controller module (Model 4000 remote and base or similar), an X10 wireless motion sensor (Model MS13A or similar), two plug-in control modules (Model 2000 or similar), two lamps or other plug-in lights, and a room with at least three wall outlets.

1. Repeat Steps 1 through 5 in Project 11-1 to set up the control modules and lamps for this project. Set the house and unit codes for the control modules to A3 and A4 as specified in the instruction.

2. Plug the controller receiver module into the third outlet. Turn it on.

3. On the controller, set the lower select switch to the left (modules 1–8 setting).

4. Open the cover of the motion sensor and set it to transmit motion detected signals only if it is in darkness. To make this setting do the following:

   a. Press the Unit/off button once.

   b. When the red light flashes, press and hold down the House/on button. The green light turns on.

   c. After three seconds, the red light blinks twice, indicating the motion sensor is set for darkness transmit only.

   d. If the red light blinks only once, the sensor is still set for daylight and darkness operation. Repeat Step 4 until the red light blinks twice.

5. Place the motion sensor at least six feet off the ground in one corner of the room in which you're working.

6. Wait a minute or so without moving, then walk in front of the sensor. Lamp A3 should not turn on because the room is lit. If it does, reset the sensor for darkness–only operation by repeating Step 4. If lamp A3 doesn't turn on, go on to Step 7.

7. Darken the room by turning off the lights and covering any windows.

8. Wait a minute or so without moving, then walk in front of the sensor. Lamp A3 should turn on, but lamp A4 should remain off. After one minute, lamp A3 should turn off in response to an off command from the sensor because it detected no further motion.

9. Use the command controller to turn both lamps on and wait for a minute without moving. Does lamp A3 turn off in response to an off command from the sensor. Why do you think it did or didn't?

11

Project 11-5: Install a Split X10-controlled Receptacle

In this project you install an X10 split receptacle into an outlet box that has been roughed in for new wiring or already contains a standard outlet receptacle. For this project you need access to a simulated electric circuit set up in a classroom or an existing AC circuit with an outlet receptacle that you can replace. You also need a Leviton DHC split receptacle or similar, a cover plate for the receptacle, 2 lamps or other plug-in lights, and an X10 mini-controller.

1. Turn off the power to the circuit you're working on.

2. Test the circuit with a two-prong circuit tester to confirm that the power is shut off.

3. If the circuit has a receptacle that you're replacing, remove the cover plate from the receptacle and then take the receptacle out of its wall box by removing the holding screws at the top and bottom of the receptacle.

4. Disconnect the wires from the receptacle. If they're held with screws, loosen them and remove each wire. If they're the push in type, use a flat-bladed screwdriver in the release slot of each wire to depress the retainer clip and release the wire.

5. Connect the green lead from the X10 receptacle to the ground wire or a grounding screw in the outlet box. Secure the connection with a twist-on connector, if necessary.

6. Connect the white lead from the X10 receptacle to the white wire or wires in the outlet box. Secure the connection with a twist-on connector. A second white wire leading to another outlet can be connected to the receptacle without affecting the operation of the X10 receptacle or the other one connected to it.

7. Connect the black wire or wires to the black lead of the X10 receptacle. Secure the connection with a twist-on electrical connector.

8. Install the receptacle in the outlet box using the screws provided with it. Install the cover plate.

9. Set the house code on the left set wheel of the receptacle to C. Set the unit code on the right set wheel to 3.

10. Turn the power in the circuit back on.

11. Connect a lamp to the lower (always-on) outlet of the X10 receptacle. Turn the lamp on and leave it on while you unplug the lamp. Plug the lamp into the top (controlled) outlet of the receptacle. The lamp may come on again or remain off, as it is now being controlled by the X10 receptacle. Plug a second lamp into the always-on outlet of the receptacle and turn it on. Both lamps should now be illuminated.

12. Plug the mini-controller into another receptacle on the same AC power system as the circuit you've been working on.

13. Send a command from the mini-controller to turn C3 off. The controlled lamp should go off and the other remain on.

14. Try a dimming command. Does it work? Why or why not? How about an All On command? All Off? Is the second, uncontrolled lamp affected by any of these commands?

Project 11-6: Install Three-way X10 Switches

In this project you install an X10 three-way master switch and slave switch into an existing roughed-in, new wiring, three-way circuit or an existing three-way circuit. For this project you need access to a simulated three-way electric circuit set up in a classroom or an existing three-way AC circuit with switches that you can replace. You also need a Leviton 2202W DHC X10 500-watt dimmer switch, a Leviton 22081 slave switch, two cover plates for the switches, and an X10 mini-controller.

1. Turn off the power to the circuit you're working on.

2. Test the circuit with a two-prong circuit tester to confirm that the power is shut off.

3. If the circuit has three-way switches that you're replacing, remove the cover plates from the switches and then take the switches out of their wall boxes by removing the holding screws at the top and bottom of the switches.

4. Disconnect the wires from the switches. If they're held with screws, loosen them and remove each wire. If they're the push-in type, use a flat-bladed screwdriver in the release slot of each wire to depress the retainer clip and release each wire.

5. Check which of the three-way switches you removed was wired directly to the light fixture. In the X10 controlled switch setup, this switch must be the master switch. The switch wired directly to the power supply must be the slave switch.

6. Install the slave switch first. Connect the black (hot) lead and the black traveler lead both to the black lead from the X10 slave switch. Secure the connection with a twist-on connector.

7. Connect the red traveler wire to the red lead from the X10 slave switch. Secure the connection with a twist-on connector.

8. Connect the two white (neutral) leads in the box to one another. Secure the connection with a twist-on connector.

9. Now install the master switch. Connect the two white leads in the box to one another. Secure the connection with a twist-on connector.

10. Connect the black traveler wire to the black lead of the X10 master switch. Secure the connection with a twist-on electrical connector.

11. Connect the red traveler wire to the red lead of the X10 master switch. Secure the connection with a twist-on electrical connector.

12. Connect the black wire going to the light to the blue lead of the X10 master switch. Secure the connection with a twist-on electrical connector.

11

13. Use a small screwdriver to remove the plate from the master switch and expose the setting wheels. Use the screwdriver to set the house code on the left set wheel of the switch to D. Set the unit code on the right set wheel to 3. Replace the plate by pressing it in place.

14. Install both switches in their respective boxes using the screws provided with them. Install the cover plates.

15. Turn the power in the circuit back on.

16. Manually turn the master switch to the on position to turn the controlled light on.

17. Plug the mini-controller into another receptacle on the same AC power system as the circuit you've been working on.

18. Send a command from the mini-controller to turn D3 off. The controlled light should go off.

19. Try a dimming command. Does it work? Why or why not? How about an All On command? All Off?

20. Test the master and slave switches manually to be sure they function correctly in that mode.

CASE PROJECTS

Case Project 11-1: Design Lighting Automation for a Garage and Driveway

A client wants you to install automated lighting in his garage and outside lighting to illuminate the driveway. The home's garage is attached to the house and is entered from the house through an interior door. The overhead garage doors each have electric openers on them which can be activated by switch buttons near the interior door or by an RF opener in each of the family cars (one opener in each car opens one garage door). The client wants the interior lights in the garage to turn on whenever someone enters the garage from the house or when either of the garage doors is raised to allow a car to enter. She also wants the outside driveway lights to turn on when either garage door opens, but not when someone enters the garage from inside the home. Diagram an automatic lighting solution that accomplishes the lighting the client wants as simply as possible. Note the hardware pieces that are needed and how each is to be connected and set so that it performs as needed. For this exercise, assume that there are no other automated lighting zones in the home.

Case Project 11-2: Design an Automated Room Lighting Zone

You are installing a home lighting system in a living room that has two overhead lights, both controlled by three-way switches at opposite ends of the room. It also has three lamps all plugged into split duplex outlets and all controlled as a group by two three-way switches at opposite ends of the room. How would you design the lighting control for this room so that both overhead lights and lamps are controlled as a unified zone, and the overhead lights can also be operated manually from their switches? Draw a design using RadioRA control modules and other hardware to control the lighting and conform to UL electrical safety standards.

CASE PROJECTS

Case Project 11-3: Find a Programmable X10 Controller

One of your clients wants a programmed home lighting system, but doesn't want to run it from her computer. She wants a small controller that can be permanently located in the home's master bedroom and direct the lighting system from there. She would like to be able to program the system from a graphic interface using a keyboard or a touch screen. The lighting system in her home has both X10 modules and wireless modules controlling some of the lights. The system has eight zones and each has up to four control modules in each zone. Visit some X10 Web sites (*www.x10.com* and *www.smarthome.com* are two to start with) and see what you can find that's available to meet her requirements. Compare the features of the controllers available and write a recommendation on the one you think is best.

CASE PROJECTS

Case Project 11-4: Design an Automated Lighting System for a Cabin

A client has a cabin located on a remote mountain lake. Lights there are powered by a generator with battery backup. The cabin can only be reached by boat across the lake. Its dock is in a little cove with a narrow, rocky entrance that is dangerous to enter at night unless illuminated. The cabin's owner visits the cabin only about once a month and doesn't want to have lights come on nightly with a timer when he isn't there. He would like a system that turns the dock and safety lights on only when his boat (or any other boat) approaches within 200 yards of the entrance to the cove after sundown. What can you suggest that meets his need and doesn't require other visiting boats to have any special device on board to signal for the lights to come on?

11

12

HEATING, VENTILATION, AND AIR-CONDITIONING MANAGEMENT

After reading this chapter, you will be able to:

♦ Describe the design and operation of zoned and nonzoned heating and air-conditioning systems.

♦ Identify and describe the function of heating and air-conditioning components and their controls.

♦ Describe how to install a heating and air-conditioning control system.

♦ Describe how to set controls and program an HVAC control system for year-round operation.

In this chapter you will learn how heating, ventilation, and air-conditioning (HVAC) systems operate to provide comfortable environments in homes. You will learn how to identify the major components and control devices in HVAC systems and to describe how each of them functions. You will also learn how to install an automated controller for an HVAC system and how to set the controls of the system and program its control panel so that it will provide a comfortable interior environment under a variety of conditions.

DESIGN AND OPERATION OF ZONED AND NONZONED HVAC SYSTEMS

Heating, ventilation and air-conditioning (HVAC) systems in American homes vary as widely as the locations and climates in which they're located. Heating systems for low-altitude southern latitude homes may be little more than a few **space heaters** placed in strategic locations, while whole-house **air conditioning (A/C)** is a must. At the other extreme, a home in the mountains of Montana or almost anywhere in the northern tier of states may need a **central heating system** for nine months of the year and no A/C at all. And then there are many areas such as Chicago, Omaha, and Denver (to name just three of hundreds) where central A/C and central heating are both necessities for year-round home comfort.

This chapter discusses the **automated control** of central heating and A/C systems only. Most homes have at least one of these and many have both. Most automation systems are designed to work with central heating and A/C rather than room-size units.

Space Heaters, Room Air Conditioners, and Evaporative Coolers

Confining ourselves to central (whole-house) systems means passing over with just this brief mention all sizes of space heaters (electric or gas) as well as window and other room air conditioners. All of these units can be automatically controlled with thermostats or timers, but none are large enough, or have a large enough impact on a home's interior climate, to warrant a whole-house temperature control system.

Also not covered is the class of air conditioners known as **evaporative** or **"swamp" coolers** that are frequently designed to cool and humidify an entire house. These units are used mainly in dry desert climates where they can attain maximum cooling efficiency. They don't work well in high-humidity climates. They depend for their effectiveness on moving large volumes (several thousand cubic feet per minute) of evaporative-cooled air through the home, drawing it in through the cooler and expelling it out through open windows or doors. Like space heaters and room air conditioners, evaporative coolers can be automatically controlled with a thermostat or timer, but nothing more than on or off commands are needed (or possible) for them. Changes to their cooling effects are best made by adjusting the air exits (open windows or doors) rather than the operation of the cooler.

Central Heating Systems

Central heating systems are divided into two types, **forced air** and **radiant**. Forced air systems all function by drawing air from the home's interior into a furnace where it is heated and then blown out again into the home through heating **vents** connected to the furnace by metal **ducts**. All forced air-heating systems rely on the continual transfer of air from the home's interior to the **furnace** (where it's heated) and back again. They keep the air temperature in the room comfortable by heating the air itself.

A typical forced air-heating system is shown in Figure 12-1. The system is shown combined with a central A/C system, which uses the same ducts and **blower** as does the furnace. When heating is required, the furnace provides it, and the A/C unit is idle. When cooling is necessary, the furnace is idle and the air conditioner takes over.

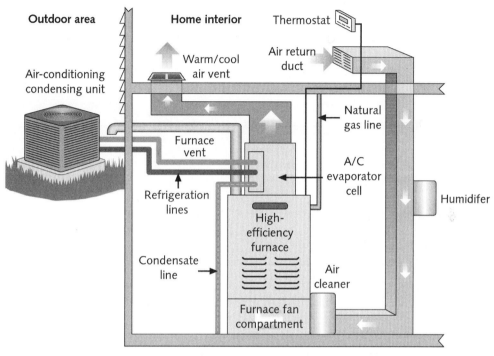

Figure 12-1   A basement-located furnace and A/C system

Radiant heating systems don't have any air movement system. They work by heating the air in the house through convection or by heating the house itself rather than the air inside it. Older radiant systems use circulating hot water or steam from a central boiler to heat standing radiators or baseboard radiators in each room of the house. These units warm the air around them which then expands and becomes lighter. The heated lighter air rises away from the radiator and is replaced by cooler air which, in turn, is heated and rises away from the radiator. Radiator heating systems do not heat evenly and are not as efficient as either radiant or forced air systems. Few, if any, of these systems are being installed in new homes, although millions still function in older homes.

Radiant heating systems now being used in newer homes consist of a large water heater connected to pipes that run at spaced intervals under the floors of the home. The heating system operates by heating water in the central boiler and then circulating the water through all the pipes beneath all the floors of the house. Heat from the pipes is absorbed into the structure of the house and radiates from there to the home's interior air, warming it to a comfortable temperature. A section of a radiant heating system is shown in Figure 12-2.

12

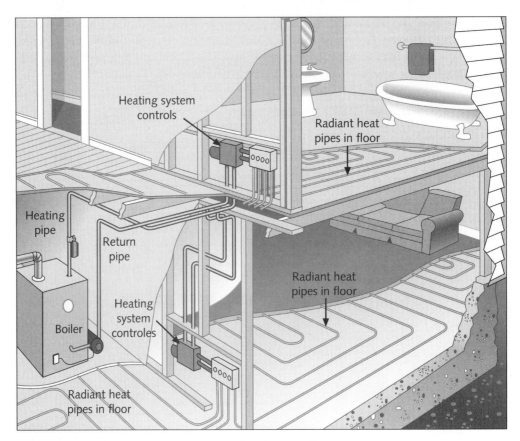

Figure 12-2 Radiant heating system with piping in floor

Although this heating methods sounds less efficient than forced air heating, it is actually more energy efficient and provides more even heat distribution throughout the home than the other type. For these reasons, radiant heating systems, though more expensive to install initially, are growing in popularity.

Fuels within Furnaces

Fuel for the combustion chambers of nearly all modern furnaces is either fuel oil or natural gas. Some coal-burning furnaces remain in use and some that were once coal-burning have been converted to burn oil. These are a declining minority, however, and all new residential furnaces use oil or gas. Oil is stored in a tank and piped from there to the furnace. Gas comes through a pipeline from a pressurized storage facility. The flow of either oil or gas fuel is not controlled as a means of regulating heat. Fuel settings are constant in furnaces as is the amount of heat produced by the unit when running. The total amount of heat produced by the system to heat the home is controlled simply by turning the furnace on or off.

Both forced air furnaces and radiant systems can be fueled by either oil or gas. The choice of which to use is usually a matter of which is available. Gas tends to be preferred wherever it's available, both because it burns cleaner (the usual combustion products are carbon dioxide and water) and because gas also leaves no ash or residue in the furnace, which must be removed periodically. Gas requires a pipeline connection for home delivery, but if lines are installed in a residential area, delivery is much simpler than pumping fuel oil from a large truck into an underground storage tank.

Central Air Conditioning (A/C)

Central air-conditioning (A/C) systems are all forced air designs. They move air in much the same way as a furnace heating system. In fact many A/C systems use the same ducts and vents as the heating system. Instead of heating the air that is drawn into the system from the home's interior, the air conditioner cools it by **refrigeration** and then blows it back into the home through the duct system.

Refrigeration cooling is provided by the A/C **condensation** and **compressor** unit, which is located outside the home. Chilled refrigerant from the condenser unit flows to the A/C unit and cools the air passing through it. Excess **humidity** condenses out of the cooled air and is carried away by a drain pipe.

A/C units are mainly electric powered and use no other fuel. The compressor in the condenser unit requires a fairly large motor to operate it and the blower unit that moves air over the cooling coil and into the home is also powered by a large electric motor. These motors make air conditioners heavy users of electric power. In most homes the A/C system is the largest user of electric power when operating, because it requires substantial power and because it operates for long periods of time.

Single and Multiple-Unit HVAC Systems

Most homes have only a single forced air furnace, which serves to heat the entire house. The larger the home is, however, the more difficult it is to heat adequately or evenly with a single furnace. Long duct runs from the centrally located furnace to the furthest rooms in the home tend to dissipate much of the heat in the air traveling through them so that by the time it reaches its destination, its temperature has dropped too low to raise the room temperature to an acceptable level. Similarly, the sheer size of many homes may exceed the heating capacity of a single furnace.

The effect of A/C systems is also limited by the distance their cooled air must travel and the size of the blower required to move it. Though blowers run more quietly than fans, they still make some noise and the noise level increases with the size of the blower. As with a single unit furnace, a point is reached where the size of the home exceeds the ability of one A/C unit to effectively cool it. A second unit is the logical answer.

The Air Conditioning Contractors of America (ACCA) publishes Manual J, which contains the industry standard for calculating heating and air-conditioning loads in residential buildings. To meet or exceed its recommended furnace capacity, many homes have two or more furnaces and A/C systems located in different parts of the structure. Whenever there are two or more furnaces and A/C systems in a home, the HVAC system is by definition divided into **zones**, each of which is heated by a different furnace and cooled by a separate A/C system. One zone, with one HVAC system handling its heating and cooling, might be, for example, the main floor of the home, while another HVAC system handles the lower floor or the second floor. The controls of each system must be programmed to work together or the efficiency of both are degraded and the home is poorly heated and cooled.

Radiant heating systems are less likely to require two or more separate heating units than forced air systems. This is because radiant home heating systems can be larger in overall capacity than forced air units and because radiant systems are more efficient in carrying heat over long distances without significant loss. Finally, radiant heating systems can be more easily divided into zones and their heat distribution adjusted for distance than forced air systems. Few homes of less than 5,000 square feet floor area have more than one radiant heating unit, and many of these systems can go to even higher capacity.

Homes with radiant heating systems often have forced air A/C systems for cooling. The two systems are completely separate, but they can be controlled by one set of thermostats and a single central controller.

Zoned and Nonzoned Systems

Heating and cooling zones are not just the result of multiple furnaces or air conditioners. They can be set up in homes with only a single furnace and A/C unit as well. The purpose of heating zones is to more evenly and efficiently distribute heat throughout the home. The two factors that make zones necessary in many home HVAC systems are distances from the central furnace to some parts of the home and the effects of outside climate, mainly sunlight.

In an HVAC system, the further heated air travels from its source (the furnace), the more heat is lost in transit so that less remains when the air finally reaches its destination. The same is true for the cooled air from an A/C system: it warms as it moves through the ducts, absorbing heat from them as it moves. In a home with only one zone and relatively equal heated air distribution to all rooms, this results in the rooms closest to the HVAC system being the warmest, and those furthest away being the coldest. If colder rooms are brought up to normal temperature, warm ones are then too hot for comfort and vice versa.

Radiant heating systems with only one zone also have this problem. The heating water cools more by the time it reaches the most distant pipes than it does before reaching the nearby ones. The result again is uneven heating.

The A/C system suffers from a similar unequal heat distribution, only this time it's caused by cool air from the air conditioner warming more as it travels to the outer parts of the home than it does for those nearer. This causes the central core of the house to be cooler than the outer, more distant (from the air conditioner) parts. The condition is made worse by the effects of summer sunlight, which can heat the southern exposed side of the home more than the northern side and thus make it even hotter. Once again equally distributed cool air results in an unequally cooled home, some parts of which are comfortable and some not.

Another factor contributing to this condition is adjacent areas, which may be hotter or colder then the home's living area by design. Even with good insulation in the walls, some **heat transfer** occurs from the warmer area to the colder one. Figure 12-3 shows how outside climate, sunlight, and adjacent areas can all contribute to unequal heating and cooling of a home with only a single zone.

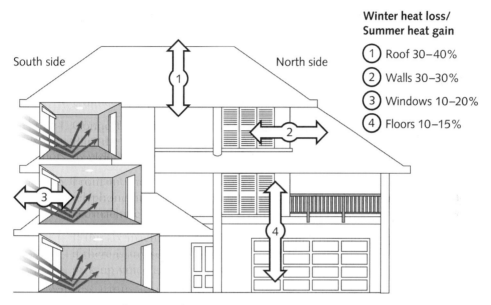

Winter heat loss/
Summer heat gain

1 Roof 30–40%

2 Walls 30–30%

3 Windows 10–20%

4 Floors 10–15%

South side   North side

Figure 12-3   How heat transfer creates uneven temperatures in a home

Dividing the heating and A/C systems into zones with separate temperature controls in each allows the system to compensate for inequalities in heating and cooling of the home by sending more or less heated or cooled air to needed areas, independent of what is happening in other zones. Each zone is treated like a separate apartment with its own HVAC system and controls. If the controls of each zone had to be continually adjusted for changing conditions by hand, the system would be too cumbersome to use effectively. Automating the HVAC system allows it to be controlled by a preset program based on input from **temperature sensors** (**thermostats**) located in each zone.

Ventilators

In addition to heating, some HVAC systems may need to provide for **ventilation**, the exchange of air in the home with outside air. Ventilation may be necessary even when the inside and outside temperatures are the same and no heating or cooling is required. If a home is well insulated and sealed against outside weather conditions, the air inside it remains cut off from outside air unless a door or window is opened. With occupants inside the home, this can result in depletion of the oxygen in the air, stagnant odors, buildup of humidity, and accumulation of dust and bacteria. Ventilation provides fresh air in the home without heating or cooling the new air it brings in. The new air may be filtered or humidified so that it doesn't add to the air-quality problems already present.

12

For ventilation to be effective, the system must have both an intake vent on the outside of the home through which outside air is drawn in and an exhaust vent through which stale inside air is expelled. In a sealed home, an intake vent without an exhaust vent won't work, and neither does the reverse. Both are required. The intake vent may be a part of the HVAC system and controlled so that it can be opened or closed as needed. The outside exhaust vent could also be part of the HVAC system's air return duct system, or it could be a separate vent or vents that exhaust air into the attic, from which it would be expelled outside by an attic fan. Figure 12-4 shows a typical A/C system with built-in outside ventilation and exhaust of room air. The amount of outside air entering the system is controlled by **dampers** (air duct doors).

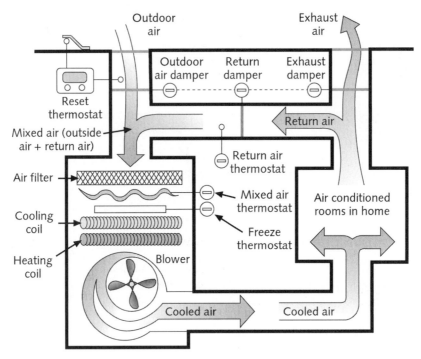

Figure 12-4   An air-conditioning system with outside ventilation

HVAC Components

HVAC systems all include the same basic components. Some of these can vary greatly in size and capacity, but their functions are standard. This section describes all of the important components of HVAC systems except for the metal ducts of forced air-heating systems and A/C systems and the piping network of radiant heating systems. The reason for not including ducts or piping is that technicians who work on the automation controls for HVAC systems rarely, if ever, install or remodel metal ducts or pipes for radiant heating. The former are made and installed by sheet metal workers who specialize in building heating and A/C duct systems. The latter are installed by plumbers and pipefitters who specialize in heating systems.

Duct systems and pipes are nearly always installed when a home is built. The control technician may install control mechanisms at the time the HVAC system is installed, or he or she may be called in later to automate a system that was originally a manual one. By installing additional control components, an HVAC system that was originally a single zone system can be converted to multizone in order to provide more even temperature control and better economy.

Furnaces

Furnaces provide the heat in an HVAC system. Forced air furnaces are controlled by a thermostat, which turns them off or on. Furnaces do not have graduated control, but only a simple on or off switch. When they're on, they produce heat at full capacity. When they're off, they produce none. Figure 12-5 shows how a forced air furnace works and the main parts of the furnace. As was shown in Figure 12-1, furnaces and air conditioners are often built as combination units using the same blowers and duct work to transport the air they heat or cool.

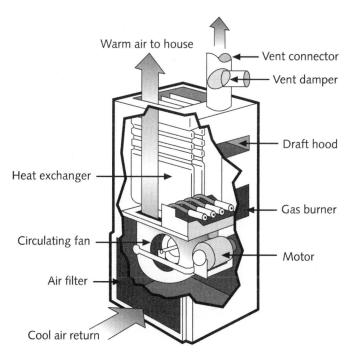

Figure 12-5   A typical forced air furnace

Gas and oil furnaces, which are connected to a gas or oil line, have a safety device called a **thermocouple**. This device is a flexible metal tube, which produces an electric current when heated. In a furnace that has a continuously burning **pilot light** (that functions to ignite the gas or oil when the furnace is turned on), the thermocouple is placed in the flame of the pilot light. As long as the pilot light flame is burning, the thermocouple produces electricity, which in turn signals a **valve** on the gas or oil line to stay open so that fuel can flow to the furnace. If the pilot light goes out, the thermocouple cools off and stops producing the electric current. This signals the gas or oil **safety control valve** to close, shutting off the gas or oil and preventing any buildup of unburned fuel, which could cause a fire or explosion.

Furnaces without continuously burning pilot lights are fired by a **spark igniter**, but they also have thermocouples as safety devices to control the flow of fuel. When the spark igniter fires the furnace, the fuel valve is open and remains open for a few seconds while the furnace fires and the pilot light begins to burn. When the pilot light starts burning, the thermocouple begins producing current and this signals the valve to stay open. If the pilot light doesn't come on, the thermocouple doesn't signal and the valve closes as soon as the delay period ends.

Radiant **boilers** also have thermocouples on their heating units to prevent any buildup of unburned fuel. On most occasions when a furnace stops working, the problem is a failed thermocouple. Other safety devices in furnaces and boilers are temperature sensors, which shut the units down if they get too hot. Heat buildup in a furnace can occur if a blower motor or drive belt fails or if a **circulating pump** on a radiant unit fails.

Refrigeration Air Conditioners

Air conditioners work like a refrigerator to cool air and circulate it. Air conditioners consist of a **condensing unit** and a cooling coil through which air is blown by a fan or blower. The condensing unit and **cooling coil** are connected by pipes or tubing so that a **refrigerant fluid** can circulate between them. The condenser unit is located outside the home so that the heat it extracts from the cooled air can be exhausted to the outside air. The cooling unit is located inside in the main air flow duct of the HVAC system where it can cool the air passing through it.

The refrigerant, which is a gas at room temperature and pressure, is held inside a sealed circulation system in the A/C unit. As the refrigerant passes through the condenser unit, it is compressed by a compressor into a liquid under high pressure. Compressing the gas makes the liquid it forms hot and it is cooled by the fan of the condenser unit as it passes through the **condenser coil**. From the coil the cooled liquid, still under high pressure, flows to the cooling coil in the air conditioner unit. There it is permitted to expand back into a gas at lower pressure and, as it does so, it absorbs a large amount of heat from the cooling coil and the surrounding air. This cools the air, which then is forced into the home by a blower. The expanded gas, which has absorbed heat from the air, flows back to the condenser unit where it is again compressed into liquid form and its heat is extracted in the condenser coil by the cooling fan of the condenser. Figure 12-6 shows how an air conditioner works.

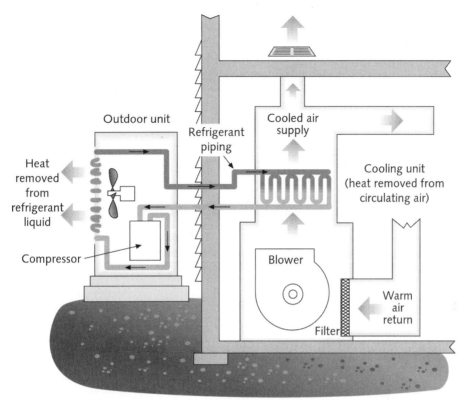

Figure 12-6   How an air conditioner works

Thermostat

A thermostat is the main control sensor used for HVAC systems. It consists of a temperature sensing device coupled to a switch. A thermostat can be set at a given temperature and whenever the temperature falls below the set temperature, the switch on the thermostat closes. This sends a signal to the furnace to turn on and raise the room temperature. When the temperature reaches the set level, the thermostat switch opens and this signals the furnace to turn off.

Thermostats can be dual-acting so that they control both heating and cooling equipment. In this case, when the room temperature falls too low and the thermostat switch closes, the furnace will turn on. When the temperature is above the set figure and the switch is open, the A/C unit turns on and cools the room until the switch closes, signaling the air conditioner to turn off. Dual-acting thermostats have a second switch, which sets them to either heat or cool mode. This prevents both the heating and A/C units from being active at the same time. The switch can be set by the user and it determines which system is operational. Without such a switch, the two systems would constantly conflict with one another, the furnace continually raising the room temperature and the A/C lowering it.

In HVAC systems that have multiple zones, a thermostat normally is installed for each zone. This allows the temperature to be maintained at a set level in each zone. The actual temperature set may be the same in each zone, but the individual thermostats are still useful

12

because they allow the system to act independently in each zone to maintain the desired temperature. Twice as much heat, for example, may be needed to maintain 70 degrees Fahrenheit (F) in a room over an unheated garage on the north side of the house, as in a sunny room on the south side. The individual thermostats can signal for the necessary heating in each zone.

Sensors

Thermostats are not thermometers. They don't signal the temperature. They only signal when one particular temperature is reached. In automated HVAC systems, temperature sensors are sometimes used, which do signal the actual room temperature. These sensors do not signal the HVAC system to turn on or off; they simply signal the existing temperature so that the system's central control can determine from that data what system to turn on and when. In a zoned system, a temperature sensor is placed in each zone so as to provide temperature information about the zone, enabling the HVAC system to act independently to maintain the correct temperature in each zone.

Another type of sensor used in HVAC systems is a **humidity detector**. This device measures the amount of moisture in the air and can be used to signal an HVAC system when to turn on or turn off a **humidifier** that adds moisture to the incoming air stream. Humidifiers are normally used only with furnaces. The act of heating air also dries it, and moisture often needs to be added for comfort in a heated room. This is especially true in normally dry climates where winter humidity levels can fall below 10%. Air-conditioning systems rarely use humidifiers because cooled air has a higher relative humidity than it did before cooling. Most A/C systems actually extract moisture from the air as they cool it. The extracted water is drained out of the system and discarded.

HVAC systems also contain safety sensors to protect the equipment and the home. For the air conditioner, the sensor is a **freeze sensor**, which signals if the cooled air is at or below the freezing point of water. This could happen if the A/C were inadvertently turned on in the winter, or the controlling thermostat failed to shut it off at the set temperature. The freeze sensor provides a safety check on the system that shuts it down before it freezes up and damages the cooling coils and dehumidifier. For the furnace, a high-temperature sensor is included that shuts the furnace down if its internal temperature rises too high. Such an event could occur if the blower motor or drive belt failed, or if the air vents were blocked so that heated air couldn't exit from the system.

Air Handlers

Air handlers might better be named air movers. They are the mechanical devices that move air in an HVAC system. There are two basic types of air handlers: fans and blowers, and each can be used in either of two ways: to force air forward from the air handler into an area by increasing pressure, or to exhaust air out of an area by decreasing the pressure.

Fans are sets of angled blades on a shaft spun by a motor. An airplane propeller is a fan, but one designed to pull or push the aircraft through the air rather than to move the air. A fan designed to move air has wider blades set at a shallow angle. Fans move air well and are widely used as cooling devices by themselves. As their size and speed increases, however, they become noisy. This is because the leading edges of the blades "bite" into the air as they turn and produce a small shock wave that can be heard as sound. In small fans, this sound is barely audible, but in large ones turning fast, it quickly becomes a roar that nobody wants to listen to for long. The sound problem for fans is made worse by the fact that the outer tips of the blades are moving much faster than the hub in the middle of the fan. In large fans rotating at high speed, the moving blade tips can actually approach the speed of sound. If they were to exceed the speed of sound, they would produce a continuous sonic boom that would be deafening to anyone nearby.

Because fans are noisy in large sizes, a second type of air handler was developed that greatly reduced this problem: blowers. A blower looks somewhat like the paddle wheel on the rear of a river boat, and it acts somewhat similarly on air as the paddle wheel does on water. The rotating wheel of a blower is closely fitted in a housing with one exit on the outside. As the wheel spins, air is drawn into its center and impelled outward by the blades of the wheel. When the air finds the exit opening in the housing, it moves into it, forced along by the moving blades.

Blowers can be made larger than fans and they move slower, rotating at 400 to 500 rpm in contrast to fans, which often spin at 3600 or 7200 rpm. Because of their slower speeds, blowers are quieter and because of their size they can move large amounts of air. Most HVAC systems use blowers rather than fans as their main air handlers.

Blowers usually push air forward, although they can be used to exhaust air as well. Fans can also push air as well as exhaust it, but most exhaust air handlers are fans. Forced air handlers work by increasing the pressure of the air, causing it to move forward where the pressure is less. Exhaust fans work by reducing the air pressure behind them as they push the air forward in front of them. The reduced pressure causes air further back in the system to move forward to where the pressure is less. HVAC systems use forced air handlers to move air through the system. If fresh air is taken into the system and used air exhausted, these functions are handled by an exhaust fan.

Damper Controls

Dampers control the flow of air in a duct by opening or closing. They act like a door that can be opened to allow the passage of air or closed to block it. Dampers are not hinged at the side like a door, however. One type is pivoted in the middle with half the damper door on one side of the pivot and half on the other. The door is fixed to the pivot rod and the rod extends outside the duct so that it can be used to open or close the damper. This arrangement makes the pivot easy to open and close because the pressure of the moving air in the duct on it is balanced: there is as much air pushing to close the door as to open it.

Another type of damper is a set of louvers like those used to close the A/C vents on the dashboard of a car. The louvers are set in the duct and an activator rod that can open or close them extends outside the duct. Dampers can be automated by small motors called servomechanisms, which are attached to the pivot rod or activator rod and open or close the damper on command. Motorized dampers usually operate on 24-volt AC power and

12

are controlled by a controller. Figure 12-7 shows a louvered damper configured for installation in a rectangular duct. The damper's motor and control are mounted on the right side of the square casing.

Figure 12-7 A motorized damper for a rectangular duct

Dampers are normally installed fully open. This means that their normal position is open and they can only be closed by a signal from a controller. If the power fails or the system shuts down, all the dampers open. It should be noted that the function of dampers is limited to blocking the flow of air in a duct. They can't increase the flow, only reduce it.

Duct Boosters

If an area in a home has too little heated or cooled air reaching it, installing a damper won't help. To get more air into the room, an auxiliary fan is needed. These fans are called duct boosters because they're placed in the duct just as a damper is and they pull more air through the duct and into the room it heats than the furnace blower alone can provide.

A duct booster has its own motor and can be controlled and operated independently of the main furnace. Duct boosters can only operate when the furnace is running because they don't have any source of heat other than the furnace. They are only fans that distribute the furnace's heat more efficiently to a specific area. If the room it serves is consistently underheated, a booster can be set to operate whenever the furnace is running in order to bring the room temperature up to normal. If lower temperature in the room is only an occasional problem, the booster can be connected to its own temperature sensor and set to operate only when the room temperature is too low.

Controller Panels

Most HVAC systems are controlled by a thermostat or multiple thermostats, if the system has zones. An HVAC system only has a control panel if it is centrally controlled from one point. The control panel can be an independent multizone controller or an interface to a computer, which provides the control through a software program.

Forced air systems typically use a controller such as an RCS brand 6-zone HVAC control, which provides all the control features needed for a multizone system. The controller does all of the following:

- Communicates directly with up to six RCSLinc units, which control 24-volt A/C, normally open, motorized zone dampers and furnace thermostats

- Communicates with an outdoor RCSLinc unit, which controls the air-conditioning compressor/condenser unit

- Sets and maintains independent temperature control of up to six zones

- Automatically changes over from heat function to cooling based on time setting or temperature setting

- Provides a built-in, short-cycle control function for the A/C compressor to prevent damage from too rapid starting and stopping cycles

- Shows visible LED status indicators on the panel for verification of the system's operations

This unit can also be interfaced with a computer through an RS232 or RS485 connection so that computer software can program its operation and provide more complete automation for the HVAC system. The control unit must be connected by low-voltage wires to each of the zone thermostats and to the zone dampers it controls. If it interfaces with a computer, the computer instructions are still implemented through the motor and temperature control connections of the controller rather than directly by the computer, so the same wired connections are needed in either case.

Multizone radiant heating systems are more easily controlled than forced air systems because each zone can be turned off or on with a single valve control in the hot water circulation system. Since all the piping exits from the system's boiler, the entire control system can be wired there. No dampers are used in these systems, but thermostats are normally wired in each zone so the controller knows the room temperature and can adjust the water controls accordingly. Figure 12-8 shows an 8-zone radiant heating system control setup with an automated valve control on each zone pipe. The water storage tank is in the foreground of the picture and the boiler is in the background. The home in which this system is located is in Park City, Utah, at an altitude of about 8000 feet, so no air conditioning is required for the system.

12

Figure 12-8   A radiant heating system with automatic controls

HVAC CONTROLLER SYSTEM INSTALLATION

HVAC systems are nearly always installed at the time the home is built. Not only the physical equipment for the systems, but also the control devices (thermostats, temperature sensors, and damper controls) and wiring for them are built into the basic structure of the home. While it's possible to retrofit an automated control system to a previously installed HVAC system, this is unusual and is likely to be both difficult and expensive.

This section describes the controller wiring and devices that need to be in place for an HVAC controller system. Also described is how the wiring connects to termination points on each of the control devices as well as the central controller. Assume that the system is centrally controlled from a controller panel, although the wiring for thermostats would be similar if they were the only control mechanism in the system.

Controller Wiring

Wiring for HVAC controllers can be done with Category 2 telephone wire. Dampers, thermostats, and temperature sensors all connect with only two wires and generally run on 24-volt AC power. Thermostats send only power on and power off signals and dampers receive only those same signals. Temperature sensors send more complex data, but still in relatively simple form and at slow speeds.

As with security system wiring, HVAC wiring can be stapled in place, bent around sharp corners, and carried near high-voltage power lines without any effect on their function. A home run wire pair must be run from each thermostat to the controller panel and from each damper to the controller panel. If the system is using temperature sensors in place of thermostats, these, too, must each have a home run wire to the control panel.

In a forced air system, heated or cooled air to each zone is controlled by a damper installed in the zone ducts coming from the main blower. At the controller panel, the thermostat located in the zone is wired to the control panel's sensor connection for that zone, and the damper is wired to the control out connection for the zone. In a radiant system, the thermostat wiring is the same as for forced air, but the power out connections for each zone go to the respective zones' water control valves located near the boiler for the system. The starter control on the furnace itself is also connected to the control panel.

Air-conditioning control wires go to the condenser/compressor unit outside the house and also to the temperature sensor inside the cooling coil enclosure. If the system has outside air ventilation, the dampers for exhaust air and incoming air must also be wired to the control panel along with the return air thermostat or sensor that helps the system determine how much fresh air is needed.

Termination Points

HVAC wiring is all connected to screws or nut posts on the devices and should be attached firmly so it is held in place over a long period of time. The wiring is AC, which means that the current flowing in it reverses direction 60 times per second, so the order in which the two wires are attached to each device doesn't matter. AC motors and solenoids operate the same, regardless of the termination point to which the "hot" lead is connected.

When wiring the control panel, wires should be carefully labeled to identify to which zone and device they are connected. Care should be taken to wire everything to the right connection point. A misplaced sensor or damper wire can cause the whole system to malfunction by turning on heat or cooling in the wrong room based on data from another zone. Once wired, the HVAC system should be manually tested and each zone physically checked to be sure the system is actually functioning as the control panel says it is. Figure 12-9 shows the typical wiring for a multiple-zone HVAC controller.

12

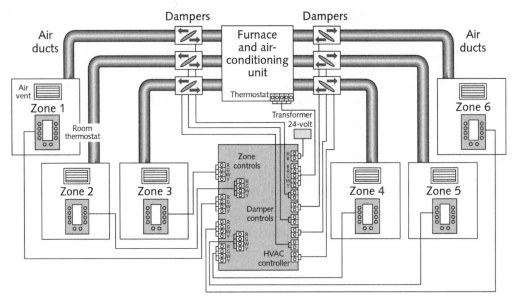

Figure 12-9   A multiple-zone HVAC controller wiring diagram

Safety sensors in both the furnace and A/C are internally wired to shut each unit down if a safety problem arises. These shutdowns override the normal operation of the control panel, which doesn't need to be connected to the freeze or overheat sensors unless the system has an emergency notification feature that alerts the homeowner to the problem.

Computer connection for an HVAC control panel is through an RS232 port on the computer and the panel. The connection requires only four wires and can be changed with an adaptor to an RJ-11 or RJ-45 connector if the computer is separated from the control panel by more than a few feet. With the smaller connectors, a cable can be run between the computer and the panel to link them.

SETTING AND PROGRAMMING HVAC CONTROLLERS AND SENSORS

Once installed, tested, and programmed, a good HVAC control system should function on its own with virtually no required input from the home owner for long periods of time. Setting and adjusting the system to function on its own may take a little time, but results in a comfortable environment over long stretches. This section describes setting the controllers and sensors to operate without additional human input.

Sensor and Thermostat Settings

Thermostats should be set to a comfortable room temperature, around 68 to 70 degrees in the winter and 75 to 78 degrees in the summer. Some people may prefer only one year-round temperature somewhere in between those given, but most feel better with two settings, and the dual range is more economical as well. Once set, thermostats can be left in the same position indefinitely.

Experience may show that some zone thermostats need to be set a few degrees higher or lower than the desired temperature in order to maintain that actual temperature in the room. This can be a function of the thermostat itself (it reads slightly above or below the actual temperature) or its location (it's placed in the room where the temperature is consistently higher or lower than the room average). There's nothing wrong with making these adjustments and they won't affect the economy of the system as long as the actual room temperature level (as contrasted with the thermostat setting) isn't increased substantially.

Zone Programming

The control panel, based on input from the thermostats, starts the HVAC system (furnace or A/C) as needed and opens or closes the dampers to each zone as required. Only those areas of the home that need heat or cooling receive it. In radiant systems, the controller opens or closes the appropriate valves on the piping system to control the flow of hot water.

Zones can be set to maintain different temperatures if desired. A garage or storage room, for example, might be kept 10 or 15 degrees colder than the rest of the home. The garage might be eliminated entirely from the A/C system. A sun room might be allowed to rise 10 degrees above the rest of the home's A/C level, and in winter to drop 10 degrees below the heated level of other rooms.

Time-of-Day Programming

Many people prefer lower heating temperatures at night and a control panel or programmable thermostat in a single-zone HVAC system usually permits such time-of-day changes. The typical system allows for four temperature changes per day, so a day's program might look like this:

- *5:30 a.m.* — Temperature up to 70 degrees prior to family awakening.

- *8:00 a.m.* — Temperature down to 55 degrees while family is at work or school.

- *4:30 p.m.* — Temperature up to 70 degrees prior to family's arrival home.

- *10:30 p.m.* — Temperature down to 65 degrees while family is asleep.

Weekend times and temperatures would probably be adjusted somewhat differently because the family's schedule would be different on those days. Figure 12-10 shows an automated thermostat for a single-zone HVAC system. A control panel has similar inputs for a zoned system.

12

Figure 12-10   An automated thermostat control

Seasonal Presets

In addition to timed temperature settings on a daily basis, control panels allow for longer range settings as well. These seasonal adjustments can include temperature changes that vary depending on the time of year and time adjustments for away periods. If the home is not occupied year-round, the HVAC system can be programmed to reduce operation to the minimum needed to avoid freezing or overheating whenever the occupants are not in the home. This can be programmed automatically (using a motion sensor and a time delay — if no motion is detected in the home for 12 hours, the minimum operation cycle starts) or it can be integrated with the home's security system (whenever the security system is armed because the family is away from the home, the HVAC system goes to minimum operation status).

Remote Access

The minimal operation function of an HVAC system, whether timed or activated by a security system or sensor, is made better by a remote access feature for the system. Since no one likes coming home to a cold (or overheated) house, being able to contact the HVAC system by telephone or by computer on the Internet enables the homeowner to call ahead so that the home temperature is normal when the family arrives. The radiant heating system pictured in Figure 12-8, for example, is in a home occupied only part of the year by a family who otherwise lives on the East Coast. When the owners are away, the HVAC system is on minimum operation. When they arrive at the Salt Lake International Airport, about an hour's drive from Park City, a telephone call and a few command inputs changes the home's HVAC system to normal operation so that by the time the owners arrive at the front door, the home is heated normally and ready to receive them.

Chapter Summary

- Central heating systems consist of forced air and radiant designs. Forced air systems heat by moving warmed air from a furnace unit to the rooms of the home. Radiant systems heat by circulating hot water from a boiler to radiators or pipes beneath the floors of the home from which warmth radiates to the interior air. Home heating systems are gas or oil fueled.

- Central air-conditioning systems are all forced air designs. They move cooled air from a cooling unit to the rooms of a home to reduce the room air temperature. Most A/C systems are electric powered, and in addition to the inside cooling unit have an outside condenser unit, which compresses the refrigerant and dissipates its heat.

- HVAC systems that are divided into zones can better heat and cool a home. The zone controls enable the system to overcome the effects of climate, sun heating, and uneven heat loss in a home and also provide for varying temperatures in each zone, if desired.

- HVAC components consist of furnaces that provide heat, air conditioners that cool air, air handlers that move air, thermostats that signal temperature changes, sensors and dampers that control the operation of the system, and controllers that automate the operation of the HVAC system.

- HVAC systems are installed when a home is built. Control systems can be installed then or later. In either case, the thermostats and dampers are wired to the control panel as are the other sensors and controls in the system.

- HVAC control panels can be programmed for automatic operation of all zones in the system. They also permit time-of-day programming, seasonal presets, and remote access to the system by telephone or Internet connection.

12

Key Terms

air conditioning (A/C) — The part of an HVAC system that provides cool air to lower the indoor air temperature.

air handlers — The mechanical devices that move air in an HVAC system. They are mainly blowers and fans.

automated control — A method for controlling HVAC systems by preset programming rather than manual setting of controls.

blower — A device that uses a rotating bladed wheel to move air in an HVAC system. Not the same thing as a fan.

boiler — A device for heating water to be used for heating a building. Not the same as a water heater.

central heating system — The part of an HVAC system that provides warm air from a central furnace to raise the indoor air temperature.

circulating pump — A device in a radiant heating system that continuously circulates the heated water through the boiler and heating pipes.

compressor — The part of an A/C system that squeezes the refrigeration gas under pressure into a smaller volume until it converts into a liquid.

condensation — The process in an A/C system by which the refrigeration gas changes back into a liquid under pressure. Also the process by which water vapor is removed from cooled air and is deposited as a liquid.

condenser coil — A coil through which hot refrigerant passes and is cooled by flowing air in the same manner as an automobile radiator cools engine coolant.

condensing unit — The part of an A/C system in which the refrigerant is converted back into a liquid from a gaseous state.

cooling coil — The part of an A/C system that cools the surrounding air by the expansion of the refrigerant in the coil, which absorbs heat from the air.

dampers — Devices that act like doors in ducts. They can be closed to block air passage or opened to allow it.

duct — A metal tube or open ended box though which air can flow. Can be rigid or flexible and of any size.

evaporative or"swamp"cooler — A type of air cooler that works by evaporation of water into air, which is thereby cooled as it passes through the cooler.

fan — A device consisting of a balanced set of angled blades on a shaft spun by a motor. Fans move air and are one type of air handler.

forced air — A type of heating or A/C system that works by blowing heated or cooled air into a home through ducts and air vents.

freeze sensor — A device that signals if the air around it is at or below the freezing point of water so that action can be taken to prevent freezing.

furnace — A device for heating air so that it can be blown into the interior of a home.

heat transfer — The process by which heat radiates from warmer objects to cooler ones.

heating, ventilation and air-conditioning (HVAC) systems — Systems that provide controlled heating, cooling, and ventilation in buildings.

humidifier — A device that adds moisture to an incoming air stream.

humidity — Moisture contained in air. All air contains some water vapor (gaseous water). The amount can vary with pressure and temperature of the air.

humidity detector — A device that measures the amount of moisture in the air around it and signals that data to a controller or computer.

pilot light — A small flame that burns continuously in a furnace to ignite the furnace's main burner when it is turned on.

radiant — A type of heating system that works by warming a home with hot water that flows to radiators in each room or in pipes beneath the floors. The radiators or floors then warm the interior air.

refrigerant fluid — A gas/liquid that circulates in an A/C system continuously extracting heat from the surrounding air as it changes from a liquid to a gas and back again.

refrigeration — A method of cooling air that uses the heat absorption of expanding gas to extract heat from the surrounding air.

safety control valve — A specialized valve on the fuel line of a furnace or other appliance that must receive a continuous electric current from a thermocouple in order to stay open. If the current stops, the valve closes, shutting off the fuel flow.

space heaters — A small heater, usually electric, but sometimes gas fired, designed to heat a small area or room. Manually controlled.

spark igniter — An electrical device that ignites the fuel in an oil or gas furnace when it starts.

temperature sensor — A device that signals the actual temperature of the air surrounding it to an HVAC controller or a computer.

thermocouple — A safety device that produces electric current when heated. Used to shut valves on gas or oil lines if the furnace fails to start or run properly.

thermostat — A special type of temperature sensor that sends a signal when air temperature reaches a preset level.

valve — A device for controlling the flow of fluids (gases or liquids) in a pipe. Can be manually or automatically controlled.

12

ventilation — The process of exchanging air in a confined room or space. Ventilation exhausts the old air out of a room and brings new air in.

vents — An opening in a wall or floor through which air flows from a connected duct into a room.

zone — In HVAC systems, a part of a home separately heated and cooled and controlled by one thermostat.

REVIEW QUESTIONS

1. A space heater is a device that:

    a. heats water in a shallow container to provide humidity

    b. heats a small area or a single room

    c. fits into a small space

    d. heats objects placed in it

2. Evaporative or "swamp" coolers can be used only in very damp humid climates. True or False?

3. The two main types of central heating system are _____ and _____.

4. What does an air handler do?

5. A radiant heating system heats by:

   a. reflected sunlight

   b. hot water pipes beneath the floors

   c. large windows that trap heat from the sun

   d. heated bricks placed around the home

6. The two main types of air handlers are _____ and _____.

7. Many furnaces were once fired by coal, but now most are fueled by either _____ or _____.

8. How does refrigeration work?

9. Most air conditioners are powered by _____.

10. If a home has more than one furnace or A/C unit, it also has more than one _____.

11. What is heat transfer?

12. Each zone in an HVAC system is independently controlled even though all may be heated and cooled by one system. True or False?

13. A thermostat and a thermometer are the same thing. True or False?

14. Ventilating a room means:

   a. installing heating and cooling vents in it

   b. closing doors so air is forced out of the vents

   c. exchanging the air in the room without heating or cooling it

   d. releasing high-pressure gas into the room

15. The function of a damper is to open or close a _____ so that air can pass or is blocked.

16. What do intake vents and exhaust vents do?

17. The device that protects a furnace from a buildup of unburned fuel is called a(n) _____.

18. Furnaces that don't have pilot lights are started by a(n) _____.

19. A boiler and a circulating pump are both devices that would be found in what type of system?

   a. air conditioning

   b. ventilating

   c. radiant heating

   d. forced air furnace

20. What does the compressor in a condenser unit compress and why?

21. A thermostat consists of a temperature sensor and a(n) _____.

22. A humidity detector detects _____ in the air.

23. Blowers are used in large HVAC systems rather than fans because fans make more _____.

24. An HVAC control panel is connected by home run wiring to which of the following?

   a. thermostats

   b. dampers

   c. both of the above

   d. neither of the above

25. Using remote access, an HVAC system can be controlled using a _____ or the _____.

12

HANDS-ON PROJECTS

HANDS-ON PROJECTS

Project 12-1: Wire a Thermostat

In this project you wire a thermostat to an electric light that serves as a simulated furnace. For this project you need a thermostat (standard or automated), a 9-volt electric light in a socket with connector screws, a 9-volt battery in a holder with connector screws, and some single-strand insulated wire to make the connections. You also need a hair dryer to test the project when you have finished wiring it.

1. Remove the battery from the holder until you have finished wiring the thermostat.

2. Strip a short length of wire at both ends and connect the positive lead of the battery holder to one connector on the light socket.

3. Strip the ends of a second length of wire and connect the negative lead of the battery holder to one connector screw on the thermostat.

4. Strip the ends of a third length of wire and connect the other connector screw on the thermostat to the open connector on the light socket.

5. Set the thermostat to 70 degrees (or just above the present room temperature) so it is on. Place the battery back in the holder. The light should go on because the thermostat is on.

6. Plug in the hair dryer and turn it on low heat. Direct the dryer's air stream on the thermostat until it opens and the light goes off.

7. Immediately turn off the dryer and see how long it takes for the thermostat to close and turn on the light.

HANDS-ON PROJECTS

Project 12-2: Program an Automatic Thermostat

In this project you program four time-of-day settings with corresponding temperatures into an automatic thermostat. For this project you need an automatic thermostat (Dayton Fuel Trimmer Model T-110 or similar).

1. Open the back of the thermostat's case and insert a 9-volt battery to power it. The thermostat can be programmed without being connected to an HVAC system

2. Set the Heat/Cool switch to Heat. Set the Master Switch to On.

3. Press the Set Day button. Use the Time Forward or Time Back button to set the day to the number (1 through 7) of today. Monday is 1, Sunday is 7.

4. Press the Set Clock button. Use the Time Forward or Time Back button to set the correct hour of the time. Be sure you get the correct setting for a.m. or p.m.

5. Press the Set Clock button again. Use the Time Forward or Time Back button to set the correct minutes of the time.

6. Press the View Program button. The program opens to the first setting.

7. Advance or back up the time to 5:30 a.m. using the Time Forward or Time Backward buttons.

8. Use the Up Arrow and Down Arrow buttons to set the temperature to 70 degrees.

9. Press the View Program button. The program opens to the second setting.

10. Advance the time to 8:00 a.m. using the Time Forward button.

11. Use the Down Arrow button to set the temperature to 55 degrees.

12. Press the View Program button. The program opens to the third setting.

13. Advance the time to 4:30 p.m. using the Time Forward button.

14. Use the Up Arrow button to set the temperature to 70 degrees.

15. Press the View Program button. The program opens to the fourth setting.

16. Advance the time to 10:30 p.m. using the Time Forward button.

17. Use the Down Arrow buttons to set the temperature to 60 degrees.

18. Press the Run Program button to close the program. You can view the program by pressing the View Program button repeatedly to advance through the settings.

Project 12-3: Compare Heat Transfer and Insulation

In this project you compare heat transfer through from different substances to see how it can affect the performance and economy of HVAC systems. For this project you need a drinking glass, a small plate (plastic or glass), a cardboard box with a lid that is large enough to hold the plate, some ice cubes, and a hair dryer.

1. Put three or four ice cubes in the glass.

2. Plug in the dryer and turn it on low heat.

3. Direct the dryer's air stream at the side of the glass (keep air from going in the top of the glass) and watch how quickly the ice begins to melt.

4. Time how long it takes to completely melt the ice cubes.

5. Put the same number of ice cubes as you had in the glass on the plate and place it in the box. Close the lid.

6. Direct the dryer's air stream at the bottom of the box (keep air from going in the top of the box).

7. After a few minutes, open the box and see if the ice has begun to melt.

8. Close the lid and continue heating the box with the dryer. Time how long it takes to melt the ice cubes in the box.

9. The glass is made of window material. The box is made of material similar to insulation in walls. Which transfers heat fastest? How would this difference in heat transfer affect an HVAC system in a home with large windows on one side?

12

Project 12-4: Wire a Thermostat to a Damper

In this project you wire a thermostat to a motorized damper that could be used as a zone control in an HVAC system. For this project you need a thermostat (standard or automated), a 24-volt motorized damper, a 24-volt output AC transformer with connector screws, and some single-strand insulated wire to make the connections. You also need a hair dryer to test the project when you have finished wiring it.

1. Unplug the transformer until you have finished wiring the thermostat and damper.

2. Strip a short length of wire at both ends and connect one lead of the transformer to one connector on the damper.

3. Strip the ends of a second length of wire and connect the other lead of the transformer to one connector screw on the thermostat.

4. Strip the ends of a third length of wire and connect the other connector screw on the thermostat to the open connector on the damper.

5. Set the thermostat to 70 degrees (or just above the present room temperature) so it is on. Plug in the transformer. The damper should open because the thermostat is on.

6. Plug in the hair dryer and turn it on low heat. Direct the dryer's air stream on the thermostat until it opens and the damper closes.

7. Immediately turn off the dryer and see how long it takes for the thermostat to close and open the damper.

CASE PROJECTS

Case Project 12-1: Design Zones for an HVAC System

You've been asked to determine the zones in a home HVAC system. The home is a two-story house with an attached double garage. All four bedrooms are upstairs, two of them over the garage. The living room, family room, and kitchen are downstairs. The owner would like heat available to the garage, but not air conditioning. The rest of the home should have heat and A/C. A maximum of four zones are available in the HVAC system. Tell how you would configure the HVAC zones so as to provide even heating and A/C in the home and heat only in the garage.

Case Project 12-2: Solve a Heat-deficiency Problem

A homeowner asks you for help solving an HVAC problem in his home. The home has a single-zone HVAC system with the furnace and A/C equipment located next to the garage on one side of the house. The two bedrooms on the other side of the home are cold when the rest of the home is normally heated. The whole house is well-insulated and sealed, but these rooms just don't receive enough heated air from the distant furnace to keep them warm. The home has an unfinished attic that is also well-insulated. Installing a second furnace or zones in the existing system would be expensive. What solution can you suggest that would draw more heated air into the two bedrooms without major expense?

Case Project 12-3: Advise a Client about a Failed Pilot Light

You receive a call late at night from a friend who has just moved into her first home, a new condominium with a state of the art HVAC system. She tells you that her furnace has stopped working and she cannot see any pilot light burning in the combustion chamber. With the pilot light out, she's concerned that natural gas could leak into the condominium and build up to explosive levels. She's opened the windows to let any gas that's present escape, but the night is cold and she doesn't want to leave the windows open until she can call a repairman in the morning. She asks what you suggest she should do for the remainder of the night. What would you tell her about the missing pilot light (remember, her furnace could use a spark igniter instead of a pilot light) and the possibility of gas leaking into her home from the stopped furnace?

Case Project 12-4: Diagnose a Malfunctioning Heating System

In a large home with a 6-zone HVAC system, Zone 3, which covers three upper-floor bedrooms, is consistently cold during cold nights. Setting the thermostat for this zone to a higher level doesn't help. The rooms' temperature doesn't rise at all. Some heat is getting to these rooms because they're definitely warmer than the outside air, but not enough to make them comfortable. When you check the radiant heating system in the utility room, you find that the water pipe leading to Zone 3 is cool to the touch, while all the other zone pipes are hot. From what you know about heat transfer and zoned heating systems, what piece of HVAC equipment would you check first to solve this problem? What piece would you check next and why?

12

13

WATER SYSTEM MANAGEMENT

After reading this chapter, you will be able to:

♦ Describe the design and operation of automatic water system controllers

♦ Identify the major components in automated water systems and describe their functions

♦ Describe the installation and programming of an automated home water system

Water systems are one of the home utilities most frequently automated. In this chapter you will learn how to design a water control system that will provide maximum convenience and flexibility to the home owner. You will learn about the major components in a water control system and how each of them functions. Finally, you will learn how to install a water control system and program it for automatic operation with a minimum of user input.

Water Control System Design

Automated home water systems are rare inside American homes, but millions are installed outside in their yards. This is actually the logical place for them because about 65% of the culinary water (drinking-quality water delivered to users through municipal systems) usage in the United States is for lawns and gardens, while only about 35% is used inside the home in bathrooms, laundries, and kitchens. Only a few inside uses of water can be automated. The rest usually require the presence of whoever is using the water and remote operation is pointless.

Outside watering, however, is ideally suited for automation both because it's time consuming to do manually and because the hours when it's most economical and beneficial to do it are hours when most people prefer to be asleep.

This section describes the design of water control systems that can do all the work of watering the entire yard and do it during the hours between midnight and dawn, thus automating the water system to eliminate both the labor and the timing problem of having to do it with the garden hose.

Zoned Water Systems

Sprinkler systems are usually installed by plumbers who specialize in outdoor watering systems. Sprinkler systems were once almost all made of metal pipe and were both expensive and difficult to install properly. Most new systems are constructed of **PVC** (polyvinylchloride, a hard plastic) pipe that is less expensive than metal and far easier to install. PVC pipe is easily cut with a small saw or a pipe cutter and is flexible enough to be bent into gentle curves. The fittings that bend it around sharp corners and allow sprinkler heads and other attachments to be joined to it are all plastic castings that cost a few cents per piece. Equally important, PVC pipe can be joined by "welding" it with a type of liquid glue that dissolves the surfaces of two parts to be joined and fuses them together in a waterproof joint that is as durable as the pipe itself. Reduced materials expense and easier installation have brought the real cost of a sprinkler system down by half in recent years and made a fully automatic system affordable for almost every homeowner.

Many sprinkler systems are installed in the yards of new homes at the time of their construction, but many others are added later when the home owner can better afford them or when changing the landscaping makes a convenient opportunity. In either case, many systems are originally installed with manual controls, a series of hand-operated valves that turn various parts of the system on and off. Each **valve** controls a **zone** in the system.

NOTE As with HVAC systems discussed in Chapter 12, neither the design or installation of sprinkler systems is covered in depth; this chapter concentrates on the control systems that direct them.

The design of sprinkler system zones is determined by two main factors. Each are discussed in turn.

The Role of the Water Service Line

How large an area a sprinkler system zone can cover in a home installation is limited by how much water is available to the home through its **water service line**. The amount of water available is, in turn, determined by the size of the pipe used for the home water line pipe and the minimum amount of pressure forcing water through that pipe. Homes may have a 1/2-inch (inside pipe diameter) water line, a 3/4-inch, a 1-inch, or occasionally an even larger line. **Water pressure** in the lines also varies greatly, depending on the community's water system design, the availability of water in the area, and how the water system is pressurized. Home water systems can have water pressure from a few pounds per square inch up to 125 pounds per square inch or even more. If pressure is much above 125 pounds, a relief valve placed in the main incoming water line is a good idea to reduce the pressure to a level that protects water heaters from leaking or bursting.

Water Pressure Counts!

The sprinkler system designer should know the average water pressure for the area and design the system's zones so that they are no larger than the maximum area that can be covered using the available water pressure. The maximum number of sprinkler heads per zone depends on the type of heads used and the area each covers, but the total water flow in each zone can't exceed the capacity of the available water supply. Zones can be smaller than the maximum because the length of time the water is on in a zone can be reduced so that it doesn't receive too much water, but there's no way to get enough water to an oversized zone. Lengthening the watering time won't do it because the water lines can't carry enough water to make the sprinkler heads reach to all parts of the zone. If the designer is in doubt, it's better to err on the side of making the zones small rather than too large. That way coverage can be adjusted with the timer and the yard won't have dry spots.

Not all areas of a yard may require the same amount of water. If an area requires less, it should be placed in a single zone, if possible, so that the watering time for the area can be adjusted to conserve water. If part of the yard, for example, needs a **drip irrigation system** for flowers and other decorative plants, while the rest requires regular sprinklers for grass, the water system should be zoned accordingly so that each type of watering can be adjusted independently. Figure 13-1 shows a sprinkler design for a home with grass and garden areas. The sprinkler system has five zones, one of which uses only small sprinkler heads and waters the garden areas. One zone waters some garden area and some grass and the other three zones use large sprinklers and water only grass areas.

13

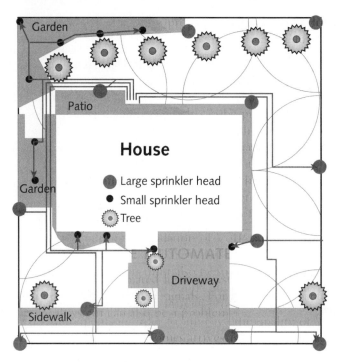

Figure 13-1   A 5-zone sprinkler system design

Interior Zones

A home with a large **atrium** or other inside garden area may want to include an interior watering zone with the yard sprinkler system. This can be done by having the control valve outside with the other zone valves in the system and running a line (usually smaller than the PVC pipe used for standard sprinkler lines) into the home through an exterior wall next to the garden area to be watered. Copper tubing is the preferred choice for piping in an interior line. A 1/4-inch tube is usually large enough for interior watering and the line should be carefully sealed where it passes through the outer wall so that insects cannot enter through the opening.

Because any failure in the sprinkler system zone inside the home is likely to cause considerable damage, safety precautions should always be added to the control program of such a zone. These should include a default automatic shutoff within a few minutes after the normal shutdown time for the zone, and a **flow valve** or **pressure valve** that shuts off water flow automatically if the amount of water moving in the line exceeds a set level. These precautions can keep an interior watering zone safe from flooding that could damage the home.

Timed Water Systems

All automatic sprinkler systems are timed to regulate the amount of water for each watering zone. If the zones divide the home's yard into landscaped areas of different water requirements, then the system can be timed to correctly water each one. Most water control systems can adjust zone times to the minute so water requirements can be very precisely defined over a period of time and the system set to meet them exactly with no wasted water and no plants withering from insufficient water.

In addition to timing each zone independently for watering, many automated controls allow seasonal adjustments to those times for each zone. Some systems have only three or four seasonal periods to work with while others allow for monthly or even more frequent adjustments. These seasonal programs allow watering periods for each zone to start short in the spring when heat is low and rain may provide much of the needed water, then grow longer (in one or two steps or half a dozen) as the year advances to mid summer. Once the hottest days of the year are past, the watering times for the zones again decrease.

Each zone can be adjusted for time upward or downward by a set percentage or number of minutes in some systems. Others require each program to be entered separately and set for a specific time to be implemented. These take longer to program than those that can be advanced or reduced as a system by a set percentage or number of minutes, but they work just as effectively once the program is entered.

The independent settings available for each zone mean that different watering patterns can also be accommodated. Drip irrigation systems typically don't need to increase their watering times as much in midsummer as sprinklers do because they lose less water to evaporation. Drip systems also require far less water pressure overall than sprinklers and can often be timed to run simultaneously with a sprinkler zone without having an adverse effect on either zone.

Watering Scenes

Drip irrigation zones and surface lawn sprinkler zones are two examples of watering scenes. Like lighting scenes defined as integrated units in a home, as discussed in Chapter 11, watering scenes are simply areas of landscaping outside that are intended to be viewed as a unit. These areas generally having similar water requirements, which can best be met by treating them as separate zones. Many landscaping designs include water features that require special water input, and these should always be set up as scenes with controlled water.

Water features in landscaped yards can be fountains, waterfalls, ponds, or combinations of these. Water features usually use recirculating water that is moved by a pump from the lowest point in the fountain or pond to the highest point and then allowed to flow down. As the water reaches the low point of the feature again, it is lifted back to the top and flows down once more. This recirculation minimizes the amount of water actually used in a water feature and eliminates the need for any continuous outlet or drain through which used water would flow.

Although recirculating water features use far less water than a continuous flow, they still use some, and they need to be "watered" regularly to replace the water they lose through evaporation or outflow. Some features also need to be flushed with a charge of fresh water so they don't become stagnant. Both replacement water and flushing with clean water can be automated as part of a watering system if the water feature is set up as a zone with its own timing and water flow.

13

Remote Access

Automatic water control systems run mainly on preset timed schedules that require little change over time. The **controller** for the system is usually located in or near the **valve box** where the wiring to the zone valves is connected. Locating the controller near the valve box minimizes the length of wiring that must be run to each of the valves. It's not always a convenient location, however, for programming or accessing the system after installation. Remote access requires only a single cable to connect the system with a computer from which it can be controlled much more easily. Moving access to the computer also means that a distant connection to the system is possible either over the Internet or through a telephone link so that in an emergency the water system can be turned off or rescheduled while the family is away.

WATER CONTROL SYSTEM COMPONENTS

The main automatic sprinkler system components are the solenoid valves that control the watering zones and the central controller on which the watering schedule is programmed. Other components are accessories to these devices. They include sensors and pumps.

Solenoid Valves

Solenoid valves are the main operating device for all automated water systems. They are simple and very reliable valves that turn water off or on by means of a solenoid that can be energized or turned off from the controller. The solenoid is a round electromagnet with a hole in its center in which is placed a metal plunger. The plunger can move within the electromagnet and its lower end functions as a small valve. Figure 13-2 shows a cross section of a solenoid valve in both the open and closed position.

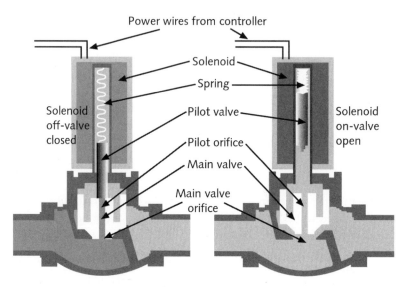

Figure 13-2   A solenoid water valve in the open (right) and closed position

As shown in Figure 13-2, the solenoid with its plunger (denoted by the pilot valve in the figure) is placed directly over the main valve so that the pilot valve sits on top of the main valve itself. A small hole through the center of the main valve serves as a pilot orifice for opening and closing the main valve. The pilot orifice is opened and closed by the solenoid's pilot valve. The main valve's operation is started by the pilot orifice opening or closing, but the valve is actually forced open or closed by water pressure in the pipe, thus leveraging the effect of the solenoid, which doesn't have to be large or powerful to control even a high-pressure valve.

When the valve is closed, the solenoid pilot valve is held down in the pilot orifice by a spring above the plunger. Water from the side orifice pressurizes the area above the pilot valve and pushes it firmly into the pilot orifice. This pressure seats the valve firmly and prevents it from leaking. As long as the pilot valve keeps the pilot orifice closed, the valve remains off.

When the solenoid is energized by the automatic controller, its magnetic force pulls the plunger up into the solenoid's electromagnet center, as seen at the right in Figure 13-2. This allows water to flow through the pilot orifice to the other side of the main valve. As the water pressure is equalized on both sides of the valve, it opens slightly and flowing water pushes it open completely allowing the full pressure of water to flow through the valve. Water continues to flow from the side orifice into the area above the main valve and down through the pilot orifice, but the water pressure above and below the valve is equal and the flowing water keeps the valve open.

When watering is completed, the controller turns off the solenoid and the pilot valve closes off the pilot orifice. Now pressure above the main valve increases because water can't flow out through the pilot orifice. The increasing pressure forces the main valve down until it closes and the water pressure above it seals it tightly in place. The valve remains closed until the activated solenoid releases water through the pilot orifice and again equalizes pressure on both sides of the valve.

A solenoid valve installed on each zone pipe of a sprinkler system enables a controller to open and close each valve in a programmed sequence. Solenoid valves are not adjustable for water flow rate. They have only two conditions possible: either closed or fully open. Total water flow in each sprinkler system zone must be adjusted by the length of time water flows to the zone, or by a separate hand-set adjustable valve in the zone line that adjusts the amount of water flowing in the line when the solenoid valve opens it.

Controller

The controller is the electronic device that controls the operation of the valves according to a timed schedule. It functions like an electric clock and calendar combination and signals each zone valve when to commence and end its watering cycle. Early controllers were electric clocks with **mechanical relays** built into them that could be adjusted for the day and time when they were to turn a water valve on or off. Today all controllers are electronic and activate each zone's solenoid valve by means of a current triggered from a relay built into the unit's circuitry. Figure 13-3 shows a control unit installed on a sheltered exterior wall (on a covered patio) that controls the sprinkler system for the yard.

13

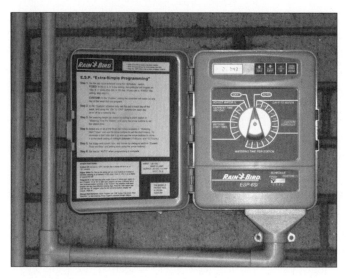

Figure 13-3   A 6-zone sprinkler system controller

The controller can be set to turn on the sprinkler system at a specified start time on specified watering days. On watering days, the sprinkler cycle begins with Zone 1 turning on at the start time. The controller then turns the zone off after the water has run for a specified number of minutes, and turns on the next zone in succession for its allotted time until all zones have been activated. The controller shown in Figure 13-3 allows two separate programs to be set for each zone so that the watering schedule can be adjusted for the season. Two schedules aren't really enough to adjust for the full range of watering needs during an entire year, but with some programming creativity, the two can provide considerably more variation.

If for example, the yard is determined to need a minimum of 40 minutes watering per zone every week during the spring and fall of the year, and a maximum of 80 minutes watering every week during the height of summer, then Schedule 1 could be set for a 10 minute watering time per zone and schedule 2 to 20 minutes watering time per zone. By varying the use of each schedule during each week, a wide range of total weekly watering times is possible over a 7-day period. An example of schedules and total watering times that can be achieved is given below in Table 13-1.

Table 13-1

Month	Day 1	Day 3	Day 5	Day 7	Total Watering Time
April	Schedule 1	Schedule 1	Schedule 1	Schedule 1	40 minutes
May	Schedule 1	Schedule 2	Schedule 1	Schedule 1	50 minutes
June	Schedule 1	Schedule 2	Schedule 1	Schedule 2	60 minutes
July	Schedule 2	Schedule 2	Schedule 1	Schedule 2	70 minutes
August	Schedule 2	Schedule 2	Schedule 2	Schedule 2	80 minutes
September	Schedule 2	Schedule 1	Schedule 2	Schedule 2	70 minutes
October	Schedule 2	Schedule 1	Schedule 2	Schedule 1	60 minutes

Additional variations are possible with this system by scheduling the sprinklers to run three days per week rather than four. Other controllers have more programmable schedules available and can be programmed on a monthly or daily calendar.

Standard automatic sprinkler controllers are designed to function independently of any networked home automation system. Once programmed, they function according to schedule without further input from the home owner or other sensory data.

A number of systems are now available that connect directly to a computer and allow the sprinkler system to be programmed, controlled, and monitored from a PC. These systems use either a full X10 technology controller or an X10 interface unit that allows the computer to communicate with and program a stand-alone controller. Either of these alternatives provides a greater measure of convenience and control for the water system and also allows for additional input from other sensors that can improve the system's performance and economy.

Rain8 is an X10-based sprinkler control system that can control up to eight sprinkler zones as a single unit and can be networked in multiple units to control up to 256 zones. This system is manufactured by a Texas firm, WGL and Associates, and can be operated in dual modes with sprinkler zone times controlled directly from a PC or with times preset in the controller and triggered by simple X10 commands. The system provides for two schedules in each zone, all of which can be independently controlled and timed.

This system also provides several fail-safe features to eliminate malfunction due to interference or dropped signals in the X10 technology. These include default limits on a sprinkler's on time that the user can set, and a program block that prevents more than one sprinkler zone from being on at a time, which the user can override. Figure 13-4 shows a programming screen from the Rain8 system. Further information on the system is available at *www.wgldesigns.com/rain8.html*.

13

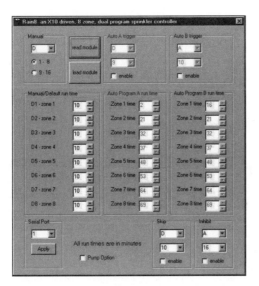

Figure 13-4   A programming screen from the Rain8 sprinkler system control software

RCI Automation also offers an X10-automated sprinkler control unit that can control up to eight sprinkler zones and interface with a number of X10 controllers that can schedule commands by time. Such controllers are made by JDS Technologies, Applied Digital, and others. The RCI system also has the fail-safe features of limiting the on time of any single zone valve (in this case to an 80-minute maximum) and blocking more than one valve from being on simultaneously (again, this feature can be bypassed, if necessary, for a watering program). By interfacing with an X10 controller, all the features of the controller itself become available for use with the watering system. These features include:

• Controls for sprinkler zones using standard X10 commands that are entered through the inside controller.

• Control that can be extended to any wireless or remote X10 unit with which the inside controller can communicate.

• Timed schedules that can be started with a single X10 command from the controller entered manually or started at a preset time by the system program.

• Watering schedules that can be temporarily suspended by use of a preset code from the controller or sent remotely.

• Watering schedules that can be weather delayed by input from sensors connected to the controller.

Figure 13-5 shows the RCI 8-zone IR8Z controller. Further information about this system and the optional sensors available with it can be found at *http://ourworld.compuserve.com/homepages/rciautomation/p6.htm.*

Figure 13-5   An RCI 8-zone X10-based sprinkler controller

Smart Electronics Corporation offers a graphical interface software and hardware package for Windows-based PCs that allows for complete control of the sprinkler system plus input from temperature, humidity, and soil moisture sensors that can further refine the watering schedules. Details about the system and prices for components are available at *www.hometoys.com/htinews/aug99/articles/vogel/vogel.htm.*

Sensors

Sensors for use with sprinkler system controllers are all weather-related devices that sense outdoor conditions and allow the computer to delay or alter the sprinkler system's schedule accordingly.

Rain sensors detect the presence of water in a small holder and signal to the controller. The controller is usually set to respond to this signal by delaying or stopping a scheduled sprinkler cycle. The amount of rain that must be present in the holder to trigger a signal can be set by the user (usually from a minimum of 1/8 inch to a maximum of one inch. This is done by simply adjusting the float mechanism in the holder so that it lifts only when the desired water level in the holder is reached. Rain sensors need to be placed where they won't be "watered" by the sprinkler system or acquire water from any source other than rain. They need to be in the open, however, so that falling rain can hit them directly. This often means that leaves and other debris can also fall into them. A screen over the collector helps prevent debris from accumulating, but the sensor should also be checked occasionally and cleaned as needed.

A **soil moisture sensor** is another type of water sensor. It works by measuring the electrical conductivity of the ground in which it's buried. Wet earth transmits electric current better than dry earth and so the sensor can detect the presence of water in the soil by measuring its conductivity. When the amount of moisture brings the current capacity up to a preset level, the sensor sends a signal to the controller. The moisture level can be adjusted on the sensor. It should be placed a few inches in the ground at a well-drained spot in the yard (a location high enough so that water from the surrounding area does not drain into it and produce false high moisture readings for the yard). Since a moisture sensor senses water in only one tiny spot and is used to represent the entire yard in the controller program, its placement should be carefully selected so that it is a fair example of the landscaped area.

A **freeze sensor** is useful for sprinkler systems located in areas where sudden low temperatures during the growing season are possible. Freeze sensors send a signal when the temperature around them falls to near freezing (37 degrees normally, although some can be set to lower or higher temperatures). As with the rain and moisture sensors, when the freeze sensor signal is received by the system controller, the response is to delay or eliminate a sprinkler cycle until the temperature warms.

Finally, a **wind sensor** can be useful for sprinkler systems, especially where water conservation is important. A wind sensor can be set to signal the controller whenever the average wind speed rises to a preset level (adjustable from 12 to 35 miles per hour). If a high wind is blowing, the controller delays the sprinkler cycle to avoid wasting water. A wind sensor should be set in an open location where it can accurately measure wind speed and where unusual gusts of wind won't be directed at it by other obstructions nearby.

13

Pumps

The majority of automatic sprinkler systems don't include any pumps because the water pressure needed to operate them is provided entirely by the utility supplying water to the home. Some systems, however, may have inadequate pressure for a sprinkler system without the aid of a pump. In these systems, the pump must normally start before the sprinkler system begins its cycle in order to build up enough pressure to operate the system.

Figure 13-6 shows a typical home water system with a pressure pump and tank. For the internal needs of the home, a pressure switch in the main incoming line controls the operation of the pump. For the sprinkler system, another pressure switch can be used in the sprinkler line or an electronic switch can be installed on the pump so that it can be programmed to activate before the sprinkler cycle begins and stay in operation until the cycle is completed. This assures adequate pressure throughout the sprinkling period.

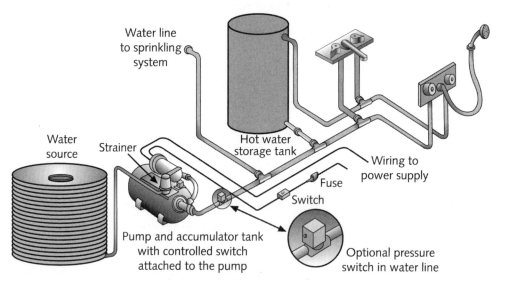

Figure 13-6   A home water system with a pressure pump and tank

In the configuration shown in Figure 13-6, the pressure switch turns the pump on whenever water pressure on the delivery side of the switch falls below a set level. But because the pressure switch is sensitive, it turns off as soon as normal pressure is restored. If water use is continued, the pressure again drops and the switch turns the pump on again. This rapid on and off cycling can continue indefinitely and is very hard on the pump and the pipe system. An automatic switch that keeps the pump on while the sprinklers are operating gives much smoother service and eliminate unnecessary wear on the pump and motor from frequent starting and stopping.

WATER CONTROL SYSTEM INSTALLATION AND PROGRAMMING

Whether an automatic control system is installed as an original part of a new sprinkler system or added to an existing system, the installation procedure is almost identical. This section describes how to install the controller and wiring for the control system and how to program its operation.

Locating the Controller

The controller for the sprinkler system must be located where it can be easily wired to each of the zone valves. If the zone valves are located in one place, then the controller can be sited near them in a sheltered position and at a height that's convenient for working at the controller box to program it. Most controllers have lids that can be closed to protect the inside electronics from the weather, but they do not lock.

If a nonlocking controller is used, it should be placed in a location where children or potential vandals won't find it easy to tamper with. This may mean placing it inside the house and running the control wiring outside to the valves in a conduit. At the least, the controller should be placed in the back yard, out of view from the street and in as sheltered a position as possible. If a locking box protects the controller from tampering, a sheltered location is still preferable, but it can be more openly positioned for convenience in wiring.

Because a wiring path from the controller to the valves is necessary, the controller should be placed so that wiring from it to the ground won't have to pass through concrete patios or sidewalks, or other obstructions that will make the installation more difficult. Before installing the controller, check the path that the wires from it to the zone valves have to follow to be sure that they can connect without major excavation or moving of landscaping. If the valves are located in two or more places, both paths should be as convenient as possible. It's often easier to relocate the controller box, than to overcome serious wiring obstacles.

The controller also requires a power source, usually 24-volt AC that can be wired from an outside power outlet or light. The controller comes equipped with a step-down transformer to reduce the voltage from 110 to 24, or one can be purchased as an accessory to go with it. Built-in transformers are part of the controller box, but separate ones may need an enclosure (covered junction box or similar) placed near the controller box and connected to it by a conduit for the wiring. The only power connection needed for a sprinkler system is the one to the controller box. Power to operate the solenoid valves is supplied through the wires connecting them to the controller.

If the controller is to be interfaced with a computer or inside control device (X10-type or wireless), then a wired or wireless path from the inside control device to the outside controller is also required. This will be a two-wire connection using telephone wire or a wireless X10 receiver connected to the outside controller by a similar two-wire connection.

13

Low-voltage Wiring

Because it's outside and mostly underground, the low-voltage wiring from the controller to the valves should always run in conduit. Most jurisdictions allow PVC pipe to be used for this purpose and require that the system be grounded only at the controller. Some codes require metal conduit and an additional ground at the valves. Before installing the wiring, check what local requirements apply in your area. Figure 13-7 shows a controller box installed on a rear wall with wiring conduit running from a nearby outlet box and up from the controller to the underside of the overhead balcony.

Figure 13-7   Sprinkler system controller with wiring conduits

Figure 13-8 shows the conduit extending down the spiral stairway support and underground to the nearby valve box. By going overhead to the outside of the patio, the wiring avoided the necessity of passing through the concrete slab or running on top of it.

Figure 13-8   Wiring conduit to sprinkler system valve box

Two wires connect each solenoid valve to the controller. All these wire pairs can be run through a single conduit, but they must be carefully color coded or labeled so that they can be correctly connected at both ends. The wires all carry AC current so there's no required order for wiring each pair, but the correct wires for each zone must connect to the zone's location in the controller or else the controller will be programmed for the wrong zones.

The power connections to the controller and to the remote access unit, if there is one, are also AC and can be wired with a single pair of wires connected in any order. All controllers have a built-in switch that turns power to the unit off so no separate power-line switch is necessary.

Once the wires have been run to the controller and from it to the valves, all the connections can be made according to the labels or color codes of the wires. The valves should always be located in a valve box, such as the one shown in Figure 13-9. This type of open-bottom box provides protection for the valves and a cover that keeps water away from the electrical connections. Figure 13-9 shows the valve wiring connections made with twist-on connectors. These should only be used if the wiring will not be submerged in water. If there is any danger of the wiring getting wet, either from the sprinklers or from outside weather, the connections should be soldered and carefully taped to keep moisture out.

Figure 13-9   A 5-zone sprinkler system valve set in a valve box

Programming

When the sprinkler system is wired, it should be tested by manually activating each zone to be certain that all zones are wired correctly. If the sprinkler system is a new installation, this testing can also extend to checking that all the sprinklers function correctly. The sprinklers can also be adjusted for area coverage. Once the system checks out, then it can be programmed to function automatically.

Time-of-day Settings

The first programming for the system is to set the time of day and the calendar date, if the controller has one. All the zone times key from the base time setting in the controller.

The next scheduling selection is to choose the overall watering schedule, the days on which the sprinkler system activates. Controllers can be set to activate the system every day, every other day, or another schedule custom programmed by the user. Whatever schedule is selected, the final input for it is to select a "day one" from which the system times its schedule. If the schedule calls for watering every three days, for example, and Sunday is selected as day 1, the system activates on Sunday, then on Wednesday, then on Saturday, and the following week starts the schedule on Tuesday, the third day after the preceding Saturday.

The set schedule usually applies to all zones. Controllers don't permit individual watering day schedules for zones. Those that have multiple schedules available, however, can often be programmed so that half of the zones function on one schedule and half on another, or a similar arrangement. All the zones will actually function on both schedules, but the watering times of those not wanted on a schedule can simply be set to zero for that schedule. The system then bypasses them and activates only those zones with set times. On days when the second schedule runs, the zones set to zero time in the first schedule are set to normal watering times, and those that are activated in the first schedule are set to zero and bypassed.

Seasonal Presets

Controllers that can be programmed with multiple schedules usually also have calendar timers that allow each schedule to be set for activation on a specific date. Schedule 1 might activate starting April 15, for example, and Schedule 2 on June 1. Other schedules, if available, could have other activation dates. In most controllers, activating a second schedule does not deactivate the one already running. Each schedule needs an off date, as well as an on date, to avoid overlapping.

Zones

With the daily schedule and seasonal presets established, all that remains to complete the sprinkler system programming is to set times for the individual zones. This is somewhat a trial-and-error process. The system should provide enough water for all zones, but not too much. Finding that level for each zone may take several time adjustments during the first year of the system's operation.

Setting watering times can be assisted by testing how much water the sprinklers distribute in each zone. This can be done while the system itself is being manually tested for functionality. A flat-bottomed plastic bucket can be placed in the center area of each zone and allowed to fill from the sprinklers to a depth of one inch (using a translucent bucket with the 1-inch depth marked on the outside and a few drops of food coloring in the bucket to color the water makes the measurement easy).

Once you know how long the sprinklers require to distribute an inch of water, you can compare this amount with the weekly or monthly water needed for lawns in the local area. Then time the sprinklers in each zone to stay on for the proper length of time to get the amount of water required. This procedure allows you to set the zone times close to the ideal. If dry spots show up as the season progresses, the times can be adjusted upward. If areas of the yard appear to stay too wet, some downward adjustment may be in order.

CHAPTER SUMMARY

- Automatic water systems are usually installed by plumbers who specialize in sprinkler systems. They can be automated at the time of installation or later.

- Nearly all sprinkler systems are divided into zones, which are areas within a yard that require similar water amounts and are small enough to be watered by a group of sprinklers controlled by one valve.

- A sprinkler system can be programmed to time each zone independently. This allows for customized watering schedules for specialized zones such as water features and interior garden areas.

- Sprinkler system zones are controlled by solenoid valves that are electrically operated and are activated individually by signals from a central controller.

- A sprinkler controller is an electronic device that controls the operation of the solenoid valves according to a timed schedule. It functions like an electric clock and calendar combination and signals each zone valve when to commence and end its watering cycle.

- Controllers can be programmed to function automatically or they can be interfaced with a computer or remote control device for programming and control.

- Home water systems without sufficient water pressure may need to have a pressure pump installed as an accessory for a sprinkler system. Other system accessory devices include rain sensors, wind sensors, soil moisture sensors, and freeze sensors.

- Sprinkler systems are wired with single-pair telephone wire. Underground and outdoor portions of wiring should be placed in plastic or metal conduit according to local code requirements.

- Programming for controllers includes time of day and calendar date settings, seasonal presets, zone times, start times, and multiple schedule settings, if these are used for the individual system.

13

KEY TERMS

atrium — An area within a home that is open to the outside or walled in glass, in which plants can grow as in the outside yard.

controller — The electronic device that controls the operation of sprinkler system zone valves through a preset, timed schedule.

drip irrigation system — A type of irrigation system in which small tubes deliver water flow directly to individual plants or plots of ground without spraying. The system conserves water compared to spraying sprinkler systems.

flow valve — A type of valve that measures the amount of water flowing through it and can adjust that flow automatically.

freeze sensor — A device that sends a signal when the temperature around it falls to near freezing (37 degrees normally, although some can be set to lower or higher temperatures).

mechanical relay — An electrical device activated by an electromagnet being energized that functions as a switch to turn a control current on or off; an automatic, remote-controllable switch.

pressure valve — A type of valve that shuts off water flow automatically if pressure in the pipe drops below a set minimum, indicating that there is a leak or break in the pipe.

PVC — Polyvinylchloride, a hard, strong plastic used to make pipe and many other products.

rain sensor — A device that detects the presence of rain water in a small holder and signals to the controller when a preset level is reached.

soil moisture sensor — A device that can measure the electrical conductivity of the ground in which it's buried. This measurement allows it to detect the amount of water in the soil.

solenoid valve — An automatic valve operated by an electromagnet that can be energized or turned off to open or close the valve. It is the main control device in automated water systems.

valve — A device for controlling the flow of water or other liquid in a pipe; can be turned on to permit flow or off to stop it.

valve box — An open-bottom box sunk to its lid in the ground where the zone valves and sometimes the controller of a sprinkler system are located.

water pressure — The force that impels water through a pipe. Water pressure is produced by gravity (the weight of water pushing down from higher elevation to a lower one) or by artificially pressurizing a sealed water system, usually with compressed air.

water service line — The pipe that supplies water to a residence from a public utility. It enters the home and connects to the interior plumbing and exterior water system

wind sensor — A device that can be set to signal a controller whenever the average wind speed rises to a preset level (adjustable from 12 to 35 miles per hour). Used to shut off sprinkler systems in high wind conditions.

zone — In sprinkler systems, multiple sprinkler heads in an area that are controlled by one valve.

REVIEW QUESTIONS

1. Home sprinkler system zones should be sized according to how large an area the home water system can water at one time. True or False?

2. Drip irrigation systems typically use _____ water than regular sprinkler systems.

3. The total amount of water flowing to a water system zone is usually adjusted by changing the:

   a. area of the zone

   b. length of time that water flows

   c. size of pipe to the zone

   d. time of day for watering

4. Water features such as ponds and fountains usually use _____ water that is moved by a pump.

5. A solenoid valve is operated by _____.

   a. a motor

   b. a spring

   c. an electromagnet

   d. air pressure

6. The setting on a sprinkler controller that determines the time when Zone 1 begins watering is the:

   a. time-of-day setting

   b. length-of-watering setting

   c. start setting

   d. seasonal preset

13

7. To reduce the amount of water going to a zone, the solenoid valve for that zone can be set to 50% open instead of fully open. True or False?

8. Why are multiple schedules in a water system controller useful?

9. How many zones in a controlled sprinkler system can be on simultaneously?

   a. one

   b. two

   c. three

   d. four

10. Computer software and interfaces are available for sprinkler controllers using _____ technology as the method of data transmission.

11. How is a soil moisture sensor used in a sprinkler control system?

12. A(n) _____ sensor could be used to help control a standard sprinkler system, but wouldn't be helpful with a drip irrigation system.

13. A rain sensor senses when the sprinklers in a zone have run long enough. True or False?

14. How would a freeze sensor function in an automatic sprinkler system?

15. What is the purpose of a pressure pump in the water line running to a sprinkler system?

16. Most automatic sprinkler controllers operate on _____ power.

17. The power supply for a controller is usually:

    a. batteries

    b. solar panel

    c. AC step-down transformer

    d. storage capacitor

18. Wiring for sprinkler system components requires what type of wire?

    a. 110-volt AC cable

    b. Cat5 cable

    c. single-pair telephone wire

    d. armored cable

19. The first item that should be programmed on a water system controller is the _____ setting. The second item is the _____ setting, if the controller has one.

20. In a 2-schedule controller with four zones, how would you program Zone 3 to water only once a week, Zone 2 twice a week, and Zones 1 and 4 three times a week?

HANDS-ON PROJECTS

Project 13-1: Divide a Sprinkler System into Zones

In this project you divide the sprinkler system for the large home and yard shown in Figure 13-10 into zones for automatic control. Make several copies of Figure 13-10 (enlarged, if possible) so that you can draw zone divisions for the system on the copies.

1. The sprinkler system has large and small sprinkler heads. Each zone can include a maximum of six full-circle large sprinkler heads or twelve full-circle small sprinkler heads. Two half-circle heads or four quarter-circle heads equal one full-circle head in either size. Each zone must include the equivalent of two full-circle large heads or four full-circle small heads.

2. Divide the system into the minimum number of zones you can (use no more than eight).

3. It's preferable that both large heads and small heads not be in the same zone, so keep them separated as much as you can.

4. When you finish designing one set of zones that works for this system, try again and see if you can automate the system with one less zone than you used on your first try.

Project 13-2: Wire a Controller for a Zone Sprinkler System

In this project you wire an automatic sprinkler controller to control a 4-zone sprinkler system. For this project you use a light to simulate each of the sprinkler system zone valves so that you can wire the system in a classroom rather than outside in a yard. For this project you need an automatic sprinkler controller (Rain Bird ESP 6Si or similar) with a 24-volt transformer, a standard 110-volt AC plug, four 24-volt lights in sockets that can be wired individually, 20 small twist-on wire connectors, and a roll of telephone wire (single-pair).

1. Connect the pair of wire leads for Zone 1 that extend out of the bottom of the controller to the connector posts or screws on one of the lights. Add a length of telephone wire to both of the colored leads before connecting them to the light so the wires are long enough to place the light two or three feet from the controller. Use twist-on connectors to connect the new length of wire to each lead from the controller, and then connect the new wires to the light.

2. Repeat Step 1 to connect another light to the Zone 2 leads, then Zone 3 and Zone 4. Finish one zone completely before starting the next so you don't get the wire leads mixed up.

3. Attach the two power leads from the controller to an 8-foot length of telephone wire. Connect the other end of the wire to the 24-volt transformer's output wires.

4. Connect the input wires of the transformer to a standard AC plug that can be plugged into a 110-volt AC outlet.

5. Set the controller and the connected lights on a table and plug the power cord of the transformer into a wall outlet. When the controller is plugged in to power, the display window should begin to blink.

6. Test the wiring by following these steps:

7. Set the twist dial to the Auto position.

8. Set the Schedule switch at the bottom of the controller to the 2 position.

9. Press the Manual Start (Man Start) button in the top-right corner of the controller once. The Zone 1 light should go on. If it does, proceed with the test. If it doesn't, unplug the controller and check the wiring to the lights.

10. Press the Manual Start button again. The Zone 2 light should come on and the Zone 1 light should go off.

11. Press the Manual Start button again. The Zone 3 light should come on and the Zone 2 light should go off.

13

12. Press the Manual Start button again. The Zone 4 light should come on and the Zone 3 light should go off.

Project 13-3: Program a Controller for Date, Time, and Schedule

In this project you program an automatic sprinkler controller for the correct date and time. You then program start times for a watering cycle and test the program. For this project use the same sprinkler controller and wired lights you used in Project 13-2.

1. Plug the controller into a power outlet.

2. Set the Schedule Switch to the Fixed/2 position. This sets the watering schedule to water every two days.

3. Check the display window on the upper-left side of the controller. The display should say PGM A (Program A) to the left of the time and day display. If it says PGM B, press the A/B button once to change it to PGM A.

4. Turn the controller dial to the Current Time and Day/Day position.

5. Press the Up Arrow or Down Arrow button at the top of the controller to set the day. This controller doesn't have a calendar function, so the day is either Day 1 or Day 2. Set the timer to Day 1.

6. Turn the controller dial to the Current Time and Day/HR (Hour) position.

7. Press the Up Arrow or Down Arrow buttons at the top of the controller to set the correct hour (be sure to include a.m. or p.m. in your setting).

8. Turn the controller dial to the Current Time and Day/MIN (Minute) position.

9. Press the Up Arrow or Down Arrow button at the top of the controller to set the correct minutes.

10. Turn the dial to the Watering Time Per Station/1 position. Use the Up Arrow button to set the watering time at 1 minute.

11. Repeat Step 10 for each of the other three stations. Set all the watering times for one minute.

12. Turn the dial to the Watering Start Times/1 position. Use the Up Arrow button to set the watering start time a few minutes ahead of the current time. The start times can only be adjusted in 15 minute increments, so set the start time to the time at least three minutes, but not more than 18 minutes, ahead of the current time.

13. Turn the dial to the Auto position and wait to see if the controller turns on each of the lights at 1-minute intervals when the time reaches the start time.

14. If the test doesn't work correctly, follow the steps above again to reset the program. Check carefully to be sure you are setting each function correctly. Test the program again.

Project 13-4: Program a Controller for a Dual Schedule

In this project you program an automatic sprinkler controller for a dual schedule. You then test the dual program to see if it functions correctly. For this project use the same sprinkler controller and wired lights you used in Project 13-3.

1. If the Program A you entered in the controller in Project 13-3 is not still in place, repeat the Project 13-3 steps to enter that Program A into the controller, then continue with this project.

2. Verify that the Schedule Switch is still set to the Fixed/2 position. This sets the watering schedule to water every two days.

3. Check the display window on the upper-left side of the controller. If the display does not say PGM B to the left of the time-and-day display, press the A/B button once to change it to PGM B.

4. Turn the dial to the Watering Time Per Station/1 position. Use the Up Arrow button to set the watering time at one minute.

5. Repeat Step 4 for Station 3. Set its watering time for one minute.

6. Repeat Step 4 for Stations 2 and 4. Set their watering times for two minutes.

7. Press the A/B button once to change back to Schedule A.

8. Repeat Step 4 for Stations 2 and 4 in Program A. Set their watering times for zero minutes.

9. Turn the dial to the Watering Start Times/1 position (This sets the start time for Program A). Use the Up Arrow button to set the watering start time a few minutes ahead of the current time. The start times can only be adjusted in 15 minute increments, so set the start time to the time at least three minutes, but not more than 18 minutes, ahead of the current time.

10. Turn the dial to the Watering Start Times/2 position (This sets the start time for Program B). Use the Up Arrow button to set the watering start time 15 minutes ahead of the time you set for Program A to start. Both Program A and B should start on Day 1, 15 minutes apart. This enables you to test both programs one right after the other. In an actual sprinkler system, the two programs would run on different days.

11. Turn the dial to the Auto position and wait to see if the controller turns on each of the lights at 1-minute intervals when the timer reaches the start time.

12. If the test doesn't work correctly, follow the steps above again to reset the programs. Check carefully to be sure you are setting each function correctly. Test the program again.

CASE PROJECTS

Case Project 13-1: Consult with a Client about a Pressure Tank

A client wants to have an automatic sprinkler system installed, but the water pressure available in his area is not sufficient to drive it. He asks you about the expense of installing a pressure tank and pump in the attic of his two story home, the only location he says, where it would be high enough for the force of gravity to increase water pressure in the home. Is the attic really a good location for a pressure tank? Will it help increase the water pressure to put it there? Write a short report to advise this client about installing a pressure tank, how it works, and where it should be located.

Case Project 13-2: Reprogram a Sprinkler System to Meet Restrictions

The town where a home with a sprinkler system is located is suffering from a drought. To conserve water, the town council has restricted lawn watering to a maximum of two hours on each of four days of the week only (Monday, Wednesday, Friday, Sunday). The home's 8-zone sprinkler system is set to operate every third day, but it requires four hours to complete its full 8-zone cycle (30 minutes per zone). How would you reprogram the sprinkler system so that it would be in compliance with the water restrictions, none of the zone watering times would be shortened, and the system would make maximum use of the available watering times?

Case Project 13-3: Solve a Water Seepage Problem

A client has an automatic sprinkler system in the yard of a summer home that his family occupies only intermittently. When they're away, the sprinkler system keeps the yard watered, but the owner has noticed a problem with the system. If the sprinkler system waters during a rainstorm or within two days following one, too much water builds up in the soil of the yard and water seeps into the home's basement window wells, and from there into the home where it damages the interior. Suggest two solutions that could solve this problem for the homeowner and still keep the yard adequately watered.

Case Project 13-4: Solve a Water Deficiency Problem

A house that was recently purchased has a sprinkler system installed in the yard, but the new owner finds that it doesn't work very well. There is not enough water pressure to operate the six sprinkler heads that are included in each of the system's four zones. The low pressure is caused by the small (½-inch) water service pipe that comes into the home. It just can't carry enough water for six sprinkler heads. The homeowner finds that the size of the incoming pipe can't be enlarged because a local ordinance specifies a ½-inch line as the maximum allowed for a residence. The homeowner wants to put all new landscaping in the yard, but is reluctant to do so without the sprinkling system. Hand-watering would be very time consuming. Can you suggest a way that the sprinkling system could be altered so that it would work with the available water pressure? (*Hint*: A pressure pump won't help because the small water line can't supply it any more water than it does the sprinkler system. If there's no way to get more water, you must use less at one time.)

13

MISCELLANEOUS AUTOMATED CONTROL SYSTEMS

After reading this chapter, you will be able to:

♦ Describe the basic design, operation, and installation of automated furnishings

♦ Explain how the operation of doors, windows, and window treatments can be automated

♦ Describe the basic design, function, and installation of lift systems

♦ Identify some indoor and outdoor heating system controls and how they are installed and used

In this final chapter, you'll learn some of the other home systems that can be automated or controlled through technology. You'll learn about the design, operation, and installation of automated furnishings in a home. You'll learn about automatic window and door openers as well as automated window coverings and ventilation fans. You'll also learn about the basic design and operation of lift systems for people and objects and how they can be installed in homes. Finally, you'll learn the basics of some indoor and outdoor heating system controls.

AUTOMATED INTERIOR FURNISHINGS

Many home furnishings, appliances, fittings, and decorations can be automated in addition to the major systems discussed in previous chapters. This final chapter covers some of the other home automation options available. Home owners may want to automate these items simply for greater convenience or because they are difficult or impossible to operate manually. If one or more of the home's occupants has limited physical mobility, some of these automations may be much more essential for comfortable living than for persons without any disability.

Automated Audio and Video Furniture

Many audio and video systems can be concealed in closed cabinets that open on command to reveal the equipment and move it into position for viewing and listening. This type of **automated furniture** can provide convenience in displaying and using electronic equipment, save space in a crowded area, and supply a dramatic introduction to an audio or video session. The variety of automated systems is limited only by the imagination of the designer. A few examples illustrate how innovative they can be:

- A video projector is concealed in the ceiling of a home living room on a platform whose bottom panel exactly matches the ceiling decor of the room. When the projector is turned on, the platform automatically lowers it down into position to project on a screen that lowers from another concealed position near one wall. Screen and projector retract into the ceiling again when not in use.

- A framed picture on a wall lifts upward to reveal a similar-size concealed television screen behind it.

- A flat screen television display is concealed face down in the top of a coffee table. When activated, the hinged table top pivots up revealing the screen, which positions itself on the back side of the coffee table at an angle suitable for direct viewing by those seated on the sofa in front of the table. The TV remote control is revealed in a recessed area beneath the raised table top/screen.

- A coffee table top elevates to dining table height and hidden leaves swing out and pivot into place to triple the size of the table top so that it can be used for dining or games. When not in use, the top retracts back to coffee table size and height.

- A concealed television lifts out of an antique quilt chest positioned at the foot of a bed. In addition to television viewing, the home's lighting and security systems can be viewed on the screen and controlled from the bedside remote master control.

- A floor-to-ceiling bookcase pivots inward to reveal a hidden room behind it where the owner's coin collection is displayed in secure cabinets.

- Sliding wood panels on a family room wall retract to both sides to reveal a small room behind them that contains the family's model railroad system.

- A tapestry hung on a horizontal pole travels to one side to reveal a television screen set in the wall behind it.

While each of these systems was custom designed for the individual application, the **motorized drive** systems, **cable pulls**, and other hardware devices from which they are constructed are available from a number of manufacturers. Figure 14 – 1 shows the construction of an entertainment center with **automated doors**. The door hardware, motor unit, and **track** can be adapted to any pair of 21-inch doors covering a 40-inch-wide opening.

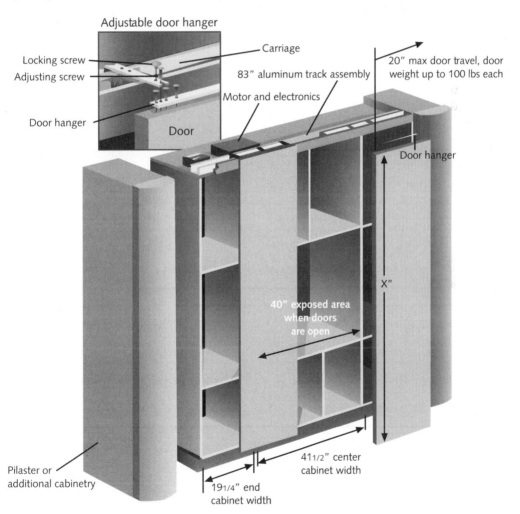

Figure 14-1   Automated doors can be adapted to many entertainment centers

14

Other hardware sets can be used to create a variety of automated furniture pieces, wall mounts, and motorized devices. Among the standard hardware sets available are the following:

- A **television lift** is a motorized platform with holding brackets for the television set. The lift base is driven vertically by cables or chains that run in side tracks. Lifts are available for television sets up to 42-inch screen size and weighing 300 pounds. They have vertical movements up to 36 inches.

- A **projector lift** is generally smaller than a television lift, but operates similarly to raise the projector into operating position. The lift has holding brackets for the projector.

- A **picture frame lift** mounts on a wall and lifts a framed picture vertically to reveal something behind it. Picture lifts are available in sizes up to 72-inches wide and with 100-pound lifting ability. They mount near the top of the opening to be covered and grip the top of the picture frame in the center so that it is actually hung on the lift bracket. The vertical movement of the lift can't exceed the height of the picture frame less a couple of inches.

- **Platform lifts** and wall lifts both can be adapted for use with other equipment. They can serve as speaker lifts, table top lifts, and drapery lifts.

- Television sets, speakers, and other equipment can be automatically maneuvered in a number of ways by mechanical devices. Among the **off-the-shelf hardware** sets available to achieve specific movements are pullout mechanisms that move a device in and out of an enclosure, **swivel mechanisms** that rotate equipment into a specific position for viewing or operation, and **tilt mechanisms** that raise a device from concealment into operating position by pivoting it or adjusting the angle of equipment for better viewing or listening.

- Door drive mechanisms slide doors or other panels along tracks. The door panels and the tracks can be large in size and quite heavy. The tracks can also curve so that doors or panels can be concealed in pockets or moved around a corner.

- **Drop-down mechanisms** and **pivot-down mechanisms** are both used to move projectors concealed in a ceiling down into operating position.

Figure 14-2 shows a drop-down projector mechanism in the open and closed position. The projector enclosure can be mounted below the ceiling, or **recessed** so that its base is flush with and concealed in the ceiling.

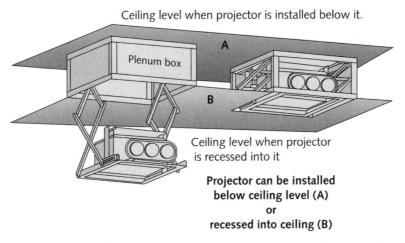

Ceiling level when projector is installed below it.

A

Plenum box

B

Ceiling level when projector
is recessed into it

**Projector can be installed
below ceiling level (A)
or
recessed into ceiling (B)**

Figure 14-2 A drop-down projector housing conceals the unit when not in use

Installation of Mechanical Systems

Installing automated platforms, doors, and other mechanical systems can be done during new construction or after the home is completed. If the automated system is built as a part of the home's basic structure, then the design of the building must accommodate it. The mechanical parts of an automated system are normally installed after home construction is complete, but door openings, **concealed enclosures**, **shafts**, electrical circuits, wiring conduits, and similar units must be framed into the structure of the house. This can be done after construction, but it's much easier and less expensive to do it while the house is being built.

Most automated interior systems can be constructed using mechanical parts that are available as off-the-shelf hardware. When designing automated systems, it's a good idea to first become familiar with the automation devices and components that are readily available and require no engineering. Adapting these existing units to the design of a custom automation project is much easier than developing individual custom mechanical systems.

AC power outlets, from which mechanized systems can draw electricity, are nearly always installed where audio and video equipment will be used, but some automated devices shouldn't be connected to the same circuit as audio, video, or other electronic equipment. The mechanical system's motors may produce interference when operating under load (as when lifting heavy equipment) or may draw enough power to affect the voltage in the circuit. If the mechanized system operates only before or after the electronic gear, it's not likely to do harm, but if both are live on the same circuit at the same time, power surges, interference and other electrical anomalies are possible. To avoid the necessity of wiring a separate circuit for the mechanical system, it's best to interlock switches on the two systems so that both can't be on together.

CAUTION

If new high-voltage wiring is required for an automated mechanical system, or alterations to existing circuits are necessary, these should only be installed by a qualified electrician.

14

AUTOMATED WINDOW AND DOOR SYSTEMS

This section discusses how some doors and windows can be automated and how many window coverings can be made more functional and convenient by automation. Doors can be powered, but not remote controlled. Windows can be both powered and remotely controlled. Window shades, drapes, and other decorative items can be controlled remotely or directed by timers or sensors for increased effectiveness.

Window Shades and Blinds

Window shades and blinds are often automated when the hand controls on them are difficult to reach or operate. Automation consists of a motor unit activated by a remote control. The motor unit can often be fitted to a manually operated blind or shade so that existing window treatments can be converted to automatic operation.

Vertical and horizontal slat blinds are usually opened and closed by turning an octagonal plastic rod on one side of the shade. The turning rod operates a gear and pulley arrangement in the top frame of the shade to open or close the slats. The gear system requires several turns of the control rod to completely open or close the shades. This slow movement allows the shades to be precisely adjusted and also keeps the force required to turn the control rod low.

Such rod-controlled shades are easily automated by adding a motorized turning device into which the end of the control rod is fitted. The **shade controller** unit contains a wireless receiver and is activated by a handheld remote transmitter. The blind controller can be directed to turn in either direction, thus opening or closing the blind on command. The motor and receiver unit is battery operated and so requires no wiring either for motor power or control. The controller unit also has push buttons on it, which allow manual control of the shade without the remote unit. The remote unit can control a single window shade controller or several set to the same X10 house and unit codes. The controller units can also be controlled with any of the X10 wireless master control systems. Figure 14-3 shows a controller installed on a rod-controlled blind and the remote control unit that directs it. These units fit almost any vertical or horizontal blind that is opened with a turning rod.

Figure 14-3   Automatic blind controller and remote

Drape and Shade Pulls

Blinds require a stronger motor to lift them open or pull them back than is necessary to just turn their slats in one direction or the other. They can be automatically lifted or opened by the same systems used to open and close drapes. **Drape pull mechanisms** typically have the ability to pull up to 60 pounds of fabric or blinds. Some heavy-duty units can pull 75 pounds. Both require an AC motor for their operation, however, as the current load is too heavy for batteries. This means that the motor unit must be mounted within a few feet of an AC power outlet into which it can be plugged, or an AC power line must be installed in the wall to power it.

AC-powered drape pulls can be attached to any blind or drape fixture that has a **loop pull cord** or chain. The motorized controller is mounted at a level even with the bottom of the loop below one end of the drape rod or blind. The loop is then fitted into the controller's pulley and tension on the pull cord is adjusted at the rod. The motor is bidirectional and so can open or close the drapes or blinds on command.

Because drape controllers are all AC powered, they use X10 power-line commands for control. The commands can be sent by a standard X10 power-line controller connected to the AC wiring or by a wireless remote which sends commands to a receiver connected to the AC system. The wireless receiver doesn't need to be near the drape controller because it relays the commands it receives from the remote throughout the AC power lines and the drape controller can receive the commands through its power line. As with blind controllers, several drape controllers can be set to operate together by using the same X10 house and unit codes for them. Figure 14-4 shows two handheld remotes and a master wireless controller for automated window coverings.

14

Figure 14-4   Remote controls for window coverings

Shade Lifts

Horizontal window shades can also be automated and remote controlled. Because manually operated shades usually have pull cords without loops, they can't be retrofitted with motorized controllers. The controller must be built into the shade's top frame and the pull cords for the shade permanently connected to it. The remote control is also built into the shade frame and is directed by the same type of handheld remote as other blind and drape controllers.

These types of shades are often used on windows that have no easy access for manual control and where it's desirable to have the window completely unobstructed some of the time. Figure 14-5 shows a set of widows with automated shades attached. The highest of these windows is over 20 feet above the floor, making them totally impractical for manual shades. In this window treatment, the shades in each pair of windows on the same level are operated together on a single set of codes so that four unit codes are required to operate the full set of controllers. All the shades can also be operated together using a controller that can address multiple codes.

Figure 14-5   Automated shades in a home with high windows

All of these window covering controllers can be set on timers will open or close them at specific times. Timed opening and closing of the shades or drapes is particularly useful for south-facing windows where sunlight can damage furnishings if the windows are left uncovered during periods of intense daylight. Master controllers can also be programmed to close all shades and drapes when the home is not occupied as part of the security system arming procedure.

Door Openers

Automatic door openers are available for two types of doors: sliding glass patio doors and hinged doors. Neither type includes a locking mechanism as part of the opener, so a door lock must be provided and operated separately for these devices.

Patio door openers are motorized units which attach to the base of a sliding door at floor level. They are not weatherproof and so cannot be mounted outdoors in order to pull open a door that slides on the outside of the adjacent stationary patio window. They are only suitable for doors that slide on the inside of the adjacent window. The motorized opener attaches to the door itself and runs back and forth along a **geared rack** attached to the floor to open and close the door. The opener requires an AC power connection and can fully open a 32-inch glass door.

Door closers are activated by a handheld wireless remote that transmits to an X10 receiver in a wall outlet. The receiver relays the command signals through the AC wiring to the opener. The opener has a built in **operation cycle** which activates on the open command. It opens the door, pauses for a few seconds, then closes it. Only the single command is needed. If the door encounters resistance while closing (an obstruction in the doorway), it reverses direction and opens again. After a pause, it again closes, but the obstruction part

14

of the cycle can repeat as often as necessary until the doorway opening is clear. A sensor can be added on either side of the door so that it also opens for a pet. On some doors, the pet open cycle can be set so that the door opens only enough to let a pet pass through.

The rack and gear system which opens the sliding door also holds it closed when the device is not operating, but it doesn't have the security of a door lock. The door opener can be disengaged from the inside so that the door can be opened manually in case of power failure or other emergency. For good security, any door with an automatic opener should also have a lock which can be set independently of the opener to secure the door.

Hinged door openers are either hydraulic arms similar to outside gate openers or cable pull openers used in combination with a **spring-loaded door closer** such as those found on many doors in commercial settings. Hydraulic arm-type openers are expensive and seldom used for inside doors.

Cable pull openers are motorized units similar to drape openers. They operate by pulling a looped cord to open the door, then reversing the pull so that the spring-loaded closer can close it. They don't have an open/close cycle built in as the sliding door openers do. They must receive separate commands to open the door and to close it. They also do not have an obstruction detector built in so that they reverse if an object blocks their motion. The 50-pound maximum pull that the opener has is not sufficient to cause injury when opening the door slowly (as all door openers do), and an obstruction simply stops the motorized unit.

Door openers are activated by remotes in the same manner as drape openers. The remote is an X10 transmitter that transmits to an outlet-mounted receiver, which relays the signal through the power lines to the motorized unit.

Skylights

Skylights, which can face the sun all day, can be controlled for heat and light with automated shades and motorized remote controlled openers. Opening skylights to release summer heat that rises up toward them is a good way of ventilating homes that don't have air conditioning. A skylight can be equipped with a heat sensor that activates the shade when sunlight reaches a preset level. A rain sensor can also be installed that automatically closes the skylight in the event of rain. Figure 14-6 shows the control configuration for an automated skylight and the wall-mounted control panel that can override the preset controls to open or close the skylight.

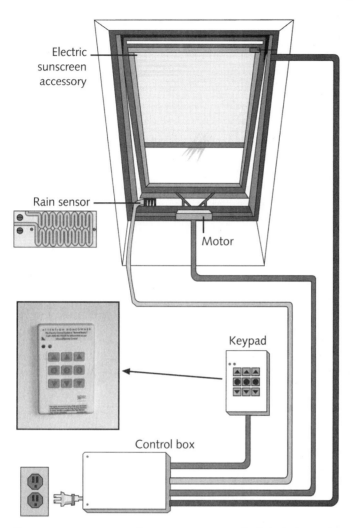

Electric
sunscreen
accessory

Rain sensor

Motor

Keypad

Control box

Figure 14-6   Design for a sensor-controlled skylight with opener and shade

14

Skylight automation systems require AC power to operate and a wired controller. The wiring needed for both power and control should be installed as part of the home's structural wiring during construction because it is much more difficult to do as a retrofit afterward. If the heat and rain sensors are used as part of the control system, they should not be relied on when the homeowner is not available to check on their operation. A skylight is a dividing barrier between inside and outside climate conditions. When the skylight is open, the two systems mix at the opening where the sensors are also located. This can cause disruption in their function under some conditions. Drafts coming out of the house may blow rain away from the sensor, for example, and hot air escaping may keep the skylight open when falling rain should cause it to close. The keypad control should always be used to close the skylights when the home owner is away.

Automated Fan

Sensor-controlled or timer-controlled fans can be installed in a home to provide ventilation when the central heating system or air conditioning isn't operating, or in homes that don't have either of these systems. Fans can be either of the exhaust type (pulling air from the inside of the home and exhausting it outside) or the intake type (pulling air in from the outside and blowing it into the home). In either case, new air from outside is brought into the home. With an intake fan, the air only enters through the fan. With an exhaust fan, new air is drawn in wherever there is an opening to the outside. Such openings can be created where incoming air is wanted in the home by opening a window in that area through which the air can flow. By opening several windows slightly, an exhaust fan can circulate air through the entire home, pulled in through the various openings and drawn to the exhaust fan.

A fan should be installed in an exterior wall and its outside face should be carefully covered with screen to keep out insects when the fan isn't operating. The fan should also have an automatic shutter system that closes the fan opening when the unit is not operating. The shutters are spring loaded to remain firmly closed unless pulled open by a solenoid mechanism or a small motor wired in parallel with the fan motor.

Fans require AC current and so must have a power outlet nearby to which they can connect. Alternatively, a power line can be run to the fan from the nearest outlet, either inside the wall or in a surface-mounted raceway. Large fans should always have a manually operated switch that can override any automated control to turn them on or off. The switch can be on the power outlet in which the fan is plugged or an X10 remote on-off module controlled by a wireless remote or a master controller. Fans can also be automated by wiring an adjustable temperature sensor into the power circuit. If this is done, then the manual switch is left on unless it is needed to override the sensor.

Smaller exhaust fans that vent heat, humidity, and odors are often installed in kitchens and bathrooms and activated manually by a switch. These fans can be automated with a temperature sensor, or a motion detector, depending on their location.

AUTOMATED LIFT SYSTEMS

There are at least four types of **automated lift** system now available for home installation. Each has specific applications, although some of their functions overlap. Lift systems are intended to elevate people or objects from one level to another in a home. Because they are all technically "vertically moving vehicles," they have stringent safety standards designed to prevent people from falling in a lift system or falling from one, as well as to prevent harm to anyone from objects (or people) falling on them from a lift system. This section describes the various kinds of lift systems, how they operate, and the safety requirements for each, and then concludes with a discussion about the installation of lifts.

Dumbwaiter

A **dumbwaiter** is actually a small elevator designed to carry objects from one floor to another in a building. Early ones were operated by ropes turned by hand cranks and were used to deliver hot food from outside kitchens to dining rooms on upper floors. The name comes from this original use (dumbwaiter is also the name of a piece of furniture used in early dining rooms, but this item should not be confused with the lift type).

Modern dumbwaiters are motorized and can lift up to 500 pounds, making them very handy devices for moving heavy objects of any variety to upper floors in a home. The design and construction of a dumbwaiter are very similar to that of an **elevator**. It consists of a box with an open front mounted on rails on which it can slide up or down from one floor to another in the home. The box is attached to a cable which runs up to a motor assembly at the top of the shaft in which the dumbwaiter's rails are mounted. The shaft can be enclosed or open. It is merely the space in which the dumbwaiter moves. Its walls, if it has any, do not provide support for the dumbwaiter's rails, which are independently mounted. Figure 14-7 shows the design of a dumbwaiter in a three-story shaft with control panels and openings for loading and unloading on each floor.

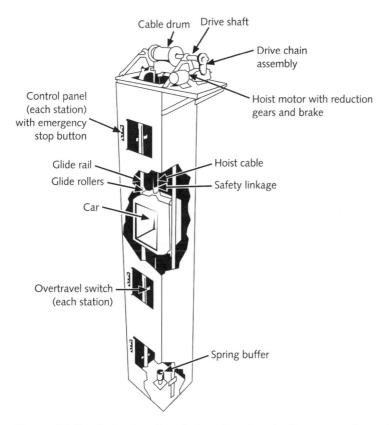

Figure 14-7   A dumbwaiter design showing shaft, car on rails, and motor drive assembly

The openings in the shaft on each floor all have doors that close and lock when not in use. This is necessary to prevent anyone or anything from falling down the shaft when the dumbwaiter is above or below an opening. The dumbwaiter itself may or may not have a door on its open front side. Most codes don't require a door on the car because it doesn't carry people as an elevator does.

Dumbwaiters have low-geared electric drive motors to lift and lower them. The motor is controlled by the control panels on the outside of each floor opening. Unlike an elevator, there are no controls on the inside of the car. The outside controls start the dumbwaiter moving up or down and it is stopped at the next floor above or below by a **trip switch** that the car strikes as it ascends or descends. The drive motor for the dumbwaiter is geared low so that it moves the dumbwaiter relatively slowly and, if stopped, can hold the car in place wherever it is inside the shaft, regardless of the load it may be carrying. The motor also has a safety brake on it which activates if the motor moves too fast, indicating that the dumbwaiter is falling. A dumbwaiter is capable of carrying a person, but should not do so because it doesn't have all the safety devices on its drive mechanism that an elevator and **stairway lift** have. A dumbwaiter may not have a door on the car and may move in an open shaft, both of which are serious potential safety hazards if the unit is used to carry people.

For safety reasons, dumbwaiters are not controlled remotely. Their start buttons must be interlocked with all the access doors in the shaft to assure that these are closed and locked before the car can be moved. An emergency stop button on each of the control panels allows the car to be stopped at any time by an operator in the event of a malfunction. One person can operate a dumbwaiter safely because the controls on each floor are interlocked and cannot function unless all access doors are closed and locked. The control panel can only start the car moving up or down. The car stops automatically at the next floor, whether up or down. The stop points for each floor are determined by the placement of the trip switches, as the operator cannot see inside the shaft to observe the car's position when the doors are closed.

Figure 14-8 shows a dumbwaiter stopped at an access door. This unit has an expanding grid door on both the front and rear of the car, which indicates that on at least one floor it has an access door on the rear side. The control unit is mounted at the upper-left inside the outer access door and has a safety switch which must be held closed by the door once it is closed and locked or the dumbwaiter cannot move. On this dumbwaiter's control, the up or down switch is pressed, then the access door is closed and latched. Only then does the car begin to move.

Figure 14-8   Loaded dumbwaiter with inside grid doors

Dumbwaiters are nearly always installed as part of a home's original construction. While retrofitting one in an existing home is possible, it's very difficult and expensive because of the need to install the shaft for the dumbwaiter by cutting openings in the floors of the building and adding sidewalls between floors.

Elevators

Because of their cost, home elevators are still not a common feature of homes, but where disabilities or health concerns require transporting people between floors without climbing stairs, an elevator is often the best solution. Elevators are enlarged versions of dumbwaiters with higher carrying capacity in both weight and size, and additional safety features to protect the riders. Cost for an elevator starts at about $15,000, and varies widely depending on the unit's size and decor.

A home elevator usually has a capacity of 750 to 1,000 pounds and runs at a speed of about 40 feet per minute. This allows it to move between two floors in about 15 seconds. Size for an elevator varies from a minimum footprint of about 36 by 50 inches upward to some units twice that size. Many elevators are fully enclosed cars or cabs that are hoisted up and down on side rails by cables connected to overhead motors. But recently designed models sometimes vary considerably from this traditional design.

Figure 14-9 shows an elevator which moves on a single track located at the back of the unit. The elevator is installed in an open stairwell in a shaft space with almost completely open sides. The glass-walled elevator allows entry from doors on either side on the various landings and is powered by a rack and gear drive system mounted below the cab so that no cables are used at all. This elevator uses the stairway railing as a safety barrier to prevent falls through access points when the elevator is on another floor.

14

Figure 14-9   A glass-walled home elevator installed in a stair well

This type of unit can also be mounted in an enclosed shaft, if one is available, but the open construction allows for retrofit installation in a stair well or on an upper-story landing much more easily than is possible with the older elevator designs with dual side rails. These units usually require a small machine room below the elevator's lowest station or above its top one.

To better accommodate heavy loads, most elevators use **counterweights** to balance part or all of the elevator cab's weight. These counterweights are connected to the elevator cab by a cable that runs from the cab over a support wheel at the top of the rail assembly and down to the counterweights. The counterweights are also mounted on rails and move with the cab, but in the opposite direction. When the cab moves up, the cable allows the counterweights to move down, and vice versa. The counterbalancing weights mean that the drive motor on the elevator doesn't have to lift the weight of the cab and its occupants, but only the weight of the occupants. The cab weight is balanced by the counterweights so that the empty cab could be moved up and down on its rail by a very small force. Figure 14-10 shows a design for a single rail, overhead-powered elevator with counterweights running on the same rail assembly to balance the weight of the elevator cab.

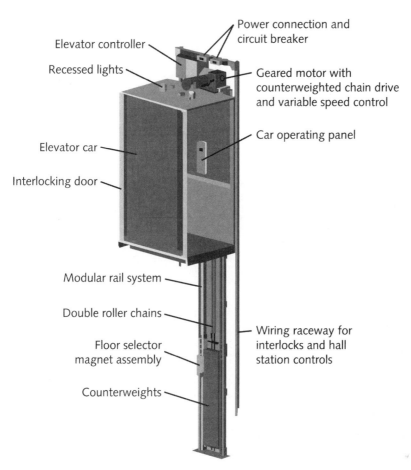

Power connection and circuit breaker

Elevator controller

Recessed lights

Geared motor with counterweighted chain drive and variable speed control

Car operating panel

Elevator car

Interlocking door

Modular rail system

Double roller chains

Floor selector magnet assembly

Wiring raceway for interlocks and hall station controls

Counterweights

Figure 14-10   A counterbalanced, single rail elevator design

Like dumbwaiters, elevators are not remotely controlled. They have call buttons located on the outside of the elevator on each floor served, but the main control panel for an elevator is inside the cab. The outside buttons can only call the elevator to their floor station. When the occupants are inside the cab, the unit is started from within. Nearly all home elevators, when started up or down, follow an operation cycle that automatically stops them at the next floor without further control input by those inside. If the elevator traverses more than two floors, the inside control allows it to bypass a floor, but the stop cycle is still automatic at the selected floor so that no adjustment or other action by the occupants is required to get the elevator correctly positioned for exit.

Hydraulic Lifts

Hydraulic lifts are a special class of elevator designed to raise a person or object a shorter distance than a full floor. They're usually installed to bypass a short stairway at the entrance into a home. An **inclined ramp** can often permit wheelchair access up three or four steps, but if there is not sufficient space for a ramp, a vertical lift is an alternate solution.

14

Because they don't rise more than three or four feet, lifts don't often use cables and motors or rack and gear drives commonly found in elevators for power. Most rely on **hydraulic cylinders** with high-pressure pumps that work much like an automobile lift in a car repair facility. The hydraulic cylinders are attached at the sides of the lift. When the pump is activated, hydraulic fluid is forced into the bottom of the cylinders under high pressure. The fluid forces piston rods to move out of the tops of the cylinders. Since the ends of the rods are attached to the lift platform, when the rods are forced out of the cylinders, they lift the platform. To lower the platform again, the process is reversed and fluid is allowed to bleed out of the cylinders. The rods retract and the platform lowers.

Lifts usually have a capacity of about 500 pounds, which allows them to raise two average people without difficulty. They require fewer safety protection devices because they don't lift nearly as far as elevators and the hydraulic cylinders that power them rarely fail. If they do, the result is only a slow descent of the lift as hydraulic fluid drains from the cylinders.

Stair Lift

Where a home doesn't have room for an elevator and only one person at a time needs to move between floors, a stair lift is often a workable alternate solution. A stair lift is a small elevator mounted at an angle so that it can fit on one side of a stairway. Stair lifts can be rack and gear driven or cable powered. They are usually not counterweighted, but have a lifting capacity of about 500 pounds. The user sits on a chair, which is mounted to the lift rail or rails, and controls the lift's operation with a hand rest-mounted controller. Wall-mounted call buttons at the top and bottom of the stairs allow the stair lift to be summoned to either position, but control when the unit is in use is always with the rider. Figure 14-11 shows a stair lift mounted on a straight stairway.

Figure 14-11   Stair lift mounted on a straight stairway

Stair lifts can be adjusted to fit the angle of rise of a stairway and some models can be accommodated to a curved stairway. They can't reverse their direction of travel, however, and so cannot be used on split stairways. One type of stair lift travels on hand rails set two to three feet above the stairs and this unit can adapt to reversing stairways. Like other lift devices, stair lifts have built-in safety sensors that hold them in place in the event of a power or motor failure, and that stop them if they begin to descend too rapidly.

Installation of Lifts

All types of lifts require some degree of custom installation. Their AC motors draw fairly large amounts of power and should, wherever possible, be wired to an independent circuit that has no other devices on it. This helps protect against accidental tripping of the circuit breaker caused by a power overload from some other device in combination with the lift system's motor.

The safety devices that are always included with lifts must be installed and tested to be sure they function correctly. Lifts are often used by persons with limited mobility and sensory perception who rely on the technology of the system to protect them from harm even more that the average person might. Most lifts are intentionally over-engineered for safety so that even persons with minimal physical abilities can use them safely. Installation of lifts should also reflect this primary concern with safety.

14

AUTOMATED HEATING SYSTEMS

In addition to the central heating systems most homes have, many have other smaller heating devices for specialized purposes. These smaller heating devices are not needed continuously and are often automated so that they turn on only when directed to do so by sensors or timers. This section covers some of the control mechanisms used to automate the function of small heating devices.

Fireplace Igniter

Many fireplaces are gas fired rather than wood or coal burning. Even some of those that do burn solid fuels have gas flame jets that are used to start the wood or coal fire in the fireplace. Natural gas burns more cleanly than wood or coal and produces no ashes, so it has become a popular fuel for home fireplaces.

Some gas-fueled fireplaces must be lit with a match after the gas is turned on by hand, but this method is being replaced by automatic **fireplace igniters** that also offer improved safety for the user. Many of the hand-operated gas jets in fireplaces did not include a **thermocouple** and safety flame, which meant that if the gas flame was extinguished for any reason, unburned gas would continue to flow into the fireplace and could easily produce an explosion.

Automatic igniters always include a thermocouple and safety flame as part of the ignition assembly. The thermocouple is a metal tube that produces an electric current when heated in a flame. The electric current keeps the gas valve that feeds fuel to the fireplace open. If the flame in the fireplace is extinguished, the thermocouple stops producing current and the gas valve closes, cutting off the gas glow and eliminating any chance of fire or explosion. All gas-fueled appliances have thermocouples and all gas fueled fireplaces should.

In a gas-fired fireplace, the thermocouple and safety flame nozzle are part of an assembly that also includes a spark igniter. A separate second igniter for starting the fireplace may also be installed in a more convenient location near the front of the fireplace. The igniter is an electric device which produces a spark similar to that of a spark plug in a car. When the gas fuel valve is turned on (this can be done manually or automatically with a remote controlled valve) the spark igniter sparks and ignites the gas as it flows into the fireplace. The gas fuels the safety flame which burns directly under the thermocouple. The thermocouple heats and begins producing current which keeps the gas valve open and allows the fire to continue burning.

The igniter and thermocouple assembly are always a built-in part of the gas flame unit that is inserted in a fireplace. This assembly is usually hidden at the bottom of the flame unit beneath stone clinkers or decorative concrete "logs" that form part of the gas flame unit. Even if the unit burns wood or coal, the igniter assembly is probably beneath the fire grate which holds the solid fuel. HTI technicians almost never install gas flame units in fireplaces because they are usually a part of the home's original construction or are installed by aftermarket specialists who sell them. Once installed, these devices are reliable and durable, except for the spark igniter and the thermocouple. Both of these devices wear out with use and must be replaced when they fail to operate correctly. Replacing an igniter or thermocouple is a task any technician may be commonly asked to do.

There are many types of fireplace units and dozens of different brands, but the general procedure for replacing a spark igniter or thermocouple is similar for most of them. The first requirement is to expose the igniter and thermocouple assembly by removing the decorative parts of the unit that cover it. An instruction manual for the individual brand of fireplace unit is helpful, but if it's not available, the technician must simply find the fasteners which hold the decorative parts of the unit in place and remove them. These parts may include stone coals, concrete logs, and a shield that prevents debris from falling into the safety flame.

Once the igniter and thermocouple assembly are exposed, either can be changed quickly with hand tools. The thermocouple, safety flame jet, electrode, and often a flame spreader are replaced as a single unified assembly. They are constructed together with precise spacing and adjustment that is critical to their operation and should not be replaced separately. The spark igniter can be replaced as a separate unit, but should be adjusted to the same position as the original so that it functions correctly. Figure 14-12 shows the main parts of a typical fireplace insert and where the thermocouple assembly and spark igniter may be placed.

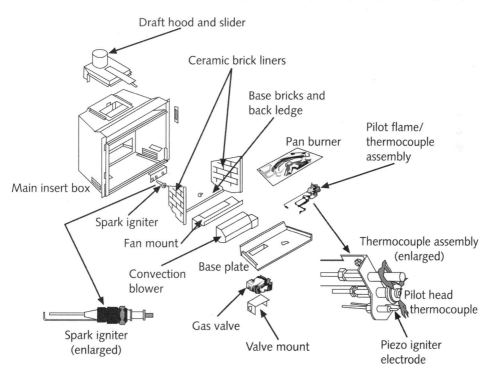

Figure 14-12   Exploded view of gas fireplace insert showing igniter and thermocouple

Once the new igniter or thermocouple assembly is in place and the shield is reinstalled, the gas can be turned on and the unit tested to see that it ignites and flames properly. When operation is confirmed, the gas should be shut off again and the unit allowed to cool down.

Then the decorative parts can be reassembled to the original finished appearance. After that, the gas should be turned on and a second test conducted to be sure the unit still functions as it should.

Heating Cables

A **heating cable** is an electric cord which has high resistance to electricity. The resistance of the metal wire in the cord to the passage of electricity causes some of the current to be transformed into heat. This heat, produced continuously as long as the cable is powered, radiates out from the cable. The operation of heating cables can be automated by use of a temperature sensor or a timer wired into the cable circuit. Heating cables have a variety of applications, mostly exterior, around the home. Among these are:

- To prevent pipes from freezing during periods of low temperature, a heating cable can be run parallel to the pipe, or wrapped around it.

- To keep rain gutters and downspouts clear of ice, heating cables can be laid in the gutters and run down the inside of the spouts.

- To keep roof edges free of ice and snow buildup, heating cable can be attached to the roof in a zigzag pattern of sufficient size to melt off ice and prevent damage.

- To keep ice and snow from remaining on sidewalks and stairs, heating cables can be laid under the concrete before it is poured. The cables transfer enough heat to the concrete to keep it above freezing temperature so that snow melts off and ice cannot form.

- To keep outside drains from freezing over, heating cable can be laid around the drain and, if necessary, run down the drain to a point below the freeze line to prevent ice from blocking the drain.

- To keep garden areas from freezing or to keep the temperature at a level that encourages early plant growth, heating cable can be laid in parallel rows under the soil.

- To keep a pet house above freezing, heating cable can be installed under its floor.

Heating cable comes in a variety of sizes, which is to say that it has a variety of heat output ratings, which depend on the size and type of wire used. Heating cable's heat output is measured by the amount of current that is transformed into heat in each foot of cable length. This output is rated in watts per foot. Low heat cable consumes about three watts of current per foot of cable. High output cable consumes eight watts per foot. Even the higher figure may not seem like a large rate of power consumption, but as the length of cable used multiplies, the power requirement quickly increases. A 12-foot cable with an eight watt per foot rating consumes almost 100 watts of power. A 100-foot cable consumes 800 watts. Two cables of this size use the capacity of a 20-amp circuit.

When used in rain gutters, downspouts, and small-diameter pipes (one inch outside diameter or less), a single strand of heating cable is generally sufficient to prevent freezing. The heat rating of the cable used must be determined by the lowest potential outside temperature to which the heated area will be exposed. If the temperature won't ever fall more than a few degrees below freezing, low heat cable will suffice. If below zero temperatures are a possibility, high heat cable is necessary.

Large-diameter pipes should be wrapped with heating cable. The angle of the wrap should be determined by the low temperature potential. On small diameter pipe, a single strand of cable run along the bottom of the pipe (and kept in close contact with it by tape or fabric wrapping) warms the bottom of the pipe and the rising heat spreads through the rest of the pipe and its contents. On larger pipes, the heat diffusion won't be sufficient to prevent freezing unless the heating cable is wrapped around the entire pipe and again held in contact with it by outer wrapping.

Roof-mounted heating cable installations requires considerably more cable than straight runs because of the zigzag pattern that must be used to keep a sufficient area of the roof edge warmed. Figure 14-13 shows a typical roof layout pattern for heating cable. The loops on the lower points of the cable pattern are drip loops that provide easy drainage for melt water running down the cable. The dotted line indicates where another heat cable should be run in the rain gutter and downspout. To lay cable in this pattern eight-inches wide requires two feet of cable for every foot of roof width. If the pattern is 12-inches wide, 3 feet of cable per foot of roof is required.

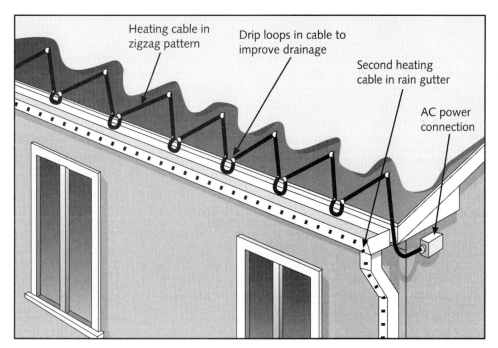

Figure 14-13   A zigzag heating cable pattern on a roof edge

Heating cable can be attached to a roof with loop brackets fitted with screws. The cable is easily bent to the pattern required. The most difficult part of the installation is usually getting the necessary AC power connection to the cable. If a heating cable installation needs more than 500 watts of power, a separate circuit for the cable is preferable. If the installation needs 1,000 watts or more, the separate circuit is essential and nothing else should be wired on it that will be operating at the same time as the heating cable. Winter-used heating cables can be run from the same circuit that powers the summer air conditioner, provided that a switch or timer prevents both from being turned on together.

Since power connections for heating cable in rain gutters or on the roof need to terminate in a high outside outlet, it's usually best to bring a new circuit wire up into the home's attic and then run it to an outside exit point near where the outlet can be placed. Running the wire through a hole drilled in the exterior wall is the best method of installing the circuit, but if that's not possible, the wire can be brought out through a roof gable, a vent, or even through the roof itself. On the outside, the wire must be in conduit and the opening through which it exits must be sealed, particularly if it's on the roof where the potential for water leaking into it is high.

The outside circuit wire should terminate in a waterproof outlet or junction box where the heating cable can be connected. Most heating cables have plugs attached, but some wire directly to the AC cable. In either case, the cable connection should be carefully sealed against water and grounded.

Heating cable run on or under the ground for gardens, sidewalks, or similar areas, must also have sealed, grounded connections. These installations are usually made at the time the home is built, but if they are retrofitted, the power circuit for them probably has to be added in the same manner as one for a roof installation.

Heating cables can be purchased with connecting plugs attached in specified lengths up to 100 feet. Cable can also be purchased by the foot without a connecting plug. The cable is simply cut to the desired length in the same manner as ordinary AC two-conductor cable and a plug is attached to one end. A terminator must also be attached to the other end of the cable to complete the circuit through it.

Heating cables are usually controlled by a temperature sensor that activates them when the air temperature drops to near freezing or below. Temperature sensors are often built into finished cables, but must be added in the circuit of those that are cut to length. The temperature sensors tend to be more expensive than those used for other automated devices because they are heavy duty (activate a large capacity circuit) and must be strongly weatherproofed to withstand installation in exposed outside areas.

Almost any number of heating cables can be installed on a home or in a yard, but when the total watts consumed by such cables exceeds 1,000, other methods of preventing freezing start to become more economical. In many homes that have radiant heating systems, heating pipes can be run to the driveway and sidewalk areas as well as the home's interior. The outside heating pipes are installed as a separate zone with a thermostat that activates the zone only when low temperatures require it. This type of radiant heat, if available, is more economical than large scale electric outdoor heating with cables.

CHAPTER SUMMARY

❏ Many home appliances, decorations, and pieces of furniture can be automated for greater convenience in using them, for greater accessibility by disabled persons, or for dramatic effect when using them.

❏ Among the interior automation devices are television and projector lifts, picture frame lifts, automatic doors, automated shades and blinds, powered drapery pulls, drop-down devices, automated skylights, and automatic ventilation fans.

❏ Window shades, blinds, and curtains can all be automated to open and close automatically, either on command of a remote control or according to programmed instructions sent by a controller or computer. Doors and some windows (skylights) can also be automated to open and close on command.

❏ A dumbwaiter is a small elevator that is designed to move only objects, not people. Elevators are enclosed cars that move people from one floor to another in a building. Both are types of lift that operate on programmed cycles started by the user, but neither is remotely controlled.

❏ Hydraulic lifts are sometimes used to raise people short distances such as onto a porch or landing in a home. Stair lifts are angled lifts mounted on stairways that can move one person at a time from floor to floor. They are controlled from the user's chair with hand controls.

❏ Fireplace igniters are electrical devices for sarting gas fired fireplaces. They can be remotely activated.

❏ Heating cables are electrically heated wires that serve a variety of outdoor functions. They keep pipes from freezing and other areas warmed above the freezing point so that snow or ice cannot build up on them.

KEY TERMS

14

automated doors — Doors mechanized to open and close on command by means of cable pulls or hydraulic actuators.

automated furniture — Any piece of furniture which can be remotely directed to open, move a display or object within it into a functional position, or change its own configuration by mechanical means.

automated lift — Any mechanical system designed to lift people or objects from a lower position to a higher level.

cable pull — A motor-driven mechanism that uses a looped cable to move an object horizontally or vertically.

concealed enclosure — A box or other three-dimensional shape built behind a wall or other flat surface to contain an object normally hidden from view.

counterweight — A heavy weight suspended on a cable or chain looped over a support wheel. The cable connects the counterweight to the object whose weight it is balancing. When the balanced object moves in one direction, the counterweight moves in the other.

drape pull mechanism — A device for opening or closing drapes or blinds by means of a motorized loop cord.

drop-down mechanism — A mechanical device that lowers a display or piece of equipment from a concealed overhead position to a level where it can be seen or used.

dumbwaiter — A small elevator designed to carry objects from one floor to another in a building. It is electrically powered and moves up and down on rails in an open shaft.

elevator — A large enclosed lift designed to move people from one floor to another in a building.

fireplace igniter — An electric device which lights a gas-fired fireplace by producing a spark near the gas jet which ignites the natural gas.

geared rack — A flat strip of metal geared on one side. It is mounted in a stationary position and a powered gear wheel travels along it in either direction, pulling whatever is attached to the gear.

heating cable — An electric cord which has high resistance to electricity and gets hot when current passes through it. Used to warm pipes, rain gutters, and other areas so they don't freeze.

hydraulic cylinder — A device which uses oil under high pressure to force a piston rod out of a cylinder. The moving rod lifts whatever is attached to its other end.

inclined ramp — A sloped walkway used in place of stairs. It can be traversed by wheeled vehicles as well as on foot.

loop pull cord — A continuous cord that extends through a drapery rod or blind and is used to pull the drape or blind open or closed. The cord forms an open loop on one end of the rod or frame.

motorized drive — A mechanical device that uses an electric motor and gear assembly to power a piece of equipment to perform a specific function.

off-the-shelf hardware — Mechanical assemblies already designed and built to accomplish movements in automated furniture or assist in the construction of custom systems.

operation cycle — A programmed series of commands that a device executes upon receiving a single start command. No additional commands are needed to complete the cycle.

picture frame lift — A motor-driven device that moves a picture frame upward to reveal what is behind it.

pivot-down mechanism — A mechanism that is held in position on one side by a hinge and opens by swinging downward on that hinge to reveal its contents.

platform lifts — Any motor-driven device intended to lift a piece of equipment or a display into a higher position for use or viewing.

projector lift — A motor-driven device that lifts a projector from a concealed location and positions it for projecting an image on screen.

recessed — Concealed below (or above) a flat surface, usually with a covering that matches or complements the surface.

shade controller — A device into which the end of a window shade's control rod fits, allowing the motor-driven controller to control the shade by remote commands.

shaft — Any vertical open space (sometimes enclosed with walls or by a tube) that extends through a building or the earth for some distance. Shafts provide open space for elevators to move in, or for cables, wiring, and other equipment.

spring-loaded door closer — A device with a strong spring and a hydraulic damper that slowly closes an open door. The strong spring pulls the door shut firmly, and the damper prevents it from acting too fast.

stairway lift — A motorized lift with guide rails angled to fit on a stairway so that the lift can move at an angle up and down the stairs.

swivel mechanisms — A motorized platform that can turn a display or piece of equipment left or right. Some types can rotate continuously at a steady pace.

television lift — A motor-driven device which can lift a television set out of concealment and position it for viewing.

thermocouple — An electric device that produces an electric current when heated. Used as a safety check to prevent unburned gas from flowing in any gas appliance.

tilt mechanism — A mechanical device designed to change the angle of an object for better viewing or to make its use easier.

track — In automated equipment, a metal channel with sides which guide wheels that are set in the track along a set path.

trip switch — An electric switch that turns a circuit on or off when activated by a moving object hitting it. Used as a stop switch for lifts or as a safety check to keep a lift car from moving too far up or down.

REVIEW QUESTIONS

1. Automated sliding doors for cabinets are opened and closed with a motor-driven _____.

2. A television lift is a device to:

   a. raise the quality of television reception

   b. lift the television from concealment to a viewing position

   c. increase the distance over which the signal can be received

   d. tilt the television screen downward to avoid light reflections

3. A drop-down mechanism would normally be used to house a(n) _____.

4. Why should a television lift and the television not be powered from the same circuit simultaneously?

5. A recessed device could be concealed:

   a. below the floor

   b. above the ceiling

   c. behind a wall

   d. any of the above

6. A shaft in a building is an open space that allows objects to move _____through the building.

7. A shade controller fits over the octagonal turning rod of a window shade. True or False?

8. Automatic drapery pulls can also be fitted to open vertical or horizontal _____.

9. Why can't a 60-pound drapery pull be battery powered?

10. AC-powered drapery pulls and door openers are usually controlled using what technology?

    a. hardwired

    b. WiFi

    c. HomePNA

    d. X10

11. A geared rack is a gear wheel with teeth cut on the side. True or False?

12. A dumbwaiter has interlocked controls that won't let the car move unless:

    a. everyone is out of it

    b. the load is not over 100 pounds

    c. all access doors are closed and locked

    d. the load is not over 200 pounds

13. What is the function of a counterweight on an elevator?

14. A stair lift is controlled from:

    a. the upper floor

    b. the lower floor

    c. both floors

    d. the lift chair

15. A fireplace igniter starts a gas flame burning by creating an electric spark. True or False?

16. A high heating cable consumes electric power at the rate of about _____ watts per foot.

    a. three

    b. five

    c. eight

    d. 10

17. For two 600 watt heating cables, a circuit of what minimum capacity is required?

    a. 10 amps

    b. 15 amps

    c. 20 amps

    d. 30 amps

18. A thermocouple produces an electric current when it is _____.

19. A skylight with an automatic opener on it can be activated by remote control and controlled by what two types of sensors?

14

    a. heat and motion sensors

    b. motion and humidity sensors

    c. heat and rain sensors

    d. rain and wind sensors

20. The main control panel for an elevator is always located where?

    a. on the main floor

    b. on the highest floor

    c. inside the elevator

    d. on the outer doors of the elevator

HANDS-ON PROJECTS

Project 14-1: Install a Window Blind Controller

In this project you will install an Auto-Tilt blind controller on a mounted bind. For this project you need access to a window blind mounted in a window or on a classroom simulation, an Auto-Tilt blind controller kit, 4 AA batteries for the controller and 2 AAA batteries for the remote.

1. Install the batteries in the controller receiver and the remote unit.

2. Connect the flexible connecting tube supplied as part of the Auto-Tilt kit to the bottom of the blind's control rod. Push the tube about an inch onto the rod. It will be a tight fit, but it can be forced on.

3. Hold the clear plastic mounting bracket against the inside edge of the window frame. Position the controller on the bracket so that the blind rod hangs straight down when connected to the controller's drive shaft.

4. Mark the position of the controller on the bracket and then mount the controller on the bracket in that position using the screws provided in the kit.

5. Slide the open end of the connecting tube that is on the rod over the drive shaft of the controller. Push it down an inch onto the shaft. The controller now hangs from the rod.

6. Position the controller and bracket against the window frame. Mount the bracket to the frame using the screws provided in the kit.

7. When the controller is mounted, test it with the two manual control buttons near the bottom of the unit. Press either button to turn the controller. Try closing the blind completely in one direction, then turn it back completely in the other direction. Don't run the controller too far.

8. Between the two manual buttons of the controller a number between 1 and 6 is printed. This is the controller's frequency number. Stand away from the window and point the remote toward the controller. Using one of the buttons on the remote that has the same number as the controller, open or close the blind with the remote.

Project 14-2: Install a Remote-controlled Drapery Pull

In this project you install a drapery control on a loop pull curtain rod. For this project you need access to a mounted loop pull curtain rod (the rod doesn't need to have drapes hung on it, although testing the automated unit is more realistic if it does), a SmartHome Model 44 Drapery motor kit, an X10 lamp control module, and an X10 controller.

1. Remove the snap-in plastic covers from the sides of the drapery motor so that the rope channel is open. Hang the drapery motor in the loop of the curtain rod. Let the motor rest on the loop so that its weight pulls the loop tight. Be sure the loop is seated all the way in the rope channel and on the drive wheel of the motor.

2. Place the mounting bracket behind the motor with the motor centered on the bracket. Move the bracket back against the wall with the motor still in place on it. Mark the position of the bracket on the wall.

3. Mount the bracket to the wall using the mounting hardware in the kit.

4. Snap the motor in place on the bracket at the position where the motor's weight is resting fully in the loop. Don't pull the cord tighter than the motor's weight pulls it and don't loosen it. Keep the cord tension as the weight of the motor pulls it.

5. Snap the rope channel covers back in place. Connect the motor to an AC power outlet. As soon as the motor is plugged in, it will run to open the drapery completely or close it. The motor is self-limiting and stops when it reaches a fully closed or open position. When the motor stops, unplug it.

6. Set the house code and unit code on an X10 lamp module so it can be controlled from the X10 controller. Connect the X10 lamp module in the AC outlet and plug the drapery motor into the lamp module.

7. Connect the controller to an AC outlet.

8. Send an On command to the module. The motor should reverse direction and pull the drapery to the opposite position of what it was when the motor stopped (open if the drapes were closed, closed if they were open). With a single On command the motor runs until it hits the limit of its pull, then it turns itself off.

9. Send another On command. The motor reverses and runs to the opposite limit again.

10. Send an On command and, when the curtains are halfway open or closed, send an Off command. The motor stops on the Off command. Send another On command and the motor continues in the same direction it was going until it hits the limit again. It then stops. With repeated On and Off commands, the drapery can be set in any desired position on the rod.

Project 14-3: Install an Automatic Door Mechanism

HANDS-ON
PROJECTS

In this project you mount two doors on a remote-controlled power door system. For this project you need access to a Eubank Remote Control Door Mechanism kit, and an entertainment center with 20-inch-wide sliding doors. Alternatively, in a classroom the door mechanism can be mounted on the edge of a table top and the doors hung over the side of the table.

1. Assemble the track pieces into a single track of the length needed for the doors with which you are working. The track should be twice as long as the width of both doors plus three inches.

14

2. Mount the cable end wheels in each end of the track assembly. Mount the cable on the wheels as shown in the instruction sheet drawing and position it so that it can be connected to the drive mechanism.

3. Position the motor unit on the track assembly so that its center mark is at one quarter of the distance of the track length from the left end of the track (as you face the track from the side on which the doors will hang). Attach the motor to the track with the hardware provided.

4. Feed one end of the cable on the short side of the track through the motor drive by hand turning the motor. Feed enough cable through the drive mechanism that you can clamp the two ends of the cable together on the long side of the track. Overlap the cable ends together about two inches and clamp them with the clamp provided. Don't try to put heavy tension on the cable. It only needs to be tight enough so that it can't come off the end pulley wheels.

5. Set the two door hangers in place on the track and fit their hardware in place on the track. Position the door hangers in the closed position. Clamp the left door hanger to the front side of the cable. Clamp the right door hanger to the back side of the cable.

6. Connect the motor to an AC power supply and test the track assembly to be sure the door hangers function correctly.

7. Mount the track and motor assembly on the cabinet or table top edge. Use the hardware provided. The outer edge of the track should be flush with the cabinet or table edge for the entire length of the track. The door hangers can be adjusted in or out to position the doors correctly if the track is correctly aligned.

8. Loosen the holding nuts on the door hangers and slide them off the carriages. Mount the hangers on the two doors with the back edge of the hanger flush with the back edge of each door.

9. Slide the door hangers back on the carriages and adjust their position so that the doors hang about 1/16 inch away from the edge of the cabinet or table top. Tighten the holding nuts to lock the door hangers in position.

10. Plug the motor into an AC power supply and test the door assembly using the remote control unit to see that it opens and closes the doors properly.

11. Adjust the door hangers on the carriages, if necessary, so that the doors come together squarely in the center of the track and so that they don't rub on the sides of the cabinet or table top as they open and close. Adjustment may take several tries to get the doors set perfectly, but when they are, tighten all the hardware to hold them firmly in place.

Project 14-4: Install a Heating Cable

In this project you install a heating cable on a pipe. The pipe can be set up in a classroom or actually installed in a plumbing system. It does not need to be in a location where it's subject to freezing. For this project you need an eight-foot heating cable with a built-in temperature sensor and a six-foot section of pipe with at least one bend in it. You also need a roll of fiberglass wrapping tape and several wire or plastic twists.

1. Plan how you will position the heating cable on the pipe so that the plug end of the cable can reach an AC power connection. An extension cord can be used, if necessary, but a direct connection to an outlet is better.

2. Bring the heating cable up against the bottom of the pipe. Hold it in place and start wrapping it with the fiberglass wrapping tape. Angle the tape so that it overlaps itself on each turn and pull it tight enough that the heating cable is in solid contact with the bottom side of the pipe.

3. Work the cable against the bottom of the pipe. Straighten any kinks in the cable so that it stays incontact with the pipe. Wrap it with the tape to hold it in place.

4. Bend the cable to conform to any curves or bends in the pipe and keep it on the bottom side of the pipe. Wrap the cable along the full length of the pipe.

5. Cut the wrapping tape and hold its end in place with a wire or plastic twist. Check along the length of the pipe for any places where the heating cable or the tape is loose on the pipe. Put twists on these places, if necessary, to keep the cable firmly in place.

6. Set the temperature sensor away from the pipe and in a position where the air can freely circulate around it. Connect the heating cable to an AC power outlet.

7. The cable should not come on when it's plugged in because the temperature isn't low enough. If you want to test the cable in operation, place some ice cubes around the temperature sensor and wrap a cloth around them to chill the sensor. It should turn on within a few minutes. In warm temperature areas, don't allow the heating cable to stay on more than a minute or two or it will begin to overheat.

14

CASE PROJECTS

Case Project 14-1: Recommend the Use of a Concealed Television

A beautiful and expensive home has a living room furnished in colonial style. The furnishings are mostly chairs and a pair of sofas with many pieces of the home owner's art collection hung on the walls in ornate frames. The room is used mostly for social gatherings in which conversation is the chief activity, and the décor is well-suited to that purpose. Occasionally, however, the owner would like to watch a television show or movie in the room and so would like to have a television installed. None of the large screen sets fit the room's décor at all and there's no piece of furniture large enough in which to conceal even a 27-inch screen. The ceiling of the room is too high for a drop-down projector system to be practical. What solution can you suggest that can get a television into this room without clashing with the décor?

Case Project 14-2: Automate Household Functions

A home with a good security system has had several alarms because vandals have tried to break in while the owner was away. The owner thinks the break-ins happen because the house appears to be empty most of the time. Potential thieves see that there's no activity around it and conclude that they can burglarize it unnoticed. The owner wants to automate some things inside the home that will be observable from the outside and will suggest that the home is occupied. What automation ideas can you suggest to give the impression from the outside that someone is present inside the home?

Case Project 14-3: Automate an Entrance Door

A disabled individual gets around her home using a powered wheelchair. She would like to be able to go outside into the backyard through her patio door. The door can be automated with an opener easily, but she doesn't have enough use of her hands to operate the remote used to control door openers. The most she can manage is pressing a single large button with her hand or calling out a voice command. How could the door be controlled inexpensively from either side so that it opens only when necessary and only for the homeowner?

Case Project 14-4: Improve a Ventilation System

A large mountain cabin has no central heating or cooling system because the climate where it's located is usually mild on most days of the year. The cabin has a fireplace that provides heat on the few cold days in winter and a large ventilation fan for cooling on warm summer days. The fireplace heats the room it's located in very well, but not much heat carries to other rooms. The ventilator fan cools the room where it's located very well, but other rooms in the cabin tend to remain quite stuffy and warm. What change can you suggest that would probably improve this cabin's ventilation in both winter and summer at minimal cost?

A

COMPTIA HTI+ EXAMINATION
OBJECTIVES

Objective	Chapter and Section(s)
HTI+ Residential Systems Examination Objectives	
DOMAIN 1.0: Computer Networking Fundamentals	
1.1. Identify basic network design considerations and information distribution methods through diverse media.	Chapter 1: Introduction to HTI **(Basic Components of HTI Systems)** Chapter 2: Home Technology Network Basics **(What is a LAN and How Does It Work? and Network Architecture)**
1.2. Identify the equipment location considerations when designing a computer network.	Chapter 3: Home Network Design and Configuration **(Home Information Distribution Requirements and Network Configuration and Settings for a Home Network)**
1.3. Identify the physical devices (hardware) that comprise the core networking technology.	Chapter 3: Home Network Design and Configuration **(Home Information Distribution Requirements, Wired Network Types, and Wireless Protocols and Standards)**
1.4. Identify the core configuration and setting for the networking technology hardware and software.	Chapter 3: Home Network Design and Configuration **(Wired Network Types, Wireless Protocols and Standards, and Network Configuration and Settings for a Home Network)**
1.5. Identify standard methods of device connectivity in the core networking technology.	Chapter 2: Home Technology Network Basics **(What is a LAN and How Does It Work? and Network Architecture)**
1.6. Identify the shared in-house services of the core networking technology.	Chapter 2: Home Technology Network Basics **(What is a LAN and How Does It Work? and Receiving and Sending Internal and External Information on a LAN)**
1.7. Identify and detail sources of externally provided data services found in the core networking technology.	Chapter 2: Home Technology Network Basics **(Receiving and Sending Internal and External Information on a LAN)**

Objective	Chapter and Section(s)
1.8. Identify and describe current industry standards of the core networking technology	Chapter 2: Home Technology Network Basics **(What is a LAN and How Does It Work?** and **Network Architecture)** Chapter 3: Home Network Design and Configuration **(Wired Network Types** and **Wireless Protocols and Standards)**
Domain 2.0: Audio and Video Fundamentals	
2.1. Identify and describe design considerations of a connected audio/video system	Chapter 6: Video and Audio Fundamentals **(From Analog Recording to Digital Transmission, Audio Recording and Broadcasting,** and **Television Recording and Broadcasting)**
2.2. Identify and describe audio and video equipment location considerations	Chapter 7: Audio and Video Installation and Setup **(Audio and Video System Components** and **Installation and Setup of Audio and Visual Systems)**
2.3. Identify and describe the physical audio and video products that make up the components of the core technology	Chapter 6: Video and Audio Fundamentals **(Audio Recording and Broadcasting,** and **Television Recording and Broadcasting)** Chapter 7: Audio and Video Installation and Setup **(Audio and Video System Components)**
2.4. Identify and describe the standard configuration and settings of the audio/video components of the core technology	Chapter 7: Audio and Video Installation and Setup **(Configurations and Settings for External Audio and Video** and **Configuration and Settings for Internal Video/Audio)**
2.5. Identify and describe the methods and components involved in device connectivity	Chapter 7: Audio and Video Installation and Setup **(Configuration and Settings for External Audio and Video** and **Configuration and Settings for Internal Audio and Video)**
2.6. Identify and describe the in-house services of the core technolog	Chapter 6: Video and Audio Fundamentals **(Sources of Audio and Video Services** and **Internet Video)**
2.7. Identify and describe the sources of externally provided audio and video services and their associated technologies	Chapter 6: Video and Audio Fundamentals **(Sources of Audio and Video Services** and **Internet Video)**
2.8. Identify and describe current standards and industry related organizations	Chapter 6: Video and Audio Fundamentals **(Audio Recording and Broadcasting,** and **Television Recording and Broadcasting)** Chapter 7: Audio and Video Installation and Setup **(Audio and Video System Components** and **Installation and Setup of Audio and Visual Systems)**

Objective	Chapter and Section(s)
2.9. Identify and describe installation plans and procedures for audio/video system components	Chapter 7: Audio and Video Installation and Setup **(Audio and Video System Components** and **Installation and Setup of Audio and Visual Systems)**
2.10. Identify and describe maintenance plans and procedures for audio/video system components	Chapter 7: Audio and Video Installation and Setup **(Configuration and Settings for External Audio and Video** and **Configuration and Settings for Internal Video/Audio)**
Domain 3.0: Home Security and Surveillance Systems	
3.1. Identify basic home security and fire alarm design considerations	Chapter 8: Security and Access System Fundamentals **(Security Design and Installation Factors** and **Security System Types)**
3.2. Identify the equipment location considerations when designing a security or fire alarm system	Chapter 8: Security and Access System Fundamentals **(Security System Equipment Locations)**
3.3. Identify the physical devices that comprise the security and surveillance alarm systems core technology	Chapter 8: Security and Access System Fundamentals **(Security System Components)**
3.4. Identify the core configuration and settings for the home security and surveillance alarm systems core technology	Chapter 9: Security System Installation and Setup **(Security System Programming and Settings)**
3.5. Identify standard methods of device connectivity in the home security and surveillance alarm systems' core technology	Chapter 9: Security System Installation and Setup **(Security System Programming and Settings, Security System Installation,** and **Component Installation and Setup)**
3.6. Identify the in-house services available in the home security and surveillance alarm systems' core technology	Chapter 8: Security and Access System Fundamentals **(Security System Types** and **Security System Components)**
3.7. Identify the external services available in the home security and surveillance alarm systems' core technology	Chapter 8: Security and Access System Fundamentals **(Security System Types** and **Security System Components)**
3.8. Identify and describe current industry standards relating to the home security and surveillance alarm systems' core technology	Chapter 8: Security and Access System Fundamentals **(Security Design and Installation Factors** and **Security System Types)**

Objective	Chapter and Section(s)
3.9. Identify and describe installation plans and procedures for home security and surveillance alarm systems	Chapter 9: Security System Installation and Setup **(Security System Installation** and **Component Installation and Setup)**
3.10. Identify and describe maintenance plans and procedures for home security and surveillance alarm systems	Chapter 9: Security System Installation and Setup **(Maintenance, Servicing, and Recovery)**
Domain 4.0: Telecommunications Standards	
4.1. Identify and describe the telecommunications design considerations of the home network	Chapter 10: Telecommunications Fundamentals and Installation **(Telecommunications System Types and Characteristics)**
4.2. Identify and describe telecommunication equipment location considerations when designing a home network	Chapter 10: Telecommunications Fundamentals and Installation **(Telecommunications System Types and Characteristics)**
4.3. Identify and describe the physical telecommunications products that make up the core technology of the home network	Chapter 10: Telecommunications Fundamentals and Installation **(Local Telephone Systems** and **Telephone Components and Features)**
4.4. Identify and describe the standard configurations and settings of the telecommunications components of the home network core technology	Chapter 10: Telecommunications Fundamentals and Installation **(Local Telephone Systems** and **Telephone Components and Features)**
4.5. Identify and describe the standard methods of device connectivity with telecommunications equipment in the core technology of the home network	Chapter 10: Telecommunications Fundamentals and Installation **(Telecommunications System Types and Characteristics)**
4.6. Identify and describe the in-house services available in the telecommunications core technology	Chapter 10: Telecommunications Fundamentals and Installation **(Local Telephone Systems)**
4.7. Identify and describe the external services available in the telecommunications core technology	Chapter 10: Telecommunications Fundamentals and Installation **(Telephone Components and Features)**
4.8. Identify and describe current industry standards to the telecommunications core technology	Chapter 10: Telecommunications Fundamentals and Installation **(Telephone Components and Features)**

Objective	Chapter and Section(s)
4.9. Identify and describe installation plans and procedures for home telecommunications systems	Chapter 10: Telecommunications Fundamentals and Installation **(Telephone Installation and Configuration)**
4.10. Identify and describe troubleshooting and maintenance plans and procedures for home telecommunications systems	Chapter 10: Telecommunications Fundamentals and Installation **(Telephone Installation and Configuration)**
Domain 5.0: Home Lighting Control and Management	
5.1. Identify and describe the design considerations of the networked home lighting control and management systems	Chapter 11: Home Lighting Control **(Automated Home Lighting Design** and **Automated Lighting System Types)**
5.2. Identify and describe the equipment location considerations of the networked home lighting control and management system	Chapter 11: Home Lighting Control **(Automated Home Lighting Design)**
5.3. Identify and describe the physical products that make up the networked home lighting control and management system	Chapter 11: Home Lighting Control **(Automated Lighting System Types** and **Lighting Control Components)**
5.4. Identify and describe the standard configurations and settings of the networked home lighting control and management system	Chapter 11: Home Lighting Control **(Automated Lighting System Types** and **Lighting Control Components)**
5.5. Identify and describe the standard methods of device connectivity with the networked home lighting control and management system	Chapter 11: Home Lighting Control **(Lighting Control Components** and **System Installation and Setup)**
5.6. Identify and describe current industry standards related to the home lighting control and management	Chapter 11: Home Lighting Control **(Automated Lighting System Types** and **System Installation and Setup)**
5.7. Identify and describe installation plans and procedures for home lighting control and management	Chapter 11: Home Lighting Control **(System Installation and Setup)**
5.8. Identify and describe troubleshooting and maintenance plans and procedures for the networked home lighting control and management system	Chapter 11: Home Lighting Control **(System Installation and Setup)**

Objective	Chapter and Section(s)
Domain 6.0: HVAC Management	
6.1. Identify and describe the design considerations of the home HVAC system	Chapter 12: Heating, Ventilation, and Air-Conditioning Management **(Design and Operation of Zoned and Non-zoned HVAC Systems)**
6.2. Identify and describe the equipment location considerations when designing a home HVAC system	Chapter 12: Heating, Ventilation, and Air-Conditioning Management **(Design and Operation of Zoned and Non-zoned HVAC Systems)**
6.3. Identify and describe the physical products and components that make up the core technology of the home HVAC system	Chapter 12: Heating, Ventilation, and Air-Conditioning Management **(HVAC Components)**
6.4. Identify and describe the standard configurations and settings of the products and components that make up the core technology of the home HVAC system	Chapter 12: Heating, Ventilation, and Air-Conditioning Management **(HVAC Components and HVAC Controller System Installation)**
6.5. Identify and describe the standard methods of device connectivity with the equipment and components that make up the core technology of the home HVAC system	Chapter 12: Heating, Ventilation, and Air-Conditioning Management **(HVAC Components and HVAC Controller System Installation)**
6.6. Identify and describe current industry standards related to the installation and maintenance of home HVAC systems	Chapter 12: Heating, Ventilation, and Air-Conditioning Management **(HVAC Controller System Installation)**
6.7. Identify and describe installation plans and procedures for home HVAC systems	Chapter 12: Heating, Ventilation, and Air-Conditioning Management **(HVAC Controller System Installation)**
6.8. Identify and describe troubleshooting and maintenance plans and procedures for home HVAC systems	Chapter 12: Heating, Ventilation, and Air-Conditioning Management **(HVAC Controller System Installation)**
Domain 7.0: Home Water Systems Controls and Management	
7.1. Identify and describe the design considerations of the networked home water system control and management system	Chapter 13: Water System Management **(Water Control System Design)**

Objective	Chapter and Section(s)
7.2. Identify and describe the equipment location considerations when designing a home water system control and management system.	Chapter 13: Water System Management **(Water Control System Design)**
7.3. Identify and describe the standard Configurations and settings of the core technology of the home water system control and management system.	Chapter 13: Water System Management **(Water Control System Installation and Programming)**
7.4. Identify and describe the standard methods of device connectivity with the equipment in the core technology of the home water system control and management system.	Chapter 13: Water System Management **(Water Control System Components)**
7.5. Identify and describe current industry standards related to the core technology of the home water system control and management system.	Chapter 13: Water System Management **(Water Control System Components)**
7.6. Identify and describe installation plans and procedures for the core technology of the home water system control and management system.	Chapter 13: Water System Management **(Water Control System Installation and Programming)**
7.7. Identify and describe troubleshooting and maintenance plans and procedures for the core technology of the home water system control and management system.	Chapter 13: Water System Management **(Water Control System Installation and Programming)**
DOMAIN 8.0: Home Access Controls and Management	
8.1. Identify and describe the design considerations of the home access control and management system.	Chapter 8: Security and Access System Fundamentals **(Security Design and Installation Factors)**
8.2. Identify and describe equipment and component location considerations when designing a home access control and management system.	Chapter 8: Security and Access System Fundamentals **(Security System Equipment Locations)**

Objective	Chapter and Section(s)
8.3. Identify and describe the physical products and components that make up the core technology of the home access control and management system	Chapter 8: Security and Access System Fundamentals **(Security System Components)**
8.4. Identify and describe the standard configurations and settings of the components that make up the core technology of the home access control and management system	Chapter 9: Security System Installation and Setup **(Security System Programming and Settings)**
8.5. Identify and describe the standard methods of device connectivity with equipment that make up the core technology of the home access control and management system	Chapter 9: Security System Installation and Setup **(Security System Installation** and **Component Installation and Setup)**
8.6. Identify and describe current industry standards related to the core technology of the home access control and management system	Chapter 8: Security and Access System Fundamentals **(Security Design and Installation Factors)**
8.7. Identify and describe installation plans and procedures for the core technology of the home access control and management system	Chapter 9: Security System Installation and Setup **(Security System Installation** and **Component Installation and Setup)**
8.8. Identify and describe troubleshooting and maintenance plans and procedures for the core technology of the home access control and management system	Chapter 9: Security System Installation and Setup **(Maintenance, Servicing, and Recovery)**
Domain 9.0: Miscellaneous Automated Home Features	
9.1. Identify and describe the fundamental design considerations of connected home system features	Chapter 14: Miscellaneous Automated Control Systems **(Automated Interior Furnishings, Automated Window and Door Systems, Automated Lift Systems,** and **Automated Heating Systems)**
9.2. Identify and describe telecommunication equipment location considerations when designing connected home system features	Chapter 14: Miscellaneous Automated Control Systems **(Automated Interior Furnishings, Automated Window and Door Systems, Automated Lift Systems,** and **Automated Heating Systems)**

Objective	Chapter and Section(s)
9.3. Identify and describe the physical products and components that make up the core technology of the identified connected home system features	Chapter 14: Miscellaneous Automated Control Systems **(Automated Interior Furnishings, Automated Window and Door Systems, Automated Lift Systems,** and **Automated Heating Systems)**
9.4. Identify and describe the standard configurations and settings of the components of the identified connected home system features	Chapter 14: Miscellaneous Automated Control Systems **(Automated Interior Furnishings, Automated Window and Door Systems, Automated Lift Systems,** and **Automated Heating Systems)**
9.5. Identify and describe the standard methods of device connectivity with the equipment and components of the identified connected home system features	Chapter 14: Miscellaneous Automated Control Systems **(Automated Interior Furnishings, Automated Window and Door Systems, Automated Lift Systems,** and **Automated Heating Systems)**
9.6. Identify and describe current industry standards related to the core technology of the identified connected home system features	Chapter 14: Miscellaneous Automated Control Systems **(Automated Interior Furnishings, Automated Window and Door Systems, Automated Lift Systems,** and **Automated Heating Systems)**
HTI+ Systems Infrastructure and Integration Examination Objectives	
Domain 1: Structured Wiring: 1A - Low Voltage	
1A.1. Identify standard structured wiring design considerations	Chapter 2: Home Technology Network Basics **(Network Architecture** and **Connecting a Home Network to the Internet)** Chapter 3: Home Network Design and Configuration **(Home Information Distribution Requirements, Wired Network Types,** and **Wireless Protocols and Standards)** Chapter 4: Installing Central Components and Low Voltage Wiring **(Planning a Home Network)**
1A.2. Identify standard structured wiring location considerations	Chapter 2: Home Technology Network Basics **(Network Architecture** and **Connecting a Home Network to the Internet)** Chapter 3: Home Network Design and Configuration **(Wired Network Types** and **Wireless Protocols and Standards)** Chapter 4: Installing Central Components and Low Voltage Wiring **(Planning a Home Network, Basic Central LAN Components,** and **Wiring a Home LAN)**

Objective	Chapter and Section(s)
1A.3. Identify physical structured wiring connection components	Chapter 2: Home Technology Network Basics **(Network Architecture and Major Hardware Components of a Home Network)** Chapter 3: Home Network Design and Configuration **(Home Information Distribution Requirements, Wired Network Types, and Wireless Protocols and Standards)** Chapter 4: Installing Central Components and Low Voltage Wiring **(Basic Central LAN Components and Wiring a Home LAN)**
1A.4. Identify the core configuration and settings for low voltage structured wiring design	Chapter 3: Home Network Design and Configuration **(Wired Network Types, Wireless Protocols and Standards, and Network Configuration and Settings for a Home Network)** Chapter 4: Installing Central Components and Low Voltage Wiring **(Planning a Home Network and Configuring the Hardware and Cables)**
1A.5. Identify standard methods of device connectivity for low voltage structured wiring design	Chapter 3: Home Network Design and Configuration **(Wired Network Types and Wireless Protocols and Standards)** Chapter 4: Installing Central Components and Low Voltage Wiring **(Planning a Home Network, Wiring a Home LAN, and Configuring the Hardware and Cables)**
1A.6. Identify and describe current industry standards for structured wiring design	Chapter 4: Installing Central Components and Low Voltage Wiring **(Planning a Home Network and Wiring a Home LAN)** Chapter 7: Audio and Video Installation and Setup **(Installation and Setup of Audio and Visual Systems)** Chapter 9: Security System Installation and Setup **(Security System Installation and Component Installation and Setup)** Chapter 10: Telecommunications Fundamentals and Installation **(Telephone Components and Features and Telephone Installation and Configuration)**

Objective	Chapter and Section(s)
1A.7. Identify and describe standard installation plans and procedures for structured wiring design	Chapter 4: Installing Central Components and Low Voltage Wiring **(Wiring a Home LAN, Basic Central LAN Components, and Configuring the Hardware and Cables)** Chapter 7: Audio and Video Installation and Setup **(Installation and Setup of Audio and Visual Systems)** Chapter 9: Security System Installation and Setup **(Security System Installation)** Chapter 10: Telecommunications Fundamentals and Installation **(Telephone Installation and Configuration)**
1A.8. Identify and describe maintenance plans and procedures for structured wiring design	Chapter 4: Installing Central Components and Low Voltage Wiring **(Configuring the Hardware and Cables)** Chapter 7: Audio and Video Installation and Setup **(Installation and Setup of Audio and Visual Systems)** Chapter 9: Security System Installation and Setup **(Maintenance, Servicing, and Recovery)** Chapter 10: Telecommunications Fundamentals and Installation **(Telephone Installation and Configuration)**
Domain 1: Structured Wiring: 1B - High Voltage	
1B.1. Identify and describe design considerations for high voltage structured wiring	Chapter 5: High Voltage Wiring **(High Voltage Electrical Safety Standards, Calculating AC Load Requirements, and Planning and Installing New AC Circuits)**
1B.2. Identify and describe audio and video equipment location considerations	Chapter 5: High Voltage Wiring **(High Voltage Electrical Safety Standards, Calculating AC Load Requirements, and Planning and Installing New AC Circuits)**
1B.3. Identify physical high voltage structured wiring connection components	Chapter 5: High Voltage Wiring **(Planning and Installing New AC Circuits)**
1B.4. Identify the core configuration and settings for high voltage structured wiring design	Chapter 5: High Voltage Wiring **(High Voltage Electrical Safety Standards, Calculating AC Load Requirements, and Planning and Installing New AC Circuits)**
1B.5. Identify standard methods of device connectivity for high voltage structured wiring design	Chapter 5: High Voltage Wiring **(High Voltage Electrical Safety Standards, Calculating AC Load Requirements, and Planning and Installing New AC Circuits)**

Objective	Chapter and Section(s)
1B.6 Identify and describe current high voltage structured wiring standards and industry related organizations.	Chapter 5: High Voltage Wiring **(High Voltage Electrical Safety Standards and Calculating AC Load Requirements)**
1B.7. Identify and describe installation plans and procedures for high voltage structured wiring design.	Chapter 5: High Voltage Wiring **(Calculating AC Load Requirements, and Planning and Installing New AC Circuits)**
1B.8. Identify and describe maintenance plans and procedures for high voltage structured wiring design.	Chapter 5: High Voltage Wiring **(Planning and Installing New AC Circuits)**
DOMAIN 2.0: : Systems Integration	
2.1. Identify standard system integration design considerations	Chapter 2: Home Technology Network Basics **(What is a LAN and How Does It Work? and Network Architecture)** Chapter 3: Home Network Design and Configuration **(Wired Network Types, Wireless Protocols and Standards, and Network Configuration and Settings for a Home Network)** Chapter 4: Installing Central Components and Low Voltage Wiring **(Planning a Home Network)** Chapter 6: Video and Audio Fundamentals **(Audio Recording and Broadcasting, Television Recording and Broadcasting, Sources of Audio and Video Services, and Internet Video)** Chapter 8: Security and Access System Fundamentals **(Security Design and Installation Factors)** Chapter 10: Telecommunications Fundamentals and Installation **(Telecommunications System Types and Characteristics)**
2.2. Identify equipment location considerations in system integration designs.	Chapter 2: Home Technology Network Basics **(Connecting a Home Network to the Internet)** Chapter 3: Home Network Design and Configuration **(Home Information Distribution Requirements, Wired Network Types, and Wireless Protocols and Standards)** Chapter 4: Installing Central Components and Low Voltage Wiring

Objective	Chapter and Section(s)
	(Planning a Home Network) Chapter 6: Video and Audio Fundamentals **(Audio Recording and Broadcasting** and **Television Recording and Broadcasting)** Chapter 8: Security and Access System Fundamentals **(Security System Equipment Locations)** Chapter 10: Telecommunications Fundamentals and Installation **(Local Telephone Systems)**
2.3. Identify the core components found in system integration designs	Chapter 2: Home Technology Network Basics **(Major Hardware Components of a Home Network)** Chapter 3: Home Network Design and Configuration **(Wired Network Types** and **Wireless Protocols and Standards)** Chapter 4: Installing Central Components and Low Voltage Wiring **(Basic Central LAN Components)** Chapter 7: Audio and Video Installation and Setup **(Audio and Video System Components)** Chapter 8: Security and Access System Fundamentals **(Security System Components** and **Security System Equipment Locations)** Chapter 10: Telecommunications Fundamentals and Installation **(Telephone Components and Features)**
2.4. Identify the configuration and settings for the components found in system integration designs	Chapter 2: Home Technology Network Basics **(Connecting a Home Network to the Internet)** Chapter 3: Home Network Design and Configuration **(Network Configuration and Settings for a Home Network)** Chapter 4: Installing Central Components and Low Voltage Wiring **(Configuring the Hardware and Cables)** Chapter 7: Audio and Video Installation and Setup **(Configuration and Settings for External Audio and Video** and **Configuration and Settings for Internal Video/Audio)** Chapter 9: Security System Installation and Setup **(Security System Programming and Settings)** Chapter 10: Telecommunications Fundamentals and Installation **(Telephone Installation and Configuration)**

Objective	Chapter and Section(s)
2.5. Identify methods of device connectivity for the components found in system integration designs	Chapter 2: Home Technology Network Basics **(Network Architecture, Connecting a Home Network to the Internet, and Major Hardware Components of a Home Network)** Chapter 3: Home Network Design and Configuration **(Wired Network Types, Wireless Protocols and Standards, and Network Configuration and Settings for a Home Network)** Chapter 4: Installing Central Components and Low Voltage Wiring **(Wiring a Home LAN and Configuring the Hardware and Cables)** Chapter 9: Security System Installation and Setup **(Security System Installation and Component Installation and Setup)** Chapter 10: Telecommunications Fundamentals and Installation **(Telecommunications System Types and Characteristics)**
2.6. Identify and describe current industry standards for system integration designs	Chapter 2: Home Technology Network Basics **(What is a LAN and How Does It Work?, Network Architecture, and Connecting a Home Network to the Internet)** Chapter 3: Home Network Design and Configuration **(Wired Network Types, Wireless Protocols and Standards, and Network Configuration and Settings for a Home Network)** Chapter 6: Video and Audio Fundamentals **(Sources of Audio and Video Services and Internet Video)** Chapter 8: Security and Access System Fundamentals **(Security System Types)** Chapter 9: Security System Installation and Setup **(Security System Programming and Settings)** Chapter 10: Telecommunications Fundamentals and Installation **(Telecommunications System Types and Characteristics)**

Objective	Chapter and Section(s)
2.7. Identify and describe standard installation plans and procedures for structured wiring design	Chapter 2: Home Technology Network Basics **(Network Architecture and Connecting a Home Network to the Internet)** Chapter 3: Home Network Design and Configuration **(Wired Network Types, Wireless Protocols and Standards, and Network Configuration and Settings for a Home Network)** Chapter 4: Installing Central Components and Low Voltage Wiring **(Wiring a Home LAN)** Chapter 7: Audio and Video Installation and Setup **(Installation and Setup of Audio and Visual Systems)** Chapter 9: Security System Installation and Setup **(Security System Installation and Component Installation and Setup)** Chapter 10: Telecommunications Fundamentals and Installation **(Telephone Components and Features)**
2.8. Identify and describe maintenance plans and procedures for structured wiring design	Chapter 2: Home Technology Network Basics **(Network Architecture and Connecting a Home Network to the Internet)** Chapter 3: Home Network Design and Configuration **(Wired Network Types, Wireless Protocols and Standards, and Network Configuration and Settings for Home Network)** Chapter 7: Audio and Video Installation and Setup **(Installation and Setup of Audio and Visual Systems)** Chapter 9: Security System Installation and Setup **(Maintenance, Servicing, and Recovery)** Chapter 10: Telecommunications Fundamentals and Installation **(Telephone Installation and Configuration)**

B

STATE CODES AND STANDARDS

Before working with high-voltage electrical wiring, you must be certain that you meet the required knowledge and licensing requirements for the state and local area in which you're working. You should also know what inspection procedure, if any, your work must pass before going into service.

State electrical contracting and licensing requirements vary greatly, from New York and Texas, which have no statewide electrical code laws, to California and Connecticut, which require all electrical contractors to be licensed and all electrical work to conform to the National Electric Code.

You can learn about the requirements for a specific state by contacting the individual regulatory agencies in that state. To obtain a list of these agencies for all states, go to the National Electrical Contractors Association Web site at *www.necanet.org/store/index.cfm?fuseaction=search_results&index_number=5060*. There, you can download their free publication: "State Electrical Regulations: Guide to Electrical Codes, Enforcement and Licensing (2002)." This 49-page booklet is available without charge as a PDF file download.

The guide lists only the state agencies that regulate electrical work and workers. Many local jurisdictions (cities and counties) have their own requirements, especially in states where there are no statewide laws governing the electrical profession. Be sure to find out if there are local codes and licenses in your area as well.

C

INTEGRATION CASE STUDIES

This appendix gives multiple case studies that you can use for study and group discussion. The real-world context of the cases should give you a good idea of what you might encounter in the workplace. The ultimate goal of the case studies is to encapsulate all that you have learned to date, and to provide real industry application of the skills you've learned.

CASE STUDY #1: DISCUSSION

A customer of yours calls. This customer lives in a brand new home in which your company installed structured wiring. The structured wiring has been tested and certified to meet or exceed industry standards. The customer has moved into the new home and plugged in telephone equipment that she had in her previous home. This equipment includes a number of cordless phones, an answering machine, and a fax machine.

The customer complains that the phones are not ringing when someone calls. Family members can receive faxes, they can make outgoing phone calls, and if, by coincidence, they pick up the phone when someone is calling, they can speak to them. The fax machine is on a separate line from the main phones in the house.

What steps would you take to solve this problem?

Is there any other information that you need to know?

What tools would you need?

CASE STUDY #1: SOLUTION

This has become a very common problem when a new home is built and many phone extensions are installed. The problem is caused by the ringer equivalency voltage (REN) being too low. To evaluate the problem, you must measure the voltage using a volt-ohm meter; the voltage should be measured with no phones off the hook and then when the phone is ringing. If the voltage is too low, the phones will not ring. The phone company, the structured wire panel, or the number of phones in the house can cause this problem. Each phone has a REN value printed on the bottom of the phone; add these numbers to get the total value of the REN for the home and then check with your local provider to see if it exceeds their equipment.

CASE STUDY #2: DISCUSSION

You are putting the finishing touches on a security system. During this process you test each door and window to verify that it reads as open on the keypad when it is in the open position. Everything seems to be working except one window. When you open that window, the security keypad does not show it as open. You check the placement of the magnet and the sensor and they appear to be correct. You test the wire for continuity and it checks out.

What is the process to solve the problem?

What tools do you need?

What other information would be important to help solve this problem?

CASE STUDY #2: SOLUTION

The problem is more than likely caused by a nail or screw shorting out the wire somewhere behind the wall. The first thing to try is to disconnect the sensor and test the wire from that side; it should still show that it is shorted. A line tester can then be used to determine the distance from the end of the wire to the short. This is why it is important to have good documentation about how the wires are run in the home and the direction they take. Once the tester tells you the distance, then the wire can be traced and the short found. The drywall will have to be opened and the offending screw or nail removed.

This problem should be reported immediately to the field supervisor so that the trade worker who shorted the wire can be alerted to the problem so that it does not happen again.

CASE STUDY #3: DISCUSSION

You install a power line carrier lighting control system in a new home. After your client moves in, he reports that the family room light goes on every night at 5 pm, when it is programmed to go on at 6:30 pm. After checking the programming, you verify that it states that the light should go on at 6:30 pm and off at 11 pm. It is going off normally and no other lights are programmed to go on at 5 pm.

What is the problem?

How do you solve it?

How do you prevent similar problems from occurring?

CASE STUDY #3: SOLUTION

The problem is interference from outside the house. Install a filter at the service panel of the home. This accomplishes two things: first, it stops unwanted signals from entering the home and second, it stops signals from leaving the home and affecting the neighbors. By installing the filter, you will solve most of the installation issues associated with power line carrier lighting control systems. If the problem persists, test the "noisy" items in the house. These would include, but are not limited to, TVs, computers, stereo equipment, hair dryers, or any other device that can create RF on the power line. However, in this scenario, it would be unlikely that the interference would be caused at precisely 5 pm every day.

CASE STUDY #4: DISCUSSION

After installing a new camera in a home, none of the existing TVs display the signal, even though you have programmed the modulator properly and checked all of the connections.

What is the problem?

What other diagnostic procedures should be done?

How can this problem be prevented?

CASE STUDY #4: SOLUTION

The first task that should be done is to hook up a monitor directly to the camera to verify that it is operating properly. Next, check for digital or "high-speed" services that are provided by the cable company. These can block other signals from modulators. The solution to the problem is to install a high-pass filter before the signal is distributed around the home or combined with the camera signal. The high-pass filter blocks the signals associated with digital or high-speed service so it should be installed in a manner that does not block those signals tracking to the areas that they need to be, for example, to the cable modem.

CASE STUDY #5: DISCUSSION

You've recently installed an eight-zone controller on an existing sprinkling system. Only six of the controller's zone controls are actually used because the system was only divided into that number of zones. Wiring leads for the last two were simply taped over and left unattached. The new controller works well, but the grass covered by sprinklers in Zone 6 is dying. The home owner has increased the watering time for this zone repeatedly until it's now up to 60 minutes, but the grass is still dying. The sprinklers are timed to come on at night and there's water evident on the grass in Zone 6 in the mornings, so the sprinklers there are activating.

What's causing the problem in Zone 6?

How can you find out if the sprinkler controller is somehow malfunctioning in the night?

If it is, how do you correct it?

CASE STUDY #5: SOLUTION

Zone 6 is getting some water (evident in the mornings), but not enough to keep the grass alive. If increasing the watering time isn't helping, then the increase must not be actually occurring. The most probable cause is that Zone 6 is miswired in the controller, either to one of the unused zones (7 and 8) or crossed with one of the other used zones. With this miswiring, the homeowner is increasing the watering time in a zone that doesn't need it or in one that's not connected to the system at all. Watering time for Zone 6 isn't being changed at all.

To confirm this, run a zone test on the controller. Advance the controller manually through each zone and observe which sprinklers actually come on for each zone setting. If Zone 6 is found to be wired to another zone, no rewiring is necessary. The problem can be solved by simply renumbering the zones according to the way they're actually wired. Then the homeowner can adjust the watering time of the dry zone by resetting the correct zone number for it on the controller.

CASE STUDY #6: DISCUSSION

A client for whom you've recently installed a video system complains that the television set in his daughter's bedroom has serious audio problems. This is an analog set that's connected to the satellite digital decoder/converter, but it displays its picture and sound only in analog format. The client has added a DVD player to this television station, connecting it to the television's input jacks with RCA cables. The problem is that the audio volume for satellite reception is normal, but sound from the DVD player varies tremendously at a single setting. Sometimes it's normal, sometimes too loud, and sometimes so low that it can't be heard.

You check the wiring setup and confirm that the television has only monaural sound capability. It's connected to the decoder via a single coaxial cable input. The DVD player's left side audio output is wired via an RCA cable to the monaural audio input jack on the television. A second RCA cable connects the composite video from the DVD player to the input jack on the television.

Why is the DVD sound varying so much?

What simple solution can correct this problem?

CASE STUDY #6: SOLUTION

The variation in sound output from the DVD player is caused by the fact that only half of its audio output is being received by the television. DVD players all have stereo sound output. Connecting only the left side of the output to the television means that all of the right side sound is lost. This results in large volume variations that depend on the side of the stereo system from which sound output is coming. The solution is a simple RCA combination plug that has two input jacks on one end and that combines both inputs into a single plug on the other end. This plug allows both audio outputs to be combined in the television's monaural input and eliminates the sound variations caused by the missing audio output.

CASE STUDY #7: DISCUSSION

In a home where you've installed an extensive X10-based automated lighting system, the client has added some X10-controlled shade openers and drapery pulls to the system. Everything works as programmed, except that when one lamp module in the lighting system is commanded to turn on, one of the drapery pulls goes crazy. Sometimes it opens the drapes; sometimes it closes them, sometimes it moves them part way open or closed, and sometimes it appears to do nothing at all. If the lamp is turned off with another command, the movements of the drapery pull also stop. The drapery pull is normally activated with a handheld mini-controller, while the lighting system is controlled from a master controller in the family room. If the drapery pull is activated, the lamp also turns on and stays on even when the drapes stop moving.

What is wrong with the drapery pull?

How can it be easily corrected?

CASE STUDY #7: SOLUTION

Even though they are being activated by different controllers, both the lighting system and the drapery pulls use the same X10 signals. This problem is caused by having the drapery pull set to the same house and unit code as the lamp module in the lighting system. This causes both devices to activate on command from either controller. X10 drapery pulls respond only to On and Off commands. The seemingly erratic behavior of the drapery pull is actually just its normal operation. Any On command starts the pull moving to open or close the drapes and it continues moving until it reaches the totally open or totally closed position, at which point its self-limiting switch stops it and reverses its direction. If an Off command is received, the pull stops in a partially opened or closed position. The next On command starts it moving again in the same direction it was going when turned off. The apparently random drape movements are really normal (but unintended) operation.

The problem can be corrected by changing the house or unit code on the drapery pull to one not used by the lighting system. This separates its operation from the lamp module.

CASE STUDY #8: DISCUSSION

A client with a satellite digital television receiver wants to add a second receiver to his system. Rather than purchase or lease a second decoder from the satellite company, he suggests installing a splitter on the existing decoder's output line and simply running its signal to both television sets. This saves him the installation cost and continuing fees for additional satellite service.

Will this idea work?

Would you recommend this solution to your customers? Why or why not?

CASE STUDY #8: SOLUTION

Splitting the signal coming out of the decoder is possible, although doing it weakens the signal on both legs of the splitter and may require a signal booster if the cable connection to either television set is long. More importantly, splitting the signal after it passes through the decoder doesn't really provide another reception channel. The second television set connected to the decoder can only show the same channel that is playing on the first set. The channel can be changed only at the decoder and both television sets will always display the same channel. If one set is located in a different room from the decoder, a viewer will have to go to the decoder room to change channels because the controller for the decoder is a line-of-sight IR device that won't work from another room.

Even though this setup is possible, the customer won't be satisfied with it. A second satellite decoder should be installed for the second television set. It will be worth the cost.

STRUCTURED WIRING INSTALLATION BACKGROUND INFORMATION

In almost all of the following cases, the problem arises from the fact that there are multiple dependencies that the integrator (installer) cannot control. In every case, accurate planning and communication would solve the problem, but alas, this is not a perfect world and the integrator has to make decisions to move the project along.

Each case is something that the integrators of structured wiring products experience on a regular basis. There are usually multiple solutions, each with its own advantages and disadvantages.

CASE STUDY #9: DISCUSSION

The integrator is contracted for pre-wiring of locations for satellite service and/or high-definition pre-wires. The customer has not chosen her preferred satellite service vendor.

First, it is important to understand why there are many issues involved with this seemingly simple exercise. Depending on whether the customer has chosen or will choose high-definition, there may be up to four wires (RG-6 shielded cables) run from the proposed satellite dish location(s). The type of dish and switching equipment needed also influences the number of wires run. While most multi-satellite dishes (HDTV) utilize a built-in multi-switch with four outputs, standard or single satellite dishes have one or two outputs. In either case, the number of outputs from these dishes usually dictates the number of rooms to which satellite reception can be provided. While the use of external multi-switches and launch amplifiers can be used to multiply and distribute satellite signals to every room in the home, costs become somewhat prohibitive to most customers.

Depending on the service desired, there may be multiple satellite dishes aimed between 170–210 degrees south from the azimuth. In the western states, DirecTV satellite dishes are mounted on the southeast side of the house at 130–150 degrees.

On the other hand, Dish Network may require multiple dishes if the customer wishes to get local and international channels. The satellite dish for local channels is at 140 degrees from the azimuth. The international channel dish sits at 200 degrees from the azimuth. Note: The exact position depends on the location in the US.

You may have to install multiple cable runs to meet the customer's needs. But that's not all. If the customer plans to set up service after she moves in, she may get installation from the service provider's contractor, not you. In this case, the contractor usually routes a cable from the dish, under the eaves, and into the service location for the regular buried landline. This completely eliminates the need for any pre-wire for satellite dishes.

Finally, if the customer wants to have land-based cable or high speed DSL connections, this requirement may compete with the satellite connection because broadband sometimes comes in on cable and competes with video service for a pre-wired coaxial cable.

CASE STUDY #9: SOLUTION

If at all possible, get the customer to decide on her service before you wire! You can make the best decision if you have this information. Because sometimes the satellite installation company runs a wire around the eaves to the buried cable entry location, you would not need to install any pre-wires to the possible satellite dish location. If this is the case, explain this to the customer and don't include any pre-wires if the customer agrees.

If your contract requires a pre-wire or if the customer thinks she wants to include accommodations for the satellite dish, run the four cables to the network connection center and into the attic. Leave a coil of wires in the attic close to the south side of the house. Make sure to leave enough cable to run to the furthest possible locations on the south side of the house. Inform the customer/builder what you have done, and then leave a note in the network connection center so the installer will understand what is there.

Of course, if you are also installing the satellite dish, then you have the information you need and you can just wire it as needed.

CASE STUDY #10: DISCUSSION

Differentiating RJ-45 jacks from RJ-11 is a problem of the visual versus the technical. There are two types of connections that can work with phones: an RJ-11 (traditional 4-wire) or an RJ-45 (8-wire). The RJ-11 jack can be used for up to two phone lines, while the RJ-45 can be used for up to four. There are two wires required for each phone line or number.

The advantage of RJ-45 is that it can carry data for computer networking as well as for phone connections. It is becoming common practice for installers to use RJ-45 connections for phones, as these connections are the most flexible.

Typically, structured wiring workers do not perform their work until after the electrician. The electrician establishes the outlet heights. Sometimes electricians run the phone lines! If they do this, they usually use RJ-11 instead of the versatile RJ-45 outlet.

If the structured wiring installer is also asked to run phone lines, this is a mistake of the builder because they have requested two work orders. Figure out what's really specified and give preference to the RJ-45 connections.

You have to explain to homeowners that an RJ-45 jack can also act as a phone jack. You can actually plug an RJ-11 plug into an RJ-45 connection. Sometimes homeowners do this and wonder why they can't get a particular number to ring in a certain room. Recall that one RJ-45 (CAT-5 cable) line can have up to four numbers. If you plug an RJ-11 plug into an RJ-45 jack, you will get only lines 1 and 2. So what are you to do?

CASE STUDY #10: SOLUTION

You need a breakout box or a configurable telephone hubs package. A breakout box takes a single RJ-45 8-wire connection in and separates it into four phone lines. The customer simply plugs the phone connector into the required line. This is the easiest aftermarket solution.

Alternately, the installer could change the configuration of the punch down connection. However, this creates a nonstandard color coding that is sure to cause problems in the future.

The ideal solution is to use a configurable hub. The hub allows you to assign a particular number to any RJ-45 jack in the house using a jumper configuration. You should make sure that the homeowner understands the telephone uses and needs for each room and wire accordingly.

CASE STUDY #11: DISCUSSION

The installer shows up for installation of telephone service and the demarc has not been installed or the service is not live. The result is the customer will not get a live phone service connection when he moves into the home. Customers usually view this as an urgent situation and will call the installer.

Four parties are involved:

- The installer
- The service provider
- The service provider's installation crew
- The homeowner who has to instigate the service activation or switch

Note that the service provider will not touch the installer's wiring (the wires that go into the house). Even if the wiring is right in front of them, they will not connect it. Keeping this in mind, the installer has to watch out for the following scenarios.

Scenario 1: No Demarc Evident

The installer does his job wiring the home and must come back to connect the service. The installer leaves the wires coiled up in an opening that the contractor created for the demarc.

The installer will have to come back from time to time to check for a demarc. If you are performing services on multiple houses in the development, visit the outside of the houses in the development that you have installed and check for the demarc. It's just a few screws to open the box and connect the wires. However, this may not assure a working service if the homeowner has not activated it or if the service has not been switched on by the provider.

Scenario 2: Demarc is Evident

The installer connects the wires at the demarc. The installer comes back after homeowner has moved in and verifies that all systems are working. Sometimes the homeowner forgets to transfer the service, so even if all the wires are there, the line may be "dead."

Scenario 3: Homeowner Moves in, but Demarc Is Not There!

Sometimes the demarc is not installed even after the homeowner has moved in. In this case, the homeowner needs to contact the builder to get the demarc installed. After this installation, the integrator needs to return to connect the wiring to the demarc. Sometimes the service provider has activated the service, but the crew hasn't physically installed it.

CASE STUDY #11: SOLUTION

Have daily communication with the builder to be sure that the demarc is there. Establish a line of communication with someone at the service provider involved with scheduling the hookups.

CONTRIBUTORS TO THE CASE STUDIES

Avi Rosenthal is part of Digital Living of CompUSA. In addition, he is a board member of the Tech Home division of the Consumer Electronics Association, as well the chair of the Education Subcommittee. He has been profiled by *USA Today*, *CE-Pro Magazine*, and *Electronic House Magazine*, and he has been featured in many magazines and news programs. In addition, he is a subject matter expert for CompTIA's HTI+ Certification program. He lives in Boca Raton, Florida, with his wife and three children.

Brandon Blankenship is the director of operations for California Production at Digital Interiors, a Home Director company. (Home Director is a leading home networking company that designs, manufactures, sells, and installs home networking products.) He has 20 years of experience in the building industry, 10 of those spent with Simplex-Grinnell, a premier provider of fire and safety systems. He was an active member on the Board of Education for the California–American Fire Sprinkler Association (CAFSA) and was instrumental in setting up their guidelines and teaching curriculum.

Glossary

2-conductor wire — A high-voltage cable containing a hot wire, a neutral wire, and a ground, which is not counted as a conductor.

AC cable — Armored cable; type of cable sheathed in metal. Also, any cable used for alternating current (AC) wiring.

AC power — Alternating current electric power; the standard electric service in homes.

access control — Restriction on who has the right to use a computer system or to enter a physical location.

access point — A wireless hub or device through which a wireless node can connect to a LAN.

adaptors — Devices that change audio and video connectors from one form to another, including gender changes.

administrator — A person designated to maintain and control a computer system or subsystem.

ADSL splitter — A device attached to the NID, which splits an incoming ADSL data line, isolates other telephone lines and equipment, and allows a home run to be installed to the modem.

Advanced Television Systems Committee (ATSC) — The government-run and industry-influenced group that sets standards for the television industry.

air conditioning (A/C) — The part of an HVAC system that provides cool air to lower the indoor air temperature.

air handlers — The mechanical devices that move air in an HVAC system. They are mainly blowers and fans.

alarm — An audible warning of fire, illegal entry, or other security breach. Usually a siren, bell ringing, or similar sound.

alternating current (AC) — The type of power that almost all homes receive from the electric utility company.

always-live duplex outlet — An AC electrical outlet that is not controlled by a switch and always has current available.

American Wire Gage (AWG) — The standard for electrical wire sizes.

ampere — The unit used to measure electric current flow.

amplifier — A device that strengthens the power of an RF signal it receives from an antenna or pre-amplifier.

amplitude modulation (AM) — A method of converting sound waves to radio signals by varying the amplitude (strength) of the signal, but not its frequency.

analog — Sound or video signals that are analogous to (have patterns similar to) the actual sounds or images.

analog data — Data in nonnumeric form such as radio waves, sound waves, etc.

antenna — The component of a radio or television receiver that receives a broadcast signal from a distant transmitter.

appliance — Any piece of equipment that performs a specified task.

arm — Activate a security system so that its sensors are functioning.

aspect ratio — The ratio of a video screen's width to its height. NTSC screens have a 4:3 ratio, HDTV screens a 16:9 ratio.

atrium — An area within a home that is open to the outside or walled in glass, in which plants can grow as in the outside yard.

attenuated — Weakened by distance from the source; resistance; used to describe radio and television signals.

automated control — A method for controlling HVAC systems by preset programming rather than manual setting of controls.

automated doors — Doors mechanized to open and close on command by means of cable pulls or hydraulic actuators.

automated furniture — Any piece of furniture that can be remotely directed to open, move a display or object within it into a functional position, or change its own configuration by mechanical means.

automated lift — Any mechanical system designed to lift people or objects from a lower position to a higher level.

automation — The process of controlling a lighting or other system remotely, either with manual commands from a controller or by a programmed set of instructions from a computer. Also, performing a task or function by means of a programmed device or system without the need for human supervision.

average use — The amount of electricity used in a home over a period of time, usually a day.

bandwidth — In telecommunications, the amount of data transmission capacity in a line. In networks, the amount of data that can travel over a communication line or wireless connection in a given length of time.

baud — One complete cycle or wave in an analog transmission signal. A baud starts at zero voltage, goes up to maximum positive voltage, comes back to zero, goes to maximum negative voltage, and finally returns to zero voltage.

biometric identifiers — Unique distinguishing physical features of an individual that can be used as means of identification. They include fingerprints, eye retinas, voice prints, and facial characteristics.

blower — A device that uses a rotating bladed wheel to move air in an HVAC system. Not the same thing as a fan.

Bluetooth — A short-range (100 meters) wireless connection technology now being used for networking.

boiler — A device for heating water to be used for heating a building. Not the same as a water heater.

break switch — A sensor that monitors a closed switch and signals if the switch is opened and the circuit broken. Used on doors, windows, and containers that should remain closed as their normal state.

breaker — A safety device that is wired into a circuit to cut off current flow if the circuit becomes overloaded.

bridge — An intelligent switch that limits data flow on a LAN.

broadband — Any method of transmitting large amounts of data in a short time span. Usually accomplished by using multiple frequencies or data streams; a large (or wide) bandwidth technology.

bus topology — One form of network architecture for Ethernet.

bypass — Any means of evading a security device by making it appear to be functioning in a normal state when, in fact, conditions have changed. A window sensor, for example could be bypassed by slipping a loose plate onto its contact points to make the switch continue to signal normal (closed) even when the window is opened.

cable modem — A device that converts digital data to analog signals and connects a LAN to an ISP via the cable television connection.

cable pull — A motor driven mechanism that uses a looped cable to move an object horizontally or vertically.

cable run — A cable installed between two connecting points such as a patch panel and jack.

call restriction — A telephone system feature that allows certain calls to be blocked from incoming or outgoing lines.

Caller ID — A system in which a signal sent by the telephone company with an incoming call identifies the calling number and its registered owner. Telephones with electronics capable of reading this signal display the caller ID information on a small LCD screen.

camera — A device that creates a video image in digital or analog form. Cameras can produce still images or moving images.

carrier frequency — In radio transmission, a signal at high frequency on which a signal of lower frequency is carried.

Carrier Sense Multiple Access/Collision Avoidance (CSMA/CA) — A method of data transmission in which nodes avoid data packet collisions through use of a token or other device controlling the movement of data.

Carrier Sense Multiple Access/Collision Detection (CSMA/CD) — A method of data transmission in which data packets contend for space on the network, and nodes sense packet collisions that require resending.

Category 2 telephone wire — A low speed data wire containing two pairs of solid core insulated wires. Named for its widespread use in wiring analog telephone lines.

Category 3 wire — Low speed data wire with the same composition as Category 2 wire but having either four or six pairs of wires.

Category 5 (Cat5) cable — A high-speed eight wire UTP data cable for Ethernet.

cathode ray tube (CRT) — The electronic tube in a television set or computer monitor on which the picture or display appears.

CatX cable stripper — A tool for cutting and removing the outer jacket from Category 5 and other similar types of cable.

CD burner — A device for recording compact discs (CDs). A CD burner can also play a CD, but CD players are not always burners.

CD player — A device for playing recorded compact discs.

CD-R (CD-Recordable format) — A compact disc that can be recorded once on a CD burner, but is then a permanently fixed recording that cannot be changed.

CD-RW (CD-Rewritable format) — A CD that can be recorded multiple times with succeeding recordings added to or replacing older ones on the disc.

central heating system — The part of an HVAC system that provides warm air from a central furnace to raise the indoor air temperature.

central processor — The main computer in an HTI system or, alternately, the component in a computer that performs calculations on data.

Centrex — Central exchange, the main switching point in the telephone company where calls are connected by switching them to the line called.

certification — The process of attesting to the qualification or competence of a person to perform certain services.

checksum — A mathematical method for a receiver to determine if a data packet has been corrupted.

cipher lock — A door lock that opens only when a numeric code is entered on a keypad mounted near it. The code can also be placed on a memory card that is swiped through a reader to open the lock. Some locks can have many access codes, some only one.

circuit — A conducting "circle" in which electricity flows from a source to a device, through the device, and back to the source.

circuit-switched lines — The normal method of completing an analog call in which the calling line is physically connected to the called line by a defined path, and the path is kept open for the duration of the call.

circulating pump — A device in a radiant heating system that circulates the heated water through the boiler and heating pipes continuously.

clean power — AC current that does not contain noise, interference, surges, or spikes.

cliff effect — A description of the sudden termination of the range of digital video or radio transmissions, which can end as if they "fell off a cliff."

codec — Coding/decoding: a software program or hardware device that encodes and/or decodes digital transmissions.

command module — An X10-technology controller that sends commands (manually generated or programmed) to control modules that control lights or other devices.

compact disc (CD) — A plastic disc on which audio files or other digital data files are encoded using the pulse code modulation method.

compression — Any technique that uses math algorithms to reduce the size of digital files for storage or transmission.

compressor — The part of an A/C system that squeezes the refrigeration gas under pressure into a smaller volume until it changes into a liquid.

CompTIA — Computer Technology Industry Association, a global information technology (IT) trade association with more than 13,000 members in 89 countries. It works to advance the IT industry, promote IT public policy, and develop standards for training of professionals in the industry.

concealed enclosure — A box or other three dimensional shape built behind a wall or other flat surface to contain an object normally hidden from view.

concealed wiring — Retrofitted wiring installed within the finished walls of a structure.

condensation — The process in an A/C system by which the refrigeration gas changes back into a liquid under pressure. Also the process by which water vapor is removed from cooled air and is deposited as a liquid.

condenser coil — A coil through which hot refrigerant passes and is cooled by flowing air in the same manner as an automobile radiator cools engine coolant.

condensing unit — The part of an A/C system in which the refrigerant is converted back into a liquid from a gaseous state.

cone — The part of a speaker that vibrates in the air, producing sound.

control device — Any device that initiates a process, directs equipment to perform a function, or responds in a preset manner to remote commands.

control module — In X10 systems, any of the devices that receive control instructions from the controller and implement them by adjusting lights or activating other devices.

controller — The electronic device that controls the operation of sprinkler system zone valves through a preset, timed schedule. Also, a lighting control device that sends lighting commands to control modules in an automated lighting system.

converter — A device that changes digital signals into analog, or vice versa, in audio and video systems, or computer networks. *See* decoder.

cooling coil — The part of an A/C system that cools the surrounding air by the expansion of the refrigerant in the coil, which absorbs heat from the air.

cordless phones — Phones with transceivers (transmitters and receivers) that operate on radio frequencies. They have a limited range from the base unit, which contains another transceiver.

counterweight — A heavy weight suspended on a cable or chain looped over a support wheel. The cable connects the counterweight to the object whose weight it is balancing. When the balanced object moves in one direction, the counterweight moves in the other.

credential — A written certification that an individual has specified qualifications, abilities, or expertise.

crossover network — A wiring circuit in speaker systems that permits several speakers of different ranges to function seamlessly together.

crown molding — Angled decorative slats installed at the junction of interior walls and ceiling. It can conceal cable.

current — Flow of electricity, measured in amps.

daisy chain wiring — Wiring light fixtures in parallel one to another with only the first light being connected directly to a power supply and each of the others receiving power in succession down the chain.

dampers — Devices that act like doors in air ducts. They can be closed to block air passage or opened to allow it.

decibel (dB) — A unit for measuring sound level. Used in audio engineering.

decoder — A device for rendering data received in an encrypted form into a form that can be used by a computer or displayed by a video or audio system. Also, a device that renders digital data into analog signals or vice versa in audio and video systems. *See* converter.

demarcation point — The physical place where the incoming telephone lines from the telephone company connect to the internal wiring of the home; also known as demarc.

detection devices — Sensors that discern changes in conditions that indicate the presence or passage of a person or persons.

detector — A sensor designed to react to a certain event such as pressure, motion, heat, or light.

dial tone — A continuous tone sent on a telephone line by the PBX or the central exchange to indicate that it is available for a call.

digital — Any kind of data that is recorded in numerical (discrete) form rather than analog (continuously varying).

digital audio file — A recorded music or voice audio segment stored on a computer hard drive or other similar media.

digital audio tape (DAT) — Standard for recording uncompressed digital audio on tape at the same quality level as a CD.

digital cable ready — A government designation for television sets denoting their capability to play digital cable programs.

digital data — Data in the form used by computers consisting only of the binary numeric digits 1 and 0. Nearly all forms of information can be rendered into digital form for processing or transmission and then rendered back into a form that can be displayed or understood by people.

Digital Subscriber Line (DSL) — A telephone line used for high-speed digital data and voice transmission and always available for the subscribing user's exclusive use.

digital television (DTV) — Television signals that are in numerical format and create a picture in pixels rather than rasters as does analog TV.

digital video discs (DVDs) — Media for recording digital video.

digital video/audio switcher — A device that receives digital signals from multiple sources and routes them as instructed to multiple outputs.

Direct Sequence Spread Spectrum (DSSS) — A method of signal hopping or rapidly changing frequencies in a specified sequence to transfer data at high speed.

disarm — Deactivate a security system so its sensors are not functioning.

dish antenna — A parabolic-shaped antenna that receives satellite broadcasts.

distortion — Changes in reproduced sound waves caused by excessive power or other interference in the recording and playback processes.

distribution — The process of transmitting data throughout a system so that it is available to all components.

DNS server — Special computers on the Internet that keep databases of IP addresses and their corresponding domain names.

domain name — A unique name assigned to a network and registered with ICANN.

Domain Name Service (DNS) — A part of the TCP/IP protocol that translates domain names into their corresponding IP addresses.

dot matrix printer — A printer that prints using a matrix of small pins that strike the paper through a ribbon and combine to form characters.

dot pitch — The distance between the colored phosphor dots in a color monitor that determines the sharpness of its image.

double protection — In security systems, at least two devices monitoring a means of entry into a home so that if one is disabled or fails, the other still detects any intruder.

downlink — Digital data being transferred into a ground-based system from a satellite.

drape pull mechanism — A device for opening or closing drapes or blinds by means of a motorized loop cord.

drip irrigation system — A type of irrigation system in which small tubes deliver water flow directly to individual plants or plots of ground without spraying. The system conserves water compared to spraying sprinkler systems.

drive ring — A metal ring that can be hammered into walls to carry cable on the exterior of buildings.

drop down mechanism — A mechanical device that lowers a display or piece of equipment from a concealed overhead position to a level where it can be seen or used.

drywall — The paper-covered gypsum board that is fastened to studs to finish the walls in most homes.

duct — A metal tube or open ended box though which air can flow. Can be rigid or flexible and of any size.

dumbwaiter — A small elevator designed to carry objects from one floor to another in a building. It is electrically powered and moves up and down on rails in an open shaft.

duress code — An access code (to be used in the event a person is accosted or threatened at the door) that opens the door, but also summons help.

Dynamic Host Configuration Protocol (DHCP) — A method of automatically assigning IP addresses to nodes on a LAN.

eave — The underside of a roof that overlaps the outer walls of a building.

electric service — Electric power purchased from a utility; also the cable bringing the electricity to a home from the utility.

electromagnet — A magnet created by passing a current through a coil of wire. Used in audio speakers and many other devices.

electromagnetic field — Force field of electrons generated by high-voltage equipment and wires.

elevator — A large enclosed lift designed to move people from one floor to another in a building.

emergency response — Any assistance delivered as a result of a security system call-in. Fire department, police department, and medical teams are all emergency responses.

encoder — A device or software program for changing analog audio or video signals into digital format. Video versions are also called coders.

Enhanced Definition Television (EDTV) — An ATSC-defined television that can play both analog and SDTV digital programs.

equalizer — An audio device for balancing the levels at which sound frequencies are recorded or played back.

Ethernet — The most common form of LAN architecture. It uses bus or star topology and employs CSMA/CD to manage the flow of data on the network.

evaporative or "swamp" coolers — A type of air cooler that works by evaporation of water into air, which is thereby cooled as it passes through the cooler.

extensions — In telephone systems, an additional phone wired in parallel into a single line.

face plate — The decorative cover on wall boxes that contain data jacks or AC power outlets.

fail-safe — A theoretical term for a security system that can't be disabled or bypassed. Not possible to achieve in actual systems.

false alarms — Any security breach not produced by a genuine security threat.

fan — A device consisting of a balanced set of angled blades on a shaft spun by a motor. Fans move air and are one type of air handler.

fax machine — A digital device that operates on an analog telephone line. It sends and receives printed documents by transmitting them as bit-mapped images.

Fiber Distributed Data Interface (FDDI) — Large, fast networks that are constructed almost entirely using fiber-optic cable.

fiber-optic cable — A very high-speed means of transmitting data using light beams through glass or plastic threads or fibers.

field — One scan of an interlaced television frame which refreshes one half the frame.

filter — A device to remove interference from an electric circuit.

fire-stop — A wooden crosspiece set between studs in interior walls to retard fire.

fireplace igniter — An electric device that lights a gas-fired fireplace by producing a spark near the gas jet that ignites the natural gas.

firewall — A software program or hardware device that controls information passing from the Internet onto a LAN and from a LAN onto the Internet.

FireWire — A 1394 standard data connection for transmitting digital data at high speed between two devices or nodes on a network.

flat panel screen — An LCD monitor or television. *See* liquid crystal display (LCD).

flow meter — A device that measures the amount of water flowing in a pipe and signals its measurement to a recording device. Used to detect leaks or breaks in pipes or sprinkling systems.

flow valve — A type of valve that measures the amount of water flowing through it and can adjust that flow automatically.

fluorescent lighting — Lighting tubes that contain phosphorescent material and glow when a high-voltage current is passed through them. The tubes are made in various lengths up to eight feet.

forced air — A type of heating or A/C system that works by blowing heated or cooled air into a home through ducts and air vents.

frame — One complete refresh of a television screen, which can be two scans (fields) if interlaced, one scan if progressive.

freeze sensor — A device that sends a signal when the temperature around it falls to near freezing (37 degrees normally, although some can be set to lower or higher temperatures).

frequency division multiplexing — An analog technology for carrying multiple data streams, voice or data, on the same wires.

Frequency Hopping Spread Spectrum (FHSS) — A method of signal hopping or rapidly changing frequencies in a random sequence to transfer data at high speed.

frequency modulation (FM) — A method of broadcasting sound by varying the frequency of the carrier wave, but not its strength.

furnace — A device for heating air so that it can be blown into the interior of a home.

gas detector — A device that senses the presence of natural gas, carbon monoxide, or other poisonous gas.

geared rack — A flat strip of metal geared on one side. It is mounted in a stationary position and a powered gear wheel travels along it in either direction, pulling whatever is attached to the gear.

ground — A wire that connects an electric device to the earth so that excess current can flow to the ground rather than elsewhere.

ground start system — Local telephone system that seizes a telephone line as soon as a receiver is lifted so that no other call can transmit on the line.

HDTV tuner — A digital television tuner that receives full resolution HDTV signals in 16:9 format.

header — Data at the beginning of a data packet identifying its source and destination.

heat sink — A relatively large piece of metal or other material placed near a heat source to absorb heat from it and dissipate it into the surrounding air.

heat transfer — The process by which heat radiates from warmer objects to cooler ones.

heating cable — An electric cord that has high resistance to electricity and gets hot when current passes through it. Used to warm pipes, rain gutters, and other areas so they don't freeze.

heating, ventilation, and air-conditioning (HVAC) systems — Systems that provide controlled heating, cooling, and ventilation in buildings.

high definition television (HDTV) — Digital television format with a 16:9 aspect ratio and high resolution.

home lighting system — The entire electrical light configuration in a home, including all interior and exterior lights and the controls (manual or automated) that direct them.

home run cable — A data cable running direct from an ADSL splitter to the network modem assuring a clean incoming signal. Also, a wired connection that links a light directly to its power supply without the current to it passing through any other fixture except a switch.

home security system — An HTI subsystem of hardware and software designed to prevent unauthorized persons from entering a home or yard, using any of its data systems, or removing anything from them.

Home Technology Integration (HTI) — A connected home environment in which a computer system manages data and controls subsystems in the home.

home theater — An HTI subsystem for displaying television programs and recorded video programs.

Similar to a home entertainment center, but usually specialized primarily for video viewing.

HomePNA — A technology for networks that uses existing telephone lines for connectivity.

HomeRF (Home Radio Frequency) — A wireless network technology for home LANs.

host — Another name for a computer on a LAN.

hot wire — The wire in a cable that is connected to the source of electric potential, usually colored black.

HPNA 2.0 — Network standard currently in use for HPNA networks.

hub — A device that connects nodes on a LAN and broadcasts data received from any node to all other nodes.

Huffyuv — A lossless codec for digital video compression.

humidifier — A device that adds moisture to an incoming air stream.

humidity — Moisture contained in air. All air contains some water vapor (gaseous water). The amount can vary with pressure and temperature of the air.

humidity detector — A device that measures the amount of moisture in the air around it and signals that data to a controller or computer.

hydraulic cylinder — A device that uses oil under high pressure to force a piston rod out of a cylinder. The moving rod lifts whatever is attached to its other end.

IEEE 1394 — A fast serial protocol running from 100 to 400 Mbps.

IEEE 802.11b — Wi-Fi version of the IEEE 802.11 wireless network standard.

IEEE 802.11g — New and extremely fast version of IEEE 802.11 standard not yet in use.

inclined ramp — A sloped walkway used in place of stairs. It can be traversed by wheeled vehicles as well as on foot.

infrared (IR) devices — Devices that function as controllers by sending command signals using infrared light, which is invisible to human eyes.

infrared sensor — A device that functions by detecting heat (infrared-wavelength energy) or changes in the heat level of its surroundings.

infrastructure — Any of the wiring, conduit, connectors, wireless hubs, switches, routers, and other hardware that enable the subsystems of an HTI system to communicate with one another and the outside world.

inside arming — Code or command that activates perimeter devices in a security system and may activate some interior devices, but usually not all. Inside armed is the normal status for a security system at night while the family is asleep.

Integrated Services Digital Network (ISDN) — A technology that uses a telephone line to transmit digital data at high speed.

intercom — A line in key systems that allows any extension to connect to any other for an internal call without accessing an outside line.

interference — Any signal that corrupts or blocks an analog or digital signal.

interlaced — Method of refreshing a video screen in which only odd-numbered lines are scanned on one pass and even-numbered lines on the next.

Internet — A worldwide web of interconnected, but independent, networks over which data travels from source to destination by various routes.

Internet Corporation for Assigned Names and Numbers (ICANN) — The group that assigns and regulates domain names and IP addresses through accredited registrars.

Internet Home Alliance (IHA) — An industry group whose objective is to develop the market for home technologies that require a broadband or persistent connection to the Internet.

Internet service provider (ISP) — A company that provides Internet connections to home and business LANs.

Internetwork Packet Exchange/Sequenced Packet Exchange (IPX/SPX) — The protocol used by Novell NetWare networks.

intruder — Any unauthorized person trying to enter a secured home or yard.

IP address — Internet Protocol address, a 32-bit address consisting of four numbers separated by periods, used to uniquely identify a device on a network.

IPCONFIG — TCP/IP utility that displays the computer's adapter address, IP address, subnet mask, and default gateway, and allows the DHCP to be renewed or released by the user.

jack — A connecting device terminating a cable into which a plug is mated to connect a node.

joist — A horizontal support beam in a floor.

key system — A local telephone system in which multiple phones are connected to multiple lines by switching buttons so that any telephone can use any line.

keyboard — An alphanumeric data input device for a computer. It may contain additional keys that input specific commands or run sequences of data.

keypad — A numeric data input device for a computer or other hardware in an HTI system. Also, a numeric pad similar to a telephone dial pad that is used to input passwords to cipher locks and other security devices.

laser light — Coherent light waves transmitted in parallel beams so that they maintain their intensity over long distances. Used in light beam sensors and many other devices.

laser printer — A printer that works by picking up toner on a charged image on the surface of a rotating drum and depositing it on paper where the image is fused in place.

latchkey function — A command or code that programs a security system call-in device to notify a set telephone number when a specific door of the home is opened during set hours.

light beam sensor — A device in two pieces, one of which transmits a beam of light to the other across a distance. If the light beam is obstructed, the sensor signals its failure to arrive.

light scenes — Illuminated rooms or areas within a room that not only provide light but beautify a setting or invoke a mood.

light sensor — A device that senses the presence of light and signals it or senses the absence of light and signals it.

light-emitting diode (LED) — An electronic device, similar to a vacuum tube, which emits red light or infrared radiation.

line of sight — A term used to describe the location of wireless transmitters and receivers. It means that the receiver must be visible when viewed from the transmitter for the signal to be received.

line speed — The amount of data that can travel over a communication line or wireless connection in a given length of time.

liquid crystal display (LCD) — A thin, light-weight type of video display that uses liquid crystal material sandwiched between two layers of electrodes to create a color image.

load — In electrical systems, the amount of current (amps) flowing in the wiring at a given time.

local area network (LAN) — A regionally con-fined network consisting of computers that communicate and share data and services.

lock-down feature — A program in some security systems that allows all door locks to be deactivated during specified times so that they can't be opened from the outside at all, even with a valid access code.

loop pull cord — A continuous cord that extends through a drapery rod or blind and is used to pull the drape or blind open or closed. The cord forms an open loop on one end of the rod or frame.

loop start system — Local telephone system in which a Centrex-supplied dial tone indicates when a line is available for a call, but no line is seized until a call is actually placed.

lossless — Type of video compression in which no data is lost. Huffyuv is an example.

lossy — Type of video compression in which some data is lost, but files can be made smaller than with lossless compression.

macros — Sequences of commands in a specified order that a programmable device stores in memory and executes at preset intervals.

magnetic key — A key similar to a plastic credit card with its access information coded on a magnetic stripe that can be read by an access device.

magnetic media — Any media with a ferrous coating capable of storing analog or digital data recorded on it by a magnetic head.

magnetic recording — Any analog or digital data recorded on magnetic media.

magnetic tape — Plastic tape coated with ferrous material for recording data.

make switch — A sensor that monitors a switch that should remain open and signals if it is closed. Most commonly used as pressure pads, which are closed by weight passing over them.

MC cable — Metal clad cable used for AC wiring.

mechanical relay — An electrical device activated by an electromagnet being energized that functions as a switch to turn a control current on or off. An automatic, remote-controllable switch.

media — Any means of storing or recording audio or video information: magnetic tape, CD, DVD, and phonograph record are examples.

microphone — A device that converts sound waves into digital or analog data, which can be transmitted over distances and replayed or stored.

MIDI (Musical Instrument Digital Interface) file — A type of digital music recording in which the file stores an actual musical score. MIDI files can be played on many electronic instruments or software-equipped computers.

miniDV cassettes — A small-format recording medium used in many digital video cameras.

modem — An electronic device that converts digital data into a form that can be sent over a telephone line. Modems are the most common method of connecting a home computer to the Internet through a telephone line to a service provider.

monaural — Having only one track or sequence; not stereo. Used to describe single-track audio recording.

monitor — A screen device for displaying data in text or picture (graphic) form. Also, a sensor that monitors one or more environmental conditions.

monitored — In security systems, watched either by a person at a control console or by the electronic security panel itself, so that any change in status can be responded to.

monitoring service — A commercial service in which a company's staff continually watches a home security system via a telephone line linked to the home.

motion sensor — A device that detects any object that radiates heat moving into its range and signals the change in its surroundings.

motorized drive — A mechanical device that uses an electric motor and gear assembly to power a piece of equipment to perform a specific function.

MP3 file — A file created with an audio compression algorithm with the same name.

MP3PRO — A file created with an audio compression algorithm with the same name; higher compression than MP3, but equal in quality.

MPEG-1 — A file created with a video compression algorithm with the same name.

MPEG-2 — Video compression algorithm used for DVD video recording.

multiplexing — Combining different types of data from multiple sources on a single transmission path.

Multistation Access Unit (MAU) — Device used in a token ring star network design to which all nodes are connected.

multisystem VCR — A video player capable of playing NTSC, PAL, or SECAM video cassettes on any analog television.

narrow band — In telecommunications systems, bandwidth of 128 Kbps or less.

National Electric Code (NEC) — A safety standard for electrical wiring and installation developed by the NFPA.

National Fire Protection Association (NFPA) — Publisher of the NEC.

network — A group of computers, information sources, and peripheral devices connected by cable or radio so that they can share data and communicate with one another.

Network BIOS Extended User Interface (NetBEUI) — A Microsoft proprietary protocol commonly used for LANs.

network interface card (NIC) — A device for connecting a node to a LAN.

Network Interface Device (NID) — A device that connects the ISP service line to a home's inside telephone and data wiring.

network printer — A printer of any type connected to a LAN as a node with its own IP address.

NM cable — Nonmetallic cable used for AC wiring.

node — A computer or other device connected to a LAN by a NIC.

noninterlaced — A type of video screen refresh that renews each line of the screen in order. This method of refreshing is also called progressive.

NTSC format — Standard analog U.S. TV format with 525 scan lines and 4:3 aspect ratio.

numeric code — A group of digits that serves as a password and must be entered into a cipher lock to open it.

obstruction detector — A safety device that detects anything unusual under a descending garage door and stops the door's downward movement.

off-the-shelf hardware — Mechanical assemblies already designed and built to accomplish movements in automated furniture or assist in the construction of custom systems.

Ogg Vorbis (OGG) — An open source video compression format and hence free of any patents.

Ohm's Law — Describes the relationship among amperes (amps), or the amount of current flowing; volts, which is the electrical potential between the two ends of a circuit; and resistance within the circuit to the flow of current.

operation cycle — A programmed series of commands that a device executes upon receiving a single start command. No additional commands are needed to complete the cycle.

outlet box — A metal or plastic wall box into which an outlet receptacle or data jack is wired.

outside arming — A code or command that activates all security sensors to function while the home is unoccupied.

overload(ing) — Current flow greater than a circuit can carry without danger of burning out.

packet — A small segment into which data is divided and packaged with a header and trailer for transmission on a network.

PAL format — European analog TV standard equivalent to U.S. NTSC standard.

panning motor — An accessory device for a surveillance video camera. The panning motor slowly swings the camera right and left allowing it to cover more area than a stationary camera could.

Passport — Older and slower type of power-line technology for networking.

password — A group of letters and numbers that must be entered into a security system in a home or into a computer system to gain access.

patch panel — A device consisting of a row or block of jacks, used for connecting all components of a network.

PATHPING — An improved version of PING.

peak use — The maximum load of electrical consumption in a home.

peripheral — Any input or output device connected to a computer that sends or receives data from the processor. Examples of input peripherals are floppy drives and microphones. Examples of output peripherals are printers and control devices.

phonograph — A machine that plays analog recordings from a plastic disc embossed with grooves bearing the sound wave impressions.

picture frame lift — A motor driven device that moves a picture frame upward to reveal what is behind it.

pilot hole — A small hole drilled to locate a position or guide a larger drill bit.

pilot light — A small flame that burns continuously in a furnace to ignite the furnace's main burner when it is turned on.

PING — A TCP/IP utility that enables a user at one computer to determine if that node can communicate with another computer connected to a network.

pivot down mechanism — A mechanism that is held in position on one side by a hinge and opens by swinging downward on that hinge to reveal its contents.

pixel — A picture element in digital television; the unit of color and brightness that forms the picture in digital television.

Plain Old Telephone Service (POTS) — The most common method of home Internet connection.

platform lift — Any motor driven device intended to lift a piece of equipment or a display into a higher position for use or viewing.

plug — A terminator on the end of a cable that mates with a jack to make a connection.

potential — The flow force of electric current, measured in volts.

power failure warning sensor — A device that detects the presence of voltage (electrical pressure) in a circuit and signals its absence to a monitor.

power-line technology — Network data transmission method in which data signals are sent on AC wiring using a different frequency and voltage than the regular current flowing in the circuits.

PowerPacket — High-speed power-line technology for networking.

pre-amplifier — A device that strengthens an original signal from an antenna or other source before it goes to an amplifier.

pressure pad — A make switch that is closed when a set weight is placed on it. The sensor then signals its changed state.

pressure sensor — A device that monitors gas or liquid pressure in a pipe or tank. If pressure drops too low (or, in a steam pipe, rises too high) the sensor signals the change.

pressure valve — A type of valve that shuts off water flow automatically if pressure in the pipe drops below a set minimum, indicating that there is a leak or break in the pipe.

private branch exchange (PBX) — A local switching point where phone lines within an organization can be connected to one another or to outside lines.

program — A set of digital instructions that a computer executes in sequence to perform functions.

programmable — Capable of storing instruction sets for later execution in sequence.

progressive — Method of refreshing a video screen in which all lines are scanned in sequence.

projector lift — A motor driven device that lifts a projector from a concealed location and positions it for projecting an image on screen.

protocol — A set of rules and standards that a network uses to communicate among its nodes.

public switched telephone network (PSTN) — The commercial network of telephone lines and transmission facilities over which most telephone calls are made.

pulling cable — The process of drawing a cable through an existing structure from one connector to another.

pulse code modulation (PCM) — The method used to record compact discs using MP-2 compression. Not a magnetic process. Uses light diffraction to record data.

punchdown block — The usual means of centrally terminating telephone lines and connecting them to the trunk lines.

PVC — Polyvinylchloride, a hard, strong plastic used to make pipe and many other products.

Quicktime — An Internet and computer video file format that uses compression and is widely used by PC and Apple computers.

raceway — An enclosed track in which to run cable; the track is attached to the surface of walls.

radiant — A type of heating system that works by warming the floors of a home with hot water in pipes. The floors then warm the interior air.

radio frequency (RF) — Any electronic wave with a frequency in the radio band of the electromagnetic spectrum. Includes all radio and TV frequencies.

RadioRA — A proprietary wireless lighting control technology developed by Lutron and used for home lighting control.

rain sensor — A device that detects the presence of rain water in a small holder and signals to the controller when a preset level is reached.

rasters — The individual horizontal scan lines that make up an analog television picture.

RealVideo — A computer and Internet video compression algorithm.

receptacle — A device into which AC-powered appliances can be plugged to obtain power.

recessed — Concealed below (or above) a flat surface, usually with a covering that matches or complements the surface.

record — A plastic disc with grooves bearing sound wave impressions that can be played on a phonograph.

recorded emergency message — A message recorded on a security system call-in device; it plays after the device calls a preset telephone number and gets a connection. Some systems dial multiple numbers in succession and some can play multiple messages.

redundant protection — In a security system, having two or more sensors or detectors monitoring one area or entrance. Provides additional security to high-risk areas.

refresh rate — The number of times per second that the electron beam in a CRT repaints the entire screen.

refrigerant fluid — A gas/liquid that circulates in an A/C system continuously extracting heat from the surrounding air as it changes from a liquid to a gas and back again.

refrigeration — A method of cooling air that uses the heat absorption of expanding gas to extract heat from the surrounding air.

regenerator — A digital data amplifier that reads weakened data signals and recreates them at full strength and without noise on the transmission line.

relay — A remotely operated electric switch that is controlled by a small current, but that controls a large current flow.

remote access — Security system monitored by an outside commercial firm through a telephone or radio connection to the home control panel.

remote-control system — A combination of hardware and software that allows a person or a computer to direct the operation of a subsystem from a distance.

repeater — A device in a LAN that receives and strengthens the data signal to offset its attenuation over distance.

residential gateway — A device that connects a LAN that a WAN that is part of the Internet; the gateway controls the data coming into or going out of the LAN.

resistance — The force inhibiting the flow of electricity in a circuit, measured in ohms.

resolution — The number of pixels on a monitor that are individually addressable by software.

response devices — Security devices that can perform an action when commanded to do so by the security panel. They may sound alarms, call for assistance, activate systems, or perform other tasks.

retrofit — To add new wiring or other infrastructure to an existing building.

RJ-11 jack — The standard single line telephone connector wired with two wires.

RJ-14 jack — The standard 2-line telephone connector wired with four wires.

RJ-45 crimping tool — A tool used to attach an RJ-45 plug as a terminator on the end of a cable.

RJ-45 jack — A terminator device on a cable into which a plug is mated to make a network connection.

RJ-45 punchdown tool — A tool used to attach an RJ-45 jack as a terminator on the end of a cable.

rough-in — To install the outlet boxes and cable runs for network wiring or AC circuits.

routable — A protocol that allows data to be sent to interconnected networks on the Internet.

router — A device that connects two or more networks and directs the data traffic passing between them.

safety control valve — A specialized valve on a furnace or other appliance that must receive a continuous electric current from a thermocouple in order to stay open. If the current stops, the valve closes, shutting off the fuel flow.

sampling — A technique for converting analog signals into digital form by taking quantified samples of the analog data.

satellite link — An Internet connection to an ISP via a satellite through a receiver dish antenna.

satellite transmission — Digital television signals beamed to receivers on the ground from a stationary satellite orbiting Earth in space.

scan — Survey of a data set, space, or sensors to determine if particular data or a set of conditions is present.

scan rate — The number of times per second that the electron beam in a CRT repaints the screen from top to bottom. Same as refresh rate in progressive screens, equal to twice refresh rate in interlaced screens.

SDTV television — A television that receives and displays all ATSC digital formats, but not necessarily at full high resolution.

SDTV tuner — An RF receiver that receives ATSC terrestrial digital television signals and decodes all Table 3 video formats.

SECAM — A French-created European equivalent of NTSC analog standard.

security breach — An event that occurs any time a sensor signals a change of status to a security panel.

security panel — The control center of a security system to which all of the system's sensors and surveillance devices report their status. The panel may also direct responses, record data, and sound alarms.

security zone — An area in a home or its yard that is monitored by a specific group of sensors in the security system. Zones are set up with defined monitoring devices so that the location and nature of any security breach can be quickly identified.

sensor — Any device that detects or measures human activity or environmental conditions and sends data regarding its measurement to a processor.

server — A computer or device on a network that provides network services or manages network resources.

service line — The cable that brings electric power into a home from the utility.

service panel — The wall box containing a home's circuit breakers to which the service line is connected.

service provider — A company that provides data transmission service or other utility services to consumers.

shade controller — A device into which the end of a window shade's control rod fits, allowing the motor driven controller to control the shade by remote commands.

shaft — An vertical open space (sometimes enclosed with walls or by a tube) that extends through a building or the earth for some distance. Shafts provide open space for elevators to move in or for cables, wiring and other equipment.

shielding — Metal webbing around a data line that grounds noise and interference before it can reach the data line.

shock — Electric current flowing through a person.

signal-to-noise ratio (S/N ratio) — The difference in sound level between the recorded audio and the background noise on any type of audio recording.

single-pole switch — An AC basic switch that opens or closes a circuit to control power to a fixture.

smoke detector — A device that signals the presence of smoke in the air around it. It does not react to heat or flame, only to the presence of smoke particles.

softphones — Software programs that display phone features (hold button, caller ID, message waiting) on the computer screen and route calls through a handset or an earphone and microphone wired to the computer.

soil moisture sensor — A device that can measure the electrical conductivity of the ground in which it's buried. This measurement allows it to detect the amount of water in the soil.

solenoid valve — An automatic valve operated by an electromagnet that can be energized or turned off to open or close the valve. The main control device in automated water systems.

space heater — A small heater, usually electric, but sometimes gas-fired, designed to heat a small area or room. Manually controlled.

spark igniter — An electrical device that ignites the fuel in an oil or gas furnace when it starts.

spike — A large but very brief increase in voltage or current flow in a circuit.

split duplex outlets — An AC electrical outlet in which one receptacle is always live and the other is controlled by a switch.

splitters — Devices that allow two or more telephones or peripherals to be connected to a single wall jack.

spread spectrum — Spread spectrum signals constantly change frequency, a process known as hopping, to reduce the power requirements for transmission.

spring-loaded door closer — A device with a strong spring and a hydraulic damper that slowly closes an open door. The strong spring pulls the door shut firmly and the damper prevents it from acting too fast.

stairway lift — A motorized lift with guide rails angled to fit on a stairway so that the lift can move at an angle up and down the stairs.

standard definition television (SDTV) — The approved format for U.S. digital television with a 4:3 aspect ratio and a 720 by 525 pixel screen.

star topology — One type of network topology in which nodes are arranged in a star pattern.

static — Noise or interference on a telephone line that is typically heard as a background crackling sound.

stereo — Two soundtracks recorded from the left and right side of a musical performance to give balance and depth to the recording.

storage device — A computer peripheral that can record and retrieve digital data on magnetic or other media.

STP cable — Shielded twisted-pair cable used for LANs.

straight-through cable — Cable wiring that is connected to the same terminator pins at both ends of the cable.

studs — The 2 x 4 or 2 x 6 wood uprights in the walls of homes.

subsystem — A group of hardware components and software set up to perform a specific task or function within a larger, multiple-function HTI system.

suppressor — A device for blocking surges and spikes in a circuit.

surface wiring — Wiring run along the outside of a wall, usually in a raceway, although it can be bare.

surge — A brief increase in voltage or current flow in a circuit.

surveillance video camera — A small video camera used in a home security system to monitor a yard or part of the home's interior. The camera's output can be displayed or recorded or both.

swipe slot — An input device for plastic magnetic-striped keys. The plastic key is passed (swiped) through the slot in the device that reads the key code and grants access.

switch — A device for controlling the flow of electricity in a circuit Also, a device used in a LAN to direct data traffic among the nodes.

switchboard — A device to which a number of telephone lines are connected and which can switch any line to connect to any other.

switched duplex outlets — An AC electrical outlet controlled by a switch that turns current to it on or off.

switcher — A multiple video input panel with a single output to a monitor and a switch that allows the monitor to display any video input selected.

swivel mechanisms — A motorized platform that can turn a display or piece of equipment left or right. Some types can rotate continuously at a steady pace.

synchronized — Operating or playing together at the same rate. Stereo sound tracks are synchronized as are the picture and sound of a video program.

T-1 line — A high-capacity telephone trunk line capable of simultaneously handling up to 24 voice lines or 1.5 Mbps of data.

telecommunications — The general name for all communication and data functions carried on telephone lines or radio signals, or performed by telephone hardware and software.

television lift — A motor driven device that can lift a television set out of concealment and position it for viewing.

TELNET — A TCP/IP utility that allows a user in one location to access a computer in a remote location as if the user were physically sitting in front of the remote machine.

temperature sensor — A device that measures the ambient air temperature and signals it to an HVAC system or security system monitor that can compare it to programmed instructions and take appropriate action.

terminator — A device on an Ethernet that ends the data flow in a bus topology.

thermocouple — A device that transforms heat into an electrical current. Used in gas appliances to monitor the pilot light. If the light goes out, the thermocouple stops generating electricity, thereby shutting off the fuel supply. Used as a safety check to prevent unburned gas or oil from flowing in any appliance.

thermostat — A special type of temperature sensor that sends a signal when air temperature reaches a preset level.

three-way switch — A type of AC switch that is used in pairs to turn a circuit on or off from two locations.

tilt mechanism — A mechanical device designed to change the angle of an object for better viewing of it or to make its use easier.

token ring — A type of network in which data flows in a circular pattern and is controlled by a token.

TRACERT — A TCP/IP utility that shows the complete path that data packets are taking from the computer to reach any given destination.

track — In automated equipment, a metal channel with sides which guide wheels that are set in the track along a set path.

trailer — Data attached to the end of a data packet.

transformer — An electrical device for stepping voltage in a circuit up or down with an inverse increase or decrease in amperage.

translator — Another term for a decoder that converts encrypted data into a readable form for display by an output device.

transmission — The movement of data from one location to another. The data can be digital or analog and the locations close together or distant.

Transmission Control Protocol/Internet Protocol (TCP/IP) — The most common protocol used to connect networks.

triad — A set of three dots on a color monitor screen which in combination can produce all colors.

trip switch — An electric switch that turns a circuit on or off when activated by a moving object hitting it. Used as a stop switch for lifts or as a safety check to keep a lift car from moving too far up or down.

trunk line — A telephone line from a PBX to the telephone company that can be used by any of the telephones connected to the PBX.

truss — The triangular structure that supports a roof.

tuner — The device in a radio or television that sets the one station frequency to be received and excludes all others.

twisted-pair wires — A set of two wires twisted around one another in a specific manner to improve data transmission in a high-speed cable.

uncompressed original video footage — Digital video recorded without use of any algorithm to reduce file size. Produces large files that contain all digital data in sequential format.

unified messaging — A computer-based system for storing messages from multiple sources. Storage is located on a PC's hard drive and the messages include voice mail, fax, and e-mail.

Universal Serial Bus (USB) — A bidirectional, isochronous, dynamically attachable serial interface for adding devices on a single bus.

valve — A device for controlling the flow of water or other liquid in a pipe. Can be turned on to permit flow or off to stop it. Can be manually or automatically controlled.

valve box — An open bottom box sunk to its lid in the ground where the zone valves and sometimes the controller of a sprinkler system are located.

ventilation — The process of exchanging air in a confined room or space. Ventilation exhausts the old air out of a room and brings new air in.

vent — An opening in a wall or floor through which air flows from a connected duct into a room.

video — An analog or digital display of pictures such as television programs or computer screens.

video conferencing — A technology for sending full-motion picture images with a voice telephone call so that callers can both hear and see one another.

video distribution system — A wired system for distributing video programs from multiple sources to multiple viewing sites in the home.

Video Home Standard (VHS) — The U.S. standard analog video recording format used in video cassettes.

video image — Any image, analog or digital, displayed on a CRT or other type of screen.

video server — A computer set up as a storage location for video programming on a network, from which the video footage can be requested by other network nodes.

virus — A self-propagating program that is sent to a computer, remains resident in its storage, and can interfere with or disable its operation.

voice mail — A digital system that allows telephone callers to record messages that the system stores, retrieves, and plays on demand.

Voice over Internet Protocol (VoIP) — A system whereby analog phone calls are digitized and sent in packets over the Internet. At the destination,

the digital data is decoded to analog form and delivered to the receiver.

volts — The unit used to measure electric potential or flow pressure.

wall-mounted controllers — In video and audio systems, a device for controlling distributed programming in a room or for the whole system.

water pressure — The force that impels water through a pipe. Water pressure is produced by gravity (the weight of water pushing down from a higher elevation to a lower one) or by artificially pressurizing a sealed water system, usually with compressed air.

water sensor — A device that senses the presence of water and signals it to a security monitor or panel.

water service line — The pipe that supplies water to a residence from a public utility. It enters the home and connects to the interior plumbing and exterior water system.

watt — The unit of electric power, often calculated for a circuit by multiplying the number of volts by the number of amps.

WAVE file — A compression algorithm for sound files.

Wi-Fi (Wireless Fidelity) — IEEE 802.11b wireless standard with an 11 Mbps transmission rate. It is presently the most popular wireless standard.

WiFi5 — IEEE 802.11a wireless standard, a very high-speed wireless technology.

wind sensor — A device that can be set to signal a controller whenever the average wind speed rises to a preset level (adjustable from 12 to 35 miles per hour). Used to shut off sprinkler systems in high wind conditions.

Windows Media Audio (WMA) — An MPEG–4 audio compressed file.

WINIPCFG — Windows 9x version of IPCONFIG, a utility for displaying a computer's adapter address, IP address, subnet mask, and default gateway and renewing or releasing its DHCP.

wireless audio transmitter — A wireless transmitter that sends analog or digital audio signals to a computer.

wireless hub — A device to which nodes in a wireless LAN can connect using radio waves.

wireless NIC — A device in a wireless node that connects it to a hub using radio waves.

wireless technology — Any of several methods of communicating digital data by means of radio waves without the need for any wires connecting the sender and receiver.

World Wide Web (WWW) — The global system of interconnected networks over which users can share data through the use of common protocols.

X10 — A wired technology that transmits data on existing high-voltage AC power lines in the home, and thus requires no new wires for installation.

zone — A group of lights controlled together to provide a specific scene or accomplish a specific task such as security lighting. Also, in sprinkler systems, multiple sprinkler heads in an area that are controlled by one valve. Also, the area around a wireless hub which its transmission reaches and from which it can receive data from wireless nodes. Also, in HVAC systems, a part of a home separately heated and cooled and controlled by one thermostat.

Index

2-conductor wire, 161, 175
3Com, 79
3-conductor wire, 161
3-way switch, 165, 175
5-4 rule, 34
5-4-3 rule, 34
10-Mbps Ethernet, 31, 34, 210
50-ohm RG8/U coaxial, 31
50-ohm RG58/U coaxial
  cable, 31
80/20 rule, 57
100BaseFX, 31
100BaseTX, 31
100-Mbps Ethernet, 31, 210
240-volt power, 155
802.11a standard, 44, 91
802.11b standard, 44, 90–91
802.11g protocol, 91
1000-Mbps Ethernet, 31
4100 chip, 78–79
4210 chip, 78–79

A

A/C (air conditioning), 408, 427
  central, 411
  compressor unit, 411
  condensation unit, 411
  condenser coil, 416
  condensing unit, 416
  cooling coil, 416
  humidity, 411
  refrigerant fluid, 416
  refrigeration, 411, 416

AC (alternating current), 175
  calculating requirements,
    154–158
  installing wiring, 160–162
  power, 142
  power connections, 118
AC (armored cable), 159, 162,
  175, 390
AC electrical wiring, 17
AC outlets, 164–165
AC power-line networks, 80–84
ACCA (Air Conditioning
  Contractors of America), 411
access control, 3, 6, 19
access devices, 280–283
access hub, 118
access point, 36, 61
Active Voice, 350
adapter addresses, 54
adaptors, 240–241, 255
ADC (analog-to-digital
  converter), 193
administrators, 4, 19
ADSL (Asymmetric DSL),
  42, 44, 339
ADSL splitter, 135, 138–139, 142
ADT Security Systems, 270, 276
aerial, 228
air handlers, 418–419, 427
alarms, 270, 290
always-live duplex outlets,
  388, 394
AM (amplitude modulation),
  190, 213

AM radio broadcasting, 190–191
amperes (amps), 155, 175
amplifier repeater, 34
amplifiers, 229–230,
  242–243, 255
amplitude, 188
analog, 213
analog data, 41, 61
analog devices, 186
analog modems, 337
analog radio receiver, 227
analog recordings, 189
analog signals, 48, 187–188
analog technology, 186
analog telephone communication
  systems, 336–337
analog television
  antennas, 233
  components, 243
  digital programs, 203
  interference, 197
  noise, 197
  screens, 236
  signals, 197
analog tuners, 229
analog video, 197–198
analog video device
  connections, 245
analogous, 186
analog-to-digital and
  digital-to-analog audio
  conversion, 248
antennas, 227–229, 233–234,
  241, 255

Apple Computer, 90

AppleTalk protocol

CSMA/CA (Carrier Sense Multiple Access/Collision Avoidance), 33

Wi-Fi (Wireless Fidelity), 90

appliances, 2–3, 19

Application layer, 28

applications, 99

Applied Digital, 446

arming, 325

Armstrong, Edwin H., 191

ASICs (application specific integrated circuits), 92

aspect ratio, 199, 213

assisted living functions, 9

atrium, 440, 453

ATSC (Advanced Television Systems Committee), 235, 255

ATSC (Advanced Television Systems Committee) standards, 203, 237

ATSC terrestrial digital transmissions, 235

attenuated, 255

attenuated signals, 229

attenuation, 80, 197

audio, 2, 17, 188

amplifiers, 242

analog-to-digital and digital-to-analog audio conversion, 248

cables, 241

components, 241–243

configuration for internal, 252–253

connections, 242

connectors, 243

grounding, 243

interference, 243

media, 232

reception and distribution, 5

recording, 189

audio cassette players, 233

audio devices, wiring, 242

audio files, 212

audio players, 232–233

audio servers, 55

audio signals, 227

audio systems

amplifiers, 229–230

antennas, 228–229

cables, 239–240

coaxial cable, 238

components, 226, 227–232

condensation, 254

configuration and settings for external, 247–251

connecting to Ethernet network, 248

connecting to networks, 247–249

dirt, 254

equalizers, 231–232

heat, 253

input and output jacks, 247

installation and setup, 238–246

monaural (single track) devices, 227

monitoring and maintaining, 253–254

multiple sound tracks, 227

new construction installations, 238

power fluctuations, 254

receiving components, 241

retrofitted installations, 238

shielded coaxial cable, 241

stereo, 227

termination points, 239–241

tuners, 229

audio/video connected-system design, 210–212

automated audio and video furniture, 464–466

automated controls, 427

automated doors, 465, 487

automated fans, 474

automated furniture, 487

automated heating systems

fireplace igniters, 482–484

heating cables, 484–486

automated home lighting design

daisy chain wiring, 377–378

home run connection, 377–378

lighting scenes, 375–376

lighting zones, 375–376

load requirements and grounding, 372–374

automated interior furnishings, 464–467

automated lift systems, 474

dumbwaiters, 475–477

elevators, 477–479

hydraulic lifts, 479–480

installation of lifts, 481

stair lifts, 480–481

automated lifts, 487

automated lighting systems

connecting lighting components, 388

installation and setup, 388–390

installing lighting zones, 388–390

power-line control systems, 380–382

programming, 390–392

troubleshooting, 392–393

types, 379–383

wire runs, 383

wireless lighting controls, 382

wireless zones, 383
wiring, 388
automated window and door systems
  automated fans, 474
  door openers, 471–472
  drape and shade pulls, 469
  shade lifts, 470–471
  skylights, 472–473
  window shades and blinds, 468
automated window treatments, 387
automation, 19, 394
average use, 156, 175
AWG (American Wire Gauge), 161, 175

B

baby monitors, 7
backup servers, 55
backups for security systems, 319–320
ballast, 172
bandwidth, 4, 19, 32, 61, 338, 360
  digital data transmission, 41
  technologies, 44
  telephone lines, 77
  video conferencing, 349
baseboard moldings, 132
battery-operated keypads, 277
baud, 337, 360
Bell, Alexander Graham, 186
bidirectional printing, 83
biometric identification, 283
biometric identifiers, 292
black-and-white laser printers, 51–52
blinds, 468
blowers, 409, 419, 427
Bluetooth, 89–90, 92–93, 104, 117, 126

BNC connectors, 242, 245
body identifiers, 283
boilers, 416, 427
bps (bits per second), 41
break switch, 292, 306, 325
break switch sensors, 285–286
breakers, 156, 175
BRI (Basic Rate Interface), 42
bridge tables, 56
bridges, 30, 61, 118
Brinks, 276
broadband, 17, 19, 126
broadcasting
  AM radio, 190–191
  antennas, 241
  digital, 204
  television, 196–203
Broadcom, 79
bus topology, 31–32, 34, 61, 125
bypassed, 292, 325

C

cable modems, 4, 42, 44, 61
cable pull openers, 472
cable pulls, 465, 487
cable run, 119–120, 142
cable television, 5, 203, 205–207
cables, 13, 17, 241
  audio systems, 239–240
  configuring, 140
  connector standards, 132–133
  connectors, 240
  crossover, 124–125
  decoder, 5
  fiber-optic lines, 120–121
  hookups, 5
  installing, 160–162
  labor to install, 120
  pulling, 129
  rollover, 124

shielding, 173
straight-through, 124–125
translator, 5
types, 120
video systems, 239–240
call blocking, 358
call conferencing, 349
call restriction, 349–350, 360
call waiting, 358
Caller ID (caller line identification), 348, 357, 360
call-in devices, 290–291
CAM (content addressable memory) tables, 56
cameras, 12, 20
  heat or water, 280
  inside home, 279–280
  location of, 279–280
  panning, 279
  panning motor, 284
  security systems, 283–284
  stationary, 284
  wired security systems, 310
carrier frequency, 246, 255
carrier wave, 190
cassette tapes, 189
Cat5 (Category 5) cable, 72, 119–120, 125, 142, 238
  pulling, 130
  size, 128
Category 2 telephone wires, 304–305, 325
Category 3 wire, 325
category 3 wire, 305
CatX cable, terminating, 134
CatX cable stripper tool, 133, 142
CD (compact discs), 213
CD audio, recording, 194–195
CD burners, 232, 255

CD players, 232, 242, 255

CD-R (CD-Recordable format), 237, 255

CD-ROM drives, 232

CD-RW (CD-Rewritable format), 237, 256

CDs (compact discs), 16, 189, 194, 237

central air conditioning (A/C) systems, 411

central computer, 45–46

central heating systems, 427
  blower, 409
  ducts, 408–409
  forced air, 408
  fuels for furnaces, 410–411
  furnace, 408–409
  radiant, 408–410
  vents, 408

central hub, 115

central processors, 14, 20

Centrex (central switching exchange), 339–340, 350, 360

certification, 20

chair rails, 132

checksum, 29–30, 61

chemical sensors, 15

Cinepak, 201

cipher locks, 6, 20, 281, 292

circuit breaker, 156

circuits, 151, 175
  grounding, 169
  load requirements, 154
  planning electrical system upgrade, 158–159
  protection, 169
  spikes, 169–171
  surges, 169–171
  wiring, 163–164

circuit-switched lines, 343, 360

circulating pump, 416, 428

clean power, 156, 175

cliff effect, 200, 213

coaxial cable, 73, 238, 244

code regulations, 274

codecs (compression/decompression), 201, 213

color laser printers, 51–52

combo cards, 53

command modules, 384–385, 394
  X10 systems, 380–382

commercial wiring and cabling, 3

communication links, 13

communications network, 3

Compaq, 92

components
  accessories for security system, 317–319
  audio, 241–243
  audio system, 227–232
  BNC connectors, 245
  heat, 253
  HVAC systems, 414–421
  lighting control, 384–388
  RCA connectors, 245
  security systems, 280, 309–316
  stacking, 253
  telephones, 345–351
  television systems, 233–237
  VGA-type connector, 245
  video, 243–246
  water control systems, 442–448
  wired security systems, 309–312
  wireless security systems, 312–314
  X10 security system, 314–316

composite video signals, 243

compressed video, 210

compression, 200–202, 214

compressor unit, 411

compressors, 428

CompTIA (Computer Technology Industry Association), 17, 20

CompTIA HTI+ Certificate, 17

CompTIA Web site, 3

computer networks, 17

computer screens, 236

computers, 45–46
  antivirus software, 102
  central processing unit, 12
  communication links, 13
  digital sounds and images, 188
  hackers, 4
  interface, 381
  recording audio, 195–196
  as splitter extension, 347–348

concealed enclosures, 467, 487

concealed wiring, 129–130, 142

condensation, 428

condensation unit, 411

condenser coil, 416, 428

condensing unit, 416, 428

conduit, 161

cone, 230–231, 256

connection blocks for telephones, 356–357

connectors, 13, 132–135
  adaptors, 240
  video distribution systems, 250

contention-based system, 33

continuity lights, 16

control components, 246

control devices, 15, 20

control modules, 394
  RadioRA, 389–390
  X10 technology, 380–382, 389–390

controlled access components, 317–318

controlled outlets, 164–165

controller panels for HVAC systems, 420–421

controllers, 395, 453
  lighting, 373
  lighting control components, 384–385
  locating, 448–449
  mechanical relays, 443
  power source, 449
  programming, 424–426
  setting and programming, 424–426
  sprinkler systems, 444–445
  water control systems, 442, 443–446
  X10 technology, 445–446

converters, 208, 214, 227, 256

cooling coil, 416, 428

cordless phones, 345, 360

corrupted packets, 30

counterweights, 478, 488

cps (cycles per second), 231

credentials, 3, 20

crossover cables, 124–125

crossover network, 231, 256

crown molding, 131, 142

CRTs (cathode ray tubes), 46, 61, 197, 213, 236

CSMA/CA (Carrier Sense Multiple Access/Collision Avoidance), 33, 38, 61, 92

CSMA/CD (Carrier Sense Multiple Access/Collision Detection), 33, 61

current, 153, 175

curtains, control of, 7

D

daisy chain wiring, 377–378, 395

dampers, 414, 419–420, 428

DAT (digital audio tape), 193–194, 214

data
  Ethernet control, 33
  scanning for viruses, 4
  sending and receiving, 39–45
  token ring control, 35–36
  traveling on Internet, 39

Data Link layer, 29

data packets. *See* packets

database servers, 55

DataLabsUSA, 342

dB (decibel), 195, 214

decoder, 5, 20, 205, 214, 227, 256

demarcation point, 340, 360

denial of service, 99

Denon DVD-9000, 237

Denon Web site, 237

desktop computers, 10–11

destination IP address, 59

destination TCP/UDP port, 59

detection devices, 270, 292

detector, 20

DHCP (Dynamic Host Configuration Protocol), 97, 104, 127

DHCP servers, 91, 127

diagram of LANs (local area networks)
  areas for pulling wire, 122
  correctly labeling, 122–123
  gateway, 121
  location for patch panel and equipment in unfinished area, 122
  NID (Network Interface Device), 122
  nodes, 121
  patch panel, 121
  wall jacks, 121

dial tones, 341, 360

Diamond, 79

digital, 186–187, 214

digital audio, recording, 193–194

digital audio files, 232, 256

digital broadcasting, 204

digital cable ready, 214

digital cable ready television receivers, 206–207

digital cameras, 252

digital converters, 208

digital data, 2, 20, 41, 61, 187–188

digital decoders, 205

digital encoder, 233

digital images, 188

digital radio receiver, 227

digital radios, 192–193, 205, 228

digital recordings, 187–188

digital satellite television, 207–208

digital signals, 48, 338

digital telephone communication systems, 338–339

digital television, 200–202, 205–206

digital television displays, 236

digital television tuners, 236

digital thermometer, 12

digital transmission, 234

digital tuners, 229

digital video, 199, 202

digital video programs, 198

digital video/audio switcher, 249, 256

Digital-S, 201

dimmers, 386

dimming modules, 166

disarming, 325

dish antennas, 207–208, 214, 234

disinformation, 100

displays, 15–16, 236

distortion, 230, 256

distribution, 2, 20

D-Link, 79

D-Link DI-804, 127

DNS (Domain Name Service), 104

DNS servers, 96, 104

Dolby Digital audio, 235

domain names, 104

  filters, 101

  qualifiers, 96–97

door closers, 471–472

door openers, 471–472

dot matrix printers, 50, 62

dot pitch, 47, 62

double protection, 319, 325

double-cut mechanical key, 282

downlink, 5, 20

drape pull mechanisms, 469, 488

drip irrigation systems, 439, 441, 453

drip irrigation zones, 441

drive rings, 137, 142

drop-down mechanisms, 466, 488

drywall, 129, 143

DSL (Digital Subscriber Line), 6, 10, 20, 42, 61, 338–339

DSL Lite, 339

DSL Lite or G.Lite, 44

DSL (Digital Subscriber Line) modems, 4

DSSS (Direct Sequence Spread Spectrum), 90, 104

DTCP (Digital Transmission Content Protection), 246

DTV (digital television), 203, 214

dual-acting thermostats, 417

duct boosters, 420

ducts, 408–409, 414–415

dumbwaiters, 475–477, 488

duress code, 320, 325

DV, 201

DVB (Digital Video Broadcasting) standards, 203

DVD players, 237, 244–245

DVD-R/RW (DVD-Recordable and Rewritable formats), 237

DVDs (digital video discs), 16, 209–210, 212, 214, 234, 256

DVI (Digital Video Interface) connectors, 245

dynamic NAT (Network Addressing Translation), 98

E

earphones, 16

eaves, 137, 143

EBN (Entrance Bridge Network) demarcation point, 138

Edison, Thomas, 189

EDTV (Enhanced Definition Television), 237, 256

EDTV (Enhanced Definition Television) monitor, 235

EIA (Electronic Industries Alliance), 153

EIA Web site, 153

EIA/TIA-568-A standard, 132

electric appliances, control of, 7

electric service, 155, 175

electrical components, high-voltage, 164–166

electrical relays, 15

electrical safety hazards, 153–154

electrical standards, organizations that develop, 152–153

electrical system monitoring, 272

electrical use, 155

electricity

  average use, 156

  overloading, 372–373

  peak use, 156

  planning system upgrade, 158–159

  potential volts, 155

electromagnet, 230, 256

electromagnetic fields, 120, 143

electromagnetic mechanisms, 15

electromagnetic valve controls, 15

electronic keys, 282–283

electronic locks, 318

elevators, 475, 477–479, 488

e-mail bombs, 99

emergency response, 310, 326

emergency response system, 358–359

EMI (electromagnetic induction), 172

EMT (electrical metallic tubing), 161

encoders, 232, 256

entertainment network, 3

entertainment video, 212

environmental sensors, 14

equalizers, 231–232, 256

error correction algorithm, 188

ESD (electrostatic discharge), 171

Ethernet, 3, 27, 44, 62, 72–76, 126

  5-4 rule, 34

  5-4-3 rule, 34

  addresses, 54

  amplification of data signals, 34

  bus topology, 31–32

  cabling, 74

  connecting audio system to networks, 248

  data control, 33–34

  fiber-optic cable, 31

  hubs, 31–32

  NICs (network interface cards), 53

passive designs, 33–34

repeaters, 34

star topology, 31–32

terminator, 31–32

twisted-pair cable, 31

unshielded twisted-pair cable, 31

wiring, 72–76

Ethernet IEEE 802.3, 31

evaporative coolers, 408, 428

extension dialing, 347

extensions, 339, 360

exterior door locks, 317–318

exterior walls, 116

F

face plates, 128, 130, 143

fail-safe, 326

fail-safe systems, 319–320

fall alarms, 7

false alarms, 324, 326

fans, 418–419, 428

Farnsworth, Philo T., 186

Fast Ethernet, 31, 34

fax machines, 351, 360

FCC (Federal Communications Commission), 89, 90

FDDI (Fiber Distributed Data Interface), 39, 44, 53, 62

FDM (frequency-division multiplexing), 77

FHSS (Frequency Hopping Spread Spectrum), 90, 104

fiber-optic cable networks, 39

fiber-optic cables, 31, 62, 73

fiber-optic lines, 120–121

fields, 199, 214

file servers, 55

filters, 170, 175

    domain names, 101

    firewalls, 101–102

    interference, 173–174

IP addresses, 101

    protocols, 101–102

fingerprints, 283

finished areas, 116

fireplace igniters, 482–484, 488

fires, 153–154, 322–323

fire-stops, 129, 143

firewalls, 4, 20, 45, 58–60, 62, 99, 100, 104

    dynamic packet processing, 59

    filters, 101–102

    packet filtering, 101

    ports, 102

    protocols, 101–102

    proxy servers, 103

    proxy services, 101

    specific words and phrases, 102

    stateful inspection, 101

    viruses, 60

FireWire, 89, 256

FireWire connectors, 245–246

fixtures, 166, 372, 387

flat panel screens, 27, 48–49, 62, 236

floppy disks, 16

flow meter, 273, 292

flow valve, 440, 453

fluorescent lighting, 374, 395

FM (frequency modulation), 214

FM radio, 191–192

FM (frequency modulated) wave, 192

forced air, 408, 428

forced-air furnaces, 415–416

forwarding tables, 56

frames, 199, 214

freeze sensors, 418, 428, 447, 453

frequency, 186, 188, 231

frequency division multiplexing, 337, 360

FSK (frequency-shift keying), 83

FTP (File Transfer Protocol), 102

fuels for furnaces, 410–411

furnaces, 408–409, 428

    forced-air, 415–416

    fuels, 410–411

    pilot light, 415

    safety control valve, 416

    spark igniter, 416

    thermocouples, 415–416

    valves, 415

fuse, 156

G

garage door openers, 317–318

gas detector, 273, 292

gas-fired fireplaces, 482–483

gate controls, 318–319

gateway, 121

GE, 84

geared rack, 471, 488

geosynchronous orbits, 207

ghosting, 234

Gigabit Ethernet, 31

glassbreak detector, 310

ground, 175, 227

ground connections, 169

ground start systems, 341, 360

ground wires, 154

grounding

    audio components, 243

    high-voltage fixtures, 374

G.SHDSL, 339

H

hackers, 4, 99–100

hard drives, 16

hardware

    bridges, 56–58

    computers, 45–46

    concealed wiring, 129–130

configuring, 140

firewalls, 58–60

monitors, 46–49

NICs (network interface cards), 53–54

patch panel, 123–124

power consumption, 156

printers, 49–53

residential gateways, 126–127

routers, 55–56

servers, 55

surface wiring, 130–132

switches, 56–58

wireless access hubs, 58

wiring, 127–140

hardware firewalls, 100–102

hardwired home security system, 275

HAVi (Home Audio Video interoperability), 127

HDSL (High-bit-rate DSL), 44, 339

HDTV (high definition television), 62, 203, 212, 214, 235

HDTV devices, 245

HDTV monitors, 47, 237

HDTV televisions, 236

HDTV tuners, 236, 256

headers, 29, 62

heat sensors, 6, 15, 279, 287–288

heat sinks, 253, 256

heat transfer, 413

heating cables, 484–486, 488

high-frequency response speakers, 231

high-quality sound reproduction, 230

high-resolution photographic images, 16

high-speed Internet connection, 211–212

high-temperature sensors, 288

high-voltage electrical components, 164–166

high-voltage electrical safety standards, 152–158

high-voltage fixtures, 374

high-voltage interference, 171–174

high-voltage wiring, 372

home automation and control, 7

home control network, 3

home LANs (local area networks)
    See also LANs
    HomePNA, 76–77
    lighting control segment, 14
    programming system parameters, 14

home lighting systems, 372–378, 395

home networks
    See also networks
    cable modems, 42
    central computer, 45–46
    configuration, 94–103
    connecting to Internet, 41–43
    DSL (Digital Subscriber Line), 42
    hardware, 45–60
    home security system, 117
    integrating security systems with, 304
    ISDN (Integrated Services Digital Network), 41–42
    ISPs (Internet service providers), 41
    peripherals, 4
    planning, 114–123
    POTS (Plain Old Telephone Service), 41

routers, 56

satellite link, 42

servers, 55

settings, 94–103

sources of audio and video services, 204–208

switches, 56–58

utility management systems, 117

varying bandwidths, 41

wired and wireless segments, 74–75

wireless Internet access, 43

home office enhancement, 9–10

Home Plug system, 13

Home Radio Frequency Working Group, 91

home run cable, 143
    ADSL splitter, 135
    drive rings, 137
    installing splitter, 138
    interference, 137
    jack connection, 138
    NID (Network Interface Device), 136
    patch cord connection, 138
    patch panel, 136
    planning and preparing route, 135–137
    running, 137–138
    wiring splitter, 138–139

home run connection, 377–378, 395

home security, 3, 6, 17, 268

home security systems. See security systems

home theater system, 8, 21

Home Toys Web site, 446

HomePlug, 117, 210
    connecting devices, 118
    home security devices, 275
    wireless security systems, 308

HomePlug Alliance, 80
HomePlug Web site, 117
HomePNAs, 13, 104, 117, 126, 210
  4100 chip, 78–79
  4210 chip, 78–79
  analog signals, 79
  attenuation, 80
  connecting devices, 118
  FDM (frequency-division multiplexing), 77
  features, 76–77
  filters, 79
  installing, 79–80
  limitations, 77
  noise on line, 79
  operation of, 77–79
  PCI (Peripheral Component Interconnect) cards, 78
  peer-to-peer system, 79–80
  security system use, 275
  slow rate of data transfer, 79
  starter kit, 78
  telephone jacks, 79
  USB (Universal Serial Bus) adapters, 78
  wireless security systems, 308
HomeRF (Home Radio Frequency), 88, 91–93, 104, 210
  FHSS (Frequency Hopping Spread Spectrum), 90
  wireless security systems, 308
homes
  electrical use, 155
  exterior walls, 116
  finished areas, 116
  installing wiring, 76
  load requirements, 154
  unfinished areas, 116
Honeywell, 308

horizontal sync, 197
hosts, 30, 62
hot wires, 154, 175
HP, 92
HPNA (Home Phone Networking Alliance), 76
HPNA 2.0 specification, 76, 105
HTI (Home Technology Integration), 1, 21
  assisted living functions, 9
  benefits of, 8–10
  centralized processing, 12
  communication and data sharing, 8
  control, 2
  defining, 2–3
  home office enhancement, 9–10
  management, 2
  necessary amount of, 18
  protection for children, 9
  security, 9
  technology on demand, 8
  technology to save money, 9
  technology to save time, 8–9
  wireless connection, 13
HTI+ certification, 3
HTI+ Certified Professional, 3
HTI+ credential, 17
HTI professionals, 3
  CompTIA HTI+ Certificate, 17
  need for, 16
HTI+ Residential Systems exam, 3
HTI sensors, 15–16
HTI systems
  access control, 3, 6
  appliance automation and control, 3
  audio, 2
  audio and video reception and distribution, 5

basic components, 10–17
communication links, 13
data line, 6
designing and installing, 16–17
desktop computers, 10–11
home automation and control, 7
home security, 3, 6
home security system, 6
Internet, 2
Internet connectivity, 4
keypads, 14
laptop computers, 10–11
networks, 2
overall design, 18
processors, 12
recording and storage devices, 16
sensors, 13–15
subsystems, 2
swimming pools, 8
telecommunications, 3, 5–6
telephones, 5
utility and resource management, 7–8
utility management, 3
video, 2
HTI+ Systems Infrastructure and Integration, 3
HTML (Hypertext Markup Language), 95
HTTP (Hypertext Transfer Protocol), 95, 101
hubs, 31–32, 56–57, 62, 125
  as signal-regenerating repeater, 34
  wireless networks, 37
Huffyuv, 201, 214
humidifiers, 418, 428
humidity, 411, 428

humidity detector, 418, 428

HVAC (heating, ventilation, and air-conditioning systems), 17, 20, 407, 428

A/C (air conditioning), 408

air handlers, 418–419

blowers, 419

boilers, 416

central air conditioning (A/C) systems, 411

central heating systems, 408–410

circulating pump, 416

components, 414–421

controller installation, 422–424

controller panels, 420–421

dampers, 414, 419–420

duct boosters, 420

ducts, 414–415

evaporative coolers, 408

fans, 418–419

freeze sensor, 418

furnaces, 415–416

heat transfer, 413

humidifiers, 418

humidity detector, 418

multiple-unit, 411–412

pipes, 414–415

refrigeration air conditioners, 416

remote access, 426

room air conditioners, 408

seasonal presets, 426

sensors, 418

setting and programming controllers and sensors, 424–426

single unit, 411–412

space heaters, 408

termination points, 423–424

thermostats, 417–418

time-of-day programming, 425

ventilators, 413–414

wiring controllers, 422–423

zone programming, 425

zoned and nonzoned, 408–414

zones, 411–412

hydraulic cylinders, 480, 488

hydraulic lifts, 479–480

Hz (Hertz), 231

I

IANA Web site, 96

IBM, 84, 92

IBOC (In-Band On-Channel) digital radio broadcasting, 192–193

ICANN (Internet Corporation for Assigned Names and Numbers), 96, 105

ICMP, 59

identifier pads, 278

identifiers, 281

IDSL (ISDN Digital Subscriber Line), 44

IEEE (Institute of Electrical and Electronics Engineers), 153

IEEE 802 standard, 89

IEEE 802.11b standard, 88, 105

IEEE 802.11g, 89, 105

IEEE 802a standard, 89

IEEE 1394 standard, 89, 105

IEEE standards, 153

IHA (Internet Home Alliance), 17, 21

IHA (Internet Home Alliance) Web site, 3

iHG (Internet Home Gateway), 127

i.LINK, 89

impact printers, 50

inadequate wiring, 157–158

inclined ramp, 479, 488

Indeo, 201

infrastructure, 2, 21

ink jet printers, 52–53

input jacks, 242

inside arming, 321, 326

Intel, 79, 92

Intelogis, 80

intercom, 348, 360

intercom button, 343

interference, 75, 105, 151, 156–157, 175

analog television signals, 197

audio components, 243

control components, 246

digital data, 187

digital television, 200

filters, 173–174

minimizing high-voltage, 171–174

inter-frame compression, 201–202

interlaced, 62, 199, 214

interlaced monitors, 47

interlaced programs, 199

interlaced scans, 197

Internet, 2, 27, 62

bandwidth, 4

data traveling on, 39

dial-up connections, 97

growth of, 97

home network connections, 41–43

HomeRF (Home Radio frequency), 91

LANs (local area networks), 28

managing services, 4

other computers accessing, 4

TCP/IP (Transmission Control Protocol/Internet Protocol), 94–96 transmission, 4

video files, 208–209

WANs, 39

Internet connections, 4

cable modems, 42

DSL (Digital Subscriber Line), 42

high-speed, 211–212

ISDN (Integrated Services Digital Network), 41–42

POTS (Plain Old Telephone Service), 41

PowerPacket, 82

satellite link, 42

wireless access, 43

Internet sites, password-protecting access, 4

intra-frame compression, 201–202

intruders, 310, 322, 326

IP (Internet Protocol), 59, 101

IP (Internet Protocol) addresses, 39, 62, 94, 98, 105

filters, 101

routers, 40–41

IPCONFIG, 95, 105

IPX/SPX (Internetwork Packet Exchange/Sequenced Packet Exchange), 40, 62

IR (infrared) devices, 246, 256, 287, 292

IR8Z controller, 446

ISDN (Integrated Services Digital Network), 41–42, 44, 62

ISM radio band, 89–90

ISO (International Standards Organization), 28

ISPs (Internet service providers), 41, 62

J

jacks, 118, 121, 143

JDS Technologies, 446

joists, 128, 143

K

Kbps (kilobit), 41

key systems, 339, 360

call conferencing, 349

call restriction, 349–350

circuit-switched lines, 343

intercom button, 343

loop start systems, 342

voice mail, 350

keyboards, 12–14, 21

keypad access devices, 320–321

keypads, 6, 14, 21, 277–278, 281, 292

keys, 281–283

kinescope recording, 197

L

LANs (local area networks), 27, 63

802.11b standard, 90–91

bandwidth, 32

basic components, 123–127

bridges, 56–57

definition of, 28

firewalls, 45

Internet, 28

large, high-speed, 31

large home, 34

network administrators, 44–45

nodes, 27

packets, 29

patch panel, 123–124

receiving and sending information, 39–45

residential gateways, 126–127

straight-through and crossover cables, 124–125

switches, 57–58

TCP/IP (Transmission Control Protocol/Internet Protocol), 39

topology, 3

transmitting internal information on, 44–45

wireless Internet connection, 43

wiring, 127–140

WWW (World Wide Web), 28

laptop computers, 10–11, 78

laser light, 287, 292

laser printers, 50–52, 62

latchkey function, 322, 326

LCD (liquid crystal display), 63

LCD (liquid crystal display) panels, 48–49

LCD projection systems, 236

LEDs (light-emitting diodes), 246, 256

light beam sensors, 287–288, 292

light fixtures, 166

light scenes, 372, 375–376, 395

light sensors, 14, 273, 292

light switches, 386

lighting

centralized control of, 7

controllers, 373

daisy chain wiring, 377–378

fixture installation, 372

fluorescent, 374

high-voltage wiring, 372

home run connection, 377–378

inadequate wiring, 373

lighting scenes, 375–376

overloading electricity, 372–373

track lighting, 383

upgrading or altering, 372

wireless controls, 382

zones, 373, 375–376

lighting control components

automated window treatments, 387

command modules, 384–385

controllers, 384–385

dimmers, 386

fixtures, 387

light switches, 386

macros, 385

outlets, 386

programmable components, 385

remote-access controllers, 385–386

sensors, 387–388

lighting systems types, 379–383

lighting zones, 388–390

line of sight, 308, 326

line speed, 41, 62

Linksys, 79

Linux NIC Installation: Guide to Linux Installation and Administration (Wells), 94

load, 175, 372, 395

local telephone systems, 339

lock-down feature, 281, 292

locks, 282–283

loop pull cord, 469, 488

loop start systems, 342, 361

lossless, 214

lossless compression, 200–201

Lossless JPEG, 201

lossy, 214

lossy compression, 200–201

low-frequency responsive speakers, 231

low-frequency sounds, 229–230

low-temperature sensors, 288–289

low-voltage wiring, 304–307

Lutron, 382

M

MAC (Media Access Control) addresses, 54

macros, 99, 385, 395

magnetic keys, 278, 293

magnetic lock controls, 15

magnetic media, 194, 214

magnetic recording, 189, 214

magnetic recording head, 189

magnetic tape, 189, 214

make switch sensors, 285–286, 293

Marconi, Guglielmo, 186

Marlock key, 282

MAU (Multistation Access Unit), 35–36, 63

Mbps, 41

MC (metal clad) cable, 162, 176, 390

mechanical relays, 443, 454

mechanical systems installation, 467

media, 232, 257

memory sticks, 16

microphones, 12, 14, 21

Microsoft, 92

MIDI (Musical Instrument Digital Interface) files, 232, 257

mini-controllers, 381

miniDV cassettes, 252, 257

minimizing high-voltage interference, 171–174

modems, 4, 21

monaural, 257

monaural (single track) devices, 227

monitored, 326

monitoring devices, 15–16

monitoring sensors, 305

monitoring service, 309, 326

monitors, 21, 27, 46–49, 63

security systems, 285

video camera cables, 307

motion detectors, 312

motion sensors, 6, 15, 279, 287–288, 293

motion/vibration detectors, 6

motorized drives, 465, 488

Motorola, 92

MP3 files, 195, 212, 215

MP3PRO, 196, 215

MPEG-1, 201, 208–209, 215

MPEG-2, 201, 203, 210, 215

MPEG-4, 201, 209

multiple-unit HVAC systems, 411–412

multiple-wire cable, 130

multiplexing, 349, 361

multisystem VCRs, 237, 257

N

narrow band, 338, 361

NAT (Network Addressing Translation), 91, 97–98

NAT agent router, 98

National Semiconductor, 92

natural gas service monitoring, 273

NEC (National Electrical Code), 152, 176, 274

Necanet Web site, 152

NetBEUI (Network BIOS Extended User Interface), 40–41, 63

network administrators, 44–45

network architectures

Ethernet, 31–33

fiber-optic cable networks, 39

token ring, 35–36

wireless networks, 36–38

Network layer, 28

network printers, 53, 63

networked entertainment video, 210

networks, 1–2, 21

access hub, 118

bridges, 118

connecting audio systems to, 247–249

connecting television systems to, 249–251

contention-based system, 33

grounding devices, 169

hosts, 30

interference, 75, 156–157

nodes, 30, 116–117

not operating consistently at maximum rated speeds, 210

packets, 344

protocols, 29

routers, 40–41

security, 99

speed, 210

UPS (uninterruptible power supply), 159

wireless hubs, 119

new construction wiring, 128–129

NFPA (National Fire Protection Association), 152, 176

NFPA Code #70, 152

NICs (network interface cards), 29, 36, 53–54, 63

NID (Network Interface Device), 122, 136, 138, 143

NM (nonmetallic) cable, 161–163, 176

nodes, 27, 30, 35, 63

AC power connections, 118

access point, 36

cable run, 119–120

connections for, 119–121

diagram of LANs (local area networks), 121

jacks, 118

location of, 118–119

planning home networks, 116–117

talking to other nodes, 44–45

wireless hub, 36

wireless networks, 37

noise

analog television signals, 197

digital data, 187

digital television, 200

filters, 170

noninterlaced, 63

noninterlaced monitors, 47

noninterlaced programs, 199

nonmetallic raceways, 161–162

NTSC format, 199, 215

NTSC (National Television Standards Committee) standard, 196, 203

NTSC television aspect ratio, 199

numeric codes, 6, 21

O

obstruction detectors, 318, 326

OFDM (orthogonal frequency-division multiplexing), 81–82

off-the-shelf hardware, 466, 488

OGG (Ogg Vorbis), 196, 215

Ohm's Law, 155, 176

Onkyo TXNR900 7 Channel Receiver with Ethernet Connection, 248

operating system backdoors, 100

operation cycle, 471, 488

organizations that develop electrical standards, 152–153

OSGi (Open Services Gateway initiative), 127

OSI model (Open Systems Interconnect model), 28–29

outdoor sensors, 279

outlet boxes, 123, 143, 159, 176

outlets, 159, 163–164

always-on configuration, 164

controlled, 164–165

installing, 159–160

lighting control components, 386

split, 165

uncontrolled, 164–165

wired in parallel, 164

output jacks, 242

outside alarms, 317

outside arming, 321, 326

overload, 156, 176

overloading, 372–373, 395

P

packets, 63, 344

checksum, 29–30

controlling flow, 30

corrupted, 30

filtering, 101

headers, 29

NetBEUI, 40–41

routing, 55–56

trailers, 29

transmission speed, 30

X10, 86–87

paging, 348

PAL format, 196, 215

panning cameras, 279

panning motor, 284, 293

Passport, 80–81, 83–84, 105

password-protecting access to Web sites, 4

passwords, 21, 281–282

PAT (Port Address Translation), 98

patch panel, 115, 121, 123–124, 143

home run cable, 136

location of, 122

telephones, 356–357

PATHPING, 95, 105

patio door openers, 471

PBCC 22 Mbps standard, 91

PBX (private branch exchange), 339, 361

call conferencing, 349

call restriction, 349–350

circuit-switched lines, 343

demarcation point, 340

dial tones, 341
extension dialing, 347
ground start systems, 341
telephones, 341
trunk lines, 341
voice mail, 350
PCI (Peripheral Component Interconnect) cards, 78
PCM (pulse code modulation), 194, 215
peak use, 156, 176
peripherals, 4, 21
personal safety devices management, 7
pet-immune motion sensor, 310
phone-line extensions, 347–348
phone-line networks, 76–80
phonograph turntables, 242
phonographic record players, 233
phonographs, 189, 215
physical addresses, 54
Physical layer, 29
picture frame lifts, 466, 488
pilot hole, 129, 143
pilot light, 415, 428
PING, 95, 105
pipes, 414–415
pitch, 186, 188
pivot-down mechanisms, 466, 488
pixels (picture elements), 47–48, 215
  digital video, 199
  NTSC standard, 199
  television, 196
  television screens, 236
plain paper fax machines, 351
planning home networks, 114
  connections for nodes, 119–121
  diagram of LANs (local area networks), 121–122

finished areas, 116
labeling LAN diagram, 122–123
location of nodes, 118–119
nodes, 116–117
prewired new construction, 115
remodeling, 115
retrofitting existing structures, 115–116
schematic drawing of existing wiring, 115
unfinished areas, 116
wireless hubs, 117
platform lifts, 466, 489
plugs, 121, 143
ports, 102
potential, 176
potential volts, 155
POTS (Plain Old Telephone Service), 41, 44, 63, 336
Poulsen, Valdemar, 189
power amplifiers (amps), 229–230
power failure warning sensor, 273, 293
power-line control systems, 380–382
power-line filters, 173
power-line networks, 80–84, 105
power-line technology, 395
PowerPacket, 80, 81–83, 105
PowerPlug, 126
PPP (Point-to-Point Protocol), 97
pre-amplifiers (pre-amps), 229–230, 257
Presentation layer, 28
pressure or weight pads, 15
pressure pads, 286, 293
pressure sensor, 273
pressure valves, 440, 454
pressure-sensitive pads, 6
prewired new construction, 115
Primary Service Interface, 42

print servers, 55
printers, 27, 49–53
  dot matrix, 50
  impact, 50
  ink jet, 52–53
  laser, 50–52
  network, 53
processors, 12
program, 21
programmable, 395
programmable controllers, 381
programming
  automated lighting system, 390–392
  controllers, 424–426
  keypad access devices, 320–321
  LANs (local area networks), 14
  security systems, 320–322
  sensors, 424–426
  water control system, 451–452
progressive, 215
progressive-scanned programs, 199
projector lifts, 466, 489
protection for children, 9
protocols, 63
  filters, 101–102
  firewalls, 101–102
  NetBEUI (Network BIOS Extended User Interface), 30
  packets, 29
  routable, 30
  telephone systems, 344–345
Proxim, 92
proxy servers, 103
proxy services, 101
PSTN (Public Switched Telephone Network), 91, 92, 105, 344
pulling cable, 129, 143
pumps, 447–448
punchdown blocks, 356–357, 361

PVC (polyvinylchloride) pipes, 161, 438, 454

Q
QuickTime, 209
Quicktime, 201, 215

R
raceway, 130–131, 143
radiant, 429
radiant heating systems, 408–410, 412
Radio Shack, 84
radio stations, 204–205
radio tuners, 229
radio wave, 190
radio-based X10 devices, 86
RadioRA, 382, 395
    command modules, 385
    control modules, 389–390
    dimmers, 386
    light switches, 386
    manual dimming modules, 166
    outlets, 386
    remote controllers, 385–386
    sensors, 387–388
    troubleshooting automated lighting system, 392–393
rain sensors, 447, 454
Rain8, 445
RAS (Remote Access Server), 55
rasters, 197, 215, 236, 257
RCA connector cables, 242, 243
RCA connector jacks, 245
RCA connectors, 244–245
RCI Automation, 446
RCI Automation Web site, 446
Real media format, 209
RealOne Player, 209
RealPlayer, 209
RealVideo, 201, 215
receivers, 13

receiving components, 241
receptacles, 159, 176
reception, 2
recessed, 466, 489
recorded emergency message, 313, 326
recorders, 283–284
recording
    analog video, 197–198
    audio, 189
    CD audio, 194–195
    computer audio, 195–196
    digital audio, 193–194
    television, 196–203
recording devices, 16
records, 189, 215
recovery of security systems, 323–324
redirect bombs, 100
redundant protection, 270, 293
reel tape recording, 189
refresh rate, 47, 63
refrigerant fluid, 416, 429
refrigeration, 411, 429
refrigeration air conditioners, 416
regenerator, 338, 361
registered IP addresses, 98
relay, 21
remodeling, 115
remote access, 293
    security systems, 276
    water control system, 442
remote controls, 246
remote login, 100
remote-access controllers, 385–386
remote-control system, 21
remote-controlled systems, 7
repeaters, 34, 63
residential gateways, 126–127, 143

resistance, 153, 176
resolution, 47–48, 63
resource management, 7–8
response devices, 307, 323, 326
retinal scans, 283
retrofit, 143
retrofit wiring, 122
retrofitting existing structures, 115–116
retrofitting home for HTI, 13
RF (radio frequency), 186, 197, 215
RFI (radio frequency interference), 173
RGB+H/V (component video plus horizontal and vertical sync) connectors, 245
risk, 268–269
RJ-11 connections, 354–356
RJ-11 jacks, 135, 361
RJ-14 jacks, 354–355, 361
RJ-45 connectors, 132–133
RJ-45 crimping tool, 133–134, 143
RJ-45 jacks, 134–135, 143
RJ-45 plug, 133–134
RJ-45 punchdown tool, 134, 143
rollover cables, 124
Romex, 161–162, 163
room air conditioners, 408
rough-in, 128, 143
routable, 30, 63
routers, 13, 30, 40–41, 55–56, 63, 95

S
safety, 274
safety control valve, 416, 429
safety systems, control of, 7
sampling, 187, 193, 215
Samsung, 92
satellite, 5, 17

satellite antennas, 234

satellite decoder, 243–244

satellite link, 42, 63

satellite television, 5, 203, 207–208

satellite transmission, 5, 22

saving money, 9

saving time, 8–9

scan, 22

scan rate, 47, 63

scanning for viruses, 4

SDSL (Symmetric DSL), 44, 339

SDTV (standard definition television), 203, 212, 215, 235, 237, 257

SDTV tuners, 235, 257

Sears, 84

seasonal presets, 426, 452

SECAM format, 196, 215

security, 9

  application backdoors, 99

  denial of service, 99

  disinformation, 100

  e-mail bombs, 99

  firewalls, 58–60, 100–102

  hardware firewalls, 100–102

  highest level of, 102

  macros, 99

  operating system backdoors, 100

  proxy servers, 103

  redirect bombs, 100

  remote login, 100

  risk, 268–269

  software firewalls, 100–102

  spam, 100

  threats, 99–102

  viruses, 100

  wireless networks, 38

security breach, 305, 310, 326

security network, 3

security panels, 269, 289–290, 293, 306, 321–323

security systems, 6, 20, 117, 267–268

  access devices, 280–283

  accessory components, 317–319

  alarms, 270, 290

  backups, 319–320

  biometric identification, 283

  bypassing, 269

  call-in devices, 290–291

  camera locations, 279–280

  cameras, 283–284

  category 2 telephone wires, 304–305

  category 3 wire, 305

  code regulations, 274

  components, 280, 309–316

  concealed wiring, 305–306

  controlled access components, 317–318

  design and installation factors, 268–274

  detection devices, 270

  double protection, 319

  electrical system monitoring, 272

  electronic locks, 318

  emergency response system, 358–359

  equipment locations, 277–280

  existing home and new construction environments, 269

  exterior door locks, 317–318

  fail-safe systems, 319–320

  false alarms, 324

  fire, 322

  fire damage, 323–324

  garage door openers, 317–318

  gate controls, 318–319

  hardwired systems, 269, 275

  hybrid, 314–316

  identifiers, 281

  installing, 304–309

  integrating with home networks, 304

  integration with utility systems, 273

  intruders, 322

  keypads, 281

  keys, 281–283

  latchkey function, 322

  lock and keypad locations, 277–278

  low-voltage wiring, 304–307

  maintenance, 322–323

  monitoring sensors, 305

  monitors, 285

  natural gas service monitoring, 273

  obstruction detectors, 318

  outside alarms, 317

  passwords, 281

  professionally installed, 275

  programming, 320–322

  protecting occupants, people and property, 268

  recorders, 283–284

  recovery, 323–324

  redundant protection, 270

  remote access, 276

  response devices, 307

  safety, 274

  security panels, 289–290, 306

  security zones, 270–271

  sensor locations, 278–279

  sensors, 270, 285–289

  service, 322–323

  settings, 320–322

  standardization, 304

  starter kits, 304

time and notification settings, 322
time coding, 283
types, 274–275
UPS (uninterruptible power supply), 319
utility specifications and capacity, 272–273
water sensors, 273
wireless, 269, 276
wiring, 275
X10, 308–309
yard sign and decals, 310
security zones, 270–271, 293, 390
sensors, 6–7, 12, 13, 22, 270, 293
break switch, 285–286
bypassing, 305
central processor, 14
chemical sensors, 15
environmental, 14
false reports, 279
fire, 323
heat, 287–288
heat (infrared) sensors, 15
HVAC systems, 418
keyboards, 13–14
light beam, 287–288
lighting control components, 387–388
location of, 278–279
make switch, 285–286
microphones, 14
monitoring, 306
motion, 287–288
motion (vibration) sensors, 15
outdoor, 279
pressure or weight pads, 15
programming, 424–426
security breach, 305
security systems, 285–289

self-monitoring, 322–323
service and maintenance, 322–323
setting and programming, 424–426
smoke detectors, 15
tampering with, 278
temperature, 288–289
water, 289
water control system, 446–447
water level sensors, 15
wired, 279
wired security systems, 312
wireless security systems, 313–314
servers, 64
heavy-traffic connections, 31
home networks, 55
ports, 102
service lines, 167, 176
service panels, 158, 167–168, 176
service provider wiring (external), 17
service providers, 4, 22
services and subscriptions, 3
Session layer, 28
shade controllers, 468, 489
shade lifts, 470–471
shade pulls, 469
shafts, 467, 489
shielded coaxial cable, 241
shielding, 176
shielding cables, 173
shock, 153, 176
short circuits, 154
Siemens, 92
signal-regenerating repeater, 34
sine waves, 188, 190
single unit HVAC systems, 411–412

single-pole switches, 389, 395
skylights, 472–473
SkyLink, 308
SkyLink Home Security, 312–313
Smart Electronics Corporation, 446
SmartHome, 315
SMC, 79
smoke detectors, 15, 279, 289, 293, 310
SMTP (Simple Mail Transport Protocol), 102
S/N (signal-to-noise) ratio, 195, 215
SNMP (Simple Network Management Protocol), 102
softphones, 344–345, 361
software firewalls, 100–102
soil moisture sensors, 447, 454
solenoid valves, 442–443, 454
Sorenson, 201
sound systems and speakers, 230–231
sound waves, 187, 188
sounds, 186, 188
high-quality reproduction, 230
low-frequency, 229–230
source IP address, 59
source TCP/UDP port, 59
space heaters, 408, 429
space monitors, 16
spam, 100, 102
spark igniter, 416, 429
speakers, 16, 227, 230–231
connections, 243
output, 247
spikes, 169–171, 176
split duplex outlets, 389, 395
split outlets, 165
splitters, 347–348, 361
spread spectrum, 105

spread spectrum radio technology, 90
spring-loaded door closer, 472, 489
sprinkler systems
  controllers, 444–445
  drip irrigation system, 439
  locating controller, 448–449
  pumps, 447–448
  solenoid valves, 443
  timed water systems, 440–441
  valves, 438
  water pressure, 439
  water service line, 439
  zones, 438–439, 452
Squish, 196
stair lifts, 480–481
stairway lifts, 475, 489
Stanley, 84
star ring. *See* token ring
star topology, 31–32, 35, 64
stateful inspection, 101
static, 336, 361
static charges, 171–172
static discharges, 171–172
static electricity, 171
static NAT (Network Addressing Translation), 98
stereo, 227, 257
storage devices, 16, 22
storage media, incompatibility of, 226
STP (shielded twisted-pair) cable, 36, 64, 73, 119, 173
STP wiring, 72–73, 74–75
straight-through cables, 124–125, 144
streaming digital video, 252
studs, 128, 144
subsystems, 2, 22

suppressors, 170, 176
surface lawn sprinkler zones, 441
surface metal raceways, 161–162
surface wiring, 130–132, 144
surge suppressors, 170
surges, 169–171, 176
surveillance video cameras, 283–284, 293
S-video (separated video), 244
S-video output jack, 244
swamp coolers, 408, 428
SWAP (Shared Wireless Access Protocol), 88, 91–92
swimming pools, 8
swipe slots, 278, 293
switch boxes, installing, 159–160
switchboards, 339, 361
switched duplex outlets, 388–389, 395
switchers, 307, 326
switches, 13, 15, 22, 30, 56–58, 64, 159, 176
  daisy chain wiring, 377–378
  wiring configuration, 165
swivel mechanisms, 466, 489
SYN packet filtering, 59
synchronized, 227, 257
system administrator, 4

T

T–1 line, 44, 338, 361
T568A standard, 132–133
T568B standard, 132–133
tabletop controllers, 381
tape recorders, 242
tapes, 16
TCP (Transmission Control Protocol), 59

TCP/IP (Transmission Control Protocol/Internet Protocol), 39, 64, 94–96
  routers, 40
  Wi-Fi (Wireless Fidelity), 90
TDMA (Time Division Multiple Access) service, 91–92
technology
  on demand, 8
  retaining old, 226
  to save money, 9
  to save time, 8–9
telecommunications, 3, 5–6, 17, 22
  bandwidth, 338
telecommunications systems
  analog telephone communication systems, 336–337
  digital telephone communication systems, 338–339
  narrow band, 338
  types and characteristics, 336–339
telephone communication systems
  analog, 336–337
  digital, 338–339
telephone interface, 381
telephone lines and bandwidth, 77
telephone links, 12
telephone systems
  Centrex (central switching exchange), 339–340
  hybrid systems, 343
  key systems, 339, 342–343
  local, 339–345
  PBX (private branch exchange), 339, 340–342
  protocols, 344–345
  PSTN (public switched telephone network), 344
  remote access methods, 344–345

standards, 344–345

VoIP (Voice over IP), 343–344

telephones, 5

call blocking, 358

call conferencing, 349

call restriction, 349–350

call waiting, 358

Caller ID (caller line identification), 348, 357

color codes, 353–354

components, 345–351

computer as splitter extension, 347–348

connecting equipment, 352–354

connection blocks, 356–357

data transmission, 5

emergency response system, 358–359

extension dialing, 347

extensions, 339

external services, 357–359

fax machines, 351

features, 345–351

frequency division multiplexing, 337

fundamentals, 345–346

handset, 346

hardwired extensions, 5

hook switch, 346

installation and configuration, 352–357

intercom, 348

Internet access, 5

operation of, 345–346

paging, 348

patch panel, 356–357

PBX (private branch exchange), 341

phone-line extensions, 347–348

punchdown blocks, 356–357

ring wire, 353

RJ-11 connections, 354–356

RJ-14 jack, 354–355

splitters, 347–348

static, 336

switchboards, 339

three-way calling, 358

tip wire, 353

video conferencing, 349

voice mail, 350

voice transmission signals, 336

wireless technology, 5

wires, 352–354

wiring, 355–356

television lifts, 466, 489

television monitors, 47, 236

television stations, 204–208

television systems

antennas, 233–234

components, 233–237

connecting to networks, 249–251

television transmission satellites, 207

televisions

analog, 197, 252

broadcasting, 196–203

built-in digital tuner, 205

CRTs (cathode ray tubes), 236

digital, 252

digital decoders for cable or broadcast, 206

digital programs, 205

digital signals, 234

digital-ready, 205

DVD players, 237

flat panel displays, 236

ghosting, 234

interlaced scans, 197

LCD projection systems, 236

PAL format, 196

pixels, 196

rasters, 197

RCA connectors, 244

recording, 196–203

remote controls, 246

RF (radio frequency) signal, 197

SECAM format, 196

tuners, 234–236

video recorder/players, 236

TELNET, 95, 102, 105

temperature sensors, 288–289, 294, 413, 418, 429

terminating jacks, 132–135

termination points, 239–241, 423–424

terminator, 31, 32, 64

thermal printing, 351

thermocouples, 273, 294, 415–416, 429, 482–483, 489

thermostats, 429

setting, 424–425

zones, 417–418

thick Ethernet, 31, 33

thin Ethernet, 31, 33

three-way calling, 358

three-way switches, 389, 395

TIA (Telecommunication Industry Association), 153

TIA Online Web site, 153

tilt mechanisms, 466, 489

time and notification settings, 322

time coding, 283

timed water systems, 440–441

time-of-day programming, 425

time-of-day settings, 451–452

timers, 7

token ring, 3, 27, 35–36, 44, 64, 72–76

NICs (network interface cards), 53

UTP or STP wiring, 72
wiring, 72–76
tokens, 35–36, 38
touch-panel interface, 381
TRACERT, 95, 105
track lighting, 383
tracks, 227, 465, 489
trailers, 29, 64
transceiver (transmitter/
receiver), 53
transformer, 277, 294
translator, 5, 22
transmission, 4, 22
transmitting internal information
on LAN, 44–45
Transport layer, 28
triad, 47, 64
trip switch, 475, 489
trunk lines, 341, 361
trusses, 128, 144
tuners, 227, 229, 234–236, 257
tweeters, 231
twisted-pair wires, 31, 133, 144

U

UDP (User Datagram Protocol),
59, 102
UGate–3200 gateway, 127
UL (Underwriters
Laboratories, Inc.) Web site, 153
uncompressed original video
footage, 252, 257
uncontrolled outlets, 164–165
unfinished areas, 116
unified messaging, 350, 361
unregistered IP addresses, 98
unshielded twisted-pair, 73
unshielded twisted-pair cable, 31
UPS (uninterruptible power
supply), 159, 319

USB (Universal Serial Bus),
89, 105
USB (Universal Serial Bus)
adapters, 78
USB-to-parallel port adapter, 78
USB-to-PCMCIA adapter, 78
USOC (Universal Service
Ordering Codes), 354
utilities
integration with security
system, 273
management, 7–8
specifications and capacity,
272–273
utility management, 3
utility sensors, 273
UTP, 36
UTP cable, 119
UTP wiring, 72–73, 74–75

V

valve boxes, 442, 454
valves, 415, 429, 438, 454
VCRs, 236–237, 243–244
Venator, John, 17
ventilation, 413–414, 429
ventilators, 413–414
vents, 408, 429
vertical sync, 197
VGA-type connector, 245
VHS (Video Home Standard), 215
VHS cassettes, 209, 237
video, 2, 17, 22
cable hookup, 5
cables, 241
components, 243–246
compressed, 210
compressing, 252–253
configuration for internal,
252–253
editing, 252–253

files and formats, 208–210
reception and distribution, 5
satellite transmission, 5
stored media, 209–210
video cameras, 252, 308
video conferencing, 349, 361
video devices, 243
video distribution systems,
249–251, 257
video editing systems, 252
video files, 208–209
video formats, 203
video images, 188, 216
video programs, 16, 212
video recorder/players, 236
video recorders, 283
video servers, 55, 252, 257
video signals, 243
video streaming, 203
video surveillance, 313
video surveillance cameras, 6
video systems
cables, 239–240
coaxial cable, 238
components, 226
condensation, 254
configuration and settings for
external, 247–251
dirt, 254
heat, 253
installation and setup, 238–246
monitoring and maintaining,
253–254
new construction
installations, 238
power fluctuations, 254
receiving components, 241
retrofitted installations, 238
shielded coaxial cable, 241
termination points, 239–241

videotape cassettes, 16

viruses, 4, 22, 60, 100, 102

visual images, 186–187

vital sign monitors, 7

VMX Corporation, 350

voice coil, 230

voice mail, 350, 361

VoIP (Voice over IP),
    343–344, 362

volts, 176

W

wall-mounted controllers,
    251, 257

WANs (wide area networks),
    28, 39, 95

water control systems
    components, 442–448
    controllers, 442–446
    design, 438–442
    flow valve, 440
    installing, 448–451
    interior zones, 440
    locating controller, 448–449
    low-voltage wiring, 449–451
    pressure valve, 440
    programming, 451–452
    pumps, 447–448
    remote access, 442
    seasonal presets, 452
    sensors, 446–447
    solenoid valves, 442–443
    timed water systems, 440–441
    time-of-day settings, 451–452
    valve box, 442
    watering scenes, 441
    zoned water systems, 438–439
    zones, 452

water features, 441

water level sensors, 15

water pressure, 439, 454

water sensors, 273, 289, 294, 324

water service line, 439, 454

watering scenes, 441

watts, 155, 176

WAV files, 195, 216

waves, 190

Web sites, streaming digital radio
    signals, 193

Web-based radio streaming
    sites, 193

WECA (Wireless Ethernet
    Compatibility Alliance), 91

WGL Designs Web site, 445

whole-house connectivity, 8–9

WiFi (Wireless Fidelity), 88,
    90–91, 93, 106, 210, 308

WiFi5, 89, 92–93, 105

wind sensors, 447, 454

window shades, 7, 468

*Windows 9x Installation: A+ Guide
    to Hardware* (Andrews), 94

Windows Media Player, 209

WINIPCFG, 95, 105

wired networks
    AC power-line networks, 80–84
    AC wiring, 84
    Ethernet, 72–76
    HomePNA, 76–80
    token ring, 72–76
    types, 72–87
    X10, 84–87

wired security systems
    arming and disarming, 309
    cameras, 310
    category 2 telephone wires,
        304–305
    category 3 wire, 305
    components, 309–312
    concealed wiring, 305–306, 311
    door sensors, 312
    emergency buttons, 312

emergency response, 310

fees, 310

glassbreak detector, 310

installation, 310–312

intruders, 310

low-voltage wiring, 304–307

monitoring sensors, 305

monitoring service, 309

motion detectors, 312

pet-immune motion sensor, 310

response devices, 307

security breach, 310

security panels, 306

sensors, 312

smoke detector, 310

splicing wires, 305

surface wiring, 311–312

wireless keys, 310

wired sensors, 279, 305

wireless access hubs, 58

wireless audio transmitters,
    249, 257

wireless frequencies, 89–90

wireless hubs, 36, 64, 117, 119

wireless keypads, 277

wireless keys, 310

wireless LANs (wireless area
    networks), 36–38

wireless lighting controls, 382

wireless mini-controllers, 381

wireless networks, 36–38, 58, 87,
    89–90, 126

wireless NIC (network interface
    card), 36, 64

wireless protocols, 87–89
    Bluetooth, 89

wireless security systems, 276
    alarm siren, 313
    batteries, 307
    call-in dialer, 314

components, 312–314

HomePlug, 308

HomePNA, 308

HomeRF, 308

installation, 313–314

power usage, 307

recorded emergency
message, 313

related technologies, 308

sensors, 313–314

signal transmission, 307–308

standards organizations, 308

video surveillance, 313

WiFi, 308

wireless video cameras, 308

wireless sensors, 269

wireless technologies, 5, 22, 93–94

wireless transmitters, 13

wireless video cameras, 308

wires, 13

audio devices, 242

AWG (American Wire
Gauge), 161

ground, 154

hot, 154

sizes, 161

telephones, 352–354

wiring

automated lighting system, 388

central hub, 115

checks for inadequate, 157–158

circuits, 163–164

concealed, 129–130

connectors, 132–135

Ethernet, 72–76

hardware, 127–140

home run cable, 135–139

home security system, 275

HVAC system controllers,
422–423

inadequate, 373

installing, 76, 160–162

LANs (local area networks),
127–140

low-voltage, 304–307

new construction, 128–129

path panel, 115

planning electrical system
upgrade, 158–159

pulling cable, 129

retrofit, 122

surface wiring, 130–132

telephones, 355–356

terminating jacks, 132–135

token ring, 72–76

video distribution systems, 250

water control system, 449–451

WMAN (Windows Media
Audio), 195–196, 216

woofers, 231

WOR radio station, 192–193

workstations, 46

WPANs (wireless personal area
networks), 92

WWW (World Wide Web), 4,
22, 28

X

X10 security systems, 308–309

components, 314–316

installation, 315–316

X10 systems, 13, 380–382

X10 technology, 22, 84–87, 106,
117, 210

appliance modules, 86

automated window
treatments, 387

command modules, 385

commands, 85

common AC power grid, 86

computer interfaces, 86

connecting devices, 118

control modules, 389–390

control panels, 84–85

controllers, 445–446

controlling lamps, 84–86

dimmers, 386

fixtures, 387

home security devices, 275

house code, 86

interfacing with Ethernet, 86

lamp modules, 86

light switches, 386

manual dimming modules, 166

modules, 84–86

no signal verification, 86

operation of, 84–86

outlets, 386

packets, 86–87

radio-based X10 devices, 86

remote controllers, 386

sensors, 387–388

troubleshooting automated
lighting system, 392–393

unit codes, 86

X10 Web site, 117

Z

Zenith, 84

Zip disks, 16

zoned water systems, 438–439

zones, 58, 64, 395, 429, 454

HVAC system, 411–412

lighting, 373, 375–376

programming, 425

security, 270–271

sprinkler systems, 438–439

temperature sensors
(thermostats), 413

thermostats, 417–418

water control systems, 452